Hannes Černy's book provides a deeply thoughtful, extremely well-written and meticulously sourced analysis of international relations theories' problems when it comes to talking about 'ethnic conflict'. His case study on relations between Kurdish groups in Syria, Turkey and Iraq neatly demonstrates how the 'ethnic group' or 'nation' cannot serve as a static stand-in for states, whose treatment as unitary actors in much of IR theory is already problematic. Readers interested in either IR theory or the Kurdish issue should find this work very refreshing and rewarding.

David Romano, *Thomas G. Strong Chair in Middle East Politics at Missouri State University; author of* The Kurdish Nationalist Movement *and co-editor of* Conflict, Democratization and the Kurds in the Middle East

Theoretically grounded and empirically detailed, Hannes Černy's book makes an insightful contribution to the study of Kurdish ethno-nationalism in the Middle East.

Stefan Wolff, *Professor of International Security, University of Birmingham; author of* Ethnic Conflict *and co-editor of* The Routledge Handbook of Ethnic Conflict

Hannes Černy brilliantly deconstructs ethno-nationalism in international relations theory. While explaining the motives and behavior shaping the strained relations between the Kurdish political parties KDP, PUK and PKK, he delivers a compelling critique of state-centrist and essentialist ontologies in explanatory theory.

Joost Jongerden, *Assistant Professor in Sociology at Wageningen University and Endowed Professor at the Asian Platform for Global Sustainability and Transcultural Studies at Kyoto University; associate editor of* Kurdish Studies

Hannes Černy provides insight on the growing importance of Kurds in the Middle East. He has a deep understanding of the balance of power and the role of Iraqi Kurds as security partners and a positive force for democratization and stability.

David L. Phillips, *Director, Program on Peace-building and Rights, Columbia University; author of* Losing Iraq and The Kurdish Spring

Iraqi Kurdistan, the PKK and International Relations

Due to its primacy in explaining issues of war and peace in the international arena, the discipline of International Relations (IR) looms large in analyses of and responses to ethnic conflict in academia, politics and popular media – in particular with respect to contemporary conflicts in the Middle East.

Grounded in constitutive theory, this book challenges how ethnic/ethnonationalist conflict is represented in explanatory IR by deconstructing its most prominent state-centric models, frameworks and analytical concepts. As much a critique of contemporary scholarship on Kurdish ethno-nationalism as a detailed analysis of the most prominent Kurdish ethno-nationalist actors, the book provides the first in-depth investigation into the relations between the PKK and the main Iraqi Kurdish political parties from the 1980s to the present. It situates this inquiry within the wider context of the ambiguous political status of the Kurdistan Region of Iraq, its relations with Turkey, and the role Kurdish parties and insurgencies play in the war against ISIS in Iraq and Syria. Appreciating these complex dynamics and how they are portrayed in Western scholarship is essential for understanding current developments in the Iraqi and Syrian theatres of war, and for making sense of discussions about a potential independent Kurdish state to emerge in Iraq.

Iraqi Kurdistan, the PKK and International Relations provides a comprehensive and critical discussion of the state-centric and essentializing epistemologies, ontologies and methodologies of the three main paradigms of explanatory IR, as well as their analytical models and frameworks on ethnic identity and conflict in the Middle East and beyond. It will therefore be a valuable resource for anyone studying ethnicity and nationalism, International Relations or Middle East Politics.

Hannes Černy is Visiting Professor at the Department of International Relations, Central European University, and he previously taught at the universities of Hull, Exeter and Passau. His research focuses on issues of identity and sovereignty and their representation in IR scholarship.

Exeter Studies in Ethno Politics
Series Editor: Gareth Stansfield
University of Exeter, UK

Iraqi Kurdistan, the PKK and International Relations
Theory and Ethnic Conflict

Hannes Černy

Routledge
Taylor & Francis Group

LONDON AND NEW YORK

First published 2018
by Routledge
2 Park Square, Milton Park, Abingdon, Oxon OX14 4RN

and by Routledge
711 Third Avenue, New York, NY 10017

Routledge is an imprint of the Taylor & Francis Group, an informa business

© 2018 Hannes Černy

The right of Hannes Černy to be identified as author of this work has been asserted by him in accordance with sections 77 and 78 of the Copyright, Designs and Patents Act 1988.

British Library Cataloguing in Publication Data
A catalogue record for this book is available from the British Library

Library of Congress Cataloging in Publication Data
Names: Černy, Hannes, author
Title: Iraqi Kurdistan, the PKK and international relations : theory and ethnic conflict / Hannes Černy.
Description: Milton Park, Abingdon, Oxon : Routledge, 2018. | Series: Exeter studies in ethno politics
Identifiers: LCCN 2017005963 | ISBN 9781138676176 (hardback) | ISBN 9781315560212 (ebook)
Subjects: LCSH: Ethnic conflict–Iraq–Kurdistån. | Nationalism–Iraq–Kurdistan. | Ethnic conflict–Turkey. | Nationalism–Turkey. | Kurdistan (Iraq)–Politics and government. | Kurdistån (Iraq)–Ethnic relations. | Turkey–Ethnic relations. | Kurds–Politics and government. | International relations–Philosophy. | Partiya Karkerãen Kurdistanãe.
Classification: LCC DS79.89.K87 C47 2018 | DDC 327.567/2–dc23
LC record available at https://lccn.loc.gov/2017005963

ISBN: 978-1-138-67617-6 (hbk)
ISBN: 978-1-315-56021-2 (ebk)

Typeset in Times New Roman
by Wearset Ltd, Boldon, Tyne and Wear

For Sarah,
my partner in everything

Contents

Preface and acknowledgements

The comedian Stephen Colbert once said of President George W. Bush:

> The greatest thing about this man is he's steady. You know where he stands. He believes the same thing Wednesday that he believed on Monday, no matter what happened on Tuesday. Events can change; this man's beliefs never will.[1]

While steadiness of character and conviction in principle are no doubt admirable qualities, I believe that, as in life in general, for intellectual enquiry the opposite of what Colbert mockingly lauded in Bush should be the case. Solid scholarly research should be distinguished by the very fact that there are no irrefutable truths, that there is a vast multiplicity of realities out there, that one's beliefs should be a reflection of the natural volatility of events, that our investigations should yield more questions than answers, and certainly challenge pre-conceived notions about the social world we inhabit and take part in shaping every day.

A certain kind of intellectual conversion then surely happened to me between the time I first developed an interest in the historic struggle of the Kurdish people in Iraq and Turkey for national self-determination and today, as I write these lines. My first inroads into the subject were inspired by the many talks I had with Kurdish friends in the smoky cafés of Vienna in 2004 and my travels in south-eastern Anatolia in the following year. Most Kurds I encountered had become enthralled by the exalting experience of Iraqi Kurds gaining the freest political entity in Kurdish history enshrined in the Iraqi Constitution, and hoped for this entity and its leaders to become champions of Kurdish cultural rights, freedoms and national self-determination in all parts of what is called wider Kurdistan. For a people who had suffered so much throughout the twentieth century it was an exhilarating image, one I adopted without much questioning for my political novel, *The Writing on the Wall*, published in 2007. Only once I looked into the relations between the various Kurdish ethno-nationalist parties more critically in the context of having started my PhD studies at the University of Exeter, UK, and had conducted actual field research in Iraqi Kurdistan, did I realize that matters are more complex, ambiguous, and contradictory, and that the pre-conceived notions I had held on Monday were soundly challenged on Tuesday.

In this respect then, this study is, if you like, a roundup of the way I interpret, on Wednesday, the various forms of Kurdish identity that are enacted in the political space of Iraqi Kurdistan and beyond, as well as a roundup of the role of explanatory IR theory in shaping ethnic conflicts, issues of sovereignty and national self-determination. As much as a snapshot of my thinking or beliefs, I would like this study to be understood then as an invitation for reflection and dialogue on the issues addressed herein, in the hope that these exchanges will lead to an even more matured position on Thursday.

One person, more than any other, has inspired and challenged me to think more critically about the social world we all inhabit and take part in shaping every day, my wife and partner in everything, Sarah Keeler. With her crucial aid in facilitating contacts in Iraqi Kurdistan, intellectual input, encouragement in difficult times, tireless support, and keen eye as well as sharp mind improving countless earlier drafts of this book, it is only natural that I dedicate the fruits of what is essentially our combined efforts to her. I also owe a big hug to our baby-daughter, Tikva, who has shown a level of tolerance and support remarkable for a two-year-old during her dad's countless hours at the computer when all she wanted was to play. My profound appreciation goes to my supervisor at Exeter, Gareth Stansfield, as well as to Brendan O'Leary at UPenn, where I had the unique opportunity to spend a doctoral fellowship – while I may differ with them on opinions of the nature of IR scholarship in general, and in my interpretations of Kurdish identity and the political space in Iraqi Kurdistan in particular, I always valued our discussions on these matters, and their support of my research was crucial to its success. The fact that Gareth has encouraged me to publish this study as part of his *Exeter Series in Ethno Politics* is testimony to his open-mindedness to diversities of opinion and his promotion of critical scholarship, even where it directly challenges his own positions. I am as appreciative of his receptiveness towards my heterodoxies as I am grateful for the many opportunities he has given me to intellectually and practically pursue them during all these years.

Outside Iraqi Kurdistan, I want to thank Selahettin Çelik, Abbas Vali, Bob Olson, Michael Gunter, Denise Natali, Nina Caspersen, Hugh Pope, Doğu Ergil, Siamend Hajo, and James Harvey for sharing their personal insights and expertise with me. In Iraqi Kurdistan, without the help of Omar Sheikhmous, who generously facilitated a great number of my contacts there, my field research would never have got off the ground. I also want to acknowledge the services of the Department of Foreign Relations of the KRG, and in particular its head, Falah Mustafa Bakir, who opened many doors for me during my stays there. Likewise, I am indebted to my tireless 'fixer' and translator during my research in Iraqi Kurdistan, Niaz Zangana, as well as to several journalists there who, due to the rapidly deteriorating human rights situation and for their own safety, I have decided not to name in this study. Ample thanks are also due to the editorial team at Routledge, first and foremost Joe Whiting and Emma Tyce; one cannot wish for a more helpful team of editors during the publication process. Finally, I want to thank my parents and Jane Keeler for the countless ways in which they have supported me personally, my family, and my research during all these years.

For the sake of full disclosure I want to record that my research has been partly funded by a Centre for Kurdish Studies Scholarship of the University of Exeter. I received further funding from a research grant from *the British Institute for the Study of Iraq*, and a Marie Curie doctoral fellowship in Sustainable Peacebuilding as part of the VII EU Marie Curie framework that allowed me to continue my field research in Iraqi Kurdistan and Turkey as well as to spend a year as a doctoral fellow at the University of Coimbra in Portugal. While all these institutions and individuals have contributed to my research in many ways, it goes without saying that all errors and omissions in this study are entirely mine.

Hannes Černy
Budapest, Hungary
December 2016

Note

1 Comedy routine at the annual White House Correspondents' Dinner 2006.

Abbreviations

ADYÖD	Ankara Democratic Higher Education Association (*Ankara Demokratik Yüksek Öğretim Derneği*)
AKP	Justice and Development Party (*Adalet ve Kalkınma Partisi*)
ARGK	People's Liberation Army of Kurdistan (*Arteşa Rizgariya Netewa Kurdistan*)
BDP	Peace and Democracy Party (*Barış ve Demokrasi Partisi*)
BISA	British International Studies Association
CENTCOM	United States Central Command
CHP	Republican People's Party (*Cumhuriyet Halk Partisi*)
CJCS	Chairman of the Joint Chiefs of Staff
CPA	Coalition Provisional Authority
CUP	Committee for Union and Progress (*İttihat ve Terakki Cemiyeti*)
DEP	Democracy Party (*Demokrasi Partisi*)
DFLP	Democratic Front for the Liberation of Palestine
DP	Democratic Party (*Demokrat Parti*)
DTP	Democratic Society Party (*Demokratik Toplum Partisi*)
GAP	South-eastern Anatolia Project (*Güneydoğu Anadolu Projesi*)
HADEP	People's Democracy Party (*Halkın Demokrasi Partisi*)
HDP	Peoples' Democratic Party (*Halkların Demokratik Partisi*)
HEP	People's Labour Party (*Halkın Emek Partisi*)
HRK	Kurdistan Freedom Unit (*Hezen Rizgariya Kurdistan*)
ICP	Iraqi Communist Party
IKF	Iraqi Kurdistan Front
ISIS	Islamic State of Iraq and al-Sham (*ad-Dawlah al-Islāmiyah fī 'l-ʿIrāq wa-sh-Shām*)
ITF	Iraqi Turkmen Front (*Irak Türkmen Cephesi*)
JİTEM	Gendarmerie Intelligence and Counter-Terrorism Organisation (*Jandarma İstihbarat ve Terörle Mücadele*)
KADEK	Kurdistan Freedom and Democracy Congress (*Kongreya Azadî û Demokrasiya Kurdistanê*)
KCK	Kurdistan Democratic Confederation (*Koma Civaken Kurdistan*)
KDP	Kurdistan Democratic Party (*Partîya Demokrata Kurdistan*)
KDP-I	Kurdish Democratic Party of Iran

KDP-T	Democratic Party of Turkish Kurdistan
KNC	Kurdish National Council
Kongra-Gel	People's Congress of Kurdistan (*Kongra Gelê Kurdistan*)
KRG	Kurdistan Regional Government
MEK	People's Mujahideen of Iran (*Mojahedin-e-Khalq*)
MERIP	Middle East Research and Information Project
MHP	Nationalist Action Party (*Milliyetçi Hareket Partisi*)
MIT	National Intelligence Agency (*Milli İstihbarat Teşkilatı*)
NLM	National Liberation Movement
NSC	National Security Council
PAK	Kurdistan Liberation Party (*Partiya Azadiya Kurdistan*)
PCDK	Kurdistan Democratic Solution Party (*Partiya Careseriya Demokratik a Kurdistane*)
PJAK	Kurdistan Free Life Party (*Partiya Jiyani Azadi Kurdistan*)
PKK	Kurdistan Workers' Party (*Partiya Karkerên Kurdistan*)
PUK	Patriotic Union of Kurdistan (*Yeketî Niştîmanî Kurdistan*)
PWD	Patriotic and Democratic Party of Kurdistan (*Partîya Welatparêzên Demokratên Kuristan*)
PYD	Democratic Union Party (*Partiya Yekita ya Demokratik*)
RCT	Rational Choice Theory
SCIRI	Islamic Supreme Council of Iraq
SHP	Social Democratic Populist Party (*Sosyaldemokrat Halkçı Parti*)
TAK	Kurdistan Freedom Falcons (*Teyrêbazên Azadiya Kurdistan*)
TAL	Transitional Administrative Law
TESEV	Turkish Economic and Social Studies Foundation (*Türkiye Ekonomik ve Sosyal Etüdler Vakfı*)
TKSP	Socialist Party of Turkish Kurdistan (*Türkiye Kürdistan Sosyalist Partisi*)
TWP	Workers Party of Turkey (*Türkiye İşçi Partisi*)
YPG	Peoples' Protection Units (*Yekîneyên Parastina Gel*)

Introduction

Constitutive versus explanatory theory

In one of the most widely used primers on International Relations (IR), Colin Wight (2010) discusses the epistemological debates preoccupying the discipline, first and foremost the rift between explanatory and constitutive theory, a schism that, according to Milja Kurki (2008), divides contemporary IR like no other. Already, back in 1995, when the post-positivist challenge to traditional theories of IR was in full vogue, Steve Smith wrote:

> In my view this is the main meta-theoretical issue facing international theory today. The emerging fundamental division in the discipline is between those theories that seek to offer explanatory accounts of international relations, and those that see theory as constitutive of that reality. At base this boils down to a difference over what the social world is like; is it to be seen as scientists think of the 'natural' world, that is to say as something outside of our theories, or is the social world what we make it? Radically different types of theory are needed to deal with each of these cases, and these theories are not combinable so as to form one overarching theory of the social world ... In my judgement this really is a fundamental divide within social theory.
>
> (Smith 1995: 26–27)[1]

In response to this assessment Wight retorts:

> But just whom does the 'we' refer to here? Setting this distinction in opposition to explanatory theory that attempts to explain international relations, we can presume that Smith means 'we' IR theorists, not 'we' members of society. But this seems implausible. It seems to suggest that 'we' IR theorists make the world of international relations.
>
> (Wight 2010: 43)

To me Smith's argument is not implausible. On the contrary, not only is it the central distinguishing feature of constitutive theory, it is also the key argument of this study that we IR theorists as categorizers and analysts, are co-protagonists of the social phenomena and processes we set out to describe; we do not 'make' the world of international relations, but, like the actors that are the subject of our analysis, we take part in influencing and shaping it. In clear rejection of the scientific objectivism and rational positivism of explanatory theories, this study commits to a constitutive theory of IR that renders us analysts as much part of social discourse on the issue to be analysed, and therefore the subject of analysis, as the social groups and actors we categorize and examine. We all are part of the social world we analysts try to understand and explain, and, in my opinion, what would be implausible is to assume that our explanations have no impact on the processes and discourses we study, that we can remain objective, neutral and detached to them, while in fact we arguably can be as subjective, involved, biased, prejudiced and party to them as our subjects of analysis.

The social phenomenon that is the object of analysis of this study is ethnic and ethno-nationalist conflict, and its subject of analysis are those ethno-nationalist entrepreneurs that engage in an ethnicized discourse, advance and thrive on it, as well as we IR theorists that seek to understand and explain their actions alike. While it would be implausible to argue that ethno-nationalist entrepreneurs, be it in reference to our case study, Kurdish nationalist leaders or members of the Turkish military-intelligence apparatus, have read either Smith or any other IR theorist for that matter, to let highly theoretical deliberations guide their thinking and policies, it would be equally implausible to posit that our thought processes occur in a social vacuum, are not filtered down through the media, the advocacy of think tanks via political decision makers, and the exchange in personnel between the scientific community and public servants, to name just a few, until they reach, in a more accessible form, politicians and the general public. Ironically, on the contrary, academia in the twenty-first century is mostly concerned with proving the impact factor of its deliberations to business, philanthropic donors, the ministers holding the purses of the higher education budgets, students expected to pay ever higher tuition fees, and the general public. How can we IR theorists proudly demonstrate these impact factors in every grant proposal we pen, yet at the same time cling to the fallacy of a detached scientific objectivism that posits us outside the social discourse we seek to explain?

As far as IR scholars' impact on the understanding of, and policies adopted in response to ethnic conflict by decision makers is concerned, one does not have to belabour the prominent example of President Clinton, allegedly declaring Robert Kaplan's infamous *Balkan Ghosts* (1994) required reading for members of his administration in dealing with the conflicts of the former Yugoslavia in the 1990s (Joras & Schetter 2004); the very *Balkan Ghosts* that is often said to have established the unfortunate and fallacious narrative of 'ancient ethnic hatreds' dominating Western representations of the wars in Bosnia, Croatia, and Kosovo. What is one of the subjects of this study, the Iraq War and the ethno-sectarian conflicts it triggered, offers a plethora of examples of IR scholars influencing the positions and policies of regional and international actors – from the 'Six Wise Men', British academics that counselled Tony Blair against invading Iraq in 2003 (Moreton 2015), to countless neo-conservative scholars in the US, Francis

Fukuyama and Bernard Lewis among them, doing the opposite with the Bush administration. What is more, in the decade since the invasion of Iraq hardly a week has passed without academics being questioned on developments in the war-torn country by journalists, in expert testimonials before parliamentary inquiries or, on their own accord, penning another op-ed to gain a wider audience for their analyses.

The prominence of IR in accounts of ethnic conflict, I would argue, stems from the widely held perception of the discipline to be most qualified to explain issues of war and peace in the international arena. 'The study of international relations can tell us much about ethnic conflict,' argue Jesse and Williams (2011: 15) in advocating for a primacy of IR and its 'theories and approaches to explain ethnic conflict'. In another primer on ethnic conflict Cordell and Wolff (2009: 14) take the same line when observing, 'theories of international relations offer useful tools and insights in the study of ethnic conflict and conflict settlement'.[2] More than any other discipline, they continue, 'IR theory is primarily concerned with issues of war and peace' in world politics, and state behaviour has a significant impact on the origins, development and duration of ethnic conflicts – whether causal, escalating or mitigating – as do norms, values, practices, institutions, legislations and forms of governance at the local, regional and international level. Although the reasons they offer for IR's primacy in explaining the complex dynamics of ethnic conflict appear compelling, others would argue that IR is not particularly well equipped for the analysis of identity conflicts. IR is a notorious latecomer to debates on questions of identity – the concept did not feature prominently as an eminent category in IR-specific approaches until the so-called 'fourth great debate' and the post-positivist challenge of the early 1990s (Zalewski & Enloe 1995). One would not have to go so far as John Stack's observations that, 'ethnicity is as alien to the study of international relations as would be Sigmund Freud's musings in *Civilization and Its Discontents*' (Stack 1997: 11), to ascertain that explanatory IR's theoretical approaches to identity are epistemologically grossly underdeveloped. Zalewski and Enloe sum it up aptly when concluding, 'all three paradigms [neo-realism, neo-liberalism, structuralism] are too restricted ontologically, methodologically, and epistemologically, and in ways which ultimately render them unable to theorize or think adequately about identity' (Zalewski & Enloe 1995: 297).

The main argumentative thrust of this study is to take up this critique of the approach to ethnic conflict of the three major explanatory theories of IR – (neo-)realism, (neo-)liberalism and systemic constructivism – and to provide a detailed critical examination of the epistemologies, ontologies, models, and frameworks they employ in their analysis of ethnic conflict.[3] The epistemological and ontological point of departure here is this: as will be shown, in the late 1980s/early 1990s, constitutive theorists such as Richard Ashley, Rob Walker, David Campbell and others led the charge in deconstructing the sovereign state in IR theory both by discussing the sovereign state as a discursive formation rather than a factual, clearly bounded, timeless and ontologically unproblematic, i.e. taken-for-granted, entity in global politics and by exposing explanatory IR's role in contributing to its reproduction as a unitary actor and as supreme in the international system by virtue of these essentialized properties. At the same time, Craig Calhoun also argued for the nation, and by implication the ethnic group, to be understood as a discursive formation rather than the factual precursor of the state, as modernist theory would have it. What I intend to do in this study, inspired by these pioneers of constitutive theory and after adopting their conceptualization of ethnic group, nation, and state as discursive formations, is to show how explanatory IR has contributed to the essentialization of the former two (that is, ethnic group and nation) by analytically equating them with the latter (that is, the state) and how this has in turn led to the reproduction and substantialization of the lines of division between self and other that form the basis of an ethnicized discourse – a theme David Campbell has already touched on in his seminal *National Deconstruction* (1998a), yet which I intend to problematize in greater depth. In fact, it is the ontological, methodological, and epistemological restrictions cursorily identified by Zalewski and Enloe above that are the main focus of this study. In this sense then, the conception of this study as a contribution to a constitutive IR theory of ethnic conflict, first and foremost, is an epistemological and ontological critique of how explanatory theories of IR perceive of, explain, and deal with ethnic conflict. This will be done, after outlining explanatory IR's approach to ethnic identity, ethnic conflict, and nationalism in general terms, by deconstructing the main concepts and frameworks, explanatory IR has contributed to or utilizes in the analysis of ethnic conflict: state-centrism, the 'ethnic security dilemma', the 'ethnic alliance model'[4] and, drawing on other disciplines, instrumentalism.

To be clear about this study's ambition, though, not only would it be impossible to show how certain texts of explanatory IR theory shape the world views and actions of individual ethnic entrepreneurs, ethno-nationalist leaders or decision makers engaging in and advancing an ethnicized discourse, but to do so would run counter to the self-perception of this study as constitutive theory, which is defined precisely by eschewing and confuting universal claims to causality; it would become guilty of the very attempt to harness constitutive theory for causal or explanatory theory that Smith (2000) criticizes in Wendt's work. On this distinction Lene Hansen elaborates:

> Mainstream approaches [i.e. explanatory theories] adopt a positivist epistemology. They strive to find the causal relations that 'rule' world politics, working with dependent and independent variables ... [Constitutive theories], by contrast, embrace a post-positivist epistemology as they argue that the social world is so far removed from the hard sciences where causal epistemologies originate that we cannot understand world politics through causal cause-effect relationships ... Constitutive theories are still theories, not just descriptions or stories about the world, because they define theoretical concepts, explain how they hang together, and instruct us on how to use them in analysis of world politics.
>
> (Hansen 2013: 171)

With that aspiration in mind, I argue that IR, more than any other discipline, is prone to what Rogers Brubaker (2004) calls 'groupism' and a 'clichéd constructivism' when dealing with identity politics in the social sciences, a constructivism in name only – limited to the introductory section or expressed in customary yet seemingly perfunctory disclaimers – but the main analysis, at large, continues to be done under essentialist and substantialist presumptions of ethnic identities, often bordering a primordialism slipping in through the backdoor. Despite advances to the contrary in sociology and anthropology, and two generations of critical theory scholarship, the three dominant schools of thought in IR still tend to treat ethnic groups as organic, static, substantive, distinct, homogeneous and bounded units and largely equate conflicts between said groups with conflicts between states. The essentialist and substantialist presumptions of groupism in how explanatory IR approaches ethnicity and ethnic conflict, I hypothesize in what is the core argument of this study, manifest themselves on three levels: (1) operationalizing ethnicity as either the dependent variable, that is perceiving it as exogenous to the social phenomena studied and reducing it to merely a political tool, or the independent variable and therewith according it with pre-eminent explanatory power; (2) equating ethnic groups with states; and (3) as a consequence thereof, all too often equating ethnic conflict with ethno-nationalist conflict by postulating that a disenfranchized group's desire for the control of territory and in the long run sovereign statehood is the prime cause of the conflict at hand.

To *herausarbeiten* – in the sense of elaborating an argument by teasing out information, by chipping away the surfaces like a carver who reveals the features and contours of a statue cut-by-cut – the workings, effects and rationale behind such groupism in the discourses on ethnic conflict and sovereignty of explanatory IR is the prime objective of this study. While these are discussed in great depth in theory in Part I, such a debate cannot and should never remain at the theoretical level since the essentialist practices criticized here have very direct and often dramatic implications on the conflicts we analysts set out to study and for the people who are its main protagonists and victims. For this reason, and in order to substantiate and illustrate the arguments made here by way of the example of one of the most widely analysed ethnic and ethno-nationalist conflicts of our times, ample room is given to the empirical case study. As elaborated below, the case of the relations between the *Kurdistan Workers' Party* (PKK, *Partiya Karkerên Kurdistan*) and the Iraqi Kurdish ethno-nationalist parties, the *Kurdistan Democratic Party* (KDP, *Partîya Demokrata Kurdistan*) and the *Patriotic Union of Kurdistan* (PUK, *Yeketî Niştîmanî Kurdistan*), as well as on the political identity cum current status of the Kurdistan Region of Iraq, constitute an ideal case with which to examine the workings and effects of groupism in explanatory IR discourses on ethnic conflict and sovereignty. As a matter of fact, it very well has the potential to serve as the cautionary tale par excellence about the epistemological, ontological and methodological flaws of such essentialist approaches in explanatory IR scholarship.

The above three contentions of the key argument of this study, put differently, encompass the two main points of critique herein levelled at how explanatory IR perceives and explains ethnicity and ethnic conflict. First, that in its epistemology, ontology and methodology when dealing with ethnic identity and ethnic conflict, explanatory IR is guilty of reification, and second, that its system-immanent normative determinism of state-centrism creates a reality that, intentionally or not, accentuates the ethnicized discourse and exacerbates the ethnic lines of division it originally set out to study. Reification, one of the cardinal errors in social research, can be defined as 'the apprehension of human phenomena as if they were things, that is, in non-human or possible supra terms' (Berger & Luckmann 1991: 106); or in the words of Anthony Giddens (1984: 180), the 'reified discourse refers the "facticity" with which social phenomena confront individual actors in such a way as to ignore how they are produced and reproduced through human agency'. For the tendency to reify ethnic groups in particular, Craig Calhoun remarks:

> We habitually refer to ethnic groups, races, tribes, and languages as though they were clearly unities, only occasionally recalling to ourselves the ambiguity of their definitions, the porousness of their boundaries, and the situational dependency of their use in practice. The point is not that such categorical identities are not real, any more than the nations are not real, it is, rather, that they are not fixed but both fluid and manipulatable. Cultural and physical differences exist, but their discreetness, their identification, and their invocation are all variable.[5]

The primary site of reification in explanatory IR's dealing with ethnic conflict I identify is state-centrism. While explanatory IR's state-centric ontology will be discussed in great detail in the theory section,[6] suffice it to say for now that 'state-centric theories of international relations assume that states are the primary actors in world politics ... the claim is that states ... are sufficiently important actors that any positive theory of international relations must place them at its core' (Lake 2008: 42). Yet this assumption about the primacy of the state in IR theory comes with considerable epistemological and ontological baggage. First and foremost, state-centrism in mainstream IR 'reduce[s] the essence of international relations to state-centred interpretations' (Youngs 1999: 34). State-centrism thus explains international relations almost exclusively – at best it inserts the above mentioned clichéd constructivist caveats – through the prism of the state, a state whose existence ontologically predates the system of which it is part; in other words,

> as an ontologically abstract category, the state, through the state-centric prism, becomes also a static category. International relations is reduced via the state-centric prism to an individualistically conceived collection of its parts – that is states – and thus as a collection of static entities.
>
> (Youngs 1999: 35)

I argue in this study that explanatory IR – for reasons that will be elaborated in detail – by equating the ethnic group with the state, has translated from the state onto the ethnic group this static conceptualization of social units as clearly bounded, organic, substantive, distinct, homogeneous and static categories endowed with social agency, whose properties and genesis are not problematized but treated as given – or to be more precise, by doing so, as with the state, it has contributed to reifying the ethnic group through its narratives. This equation of state with ethnic or ethno-nationalist group that was made possible, in modernist fashion, by ascribing the nation with the defining objective of becoming a state, brings with it then for the study of ethnic or ethno-nationalist conflict the same epistemological and ontological fallacies of reification as state-centrism does in general for the study of the state and international relations at large.

Given the centrality of the state in explanatory IR's analysis of ethnic and ethno-nationalist conflict, both as the social unit with which explanatory IR equates the ethnic group as a unitary actor and as the ultimate objective to be attained, therewith defining the ethno-nationalist group, it becomes imperative to dedicate ample room to a critical analysis of the concept of sovereign statehood in explanatory IR. Yet, it is a conjuncture dictated by the representation of both concepts and categories in explanatory IR which establishes this linkage in the first place. Consequently, I argue, any deconstruction of how explanatory IR explains ethnic and ethno-nationalist conflict would be wholly incomplete if not accompanied by a deconstruction of sovereign statehood, which, allegedly, the former is all about.

Some may argue that by denouncing explanatory IR's approach to ethnic conflict as groupist, essentialist and state-centric, this study is also guilty of reification and groupism. After all, when identifying explanatory IR scholars as co-protagonists of the ethnic conflicts they set out to describe who unquestioningly adopt the strategic essentialisms of ethno-nationalist elites as factual for their analysis, which can lead to a reification, substantialization and legitimization of those elites' claims to leadership and territory as well as to deepening the ethnic lines of division on which they strive, it may appear as if here a social group, namely explanatory IR, gets essentialized and wrongly ascribed with social agency. Anticipating this potential critique, I feel it necessary to clarify the following: International Relations theory, for the purposes of this study and drawing on Hamati-Attaya (2012), is conceptualized as a social field in the Bourdieuian sense. While a Coxian cum Bourdieuian conceptualization of explanatory IR will be discussed at greater length in Chapter 3, suffice it to say for the moment that a field, according to Bourdieu, is a two-dimensional social space,

> both as a field of forces, whose necessity is imposed on agents who are engaged in it, and as a field of struggles within which agents confront each other with differentiated means and ends according to their position within the structure of the field of forces, thus contributing to conserving or transforming its structure.
>
> (Bourdieu 1998a: 32)

Any society consists of multiple sets of fields that can overlap and complement each other; yet, as will be elaborated later, all fields are subordinated to the field of power – material and symbolic – within the Foucauldian power-knowledge nexus. From the above definition it is clear that the field itself, of course, has no agency, nor is it clearly bound, fixed or homogeneous. Within the field of International Relations theory, for example, that can be understood as a subfield of the field of science in general, the field of education or, when focusing on how theory informs political decision making, the political field, social agency rests with individual scholars, their habitus (see below) and social capital. All those fields and their sub-units are conditioned by the specific norms and culture inherent to each field – thus emphasizing the individual and collective dimension of the Bourdieuian social field (Bourdieu 1977, 1990, 1998a, 1998b; Bigo 2011; Jenkins 2002; Thomson 2014). Likewise, the above quote specifies that any field features a considerable degree of diversity, illustrated, for example, by the divide between explanatory and constitutive theory within the field of International Relations theory. As will be shown, the former contributes to conserving the dominant structure, while the latter seeks to transform it. Their relations within the field are thus defined by the above identified struggle, a 'struggle for the power to impose universalist claims' (Bourdieu 2000: 181) of what is 'the legitimate vision of the social world which has on its side all the collective … common sense' (Bourdieu 1991: 239) and the refutation of universalist claims to knowledge. Indeed, even within explanatory IR – given that it is constituted by the often contradictory paradigms of (neo-)realism, (neo-)liberalism and systemic constructivism – there is appreciable difference, exemplified, for example, by the fact that some approaches treat ethnic identity as the dependent, while others operationalize it as the independent variable. Yet, what unites and distinguishes explanatory IR within the field of International Relations theory is its epistemological, ontological, and methodological adherence to groupism, state-centrism and positivism.

In sum then, this study can be understood as a critical reading and deconstruction of ethnic identity (and consequently ethnic and ethno-nationalist conflict), together with the interrelated concept of the sovereign nation state in explanatory IR. The main thrust of critique centres on the argument that by portraying ethnic conflict in a groupist and deterministic way – that is, by depicting ethnic groups as organic, static, substantive, distinct, homogeneous and bounded units with social agency, as unitary or unitarily acting doers that can be equated with states whose defining objective is to become a state, to acquire exclusive control, i.e. sovereignty over a territory and population – explanatory IR scholars in their state-centrist ontology and through the practice of reification contribute to creating the very reality they set out to describe. In other words, I argue explicitly here that explanatory IR scholars as co-protagonists of ethnic conflict not only play into the hands of ethnic elites by unquestioningly adopting their 'strategic essentialisms' (Spivak 1987) as factual for their analysis, but that they often take part, through their scholarship, in writing into existence in the first place the ethnic lines of division, the 'us' versus 'them' worldview that constitutes them, on which these ethnic elites thrive. These theoretical deliberations are then taken up in the empirical section of the study where, in order to substantiate them, I will deconstruct the (strategic) essentialisms of ethnic elites by way of the case of relations between the PKK and the Iraqi Kurdish ethno-nationalist parties, the KDP and the PUK, as well as on the political identity cum current status of the Kurdistan Region of Iraq, illustrating why the previously deconstructed frameworks of explanatory IR – ethnic security dilemma, ethnic alliance model, instrumentalism – not only fail to explain their relations and ethnic conflict in general but, what is more, substantially misrepresent and distort realities on the ground. Instead, drawing on Karin Fierke (2005, 2007), it will be shown why and how a fluid matrix of identities and interests, that acknowledges both as socially constructed and explicitly does not operationalize ethnic identity as either dependent or independent variables, better captures the parties' relations and, I would argue, ethnic identity and conflict in general.

Methodology and case study

These ambitions necessitate a brief clarification of what is meant here by discourse and deconstruction. Norman Fairclough (2010: 3) reminds us that 'discourse is not simply an entity we can define independently: we can only arrive at an understanding of it by analysing sets of relations'. He continues:

> Discourse is itself a complex set of relations including relations of communication between people who talk, write, and in other ways communicate with each other, but also … describe relations between concrete communicative events (conversations, newspaper articles etc.) and more abstract and enduring complex discursive 'objects' (with their own complex relations) like languages, discourses and genres. But there are also relations between discourse and other such complex 'objects' including objects in the physical world, persons, power relations and institutions, which are interconnected elements in social activity or praxis.
>
> (Fairclough 2010: 3)

Michel Foucault bases his assessment of knowledge production on how he conceptualizes discourse, in particular that 'nothing has any meaning outside discourse' (Foucault 1972: 132), that matters in the social world only gain meaning through discourse, or in the words of Laclau and Mouffe, 'we use discourse to emphasize the fact that every social configuration is *meaningful*' (1990: 100, emphasis in original). Discourse therefore may be understood as 'a specific series of representations and practices through which meanings are produced, identities constituted, social relations established and political and ethical outcomes made more or less possible' (Campbell 2009: 166). In *Archaeology of Knowledge* (1972) Foucault further developed the concept of 'discursive formations' that not only included the objects under discussion but also demarcated how these discussions were structured, who was seen as in a position to discuss these objects authoritatively, and ultimately the value that individual statements within the discussion were given. 'The types of objects in their domains were not already demarcated, but came into existence only contemporaneous with the discursive formations that made it possible to talk about them' (Rouse 2005: 96); in fact, discourses 'shape the contours of the taken-for-granted world, naturalizing and universalizing a particular subject formation and view of the world' (Campbell 2009: 167). Since, for Foucault, power and knowledge are closely interconnected in all social interactions and relations expressed through discourse, a comprehensive understanding of discourse therefore must not only capture the 'systems of thoughts composed of ideas, attitudes, courses of action, beliefs and practices that systematically construct the subjects and the worlds of which they speak' (Lessa 2006: 285) but also ought to address questions of structure and agency that form the basis of every discursive relation, formation and field together with the systems of power and knowledge by which they are constituted. Of equal importance though, as Iver Neumann reminds us, is that discourse should not be seen as distinct from practice. Neumann, in his work on narratives and practices in the field of international diplomacy (2002, 2007, 2012), admits to having grown impatient

> with what could, perhaps unkindly, be called 'armchair analysis' … text-based analysis of global politics that are not complemented by different kinds of contextual data from the field, data that may illuminate how foreign policy and global politics are experienced as lived practices.
>
> (Neumann 2002: 628)

Neumann draws a wide argumentative arc from Emile Durkheim to Marcel Mauss, to Claude Lévi-Strauss, to Michel Foucault to argue why the so-called 'linguistic turn' in IR is mistaken in all too often reducing discourse analysis to mere textual analysis. Discourse cannot and should never be understood as independent from practice. For Neumann (2012: 57),

> at any one time, discourse is the precondition for action. Discourses offer a distinct set of socially recognised actions, as well as means of recognising when they are appropriate and how they should be performed. The concept that captures actions so patterned by discourse is practice.

Thus, since 'practices are discursive, both in the sense that some practices involve speech-acts and in the sense that practices cannot be thought of "outside" of discourse' (Neumann 2012: 58), by extrapolation, if one wants to understand a given discourse, it would not make sense to study it as separate from the action that 'embodies, enacts, and reifies [that knowledge] all at once' (Adler & Pouliot 2011: 8), the very practice that is an expression of this discourse.[7] In this vein then, this study, logically, has both discourse and practice as its objects of analysis, with a focus in the theory section on how explanatory IR reifies an ethnicized discourse, and in the empirical section on how an ethnicized discourse is lived as practice by the ethno-nationalist elites in their relations with each other.

What has been said here should also make clear that to recognize identities as social constructs and discursive formations is not to say that they are not real. On the contrary, they are very real, but only insofar as they are constituted by discourse; they have no meaning prior and exogenous to discourse as this widely quoted analogy from Laclau and Mouffe (1985: 108) illustrates:

> The fact that every object is constituted as an object of discourse has nothing to do with whether there is a world external to thought ... An earthquake or the falling of a brick is an event that certainly exists, in the sense that it occurs here and now, independent of my will. But whether their specificity as objects is constructed in terms of natural phenomena or expressions of the wrath of God depends upon the structuring of a discursive field.

Much has been written on whether deconstruction can be understood as method or not.[8] Jaques Derrida (2004: 78) himself has described it as '*pas de methode*', yet as Martin McQuillan (2009: 5) reminds us,

> the word *pas* in French means both 'not' and 'step', so this ambiguous phrase can be translated as either 'not a method' or 'a methodological step'. Thus, deconstruction is simultaneously ... not a method and a step in, or towards, a methodology

If it is already a challenge to consummately capture the essence of discourse, to put deconstruction in a nutshell becomes even more toilsome, all the more since 'one might even say that cracking nutshells is what deconstruction is' (Caputo 1997: 32). Originating in the structuralist theory of linguist Ferdinand de Saussure, the notion that Western philosophy and with it most of our discursive objects are structured along a series of binary opposites in a hierarchical relationship with each other – in which 'the second term in each pair is considered the negative, corrupt, undesirable version of the first' (Johnson 1981: VIII) – such as presence/absence, inside/outside, speech/writing, identity/difference, domestic/foreign, hierarchy/anarchy, order/chaos, is the basis of Jaques Derrida's deconstructive approach (Derrida 1978, 1981a, 1981b, 1982, 1998, 2004; Edkins 1999; McQuillan 2009; Norris 2002; Hansen 2006; Fagan *et al.* 2007; Zehfuss 2009). Each element of these dichotomies is co-constitutive of the other; that is, one cannot make sense of what presence means without having an understanding of absence and vice versa. One cannot conceptualize the self of one's identity without reference to the other, from who the self is set apart. Yet, these 'binary opposites are not the way things really are but the way they are represented by Western thought and through the habitualization and sedimentation of this thought are presented as natural' (McQuillan 2009: 9). In an attempted nutshell then – if it has to be put into one – a 'deconstructive approach' for the purpose of this study means 'critically examining the discursive processes of materialization that produce settlements; such as the idea of pre-given subjects – upon which the criteria for judgement are based' (Campbell 1998a: 30), or to put into question what is presented in discourses as natural by scrutinizing the binary opposites on which this representation is based. In this study then, when analysing the strategic essentialisms of ethnic elites or the writings of explanatory IR scholars on ethnic conflict as texts within a wider discourse 'the question asked is not, "what does [the text] mean?" but "what does it presuppose?"' (Edkins 1999: 74). By *herausarbeiten* that a representation in a certain text as part of a wider discourse does not reflect natural facts but is based on ideologized presumptions, by showing that it depicts not reality but *one particular* reality, and by examining the systems of power and knowledge that constitute the wider discourse of which it is part, that text becomes deconstructed. And what explanatory IR presupposes in how it makes sense of ethnic conflict is groupness, for ethnicity to be either exogenous or the pre-eminent, determining variable in relations between and within assumed ethnic groups, and to ontologically equate those presupposed ethnic groups with states in their analyses of ethnic and ethno-nationalist conflicts.

This deconstructive approach highlights why certain key concepts – in this case groupness or state-centrism – are no longer serviceable within the paradigms in which they were originally developed, yet at the same time, somewhat paradoxically, instead of being replaced, their use is continued in their now deconstructed form (Hall 1995, 1996). 'By means of this double, stratified, dislodged and dislodging writing', in the words of Derrida (1981b: 42), 'we must also mark the interval between inversion, which brings low what was high, and the eruptive emergence of a new "concept", a concept that can no longer be and never could be, included in the previous regime'. Consequently, the aim of deconstruction is never to develop new meta-theories, models or frameworks that replace the ones that have been identified as no longer serviceable, that is 'the production of [truer] positive knowledge' (Hall 1996: 1), but, after *herausarbeiten* the social context and discourse in which they were generated, to continue operationalizing them with the caveat of the insights deconstruction has yielded with regard to their production and utilization. In other words, deconstruction should be understood as a moment of passage from one concept to another, in which, in lieu of a 'better' concept, the concept is still used 'under erasure' (Derrida 1981b) until a new one has been developed – which cannot be the task of deconstruction, since to do so would violate its very principles, that is its inherently critical attitude to any kind of meta-theory.

While committed to a constitutive epistemology and applying deconstruction as a 'step towards a methodology', and while heeding Fierke's call for a 'constitutive discourse analysis' that requires for us to '"look and see" the matrix of identities and interests and the process by which they are gradually transformed through historical interactions' (Fierke 2007: 81), this study makes no pretence of comprehensively adopting discourse analysis for its methodology.[9] To make such a claim I would have had to apply the same degree of textual analysis to the empirical case study as to the theory section. While for the theory section the objective is to show how closely aligned the narratives of ethnic conflict of explanatory IR and ethnic entrepreneurs are, for which textual analysis and discourse analysis appear appropriate, they would not fit the empirical case study, where I illustrate why a matrix of identities and interests better captures the realities of relations between Kurdish ethno-nationalist parties and to explain ethnic conflict in general than operationalizing ethnic identities as dependent or independent variables, and by doing so seek to substantiate the argument made in the theory section.

As far as the role of ethnic elites is concerned, in simplified terms, there are two ways to go about empirically deconstructing an ethnicized discourse of supposed ethnic groups in conflict. One could demonstrate that the binary opposites, the 'us' versus 'them' dichotomies that constitute this discourse are constructed by questioning the fixedness of purportedly impermeable, unalterable, and inveterate ideational boundaries and divides between groups, thus disputing at large the categorization into groups based on these boundaries and divides. This, what is often misleadingly called an 'inter-group' approach, has, for example, been masterfully deconstructed for the former Yugoslavia in the 1990s by Gagnon (2004). Alternately, one could focus on the so-called 'intra-group' dimension, the supposed coherence of, and solidarity among, an assumed group in face of an alleged common enemy. It is the latter approach that has been chosen for the empirical section of this study, which sets out to analyse the relations between the PKK and the Iraqi Kurdish ethno-nationalist parties, the KDP and the PUK, in particular in light of the sanctuary the former enjoys on the territory of the latter since the early 1980s. At each stage of their relations I show the social constructedness of Kurdish ethno-nationalist identity by *herausarbeiten* that, rather than a clear sequence of identities and interests as explanatory IR wants to make us believe, they constitute a complex, ever-shifting and non-sequential matrix of identities and interests. By illustrating the ambiguities and complexities of relations between these three parties that were more often outright antagonistic than they were showing solidarity and that do not fit the simplistic explananda of either instrumentalism or of taking 'common' ethnicity as the independent variable in analysing 'intra-group' relations, I intend not only to draw into question the portrayal of Kurdish groupness in the literature but also to challenge at large the categorization in explanatory IR texts of the Kurds as one ethnic group or nation. This segment of the case study constitutes the as-of-yet most detailed analysis of relations between KDP/PUK and the PKK available in the extant literature. It goes without saying, though, that the picture would ultimately not be complete without bringing Turkey into the equation, which is why also Turkish–Iraqi Kurdish relations are given ample room for analysis in the case study.

The case study of their relations in the wider context of the status and identity of the Kurdistan Region of Iraq was chosen for three reasons. First, the so called 'Kurdish Question' constitutes the most internationalized ethnic conflict in the Middle East, affecting four nationalizing states[10] – Turkey, Iraq, Iran and Syria – in one of the world's most strategically and economically important regions. Also, and for the purposes of this study most significantly, the PKK sanctuary in Iraqi Kurdistan is routinely referred to in the literature as a textbook example of common ethnicity determining the conflict behaviour of actors in the internationalization of an ethnic conflict, that is parties or *National Liberation Movements* (NLMs) of supposedly the same ethnic group forming a so-called 'ethnic alliance' against a 'common' enemy or, less explicitly, collaborating across borders against the 'mutual' foe with their behaviour and actions being predominantly rooted in group cohesion and solidarity. This prominence in the literature then renders it a case study ideally suited to deconstructing models that take ethnicity as the independent, if not determining variable to explain social agents' behaviour in ethnic conflicts and to empirically illustrate the theoretical flaws in this approach.

Second, the rapidly shifting fortunes of the Iraqi Kurdish NLMs from ragtag guerrilla to presiding over the so-called Kurdish de facto state, to governing the freest political entity in Kurdish history as part of federally structured Iraq, to playing the role of kingmaker in inner-Iraqi power struggles during and after the US occupation, all over the course of a mere 15 years, allows us to study the transformative processes of ethno-nationalism, the fluctuations in the ethnicized discourse and how the gaining of political status affects not only a nation's self-perception but also how these shifts in political identity alter its relations to its supposed ethnic kin during a relatively short and thus more easily observable period of time. Third, the Kurdistan Region of Iraq with its ambiguous political status and contested sovereignty provides a better study subject than so-called 'established' states to examine state sovereignty as a historical process, as socially constructed, situational and never fully completed. By the same token, with its status in permanent flux, one can also better relate to the processual interplay of identities, interests and political status that are co-constitutive of each other than in 'established' and recognized states, where these developments are often wrongly seen as having reached some form of (at least temporary) completion.

At this point readers may interject that a single case study is hardly sufficient to disprove an entire set of established theories. Bearing these limitations in mind, I understand the case study of PKK-KDP/PUK relations together with the political status cum identity of the Kurdistan Region of Iraq as an 'extroverted case study with generic concepts', an approach introduced by Richard Rose, who, referring to Toqueville's *Democracy in America* as a classic example, calls it 'the most frequent form of analysis in comparative politics' (Rose 1991: 454). The crucial point here is that such a case study 'is not explicitly comparative, but comparable' (ibid.), if it is intended and possible to come to theoretical or conceptual generalizations from the single case study that can be applied to other cases. Or in the words of Peters (1998: 62), 'the purpose of the extroverted case-study then becomes to explore fully this one case with the existing theory in mind, with the expectation of elaborating or expanding that body of theory with the resulting data'. What I set out to achieve with this study, though, is to go beyond just expanding a body of theory but, after first having applied a deconstructive reading of the theories in question, to use the extroverted case study to empirically substantiate this deconstruction of the theory in question.

Ultimately, all theory should be a function of the empirical data, though. The data for the empirical part of this study, the extroverted case study on the relations between the PKK and the Iraqi Kurdish nationalist movements from the late 1970s until the present and on the current status cum political identity of the Kurdistan Region, was assembled over the course of five years. In line with the research foci of this study, equal emphasis is given to a critical reading of the actions, declarations, motives, and writings by Kurdish ethno-nationalist elites and scholars analysing the subject alike, both employed as expressions of the ethnicized discourse studied here. This results in a limited applicability of the customary distinction between primary and secondary sources in this study, since secondary sources by scholars or journalists on Kurdish ethno-nationalism constitute primary sources for this study's purpose of critically examining the role of these scholars as co-protagonists of the ethnicized discourse and conflict under investigation. Thus, in addition to already published material, ranging from monographs to the output of research institutes and think tanks to media coverage in print, radio and film, including interviews with decision makers, the nucleus of the qualitative, empirical research are interviews conducted in the field between 2010 and 2012. In all, I have conducted approximately 40 interviews with former and active decision makers of the three Kurdish NLMs in question, scholars, and journalists across Iraqi Kurdistan, Turkey, Europe and the United States. Due to the rapidly deteriorating human rights situation and for their own safety, I decided not to disclose the identity of those journalists and NGO workers interviewed in Iraqi Kurdistan. The method employed for the selection and recruitment of the interview participants is 'snowball sampling', widely-used in:

> sociological studies into hidden populations who may be involved in sensitive issues or illegal activities ... Yet the method is also used in political science and the study of elites, where the most influential political actors are not always those whose identities are publicly known.
>
> (Tansey 2009: 492)

Originally, a representative number of 'gatekeepers' were identified, whose accessibility as well as their extensive networks and reputations in the respective organization or among the diaspora showed great promise for making inroads into often particularly occlusive and close-mouthed groups. These 'gatekeepers', after having established a requisite level of trust, suggested a number of interviewees from within the organization they represented who then, upon having been approached and interviewed, indicated a third level of possible participants, and so on (Goodman 1961). The problem with this method is that the participants themselves determine the sample and thus have a disproportional influence on the data collected, which in the worst case could lead to an unwholesome bias of the study at large. I tried to counter this tendency by including as many and, often, as diametrically opposed groups as possible, such as current KDP/PUK members versus former members who had renounced their parties, and by then collating the data from one party with the other as well as secondary sources whenever available. Where applicable, these data are enriched by personal ethnographic observations from the field research in Iraqi Kurdistan and Turkey.

As, alas, with most works in political science, this analysis too focuses primarily on elites. This fact is particularly deplorable for the studies of nationalism and ethnic conflict, where pretence dictates for any 'adequate theory of ethnic conflict [to] be able to explain both elite and mass behaviour' (Horowitz 2001: 226), yet execution routinely focuses on the former to the detriment of a thorough analysis of the latter – despite the fact that, in line with what is being said in Chapter 1, a nation or ethnic group is first of all constituted by the people's belief in it. Yet this study, although well aware of this shortcoming, cannot be the place to comprehensively make up for this deficit, and, as with additional case studies substantiating the findings made here, it remains to be hoped that future research will give a more comprehensive account of all strata of Kurdish society in the present ethnicized discourse in Iraq and Turkey.

Chapter outline

The book is divided into three parts, of which the first (Chapters 1 to 3) is a theoretical analysis of how explanatory IR conceptualizes ethnic conflict, the motives behind its reifying, state-centric and essentializing representation of ethnic identity, ethnic conflict and sovereignty, together with an introduction into alternative modes of representation from critical theory and post-structuralist approaches. The second part (Chapters 4 and 5) is mostly descriptive, while in the third, empirical section (Chapters 6 to 10) the themes examined in Part I are again taken up and put in the context of the empirical case study.

Chapter 1, drawing on the classics from sociology and anthropology, such as Max Weber and Frederick Barth, but also contemporary theories such as Craig Calhoun's conceptualization of the nation as a discursive formation, gives a definition of what is meant in this study by ethnicity and nation, highlights differences between essentialism/primordialism and modernism, delineates ethnic elites' strategic essentialisms and characterizes in greater detail the concept of groupism in order to then demonstrate how it manifests itself in the approaches to ethnic conflict of neo-realism, neo-liberalism, and systemic constructivism. This problematization of these paradigms' inherent essentialism is augmented in Chapter 2 by a comprehensive overview of the concepts, models, and frameworks that the three paradigms employ in analysing and explaining ethnic and ethno-nationalist conflict together with the latter's supposed objective of acquiring and maintaining statehood by critically examining and double-reading explanatory frameworks, such as the 'ethnic security dilemma', the 'ethnic alliance model', and instrumentalism as well as the concept at the core of explanatory IR, state-centrism. Chapter 3 summarizes the effects of groupism, and drawing on the writings of Robert Cox, Michel Foucault, Jaques Derrida and Pierre Bourdieu hypothesizes on the motives behind it, and ultimately tries to suggest an alternative reading of ethnic identity as a fluid matrix of identities and interests, introducing the theoretical lens under which the case study will be examined.

The second part commences with critical reflections on the origins, nature, and inherent tendencies to 'pathological homogenisation' (Rae 2002) of the two nationalizing states in question in this study, Turkey and Iraq, and juxtaposes their nationalist discourses with each other as well as with the evolution of Kurdish ethno-nationalism in both countries up to the 1970s. This admittedly cursory review of the nationalist state discourses and of those supposedly pitted against them in pursuit of national self-determination allows us to re-examine the modernist definitions of ethnic and ethno-nationalist conflict given in Chapter 1 and to dispel some common myths about Kurdish ethno-nationalism that are routinely employed by the nationalizing states as well as some scholars directly or indirectly legitimizing these misconceptions and prejudices. Chapter 6 is then dedicated to an introduction of the main social agents discussed in this study, the most prominent Kurdish ethno-nationalist parties in Iraq and Turkey, the KDP, PUK and PKK.

Part III constitutes the main body of the extroverted case study on the relations between the PKK and KDP/PUK and the status as well as identity of the Kurdistan Region of Iraq, with Chapter 6 focusing on the origins of relations between the three Kurdish ethno-nationalist parties up to the *Anfal* campaign during the Iran–Iraq War. Here, it already becomes apparent that the strict hierarchical causality of identity and interests that explanatory IR purports in the study of the behaviour and actions of parties in ethnic conflicts is not tenable, and that the relations between the three parties are better conceived of as a complex matrix of identities and interests without a hierarchical sequence or the one generating the other. The workings and dynamics of this matrix are further illustrated in Chapter 7, which discusses their relations during the 1990s, with the birth hour of the so-called Kurdish de facto state in Iraq and the Kurdish civil war as the most prominent themes under investigation. Chapter 8 critically examines US-imposed nation- cum state-building in Iraq after the 2003 invasion and during the occupation, how Iraqi Kurdistan came to benefit from a state-centric reading of Iraq's post-Saddam political landscape, and the influence of explanatory IR scholars' essentialist representations on this process, culminating in the principle of regional federalism – a mere euphemism for ethnic partition while keeping the territorial integrity of Iraq intact. A second strand of inquiry is dedicated to a discussion of the sea change in the nationalist discourse of the PKK after the capture of Abdullah Öcalan. Chapter 9 shifts focus to problematizing the origins of the rapprochement between the *Kurdistan Regional Government* (KRG) and the *Justice and Development Party* (AKP, *Adalet ve Kalkınma Partisi*) government in Turkey after the US invasion of Iraq, and to how the emerging strategic alliance between the KRG and Turkey affected relations between the PKK and the Iraqi Kurdish ethno-nationalist parties. With Chapter 10, we reach the present and the role of Iraqi Kurdistan and, indirectly, the PKK, via its regional affiliate, the *Democratic Union Party* (PYD, *Partiya Yekita ya Demokratik*), as key allies in the international coalition's war against the Islamist insurgency of the Islamic State of Iraq and al-Sham (ISIS, *ad-Dawlah al-Islāmiyah fī'l-'Irāq wa-sh-Shām*). The implosion of both states as a result of the ISIS assault on Mosul and central Iraq, together with the civil war in neighbouring Syria, propels us to revisit and re-evaluate the political status of the Kurdistan Region of Iraq, the discourses on national self-determination there as well as their representation in international scholarship and the media, to critically examine the struggle for autonomy within the wider doctrine of democratic confederalism of the PYD in Syria, and how these discourses and resulting practices have been affected by Turkey.

The book concludes with deliberations on what this study's portrayal of the Kurdistan Region's status and identity can tell us about ethnicity, nationhood and sovereign statehood as socio-political constructs and discursive formations at large, about the nature of ethno-nationalist conflict in general, and recapitulates the major findings of the deconstruction of explanatory IR's groupist, essentialist and state-centric representation of ethnic groups and nations, now enhanced by the insights gained from the empirical case study. It closes with the hope that the contribution to the discussion of these subjects made here will trigger a rethink in our discipline of its epistemologies, ontologies and methodologies, ideally leading to us categorizers and analysts, while always remaining co-protagonists of the social world we describe, at least refraining from exacerbating its deepest divisions and most violent expressions.

A study this wide in scope and ambition with such complex themes as ethnic identity and conflict and state sovereignty, together with a wide host of sub-themes, will, by its very nature, always remain incomplete. Some of the sub-themes, while of evident relevance, are touched upon here only cursorily, and references are made to the extensive array of contributions in the literature on topics such as, for example, the nuances of the post-structuralist body of thought in relation to social identities, the legal aspects of national self-determination, strategies and tools of state-building, or on the complexities of the socio-political composition of Iraq beyond the Kurdistan Region. These limitations, like the restriction to a single significant case study, were necessary in order to remain focused on the core arguments of the inquiry, yet, in the spirit of the study as a whole, should be understood as possible points of departure for future research.

Notes

1 He further expands his thoughts on this epistemological division in his reply to Alexander Wendt's (1999) *Social Theory of International Politics*, in Smith (2000).
2 Another example for a distinct IR approach to a primer on ethnic conflict would be Taras and Ganguly (2006). In this instance, one of the authors, Rajat Ganguly, professes to an openly primordialist understanding of ethnicity and nationalism (Ganguly 1998).
3 Some of the arguments here, in particular pertaining to neo-realism and neo-liberalism, can already be found in Cederman (1997); as I will demonstrate, though, Cederman's constructivism itself features some of the shortcomings and fallacies he criticizes in neo-realist and neo-liberal approaches to nationalism, ethnicity and ethno-nationalist conflict.

4 The ethnic alliance model in particular has already been deconstructed in Černy (2014a).
5 Calhoun (1992) quoted in Cederman (1997: 21).
6 For a detailed overview on the various state-centric versus non state-centric debates in IR see, for example, Hobson (2000).
7 See also Pouliot (2008).
8 For a consummate analysis of this debate, see Hansen (2006).
9 On Critical Discourse Analysis (CDA), see van Dijk (1993, 2008), Fairclough (2001a, 2001b, 2003, 2010), Fairclough and Wodak (1997), Fairclough and Fairclough (2012), Chouliaraki and Fairclough (1999), Wodak (2001), Locke (2004), Blommaert (2005), Simpson and Mayr (2010), Egan-Sjölander and Gunnarsson-Payne (2011). For excellent applications of CDA in the context of ethnic conflict, see Campbell (1998a) and Hansen (2006).
10 Echoing Hutchinson (2004), here, rather than 'nation state', I use the term 'nationalizing state', not only to indicate that the four states in the context of this article – Turkey, Iraq, Iran, and Syria – are home to more than one nation, but also to allude to the often brutal process of assimilation during their ongoing state formation.

Part I

—

1 Explaining ethnic and ethno-nationalist conflict

Ethnic groups and nations

Since the Gulf War of 1991 sparked global interest in their fate of the Kurds, most writers, both scholarly and popular, have denoted the Kurds as the world's largest ethnic group without a state and the world's largest stateless nation.[1] This designation seems to rest on two presumptions: first, that Kurds from the four parts of what is subjectively or colloquially called Kurdistan are one organic, substantive, distinct, homogeneous, bounded group, identifying themselves and perceived as a social unit. Second, it suggests – how implicit or legitimate, whether active or symbolic is debatable – a claim to statehood. Within academia, such normative presumptions are erroneously thought to be the preserve of scholars of an essentialist or primordialist view on ethnic groups and nations, which is claimed to be largely démodé and obsolete today (Özkirimli 2010). Primordialists hold 'that nations [are] around "from the first time" and [are] inherent in the human condition, if not in nature itself ... Nations [are] seen as forms of extended kinship and as such [are] ubiquitous and coeval with the family' (Smith 2009: 8). In the Kurdish case this can be illustrated by one scholar contending that the thousand year span from the fifth century BC until the sixth century AD, 'marks the homogenisation and consolidation of the modern Kurdish national identity, [t]he ethnic designator *Kurd* is established finally, and applied to all segments of the nation' (Izady 1992: 34, emphasis in original). Given such extravagant claims unaffected by historical facts, it is hardly surprising that Anthony Smith comes to the conclusion, 'primordialism has either a flawed theory or none, and little or no history, being reductionist or largely speculative and ahistorical' (Smith 2004: 61). And yet, despite its obvious ontological flaws, primordialism, contrary to some claims (Brubaker 1996; Wimmer 2008; Özkirimli 2010), has not altogether fallen out of favour in the social sciences. On the contrary, primordialism or, what it is often referred to in contemporary parlance as essentialism (Varshney 2002), still enjoys considerable popularity in the social sciences, in particular in the discipline of IR. In addition to the socio-biologist approach (van den Berghe 1978, 1981, 1999), one of the key texts on ethno-nationalism (Connor 1993),[2] and, with some restrictions, today's most widely referenced work on ethnic conflict, Donald Horowitz'

Ethnic Groups in Conflict (2001), either directly advocates or can be associated with an essentialist understanding of ethnicity and nation. Here, ethnic groups are viewed as organic, static, substantive, distinct, homogeneous and bounded units whose objective characteristics or identity markers that simultaneously define them and set them apart from other groups are observable and, to a certain extent, empirically measurable. Consequently, an essentialist definition of ethnicity 'embraces groups differentiated by colour, language, and religion; it covers "tribes", "races", "nationalities", and "castes"', and membership within these groups 'is typically not chosen but given' (Horowitz 2001: 95, 96). This notion of kinship 'makes it possible for ethnic groups to think in terms of family resemblances' (Horowitz 2001: 57), and the cohesion of such a group is usually measured through the variable of inner-group solidarity among its members. In addition to its prominence among a wide range of scholars, primordialist/essentialist portrayals of ethno-nationalist conflict dominate the popular and political discourse in the media and among policy makers, and, naturally and most significantly, are the preserve of nationalist elites:

> For the nationalists, nationality is an inherent attribute of the human condition…. They believe that humanity is divided into distinct, objectively identifiable nations. Human beings can only fulfil themselves and flourish if they belong to a national community, the membership of which overrides all other forms of belonging. The nation is the sole depository of sovereignty and the only source of political power and legitimacy. This comes with a host of temporal and spatial claims – to a unique history and destiny, and a historic homeland.
>
> (Özkirimli 2010: 51)

In the Kurdish case, such essentialist claims by nationalist elites to the unity, cohesion and destiny of the nation, irrespective of the divisions that modern nationalizing states have imposed on its members, are illustrated by, for example, the prominent Kurdish politician and human rights activist Leyla Zana (2009) claiming the Kurdish nation to be represented by three leaders: Abdullah Öcalan, Massoud Barzani and Jalal Talabani. This triumvirate of nationalist leaders is declared to control the fates of all Kurds, whether they hail from Turkey, Iraq, Iran, Syria or the diaspora. Those leaders are averred to authoritatively speak on behalf of all Kurds, as, for example, when Masrour Barzani, groomed to one day succeed his father Massoud as President of the Kurdistan Region of Iraq, recently declared:

> If I tell you that you can find a Kurd that doesn't have a dream of having his own state, I think I wouldn't be telling you the truth. And I think the Kurds deserve to have their own independent state, like any other nation.[3]

Yet, contrary to what we are told in the literature, where in the social sciences we are made to believe that 'we are all', to a greater or lesser extent, 'constructivists now' (Brubaker 2009: 28), primordialist/essentialist understandings of ethnicity, and consequently ethnic and ethno-nationalist conflict, not only survive in the public and political but also in the scholarly discourse. This persistence of essentialism in the study of ethno-nationalist conflict, I argue, can to no small degree, be ascribed to the dominance of explanatory IR in explaining issues of war and peace in the international domain and to its pre-eminence in informing policies in response to ethno-nationalist conflicts. To trace and deconstruct these narratives of ethno-nationalist conflict in explanatory IR is the prime objective of this study.

For presumptions about the unity, social cohesion, solidarity, and ultimately destiny of a nation are not limited to a primordialist view of ethnicity. As will be shown, they also feature prominently in the paradigm that is imputed to be the diametrical opposite of primordialism/essentialism: modernism. Modernism as applied to these questions can be understood as a very loose umbrella term for a variety of quite diverse perspectives on ethnicity and nationalism (Nairn 1981; Brass 1985, 1991; Giddens 1985; Hobsbawm 1990; Breuilly 1993; Mann 1993; Kedourie 1994; Hechter 1998, 2001; Anderson 2006; Gellner 2006), many of which will be discussed in turn. Suffice it to say here, even at the risk of gross simplification, that for modernism 'nationalism, in short, is a product of *modernity* … and so [are] nations, national states, national identities, and the whole "inter-national" community' (Smith 2004: 46–47, emphasis in original). Individual scholars' perspectives may differ on nuances, on whether nationalism can be understood as a reaction to the uneven development and class divisions that accompany the novel form of production that is industrial capitalism; whether nationalism is an expression of an increasingly liberal, literate and educated bourgeoisie that oppose the *ancien régime* of absolutist monarchies, which then makes it inseparably interlinked to the idea of the modern, sovereign and inevitably democratic state based on a constitutional order rather than royal prerogative; whether it can be traced to the Kantian principle of self-determination within the larger context of the European Enlightenment propagating individual and societal freedoms; or whether nations are a product of social engineering of modern elites in an attempt to homogenize and control the masses, but what they all share is 'a belief in the inherently national, and nationalist nature of modernity … in this view, modernity necessarily took the form of nations and just as inevitably produced nationalist ideologies and movements' (Smith 2004: 47–49). The modern era is therefore inseparably linked to the new ideology of nationalism, to this new form of humans organizing themselves in communities and polities grounded in a new kind of collective identity, and thereby creating a new global order.

The final point made here is of particular importance in the context of how explanatory IR explains identity and state formation: the concomitance, almost equation of the modern, sovereign state with the nation, where one is contingent on the other in an almost symbiotic relationship. This view is distinctly expressed in the definition of nationalism of Ernest Gellner, who famously declared, 'nationalism is primarily a political principle, which holds that the political and the national unit should be congruent' (Gellner 2006: 1). It is even more explicit in the works of Anthony Giddens (1985), Michael Mann (1993), and John Breuilly, where the latter stipulated that nationalisms are 'political movements seeking or exercising state power and justifying such action with nationalist arguments' (Breuilly 2001: 32). For him the principal of these nationalist arguments, that 'the nation must be as independent as possible, [t]his usually requires at least the attainment of political sovereignty' (Breuilly 1993: 2), is the defining criterion for a nation.[4] Perhaps most explicit in his state-centrism is Anthony Giddens, when contending,

> by a 'nation' I refer to a collectivity existing within a clearly demarcated territory, which is subject to a unitary administration, reflexively monitored by both the internal state apparatus and those of other states ... A 'nation', as I use the term here, only exists when a state has a unified administrative reach over the territory over which its sovereignty is claimed.
>
> (Giddens 1985: 116)

In the Kurdish case then, the Kurds failure to achieve statehood is seen as a result of their not having progressed far enough on the rocky but supposedly redeeming path of modernity. Authors such as Hussein Tahiri (2007) who repeatedly stigmatizes Kurdish society as 'too backward' and 'not ready yet' to constitute a nation, and Ali Kemal Özcan who identifies ' "treason" as an inseparable element of the Kurdish ethnic personality' (Özcan 2006: 5), decry the tribalist segmentarization of Kurdish society and their political leaders' petty particularisms that have led to *birakuji*, the interminable series of 'fratricidal' wars in which Kurdish NLMs are often reduced to proxies of external powers, as the root causes for the Kurdish failure to achieve statehood. These scholars, mostly, although not exclusively, Kurdish graduates of Western universities and thus, often part of the diasporic discourse, appear to vent their personal frustrations when they suggest that if only the Kurdish leaders adopt a more universalist outlook and the Kurdish people feel and act more in pan-Kurdish solidarity, they may eventually be rewarded with the ultimate prize modernity has to offer: statehood. Such normative determinism not only carries forward the Orientalism of which Western authors are usually accused,[5] denying the Kurdish parties autonomous agency and condemning them to perpetual victimhood – victims of the tribalist structure they are too 'backward' to overcome, or pawns of external exploitations and machinations (Tahiri 2007); in the majority of cases analysed, they are claimed to be a combination of both. What is more, the nation's sole destiny, one may even say its purpose, is reduced to acquiring and maintaining sovereign statehood. If it fails in this defining objective it is either because of external factors, such as when the forces opposing national self-determination prove overwhelming, or because it is deemed not sufficiently modern; that is, it consequentially does not merit the designation as a nation.

It seems then as if the major difference between primordialism and modernism lies in the question, 'when is a nation?', and related to that but to a lesser degree, 'what is a nation?', but that on the question 'what is a nation's raison d'être?', in our present state-centric world, both major paradigms are in accordance: the quest for sovereign statehood defines the nation in our times. This congruence between primordialism and modernism in what the nation ultimately means cannot be emphasized strongly enough; it will form the basis for this study's critical reading of how explanatory IR explains ethno-nationalist conflict as implicitly a conflict about national self-determination, about an ethnically defined nation acquiring sovereign statehood. Before developing this thought further though, one needs to turn to the other, related sociological concept that forms the theoretical basis of the ethnically defined nation in ethno-nationalist conflicts: the ethnic group.

With a concept as complex as ethnicity that has preoccupied the social sciences for at least the better part of the past century and in order to provide a solid theoretical foundation for the subsequent critical reading of how explanatory IR explains ethnic and ethno-nationalist conflict, it seems prudent to start with the origins of the concept, to return to the classic theorists who first discussed it. One of the founding fathers of modern sociology, Max Weber, famously defined ethnic groups as:

> those human groups that entertain a subjective belief in their common descent because of similarities of physical type or of customs or both, or because of memories of colonisation and migration; conversely, it does not matter whether or not an objective blood relationship exists.
>
> (Weber 1978 [1922]: 389)

This definition is an unambiguous rejection of primordialism/essentialism that understands ethnic groups and nations as actual forms of extended kinship, as Weber explicitly states further on when clarifying that 'it differs from the kinship group precisely by being a presumed identity' (Weber 1978 [1922]: 389). What constitutes the ethnic group then in the truest sense of the word is the *belief* in common descent by the group, and without such belief there can be no ethnic group. Like an ideology,[6] the group identity is sustained by this shared belief system, a belief in common ancestry and kinship bonds that is constantly reinforced, renegotiated and reconfirmed by collective memories, narratives, symbols, and importantly also political action.[7] For, Weber continues, 'ethnic membership does not constitute a group; it only facilitates group formation of any kind, particularly in the political sphere … it is primarily the political community, no matter how artificially organised, that inspires the belief in common ethnicity' (Weber 1978 [1922]: 389). Weber seems to suggest here

> that the belief in common ancestry is likely to be a *consequence* of collective political action rather than its *cause*; people come to see themselves as *belonging* together … as a consequence of *acting* together. Collective interests thus do not simply reflect or follow from perceived similarities and differences between people; the active pursuit of collective interests does, however, encourage ethnic identification.
>
> (Jenkins 2008a: 10, emphasis in original)

This debate about causes and consequences will be revisited when discussing the major differences between the main paradigms of explanatory IR and how they conceptualize identity and the social group.

Since political action does not occur in a social vacuum, this emphasis on collective political action, directed inward and outward, as a defining criterion for an ethnic group leads to the second classic theoretical contribution to understanding ethnicity. In one of the key texts of modern anthropology Frederick Barth observes,

> the critical focus of investigation from this point of view becomes the ethnic boundary that defines the group, not the cultural stuff it encloses ... If a group maintains its identity when members interact with others, this entails criteria for determining membership and ways of signalling membership and exclusion.
>
> (Barth 1998 [1969]: 15)

Siniša Malešević highlights the importance and novelty of Barth's approach:

> Before Barth, cultural difference was traditionally explained from the inside out – social groups possess different cultural characteristics which make them unique and distinct ... Culture was perceived as something relatively or firmly stable, persistent and exact. Cultural difference was understood in terms of a group's property ... Barth turned the traditional understanding of cultural difference on its head. He defined and explained ethnicity from the outside in: it is not the 'possession' of cultural characteristics that makes social groups distinct but rather it is the social interaction with other groups that makes that difference possible, visible, and socially meaningful.
>
> (Malešević 2004: 2–3)[8]

Barth thus directs attention away from what he calls 'cultural stuff' as constitutive of an ethnic group to – drawing on Weber's collective political action – the group setting itself apart from others through interaction with them, through interactive processes of differentiation that not only give meaning to the others but also to the group itself. 'Cultural difference per se does not create ethnic collectives: it is the social contact with others that leads to definition and categorization of an "us" and a "them"' (Malešević 2004: 3). Thus, ethnic groups are 'in a sense *created* through that very contact [with other groups]. Group identities must always be defined in relation to that which they are not – in other words to non-members of the group' (Eriksen 2002: 10, emphasis in original). In this vein, ethnic identity is contextual and circumstantial. What is more constitutive for the process of ethnic identification is not the social and cultural features of a perceived group but external influences (Nagata 1981). They determine whether a certain form of identity matters, that is becomes activated, or remains dormant. These questions of identity formation will be further elaborated throughout this first part of the study, but for the moment, in order to analyse how explanatory IR operationalizes these concepts, one may summarize these classic definitions of ethnicity as follows: when taking the ethnic group as the unit of analysis in explanations of ethnic and ethno-nationalist conflict, what scholars are supposedly studying are actually belief systems constituted through inter-ethnic processes of differentiation with others. In this instance the classic texts on ethnicity resonate in Benedict Anderson's conceptualization of the nation as an 'imagined community'. For Anderson, the nation is

> *imagined* because [its] members will never know most of their fellow-members ... yet in the minds of each lives the image of their communion ...; it is *limited* because even the largest ... has finite, if elastic, boundaries beyond which lie other nations ...; it is imagined as *sovereign* because the concept was born in an age [of] Enlightenment and Revolution ... nations dream of being free, and ... directly so. The gage and emblem of this freedom is the sovereign state; finally, it is imagined as a *community*, because, regardless of the actual inequality and exploitation that may prevail in each, the nation is always conceived as a deep, horizontal comradeship.
>
> (Anderson 2006: 6–7, emphasis in original)

Thus, ethnic group and the nation are two quite closely related social concepts, since, as has been detailed, both ethnic group and nation are social groups defined by a shared belief system or ideology and political action directed inward as well as outward. However, from a modernist perspective they fundamentally differ in the nature of that political action. As Steve Fenton puts it, ' "ethnie" shares much with "nation" but lacks the sense of self governing entity; if an ethnic group (ethnie) wishes to rule itself it needs to start calling itself a *nation*' (Fenton 2010: 52, emphasis in original). A similar distinction is made by Barrington (1997: 712) who states, 'a nation is more than an ethnic group, differing from such a group because of a nation's belief in its right to territorial control'. The two main paradigms, primordialism/essentialism and modernism, but the latter in particular, in our contemporary world considers the desire for self-government, for national self-determination, as constitutive of a nation; and in the state centric system of modernity, it is argued, such self-government can only ultimately mean sovereign statehood. The distinguishing criterion of the aims of conflict, central to the subsequent reading of how IR explains ethnic and ethno-nationalist conflict, is summed up aptly by Varshney (2003: 86), 'ethnic groups ... can live without a state of their own, making do with some cultural rights (e.g. use of mother tongue in schools) or affirmative action, but the nation means bringing ethnicity and statehood together'. From a modernist perspective then, an ethno-nationalist conflict can therefore be understood as a violent conflict between two (or more) ethnically defined nations about acquiring sovereign statehood; an ethnic conflict, on the other hand, is a political conflict turned violent between two ethnic groups about a certain issue, usually political status, that does not necessarily feature acquiring statehood as the objective of one party. According to this reading of ethnic and nationalist identities, the two categories are not the same, and they should not be used interchangeably.

And yet, although on the whole embracing a modernist understanding of nationalism, explanatory IR habitually uses the concepts of ethnic and ethno-nationalist conflict interchangeably. This is evident in the Kurdish case when, for example (and in addition to other studies discussed below), Nader Entessar (1992) entitles his standard work on Kurdish nationalist movements in Turkey, Iraq, Iran and Syria, *Kurdish Ethnonationalism*. As will be detailed in Part II, though, until the mid-2000s, of all Kurdish nationalist movements throughout history and in all four respective countries, only one party, the PKK, pursued a strictly ethno-nationalist – that is, an irredentist and secessionist – agenda with the declared objective of creating an independent Kurdish state; all other so-called ethno-nationalist movements sought an accommodation on cultural and political rights with the respective central government and within the existing state structure. From a strictly modernist perspective then, these NLMs should not be categorized as ethno-nationalist since their objective was not 'to bring ethnicity and statehood together' (Varshney 2003: 86); sovereign, that is exclusive, territorial control, was not part of their political programme. By the same token, should Kurds in Turkey be categorized as a nation just because of the PKK's secessionist agenda, at the expense of taking into account all the other Kurdish movements, parties and organizations that did not advocate secession? Would that not concede to the PKK an undue prerogative of representation, would it not, as it happens all too often, admit preponderance in the discourse to the loudest, most radical voice? And finally, once the PKK abandoned its secessionist claims in the early 1990s and since then has sought political accommodation of their demands for national self-determination *within* and in negotiations with the Turkish state, did Kurds in Turkey cease to be a nation and revert to the category of ethnic group by reason of the PKK leadership adapting their demands to what was politically achievable? Just this brief example from the case study reveals the ontological flaws, and in fact practical infeasibility, of a clear-cut distinction between ethnic group and nation as propagated in modernism and then taken up by explanatory IR for the purpose of categorization.

Such questionable categories and inaccuracies of definition mean explanatory IR's categorizations of ethnic and ethno-nationalist conflict appear more grounded in ideologically based presumptions and normative value judgements than in clearly designated criteria; some ethnic groups, often based on their geostrategic importance, are termed a nation, while others are not, long before their empowered incumbents have even voiced the desire to become one. Yet by doing so, by letting their presumptions about their object of analysis guide their categorization, by anticipating ethnic elites' future demands, these scholars of explanatory IR not only reify those demands, they may actually even write them into existence and thus become co-protagonists of the ethnic conflict they set out to study.

Having highlighted this ontological flaw in explanatory IR's categorization of ethnic and ethno-nationalist conflict, whose far-reaching consequences will be detailed in depth below, I would argue, though, that the exacting modernist distinction between ethnic group and nation is analytically untenable in any event. In most cases it would be exceedingly difficult, if not impossible, to precisely determine the moment when demands for statehood are made for the first time – a watershed that, in my opinion, can often only be identified ex post – and whether the actor making these demands could claim to speak on behalf of the entire community; that is, when an ethnic group becomes a nation or an ethnic conflict turns ethno-nationalist. If, on the other hand, instead of such rigid parameters, ethnic identity and nationhood are understood as socio-political constructs and therefore by their very nature as dynamic, fluctuant, contextual, as 'points of temporary attachment to the subject positions which discursive practices construct for us' (Hall 1996: 6), that are 'never a final or settled matter' (Jenkins 2008b: 5), are 'decentred, fragmented by contradictory discourses and by the pull of other identities' (Rattansi 1999: 84), there would be no need for such artificial and, as suggested, highly normative settings of debatable benchmarks. Ethno-nationalist demands for statehood or demands for cultural and political rights based on an ethnic definition of the community would both be understood as expressions of an overall ethnicized discourse, a dynamic discourse that is accentuated or attenuated according to context, that can wax and wane between maximalist and moderate positions, that changes back and forth with circumstance; a discourse that, contrary to the rigid but inconsistently applied distinction used in explanatory IR, can ultimately be understood to be ethnic as well as ethno-nationalist precisely because these terms do not denote invariant points on a linear trajectory from ethnic group to nation, to statehood – as the modernist paradigm would want it to be – but intermittent moments of a forever dynamic and never completed discourse. For this reason, in explicit refutation of the normative equation of ethnic group with nation and à la longue with the state common in explanatory IR discourses, this study has deliberately adopted the term ethnic/ethno-nationalist conflict with the caveat of emphasizing its discursive, instead of clearly demarcated and linearly progressing, nature. In doing so it adheres to what has been said in the Introduction, that the goal of a deconstructive approach is not to invent a novel terminology or new concepts but to continue using those discussed in their now deconstructed form.

In this vein, nationhood and ethnicity in this study are understood as more than forms of identity or ideologies but, drawing on Craig Calhoun (1997), more precisely as discursive formations. Originating in Michel Foucault's *Archaeology of Knowledge* (1972), discursive formations, simply put, are the ways in which a set of speech acts, texts, statements, or a rhetoric are organized with respect to their relation to each other. As such, discursive formations, aside from their material existence, first and foremost have ideational, and behavioural qualities. The fact that they are organized in a particular way and not in an alternative fashion must be based on a certain logic, a distinct way of thinking, a particular set of values or norms; adhering to this logic, values and norms in themselves constitute a social practice but also condition subsequent social behaviour guided by the organizing principle of these speech acts, texts or rhetoric, since their consumers, in turn, can 'manipulate, use, transform, exchange, combine, decompose, and recompose, and possibly destroy' the texts as well as the principle in which they are organized (Foucault 1972: 105). Foucault focused his analysis on these, what he called 'regularities of dispersion', since to understand the logic or way of thinking that constitutes a certain discourse, i.e. the unifying principle bringing the various elements of discourse together, is key to understanding the discourse itself.

> We must ... question those divisions or groupings with which we have become so familiar ... These divisions – whether our own, or those contemporary with the discourse under discussion – are always themselves reflexive categories, principles of classification, normative rules, institutionalized types; they, in turn, are facts of discourse that deserve to be analyzed beside others.
>
> (Foucault 1972: 22)

While the meta-theorist Foucault rejected reference to the same object, common style, constancy of concepts, and reference to a common theme as unifying principles of a discursive formation and concentrated on the regularities of dispersion (Laclau & Mouffe 2001), our concern here, following Michel Pecheux, is precisely with the ideological dimension of discursive formations. Pecheux (1982: 111) elaborates, 'words, expressions, propositions, etc. change their meanings according to the positions held by those who use them, which signifies that they find their meaning by reference to the ideological formations in which those positions are inscribed'. He proceeds to define a discursive formation as 'that which in a given ideological formation, i.e. from a given position in a given conjuncture ... determines *what and should be said*' (Pecheux 1982: 111, emphasis in original). From that follows, according to Pecheux, that 'every discursive formation, by the transparency of the meaning constituted in it, conceals its dependence on the complex whole in dominance of discursive formations, itself imbricated with the complex of ideological formations' (Pecheux 1982: 113). If every discursive formation is 'imbricated' in an ideological formation, both are made more tangible in the sense that we can study one by way of the other through their mutually constitutive dialectic and relationship, which, translated to the subject of analysis here, means the rhetoric of nationalism or ethnicity as both an expression and constitutive element of the ideology of nationalism or ethnicity.

Concerned by the tendencies towards reification and essentialization of nations in the social sciences and adapting Foucault, Calhoun identifies the discursive formation that is the nation as 'a way of speaking that shapes our consciousness, but also is problematic enough that it keeps generating more issues and questions, keeps propelling us into further talk, keeps producing debates over how to think about it' (Calhoun 1997: 3). He then proceeds to itemize ten features common to the rhetoric of nation that set this specific form of social identification, as a nation, apart from others. He prominently lists 'boundaries, of territory, population, or both' and 'sovereignty, or at least the aspiration to sovereignty, and thus formal equality with other nations, usually as an autonomous and putative self-sufficient state' (Calhoun 1997: 4–5) among these criteria. However, in stark and deliberate contrast to John Breuilly, Anthony Giddens or Ernest Gellner, for whom the aspiration of the nation to territory and sovereignty is factual and the single most important defining criterion, Calhoun immediately stresses that 'these are features of the rhetoric of nation, claims that are commonly made in describing nations', and emphasizes that 'nations cannot be defined by empirical measures of whether they are actually able to achieve sovereignty' (Calhoun 1997: 5). He explicitly refutes Gellner by stating, 'to limit nationalism simply to a political doctrine – or, in Gellner's pithy summary, "a political principle which holds that the political and the national unit should be congruent" – is to narrow our understanding of it too much' (Calhoun 1997: 11). Referring to Anderson, Calhoun elaborates on what is meant by 'imagined as sovereign', namely a particular 'way of constructing identity [by] posit[ing] temporal depth and internal integration' as well as upholding an 'ethical imperative [such as that] national boundaries *ought* to coincide with state boundaries' (Calhoun 1997: 11, 6, emphasis in original). The emphasis here is rightly on 'ought', since territory and sovereignty are one way of talking, thinking and conceiving of the nation, a process of imagination that need not be based on empirically measurable fact nor necessarily be the preeminent way of devising the nation.

> Nations are constituted by the claims themselves, by the way of talking and thinking and acting that relies on these sorts of claims to produce collective identity, to mobilize people for collective projects, and to evaluate peoples and practices. There is no perfect list; we are identifying a common pattern, not a precise definition of nation. The points listed can help us to develop an "ideal type", but this is an aid to conceptualization, not an operational definition or an empirically testable description.
>
> (Calhoun 1997: 5)

Calhoun then provides several examples of nations that are perfectly content or have come to terms with not aspiring towards statehood or seeking unequivocal control of a clearly defined territory – in fact to do so would be anathema to their understanding of themselves as nations. With this line of argument, Calhoun not only convincingly challenges the supposedly clear-cut distinction between nation and ethnic group but rejects altogether the ontological basis for explanatory IR's analytical equation of nation and state.[9]

A key question that remains after these introductory deliberations is why, when the above-discussed classic texts of sociology and anthropology, and their contemporary derivates offer so clearly a rejection to essentialist understandings of ethnicity and nationhood, they feature so prominently in common-sense views as well as political and scholarly discourses on ethnic/ethno-nationalist conflict, in particular in the discipline of IR?

Groupism

This question, fundamental to how ethnic conflict is understood and explained in IR, can be rephrased to make the inherent problem that scholars are struggling with more explicit: since the basis of these social groups, ethnic group or nation, is a belief system, a form of identity or an ideology, to what extent can the groups then be treated as real, as substantial, and ultimately as actors in ethnic conflicts? This question has been problematized extensively over the past decade by Rogers Brubaker who uses the term 'groupism' to describe the tendency in the social sciences to treat social groups as real and substantial. Since the groupist challenge to how explanatory IR explains ethnic and ethno-nationalist conflict informs one of the major points of critique of this study, Brubaker's considerations will be given sufficiently large room here to subsequently raise some important caveats to his argument. By groupism he means:

> [T]he tendency to take discrete, bounded groups as basic constituents of social life, chief protagonists of social conflicts, and fundamental units of social analysis ... to treat ethnic groups, nations, and races as substantial entities to which interests and agency can be attributed ... to reify such groups, speaking of Serbs, Croats, Muslims, Albanians in the former Yugoslavia, of Catholics and Protestants in Northern Ireland, of Jews and Palestinians in Israel and the occupied territories, of Turks and Kurds in Turkey, or of Blacks, Whites, Asians, Hispanics and Native Americans in the United States as if they were internally homogeneous, externally bounded groups, even unitary collective actors with common purpose.
>
> (Brubaker 2004: 8)

But of course we do this, one may interject here, since we have just established that the common purpose of acquiring sovereign statehood defines a nation, as do cultural markers such as language, religion, myths, symbols and narratives that are established as constructed boundaries in interaction with others who define the ethnic group. But since belief systems are never universally held, what then of those members of the group who do not share these markers, who do not believe in this common purpose of acquiring sovereign statehood; are they then by definition not members of the group or nation? What, for example, of those Kurds who do not feel that Abdullah Öcalan, Massoud Barzani and Jalal Talabani can speak with authority on their behalf, and what about Abdullah Öcalan, the leader of the biggest Kurdish guerrilla movement, who himself until late in his life only spoke a very broken Kurdish? Are they by definition then not Kurds, because they do not share these cultural markers or beliefs? In his critique of groupism, Brubaker then not only highlights the fact that identities in the real social world are never as clear cut as some theories would have them to be – that in itself should be considered common sense in the twenty-first century, but unfortunately all too often is not, and will be discussed in great detail in Chapter 3 – but raises the equally important question of representation. For what he criticizes is not how these individuals are seen by other members of the group and how they are categorized within that ethnic group or nation, but how we, supposedly detached, social scientists deal with them.

To be sure, for ethnic elites, homogeneity, group cohesion and solidarity and the undivided allegiance of its members to the ethnic principle is as much a defining criterion as the polarizing principles of identity formation based on 'us' versus 'them' dichotomies. As a matter of fact they not only complement but constitute each other, based on the principle 'amity inside, enmity outside' (Kecmanovic 2002: 141). A similar point was already made by Sampson (1968: 33), when 'any increase in group cohesion seems to be gained at the price of heightened hostility towards outgroups'. Kecmanovic elaborates further that 'the identification of the group enemy smoothes, buffers, or completely neutralizes intragroup antagonisms. Discriminative aggressiveness against strangers and the strengthening of bonds among group members go hand in hand and mutually reinforce each other.' In conclusion, one may even go so far as to 'say that there is no closeness within the group without an enemy from without the group' (Kecmanovic 1996: 36).

To be sure, this understanding of identity based on difference, even enmity, made most explicit in Julia Kristeva's famous assertion that the exclusion of others 'binds the identity of a clan, a sect, a party, or a nation', being both at the same time, 'the source of the pleasure of identification ("this is what we are, therefore this is what I am"), and of barbaric persecution ("that is foreign to me, therefore I throw it out, hunt it down, or massacre it")' (Kristeva 1993: 50), is not without controversy or disagreement and will be taken up again in Chapter 3. For the moment it is important to record that such 'strategic essentialisms' in the terminology of Gayatri Spivak (1987), are understandable, even normal in an ethnicized discourse. The use of an essentialized version of oneself – individual or group – for the sake of self-representation in order to achieve political gains, while not without internal and external controversy, is part of their job description. In the eyes of ethno-nationalist elites, unity, or at least maintaining the pretence of it, is the single most important goal and interest that constitutes and defines a nation or ethnic community. Yet strategic essentialism should not be understood as fake, as theatrical performance, as nothing but a show put on to mend internal fences, as I often encountered in discussions. Since those ethnic elites often have grown up within an already heavily ethnicized discourse and among cultural markers such as myths of origin or narratives of ancient hatreds between groups in which they genuinely believe, a phenomenon Anthony Smith (1998: 158) calls the 'participants' primordialism', these essentialisms, while strategically employed, may appear thoroughly normal to them, as the natural way things are and are meant to be. And even if they did not share all of these notions, it is not difficult to see how the role they perform every day, propagating these beliefs of unity, cohesion, solidarity, and common purpose, can readily translate into a habitus. While such preconditions and transformations are easily traceable, 'for Spivak the concomitant risk is that the essentialist use of master [concepts] such as woman, worker or nationalist to mobilize the disempowered groups may ossify into a fixed identity' (Morton 2007: 127–128). If ethnic group formation is based on an 'us' versus 'them' dichotomy, on politics of differentiation, and on maintaining and reconstituting cultural boundaries in an ethnicized discourse, these politics typically involve acts of exclusion, not only against the easily identifiable other, but also against those within the group that do not fully share the group's essentialized beliefs, a process of segregation that ultimately has them becoming part of the other. Such acts of separation, one may say, are the lamentable but nonetheless commonplace product of identity politics or an ethnicized discourse.

Yet, for us social scientists, our requirements like our aims, should be different.

> Ethnic common sense – the tendency to partition the social world into putatively deeply constituted, quasi-natural intrinsic kinds … is a key part of what we want to explain, not what we want to explain things with; it belongs to our empirical data, not to our analytical toolkit … We obviously cannot ignore such commonsense primordialism. But that does not mean we should simply replicate it in our scholarly analysis or policy assessments.
>
> (Brubaker 2004: 9)

When we scholars uncritically accept the rhetoric of ethno-nationalist elites, we run the risk of becoming complicit in their attempts to ethnicize the discourse. If we scholars, rather than calling it into question, adopt the ethnic or nationalists elites' strategic essentialism as the basis of our enquiries or take on '*categories of ethnopolitical practice as our categories of social analysis*' (Brubaker 2004: 10, emphasis in original), we contribute to the reification and substantialization of the those elites' primordialism and to the reproduction of its logic (Brubaker 1996, 2004, 2009; Fenton 2004; Gagnon 2004). To be sure,

> as analysts we should certainly try to account for the ways in which – and the conditions under which this practice of reification, this powerful crystallization of group feeling, can work. But we should avoid unintentionally doubling or reinforcing the reification of ethnic groups in ethnopolitical practice with a reification of such groups in social analysis.
>
> (Brubaker 2004: 10)

In sum, and to put not too fine a point on it, one may conclude, while ethnic elites, by essentializing the group they claim to represent, are acting within the confines of their supposed social roles, we as scholars and analysts, by subscribing to their claims without challenging these strategic essentialisms, fail, I would argue, in our duty to critically analyse them; and it is this failure that is the main point of critique of this study.

Neo-realism and neo-liberalism

I would argue that explanatory IR is particularly prone to such groupist practice. In reiteration of what has been stated in the Introduction, I contend that in explanatory IR's approaches to ethnicity the essentialist and substantialist presumptions of groupism manifest themselves on three levels: (1) operationalizing ethnicity as the dependent or independent variable and therewith according it with limited or pre-eminent explanatory power; (2) equating ethnic groups with states; and (3), as a consequence thereof, all too often equating ethnic conflict with ethno-nationalist conflict by postulating that a desire for sovereign statehood of a disenfranchized group is the cause of the conflict at hand and the disenfranchized group's aspiration. As will be shown throughout this study, these levels and the inherent presumptions that inform them lead to the reification of ethnicized discourses, politicized ethnicity, ethnic divisions, and the 'us' versus 'them' dichotomies that often form the basis of ethnicized discourses.

Concurrent with or instigated by Brubaker's critique, scholars have problematized the quantification of ethnicity in large n-studies on intra- and/or inter-state conflicts – usually based on record sets such as Ted Robert Gurr's *Minorities at Risk* (MAR) project or the *Ethno-Linguistic Fractionalization* (ELF) dataset – that operationalize the ethnic group as their unit of analysis as if it were a substantial entity and not a socio-political construct, and in consequence explain its actions as derivative of the fact that ethnicity is the element defining and cohering the group (Laitin & Posner 2001; Fearon 2003; Posner 2005a; Brown & Langer 2010). In such studies, the action of the respective parties, antagonistic or collaborative – the dependent variable – is a function of their being part of an ethnic group – the independent variable – and follows and reifies the same ethnicized logic: a logic of presupposed internal homogeneity, cohesion, solidarity, unity and common purpose in opposition to the constructed other, that is groups of the same qualities yet of a different ethnic ascription. What is particularly conspicuous here is that these essentialist approaches operationalize ethnicity as the independent variable in explaining ethnic conflicts and, by implication, accept the conversion of ethnicity as the independent variable into the determining one; that is, ultimately, if groupist-think is brought to its tautological conclusion, ethnic and ethno-nationalist conflicts are explained with ethnicity. An illustration of such flawed and potentially harmful reasoning would be the infamous 'ancient hatreds' that Robert Kaplan (1994) claims to have identified as the root cause for conflicts of the 1990s in the Balkans.[10]

The second dimension of groupism and the selection of the ethnic group as unit of analysis in the study of ethnic and ethno-nationalist conflict is the belief in the unitary actor.

> Although participants' rhetoric and commonsense accounts treat ethnic groups as the protagonists of ethnic conflict, in fact the chief protagonists of most ethnic conflict ... are not ethnic groups as such but various kinds of organizations ... and their empowered and authorized incumbents.
>
> (Brubaker 2004: 14)

These organizations, in the broadest sense, can be states and autonomous polities that can be further subdivided into branches of government, ministries, political parties law enforcement and intelligence agencies, the armed forces, etc.; they can be insurgencies, paramilitary groups, terrorist organizations, armed bands and gangs, etc.; they can also include social movement organizations, NGOs, churches and other religious communities, unions and advocacy groups, various branches of the media, in the widest sense, even loosely structured Facebook groups. But these organizations

cannot be equated with ethnic groups. It is because and insofar as they are organizations, and possess certain material and organizational resources, that they (or more precisely their incumbents) are capable of organized action, and thereby of acting as more or less coherent protagonists in ethnic conflict. Although common sense and participants' rhetoric attribute discrete existence, boundedness, coherence, identity, interest, and agency to ethnic groups, these attributes are in fact characteristic of organizations.

(Brubaker 2004: 15)

In sum, Brubaker holds that the actors in ethnic conflict are not ethnic groups but individuals and organizations who ethnicize the political discourse. For, echoing Weber and Barth, ethnicity is a belief system, a way of seeing the world, a point of view of these individuals and organizations, but not substantially real, or only real as part of a discourse and for as long as they are imagined and believed in. 'In this sense identity does not, and cannot, make people do anything; it is, rather, people who make and do identity, for their own reasons and purposes' (Jenkins 2008b: 9). Consequently, social groups 'do not have the same onto-logical status as individuals. Human individuals are actual entities; groups are not. They cannot behave or act, and they do not have a definitive, bounded, material existence in time and space' (Jenkins 2008b: 10).

And yet for neo-realists in IR, not unlike ethnic elites, one may say, in admittedly simplified terms, national cohesion and the anthromorphizing of their unit of analysis are supposed to be pre-givens not further questioned. At the level of the state, not only do domestic politics rarely matter, sovereign nation states are perceived and treated like a 'black box' (Singer 1961), as unitary, rational actors in an anarchic international system. This focus on the 'third image' of realism in IR, the structure of the international system, at the expense of the other two, the individual and the state, has not always been the case. On the contrary, they feature prominently in the writings of such classic realist thinkers as Machiavelli and Hobbes and are still given ample room in Kenneth Waltz's *Man, the State, and War* (2001 [1959]). This changed, though, with his *Theory of International Politics* (1979), which, is widely con-sidered to be the founding text of structural or neo-realism. In it, Waltz posits that differences between states, like differences between individuals, 'are of capability, not function' (Waltz 1979: 96), and that 'international politics con-sists of like units duplicating one another's activities' (Waltz: 97). What matters from this perspective are no longer the different characters of actors in the international system – they are seen as quintessentially the same, as 'like units', and egoistic maximizers of material interests – but the anarchic nature of the international system, and what forms of behaviour this anarchic structure induces. With this narrow lens on international relations becoming salient in the 1970s, questions of identity, that is the character of actors in the international system, became neglected in explanatory IR to our discipline's detriment.[11] In sum, with domestic factors and the identity of actors considered less relevant, neo-realism perceives of the state as a unitary, substantive, distinct, homogeneous, bounded actor in the international system. One of the most eminent critics of neo-realism, Richard Ashley, wrote about neo-realism's general tendency for reification:

> The state must be treated as an unproblematic unity: an entity whose existence, boundaries, identifying structures, constituencies, legitimacies, interests, and capacities to make self-regarding decisions can be treated as a given, independent of transnational class and human interests, and undisputed (except, perhaps by other states)
>
> (Ashley 1984: 268)

Drawing on what has been observed already by Lars Erik Cederman (1997), I argue – and will illustrate this assertion when discussing, in the following chapter, the frameworks that explanatory IR has contributed to the study of ethno-nationalist conflict – that the same tendency for reification, and therewith groupism, also characterizes neo-realism's approach to ethnic and ethno-nationalist conflict when analytically equating nations and ethnic groups with states. In one classic reader on IR theory, groupism is even declared to be one of the 'three core assumptions' on which the (neo-)realist paradigm is based:

> Groupism: Humans face one another mainly as members of groups … people need the cohesion provided by group solidarity, yet that very same in-group cohesion generates the potential for conflict with other groups. Today the most important human groups are nation states, and the most important source of in-group cohesion is nationalism.
>
> (Wohlforth 2012: 36)

As will be shown, neo-realism and neo-liberalism still enjoy prodigious influence in explanatory IR, in particular in North American scholarship. Interestingly, neo-liberalism originated from a pluralist critique of structural or neo-realism that took issue with its conceptualization of states as unitary and rational actors and strove to give the role of transnational and non-state actors greater room in analysis (Sterling-Folker 2013). These pluralistic traditions were relegated to the background, though, in Robert Keohane and Joseph Nye's *Power and Interdependence* (2001) that tried to play neo-realism at its own game. On the one hand Keohane and Nye adopted the neo-realist tenet of the state as the unitary actor, yet on the other they tried to demonstrate via regime theory that cooperation between states in an anarchic international structure not only is possible but, drawing on the theory of Kant's 'liberal zones of peace', actually quite common – an intellectual thrust that was further fleshed out in Stephen Krasner's *International Regimes* (1983) and Robert Keohane's *After Hegemony* (1984). It is no less state-centric than neo-realism, though:

> Neoliberalism is a variant of liberal IR theory that focuses on the role international institutions play in obtaining international collective outcomes … In order to examine international cooperation, neo-liberalism subscribes to a state-centric perspective which, like structural realism, considers states to be unitary, rational, utility-maximizing actors … that is, states are treated as unified entities with particular, specific goals rather than composites of many different domestic actors and competing interests.
>
> (Sterling-Folker 2013: 115)

That means, as for neo-realists, that the sovereign nation state in the anarchic international system is the main unit of analysis for scholars in the neo-liberal paradigm, yet unlike neo-realists and echoing somewhat the classic liberal/pluralist tradition, the importance of the domestic decision making process is acknowledged. However, this acknowledgement amounts to very little since domestic pluralism is confined to a homogenizing corset of hierarchical decision making that, in the end, has the state speaking with one voice in the international arena in the rational pursuit of its national self-interest; the state may not be a unitary actor but its policies are ultimately unitary. 'Despite their willingness to rely on domestic level explanations and a more inclusive set of actor types than realists do, most neoliberals also tacitly adhere to a reified approach to agency' (Cederman 1997: 20). Indeed, the so-called 'neo-neo debate' between neo-realism and neo-liberalism in the 1980s, highlighted the similarities, more than the differences, between both paradigms. In particular, their state-centrism and rigorous empiricist positivism (Little 1997; Wæver 1997, 2007; Hobson 2000; Lacher 2003; Brown & Ainley 2009; Steans *et al.* 2010; Sterling-Folker 2013). In the words of Lacher (2003: 521), 'no aspect, of the neorealist/neoliberal mainstream of International Relations scholarship, apart perhaps from its positivist orientation, has provoked its critics more than the commitment to the analytical centrality of the state in the study of world politics'. Given the attempts from scholars of both paradigms in the 1980s to explicitly generate a common epistemological and ontological ground (Ruggie 1983; Keohane 1989; Buzan *et al.* 1993), I concur with Wæver (1997) who rather than a 'neo-neo debate' identifies a 'neo-neo synthesis' with state-centrism and the conceptualization of the state as a unitary actor among the defining commonalities. In sum,

> what is clear is that neoliberals and neorealists are much closer together than their neo-neo forebears [classic realism and liberalism] … the 'neos' both

rest their position on what are taken to be the facts of anarchy and the rational egoism of states ... certainly the two positions are close enough to be seen as offering different understandings of what is essentially the same (rational choice) research programme.

(Brown & Ainley 2009: 47)

As will be shown when discussing explanatory frameworks and models in the next chapter, like neo-realism, neo-liberalism, at the unit of analysis level treats ethnic groups or nations the same as states, that is as rational, unitary – or unitarily acting – agents in pursuit of self-interests in a predominantly hostile international system (Rose 1998; Bush 2003; Bush & Keyman 1997; Sterling-Folker 2013). In the case of ethnic groups, ethnic conflict is explained through the lens of groupism; that is, group cohesion, group solidarity and the portrayal of the ethnic group, like a state, as a unitary actor. Kenneth Bush observes:

Communal groups are *represented* as the functional equivalent of states: unitary, power-seeking [...] actors in a Hobbesian world In other words, communal groups are viewed as being analogous to the state epistemologically and ontologically. Like states, such groups are seen to constitute stable and unified entities, and to act as coherent and separate totalities.

(Bush 2003: 5, emphasis in original)

Drawing on the famous billiard ball analogy, originally coined by Arnold Wolfers (1962), that illustrates how explanatory IR theory has focused exclusively on the 'third image', the international system', at the expense of the 'second image', the domestic composition of states – in a billiard game what matters are not the individual properties of the balls, which essentially are the same, but their external dimension, their interaction with each other – Bush argues that explanatory IR theory in its analysis of ethnic conflict has simply made the new unit of analysis fit its already existing epistemological and ontological framework.

Thus, the billiard ball model, which is based on relations between separate states as unified entities, now includes interethnic group relations, each of which constitutes a unified and separate totality – that is, self-contained and self-propelling entities. In effect, realism simply adds the notion of ethnic identity to its basic assumption that the position of a collectivity, whether it be a state or a group, in an anarchical system is the primary causal variable in the area of security.

(Bush & Keyman 1997: 313)

As will be discussed at great length in the following chapter, the examples of the two main explanatory frameworks neo-realism and neo-liberalism in IR have contributed to the study of ethnic conflict – Barry Posen's ethnic security dilemma and David Davis and Will Moore's ethnic alliance model – attest to this presumption. Davis and Moore (1998: 93), for example, state 'we contend that it is useful to conceptualise ethnic linkages among people across state boundaries as functionally equivalent to alliances between states', and 'these alliances should behave much as alliances between states have been hypothesized to behave in international relations' (Davis & Moore 1998: 92).

As for the third level of groupism in explanatory IR, the equation of ethnic conflict with ethno-nationalist conflict and postulating a pursuit of national self-determination – understood as gaining independence and sovereign statehood – here, neo-realism and neo-liberalism share the essentialist determinism of modernism elaborated above. Again, for two paradigms (neo-realism and neo-liberalism) so inseparably wed to a normative and deterministic state centrism, and which routinely equate ethnic groups with states in their analysis, it is not at all surprising that they often erroneously reduce ethnic conflict to a mere pursuit of sovereign statehood. Before elaborating this thought further when discussing sovereignty and state centrism in IR in greater detail, it is imperative to turn our attention to the third major paradigm of explanatory IR: constructivism and its approach to ethnic and ethno-nationalist conflict.

Systemic constructivism

All that has been discussed here so far could easily be interpreted as making a case for a constructivist understanding of identity. Unquestionably there are profound merits to a constructivist reading of ethnic conflict, primarily because constructivism, in contrast to the materialist rationalism of neo-realism and neo-liberalism, puts the identity of the subject at the centre of its analysis. Constructivism was first and foremost born out of a critique of materialist rationalism (Hurd 2008; Reus-Smit 2009; Fierke 2010; Jackson & Sørensen 2012; Daddow 2013), replacing its 'logic of consequences'; that is, a group's rational pursuit of a goal for the maximization of, in the widest sense, a materialistically defined interest, with a 'logic of appropriateness' – the pursuit of interests that are seen as a function of the subject's identity shaped by beliefs, shared values, norms, and through practices and interaction with others. While neo-realism and neo-liberalism assume the identity of the subject of their analysis at large as resulting from those interests, as pre-given, since, in simplified terms, we are who we are because of what we want, constructivists advocate the exact opposite: we want what we want because of who we are (Kowert 2012), or in the words of Alexander Wendt, the pioneer of constructivism in IR, 'interests presuppose identities because an actor cannot know what it wants until it knows who it is, and since identities have varying degrees of cultural content so will interests' (Wendt 1999: 231). And who we are, is 'shaped by the cultural, social, and political – as well as material – circumstances in which [we] are embedded' (Fierke 2010: 171), that is, first and foremost, through our interaction with others in a social relationship, and how we give meaning to things, and implicitly ourselves, through dialogue, through 'collective interpretations, practices, and institutions' (Adler 1997: 326) that result in norms and become institutionalized.

'A fundamental principle of constructivist social theory is that people act toward objects, including other actors, on the basis of the meanings that the objects have for them' (Wendt 1992: 396–397); yet these meanings or ideas, and the practices that follow from them, are not only contextual and situational (that is, they can change over time and space), they are also 'not so much mental as symbolic and organizational, they are embedded not only in human brains but also in the "collective memories", government procedures, educational systems, and the rhetoric of statecraft' (Legro 2005: 6). They are, in sum, 'social facts, rather than purely material ones, that exist because of the meaning and value attributed to them' (Fierke 2010: 171). And if ideas and meanings are socially constructed, so are identities and, consequently, also interests, which they inform; an insight that corresponds with the classics on ethnic identity by Weber and Barth, discussed earlier.

The role of identity is key to the constructivist approach to society, and its pioneer in IR, Alexander Wendt conceptualized four forms of identity (Wendt 1999, 2003; Reus-Smit 2009; Aalberts 2012). The first, *role identity*, has no intrinsic properties but derives its meaning from interaction with others, as elaborated above, and in accordance with Barth. 'Only through recognition can people acquire and maintain a distinct identity. One becomes a Self, in short, via the Other' (Wendt 2003: 511). This mutual recognition co-constitutive of self and other leads to generalizations of self and other and to the second form of identity that Wendt calls *collective identity*, where the meanings and properties of 'a generalized Other [form] part of their understanding of [a generalized] Self' (Wendt 1999: 337). Again, the process of identification occurs through differentiation, but on this second level on a wider basis that extends beyond the original group to similar selves via different others; for example, the perception of NATO as a military alliance of democratic states within a certain region in juxtaposition to non-democratic states that do not adhere to the principles of human rights, etc. (Zehfuss 2002). This example is particularly applicable in light of the importance constructivists give to norms in processes of identity formation, what above has been called a 'logic of appropriateness', where 'what is rational is a function of legitimacy, defined by shared values and norms within institutions or other social structures' (Fierke 2010: 170). The third and fourth level, *type identity* and *corporate identity*, are grounded in Wendt's distinction between 'social terms of individuality' and 'individuality per se' (Wendt 1999: 181–183), where he identifies certain properties of identity that are claimed to be pre-social. Those are called *corporate identities* with intrinsic values and 'self-organizing, homeostatic structures that make actors distinct entities' (Wendt 1999: 224–225), an essence or core of identities that these entities 'in all times and places have in common' (Wendt 1999: 201), yet that only derive a wider meaning in the social context through interaction and intersubjective understanding, and as such are contingent.

The former [social terms of identity] refers to the features of the Self that depend on recognition by the Other ... The latter connotes to the self-organizing properties of the entity, existing independent of and prior to the social system.

(Aalberts 2012: 75)

It is the last forms of identity that turn out most problematic in Wendt's framework since they evidently contradict the first three levels and, to a certain extent, the entire constructivist concept of identities as social constructs (Campbell 1998a; Zehfuss 2002, 2006; Reus-Smit 2009; Weber 2010; Aalberts 2012; Daddow 2013).

On the surface, though, the constructivist challenge to the essentialist and materialist rationalism of neo-realism and neo-liberalism is formidable and its key tenets are claimed today to be 'largely internalized in the discipline of IR' (Hurd 2008: 301). In recapitulation, they are: (1) the social constructiveness of ideas, meanings, norms, identities, and interests; (2) a sound rejection of rationalism and positivism, since, if the above are social facts, they are difficult to measure empirically and it is next to impossible to clearly distinguish between facts and values; (3) an adjustment of the structure-bias of neo-realism and neo-liberalism towards a more balanced understanding of the interplay between agency and structure in the analysis of the social world. In his ground-breaking critique of neo-realist and neo-liberal conceptualizations of the inherently anarchic international system, 'Anarchy Is What States Make of It', Wendt declares:

Self-help and power politics do not follow either logically or causally from anarchy and that if today we find ourselves in a self-help world, this is due to process, not structure. There is no 'logic' of anarchy apart from the practices that create and instantiate one structure of identities and interests rather than another; structure has no existence or causal powers apart from process. Self-help and power politics are institutions, not essential features of anarchy. Anarchy is what states make of it.

(Wendt 1992: 394–395)

Here and in an earlier essay (1987), Wendt, drawing on Gidden's theory of structuration (Giddens 1979, 1984), takes great pains to 'make the actual behaviour and properties of states "problematic" rather than simply accepting them as a given' (Wendt 1987: 363) and to demonstrate how 'a social structure leaves more space for agency, that is for the individual or state to influence their environment, as well as to be influenced by it' (Fierke 2010: 170). This is to say that in refutation of the Waltzian neo-realist dictum of 'the structure as an independent force external to the acting unit' (McSweeney 1999: 123), of the structure determining the actors, Wendt portrays them as mutually constitutive, as the product of the inter-subjective interaction between actors on a structural level. In sum, agents and structures have 'equal ontological status' (Wendt 1987: 339).[12] It therefore seems patently reasonable when Lars-Erik Cederman (1997: 20) claims that, in contrast to neo-realism and neo-liberalism, 'to find exceptions from reified actors [in IR], one has to turn to … constructivist theory' and in particular the writings of Alexander Wendt'.

Alas, the very opposite is the case. In fact, what is often called a 'systemic' (Reus-Smit 2009), 'thin' (Daddow 2013), after its key theorist, Wendtian constructivism arguably may become as guilty of essentializing and of reifying the actor as its neo-realist and neo-liberal counterparts. The reason for this tendency lies in the above-mentioned fourth level of Wendt's conceptualization of identity that openly contradicts the previous three. This contradiction stems from Wendt's attempts to charter a 'media via' (Wendt 1999: 40, 47) through the debate between what is commonly referred to in IR as 'rationalists' and 'reflectivist', to carve out for constructivism a 'true middle ground' between these two approaches (Adler 1997: 322), 'to bridge the still vast divide separating the majority of IR theorists from postmodernists' (Checkel 1998: 327), by combining a positivist epistemology with a post-positivist ontology – an experiment in having it both ways that inevitably has to fail, leading Maja Zehfuss (2006: 116) to conclude, 'Wendt's constructivism does not work'. The crux of the problem with Wendt's balancing act on identity is that he conceives of state identity as at the same time constructed and changeable, as an expression of role, collective and type identity, but also as a pre-social, pre-given stable corporate identity, and after having taken literally hundreds of pages in *Social Theory of International Politics* elaborating that identities resulting from social interaction are more basic than interests, he declares that he is less interested in 'state identity formation' than in the workings of the state system, 'the structure and effects of states (or "international") systems' (Wendt 1999: 11), where states have essential properties 'prior to and independent from social context', thus not 'considering the constitution of states in the first place' (Zehfuss 2002: 89).

> From this perspective, it is impossible to explain how fundamental changes occur, either in the nature of international society or in the nature of state identity. By bracketing everything domestic, Wendt excludes by theoretical fiat most of the normative and ideational forces that might prompt such change.
>
> (Reus-Smit 2009: 224)

Ultimately, in effect then, Wendt's systemic constructivism does not differ much in its rationalist positivist and state-centric meta-narrative on identity from neo-realism and neo-liberalism.

Wendt's flip-flopping on identity has confused scholars and students of IR ever since then, but Christian Reus-Smit errs when he critically remarks that 'Wendt's writings represent the only true form of this rarefied example of constructivism' (Reus-Smit 2009: 223). On the contrary, voicing a commitment to the constructed nature of identity but then proceeding to treat identities as relatively stable pre-givens, thus refusing to incorporate in their ontologies what the social constructedness of identities actually means, that they are the product of social discourses and that there cannot be identities prior to these discourses, is a tendency strikingly common in the social sciences. This 'clichéd constructivism' (Brubaker 2004), a constructivism in name only – limited to the introductory section of texts or expressed in customary yet seemingly perfunctory disclaimers – but where the main analysis, at large, continues to be done under essentialist and substantialist presumptions of ethnic identities, often bordering a primordialism slipping in through the backdoor, is particularly pervasive in explanatory IR's writings on ethnic conflict. This becomes for example evident in a series of recent prominent large-*n* studies based on the *Ethnic Power Relations* dataset at the University of California, Los Angeles, and the related *Ethnic Armed Conflict* dataset at Harvard University (Cederman & Girardin 2007; Buhaug *et al.* 2008; Cederman *et al.* 2009a, 2009b, 2010, 2013; Wimmer *et al.* 2009). Not only is it telling that the *GeoSim* agent-based models developed by Lars-Erik Cederman that form the core of his team's survey of ethnic conflicts was first developed to simulate interstate relations, similar presumptions about unitarily acting ethnic groups that form the basis of neo-realist/neo-liberal readings of ethnic conflict and group solidarity also characterize these n-studies' narrow constructivist understanding of ethnic identity. On the one hand the authors want ethnicity to be understood as 'a subjectively experienced sense of commonality based on a belief in common ancestry and shared culture', that is, socially constructed, but then proceed to caution, 'we do not distinguish between degrees of representativity of political actors who claim to speak for an ethnic group, nor do we code the heterogeneity of political positions of leaders claiming to represent the same community' (Wimmer *et al.* 2009: 316–317); thus the authors, like Wendt, not only bracket the 'domestic component', i.e. the social discourse that brought about these ethnic identities, but, what is more, their studies, like neo-realist and neo-liberal approaches, treat ethnic groups as unitary actors and indirectly equate them ontologically with states. In a nutshell, they share the same meta-narrative.[13]

The discussion so far of the groupist pitfalls of systemic constructivism has already called attention to the conjuncture that their deficiencies are not limited to the ontological realm but also extend to its epistemology. By reducing identity to a pre-given and static *corporate identity* that, due to its exogenous character, has little explanatory value to account for variations in actors' behaviour, state or group conduct, is again, as in the neo-realist and neo-liberal paradigms, explained through rational and material interests, where questions of identity are relegated to the repertoire of political rhetoric of elites. By 'bracketing out' the other three dimensions of identity, this form of constructivism hardly differs from neo-realism and neo-liberalism, and via Wendt's 'scientific realism' ironically adopts their positivist and empiricist methodology that constructivism originally set out to refute. With positivism comes the belief in scientific objectivism, the myth of the detached analyst empirically studying, recording and explaining social conduct without having a stake or taking part in it,[14] which forms my main point of critique in the approach of Brubaker discussed earlier.[15] Brubaker correctly cautions against the process of reification in the social sciences when taking social – in this context ethnic – groups as units of analysis. Yet, when trying to draw clear lines between identity and process of identification, not only does he struggle to impose a theoretical and, I would argue with

Jenkins, fictitious order on a 'human world in which indeterminacy, ambiguity, and paradox are part of the normal pattern of everyday life' (Jenkins 2008b: 9), running the risk of superseding the 'reality of the model' with a 'model of reality' (Bourdieu 1990: 39), he also appears to worship the false idol of scientific objectivism. When warning that essentialist reifications of identity groups in the scholarly discourse 'reflects the dual orientation of many academic identitarians as both *analysts* and *protagonists* of identity politics' (Brubaker 2004: 33, emphasis in original), he seems to imply that by not taking '*categories of ethno-political practice as our categories of social analysis*' (Brubaker 2004: 10, emphasis in original), we can remain neutral, detached and objective observers of identity politics who stay clear of taking any part in it. He clearly and correctly distinguishes between groups – how members of a collective identify themselves – and categories[16] – how they are defined by others – but then seems to overlook the fact that,

> categorization is as much part of identity as self-identification … categorization makes a powerful contribution to the everyday reality – the realization … of groups. Attributions of group membership feature routinely in how we categorize others, and the categorization of out-groups is intrinsic to in-group identification. Who we think we are, is intimately related to who we think others are, and vice versa.
>
> (Jenkins 2008b: 12)

This process of categorization as co-constitutive of the process of self-identification, however, is not limited to the social groups from which a certain group sets itself apart, the direct (as it has been called here), constitutive other. If group identification goes hand in hand with group categorization, it would be evidently illogical to assume that the way we as scholars, together with international politics and the media, categorize a collective would have no impact on how this collective sees itself, on its process of self-identification. Yet this is precisely what the myth of positivism and scientific objectivism wants us to believe, that a clear line can be drawn between the scholarly categorizer and the categorized, that they are two social spheres apart, where the one engages in identity politics and the other discretely and dispassionately records, analyses and explains those identity politics – an artificial segmentation of the social world that is not only demonstrably fallacious but also patently absurd.

In this study, on the other hand, inclined to a post-positivist tradition that clearly rejects the notion of scientific objectivism, knowledge production, which includes processes of categorization, is always seen as inseparably interlinked with modes of power and politics of representation (Foucault 1974, 1980; Derrida 1978, 1981a, 1981b, 1998; Shapiro 1981, 1988, 2003; Laclau & Mouffe 1985; Deleuze 1988; Edkins 1999; Hall 2003a, 2003b; Said 2003 [1978]).[17] From this perspective, we scholars as categorizers, whether we engage in reification or not, inherently matter to the categorized, we inevitably are protagonists of identity politics. It is the very nature of identity and identity discourses, as defined above, that renders us categorizers and explainers part of it, makes us subjects of the identity discourse we seek to describe, irrespective of our intellectual or ideological position, political or scholarly agenda, or adherence to imaginary principles of scientific objectivism. To believe anything else would be a failure to recognize our nature as human beings in interaction with others and our role in the social world of which we are part. Consequently, to critically examine the role of explanatory IR scholars as protagonists of ethnic conflict is one of the aspirations central to this study.

Notes

1 The category of stateless nation is discussed at length in Guibernau 2000.
2 Walker Connor's contributions to the study of ethnicity and nationalism are located within the wider scholarly debate on primordialism/essentialism in Conversi (2004).
3 Masrour Barzani in an interview with James Calderwood, quoted in Calderwood (2011).
4 It should be pointed out that Breuilly (1993) objects to the notion of a single grand theory or narrative on nationalism since the various nationalisms Breuilly studies in his book are too diverse, spanning two centuries and five continents, to be captured by a one size-fit-all framework; instead, he argues for researchers to develop a typology of the various forms of nationalism. Having said that, all his types of nationalism – whether unifying, such as the Italian Risorgimento or Pan-Africanism, or secessionist, such as the Basques in Spain or the Igbo in Biafra – are developed by way of their relationship to the nation state and his entire approach, as already mentioned, is forthrightly state-centric.
5 This notion has been problematized for the Kurdish context by Houston (2009).
6 For a conceptualization of identity as a form of ideology see Malešević (2006a).
7 The importance of symbols, narratives of origin, cultural artefacts, etc., in the production and reproduction of the nation is at the core of Anthony Smith's ethno-symbolist approach to nationalism. See Smith (1999, 2000, 2008, 2009), Hutchinson (2004), Guibernau and Hutchinson (2004), Leoussi and Grosby (2006).
8 It can be argued, though, that a similar point was already made two decades before Barth by Everett Hughes, see Jenkins (2008a: 11).
9 He expands on the relationship between nationalism and ethnicity in Calhoun (1993) where he emphasizes caveats to the notion that nations seek to evolve into sovereign states while ethnic groups merely struggle for recognition of vaguely defined cultural rights, and concludes that 'the two sorts of categorical identities are often invoked in similar ways' (Calhoun 1993: 235).
10 For a similar primordialist understanding of identity and culture in explanatory IR, see also Samuel Huntington's infamous *Clash of Civilizations* (2002) or Suny (1993).
11 One may say that classic realism since the 1990s is experiencing somewhat of a revival with the works of Snyder (1991), Wohlforth (1993) and Schweller (2006) refocusing on a unit-level analysis that gives greater room to questions about the internal properties of states, the latter in particular focusing on elite cohesion and therefore of interest for this study.
12 A comprehensive discussion of the structure-agency problem in IR is given in Doty (1997), Friedman and Starr (2006) and Wight (2006). For an overview of the current state of the debate within constructivism see Adler (2010).
13 In general, one should be sceptical of the suitability of quantitative analyses for capturing the complexities of ethnic conflicts. On its limitations, see an excellent symposium in *Ethnopolitics* 7 (2–3) with contributions by Shale Horowitz, Pieter van Houten, Patrick James, Stuart Kaufman *et al.* In the annotations, only the article by Horowitz (2008) is referenced but the entire exchange is to be recommended.

14 The notion of scientific objectivism is critically discussed in Kuhn (1996 [1962]), Haraway (1988), Porter (1995), and Daston and Galison (2007). Together with 'presentism' and 'culturalism' Ken Booth (1999) has famously identified 'scientific objectivism' and/or 'positivism' as one of the 'three tyrannies' impairing scientific inquiry in the social sciences.

15 Another, more technical point of critique would be that, although trying to beware of reification, a realistic description of the social world is difficult without referring to common parlance, abstract shorthand terms that trace how people think and identify in social contexts. Whether this is doable without any generalizing terminology at all is debatable, and, as has been observed (Malešević 2006b; Jenkins 2008b), Brubaker himself in his writings lacks consistency here.

16 The most widely used definition of social categories is given by Mann (1983: 34) as 'a class whose nature and composition is decided by the person who defines the category ... a category is therefore to be contrasted with a group, defined by the nature of the relations between the members'. Alternatively, Jenkins (2008b: 105) sums the distinction between group and category up as 'collective internal definition' versus 'collective external definition'.

17 The recognition that knowledge production is a function of modes of power and politics of representation constitutes a core insight of post-structuralism and is part of the standard repertoire of any post-structuralist text in IR, of which to give a comprehensive list here would not only be of little value but also simply impossible given the sheer number.

2 Concepts, models and frameworks

State centrism

Together with categorizing ethnicity as the independent variable, the primary site of reification in explanatory IR's dealing with ethnic and ethno-nationalist conflict that I identify is state-centrism.[1] A state-centric ontology, in a nutshell, is based on the assumption 'that states are the primary actors in world politics … the claim is that states … are sufficiently important actors that any positive theory of international relations must place them at its core' (Lake 2008: 42). Yet this assumption about the primacy of the state in IR theory comes with considerable epistemological and ontological baggage. First and foremost, state-centrism in explanatory IR 'reduce[s] the essence of international relations to state-centred interpretations' (Youngs 1999: 34). As Richard Ashley has famously observed for neo-realism:

> For the neorealist, the state is *ontologically prior* to the international system. The system's structure is produced by defining states as individual unities and *then* by noting properties that emerge when several such unities are brought into mutual reference. For the neorealist, it is impossible to describe international structures without first fashioning a concept of the state-as-actor … The state must be treated as an unproblematic unity: an entity whose existence, boundaries, identifying structures, constituencies, legitimacies, interests, and capacities to make self-regarding decisions can be treated as a given, independent of transnational class and human interests, and undisputed (except, perhaps by other states).
>
> (Ashley 1984: 240, 268; emphasis in original)

State-centrism thus explains international relations almost exclusively – at best it inserts the above-mentioned clichéd constructivist caveats – through the prism of the state, a state whose existence ontologically predates the system of which it is part; in other words,

> as an ontologically abstract category, the state, through the state-centric prism, becomes also a static category. International relations is reduced via

the state-centric prism to an individualistically conceived collection of its parts – that is states – and thus as a collection of static entities.

(Youngs 1999: 35)

I argue in this study that explanatory IR, by equating the ethnic group with the state, has translated from the state onto the ethnic group and nation this static conceptualization of social units as clearly bounded, organic, substantive, distinct, homogeneous and static categories endowed with social agency, whose properties and genesis are not problematized but treated as given – or to be more precise, by doing so, as with the state, it has contributed to reifying the ethnic group and nation through their narratives. This equation of state with ethnic or ethno-nationalist group that is made possible, in modernist fashion, by ascribing the nation with the defining objective of becoming a state, brings with it then for the study of ethnic or ethno-nationalist conflict the same epistemological and ontological fallacies of reification as state-centrism does in general for the study of the state and international relations at large.

Most critiques of state-centrism in IR focus on these epistemological and ontological fallacies, which the state as a social construct cannot and should not be treated as a fixed, clearly bounded and static unit and unitary actor in the international arena. They rarely venture in their critique beyond the state, i.e. they hardly ever problematize what it means when state-centrism clouds the ontological perception of social units other than the state by analytically equating these units with states. To do precisely that by highlighting how perceptions of the ethnic group and nation are affected and shaped by the epistemologies and ontologies of state-centrism, is one core objective of this study. At first, though, given that the centrality of the state in explanatory IR's analysis of ethnic and ethno-nationalist conflict, both as the social unit with which explanatory IR equates the ethnic group as a unitary actor and as the ultimate objective to be attained, defines the ethno-nationalist group, it becomes imperative to dedicate ample room to a critical analysis of the concept of sovereign statehood in explanatory IR. Yet, it cannot be emphasized strongly enough that the conjuncture of state and ethnic group and/or nation here is not made because it is ontologically tenable; on the contrary, discussing their correlation in this study is dictated by the representation of both concepts and categories in explanatory IR that erroneously establishes this linkage in the first place. Consequently, I argue, any deconstruction of how explanatory IR explains ethnic and ethno-nationalist conflict would be fatally incomplete if not accompanied by a deconstruction of sovereign statehood, which, allegedly, the former is all about.

As has been elaborated in the Introduction and in the previous chapter, the concept of the sovereign nation state as the main unit of analysis and constitutive element of the modern, anarchic (that is, non-hierarchical), international system is central to the three paradigms of explanatory IR: neo-realism, neo-liberalism and systemic constructivism. Extrapolating from one of explanatory IR's key thinkers, Hedley Bull (2002 [1977]), one might even say, 'IR is a discipline founded on the existence of state sovereignty at both a normative and a factual level' (Esmark 2004: 121). In a similar vein one of the most prominent critics of explanatory IR's state-centrism, Richard Ashley, notes:

> For the neorealist, the state is *ontologically prior* to the international system. The system's structure is produced by defining states as individual unities and *then* by noting properties that emerge when several such unities are brought into mutual reference. For the neorealist, it is impossible to describe international structures without first fashioning a concept of the state-as-actor.
>
> (Ashley 1984: 240, emphasis in original)

And the essential quality of explanatory IR's conceptualization of the state-as-actor is sovereignty, or in the words of Gillian Youngs (1999: 25), 'what matters is that the state is an identifiable entity, thus clearly bounded. In order to act, it has to be considered sovereign, that is, possessing the power to act'. Sovereign nation states are seen as the logical consequence, the product of the ideology of nationalism; as has also been shown in the previous chapter, the modernist understanding of nationalism can essentially be defined as the doctrine about acquiring statehood for the nation, statehood as the objective constituting the defining criterion for a nation. The essential qualities of this sovereign statehood are for it to be absolute and exclusive, expressed in Max Weber's famous definition of the state 'as a human community that (successfully) claims the *monopoly of the legitimate use of physical force* within a given territory' (Weber 1970 [1919]: 78, emphasis in original). This understanding of sovereignty as 'Janus-faced' (Aalberts 2012: 14), as having an internal and at the same time external components that are mutually constitutive is summarized by Hinsley:

> [Internal and external sovereignty] are complementary. They are the inward and outward expressions, the obverse and reverse sides of the same idea … the idea that there is a final and absolute political authority in the political community … and no final and absolute authority exists elsewhere.
>
> (Hinsley 1986: 158, 26)

In other words, state sovereignty not only connotes the presence of absolute authority at the domestic level and its absence at the international level, it is defined by this very corollary. In the anarchic international system all states are seen as equal in international law, not in the degree of power they can exert but in the inviolability of their sovereignty over the territory they claim, or as Frankel (1973: 38) puts it, 'irrespective of their power and size, in legal theory all states enjoy sovereignty in equal measure'. If a state chooses to share its sovereignty with another international body or evolve aspects of it in, for example, the supra-national European Union, it does so of its own vocation and can withdraw from this legal arrangement if and when it pleases. Yet, any divisibility of sovereignty over its territory against the state's will is understood to be illegitimate; in the end, in Morgenthau's (2005 [1951]: 258–259) words, 'if sovereignty means supreme authority, it stands to reason that two or more entities ... cannot be sovereign within the same time and space'. This view, at the core of the classic canon of explanatory IR, summarized in the dictum, 'the state, as a subject of international law, possess sovereign power' (Tiunov 1993: 326), endorses the absoluteness and exclusivity of sovereign statehood in the Weberian sense. It then is a community's monopoly on the legitimate use of force, read jurisdiction, over the territory it controls, from which the right to non-interference is deduced:

> If a state has a right to sovereignty, this implies that other states have a duty to respect that right by, among other things, refraining from intervention in its domestic affairs ... The function of the principle of nonintervention in international relations might be said, then, to be one of protecting the principle of state sovereignty.
>
> (Vincent 1974: 14)

Concomitant with its dual dimensionality, sovereignty is also a principle of international law, where it is conceived as an institution constituted by two sides of the same coin, 'sovereignty as an organizational rule to regulate the international traffic between states ...; and its role in the identification of political entities as actors on the international plane' (Aalberts 2012: 62–63). Much has been written in IR on the differentiation of sovereignty as a political and as a legal principle,[2] a somewhat artificial distinction, I would argue with Simpson (2008), since all law is man-made and therefore inherently political, a point already made by Morgenthau (2005 [1951]: 34) when he observed, 'there is a profound and neglected truth hidden in Hobbes' extreme dictum that the state creates morality as well as law, and there is neither morality nor law outside the state'. Consequently, '[the state's] privileged status and power as international legal persons is defined by the legal order, while sovereign states as its main subjects can define the contours of that very order' (Aalberts 2012: 64). This perspective, in which sovereignty can simply be ascertained to factually exist or not,[3] and in which states constitute the main subjects of international law, also determines the exclusivist norms of international law to justify and ensure the continuation of their existence. In other words, international law and the international system which it is supposed to regulate, is made by states for states.

Explanatory IR acknowledges that this modern state system and the sovereign nation state that constitutes it are the product of historical change; it goes to great length in tracing its development from Medieval feudalism to the early modern Treaties of Westphalia, to the Congress of Vienna, to how the doctrine of self-determination spawned decolonization (Anderson 1974; Claude 1989; Little 1989; Schroeder 1989; Craig & George 1995; Hall 1999; Knutsen 1999; Buzan & Little 2000; Carr 2001 [1939]; Mearsheimer 2001; Kissinger 2003), and it recognizes the process of state-formation and nationalism. As has been outlined, incorporating modernist theory, explanatory IR understands acquiring statehood and attaining sovereignty to be the defining objective of the nation, its main purpose. This processual character of the state is evident when Alexander Wendt, for example, describes the state as 'an ongoing political program designed to produce and reproduce a monopoly on the potential for organized violence' (Wendt 1999: 9), yet on the same page he declares, 'since states are the dominant form of subjectivity in contemporary world politics this means that they should be the primary unit of analysis for thinking about the global regulation of violence' (Wendt 1999: 9). Like neo-realism and neo-liberalism, despite acknowledging its historical evolution, which should give reason to conceive of differing historical trajectories, Wendtian constructivism conceptualizes all states as essentially the same in the contemporary international system (Biersteker 2010). Not unlike Francis Fukuyama in 'The End of History', who portrayed Western liberal democracy as 'the end point of mankind's ideological evolution and the universalization of Western liberal democracy as the final form of human government' (Fukuyama 1989: 4), the modern sovereign nation state is seen as the culmination, the end-product of a linear historical process of state-formation that today, in essentially the same form, spans the entire globe and whose evident perfect nature renders it conceptually ever-lasting. In this sense then, Biersteker identifies this generalizing and essentializing principle, 'the tendency to treat states as fundamentally similar units across time and place' (Biersteker 2010: 158), as one of the key characteristics the three paradigms of explanatory IR have in common, expressed in, for example, Kenneth Waltz's notorious claim that the state of anarchy in the international system renders any differentiation between states unnecessary. He declares, 'anarchy entails relations of coordination among a system's units, and that implies their sameness ... so long as anarchy endures, states remain like units' (Waltz 1979: 93), that is 'autonomous political units' (Waltz 1979: 95) with the same objectives. This presumption of the sameness of all states in the contemporary international system as a result of the system's anarchic structure obscures the processual, evolving character of the state; put differently, 'it would appear that the sovereignty principle has served to reify the state and abstract it from reality, thereby obscuring its role as both agent and product of a dynamic and still unfolding historical process' (Camilleri 2008: 35).

To be sure, IR again acknowledges some degree of historical evolution of sovereignty (Fowler & Bunk 1995; Jackson 2007; Krasner 2009; Buzan 2015) – see below in more detail – as for example the sprawling literature on globalization (Held 1995, 2000; Castells 1996, 1997, 1998; Youngs 1999; Youngs & Kofman 2008; Cameron *et al.* 2006; Agnew 2009; Cohen 2012) and (humanitarian) intervention (Weber 1995; Holzgrefe & Keohane 2003; Welsh 2003; Malmvig 2006; Bellamy 2009; Cunliffe 2011) attests, and Stephen Krasner (1999) goes so far as to declare the sovereignty principle an 'organized hypocrisy', demonstrating that intervention in another state's internal affairs has always been a quintessential part of international politics. Yet again, indicative of explanatory IR's generalizing and essentializing approach to the international system of sovereign nation states, Krasner's conceptualization of sovereignty remains static:

It does not help us comprehend the possibility of change in the operational meaning of sovereignty, and it does not suggest (or allow for) any typology for the different forms of sovereignty over time and across place. Like the tendency to treat states as fundamentally like units, Krasner's conceptualization of sovereignty is essentially fixed and unchanging. It does not help us understand the significance of challenges to sovereignty or the possibility of its transformation.

(Biersteker 2010: 162)

In fact, IR's 'fascination' (Malmvig 2006: 13) with state sovereignty as a universal and consistent principle of international order is so deeply ingrained that even a post-structuralist like R. B. J. Walker – see below – whose work is dedicated to the deconstruction of sovereignty, finds it in the end quite difficult to 'envisag[e] alternative political identities'.[4]

A minority view in IR, on the other hand, holds that sovereignty is a socio-political construct:

We agree with other scholars … that territory, population, and authority – in addition to recognition – are important aspects of state sovereignty. Unlike most scholars, however, we contend that each of these components of state sovereignty is also socially constructed, as is the modern state system. The modern state system is not based on some timeless principle of sovereignty, but on the production of a normative conception that links authority, territory, population (society, nation), and recognition in a unique way, and in a particular place.

(Biersteker & Weber 1996: 3)

If one conceives of the nation as an ideological basis for the state as a socio-political construct, an ideational factor, a way of seeing the world, as discussed in the previous chapter, it leads one to ponder on whether the objective of that socio-political construct, its realization is not a construct in itself, whether Biersteker and Weber are not justified in understanding it as the product 'of a normative conception' rather than a fixed and pre-given political entity.

This notion of state sovereignty as social construct has been developed, among others, by R. B. J. Walker (1993), Jens Bartelson (1995), and Cynthia Weber (1995), who, in contrast to treating it as an ontological given, understand sovereignty and with it the perception of the modern state, like the nation discussed earlier, as a discursive formation, a 'site of political struggle' (Weber 1995: 3), whose meaning is not only historically contingent – and thus changing over time, not fixed either in the present or future – but also shaped by representations of it in our discipline of IR. Walker first famously identified the binary opposites that form the basis for the construction of sovereignty and then proceeded to deconstruct them. The eponymous *Inside/Outside* extends to more than merely the binary opposite of domestic versus foreign, also containing the dichotomies of time and space, universal and particular, and self versus other.

The timelessness of sovereignty as an organizing principle of political reality culminated in the territorial space of the modern nation state, a purportedly universal principle that while establishing sameness at the international level not only allowed for but supposedly upheld plurality at the domestic level, where a society's particularities were peacefully lived out and resolved in democratic competition. Any disenfranchised minority in any given state can readily attest to this demand on the sovereign state to be imperfectly realized at best, or in more cynical fashion, to be merely fiction. As Walker elaborates, though, it is more than fiction or a matter of imperfect realization. The question is not whether sovereignty can fulfil this function, and if not, what ought to be done so that it can; the demand in itself is a presupposition – a presupposition that together with others such as the sameness, timelessness and universality of the sovereign state constitutes the discursive formation about it. Yet, what is more, as Walker is all too keenly aware, this demand on the state results in brutally demarcated lines of division that separate us from them, self from other, citizens from humanity, with the former born into privilege, while the latter has to eternally remain at the state's gates and never will come to enjoy the blessings of sovereignty.

> Outside, there are only other particulars, an absence of cohesive community, a pure anarchy, according to some, a decentralized society of states according to others, but a realm, certainly, of difference, competition, insecurity, domination and conflict: a realm in which others can be turned into Other, and the Other may be subjected to the familiar practices of projection, negation, orientalism and obliteration.
>
> (Walker 1995: 321)[5]

As Connolly reminds us, though, even the blessings of inclusion are dubious, with the state relentlessly exercising its 'monopoly over the allegiances, identifications, and energies of its members' (Connolly 1991a: 479). Walker's attempt at deconstructing these binary opposites then, which seeks to 'destabilise these seemingly opposed categories by showing how they are at once mutually constitutive and yet always in the process of dissolving into each other' (Walker 1993: 25), in other words to show that they are not clearly delineated opposites, is to a large extent determined by the moral aspiration to 'show how other ways of thinking might be opened up' (Walker 1993: 23), to envision alternative realities, or, in Walker's terminology, 'a politics of becoming otherwise' (Walker 1993: 183).

Walker, and from a related angle Bartelson, then set out to show how the meaning of sovereignty has supposedly evolved from antiquity to Medieval, Renaissance, and modern Europe, to our present, and Bartelson in particular, by adopting a Foucauldian understanding of genealogy, highlights how past meanings of sovereignty are (re-)written from the vantage point of the present, with an eye on legitimizing and substantiating the present discourse about sovereignty. In other words, this Foucauldian understanding of genealogy 'affirms a perspectivism which denies the capacity to identify origins and meanings in history objectively' (Devetak 2009: 184). Bartelson clarifies,

> what genealogy purports to teach us from history is that we are historical beings all the way down; we are all but interpretations of earlier interpretations – but also that it is we and only we who do the interpretation. If genealogical history happens to be rewritten, it is because the present changes. If the present changes, it is partly because history is rewritten.
>
> (Bartelson 1995: 78)

This genealogical approach to history and representations thereof in the present allows Bartelson to challenge the linear evolutionary trajectory of sovereignty from polities in antiquity to medieval kingdoms, to Italian city states, to our contemporary sovereign nation state – and by implication its claims to being static and timeless – purported by explanatory IR[6] by demonstrating that this understanding of the historical development of sovereignty is genealogical, i.e. is rewritten in the present through the lens of the present in order to substantiate discourses of it in the present. What is more, he also directs attention to the producers of this knowledge, us scholars of IR who claim to and are acknowledged to speak with authority on matters of sovereignty. Rob Walker (1993) has already problematized the role of IR scholarship in the discursive formation of sovereignty when he included the disciplines of political science versus international relations in his sets of binary opposites that constitute this discourse, and in which the latter tends to read sovereignty from the outside, focusing on questions of how states maintain and defend their sovereignty in an anarchical international system, as well as issues of international recognition and the permissibility of (humanitarian) intervention in case states violate the obligations towards its citizenry that come with sovereignty. The latter question has been the focus of Cynthia Weber's approach to this discursive formation, in which she demonstrates how principles of sovereignty and intervention are co-constitutive of each other in a dialectic relationship where sovereignty and intervention are reproduced through simulation in a Baudrillardian sense, and she too comes to the conclusion that 'the meaning of state sovereignty is fixed historically via practices of international relation theorists and', in her case, 'practices of political intervention' (Weber 1995: 3). This concentration of reading sovereignty from the outside, however, comes at the expense of questions about what constitutes it on the inside, namely issues of authority and legitimacy of those who govern, the nature of the democratic process within the wider social contract that binds those who govern to the governed and how this social contract comes under stress in times of globalization, increasing diversity of society and competing identities of the various protagonists that participate and shape it – questions, as already highlighted earlier, explanatory IR either ignores or addresses insufficiently at its own peril. Yet, what is even more important, explanatory IR ignores the question of how the differentiation between inside and outside can be made, what the epistemological bases for its presumption about a clear distinction demarcating the inside from the outside are. It is precisely this question that Bartelson urges IR scholars to devote their attention to. For sovereignty's 'function in political discourse can only be properly understood if we detach' it from the 'essentialist conviction' about 'its power to organize political reality' (Bartelson 1995: 52), if we suspend our belief and presumption about a factual divide demarcating the inside from the outside.

> If we succeed in this, our analysis of sovereignty will no longer presuppose that the line in water between the domestic and the international has already been drawn, but it will instead help us to explain how it is *drawn* and perpetually *redrawn* inside knowledge, and how, subsequently, the domestic and the international are discursively constituted as self-evident.
>
> (Bartelson 1995: 52, emphasis in original)

Here, Bartelson again draws attention to the process of knowledge production in this discursive formation, and the central role social science scholarship plays in it, in particular IR scholarship in the discourse on sovereignty that is so central to the discipline – a process that will be further problematized in the next chapter. For now the discussion of state-centrism needs to return to the claims made about the state in explanatory IR, in particular the claim about the sameness and universality of sovereign states. For what is presupposed to be universal here is a distinct type of sovereignty.

To recapitulate, the claim to sameness and universality of the sovereign nation state rests mainly on two epistemologies: (1) the presupposed anarchical structure of the international system that, as has been shown, renders states essentially the same as far as their function, objective and value-maximizing nature within the international system is concerned; and (2) an extrapolation and generalization of the European experience of nationalist state-formation to the universal level. The latter presumption, drawing on the classics on state formation and nationalism (Tilly 1975, 1990; Smith 1995; Mann 1986, 1993; Hechter 2001; Anderson 2006; Gellner 2006), is rooted in the previously discussed modernist view of nationalism that seeks to carve out universal tendencies and generalizable patterns from the formation of nation states in eighteenth- and nineteenth-century Europe – mainly processes of industrialization and modernization, the advent of mass literacy in the local vernacular, mass mobilization of the armed forces, the spread of demands of democratic representation, bureaucratic centralization, and the refinement of systems of taxation – and to then identify the proliferation of similar tendencies and patterns across the non-European world.[7] These generalizing and essentializing presumptions have been criticized for the selectivity with which empirical cases in their support are chosen (Breuilly 2005; Wimmer 2008, 2012; Wimmer & Feinstein 2010), and on a more general level by the rich post-colonial literature, which holds that, due to the colonial experience, processes of state formation in eighteenth- and nineteenth-century Europe are not comparable with the trajectories of decolonized states in the twentieth century (Strang 1990, 1996; Chatterjee 1993,

1999; Young 1994, 2012; Escobar 1995; Hansen & Stepputat 2001; Spruyt 2005; Anghie 2007; Amin-Khan 2012; Hobson 2012).[8] Yet, 'the tendency within the field of state theory is to focus mainly on the Western capitalist state without attempting to even understand the specificity of the post-colonial state' (Amin-Khan 2012: 50). In explanatory IR this tendency to extrapolate from the European experience in state-formation to generalizable patterns in the rest of the world is particularly striking in the works of Cohen *et al.* (1981), Buzan (1991) and Huntington (2002), where, for example, Buzan draws parallels between the violent formation of states in early modern Europe with today's conflicts in the developing world.

Even a moment's reflection, though, should make plain that the narratives of state formation of Huntington, Buzan, Tilly, Mann, Anderson, Gellner and others of the modernist provenance – save European settler colonies such as the US, Canada, and Australia, etc. – are not applicable to the majority world.[9] While in Europe modern statehood was the result of centuries of violent struggles, state-hood in the majority world came in the form of the rather sudden bang of decolo-nization when the colonial powers realized that colonial rule was no longer economical and devised cheaper means of indirect rule.[10] Consequently, borders were drawn and imposed on the new states by the colonial powers, industrializa-tion and modernization was limited to a few export-oriented industries and cash crops that at large remained in the hands of investors from the former colonial powers, literacy in the vernacular – if codified at all – was the prerogative of a narrow elite, and as far as systems of bureaucratic centralization and taxation existed, they had been set up and reflected the needs of the former colonial power. What is more, the very nature and objective of the nation differed from the European experience to the majority world. While liberal secularism and increasing demands for popular representation were integral parts of European nationalism and to some extent were realized in universal suffrage,

> state sovereignty for post-colonial states, with few exceptions, has been a token expression of self-rule. The integral link between contemporary [neo] imperialism and Western capitalist development has deepened and cemented the North–South divide and has promoted uneven development within and between post-colonial states.
>
> (Amin-Khan 2012: 50)

Put differently, in the more flowery language of Crawford Young, 'a genetic code for the new states of Africa was already imprinted on its embryo within the womb of the African colonial state' (1994: 283). Perhaps the most significant feature of this 'genetic code' of the post-colonial state is the role of the local elites that championed decolonization, the same elites that earlier collaborated with the colonial power in the exploitation of local resources and the indigenous population, and that continued to do so, serving and profiteering from what Amin-Khan calls the 'capitalism-imperialism nexus'.[11] From this perspective, coined the 'excentric view' of decolonization by Robinson (1986), colonialism prospered for as long as the colonial power was able to recruit local collaborators, and these local collaborators benefited from the colonial structure; once these mutual benefits started to subside and material returns in terms of status, power and economic sinecures abated, the system proved no longer sustainable for both sides and was replaced with a more cost-efficient one, yet the structures of division, exploitation and dependence at the domestic and the international level persisted.[12] In sum,

> in most post-colonial societies, the ruling elite (composed of landholders, indigenous capitalists, and civil and military bureaucrats) were successors-in-interest of colonial rulers. The post-colonial elite … were former collaborators with colonial rulers … this had afforded them privilege during their years of collaboration … so the post-colonial elites were unwilling to abandon their tried and tested colonial state structures for fear of losing their power … by transplanting these colonial structures into the new post-colonial state, it has entrenched the capitalism-imperialism nexus … [and led to the post-colonial elites] hav[ing] become mired in even deeper collaboration with Western capital and [neo-]imperialist Western states.
>
> (Amin-Khan 2012: 32, 107)

Irrespective of whether one subscribes to this neo-Marxist reading of post-colonial elites continuing to serve Western capitalist interests or rather sees them as integral parts of a global capitalist Empire (Hardt & Negri 2000), two more features constitutive of the post-colonial state can be identified: a system-immanent authoritarianism and the nationalities question in most post-colonial states remaining unresolved which in turn leads to a proliferation of violent ethno-nationalist conflicts in the developing world. A wide host of post-colonial theorists have problematized how authoritarian regimes in the developing world can be seen as a concomitance of the authoritarian colonial legacy and the structural context of global capitalism and strategic expediencies of the Cold War, in which the West 'relied' on complicit elites that combined the modes of production, control of resources, government and military power (Alavi 1972; Bhabha 1990; Davidson 1992; Chatterjee 1993; Ayoob 1995; Hansen & Stepputat 2001; Premnath 2003; Amin-Khan 2012).[13] Complementary to authoritarianism is the colonial legacy of systems of 'divide and rule', in which the former colonial powers had privileged certain ethnic groups over others in order to assure compliance, collaboration and exploitation. The colonial restraints had not allowed questions of identity and difference to be addressed in a non-violent discourse at the indigenous level, which is why these questions erupted with the sudden bang of decolonization, often in violent conflict, when the local inequalities of the colonial era and its aftermath were settled by force – as we have come to see, for example, most tragically in Rwanda (Keane 1996; Taylor 1999; Gourevitch 2000; Melvern 2000; Mamdani 2001), and, as the case study will illustrate, in Iraq. The result of these ethno-nationalist challenges to the state were attempts at 'pathological homogenization' (Rae 2002) as a means of state-building. These can be understood as 'the methods state-builders have used to define the state as a normative order and to cultivate identification through targeting those designated as outsiders for discriminatory and often violent treatment' (Rae 2002: 4). The violence of the assimilationist nationalizing post-colonial state is then met with violent means by the oppressed ethnic minority or segment of society demanding greater pluralism leading to an ever escalating spiral of violent conflict, of which ethnic conflict as discussed in this study is but one prominent expression. 'The creation of outsiders', then, Rae continues, 'is a political process in which "difference" becomes translated into "otherness" and therefore a threat to be disposed of in one way or the other' (Rae 2002: 3), an aspect to the process of group identification that has already been addressed in Chapter 1. However, the extent to which this pathological homogenization plays a significant and, according to Rae, even constitutive part of the state- and nation-building process in post-colonial states has been overlooked in the literature, which largely contents itself with labelling these states as inherently 'weak', 'failed' (Sørensen 2001; Kreijen 2004; Rotberg 2002, 2010; Piazza 2008; Ghani & Lockhart 2009; Patrick 2011),[14] or 'quasi states', the latter being a term coined by Robert Jackson (1996), in one of the most salient examples of the Eurocentrism in explanatory IR.

> These developments of the decolonization period have prompted some observers of state and national identity formation to claim that instead of a nation(s) forming a state (as was the case in Europe), the state was created before a nation was even 'imagined' – as in a *state-nation.*
>
> (Amin-Khan 2012: 109, emphasis in original)

The concept of the 'state-nation' (Rashid & Shaheed 1993; Stepan *et al.* 2011), highlighting the fact that a state with inviolable borders was imposed on the developing world in the process of decolonization before there was a nation that could have 'imagined', in the Andersonian terminology, such a state, makes perfectly plain the different experiences of state-formation in Europe and the non-European world. The fact that explanatory IR not only fails to account for the different trajectories of European nation states and post-colonial states, and how the colonial legacy shaped the latter, but claims universal validity for the former is again illustrative of its inherent Eurocentrism.

In conclusion, the modern sovereign nation state as it emerged in nineteenth-century Europe is neither factually universal, timeless, fixed and clearly bounded, nor does it distinctly demarcate an inside from an outside, a domestic from an international sphere, anarchy from hierarchy, order from chaos. It is a social construct, a discursive formation, in which these features that are said to be its properties are presupposed, when in fact they are products of the discourse about it, not its actual attributes. And yet, instead of questioning these ontologies and their underlying epistemes, explanatory IR, with the state-centric lens through which it perceives the social world, not only reifies them but transfers these presuppositions about the state onto the level of the ethnic group and nation by explicitly analytically equating those with the state, as will be illustrated now when discussing the models and frameworks explanatory IR has contributed to the study of ethnic and ethno-nationalist conflict.

Ethnic security dilemmas and ethnic alliances

Symptomatic of the ways in which explanatory IR approaches, makes sense of, and explains ethnic conflict – ways that have been discussed in theory in the previous chapter – are the two main explanatory frameworks that explanatory IR has contributed to capturing the dynamics of the onset and development of ethnic conflicts. In both frameworks, the 'ethnic security dilemma' and the 'ethnic alliance model', supposed patterns of state behaviour are extrapolated to ethnic groups. In both, ethnic groups are equated with states as relatively substantive, distinct, homogeneous, bounded and unitary actors or unitarily acting agents. In doing so they display at least two of the key characteristics of groupism this study has identified earlier and subsequently sets out to challenge.

In the late 1980s and early 1990s IR scholars found themselves confronted with the fact that conflicts in world politics were no longer predominantly between states and that the Cold War lens, through which intra-state conflict had been explained for the better part of 50 years, namely as proxy wars of two competing power blocks, no longer held any purchase. What is more, these 'new wars' (van Creveld 1991, 2008; Münkler 2005; Kaldor 2007) appeared mostly rooted in ideational factors, were largely understood as conflicts of identity, primarily religious or ethnic, and/or emanating from the implosion of multi-ethnic, multi-religious states such as the Soviet Union or Yugoslavia.[15] This posed an ontological challenge to neo-realism, which held that domestic factors and ideational values of actors in world politics mattered little to explain their behaviour in the international arena. Instead of questioning the epistemological and ontological bases for the paradigm, neo-realist scholars responded to that challenge by approaching and explaining these 'new wars' in the same way they had already approached and explained the Cold War and every international conflict since 1815: by propounding that, when studying international conflict in the *longue durée*, ideational factors, whether nationalism, liberalism, religion, or ethnicity, were of secondary importance; what determined the behaviour, conflictual or cooperative, of actors in world politics, whether states, nations, ethnic groups or religious communities, was the egoistic pursuit of material interests. And, like individual human beings, the most fundamental material interest of any organized collective, superior to all other motives, is supposedly the interest to survive, the drive to self-preservation. On this premise, Barry Posen set out to explain the collapse of multi-ethnic and multi-religious states of the late 1980s and early 1990s when he transferred the classic neo-realist explanatory model of the 'security dilemma' from the level of states to the level of ethnic groups, treating them, as far as their behaviour and structure are concerned, as unitary actors, as ontologically convertible into states, with few epistemological and ontological reservations. Confronted with a situation of anarchy ensuing from state collapse, Posen argued,

> a group suddenly compelled to provide its own protection must ask the following questions about any neighbouring group: Is it a threat? How much of a threat? Will the threat grow or diminish over time? … The answers to these questions strongly influence the chances for war?
>
> (Posen 1993: 103)

The classic security dilemma, as developed for explaining rational state behaviour,[16] then stipulates that any action one state/group engages in to increase its own security in an unpredictable and hostile environment of anarchy could be interpreted by a neighbouring state/group as a threat to its own security, as compromising its chance of survival by placing it in a weaker position via the first group. According to neo-realism, this climate of fear almost inevitably leads to a race for ever more security and makes conflict between both states/groups more likely (Jervis 1978; Waltz 1979; Mearsheimer 2001; Gray 2009). Posen (1993) saw no reason why what is good for states, would not also be good for ethnic groups, why these patterns of state behaviour would not also apply to ethnic groups, why the explanatory framework of the security dilemma would not also explain the behaviour of ethnic groups in a system of anarchy, and consequently expanded the model and its implications – from arms races, to political mobilization in order to reinforce group cohesion, to windows of vulnerability and opportunity that make pre-emptive war more likely, to incentives for 'defensive expansion', a euphemism for politics of ethnic homogenization by force – to ethnic groups in conflict.

Notwithstanding the fact that the entire construct of the security dilemma revolves around the pre-condition of anarchy by presupposing a rationality of fear as the determining variable in explaining actors' behaviour, for which neo-realism has been criticized by generations of scholars in general[17] and Posen's 'ethnic security dilemma' in particular (Fearon & Laitin 1996; Lake & Rothchild 1996; David 1997; Kaufman 2001; Cederman 2010), Posen's model features prominently in leading neo-realist accounts of ethnic conflict.[18] It has been utilized and adapted by myriad scholars from quite diverse intellectual backgrounds,[19] and can largely be considered the standard device with which neo-realism makes sense of ethnic conflict. Yet, what concerns this study more is another presumption that the ethnic security dilemma makes: that ethnic groups can be equated with states as substantive, distinct, homogeneous, bounded and unitary actors or unitarily acting agents in international relations. Not once does Posen seem to be troubled by ontological questions as to whether it is tenable to apply a model developed to explain state behaviour to ethnic groups, and whether it is ontologically sound to analytically treat ethnic groups in the same manner as states, as unitary actors (regardless of whether states should be treated as such in the first place). These questions have concerned scholars such as Paul Roe (1999, 2004), who advocate substituting the unit of analysis in studies of state security with 'societal security', in particular in the context of ethnic conflict. The approach of settling for society, rather than the state, as the unit of analysis in security discourses originates from the wider context of securitization theory associated with what is colloquially often referred to as the 'Copenhagen School' (Wæver 1993; Buzan *et al.* 1997). As it pertains to reflections on the security dilemma, what can be registered here is that the concept of 'societal security' first shifts the analytical interest from discussing merely material interests as security issues to discussing ideational factors; for example, acknowledging threats to one's identity as a security threat. It therefore directly addresses issues that neo-realism deliberately brackets out from its analysis. Second, like neo-liberalism whose models for explaining ethnic conflict will be taken up shortly, it acknowledges a plurality of views, interests, and identities, and even actors to constitute its unit of analysis.

Echoing McSweeney (1996) and Peoples and Vaughan-Williams (2010), I argue that the concept of 'societal security', of society as the referent object of security discourses, operationalizes too static a concept of identity, failing to take sufficiently into account the constructed nature and inherent transience and fluidity of identity, and consequently is not only guilty of groupism but also, like the framework of the ethnic security dilemma at large, runs risk of reifying ethnic lines of division of 'us' versus 'them' constructed in an ethnicized discourse. Like neo-liberalism or systemic constructivism then, it mirrors too closely for comfort neo-realism's groupist presumptions – after conceding agency to it in the first place – about its unit of analysis, state or society, as an ultimately unitarily acting agent and therefore replicates many of their ontological and epistemological fallacies.

Diametrically opposed to the neo-realist approach that treats ethnicity first and foremost as a function of conflict behaviour of ethnic groups and relegates ideational factors to the mere political sphere and elites' rhetoric, is the 'ethnic alliance' model. This rather neo-liberal and systemic constructivist concept operationalizes shared ethnicity as the independent and determining variable to explain the behaviour of ethnic groups in conflict; that is, picking up an earlier observation on groupism, it tautologically explains ethnic conflict through ethnicity.

Like neo-realism, though, the ethnic alliance model first equates ethnic groups with states as relatively fixed, substantive and distinct actors invested with social agency in the international system. Davis and Moore (1997, 1998), in two articles on dyads, or a pair of states with transnational ethnic ties, of which the first was pointedly titled *Ethnicity Matters*, contend that 'transnational ethnic alliances serve as a conduit for conflict behaviour' (Davis & Moore 1997: 172). They hold that 'it is useful to conceptualise ethnic linkages among people across state boundaries as functionally equivalent to alliances between two states', and second, purport that

conflict between a state and an ethnic group will escalate to the international level when other elite members of that same ethnic group play a role in policy making in another state and that state finds the first state to be politically relevant.

(Davis & Moore 1998: 93)

In other words, the likelihood of violent conflict between two neighbouring states increases, if in one state (A) – say, in the case study, Turkey – a disenfranchised ethnic minority fights state oppression, while in the other state (B) – in the case study Iraq, then the Iraqi Kurdish 'de facto state', and after 2003 the Kurdish Autonomous Region in Iraq – a co-ethnic group of said minority holds considerable power or dominates the political structure. The policies of A via its minority then not only constitute part of B's 'Politically Relevant International Environment' (Maoz 1997), but they determine its actions via A. As a consequence, Davis and Moore claim that B and the oppressed minority in A will form an ethnic alliance against state A, and the internal conflict in state A will diffuse to the point where the likelihood of it escalating to the international level rises. The authors test this hypothesis by contrasting three dependent weighted variables – conflict, cooperation and net interaction between the dyadic states – from the *Conflict and Peace Databank* of Edward Azar (1982) that measures levels of interaction between states, with data from the *Minorities at Risk* set of Ted Robert Gurr with individual ethno-political groups as its unit of analysis (Gurr 1993; Gurr & Harff 1994). Notably, they at first caution that 'we do not believe that the ethnic composition of the dyads is the most critical determinate of such [cooperative or conflictual] behaviour' (Davis & Moore 1997: 174), and come themselves to the conclusion that the ethnic composition of dyads matters only 'at the margins' (Davis & Moore 1997: 181).[20] Then, however, in a rather difficult to comprehend attempt at creative reinterpretation, and trusting that future quantitative research with more extensive data will prove their hypotheses, they maintain that 'the impact of ethnic alliances is not spurious' (Davis & Moore 1998: 100).

There are many ways one could methodologically challenge the ethnic alliance model. First, as has already been discussed in the context of constructivism in the previous chapter, one may wonder whether the rather generalizing instrument of pure quantitative analyses is best suited to decode such highly complex, contextual, circumstantial, fluctuating and, ultimately, often constructed relations between and within presumed ethnic groups and in consequence thereof ethnically framed conflicts. Furthermore, like the large-*n* studies and datasets criticized in the previous chapter, the source of data for Davis and Moore's model, Ted Robert Gurr's *Minorities at Risk* set, operationalizes ethnic groups as substantive, distinct, homogeneous, bounded units of analysis. Then one may cite that Davis and Moore themselves admit what limited generalizations one could make from their findings as their entire set of data originates from a *single year* of reference, 1978 – more extensive and recent findings seem to at least superficially confirm them, though (Gleditsch *et al.* 2008; Cederman *et al.* 2009a, 2009b, 2013; Salehyan 2007, 2008, 2009). Third, as the authors themselves recognize, the ethnic composition of their dyads mattered only *marginally* for the measurable political behaviour and foreign policy of analysed states.

Karen Petersen re-examined Davis and Moore's model and, after modifying some variables with an improved measure of the foreign policy behaviour of the original dyads and adjusting control variables, discovered a slightly stronger amplitude towards conflict and decreased net interaction between dyads of states with one ethnic group in common, which leads her to allege that 'ethnic alliances do in fact matter' and 'may not operate at the margins' (Petersen 2004: 39).[21] Her findings concur with Saideman's, whose more nuanced utilization of the *Minorities at Risk* dataset and actual application of his hypotheses to three empirical case studies show that 'a group with kin dominating a nearby state is at least 10 percent more likely to receive support' (Saideman 2001: 181). He, too, admits, though, that generally speaking 'we cannot say with confidence that the particular identity of a group causes it to get more or less support' (Saideman 2001: 181). And yet, despite only marginal empirical evidence for such presumptions, explanatory IR scholars seem not to tire of working the bogey man of ethnic alliances forming against the status quo and ethnic minorities with irredentist aspirations acting as 'fifth columns' for the territorial ambitions of neighbouring states. Although not specifically called an ethnic alliance, group solidarity based on shared ethnicity is also the independent variable and main explanatory factor in other key texts on the internationalization of ethnic conflicts (van Evera 1994; Cetinyan 2002; Woodwell 2004; Jenne 2006, 2010; Gleditsch *et al.* 2008; Cederman *et al.* 2009a, 2009b, 2013; Salehyan 2007, 2008, 2009). They all to some degree share the ontological and epistemological fallacies of groupism, mainly to equate ethnic groups with states and to attribute them with agency as unitarily acting protagonists in conflict, then proceeding to tautologically explain this ethnic conflict with ethnicity, that is assuming the actions of these actors are dictated by the principles of group solidarity based on shared ethnicity. Here, a picture is presented in which 'ethnically intermixed areas are magnets for kin state interventions' (Jenne 2010: 123–124), and 'potential rescuers' will be tempted 'to jump through any windows of opportunity that may arise [...] to rescue [their kin] now by force' (van Evera 1994: 20). In the case of the PKK presence in Iraqi Kurdistan for example – which Salehyan (2007, 2008, 2009) lists as an archetype of common ethnicity determining the conflict behaviour of actors in the internationalization of an ethnic conflict – the myth of the PKK as a 'fifth column' without legitimate cause and controlled by foreign elements in pursuit of a region-wide pan-Kurdish secessionism was used for decades prior to 2007 by the Turkish nationalizing state to justify addressing the so called 'Kurdish Question' in Turkey by violent means and for countless military interventions into Iraq (Lundgren 2007). Like other groupist explanatory models in its attempts to make sense of ethnic conflict then, the ethnic alliance framework reifies the politics of ethnic division that are the primary root cause of the conflict they set out to interpret, thus either legitimizing the supposedly irredentist agenda of the secessionist ethnic elites or the totalitarian politics of the assimilationist nationalizing states or, as happens frequently, both. This dynamic of the explanatory models and frameworks of explanatory IR corresponding and serving the interests of *both* sides in ethnic and ethno-nationalist conflicts, the assimilationist state and the ethnic minority rebelling against it, cannot be emphasized strongly enough and will be illustrated with a host of examples in the case study of this book at various stages of the relations between the PKK, the Iraqi Kurdish ethno-nationalist parties, and Turkey.

An interesting qualitative counter-argument to the ethnic alliance model is made in Rajat Ganguly's *Kin State Intervention in Ethnic Conflicts* (1998). Ganguly – drawing on case studies from Pakistan's role in Kashmiri secession attempts, India's support for Bangladesh's secession, Afghanistan and Iran's interventions on behalf of Baluch separatism in Pakistan, Afghanistan's role in a wider so-called 'Pashtunistan', and finally India's ambivalent stance towards Tamil secessionism in Sri Lanka – categorizes the reaction of a 'kin state' to a co-ethnic insurgency in a neighbouring country in four patterns: diffusion and encouragement, isolation and suppression, reconciliation, and diffusion or isolation through inaction and non-intervention. Diffusion and encouragement, which Ganguly holds to be the most common practice of a kin state reacting to a co-ethnic insurgency in a neighbouring state, he sub-divides between direct support – through military or material means, supplying technical, logistic, and financial assistance, and in the most extreme form, granting sanctuary on its territory – and indirect support, i.e. politico-diplomatic assistance. While to him affective motives for diffusion and encouragement are easily explainable by group solidarity across borders or material reasons, such as pre-existing rivalries between the two states, in which the ethnic conflict is used as a pretext and the insurgency often as a proxy, a similar point is made by Salehyan, who terms this 'security delegation' (Salehyan 2009: 53). Other material reasons are the dynamics of domestic politics – public opinion, popular demand or 'ethnic outbidding' – as well as the context of international relations. Most interestingly, and contrary to the majority of the literature, Ganguly argues that external support from an ethnic kin state on a long-term perspective is to the disadvantage of the insurgency as the target state will respond to the enhanced challenge and elevated international attention by intensifying persecution and upping its repressive apparatus as a zero-sum mentality to the conflict takes over politico-strategic considerations. The normative international system also, as will be discussed shortly, is system-immanently hostile to any attempts at secession and has a wide arsenal of coercive measures at its disposal to exert pressure on the kin state. This pressure renders the kin state a notoriously fickle patron who hardly ever provides support in the scope required to defeat the target state (Ganguly 1998). Ganguly's more nuanced analysis of the dynamics between presumed sub-groups in ethnic conflict, in particular their cooperation and even 'intra-group' conflict across international borders is however impaired by his unadulterated primordialism that perceives ethnicity as a 'given', a 'natural phenomenon', and 'cultural attributes' shared by people as 'objective' (Ganguly 1998: 33, 34, n. 1). Consequently, due to these primordial kinship ties, and despite the variety of expressions to which relations between subgroups within an ethnic group can amount, for Ganguly, common ethnicity does not allow for a kin state's neutrality in an ethnic conflict. Even 'doing nothing' on the side of the kin state will always be seen as partisan, and remaining on the sidelines of a conflict 'usually strengthens the hand of the central government against the secessionists' (Ganguly 1998: 27, 29), i.e. the kin state is perceived to indirectly support the target state and to give it carte blanche to 'resolve' the conflict by 'methods of eliminating differences', as McGarry and O'Leary have somewhat euphemistically termed them.[22] Ganguly's deterministic portrayal of the dynamics of ethnic conflict then, despite the interesting qualifications made in some places, amounts to the same logic and narrative as the ethnic alliance model: ethnicity as a primordial pre-given that not only is not further questioned but whose stringency is subscribed to without further questioning, thus resulting in a reification of the strategic essentialism and the politics of ethnic division and group solidarity of the ethnic elites as well as their participants' primordialism.

Another explanatory model that explains ethnic conflict with ethnicity is the already-mentioned concept of 'ethnic outbidding' (Brubaker 1996; Kaufman 1996b; Saideman 1998; Horowitz 2001; De Votta 2005; Jenne 2006; Coakley 2008).

> Ethnic outbidding is a situation in which competing elites try to position themselves as the best supporters of a group's interests, each accusing the others of being too weak on ethnic nationalist issues. When conditions foster ethnic outbidding, the exit of ethnically defined supporters can change the balance of power domestically; most, if not all, politicians are compelled to take extreme stands favouring the ethnic group's interests.
>
> (Saideman 1998: 133)

These dynamics of 'outbidding' each other with ever more extreme and radical positions among ethnically defined parties and elites, according to the literature, can easily lead to the ethnicized discourse and with it the political situation spiralling out of control and gaining a momentum of its own that makes violent conflict between those presumed groups more likely. In the context of the case study, the concept of ethnic outbidding is explicitly applied to the PKK by Adamson (2013). However, aside from its demonstrated limited applicability (Gagnon 2004; Caspersen 2010), ethnic outbidding is merely an expression and manifestation of the conflict that must not be mistaken as its causes; it builds on, exacerbates and escalates an already existing ethnicized discourse within a deeply divided society along ethnic lines, and therefore can be understood as another expression of the previously discussed strategic essentialisms of ethnic elites. In addition to being distinctly tautological by explaining ethnic conflict with ethnicity, it is of very finite explanatory value since it does not address how the ethnicized discourse that constitutes it came about in the first place. As Donald Horowitz remarks himself,

> intragroup party proliferation usually awaits the emergence of an ethnic issue that spurs party formation and assures the new party some following. Such an issue generally relates to intergroup relations. Unless party

formation is practically ordained by the existence of sharp subethnic divisions, the pivotal event at the point of intraethnic party formation is usually an accusation that the existing ethnic party has sold out group interests by its excessive moderation toward other ethnic groups.

(Horowitz 2001: 354)

Again, at first sight, the 'Kurdish case', one of the most prominent examples of an internationalized ethnicized conflict, and in particular the PKK sanctuary in Iraqi Kurdistan, seem to fit the pattern of ethnic alliance formation as if taken from a textbook and is consequently routinely cited as a model case for these dynamics (Entessar 1992; Gurr & Harff 1994; Kaufmann 1996; Kirişçi & Winrow 1997; Byman 1998; Freij 1998; Helsing 2004; Husain & Shumock 2006; Milton-Edwards & Hinchcliffe 2008; Rear 2008; Salehyan 2007, 2008, 2009). Of the countless instances of banditry, pillaging raids, minor insurrections, insurgencies and rebellions that the one or the other self-proclaimed Kurdish insurgency has been involved in along the border regions of Iran, Turkey, Iraq and Syria since the First World War, hardly any has not had an international dimension or has not escalated to the international level; that is sought shelter across the border, shared intelligence, received logistical support and armaments, and joined forces on a temporary basis. All major Kurdish rebellions have been supported and sustained by affiliated or temporarily allied Kurdish insurgencies from the bordering state and many of these rebellions have escalated to regional conflagrations that not only dragged in local but also great powers such as the USSR, Israel and the USA during the Cold War.[23]

Consequently, and to counter these supposedly secessionist insurgencies, a 'balance of threat' (Walt 1985, 1990) was formed by the nationalizing states. Stephen Walt's 'balance of threat' can be understood as an adaptation of the neo-realist 'balance of power' concept (Vasquez 2003; Little 2007; Kaufman *et al.* 2007). In this instance, states form a defensive pact or alliance to counter, not a rising hegemon that could upset an existing 'balance of power', but a mutual threat to the status quo and their common interests, for example the threat of supposedly pan-Kurdish ethno-nationalism undermining the existent state structure and borders in the region. As early as 1937 then, Turkey signed the Treaty of Sa'dbad with Iraq and Iran 'to coordinate their defence policy' against Kurdish uprisings that could spill over from one state into the others' territories (Entessar 1992: 54); a coordination and collaboration among the three countries that was extended in the Baghdad Pact of 1955 and led to occasional joint military operations against Kurdish insurgencies.[24] The latter, in particular, can be understood as an actual alliance in the political sense of the term, as it established a 'mutual military assistance' clause against 'internal revolts liable to threaten common security' (Nezan 1993: 64). After Turkish-Iraqi relations had degenerated in the aftermath of the 1958 revolution, in 1983, the practice of Turkey securing from Iraq the right to pursue Kurdish insurgents onto its territory was revived under Saddam Hussein – then too weakened by the Iran-Iraq War to effectively control the Kurdish north – and, after Saddam Hussein's downfall, was one of the first concessions the Turkish government called for from the post-2003 Iraqi government (Phillips 2007). Given the sum of these cross-border counter-insurgency operations over the past 60 years with the single goal of keeping Kurdish separatism at bay, it might seem the balance of threat of the status quo preserving nationalizing states against presupposed irredentist Kurdish claims and activities, and, in converse argument, the Kurdish ethnic alliance, has been a factual reality. As I have already demonstrated elsewhere though (Artens 2012; Černy 2014a), closer scrutiny of the Kurdish case study will show that the ethnic alliance model, like its neo-realist and instrumentalist (see below) counterparts, is either ontologically untenable or falls short of comprehensively explaining the complex dynamics and processes of (self-) identification as well as protagonists' behaviour in ethnic conflict.

Instrumentalism

The above-identified 'clichéd constructivism' also becomes distinctly manifest in a school of thought commonly referred to as instrumentalism, which I locate at the transition from (neo-)realism to constructivism.[25] Here, the image of the nation as an 'imagined community' and of identity as a social construct is taken a step further towards an 'invented tradition' in the Hobsbawmian sense (Hobsbawm 1990; Hobsbawm & Ranger 1984), of identity having ultimately no intrinsic and little explanatory value. In the instrumentalist understanding of ethnicity, ethnic identities,

> are creations of elites who draw upon, distort, and sometimes fabricate materials from the cultures of the groups they wish to represent, in order to protect their well being or existence, or to gain political and economic advantage for their groups and for themselves.
>
> (Brass 1993: 111)

Analogous to Alexander Wendt's systemic constructivism, subsumed under the catchphrase 'anarchy is what states make of it', one may characterize instrumentalism as subscribing to the slogan 'ethnicity is what ethnic elites make of it'. They exploit 'national traditions' they have 'invented' for their own avails and to rally the masses to their leadership (Hobsbawm & Ranger 1984). In sum, in the eyes of instrumentalists, culture is reduced to a means to consolidate and homogenize societies; ethnic communities are merely 'informally organised interest groups' (Cohen 1974: 92);[26] and ethnicity is nothing but a replaceable political tool, a resource; there is nothing particular, nothing fundamental about it as any 'old shred and patch would have served as well' (Gellner 2006: 56). This modernism, carried to extremes, is grounded in the classic elite theories of Robert Michels (1915), Gaetano Mosca (1939), and Vilfredo Pareto (1976 [1902–1903], 2009 [1901]). Here, a view of society determined by a strict hierarchical order of a minority, disproportionately drawn 'from upper-status occupations and privileged family backgrounds' (Putnam 1976: 22), dominating a largely apathetic majority that subordinates to authority, is presented; an order that in its essence remains stable through time as it constitutes the most basic principle of society and is neither fundamentally altered by social change nor form of government. According to Pareto, the ruling minority, the oligarchy or elite, is distinguished by having the 'highest indices in their branch of activity', that is they rise well above the average in their education, accomplishments, wealth, and organizational ability that allows them to transform their common will into action; a cohesive, bureaucratic organization that was first established with the purpose of attaining a certain objective, becomes an end in itself and persists and governs to justify and maintain its own existence (Bottomore 1964; Putnam 1976; Parry 1977; Malešević 2004, 2006a, 2010).

Instrumentalism therefore exhibits a tendency to also presume the ethnic group as a static, substantive, distinct, homogeneous and bounded unit and as a unitary actor, and like neo-realism, concedes to ethnicity no explanatory value in itself since it is merely seen as a political tool of elite manipulation for elites to justify political actions ex post. These ethnic or ethno-national elites are egoistic interest and profit maximizers who base their actions on tactical and strategic considerations and cost-benefit analyses – the most important for an elite obviously being to stay in power; they determine their policies 'first based on tactical dictates, and then look to their identity repertoire for characteristics ... that would allow for the construction of justifying narratives' (Christia 2012: 46). Yet, echoing Gellner, 'when power considerations call for it, these [well-worn narratives], communities and traditions will be cast aside and new ones imagined in their place' (Christia 2012: 47), rendering identities always subordinate to material interests and easily replaceable.

This train of thought and its ontological as well as epistemological fallacies become eminently apparent in a recent study on *Alliance Formation in Civil Wars*, in which Fotini Christia (2012) investigates patterns of alliance formation and factionalization between and within ethnic groups in Bosnia and Afghanistan, and subsequently endeavours a generalization of her findings to civil wars dating back as far as the nationalist revolutions of 1848. While I have situated instrumentalism at the transition from neo-realism to systemic constructivism, Christia sees hers solidly grounded in neo-realism, presenting it as 'essentially a neorealist account of group behaviour in multiparty civil wars. Like neorealists, I posit that alliance choices are [primarily] driven by relative power considerations' (Christia 2012: 50). With the egoistic pursuit of relative power and material interests as the main explanatory variables for alliance formation between ethnic groups in civil wars and postulating that the rationale and motives for factionalization within groups are ultimately the same as for alliance formation between groups,[27] she deploys the full arsenal of neo-realist, systemic constructivist, and instrumentalist models to substantiate her conjecture: from the ethnic security dilemma, to a 'minimum winning coalition logic' (Chandra 2004, 2006; Posner 2005b) – groups or factions not necessarily siding with the strongest alliance, but the one sufficiently powerful enough to win, yet at the same of manageable size to guarantee a share in the division of power and sinecures after the war – to 'bandwagoning', where a weaker party to a conflict realizes that the costs of opposing its adversary outweigh the benefits and succumbs to an alliance dictated by necessity, where future spoils of joined conquest are shared proportionally (Waltz 1979; Walt 1990; Mearsheimer 2001).[28]

Like neo-realists, Christia (2012: 20) also 'suppose[s] that substate actors in civil wars behave like sovereign states in the anarchic international system', and the 'ethnic, linguistic, regional, religious, and … ideological identities [that form the bases of these groups] are presumed to stay relatively fixed' (Christia 2012: 8), without further elaborating why such presuppositions can be ontologically made. Not once in her study does the question arise as to what extent it is ontologically tenable, despite decades of shifting alliances and internal factionalization, to still treat those ethnic groups in Bosnia and Afghanistan as 'relatively fixed' political entities, to attribute them with agency, and operationalize them as the main unit of analysis. Their existence and continuity is simply considered a primordialist pre-given, or as a Wendtian constructivist corporate identity. Likewise, ideational factors only feature in her analysis as elements shaping the course of conflicts as political tools employed by elites to justify their actions – alliance formation or factionalization – ex post to an apparently apathetic and docile constituency, on whose agency Christia seems not to think worth elaborating.

> Notions of shared identity … prove endogenous [only to some extent] to alliance preferences: Elites pick their allies first based on tactical dictates, and then look to their identity repertoire for characteristics they share with their [new] friends … that would allow for the construction of justifying narratives.
>
> (Christia 2012: 46)

This bracketing of ideational factors, relegating them to the political sphere only, denying them any explanatory value, begs the question, why bother at all? Why not limit one's analysis to studying purely material interests? The answer, one may hypothesize, is, that if neo-realism wants to treat ethnic groups as units of analysis and to equate them with states, then primordialist and systemic constructivist narratives of identity as a pre-given value such as the Wendtian corporate identity, provide them with the ontological coherence necessary to do so. I further posit that, in this approach, the unit of analysis is made to fit the paradigm, a cardinal error to any scientific enquiry.

The problems with such a simplistic understanding of how identity works are obvious. First, instrumentalism's logic is not only circulatory and tautological, it also fails to explain why and how these 'invented traditions' and constructed narratives that ethnic and ethno-national elites employ to justify their policies would resonate with the masses, how the feelings of communality and solidarity that constitute them as a group came about in the first place or, echoing Benedict Anderson (2006: 7), to capture 'the fraternity that makes it possible, over the past two centuries, for so many millions of people, not so much to kill, as willingly to die for such limited imaginings'. In instrumentalism, the masses are treated as 'passive creatures prone to easy manipulation ... they are largely viewed as homogeneous, ignorant, dependent conglomerates, with child-like qualities' (Malešević 2004: 123). At best then, the social reductionism of instrumentalism, by simply presupposing Wendt's *corporate identity* or the like as a pre-given order of things that elites then exploit for their own ends, can be understood as neo-realism with a small constructivist caveat: ideational factors and identities only matter in the egoistic pursuit of material interests as far as identity and culture are reduced to politics and how they can be studied as such. Consequently, many instrumentalists, like neo-realists, founder with their ontological explanations as to how it is tenable to treat ethnic groups as their unit of analysis and their theories 'are epistemologically and conceptually too thin, ... incomplete, and as such unable to provide a more comprehensive theory of ethnic relations' (Malešević 2004: 126). What is more, if ethnicity and ethnic groups are only what ethnic and ethno-nationalist elites make of them, such systemic constructivism, as has been pointed out in IR (Campbell 1998a; McSweeney 1999; Zehfuss 2002, 2006; Weber 2010), runs the risk of again indirectly reifying the structure via the agent. A systemic constructivism 'fails to deliver on its promise to take us beyond reification, because in order to escape the reified logic of anarchy, it reifies the state' (Weber 2010: 80). Applied to ethnic identities this sort of constructivism, and related approaches such as a narrow instrumentalism, in order to escape the logic of essentialized groups, reify the ethnic elites and thus indirectly their strategic essentialisms by making them omnipotent, by, paraphrasing the title of Nicholas Onuf's famous constructivist work (Onuf 1989), rendering ethnic identity discourses a world exclusively of their making. Thus, the outcome of the challenge of such systemic constructivism to the essentialisms of the neo-neo synthesis ironically all too often runs risk of repeating the mistakes of neo-liberalism: the importance and plurality of internal actors, such as elites, is acknowledged, yet by declaring these actors omnipotent in shaping the ethnicized discourse, by reifying them and conceding to them an exclusivity of representation, those actors are portrayed again as if acting unitarily. In essence, in its clichéd constructivism and by making similar presumptions about unitarily acting ethnic groups that form the basis of neo-realist and neo-liberal readings of ethnic conflict and group solidarity, systemic constructivism and a narrow instrumentalism again purport a very similar metanarrative to neo-realism and neo-liberalism, one that constructivism at least has originally set out to challenge.

A more nuanced approach to ethnic identity and what is essentially still an instrumentalist reading thereof is offered by Daniel Posner, whose team studied electoral systems, voting patterns, and ethnic diversity in relation to economic growth and public goods provision in several Central African countries (Posner 2005b; Habyarimana *et al.* 2007; Eifert *et al.* 2010). The main merits of Posner's findings in relation to this study is that he puts equal weight on analysing the motives behind political action of the masses as of elites playing the ethnic card. In his approach, the constituents of elites are no longer passive victims of elite manipulation; instead he shows them to be as instrumentalist as the elites in their utilization of ethnicity as a political tool to attain an improvement of their position. Second, he portrays identities as contextual, putting emphasis on 'ethnicity as fluid and situation bound', as 'rather than being hard wired with a single ethnic identity, individuals possess repertoires of identities whose relevance wax and wane with changes in context' (Posner 2005b: 11). In his conceptualization of identity, ethnicity is but one of a variety of identities elites and their constituents can draw on, operationalize, and instrumentalize in pursuit of their material or ideational interests, although Posner clearly has more to say on the former than the latter. Yet, in sharp contrast to Christia's deterministic instrumentalism, where, 'when power considerations call for it, these [well-worn narratives], communities and traditions will be cast aside and new ones imagined in their place' (Christia 2012: 46), Posner highlights the limits to how easily elites can 'imagine' new forms of identity by reminding us that they can only resort to an already pre-existing repertoire of identities and not simply 'imagine new ones'.

By juxtaposing Christia's approach with Posner's it becomes evident why I have localized instrumentalism at the transition from (neo-)realism to constructivism. In Christia's case, an individual or group's identity clearly is a function of their interests, and identity itself is reduced to a political tool, whereas for Posner, for whom ethnic identity is 'an admission card for membership to a coalition of particular size and a source of information about the political coalitions to which others belong' (Posner 2005b: 12), one's interests also determine what form of identity is employed in a given context, yet the repertoire of identities at one's disposal, although fluid and alternating, is limited, which puts 'his' instrumentalism closer to the constructivist tenet of identities shaping interests. Posner (2005b: 14) contends that,

> when I assert that individuals are able to change their identities strategically in response to situational incentives, I am not claiming that people can choose any identity they want. Their choices are limited to the identities that are in their repertoire,

which suggests identities pre-existent to interests. A similar point is made by Susan Olzak (2006: 36) who reminds us of the limits to identity claims since 'ethnic mobilization expressed through ethnic conflict and protest requires commitment to a particular identity over some extended time period (and costs may rise with levels of commitment)'. Again, this indicates that, contrary to the belief that new forms of identity can simply be imagined when politically expedient for elites, that ethnicity can be easily replaced with an alternative form of identity when the situation calls for it, since in the above-quoted words of Gellner, any 'old shred and patch would have served as well', but that committing to one expression of identity is a long term process that can come with considerable costs and personal investments and thus is not easily discarded. These qualifications to instrumentalism made by Posner and Olzak are crucial because, while shifting our attention from the structure to the agency of elites and their constituents in ethnic politics, they insert the crucial caveat that in their agency these elites are not omnipotent but have to act within the confines of pre-existing identity structures not only in relation to their roles but also their constituents' roles, whose identities they seek to instrumentalize to gain power and who instrumentalize their identities to align themselves with the powerful. Posner and Olzak's instrumentalism therefore can be described as more genuinely constructivist than the clichéd constructivisms identified by Brubaker; with their more nuanced approach to agency in identity formation they make a critical point whose relevance will become evident when discussing the limitations to KRG politicians' freedom of choice in post-2003 Iraqi Kurdistan.

Having said that, though, despite their constructivist disclaimers, ultimately, for Posner, as for instrumentalists in general, 'ethnic identity is simply a means to an end'. For them,

> ethnic identities will not be chosen because of the psychological attachment that actors have toward them or because of the success of some crafty political entrepreneur in convincing voters that a particular identity is more important than others. They will be chosen because the identity gains them entry into a more [beneficial] coalition than the other identities that they might have drawn upon.
>
> (Posner 2005b: 252)

As elaborated above, I do not believe matters to be that simple, that ethnicity can be reduced to merely a means to a political end. Conceiving of identities and sets of beliefs as nothing but an 'admission card' to a 'minimum winning coalition', to a group sizeable enough to affect political change in pursuit of, at the end, mostly material interests (Posner 2005b: 12), fails to explain votes for the Green Party outside Brighton in the past British election, nor does it shed light on the motives of dozens of Kurds self-immolating in the aftermath of Abdullah Öcalan's arrest, nor, I would argue, can it account for the formation of the PKK in the first place, who in the late 1970s can certainly not be described as a sizeable group or part of any 'minimum winning coalition'.

Similar to Christia's Afghan warlords and ethnic elites in Bosnia, the behaviour of the leaders of Kurdish political parties, at first sight, seem to fit the pattern of material interests, pre-eminently to secure power, superseding ideational factors and those only being utilized to justify their actions ex post. One way to look at the genesis of Kurdish ethno-nationalism in the twentieth century is to portray it as a seemingly endless sequence of shifting alliances and group factionalizations, in which Kurdish parties who felt disenfranchised or expected greater returns from switching sides struck alliances with their ideational antagonists, the nationalizing states set on quelling their struggles for self-determination. From the 1950s on, Iraqi Kurdish parties repeatedly sided with the Shah's government in suppressing Kurdish groups in Iran and the Assad regime in brutalizing Syria's Kurds in exchange for support against Saddam Hussein; during the Iran–Iraq War the KDP teamed up with Tehran in fighting the Iranian KDP and the PUK, who initially sought its fortunes with Baghdad; while Saddam Hussein's regime perpetrated chemical warfare and genocide against its own Kurdish population, the PKK intensified its contacts with the Ba'athist dictator; and in the 1990s the KDP relied on Saddam Hussein's troops to re-take Erbil for them from a PUK-PKK-Iranian alliance, just four years after fighting the central government's troops to the death in collaboration with the PUK. On the face of it, one may have to agree with Michael Gunter's (1999a: 134) assessment that 'the Kurdish people have been the victim of leaders guilty of selfish partisanship and greed', as well as with Christia's postulate that material interests supersede ideational factors in the behaviour of ethnic elites, and sympathize with those Kurdish scholars quoted earlier who see Kurdish aspirations for independence betrayed by the petty particularisms, power and profit seeking greed, and selfish materialism of their leaders. As the analysis of Kurdish ethno-nationalism and the relations between Kurdish political parties in this study will reveal, though, matters are not that simple, and the essentialist generalizations of instrumentalism, neo-realism, and systemic constructivism do not suffice to explain the rather complex social dynamics at work here that, drawing on Fierke (2007) and as mentioned in the Introduction as well as being elaborated in more detail shortly, should rather be conceptualized as a complex matrix of identities and interests.

Notes

1 For a succinct summary of the various inter-disciplinary debates within IR on state-centrism, see Hobson (2000).
2 The most prominent example is perhaps Krasner's (1999) division into (1) 'inter-dependence sovereignty' as political sovereignty, and various legal expressions of sovereignty such as (2) 'Westphalian sovereignty', in other words the exclusivity of sovereignty over a particular territory, (3) 'legal sovereignty' strictly spoken, i.e. states recognizing each other as peers in the international system, and (4) 'domestic sovereignty', that is how authority within the state is structured.
3 'Sovereignty like pregnancy, is either present or absent, never only partially realized' (James 1999: 462). Clearly, James' understanding of pregnancy is limited and almost offensively normative as the wide occurrence of 'partially realized pregnancies' due to miscarriages up to the third trimester tragically attests. How equally limited and normative his understanding of sovereignty is this study will show.
4 'However, Walker does suggest tentatively that gender, culture and class can be introduced into the theories of International Relations without reading these identities through the concept of sovereignty' (Malmvig 2006: 13).
5 On the sovereign nation state as a zone of inclusion/exclusion of citizens versus the rest of humanity see also, among others, Linklater (1990, 1996, 1998, 2001) and Connolly (1991a, 1991b).
6 By the same token Walker identifies 'a certain amnesia about the historical and culturally specific character' of sovereignty in our discipline of IR (Walker 1993: 166), and Helle Malmvig (2006: 12) asserts that this amnesia 'allows the discipline to draw a long uninterrupted line of permanence from Thucydides to Machiavelli and Hobbes, where similar patterns of international conflict can be detected again and again'.
7 In Meyer *et al.* (1997) this generalization of patterns and claims to universality of the nation state is carried to extremes when the authors contend to have identified over

the past 200 years the emergence of a 'world-culture' with the nation state template as the constitutive feature.

8 For a study in this context specific to Iraq, see Rear (2008), on which I draw in later chapters.

9 It has to be noted though that Tilly at times emphasizes the uniqueness of the European state-formation process when he writes, 'the European state-building experiences will not repeat themselves in new states. The connections of the new states to the rest of the world have changed too much' (Tilly 1975: 81). On the following page, though, he contradicts himself by identifying several parallels between state-formation processes in eighteenth/nineteenth century Europe and the non-European world in the twentieth century (Tilly 1975: 82). For a detailed discussion of Anderson in this contest see Amin-Khan (2012).

10 The different trajectories of state formation in Europe and the decolonized world were first brought to prominence by Alavi (1972).

11 This 'capitalism-imperialism nexus' in the postcolonial states Amin-Khan (2012) juxtaposes with the 'capitalism-nation state nexus' in Europe that was aimed at strengthening capitalist development in Europe.

12 This view also forms the core of the rich body of literature subsumed under 'dependency theory', of which Wallerstein (1974, 1980, 1989), Frank (1979, 1981) Cardoso and Faletto (1979), Müller and Zulehner (2000), and Harvey (2003) are but the most prominent examples.

13 On how these patterns are perpetuated in the era of globalization see, among others, Canterbury (2005) and Amin-Khan (2012).

14 See also the annual compilation, *The Failed State Index*, by the online magazine *Foreign Policy*.

15 The concept of 'new wars' is exemplarily deconstructed in Kalyvas (2001), Berdal (2003), Newman (2004) and Melander *et al.* (2009).

16 The concept of the 'security dilemma' was first put forward by John Herz (1950) and since then is part of the classic canon of neo- or structural realism.

17 For example see Weber (2010).

18 For example see Brown (1996), Wagner (1993), van Evera (1994).

19 For example see Kaufmann (1996, 1998), Roe (1999, 2004), Saideman (2001).

20 The authors found that the presence of an 'ethnic alliance' increases conflict between dyads of states by 2 weighted points on a scale from 0 to 60 (Davis & Moore 1997: 179).

21 She detected a 3.4 weighted points amplitude towards conflictual dyadic interaction on the same scale from 0 to 60 (Petersen 2004: 36).

22 Those are, on the side of the target state, genocide, forced mass population transfers, i.e. ethnic cleansing, and forced assimilation. In contrast are 'methods of managing differences' such as arbitration, federalization or power-sharing (McGarry & O'Leary 1993).

23 However, the term 'internationalization' itself might be an anachronism in an inaccessible mountain terrain beyond any attempt to enforce the law, monitor and police the borders or keep taps on comings and goings. This is to say that the concept of 'internationalization of a conflict' does not mean the same in the Kurdish mountains as at the border separating the two Koreas. Until recent advances in satellite technology, generations of mountain dwellers with clan links encompassing the entire region and with the interchangeable expertise of pastoralists, smugglers, and insurgents have moved goods, arms and drugs on hidden paths and hazardous tracks only known to their kin as freely as if in the Schengen Area. International borders have mostly existed on paper and in the heads of bureaucrats in the nationalizing and state-building capitals of Tehran, Ankara, Baghdad, and Damascus.

24 The first military application of the alliance took place in 1956 when Iranian and Iraqi forces in joint operations crushed the uprising of Djiwanroji Kurds in Iran (Nezan 1993).

25 At the same time, instrumentalism is often listed as a distinct approach to the study of ethnicity, nationalism and ethnic conflict, apart from constructivism, see for example Varshney (2002). For the reasons detailed above, here I locate it at the transition from neo-realism to a narrow constructivism. Notwithstanding the explanatory value of classic elite theory per se, I fail to see how a strict instrumentalism that in itself has very little distinct to say about identity makes a unique contribution to a more comprehensive understanding of culture and identity.

26 Consequent with such a fuzzy conception of ethnicity, Abner Cohen goes so far as to declare London City stockbrokers an 'ethnic group' and compares them to Nigerian Hausa traders at work among Yoruba communities. To him, 'city men are socio-culturally as distinct within British society' – an interest group that shares similar values and norms, and is organized in a loose network based on similar patterns of symbolic behaviour, language, etc. – 'as are the Hausa within Yoruba society' (Cohen 1974: 99).

27 Theories of factionalism in ethnic conflicts in particular are detailed in Deane (2004).

28 Another interesting fusion of instrumentalism/elite theory and the ethnic security dilemma is offered by Stuart Kaufman (1996a) who translates the classic Waltzian realist division of studying international relations via 'three images' onto ethnic conflicts, with the 'first image', originally 'the individual' and in Kaufman's application 'mass preferences', the 'second image', in Waltzian terminology 'the state' and here defined as 'elite-led violence – that is, ethnic war created by leaders of ethnic groups for their own political purposes' (Kaufman 1996a: 149–150) – and finally the 'third image', in both cases the anarchic international or inter-ethnic system epitomized by the dynamics of the security dilemma. Although Kaufman's approach commits to analysing 'how factors at all three levels interact' (Kaufman 1996a: 150), his fusion of instrumentalism and neo-realism ultimately results in ingenuously carrying over the epistemological and ontological fallacies of both approaches: from a deterministic and tautological conceptualization of social elites that fails to adequately explain how the 'interaction' of his first and second image work to presupposing ethnic groups as organic, static, substantive, distinct, homogeneous and bounded units with social agency, to analytically equating them with states operating under the presumption of a system-immanently anarchic international or inter-ethnic system.

3 Beyond groupism

The effects of groupism, ...

After having demonstrated how explanatory IR conceptually treats ethnicity, nationalism, ethno-nationalist conflict and state sovereignty, both epistemologically and ontologically as well as in terms of concepts, models and analytical frameworks, and after having established a profound tendency to groupism in explanatory IR, and before proceeding with the case study, I want to sum up the deliberations made in this study so far by establishing in no uncertain terms the effects of such groupism, calling attention to the role of explanatory IR scholars who study identity politics as co-protagonists of these identity politics, and by shining a light on the consequences of a groupist and state-centrist epistemology and ontology on their objects of study, the supposed ethnic group in conflict. Earlier it has been established that by analytically treating ethnic groups as organic, substantive, distinct, homogeneous and bounded units with social agency, explanatory IR scholars uncritically accept the rhetoric of ethno-nationalist elites; rather than calling it into question, they adopt the ethnic or nationalists elites' strategic essentialism as the basis of their enquiries and contribute to the reification and substantialization of the those elites' essentialism and to the reproduction of its logic. But what does this process of reification and substantialization mean in practice, what are its effects on the object of study for those explanatory IR scholars who study ethnic conflict, what are the very actual consequences of their adopting the strategic essentialisms and participants' primordialism of the ethno-nationalist elites they set out to study, of analytically treating ethnic groups as organic, substantive, distinct, homogeneous and bounded units with social agency, and all too often analytically equating them to states? In a first instance then, explanatory IR scholars who approach and explain an ethnic conflict in groupist terms reify, and substantialize how ethno-nationalist elites want the group to be seen by the outside world and not to put too fine a point on it, they are complicit in the solidification and substantialization of the constructed ethnic lines of division, of the imagined 'us' versus 'them' dichotomies and the resulting identity politics that form the basis of their essentialized world views. In reifying and substantializing those essentialist and primordialist (self-)perceptions of ethno-nationalist elites, explanatory IR scholars legitimize those (self-)perceptions and portrayals, this ethnicized discourse, and since the authority, the claim to leadership of ethno-nationalist elites is grounded in these constructed ethnic identities, such scholars also indirectly legitimize their leadership, their position to speak authoritatively on behalf of the group. In sum, by reifying and substantializing the ethnicized discourse, by reproducing and confirming its logic, explanatory IR scholars, inadvertently or not, do the ethno-nationalist elites' bidding by authenticating and legitimizing their claim to representation, power, leadership and authority.

What is more, explanatory IR tends to substantiate, reify, and legitimize those ethnic elites' claims for the sovereign control over a certain territory. It has been noted earlier that explanatory IR notoriously kept struggling with forms of identity in its conceptualization of the international system. However, with the rise of ideational conflicts in the 1990s, such a position of conceptual negligence was no longer tenable. While at large ignoring, as it had always done, class and religious identities and permitting gender an existence at the margins of the disciplinary discourse – it focused on the one form of identity it considered itself best situated to problematize: ethnicity. This concentration on ethnic identities at the expense of other forms of identity, I hypothesize, is not only rooted in the self-perception of IR as the social science discipline dominating the scholarly discourse on issues of war and peace in the international domain but also because ethnic identity, rather than non-territorial class, religion and gender, is presumed to be translatable into state-centric terms and rationalist positivist explanatory models. By translatable I do not refer to the nature of ethnic identity, on which explanatory IR, as has been shown, still has very little of substance to say, but rather the presumed purpose and objective of ethnic conflict – and conflict is what explanatory IR mostly deals with when studying ethnicity. If it were ontologically possible to reduce ethnic conflict to merely a power struggle over territory, as for example Monica Duffy-Toft (2005) does, classical IR, for whom power struggles over territory have been at the centre of its research agenda and expertise, could apply the same rationalist positivist models, concepts and frameworks it has applied to states, and also to ethnic groups. In this sense, Duffy-Toft argues:

Understanding ethnic war therefore requires an understanding of how two actors come to view control over the same piece of ground as an indivisible issue. For ethnic groups, the key factor is settlement patterns … [they] bind the capability and legitimacy of an ethnic group's mobilization for sovereignty. Where both capability and legitimacy are high … ethnic groups are likely to consider control over disputed territory an indivisible issue and demand sovereignty. However, states are likely to view control over a territory … as an indivisible issue whenever precedent setting effects come into play, … i.e. the state fears establishing the reputation that it allows the division of its territory. Only when both an ethnic group and a state … view the issue of territorial control as indivisible will violence erupt. If, however, the ethnic group does not demand sovereignty … ethnic war is less likely.

(Duffy-Toft 2005: 2–3)

In the paragraph that follows, Duffy-Toft clarifies that 'ethnic groups (and nations) are not states', and that 'although reducing ethnic groups to the ontological equivalent of states may make for elegant and parsimonious theories, my research makes it clear that such theories can be of only limited use' (Duffy-Toft 2005: 3). What Duffy-Toft fails to realize, though, is that indirectly she is doing precisely that, ontologically equating ethnic groups with states, since she ascribes to ethnic groups an aspiration for sovereignty, which, as outlined in the section on modernism, is seen as the prerogative of the nation and in consequence of the state. She claims that the pursuit of sovereign statehood by an ethnic group – who she also defines in groupist terms – against a state who defends the indivisibility of its territory is what turns an ethnic conflict violent. Thus, in one go, she not only ontologically equates the ethnic group with the nation but also with a proto-state, presuming not only its desire to control a territory in question in alternative terms, an autonomous region for example, but also its desire to become the unqualified sovereign of this territory, that is a new state. This chain of reasoning, of first conceptualizing ethnic groups in groupist terms, and then ontologically and analytically equating them with nations and proto-states, is not limited to Duff-Toft's work, which is only given as a particularly revealing example, but runs like a red thread through most of the explanatory IR literature on ethnic conflict and will be illustrated in detail by way of the case study. What is more, I argue, treating ethnic groups in groupist terms and ontologically equating them with nations and consequently with proto-states is the defining criterion of explanatory IR's conceptualization of ethnic groups. I further argue that this ontological equation is what allows explanatory IR to continue applying the same rationalist positivist concepts, methods and frameworks it applies for analysing states to ethnic groups. For, if ethnic conflict can be ontologically equated to inter-state conflict as a power struggle over territory, the same theories and tools for resolving these conflicts as to conventional territorial conflicts can also be applied; that is by reducing ethnic conflict to a territorial conflict, it appears to be made manageable – an observation already made by David Campbell in his seminal *National Deconstruction* (1998a), yet that needs to be discussed and deconstructed more assiduously in order to appreciate the full scope of the epistemological, and consequently ontological problems resulting from this portrayal.

What actually happens with this manner of representation is that the portrayal of ethnic groups in groupist terms, of conceptually equating them with states, becomes tantamount with a substantialization, reification and legitimization of their claims for sovereign control over a certain territory as well as their claims to speak with authority on behalf of an organic, substantive, distinct, homogeneous and bounded group. This process of legitimization, though, works both ways; that is, as discussed earlier, if we accept identity formation as a Barthian process of social differentiation between the self and the other (Neumann 1996; Barth 1998 [1969]; Rattansi 1999; Eriksen 2002; Brubaker 2004; Malešević 2004, 2006a; Jenkins 2008a, 2008b) and as a Weberian (1978 [1922]) form of collective political action, a legitimization of the territorial claims, perceptions, images, narratives and portrayals of the self implicitly leads also to a legitimization of territorial claims, perceptions, images, narratives, and portrayals of the other.[1] Yet this other is not value-neutral. As outlined in the Introduction, the notion that Western philosophy is structured along a series of binary opposites in a hierarchical relationship with each other in which 'the second term in each pair' is not only co-constitutive of the first but as such is also 'considered the negative, corrupt, undesirable version of the first' (Johnson 1981: viii), forms the basis of Jaques Derrida's method of deconstruction (Derrida 1978, 1981a. 1981b, 1982, 1998; Edkins 1999; Fagan *et al.* 2007; Zehfuss 2009). Consequently then, if one applies Derrida's logic of deconstruction, also outlined in the Introduction, to how explanatory IR analytically treats ethnic groups in conflict, by reifying, substantializing, reproducing and legitimizing the self in identity discourses, explanatory IR also reifies, substantializes, reproduces and legitimizes the negative attributes of the other, and its perception as the enemy, its vilification. Further, it has been pointed out that any study of a minority group in, for example, a state is incomplete without giving equal attention to the study of the ethnic identity of the majority group (Isajiw 2000; Jenkins 2008a). From that, it logically follows that, when applied to ethnic conflict, by reifying, substantializing, reproducing, and legitimizing the self-perception of the oppressed minority, then explanatory IR's groupism also reifies, substantializes, reproduces and legitimizes the perception of the majority and/or the nationalizing state as an assimilationist oppressor. Alternatively, by reifying, substantializing, reproducing and legitimizing the majority and/or the nationalizing state's struggle for the survival of 'its' state, then explanatory IR reifies, substantializes, reproduces, and legitimizes the perception of the minority as irredentist secessionists. In sum then, supposedly detached and scientifically objective explanatory IR scholars, in their groupist ontologies and epistemologies, in their taking ethnic groups as organic, substantive, distinct, homogeneous and bounded units possessing social agency, are complicit in the ethnicized discourse, both at the level of the supposedly secessionist minority and the supposedly assimilationist and oppressive majority and/or nationalizing state, and reify, substantialize, reproduce and legitimize both sides' politics of division – as will be illustrated in the case study by deconstructing the (self-) perceptions of the Turkish state, Iraqi Kurdistan, and of the Kurdish political parties and insurgencies.

However, there is more to the picture than explanatory IR scholars as co-protagonists in ethnic conflicts reifying, substantiating, reproducing and legitimizing already existing ethnic lines of division in an ethnicized discourse. Recapitulating what has been said in the Introduction about Foucault's (1972) concept of 'discursive formations' in the process of knowledge production, namely that objects of discourse only come into existence through their discursive formations including its inherent social configurations of power, authority and hierarchy, when talking about explanatory IR's role in shaping the discourse of ethnic conflict, these discursive formations and their inherent social configurations need to be taken into account. Explanatory IR scholars who study, analyse, explain and write on ethnic conflict are naturally part of this discursive formation, and they are, in the terminology of this study, co-protagonists of ethnic conflict by virtue of their position to speak authoritatively about issues of war and peace in the international system, as well as by virtue of their role as categorizers of the categorized, in this case the ethnic group. However, the differentiation between social group and social category as self-defined and other-defined social entities is not as clear-cut and straightforward as some primers in the social sciences or a Brubakarian constructivism – see Chapter 1 – may suggest. On the contrary,

> categorisation is as much part of identity as self-identification … categorization makes a powerful contribution to the everyday reality – the realization … of groups. Attributions of group membership feature routinely in how we categorize others, and the categorization of out-groups is intrinsic to in-group identification. Who we think we are, is intimately related to who we think others are, and vice versa.
>
> (Jenkins 2008b: 12)

Consequently, in their groupist epistemologies and ontologies on ethnic conflict, explanatory IR scholars do more than contributing to already existing ethnicized discourses, and they do even more than reifying, substantializing, reproducing, and legitimizing already existing ethnic lines of division and the 'us' versus 'them' dichotomies, together with the strategic essentialisms of ethno-nationalist elites and/or nationalizing states in which they are grounded. If the discursive formations on ethnic conflict – of which IR scholars are a constitutive part and in which they are co-protagonists – only gain meaning through the discourse itself, and if the act of categorization is constitutive of the process of self-identification, then it is IR scholars who take part in bringing these very identities into existence, who take part in their creation and construction.

Since this is the core argument of this study about how explanatory IR analytically treats ethnic conflict, these conjunctures, in complete repudiation of the positivist rationalist essentialism discussed earlier, cannot be emphasized strongly enough when identifying the effects of a groupist approach to ethnic conflict. These effects are as follows.

1   Any scholar, whether adhering to a groupist perspective or not, participating in the discourse on ethnic conflict by way of studying, analysing, categorizing, explaining, or writing about it, is intrinsically part of the discursive formation on ethnic conflict and therefore actively takes part in the construction, and creation of the forms of identity he/she sets out to study, analyse, categorize, explain or write about.

2   From that it follows that the epistemologies and ontologies under which this studying, analysing, categorizing, and writing about is done, matter profoundly; if done from a groupist perspective, that is by taking on '*categories of ethnopolitical practice as our categories of social analysis*' (Brubaker 2004: 10, emphasis in original), by analytically treating ethnic groups as

organic, substantive, distinct, homogeneous and bounded units with social agency as well as analytically equating them with states, such a portrayal reifies, substantializes, reconfirms and legitimizes the politics of division, strategic essentialisms, and 'us' versus 'them' dichotomies in which these ethnic identities are grounded as well as the categories/groups' empowered agents.

3　Since the binary opposites of 'us' versus 'them' are never value-neutral, such a reification, substantialization, reconfirmation and legitimization of the binary opposites in identity discourses themselves also intrinsically lead to a reification, substantialization, reconfirmation and legitimization of the values that come with it; that is, the negative attributes of the other, its perception as the enemy, its vilification.

At this stage, some readers may ask what harm can be done by explanatory IR scholars confined to the ivory towers of academia or journal articles that are usually read by a few dozen peers, reifying, substantializing, and legitimatizing ethnic lines of divisions, ethno-nationalist elites' claims to leadership or demands for sovereign control over a certain territory. After all, it is doubtful that Massoud Barzani, the President of the Kurdistan Region of Iraq, has ever heard of, let alone read Donald Horowitz or John Mearsheimer. Indeed, such a direct link between political decision makers and scholars who shaped their thinking would be almost impossible to establish, even though Bill Clinton allegedly declared Robert Kaplan's *Balkan Ghosts* (1993) mandatory reading for his staff while dealing with the conflicts resulting from the implosion of the former Yugoslavia (Joras & Schetter 2004). Yet, to look for such a direct link would conceive of scholars' power in the process of knowledge production in too narrow a way. Our role as co-protagonists in the ethnic and ethno-nationalist conflicts we set out to describe is of a more indirect nature.

International Relations scholars, perhaps due to the self-declared aspirations of our discipline, are widely seen by political decision makers and the media as speaking with authority on issues of war and peace in the international arena. The legendary six wise men, for example – British academics that advised Tony Blair and (unsuccessfully) cautioned against British participation in the invasion of Iraq in 2003 – were all IR scholars (Moreton 2015). The involvement of IR scholars in the political decision-making process gets further amplified on the level of personnel when individual careers seamlessly alternate between academia, political think tanks, consultancy and public administration, as is most common in the Anglo-Saxon political system, but increasingly gains global salience. By the same token, hardly a day passes without an expert from the discipline of IR being interviewed in media outlets to explain the rise of ISIS, Turkey or Saudi Arabia's questionable relations with it, the civil war in Syria, Iran and Russia's involvement there, or how to situate all these instances within the wider regional context – to name just a few examples related to the case study. What is more, at universities we IR scholars educate and train the next generation of political decision makers, journalists and bureaucrats – at my current workplace, the Central European University, they hail from more than 100 countries. In short, there can be no doubt about the supreme power, in a Foucauldian sense, that IR scholars possess in the production and dissemination of knowledge in the discourses on international conflict. Yet, what is being produced and disseminated here is not *any* kind of knowledge, but a particular kind of knowledge, as can be illustrated by a brief example.

One may debate until the end of days whether there exists something like a mainstream in IR, but there can be no doubt about not only the preponderance but even outright revival – when compared with the 1980s and 1990s – of rationalist positivism in our discipline, in particular in US academia. This is made plain by a study of the required reading lists for general IR theory courses at the PhD level of the top ten US political science departments from 2005 until 2007, as conducted by Thomas Biersteker (2009): out of 809 different publications and a total of 454 authors, 69 per cent of required readings can be categorized as unambiguously rationalist positivist, 10 per cent as Wendtian or systemic constructivist, and only two out of ten reading lists featured authors dubbed 'radical' – post-structuralist, feminist or critical constructivist; of the authors on the reading lists, between 88 per cent (lowest, Princeton) and 99 per cent (highest, Michigan) were US based.[2] When juxtaposing these results with an earlier study (Alker & Biersteker 1984), the author is led to conclude, 'in contrast to the situation in the mid-1980s, there appears to be a decreased tendency to engage theoretical traditions developed outside of North America' (Biersteker 2009: 320). In sum, the theories of explanatory IR,

> were motivated by contemporary events, potential foreign policy challenges facing the U.S., and situated in an intertextual context that motivated, shaped, and influenced their development, … [and continue to be] projections of American foreign policy concerns unmediated by perspectives or insights from other parts of the world.
>
> (Biersteker 2009: 321–322)

Thus, while it is unlikely that Massoud Barzani himself has read John Mearsheimer, it is entirely conceivable that a young Iraqi Kurd from a privileged background and educated at a prestigious Western university, now working in Barzani's administration, has learned to see the social world through a Mearsheimerian lens. Further, as will be demonstrated in the case study, explanatory IR scholars represent developments in Iraqi Kurdistan through a state-centric and groupist prism, which is then taken up, disseminated and amplified by the media for untold political decision makers and/or readers of *Vox.com*, the *New York Times* or the *Weekly Standard* to accept it as reality and, subsequently, as Gramscian common sense (Sassoon, A. 1987; Gramsci 1992; Jones 2006; Robinson 2006). Yet, it is not singular reality, but one among many realities, and a groupist and state-centric reality as such, that is produced, re-produced and consumed here and gradually comes to shape the discourse.

... hypotheses on the motives behind it, ...

Robert Cox famously asserted,

> theory is always *for* someone and *for* some purpose. All theories have a per-spective. Perspectives derive from positions in time and space, specifically political time and space. The world is seen from a standpoint defineable in terms of nation or social class, of dominance or subordination, of rising or declining power, of a sense of immobility or of present crisis, of a past experience, and of hopes and expectations for the future ... There is, accord-ingly, no such thing as theory in itself, divorced from a standpoint in time and space.
>
> (Cox 1981: 128, emphasis in original)

This maxim of Critical Theory prompts us to ask, why are nations and ethnic groups portrayed in groupist and state-centric terms in explanatory IR? Cui bono, who stands to benefit from this particular form of representation, from rei-fication and the strategic essentialisms of ethno-nationalist elites? Certainly, an obvious beneficiary are the ethno-nationalist elites themselves whose authority and claims to leadership, territory, as well as undivided allegiance and solidarity among the nation or ethnic group's members gain legitimacy. But how does explanatory IR scholarship fit into this picture? When I once posed this question at the end of a talk, someone suggested, of course explanatory IR represents ethno-nationalist conflict and ideational conflict at large in state-centric terms, otherwise they would not have anything meaningful to say about it, and lose out precious authority against other disciplines such as sociology or anthropology. In truth, when cautioning against the post-positivist trend in IR in the mid-1980s, Robert Keohane declared,

> until the reflective scholars or others sympathetic to their arguments have delineated such a research program and shown in particular studies that it can illuminate important issues in world politics, they will remain on the margins of the field, largely invisible to the preponderance of empirical researchers, most of whom explicitly or implicitly accept one or another version of rationalistic premises.
>
> (Keohane 1989: 173)

A certain siege-mentality among explanatory IR scholars when faced with post-positivist interventions and what such iconoclasm may mean for our discipline is undoubtedly discernible in Kalevi Holsti's warnings that,

> it is hard to say that there is any longer a particular core to the field ... Our field should be basically concerned with the relations between states, and relations between societies and non-state actors to the extent that those rela-tions impinge upon and affect the relations between states. When we go far

beyond these domains, we get into areas of sociology, anthropology, and social psychology that are best dealt with by people in those disciplines.

(Holsti 2002: 621)

He expanded this regrettable rejection of interdisciplinarity and affirmation of state-centrism in explanatory IR by reminding IR scholars that, 'beyond a certain point … concern with epistemology may lead us to lose sight of the subject matter. The greatest texts of our field were written by those who were deeply immersed in the subject, and not by epistemologists' (Holsti 2002: 623).[3]

Rather cynical references to turf wars among the social science disciplines may only get us so far in hypothesizing the motives behind groupism and state-centrism in explanatory IR's approach to nations and ethnic groups. Another plausible hypothesis may be that some scholars, in the course of their often career-long professional dealing with oppressed minorities and interaction with their representatives have come to take up their cause for liberation and national self-determination in their writings. Out of empathy or sympathy with the disenfranchized, marginalized and persecuted, they have become scholars cum activists who use their purported expertise, seen as speaking with authority on the socio-political conditions of a certain group, to advocate for greater awareness, recognition, and potentially even change of status on behalf of their subjects of study. Debates about the intellectual and ethical pitfalls of the 'scholar as activist', especially in anthropology, may date back as far as the days of Franz Boas and can result in what Micaela di Leonardo (1998), in her critical examination of nineteenth century anthropologists in particular, and the relationship of her discipline with its subjects of study in general, has called 'relations of rescue'.[4] This form of identification of the scholar with his/her subject of study goes vastly beyond mere advocacy but, in Orientalist fashion, amounts to paternalistic acts of appropriation through the assertion of supposedly morally and intellectually superior Western knowledge at the expense of indigenous voices; in other words, Western scholars purporting to know better about what is good for the people they study in disregard of local knowledge. In this process of appropriation and objectification, those locals in need of rescue might be seen as 'noble' but after all are habitually perceived as if not savages then certainly as underdeveloped, weak, emotional – which all too often is equated with feminine – and thus intellectually inferior to the rational, developed, enlightened and masculine Western expert, their self-declared rescuer. Yet, scholarship as advocacy does not necessarily have to exhibit such extreme forms of appropriation to be problematic in its normativism. For what we are talking about in our case is a particular kind of scholarly activism in so far as the concern of this study is with the ways in which explanatory IR scholars in their writings, lectures, expert testimonies in public inquiries and through their political influence, advocate for a certain ethnic group or nation to attain and/or be granted an autonomous political status that can go as far as independence as a sovereign nation state. Pertaining to the Iraqi Kurds, such a pattern is clearly identifiable in the works of Brendan O'Leary or Gareth Stansfield. As will be discussed at length in Part III, O'Leary self-identifies as 'honorary Kurdistanis' (O'Leary *et al.* 2005: XIX): internationals who share a deep professional and scholarly commitment to Iraqi Kurdistan, 'take[s] the existence of Kurdistan as a political entity as a desirable given' (O'Leary *et al.* 2005: XVII), and acknowledge the 'compelling moral case for Kurdish statehood' (Anderson & Stansfield 2005: 220). While the results of such normativisms will be discussed in detail later, suffice it to say here that even such attenuated forms of Western scholars coming to the rescue of their subjects of study by championing their cause for national self-determination, are inevitably tinged with a degree of Orientalism and a certain *mission civilizatrice*. In particular, if these scholars happen to come from the British Isles and the arena of their championing a local people's liberation is the Middle East, such advocacy evokes somewhat disquieting memories of T. E. Lawrence and Gertrude Bell.

However relevant for our case study, such patterns of activism remain the prerogative of some scholars. When arguing for ethnic partition of Bosnia, for example, it is doubtful that John Mearsheimer was motivated by personal sympathy for Bosniaks, Bosnian Serbs or Croats' struggle for national self-determination. For a more general line of inquiry, we may want to return to Cox's above quoted seminal article, in which he emphasizes that scholars' 'perspectives derive from positions in time and space, specifically political time and space' (Cox 1981: 128). This assertion requires further elaboration. First, it should not come as a surprise that the positions of scholars who have come to see the social world through a state-centric and groupist lens, who if you may want, have come of age intellectually within and as a product of a state-centric and groupist discourse, and who operate in practice (writing, teaching, giving expert opinion to decision makers and the media, etc.) within inherently state-centric and groupist paradigms, continue to adhere to these state-centric and groupist positions that continue to shape their perspectives. In other words, their way of seeing the social world has become internalized and institutionalized (Carayannis & Pirzadeh 2014; Hamilton 2014; Huysman 2016) – a process beyond mere cognition, in the sense of accepting certain knowledge as relevant and valid for oneself, and this perception becoming a distinct and prominent marker for self-identification, i.e. this particular kind of knowledge has become embedded within the Bourdieuian social field of IR theory. That means, I would argue, that the same qualification earlier discerned for ethno-nationalist leaders, also applies to explanatory IR scholars. When ethno-nationalist leaders apply strategic essentialism to the ethnic group or nation they claim to represent, this essentialism, it has been argued, should not be seen as fake, as merely a political act, but as a genuine belief that is the product of their exposure in a formative process to an ethnicized discourse and having come to see themselves, their role within the group, and the group itself in ethnicized terms. Likewise, explanatory IR scholars have come to genuinely believe the social world to be state-centric and groupist as a result of state-centric and groupist intellectual nurture. In going beyond the nature versus nurture debate, in so far as these shared assumptions form the bases not only for common vision, values, norms, systems, rituals, traditions, symbols, language, beliefs and habits, but also even instinctive and reflexive responses, one may go so far as to identify state-centrism and groupism as central components of a shared culture among explanatory IR scholars and an explanatory IR habitus. 'Habitus' in Bourdieuian terminology is defined as

> systems of durable, transposable dispositions, structured structures predisposed to function as structuring structures, that is, as principles which generate and organize practices and representations that can be objectively adapted to their outcomes without presupposing a conscious aiming at ends or an express mastery of the operations necessary in order to attain them.
>
> (Bourdieu 1990: 53)

On the relationship between the social field, as defined earlier, and habitus Bourdieu observed:

> The relationship between the habitus and the field is foremost one of conditioning: the field structures the habitus which is the product of the incorporation of the immanent demands of the field ... but it is also a relationship of knowledge and of constructive cognition: the habitus contributes to the field as a world of meaning, endowed with sense and value.
>
> (Bourdieu & Wacquant 1992: 119)

The relationship between habitus and field is thus bidirectional, where dispositions and structures are a function of the norms and values that define the field, yet the configuration of the field is also a result of a particular knowledge that informs and shapes these norms and values, similar to the inter-relationality between discourse and practice discussed earlier.

Second, in so far as state-centrism and groupism are accepted as common sense, as the 'natural' and 'factual' way in which today's social world is structured, in and beyond IR by the general public, and this view is being reproduced on an everyday basis in the media, taught at universities as well as adhered to and acted on by political decision makers, state-centrism and groupism have gone beyond the realm of episteme and come to approximate *doxa*. *Doxa*, going back to ancient Greek philosophy, where it is juxtaposed with episteme (knowledge), in Bourdieu's terminology are a 'set of fundamental beliefs which does not even need to be asserted in the form of an explicit, self-conscious dogma' (Bourdieu 2000: 15). In other words, *doxa* are the taken for granted assumptions or shared beliefs within and having relevance beyond the social field in question in so far as they determine the behaviour of agents within the field and society at large. The character of *doxa* within the social field cannot be emphasized strongly enough.

> *Doxa* is the cornerstone of any field to the extent that it determines the stability of the objective social structures through the way they are reproduced and reproduce themselves in the agents' perceptions and practices; in other words in their *habitus*.
>
> (Deer 2014: 115)

Those agents, structures, discourses within fields maintaining and preserving *doxa* are then called *orthodoxy*, those challenging it are the *heterodoxy* (Bourdieu 1977, 1990, 1998a, 1998b, 2000; Eagleton 1991; Jenkins 2002; Potts 2010; Deer 2014). The *orthodoxy* operates and preserves *doxa* through censorship, that is sanctions in the social arena, both within the respective field and beyond, and 'the more effective this censorship is, the less apparent it becomes, and the more it appears as the axiomatic, natural "way of the world" of *doxa*' (Jenkins 2002: 156).

Having thus established *doxa* as a constitutive element of the social field and groupism/state-centrism as common sense both within the field and society at large, as well as having related it to social practice in a similar fashion as Neumann, quoted in the Introduction, who argues that one cannot and should not see discourse as distinct from practice, Bourdieu – echoing Gramsci's cultural hegemony – continues to elaborate on the relationship between *doxa* and the symbolic power of elites and the state in particular:

> Doxa is a particular point of view, the point of view of the dominant, which presents and imposes itself as a universal point of view, the point of view of those who dominate by dominating the state and who have constituted their point of view as universal by constituting the state.
>
> (Bourdieu 1998a: 57)

Thus, in the context of the state, *doxa* can be related to symbolic power. Here, Bourdieu, who expanded Weber's classic definition of the state as the institution that 'successfully claims the monopoly of the legitimate use of physical and *symbolic* violence over a definite territory and over the totality of the corresponding population' (Bourdieu 1998a: 40), emphasizes that the symbolic component in the field of power is as important in the state's legitimate control of its territory and population as the monopoly on the use of physical force. 'Symbolic violence', through which the state exercises symbolic power, Bourdieu expands, 'is the gentle, invisible form of violence, which is never recognised as such, and is not so much undergone as chosen' (Bourdieu 1977: 192). It is this process of becoming seen as the legitimate wielder of power – occurring simultaneously with the concentration of the physical components of power such as the unification of territory and market, the military, law enforcement, systems of taxation, etc. – that Bourdieu (1994) identifies as the symbolic dimension of state power. In this conceptualization of the state, Bourdieu goes beyond Weber's classic triad of authority composed of a (1) traditional authority deriving from long-established customs, habits and social structures; (2) a rational-legal authority based on norms and laws; and (3) charismatic authority stemming from personality and qualities of individual leadership (Weber 1978 [1922]). For Bourdieu, there is also a symbolic level of authority to the state in which it generates, cultivates and perpetually reproduces the symbolic capital, over which it holds a monopoly, to legitimize its monopoly to use physical and symbolic force; in other words the state controls and keeps re-enacting the 'performative discourse on the state which, under the guise of saying what the state is, caused the state to come into being by stating what it should be' (Bourdieu 1994: 16).

Third, Bourdieu introducing social practice and agency, and in particular the state, into the debate on *doxa* brings us back to Robert Cox. In his pioneering article of 1981, Robert Cox drew on Max Horkheimer's famous distinction between 'critical' and 'traditional' theory and identified (neo-)realism and (neo-)liberalism – constructivism was still in its embryonic stage then – as traditional theories in IR, or as he put it 'problem solving theories'. As has been elaborated in the previous two chapters, these two paradigms that constitute the core of explanatory IR are characterized primarily by an empiricist positivist methodology. 'This results in the view not only that an objective world exists independently of human consciousness, but that objective knowledge of social reality is possible insofar as values are expunged from analysis' (Devetak 2009: 164). Traditional, or in Cox's terminology 'problem solving theory', thus posits what has already been discussed in the context of scientific objectivism in Brubaker's epistemology: a belief in the possibility of neatly separating the social scientist as detached and objective observer of social interactions from the social world he/she analyses, denying the scientist any interest or agenda other than scientific and objective knowledge production. According to Cox, traditional or problem solving theory then 'takes the world as it finds it, with the prevailing social and power relationships and the institutions in which they are organized, as the given framework for action' (Cox 1981: 128). Yet here Cox identifies a fundamental contradiction inherent to positivism and therewith mainstream IR's self-conceptualization and its understanding of its own methodology. For, by 'not question[ing] the present order, [problem solving theory] has the effect of legitimizing and reifying it' (Cox 1981: 128); that is, legitimizing and reifying the present order of the international system. 'By working within the given system it has a stabilizing effect, tending to preserve the existing global structure of social and political relations' (Devetak 2009: 164). By taking the present order of the international system as a given, by understanding the state 'as an a priori reality which does not need to be questioned because it constitutes the founding unit, universal in form and purpose, of the international system' (Grenier 2012: 10), by not further questioning the nature of its object of analysis, by, epistemologically speaking, presupposing the state into existence, explanatory IR legitimizes and reifies the state and the international order constituted by states. The supposedly objective and detached scientist is thus rendered very much an actor within this system, making the international system very much also a world of our making. Cox masterfully traces how certain assumptions of explanatory IR take part in the creation of the order it sets out to describe, how explanatory IR enacts the international system of sovereign nation states through the knowledge it produces about it, participates in constructing this system and bringing it into being through its very own discourse (Ashley 1987, 1988; Walker 1993; Campbell 1998a. 1998b; McSweeney 1999; Hansen 2006; Devetak 2009; Weber 2010). In the contemporary debates on the nature of the international system the discipline of IR, whose self-declared purpose it is to analyse this system, is seen as in a position to speak about this system authoritatively. Yet the modern international system is not a pre-given but has only come into existence through discourse, in which IR scholars, whose statements about the system are given great value, are influential co-protagonists; in other words the discursive process of bringing the international system into being is constituted to a large extent by IR scholars writing about it. This recognition, in clear rejection of positivist epistemology and central to this study's critique of it, renders any notion of scientific detachment and objectivity as a key principle of positivist methodology not only demonstrably fallacious but also patently absurd. Contrary to its own pretension of scientific objectivism and value-neutrality, positivism in IR is distinctly 'value-bound by virtue of the fact that it implicitly accepts the prevailing order as its own framework' (Cox 1981: 130).

Fourth, the fallacies of positivist objectivism aside, and returning to Cox's observation at the beginning of this section, Cox claims that state-centrist and groupist positivist knowledge is produced in IR deliberately and with purpose, that in their desire to produce policy relevant theories about the social world for state institutions and bureaucracies, many IR scholars intentionally serve the state. In itself, there is nothing novel or radical about this recognition; in fact, the concomitance of explanatory, positivist IR with the state as an institution and its empowered agents is acknowledged in one way or another in any decent primer's subchapter on epistemological debates within IR – we may quote a German introductory volume, where Thomas Diez observes,

> because both international politics and International Relations (as a discipline) take the state as their unproblematic point of departure, they are entangled in the same discourse … from a postmodernist perspective, in its obsessive drive to explain prevailing political conditions, a positivist science of International Relations of this kind is *an accomplice to the 'statesman' of international politics.*
>
> (Diez 2014: 290, emphasis added)

This cognition again builds onto the famous contention of Michel Foucault (1972) that power produces knowledge, and that knowledge is never neutral but a function of existing power structures. When Foucault (1977: 27) wrote, 'there is no power relation without the correlative constitution of a field of knowledge, nor any knowledge that does not presuppose and constitute at the same time power relations', he not only meant what has been discussed above as 'authoritative knowledge', that 'knowledge linked to power … assumes the authority of "the truth"' but also that this knowledge 'has the power to *make itself true*' (Hall 1997: 76; emphasis in original); for this authoritative knowledge is then applied, implemented, translated into practices and effectuated in social action. If IR as a discipline is seen as a producer of authoritative knowledge about and within the international system, it has a natural interest in the preservation of this system; an interest it shares with other actors within this discursive formation that is the international system, and, according to explanatory IR, the main actors in this international system are sovereign nation states. Hence, explanatory IR shares an interest in the preservation of the international system constitutive of sovereign nation states with the institutions of those sovereign nation states. This conformity of interests leads to a symbiotic relationship between state institutions and IR scholars where both sides ensure their mutual position of power within the discursive formation that is the contemporary international system: state institutions by conceding to IR as a discipline the position to speak with authority about the international system and prioritizing their policy relevant theories about it, and explanatory IR scholars by providing policy relevant knowledge that ensures states and their institutions and bureaucracies remain the dominant actors in the international system. This is precisely what Robert Cox meant when he called those theoretical positions of positivist IR 'problem solving theories': their main purpose is not to objectively and dispassionately explain the social world – which is a logical impossibility in any case – but to theoretically solve problems, deal with challenges, eliminate threats for and on behalf of the community of sovereign nation states and their institutions and provide recommendations for policies which determine how to practically do so. Cox observes:

> The general aim of problem-solving is to make these relationships and institutions work smoothly by dealing effectively with particular sources of trouble. Since the general pattern of institutions and relationships is not called into question, particular problems can be considered in relation to the specialised areas of activity in which they arise … The strength of the problem-solving approach lies in its ability to fix limits or parameters to a problem area and to reduce the statement of a particular problem to a limited number of variables which are amenable to relatively close and precise examination. The ceteris paribus assumption, upon which such theorising is based, makes it possible to arrive at statements of laws or regularities which appear to have general validity but which imply, of course, the institutional and relational parameters assumed in the problem solving approach … Problem-solving theory is non-historical or ahistorical, since it, in effect, posits a continuing present (the permanence of the institutions and power relations which constitute its parameters).
>
> (Cox 1981: 129)

This holds particularly true for neo-realism and explains how it can intellectually treat the sovereign nation state as a pre-given that is simply assumed into existence in a continuing present from the Peace of Westphalia in 1648 until our current times. It explains why neo-realism does not further problematize the state or the structure of the international system, since it has a system-immanent interest in portraying it as timeless and perennial, in affirming and reifying it. For this reason and to make their self-conception more explicit I would call these paradigms *status quo preserving theories* rather than 'problem-solving theories'. Their self-conception is to affirm the current structure of the international system and the units that supposedly constitute it, namely sovereign nation states, by providing the institutions of

the latter with policy-relevant theories on how to deal with challenges to their existence. This problem-solving approach, this understanding of international relations
theory serving the purpose of making the institutions of modern nation states and
the international system as a whole 'work smoothly' and to 'effectively deal with
particular sources of trouble', neo-realism has in common with neo-liberalism and a
narrow constructivism. For neo-liberalism, whose problem-solving self-conception
is perhaps even more explicit, Cox elaborates elsewhere:

> In effect liberal institutionalism [or neo-liberalism] has its starting point in
> the coexistence of state system and world capitalist economy. The problems
> with which it deals are those of rendering compatible these two global struc-
> tures and of ensuring stability and predictability to the world economy. Thus
> regime theory has much to say about economic cooperation ... of advanced
> capitalist countries with regard to problems common to them ... Indeed,
> regimes are designed to stabilize the world economy and have the effect ...
> of inhibiting and deterring states from initiating radical departures from eco-
> nomic orthodoxy.
>
> (Cox 1992: 173)

Indeed, to substantiate neo-liberalism's self-conception as a problem-solving or
status quo preserving theory, one does not have to enlist a critical theorist such
as Robert Cox, but can instead turn to one of neo-liberalism key proponents,
Robert Keohane, for witness. Keohane declared that the main objective of
regime or neo-liberal theory is to 'facilitate the smooth operation of decentralized international political systems' (Keohane 1984: 63). As elaborated in the
first chapter, the same self-conception applies to systemic constructivism whose
self-declared purpose is to facilitate a rapprochement between constructivism
and neo-realism/neo-liberalism, which, like those two theoretical approaches
treats the state, ethnic group and nation as analytical pre-givens in their analysis
of ethnic and ethno-nationalist conflict, and which shares with them the purpose
of ensuring the permanence of the international system constituted of sovereign
nation states by analysing it into existence. In summary, all three paradigms or
status quo preserving theories not only share the same meta-narrative but also
have an identical self-conception and purpose: they 'tend to work in favour of
stabilizing prevailing structures of world order and their accompanying inequalities of power and wealth' (Devetak 2009: 164). In sum, concluding this line of
argument and returning to Bourdieuian terminology, I interpret explanatory IR
scholars as agents of the *orthodoxy* within the field of IR theory, as cultivating in
concurrence with state institutions the state-centric and groupist *doxa*, as participating in its maintenance and preservation, as in fact sharing the same habitus
with state bureaucracies and systems of education.

This contention is justifiable since Bourdieu himself, in his later writings,
argued against the 'neo-liberal *doxa*' and how it is sustained by state institutions,
academia and the media (Bourdieu 2003, 2008; Lane 2012).[5] The parallel
between the cultural hegemony of economic neo-liberalism and political

state-centrism is not difficult to draw; the same logics of habitus, discourse and practice apply. In both, I argue, the *orthodoxy* within IR scholarship serves a function resembling censors in a Bourdieuian sense whose task, in congruence with state institutions, mainstream media, and the international plutocracy, is to keep the voices of *heterodoxy* at bay. Such an interpretation of the role of explanatory or rationalist IR scholars in the scholarly and social discourse is mirrored in Campbell's *Writing Security* (1998b), where he identifies these scholars as 'gate keepers' of traditional theory and orthodox knowledge, whose function is to marginalize more critical or ideational perspectives and voices. Indeed, while in recent critical IR scholarship other forms of *doxa* have been discussed – Rebecca Adler-Nissen (2011), for example, has problematized the *doxa* of ever-closer integration in discourses on the EU – Didier Bigo argues that the true value of applying Bourdieu to IR may lie in his 'redefinition of the relationship between theory and practice and to insist on the need for academics to engage with this relation in their own research practices' (Bigo 2011: 233). In this vein, Stefano Guzzini (2013) has applied Bourdieuian theory and terminology to his reading of Richard Ashley's classical deconstruction of neo-realism, and Inanna Hamati-Ataya (2012) has examined the epistemological debates between positivist and post-positivist IR via a combination of Bourdieuian theory and a *dependencia* theory-inspired core–periphery situatedness of dominant versus marginalized forms of knowledge. All these contributions suggest the role of explanatory, positivist IR and its still dominant status as arbiter of knowledge within and beyond our discipline, but the function of serving and preserving the status quo of the international system has never again been made as explicit as in Cox's seminal article, written more than three decades ago.

Having said that, in the current constellation of the discourse on the international system the orthodoxy's censorship can be confidently hands-off: by presupposing the state, the state truly 'goes without saying, because it comes without saying' (Bourdieu 1977: 169) and the preponderance of the state as the prime and unproblematic unit of the international system has gained common-sense status. For,

> the more the system is worked and occupied by those who believe in the system, the less censorship there needs to be ... The ultimate success of censorship – which ... is about what people *think* as well as about what they *say* – is to be found in its apparent abolition. Some things become impossible to say, or, if said, they are impossible to take seriously. The cultural arbitrary is legitimated and accepted not only as "the way things are" but as the way they *ought* to be. This state of affairs is founded upon the fit between the subjectivity of the habitus and the objective nature of the field or social space and its structure of positions.
>
> (Jenkins 2002: 156, italics in original)

In fact, Bourdieu singled out state bureaucracies and systems of education, where, in the latter 'one of the major powers of the state is to produce and impose (especially through the school system) categories of thought that we spontaneously apply to all things of the social world – including the state itself' (Bourdieu 1994: 1). Consequently, the role of social scientists, including IR scholars, in the hierarchy of fields that constitute the modern state is not only to provide the state with policy relevant theories to ensure its survival and prosperity but also to shape the minds of future generations to accept as legitimate and serve under the authority of that state, and therewith to reproduce its physical and symbolic capital. For Bourdieu, the bureaucratic field of civil servants, who he calls 'state nobility' (Bourdieu 1994: 16) and who are naturally a product of the state's education system, is, after government, the dominant field in the process of controlling, administering and wielding both the physical and symbolic dimension of statecraft, including the educational/research field. In other words, civil servants are the first line in the state maintaining, administering and exercising symbolic force, since they themselves are a product of this symbolic force. 'The fundamental law of bureaucratic apparatuses is that the apparatus gives everything (including power over the apparatus) to those who give it everything and expect everything from it because they themselves have nothing or are nothing outside it' (Bourdieu 1991: 216), which is how the bureaucratic field can ensure permanent adherence to and compliance with its culture, structure, norms, regulations, and world views by each individual bureaucrat.

Finally, the concomitance of explanatory IR and state bureaucracies can be illustrated in their joint attempts to 'problem-solve' ethnic conflicts. I argue that the earlier discussed analytical equation of ethnic group with nation with state is what allows explanatory IR to continue applying the same rationalist positivist concepts, methods and frameworks as applied in the analysis of states to ethnic groups. For, if ethnic conflict can be ontologically equated with inter-state conflict as a power struggle over territory, the same theories and tools for resolving these conventional territorial conflicts can also be applied; that is, by reducing ethnic conflict to a territorial conflict, it is supposedly made manageable. Concentrating on its presupposed objective, the acquisition of sovereign control over territory – at the expense of other expressions of ethnic identity – allows explanatory IR, drawing on its decades of experience in studying, analysing and explaining conventional forms of territorial conflict, to provide policy relevant theories of how to deal with, successfully manage, and ideally to problem-solve these conflicts. Yet, by doing so it not only reifies and substantializes the claims and strategic essentialisms of (ethno)-nationalist elites as well as, to some extent, legitimizing their politics of ethnic division, but what is worse, often contributes to writing those aspirations for sovereignty into existence in the first place; through its scholarship, explanatory IR takes part in constructing these ethnic lines of division. This may seem at first surprising since a territorially defined ethnic conflict and its allegedly inherent secessionism can be argued to pose one of the most fundamental threats to the modern state system; yet, as detailed below, explaining ethnic conflict in state-centric and rationalist positivist terms together with reducing it to a power struggle over the control of territory is also what supposedly makes ethnic conflict manageable and determines the nature of Western bureaucratic regimes' policies of intervention in said conflicts.

From the toolbox of Western forms of intervention, the approach to 'problem solving' and/or managing ethnic conflict that perfectly illustrates the essentializing and state-centrist approach of explanatory IR and state bureaucracies is the concept of 'ethnic partition'. One of the leading proponents of ethnic partition theory is Chaim Kaufmann, who, drawing on Barry Posen's ethnic security dilemma, claims that, not unlike Samuel Huntingdon's infamous *Clash of Civilizations* concept, ethnic groups in conflict are fixed, stable and coherent since 'ethnic identities' are more salient and difficult to change than 'ideological identities' and get 'harden[ed in ethnic conflicts] to the point that cross-ethnic appeals are unlikely to be made, and even less likely to be heard' (Kaufmann 1996: 137). With sides hardened by the infamous 'ancient ethnic hatreds' of Robert Kaplan (1994), resulting in ethnicized discourses, all-pervasive fear, a zero-sum mentality of combatants and constituents, and mass scale atrocities, ultimately culminating in ethnic cleansing and ethnocide, Kaufmann (1996, 1998) argues that political reconciliation and a negotiated peaceful solution to ethnic conflicts become impossible if not permanently enforced by the international community. However, since the international community often shies away from the costs that come with permanent peace enforcement, Kaufmann advocates enforced partition along the lines of ethnic division (Kaufmann 1996, 1998).

Many have challenged the concept of ethnic partition in general on the basis of its flawed assumption of ethnic groups as fixed, salient and stable protagonists of ethnic conflict (Kumar 1997; Sambanis 2000; Fearon 2004b; Jenne 2009, 2012), with a range of particular critiques being made, from the impracticality of creating post-conflict ethnically homogeneous entities (Kumar 1997) to the ethical dubiousness of ethnic partition rewarding ethno-nationalist elites and entrepreneurs, or, in the worst case, the perpetrators of ethnic cleansing and genocide (Fearon 2004b). And yet, it continues to influence policy-makers more than many other scholarly works on ethnic conflict, not only because its inherent groupism and territorially-based understanding of ethnic conflicts offer 'simple models of explanation' (Joras & Schetter 2004: 318) as well as implementable 'solutions' to ethnic conflicts, but also because it represents the shared world view, habitus and culture of explanatory, state-centrist, and rationalist IR scholars and the bureaucratic field.

Theoretically, the concept of ethnic partition also clashes with the principle in international law that states' international borders are sacrosanct; but, by again reducing ethnic conflict to competing claims on territory and to a territorially-based power struggle, it provides another example of how explanatory IR imagines itself in the position to provide policy-relevant theories on how to manage, and ideally to 'resolve', these conflicts. The alleged 'solution' here is to somewhat satisfy the presupposed aspirations of the ethno-nationalist group for territorial control – to which explanatory IR often has contributed by representing them as such in the first place – while at the same time keeping intact the borders of the state in question, from whom the ethnic group supposedly aspires to secede. In theory, so the logic of the proponents of ethnic partition goes, this can be achieved by granting the ethno-nationalist group with alleged secessionist ambitions quasi-sovereign control over the territory it claims; for example, by way of an autonomous region or federal structure for the overall state, as is permissible for maintaining the integrity of the state in question. In practice, though, these forms of 'ethnic solutions' to ethnic conflicts imposed on the warring societies by Western interventionist bureaucracies all too often have two results. It either merely accomplishes a postponement of secession, yet makes the process of getting there more arduous and the irredentist conflict more protracted, as was the case in Kosovo, or, as in Bosnia and Iraq, with the violent conflict exacerbated and ethnic partition imposed on the warring parties having reified and deepened ethnic lines of division, an inherently dysfunctional state is constructed that looks good on the drawing board but has no legitimacy other than the dictate of the international community. The case of Bosnia is well documented (Kumar 1997; Chandler 2000; Gagnon 2004; Hansen 2006; Sarajlic 2010), and the role IR scholarship has played in informing and shaping Western interventionist state- and nation-building in Bosnia has been problematized in David Campbell's path breaking *National Deconstruction* (1998a).[6] The case of Iraq and the unique status of Iraqi Kurdistan as within but at the same time apart from Iraq, where, similar to Bosnia, an unsustainable system of ethnic federalism – a euphemism for constrained ethnic partition while preserving the state as such – was imposed on the country and its people, will be taken up again in the case study. Before turning there, though, and before illustrating empirically what has thus far been reserved to the theoretical discussion, it is imperative to outline a possible theoretical alternative to how explanatory IR makes sense of ethnic conflict, an alternative which will then in turn be applied to the empirical case study.

… and outlines for a possible alternative to it

As cautioned in the Introduction, the aim of deconstruction is never to develop new meta-theories, models, or frameworks that replace the ones that have been deconstructed, which cannot be the task of deconstruction, since to do so would violate its very principles, that is its inherently critical attitude to any kind of meta-theory. Therefore, readers who expect at this stage the concepts and models of explanatory IR on (ethnic) identity to be replaced with a new, neater definition are bound to be disappointed; to develop new definitions is not the task of this study – as a matter of fact, it would contradict its aspiration and methodology – and consequently will be left to others.

This limitation, however, does not prevent the study from, after at first expounding the deficiencies of explanatory IR's approach to (ethnic) identity and after revealing why explanatory IR does what it does, that is contextualizing its approach – as has been done in the previous chapters – to then point out alternative conceptualizations of (ethnic) identity from IR literature that harmonize more closely with the classic understanding of ethnicity, introduced in Chapter

1, which explanatory IR chooses to neglect for the reasons diagnosed. Chapter 1 has elaborated that Max Weber describes ethnic groups as human collectives defined by their 'subjective belief in a common descent' (Weber 1978 [1922]: 389); in other words, for him ethnicity is not an essential, pre-given characteristic, as it is for most of explanatory IR, but a belief system, an ideology, a way of seeing the world that gets strengthened and solidified through collective behaviour, through acting together as a group. Likewise, it has also been shown in this passage that Frederick Barth views ethnic groups as emerging through social interaction with others, by constructing social boundaries that define as much who belongs to the group as who does not; that, in fact, the process of constructing social boundaries – understood as a system of inclusion and exclusion – is constitutive of the group formation and identification process; in other words that the self cannot exist without the other and vice versa, that they are mutually constitutive. Ethnic groups, thus, are 'in a sense *created* through that very contact [with other groups]. Group identities must always be defined in relation to that which they are not – in other words to non-members of the group' (Eriksen 2002: 10, emphasis in original). If it is the interaction with others that constitutes the ethnic group, if group formation and ethnic identification is processual, relational, circumstantial and contextual – and not, as explanatory IR portrays them, relatively stable, pre-given, substantial, bounded and, in their entirety, homogenous units that can be attributed with social agency – then ethnic identities are logically the very opposite of stable, substantial and a pre-given, but are one of multiple and dynamic identities, 'points of temporary attachment to the subject positions which discursive practices construct for us' (Hall 1996: 6), that are 'never a final or settled matter' (Jenkins 2008b: 5), are 'decentred, fragmented by contradictory discourses and by the pull of other identities' (Rattansi 1999: 84) – and are accentuated or attenuated according to context. In sum, they are not factual but socio-political constructs and 'discursive formations', in keeping with Craig Calhoun, for whom ethnic groups and

> nations are constituted largely by the claims themselves, by the way of talking and thinking and acting that relies on these sorts of claims to produce collective identity, to mobilise people for collective projects, and to evaluate peoples and practices.
>
> (Calhoun 1997: 5)

All this amounts to a sound rejection of essentialist groupism in explanatory IR, of ascribing the ethnic group with social agency, of analytically equating it with the state, and of ethnic identity as the independent variable to explain ethnic conflict. In his survey of the recent literature on ethnic conflict that operationalizes ethnic identity as the independent variable, Kanchan Chandra comes to the conclusion:

> Ethnic identity – and concepts related to ethnic identity such as ethnic diversity, ethnic riots, ethnic parties, ethnic violence, ethnic conflict, and so

on – either does not matter or has not shown to matter as an independent variable by most previous theoretical work on ethnic identity ... In most instances, the mechanisms driving our explanatory theories about the effect of ethnic identity assume properties such as the fixedness of ethnic identity, cultural homogeneity and a shared history, which are not associated with ethnic identities ... The outcomes our theories seek to explain, then, must be caused by some other variables that act independently or interact with ethnic identity.

(Chandra 2006: 399)

This assessment applies to explanatory IR frameworks, such as the ethnic alliance model that most palpably seeks to explain ethnic conflict and the formation of ethnic alliances with ethnic identity as the independent variable, thus tautologically explaining ethnic conflict with ethnicity. It also applies to the ethnic security dilemma, on which Chandra observes:

This argument assumes that ethnic categories, like states, are fixed entities. If individuals could change their ethnic identities, then one response to the collapse of the state would be to switch to less threatening identities rather than go to war. The argument also implies that ethnic groups are more likely than other types of groups to have a common history. Otherwise, the security dilemma should be an explanation for intergroup conflict in the wake of state collapse in general, rather than ethnic conflict in particular. However, neither fixity nor a common history are intrinsic properties of ethnic identities ... This argument, thus, cannot be read as an argument about the effect of ethnic identities per se. The effect of ethnic identities here is contingent on some extrinsic variable that produces fixity in ethnic identities and a perception of a common history.

(Chandra 2006: 420)

If the effects of ethnic identity are contingent on an extrinsic variable, which means that, for the occurrence of ethnic conflict, ethnic identity cannot serve as the explanans, that it has been demonstrated to fall through as the independent variable explaining the occurrence of ethnic conflict, then ethnic identity should be operationalized as the dependent variable, instrumentalism argues. As has been shown, instrumentalism covers a wide spectrum of approaches, from Christia reducing ethnic identity to merely a political tool that can easily be traded for any other form of identity if the situation calls for it – thus rendering the elites who do the trading omnipotent in shaping the discourse, and by doing so reifying the structure via the agent – to Posner and Olzak's more nuanced application of instrumentalism that puts equal emphasis on the motives of elites and masses and highlights the limitations to either of them playing the ethnic card. They show that individuals and groups, elites and masses alike, in any given context can only operationalize identities from a pre-existing repertoire and that this choice comes with costs and long-term commitments. Yet, the trouble with instrumentalism in general – aside from its positivist belief in a strict causality – remains their prioritizing of mostly material interests to dictate people's choices and calling on identities. Posner, for example, states,

> I am not denying that ethnic identities are sometimes sources of extremely strong feelings … In many contexts … viewing ethnic identity change as a product of strategic calculations about coalition size will be counter-productive and lead to misinterpretations of the motivations of social behaviour … I [do not] want to suggest that emotions such as fear, hatred, or resentment do not trump rational calculations in motivating ethnic behaviour in some contexts.
>
> (Posner 2005b: 12–13)

Yet his analysis is almost exclusively dedicated to economic incentives such as patronage systems, the expectation and distribution of sinecures and public goods provisions as the independent variables to explain why a certain type of identity has been activated in this context. Posner admits as much when clarifying,

> like ethnicity itself, the applicability of the strict instrumentalist approach I adopt is situational … My rationale for adopting a purely instrumental view of ethnicity in this study is simply that, while not appropriate for every explanation, it is appropriate for the expressly political context that this book treats.
>
> (Posner 2005b: 13)

That is all fair and fine and does not in any way diminish the contributions of Posner's work commented on earlier. What it illustrates, though, is that instru-mentalism does not provide a general theory of ethnic identity since it is only applicable in a certain, finite context. By its proponents' own admission, it fails to explain the affect-side of ethnic identity, for example why situations may arise in which someone refuses to abandon his or her ethnic identity even in exchange for material benefits or political advantages, why people may stubbornly stick to their ethnic identity against their economic or security interests, why ideational factors may outweigh cost-benefit analyses.

A possible solution to this conundrum of ethnic identity demonstrably failing to sufficiently explain the complexities of ethnic conflict as either the dependent or independent variable is offered by Andreas Wimmer, who develops an intri-cate processual multi-level approach, where ethnic boundary construction can be seen as either a dependent or independent variable, depending on context (Wimmer 2008, 2012):[7]

> A multilevel process theory does not offer a simple formula relating 'dependent' to 'independent' variables as in mainstream social sciences, for example, by predicting the degree of political salience of ethnicity from

levels of gross domestic product, democratization, or ethno-linguistic heterogeneity ... Rather, it is a generative model where variables are 'dependent' or 'independent' depending on which phase in the cycle of reproduction and transformation [of ethnic boundary making] we focus. The model thus ... emphasize[s] that in order to understand the logic of social life we should focus on the processes that generate and transform its varying forms.

(Wimmer 2008: 1009–10)

While Wimmer's contribution has much to recommend itself and shares many commonalities with the processual approach advocated in this study, two crucial reservations are to be made, both in relation to Wimmer's positivist epistemology. Wimmer's model still adheres to the principle that all social action and its underlying motives are grounded in a hierarchical sequence of cause and effect, that cause and effect can be clearly differentiated and categorized, that they can be operationalized as variables in order to explain these actions and motives, and finally that we analysts are capable of doing this differentiating, categorizing, operationalizing of variables, and explaining in a detached, objective and rational fashion.

I believe neither of this to be the case. Grounded in constitutive theory I would argue that the social world is too complex, too much in constant flux to be neatly delineated into variables, into clear-cut divisions of empirically measurable cause and effect, into distinct and finite categories, and, perhaps most importantly, that we social scientists by applying objective and rational benchmarks can adequately explain it. We are an intrinsic part of the social world we seek to explain, are co-constitutive of it, are its co-protagonists, like the actors in our studies whose actions and motives we interpret. We are biased towards a certain view long before we conceive of a research project, and our selection of variables and the results our research produces are just a reflection of this bias, of our inherent subjectivity, and therefore can only offer a personal narrative, one 'reality' among many others, at best a snapshot with very limited capacity for generalizations. This intellectual honesty implies an admission that instead of explaining the social world we can only offer a perception of it, and an admission that the causes and effects of social action are not as readily quantifiable and translatable into variables as positivist epistemology suggests. And since they are not so quantifiable and translatable, I propose – in line with constitutive theory – doing away with dependent and independent variables, hierarchical sequences of cause and effect, and clearly bound entities as categories of analysis altogether. They do not reflect the diversity, fluidity, and complexity of the social world, and neither does the fallacious notion of scientific objectivity and of the detached scientists as rational observers and equitable 'explainers'

The distinguishing marks of the constitutive approach in addressing the three fallacies of explanatory IR's approach to (ethno-)nationalist conflict, as suggested here, are:

1   In refutation of the modernist principal distinctive feature between ethnic group and nation, it is argued that these categories are not factual in the

social world but a product of discourse and practice, at the level of both social scientists analysing them and ethno-nationalist elites enacting and practising them. A definitive distinction between the two, based on the existence or absence of a claim to sovereign control of territory, is untenable, since in most cases it can only be made ex post. Thus, rather than perceiving the ethnic group as a predecessor of the nation, and the nation as a proto-state on a unidirectional trajectory, these categories are understood as stages on a fluid and malleable spectrum, where transmutation in all directions is as possible as suspension.

2   Ethnic groups, nations and states are not represented here as clearly bounded, organic, substantive, distinct, homogeneous, and static categories endowed with social agency, but as discursive formations decidedly contingent and contextual in time and space. Agency here is not with the social group or community at large but, in Brubaker's terminology, with their empowered incumbents who enact, through discourse and practice, the social identity, ideology and discursive formation of ethnicity, nation- and statehood.

3   This understanding of these categories aims to direct scholars' attention from *what* of ethnic group, nation or state to *how* they are enacted in discourse and practice. In analysing the interplay between agency and structure from this angle, identities and interests are not operationalized as dependent or independent variables, i.e. neither is given ontological priority. Instead, drawing on Karin Fierke (2007), the intention is to make a case for perceiving the process of identity formation in the social world as a fluid and complex matrix of identities and interests without hierarchical and causal sequences of identities and interests as dependent and independent variables. Fierke elaborates:

> A causal relationship requires the isolation of independent and dependent variables. A constitutive discourse analysis, by contrast, requires that we 'look and see' the matrix of identities and interests and the process by which they are gradually transformed through historical interactions. These interactions do not by definition magnify the difference between identities; they may also attempt to renegotiate a different type of relationship between self and other.
>
> (Fierke 2007: 81)[8]

Aside from presenting an alternative to the positivist principle in explanatory IR of classifying the social world into quantifiable variables and clearly bounded categories by instead allowing for a more fluid, diverse, complex and less hierarchical and standardized make-up of the social world, the alternative epistemology and ontology of constitutive theory would therefore, after deconstructing the binary opposites around which our social world is supposedly constructed, consider other forms of human coexistence, forms more grounded in congruities rather than differences. Most importantly, constitutive theory directs our attention away from the *what* question of identity, discussed ad nauseam and, as has been shown, rather unconvincingly, to the more fruitful examination of *how* identity works. Fierke continues:

> Conventional social scientific approaches treat entities as discrete and isolated … [But] identities are not isolated. They are constituted within a world populated by other identities, particular kinds of objects and particular forms of action … [Constitutive theory highlights those] by drawing out the structure of relationships, objects and actions, the everyday assumptions that constitute a world 'made strange', such that the analyst can observe its workings from more of a distance. In undertaking a study of this kind [i.e. a constitutive theory-based], the analyst is not observing 'the' world, as it exists objectively, but [is] rather looking at how 'a' world works in practice, including the power relationships and hierarchies that hold it together, the forms of legitimacy by which this power is maintained, or the challenges by which a particular constellation of identity and action is undermined and potentially transformed.
>
> (Fierke 2007: 81–82)

This constitutive perspective on ethnic identities has guided the first part of this study, putting the role of the analyst centre stage, alongside his or her attempts, grounded in positivist explanatory IR epistemologies and ontologies, to construct a world 'made strange' in order to take a step back and examine it 'objectively' from a distance. The same constitutive perspective will also instruct the empirical case study. Here, though, rather than a textual analysis, attention will shift to demonstrating why a positivist approach with identities and interests operationalized as dependent and independent variables demonstrably fails to explain the relations between Iraqi Kurdish ethno-nationalist parties and the PKK from the early 1980s until the present. At each stage of these relations we will pause and, echoing Fierke's above call for a constitutive approach and what it entails, reflect on why their relations are better viewed through the prism of a fluid and complex matrix of contingent identities and interests, how the interplay of these factors works, analysing the structures and hierarchies of power that constitute the parties' domination of the respective Kurdish discourses for self-determination, and how Kurdish identities shifted and were transformed by intrinsic and extrinsic factors during this period. Ultimately, the case study also has the objective of exposing why an analytical equation of ethnic groups with states and their presupposed predecessors is not only demonstrably untenable but should not be made in the first place.

Notes

1 The concept of the other as defining the self can be traced back to G. W. F. Hegel's master–slave dialectic and runs like a red thread through Western philosophy as analogous to asymmetric yet constitutive relations whether it is employed to explain domination through power/knowledge in a Foucauldian sense, in the post-colonial conceptualization of an Edward Said or Frantz Fanon, or for deconstructing gender

relations in a male-dominated culture. The exception is Levinasian ethics, in which the self bears a responsibility, a moral obligation towards the other inherent to us as human beings (Campbell & Shapiro 1999).

2 The study also showed that between 65 per cent (lowest, Princeton) and 92 per cent (highest, Chicago) of the authors on the reading lists were male (Biersteker 2009: 311–320).

3 Belabouring social psychology one could also interpret this siege mentality among explanatory IR scholars faced with the post-positivist challenge to their paradigms as 'defensive cognition' (Stein 1997; de Dreu & van Knippenberg 2005; Tetlock 2006). The importance of belief systems in processes of estimation and judgement, and how the exposure of these beliefs to contradictory information can result in a strengthening and hardening of these beliefs is well established (Anderson *et al.* 1980; Anderson 1983; Hirt & Sherman 1985); in other words, strongly held beliefs and preconceived notions about an object or matter have the tendency to suppress cognition of contradictory information and lead to a refusal to revise one's position the more that contradictory information points to a revision of the position. 'Defensive cognitions', Tetlock (2006: 137) argues, 'are activated when forecasters most need them'.

4 The term originates from the work of historian Peggy Pascoe (1990) who used it to describe the nineteenth century Victorian social consciousness and advocacy of urban, bourgeois, educated and highly religious women's organizations, such as the *Women's Christian Temperance Union*, to 'rescue', i.e. liberate disenfranchised women from their oppressors at home and abroad, altogether reflected in missionary activities in the majority world or advocacy for the rights and improvement of conditions of migrant and ethnic minority women, women in polygamous marriages among Mormon societies, prostitutes, single mothers, etc., in the US.

5 For an application of Bourdieu's conceptualization of neo-liberalism as *doxa* in the context of discourses on market liberalization and globalization in India, see Chopra (2003).

6 See also Campbell (1999).

7 Another example where ethnic identity is operationalized either as the dependent or independent variable according to context is the work of James Fearon and David Laitin, see Fearon and Laitin (1996, 2000), Fearon (2004a) for their individual contextual approaches.

8 See also Fierke (2005).

Part II

4 State formation and the origins of Kurdish ethno-nationalisms in Turkey and Iraq

Turkey's Sèvres Syndrome

As a result of its defeat in the First World War, the dissolution of the Ottoman Empire was the cataclysmic event of the twentieth-century Middle East. Centuries-old political and socio-economic structures were replaced by new entities, most profoundly the modern, sovereign nation-state. Over the course of less than two years, about half a dozen new states were created on drawing boards in European chancelleries, where the victors of the Great War tried to reconcile their traditional imperialistic ambitions with the popular demands of a new era, epitomized in the idealistic principles of American President Woodrow Wilson's Fourteen Points that called for the national self-determination of the peoples of the Ottoman Empire. It is this contradiction in principles, world views, and directions that determined the fragmented process of state formation in the Middle East, and its legacies form the root-cause of countless ethnic and ethno-nationalist conflicts that keep haunting the region until today.

The Armistice of Moudros on 30 October 1918 ended the hostilities between the Ottoman Empire and the Entente in the Middle Eastern theatre of the First World War. On 10 August 1920, representatives of the Ottoman Empire reluctantly signed the Treaty of Sèvres that deprived the Sublime Porte of 72 per cent of the territory it had controlled before the war. It foresaw the creation of several independent Arab as well as Armenian and Kurdish states under mandate of the League of Nations. In regard to the Ottoman Empire's Kurdish population the Treaty of Sèvres stipulated:

> Article 62: A Commission sitting at Constantinople and composed of three members appointed by the British, French and Italian Governments respectively shall draft within six months from the coming into force of the present Treaty a scheme of local autonomy for the predominantly Kurdish areas lying east of the Euphrates, south of the southern boundary of Armenia as it may be hereafter determined, and north of the frontier of Turkey with Syria and Mesopotamia …
>
> Article 64: If within one year of coming into force of the present Treaty the Kurdish peoples within the areas defined in Article 62 shall address themselves

to the Council of the League of Nations in such a manner as to show that a majority of the population of these areas desires independence from Turkey, and if the Council then considers that these people are capable of such independence and recommends that it should be granted to them, Turkey hereby agrees to execute such recommendations, and to renounce all rights and title over these areas … If and when such renunciation takes place, no objection will be raised by the Principal Allied Powers to the voluntary adhesion to such an independent Kurdish state of the Kurds inhabiting that part of Kurdistan which has hitherto been included in the Mosul vilayet.[1]

For the first time, the idea of an independent Kurdish state was realistically within the grasp of its people and enjoyed, at least in principle, international support (Brown 1924; Helmreich 1974; O'Shea 2004; Özoğlu 2004; Bozarslan 2003, 2007; McDowall 2007). Yet it was not meant to be realized.

Unlike the German Reich or the Austro-Hungarian Empire, a good part of the Turkish political establishment and army refused to accept a peace by decree and took up arms against the Entente's imperialist designs. In the Turkish War of Independence (1919–1922), the Turkish Nationalists around Mustafa Kemal 'Atatürk' not only mobilized large swaths of the population for their cause but also dealt the Greek invaders and their allies devastating blows. Needless to say, though, Turkish nationalism or Turkism did not emerge out of the blue but, like all nationalisms, had various 'precursors, proto-nationalist movements, and ideologies that prepare[d] the ground for the emergence of [Turkish] nationalism'.[2] In fact, post-First World War Turkish nationalism or Kemalism should not be understood as a clear break from Ottomanism nor from the 'Young Turk' movement that, dominating the governing *Committee for Union and Progress* (CUP), had de facto ruled the Empire since 1908 and led it to ultimate defeat. While doing away with its supposedly antiquated structures of governance, Turkism at first held out a 'new interpretation' of Ottomanism's basic principles, yet at the same time 'attribut[ed] a central role to the Turkish ethnic group within the Ottoman whole' (Hanioğlu 2006: 4).

In several important, interrelated aspects, Kemalism though, departed from traditional CUP doctrine. First, while acknowledging the primacy of education and the Turkish language,[3] Kemalism, echoing Heather Rear's 'pathological homogenisation' discussed earlier, put emphasis on the forced assimilation of religious and ethnic minorities. Every Muslim subject of the new Turkish state – 'Christians [were considered] as unsuitable material for becoming "Turkish"' (Poulton 1997: 97) and consequently expelled in a mass-exodus[4] – could be taught to become a Turk. Those who refused to adopt the Turkish *Leitkultur*, on the other hand, were treated like the non-Muslim minorities: they were expelled or eliminated in the name of a founding ideology, that, over the course of a few years, had become distinctly racist and social-Darwinist, with 'lesser people' preordained to pay their debt for the 'survival of the fittest'.[5]

The extent to which the political space became ethnicized in the early days of the Turkish Republic has to be understood as a function of the pathological paranoia inherent in the Kemalist perception of *watan*, the fatherland, or as Omer

Taspinar calls it, 'state borders nationalism' that, 'as the defining principle of Turkish nationalism', considers the indivisibility of nation and state as delineated by 'the republic's territorial borders' supreme doctrine (Taspinar 2005: 59). Consequently, any alteration of these borders, deemed sacrosanct, would immanently distort and implicitly violate the very character of the Turkish nation. This often pathological 'preoccupation with territorial sovereignty and the fear of disintegration' explains why 'the granting of ethnicity-related minority rights' would be seen 'as a betrayal of the indivisible unity between the state and its nation. As a result, even symbolic compromises regarding minority rights are considered as a prelude to separatism' (Taspinar 2005: 59).

This paranoia via ethnic and/or religious minorities, originating from the so-called 'Eastern Question' during the late days of the Ottoman Empire, First World War and the War of Independence, in which Assyrians, Armenians, Greeks, and to a lesser extent Kurds had allegedly conspired with one or an alliance of Western powers against the Empire or the viability of a Turkish *watan*, became the leitmotiv of Kemalist state and its security doctrine. Indeed, Turkish politicians and the army continue to be plagued by what has been called in the literature the 'Sèvres Syndrome' (Jung 2001; Jung & Piccoli 2001; Kirişçi 2006; Lundgren 2007; Göçek 2011). Fatma Göçek defines the 'Sèvres Syndrome' as a nexus of 'those individuals, groups or institutions in Turkey who interpret all public interactions – domestic or foreign – through a framework of fear and anxiety over the possible annihilation, abandonment or betrayal of the Turkish state by the West' (Göçek 2011: 99). Drawing on the Bourdieuian concept of habitus, Jung and Piccoli expand:

> One essential aspect of the Kemalist habitus is its perpetuation of the Kemalist experience of external conspiracy and internal betrayal. The historical culmination of this experience as well as its social transmission to the National Movement was the Treaty of Sèvres. Although never implemented, the clauses of Sèvres, calling for a territorial division of Turkey, became the incarnation of both the Ottoman defeat and the Turkish national resistance ... The Sèvres syndrome developed into a cornerstone of the Kemalist world-view, making it essential for an understanding of Kemalist perceptions of threat.
>
> (Jung & Piccoli 2001: 149–150)

What is remarkable in this context is not only the persistence of the 'Sèvres Syndrome' into our times,[6] but that Sèvres actually became a founding myth of the Turkish Republic. After all, the Turkish nationalist forces defeated the Greek invaders and their Entente allies and wrested from the West the much more favourable Treaty of Lausanne (24 July 1923), in which Turkey's enemies officially recognized the Turkish Republic that had managed to carve out double the territory than what had been stipulated at Sèvres. Why then would a moment of defeat that was never implemented rather than the victory at Lausanne become one of the defining founding myths of the Republic? Göçek speculates that the

Turkish nationalist government, torn between a population 'traumatised by a decade of wars capping a century of pain, suffering and humiliation' (Göçek 2011: 120) at the hands of the West and its own designs for imposing on this very population a project of rapid transformation and Western modernization, had to create an official, state-sanctioned valve for public sentiment to express itself – a valve that gained a momentum of its own, turned into a founding myth and became a national syndrome.

What is, for the purposes of this study, a more central aspect is the fact that the 'Sèvres Syndrome' did not remain limited to Turkey's relations with the West but became aggrandized into a general perception of 'bemoan[ing] Turkey's location in a "bad neighbourhood"', and as 'besieged by a veritable ring of evil' (Jung & Piccoli 2001: 116–117). This pathological fear of external conspiracies against the Turkish *watan*, the sacred territory of the fatherland – whether Western or regional – is accompanied by a widely held perception of any internal opposition to Turkish state doctrine being either stirred from abroad or this internal opposition actually acting as a 'fifth column' for foreign interests. This perception of domestic problems as exogenous, as instigated abroad, is particularly relevant in the context of the two major challenges the Turkish politico-military establishment has identified for the survival of the state since the 1980s: Islamism and ethnic, i.e. Kurdish separatism. The attitude towards the so-called 'Kurdish Question' in Turkey, that any political demands or dissent of its Kurdish minority are not home-grown, and therefore cannot be solved in political dialogue, that any ethnicized discourse is steered by external enemies, and that any party engaging in such a discourse is a foreign agent or acting on behalf of foreign interests, is best summed up in a statement by former President Süleyman Demirel, who categorically asserted, 'there is no other political solution to [Kurdish demands] than to render these people ineffective by force', and that the West is 'trying to involve the Sèvres Treaty to set up a Kurdish state in the region … and that was what [the West] meant by political solutions'.[7] Prime Minister Bülent Ecevit, after the capture of Abdullah Öcalan, took the same line, when declaring, 'there is no Kurdish problem in the country, but only PKK terrorism supported by the outside in order to divide Turkey'.[8] Consequently, and as will be detailed throughout the third part of this study, this perception has strongly shaped the attitude and response of the Turkish politico-military establishment to any autonomous Kurdish region in Iraq that first and foremost was seen as a safe haven for Kurdish insurgencies and as a first step towards an independent Kurdish state that would then actively pursue the reunification of all Kurdish lands and thus the division of the Turkish *watan*. What is equally noteworthy is that, by the same token, the ethnic alliance model and related groupist frameworks that operationalize group solidarity based on shared ethnicity as their independent and, as has been detailed, determining variable to explain the behaviour of parties of the same ethnic group in ethno-nationalist conflicts – in this case the Iraqi Kurdish polity and its relations with the PKK – not only buy into the pathological paranoia of the Turkish state but run the risk of actively contributing to the misrepresentation of legitimate Kurdish grievances in Turkey as exogenous. In other words, ironically, it is often Western scholarship and explanatory IR that may in the end become complicit in the Turkish politico-military establishment manipulating the myth of the 'Sèvres Syndrome' and the discourse of denial, exclusion and persecution that comes with it.

On the 'artificiality' of the Iraqi state

'Of all the major states in the Middle East, Iraq faced the most formidable obstacles to state formation', Simon Bromley (1994: 135) observes in his comparative account of the processes of state formation in the post-First World War Middle East. 'The sheer arbitrariness of the country's formation, together with the absence of any developed tradition of state stability and the degree of ethnic and religious heterogeneity ... produced an extremely refractory inheritance for state-building', he summarizes. This had been exacerbated in later years by the state's dependence on oil revenues and a societal rentier state mentality that 'further increased [the governing elites'] ability to opt for coercion over less brutal forms of mobilisation and control. The consequence has been the creation of the most controlled and repressive society in the Middle East' (Bromley 1994: 135).

It is true that Iraq, perhaps more than any other state in the Middle East, is an arbitrary creation of the imperialist designs and compromises of the First World War victors, and while in the randomness of its borders, the heterogeneous composition of its population, and its rulers' proneness to authoritarianism it resembles many post-colonial states in Africa, it arguably exceeds their inherent instability in the fact that its British imperialist overlords imposed on its society a completely alien ruling dynasty with no social or historical ties to Iraq's population whatsoever.[9] Never in the history of the lands between the Persian Gulf and the Zagros Mountain Range has there been a single, coherent, political entity of its own. From the times of Nebuchadnezzar to Mehmed VI, the last sultan to reign from the Sublime Porte, it had always been part of larger empires in which the manifold localist and often competing identities of its people were overlaid by greater unifying ideologies and *Weltanschauungen*. With these common bonds severed after the First World War, unlike Turkey – forged on the anvil of Kemalism – Iraq lacked and still wants for a founding ideology furnishing the state with internal legitimacy and evoking loyalty from its citizens. Worse, when creating Iraq, the British, eager to establish an overland connection between the Mediterranean and the Persian Gulf as a link to India, and who as the occupying force in Basra and Baghdad were seen as the logical choice for running the yet-to-be established Mandate of Mesopotamia, imposed at the Cairo Conference of March 1921 – on a majority Shi'i population – an alien Sunni ruler, their old war-time ally, Faisal, the son of Hussein bin Ali, the Sharif of Mecca (Olson 1992; Dodge 2003; Catherwood 2004; Sluglett 2007; Stansfield 2007a; Tripp 2007; Marr 2011).[10] By doing so, they established the fatal pattern characteristic for Iraq of the Sunni Arab minority ruling over and oppressing a Shi'i Arab and Sunni Kurdish majority; a pattern culminating in the reign of terror of Saddam Hussein.

The British state-building exercise on the banks of the Euphrates and Tigris – one is hard pressed to believe they ever genuinely intended to build a nation there – was flawed from its conceptualization. It was established on two overriding principles: an 'empire on the cheap' (Catherwood 2004) – to extract the maximum of profits with the minimum of input – and resulting from that, the application of 'divide-and-rule' maxims, a re-tribalization of society, and playing particularistic local interests off against each other (Dodge 2003; Natali 2005; McDowall 2007; Sluglett 2007).They set Shi'i against Sunni, Kurds against Arabs, and exploited existing feuds between tribes to their own ends. 'Rather than neutralizing ethnic and religious differences within the heterogeneous Iraqi society ... the British reinforced them by elevating Sunni Arabs over other groups' Natali concludes and observes that the British colonial administration, 'played off tribes against one another, instigating land disputes and encouraging internal hostilities (Natali 2005: 28–29). Until the mid-1940s, the British 'divide-and-rule' strategies, imported from North-western India, today's Federally Administered Tribal Areas of Pakistan (McDowall 2007; Stansfield 2007a) – at the time of the *Raj*, an as conflict-ridden land as Kurdistan – played out as expected. While the Turkish state to the north obliterated the traditional role of the sheikh and pursued an ambiguous policy towards Kurdish tribes, the British indirect rule over Iraq nurtured tribal structures and elevated the sheikhs as state-sanctioned rulers. In its short-sighted desire for 'empire on the cheap', i.e. local allies running the show for British interests instead of stationing troops there permanently at a dear price, London became paymaster in a trickle-down system of patronage, basing its control over Iraq on corrupt *aghas* and sheikhs for whom charity began and ended at home (Dawood 2003; Dodge 2003; Stansfield 2007a), particularly in Southern Kurdistan.[11]

As much as the political structure and population composition of Iraq reflected not historic and societal conditions on the ground but the strategic needs of the British quasi-colonial system – in fact, if anything they were deliberately set to work in opposite directions to weaken national cohesion and therefore minimize the potential for local resistance – so did Iraq's borders. The original Sykes-Picot Agreement, in which Britain and France had carved up the former Ottoman Empire for themselves, foresaw the *vilayet* of Mosul to be joined with the French Mandate for Syria and the Lebanon (Helmreich 1974; Catherwood 2004; Sluglett 2007; Stansfield 2007a; Tripp 2007; Fromkin 2009; Marr 2011; Barr 2012). Soon, though, Britain was forced to change its mind and persuaded France to cede control over Mosul. What ultimately tipped the scales for the incorporation of the *vilayet* of Mosul and its Kurds into the British Mandate of Mesopotamia and thus *à la longue* into Iraq may first and foremost have been military and religious factors: once Mustafa Kemal's victories in the Turkish War of Independence had thwarted any hopes for a unified Kurdish state, Britain required an easily defensible, i.e. mountainous frontier with the Republic of Turkey, perceived as aggressive in its territorial ambitions and feared to be in cahoots with Bolshevik Russia. Of equal importance for London and Baghdad were the Sunni Kurds maintaining a balance against the Shi'i sectarian dominance in newborn Iraq – their inclusion guaranteed a desperately needed religious equilibrium, an aspect King Faisal was explicitly adamant about (Olson 1992; Shields 2004; Asadi 2007; McDowall 2007; Sluglett 2007; Stansfield 2007a).[12] By incorporating the Mosul *vilayet* into the British Mandate of Mesopotamia and by establishing the 'Brussels Line', agreed on as the border between Iraq and Turkey in the Anglo-Turkish Treaty of 5 June 1926,[13] Britain drove a permanent divide between the Kurdish lands, separating communities that had lived in close contact and social interaction for centuries, cut off Mosul – a traditional thoroughfare for goods from Aleppo and Anatolia to Persia – from its natural commercial links and forced it to coexist with Baghdad and Basra to the south, who historically had always been oriented towards the Gulf and whose ethnic, religious, economic, and societal composition differed markedly from the Kurdish north (Cuthell 2004; Stansfield 2007a; Tripp 2007; Marr 2011).[14]

In sum and using Abraham Lincoln's famous analogy, when the British released Iraq into independence-on-paper-only in 1932,[15] they left a house not only internally divided against itself but built on quicksand. A shaky monarchy headed by a child-king[16] presided over a system of proverbial instability – illustrated by countless coup attempts and Britain being forced to temporarily re-occupy the country in 1941 – patronage, rampant corruption, artificially fuelled and rumbling on local conflicts, arrant social inequality, uneven modernization campaigns, the gradual transition into the status of a rentier state dependent on oil revenues, and cash-crop agriculture subject to fluctuations of the volatile 1930/1940s global market (Elliot 1996; Stansfield 2007a; Tripp 2007; Marr 2011). The quasi-colonial legacy of the Iraqi polity has given rise to a debate about the extent to which the 'artificiality' of the state created by the British imperialist power can explain Iraq's troubled history of myriad sectarian divisions, proliferation of violent conflicts, and brutal dictatorships (Fattah 2003). This debate is taken up by Stansfield who sums it up as a perception of Iraq being 'cobbled together' to satisfy the imperialistic strategic and geo-economic requirements of the British quasi-colonial power, and

> this description is then commonly used as the starting point to explain Iraq's twentieth-century development, and, as a logic conclusion to such explanations, that it is Iraq's existential fate to suffer under a succession of non-democratic governments ... From a constellation of dissociated peoples living in different geographical spaces, the modern state of Iraq was doomed to succumb to various manifestations of authoritarian rule because this was the only mechanism by which the fractious country could be held together.
>
> (Stansfield 2007a: 28–29)

He holds against this reading of the genealogy of the Iraqi state in the twentieth century that 'virtually all states are to some extent, as human constructs, "artificial"', and goes on that,

> the argument also presupposes that social and political characteristics in twentieth-century Iraq remained in a state of stasis, rather than one of

dynamism and development. Why should it be presumed that just because Iraq was artificial in the 1920s nearly a century of existence as a state should not have endowed it with some form of societal consciousness?

(Stansfield 2007a: 29)

While I agree with Stansfield that all states are social constructs – which, in my opinion and as elaborated earlier, does not make them artificial but constructed and performatively enacted realities – I do not agree with his implicit interpretation that therefore all states are the same, a constructivist variant, or 'cliched constructivism' in Brubaker's terminology, of the neo-realist view of the international system composed of states as 'like units' discussed in the previous section. This chapter's comparison between the processes of state formation in Turkey and Iraq show that their origins and the polities resulting from these formative struggles could not be more different: on the one hand a state that was forged by a widely supported nationalist struggle against imperialist invaders and occupying forces and whose founding ideology drew on a rich canon of myths of origin, and on the other hand an arbitrary creation that corresponded with the geo-strategic needs of an imperialist power but whose people had nothing in common other than the polity that was imposed upon them and its alien ruler serving these imperialist needs. In other words, one does not have to go far, does not even have to go outside the region and belabour examples of imperialist states such as Britain or France versus post-colonial states such as Iraq or Syria, to highlight their different origins and trajectories; for an empirical example that not all states are the same, that they are not 'like units', that a colonial and non-colonial past makes a profound difference for their future development one just has to turn to a comparison between Iraq and neighbouring Turkey. Stansfield is correct though, in pointing out that there was nothing predestined about Iraq's progression in the twentieth century, that it was not necessarily 'doomed' to authoritarianism and state collapse, that one should not 'presume' (Stansfield 2007a: 29) that it could not have developed differently; yet, the fact that it did not, that it succumbed to authoritarianism and sectarian violence is a result of and can be explained by its quasi-colonial legacy, of the fundaments, structures and parameters the British quasi-colonial power established (Dodge 2003; Gregory 2004). To deny these different preconditions specific to the post-colonial state, in my opinion, would not only be factually wrong but also represent a failure to recognize the role European imperialist powers have played in shaping the non-European world and the historic and moral responsibility that comes with that recognition – a recognition that, as detailed earlier, is unfortunately notoriously underdeveloped in a Eurocentric explanatory IR that often tends to whitewash its imperialist past. Finally, I would argue that Stansfield, throughout his monograph on Iraq, gives a detailed answer to his own question as to why 'nearly a century of existence as a state should not have endowed Iraq with some form of societal consciousness' (Stansfield 2007a: 29)? This is because the parameters set to ensure imperialist control and exploitation during the British Mandate of Mesopotamia persisted and were made sure to continue in the post-colonial state of Iraq, reaching from Britain's repeated military interventions there, to oil concessions that benefited foreign proprietors, to local elites collaborating and profiteering from these systems of dependence, exploitation and internal division, to the inviolability of state borders enshrined in international law and the modern international system, to the construct of the modern sovereign nation state itself.[17]

The origins of Kurdish ethno-nationalism in Iraq

In the British occupied Kurdish territories in what is today's Iraqi Kurdistan, the Kurdish rebellions in the north – see below – had the immediate effect of proving the Turkish Republic more conciliatory on the question of the future status of the former Mosul *vilayet*. For the British, who, as part of their wider redrawing of maps of the entire Middle East, had once championed an independent Kurdish state and who had been on the verge of outright war with Mustafa Kemal's nationalist forces for almost six years, this respite meant that they could close the last chapter of contention with the Turkish Republic and embark on re-shaping their share of the Middle East to their visions (Evans 1982). For the Kurds, it meant the ultimate division of their homeland when, on 5 June 1926, Britain and Turkey reached a bilateral agreement for the former *vilayet* of Mosul to be incorporated into the British Mandate of Mesopotamia (Cuthell 2004). Before this, Kurds in Southern Kurdistan had been kept in limbo for eight years on their future status. Eight years in which the prospect of independence under British suzerainty was held out, repeatedly watered down and then replaced by pledges of a special status within Iraq under British direct administration (Ibrahim 1983; Asadi 2007; McDowall 2007; Stansfield 2007a; Tripp 2007; Marr 2011; Barr 2012); yet at the same time eight years in which the Kurdish leaders' particularisms and factionalisms allowed the British and the Turks to play them off against each other (McDowall 2007). As in Turkey, the Kurdish tribal leaders in Southern Kurdistan sought their fortune with the political system of indirect rule familiar to them – a benevolent suzerain interfering in local affairs as little as possible – rather than experimenting with the unknown, an ideology that must have appeared utopian and unrealizable. It should come as little surprise then that the first Kurdish nationalist leaders in Iraq on a supra-regional stage emerged from the rows of disgruntled sheikhs who felt excluded from the cornucopia Whitehall poured over their peers and, frequently, arch-enemies.[18]

In the end, notwithstanding the fact that the League of Nations acknowledged that the Kurdish lands of the Mosul *vilayet* had historically never been part of what was called Iraq, and voicing serious doubts about the state's survivability (Asadi 2007), all Geneva held out for the Kurds was a vague form of autonomy and the guarantee of local administration and education in Kurdish as the official language in those areas predominantly inhabited by Kurds (Asadi 2007). And yet this consolation prize constitutes the prime difference between the Kurdish situations in Iraq and Turkey, and consequently accounts for the diverse paths

Kurdish ethno-nationalisms have taken in both countries. While in Turkey, until recently, the mere existence of the Kurds as an ethnic minority has been denied, Iraq's Kurds enjoyed a vague right to autonomy and local self-rule confirmed by the highest international body, the League of Nations. 'These provisions were expressed to constitute international obligations to protect the civil and political rights of the Kurds and their rights as a minority group' (Yildiz 2007: 14). As a result, the Kurdish nationalist struggle in Iraq, centred on the implementation of these guarantees, was determined by phases of on-and-off negotiations and collaboration with the central government, and, its initial stage aside, remained local in its orientation rather than pursuing a pan-Kurdish agenda. As will be repeatedly emphasized throughout this study, the Kurdish nationalist leaders in Iraq had more to gain from forcing Baghdad to accept the autonomy they could refer to in cold print, signed and sealed by the predecessor of the United Nations, than from embarking on an adventurous secessionism in pursuit of (re-)uniting the Kurdish lands. In sum, Kurdish leaders in Iraq had come to terms with the concept of the sovereign nation state almost from day one and sought to eke out a degree of self-government within these confines rather than challenging the principle by way of secession.

In the first decades of the Iraqi state there was little room for ethno-nationalist divisions, though. The fight against the excesses of an exploitative state of dependency and the common struggle against British imperialism and its puppet regime in Baghdad united all national movements in Iraq, their ethnicity in most cases coming a distant second. This unity of purpose explains the formation of seemingly impossible coalitions of Kurds with pan-Arabists, Nasserists with Ba'athists, Communists with the petty bourgeoisie, and intellectuals with day labourers against a state whose short-sighted modernization campaigns had driven them off the fields and into urban skid rows (Jwaideh 2006 [1960]). In the Kurdish case, these odd alliances were personified in the controversial figure of Mulla Mustafa Barzani – until 1943 a mere regional brigand, after the Second World War the legendary leader of Kurdish nationalism in Iraq. Although hailing from a distinguished pedigree of religious leaders associated with the Naqshbandiyya order of Sufis, he, at the end of the day, was a particularist warlord from the mountainous outback whose constituency lived off raids on neighbouring tribes, who had distinguished himself by several unsuccessful local campaigns against the central government (Gunter 1992; Jwaideh 2006 [1960]). And yet Mulla Mustafa, whose boundless personal ambition was only checked by his fickle strategic foresight, accomplished what his rebellious peers had failed to achieve: to amend their personal vendettas to a 'national' level by appealing to Kurdish national consciousness, mustering alliances with Kurdish urban leftist movements.

In the beginning, Kurdish nationalism in Iraq did not proliferate from the mountains with which it has become mythically associated, but blossomed in the cities, among urban intellectuals and impoverished day labourers. The effects of the Great Depression, a painful slump in tobacco prices (Sassoon, J. 1987), Kurdistan's prime cash crop, and their exclusion from the oil bonanza, aggravated by constant political turmoil after Faisal's death in 1933, allied the Kurdish with Arab nationalists in the *Iraqi Communist Party* (ICP), uniting them in their struggle against imperialist exploitation, governmental corruption, and the tribal chiefs and *aghas* who collaborated with and lived on the system of Britain's 'empire on the cheap' that accrued all economic and strategic benefits while offering the Iraqi people very little in return (Batatu 1978). 'Shared spaces for Arabs and Kurds within the anti-imperialist movement encouraged the Kurds' collective identity as Iraqis to become salient alongside their sense of Kurdish ethno-nationalism' (Natali 2005: 45). The anti-imperialist parties' greatest deficiency, though, was their lack of manpower; their clandestine cells in the urban centres, intellectual debating societies, and combat organs were a powerful force when it came to talking the talk; but walking the walk required rebellious tribal chiefs such as Mullah Mustafa, who could muster the manpower to challenge the imperialist order. These individual components – the ideological appeal of nationalism and Mullah Mustafa's command over the malcontent tribes – if merged, could prove a composition with the potential to unhinge the notoriously unstable Iraqi state. And merge they did.

The short, glorious and epic last stand of the Kurdish Republic of Mahabad[19] – a Kurdish Soviet-backed separatist polity born out of the chaos of post-Second World War Iran and the dawn of superpower rivalry in the Gulf – not only gave the Kurdish nationalist movement in neighbouring Iraq wings, and boosted Mulla Mustafa's stardom but once again, most dramatically, confirmed the need for tribal-nationalist cooperation. While distinguishing himself in the military defence of Mahabad, across the border in Iraq, Mulla Mustafa was unwilling to accept a subordinate role to Mahabad's *Kurdish Democratic Party* of Iran (KDP-I).[20] He envisioned the alliance he had entered with the Communist *Rizgari Kurd* (Kurdish Liberation) *Party* to act as a catch basin for the myriad embryonic Kurdish nationalist organizations that failed to make a difference on their own, with him helming the Kurdish anti-imperialist struggle in Iraq. This alliance required a new organization, which while independent from Mahabad's KDP-I, would carry on its spirit as the vanguard of Kurdish nationalism in Southern Kurdistan. This alliance was the birth hour of the KDP, the *Kurdish Democratic Party*.[21]

The union between Mullah Mustafa, who 'like any good tribal leader [...] was constantly seeking to widen his [personal] regional authority' (McDowall 2007: 293), and urban nationalists can be characterized as 'a marriage of convenience, albeit with suspicion on both sides' (Ghareeb 1981: 39). He routinely put the interests of the land-owning tribes he represented before the class struggle advocated by the urban nationalists around Ibrahim Ahmed and his son-in-law Jalal Talabani. The resulting 'conflict between the two groups [within the KDP] has become a characteristic of Kurdish politics ever since' (Stansfield 2003a: 63).

The 14 July 1958 Revolution by Nasserist Free Officers under Abd al-Karim Qassem was a watershed event for Iraq and the wider Middle East (Dann 1969; Fernea & Louis 1991; Louis & Owen 2002; Farouk-Sluglett & Sluglett 2003; Stansfield 2007a; Tripp 2007; Marr 2011). It toppled the British-backed monarchy, terminated the state of quasi-colonial dependency and, having disso-ciated the country from the Western camp, turned Iraq into a pawn in the dominant super power confrontation. For a decade it brought to power an array of (pan-)Arabist dictatorships of various political *couleures* and Cold War align-ments, each succeeding the other with increasing regularity often through more or less bloody coups. Most importantly though, the multi-ethnic alliances that had brought down the monarchy ruptured and 'the political space became more clearly ethnicised, centralised, and militant' (Natali 2005: 69). In post-1958 Iraq, competing ethno-nationalisms amplified and faced each other in an incremen-tally violent struggle over the future of Iraq, setting both Kurds against Arabs and Iraqi against pan-Arabist nationalism (Rubin 2007).

However, it would be a gross simplification to understand the Kurdish nation-alist movement as merely a reaction to (pan-)Arabist aggression in the ensuing confrontations between Kurdish nationalists and tribal alliances with the (pan-)Arabist regimes in Baghdad over autonomy, self-rule, and cultural rights for Iraqi Kurdistan that escalated into a series of full-scale Kurdish wars.[22] On the contrary, the Kurdish nationalist movement in Iraq had become a fully-fledged political actor that was instrumental in bringing down consecutive regimes, militarily stood its ground in three full-scale wars, inflicted such heavy casualties on the forces of the Iraqi government and destabilized the country to such an extent that it forced every new regime coming to power to the negoti-ation table (Ghareeb 1981; Jawad 1981; Stansfield 2003a, 2007a; Asadi 2007). A pattern emerged in which Nasserists or Ba'athists made ample concessions on Kurdish self-rule – and thus antagonized their own constituencies – not because they genuinely believed in the need for nation building, but because they real-ized that Kurdish nationalists and Mulla Mustafa's tribal alliances had the poten-tial to bog them down in costly campaigns in the mountains. Weakened in fruitless military campaigns and having lost face politically, they were toppled by their own armed forces and/or their (pan-)Arabist competitors.[23] The Kurdish nationalist movement in the 1960s was a force to be reckoned with, the purchase, pacification and integration of which the survival of the central government depended. Mulla Mustafa recognized his role as the one force capable of tipping the scales and wielded his power by calling in ever wider concessions with considerable skill. No matter how excessive his demands, he balked at claiming actual independence (Ghareeb 1981), which might have resulted in the various (pan-)Arabist ethno-nationalist factions uniting against the Kurds. Instead he shrewdly maintained his edge in the inner-Iraqi balance of power.

Another reason for Mulla Mustafa's political restraint was the fact that his Iraqi Kurdish nationalist camp was as internally divided as his (pan-)Arabist opponents in Baghdad. In 1964, long simmering tension within the KDP between Mulla Mustafa and the leftist political bureau, headed by secretary general Ibrahim Ahmed and his son in law Jalal Talabani, over the former's autocratic leadership erupted, resulting in an irrevocable split right down the party's ranks, from which a decade later the PUK would emerge (Ghareeb 1981; Entessar 1992; Stansfield 2003a; Asadi 2007).

The origins of Kurdish ethno-nationalism in Turkey

Any analysis of the origins of Kurdish ethno-nationalisms in the Middle East in general and of Kurdish ethno-nationalism in Turkey in particular is faced with the puzzling question as to why the Kurdish tribes in Eastern Anatolia notoriously failed to capitalize on the dissolution of the Ottoman Empire and the new order crafted at Sèvres. After all, Section III Articles 62–64 of the Treaty of Sèvres foresaw a Kurdistan region whose future political status was to be determined by public referendum, a region that included the *vilayet* of Mosul and indirectly held out the prospect of an independent Kurdish state (Brown 1924; Helmreich 1974; O'Shea 2004; Ozoğlu 2004; Bozarslan 2003, 2007; McDowall 2007). And yet, ironically, it was the Kurdish tribes, who would have gained most from a defeat of the Kemalist opposition to the Sèvres order, who became one of the Turkish Nationalists' staunchest confederates – a strategic choice comparable to a scenario where Czechs, Croats and Slovaks might have sided with the dying Habsburg monarchy against the prospect of independent states they were promised by the Allies at Saint Germain-en-Laye and Trianon. How come the Kurds acted so blatantly against their best national interest to play a significant part in shutting this unique window of opportunity?

The answer appears to be that in fact there was no Kurdish national interest at this time. Unlike Turkish nationalists, the Kurds had not yet reached a stage in their 'national temporality' (Bozarslan 2007: 45), which would allow them to rally the masses for a common cause behind an internally and externally legitimized leader. Indeed, most Kurdish decision makers in eastern Anatolia were staunch Ottomanists fighting for the retention of the status quo, not to revolutionize it (Ozoğlu 2004). In addition, externally fuelled, inner-Kurdish divisions and the continual re-tribalization policies of past Ottoman central governments prevented the Kurds from exploiting their alleged once-in-a-nation's-lifetime chance for statehood when the Allies signed the death certificate of the Ottoman Empire at the Treaty of Sèvres, and turned them into unfortunate late-comers in the scramble for national self-determination. Once this unique window of opportunity – the implosion of an empire – was closed, they had to take on modern nationalizing states who, protected by the principle of state sovereignty, dealt with their minorities as they saw fit.

Not long after expelling the Greek invaders with their Entente allies, having wrested from the latter a revision of the Sèvres treaty at Lausanne in July 1923 – that permanently buried any hope for a Kurdish state (Ali 1997) – the Turkish nationalists showed their true colours. In the decade after Lausanne, the Turkish state attempted to perpetrate ethnocide against its Kurdish minority; the juggernaut of Kemalism, the new nationalist doctrine of the victorious, emerging Turkish Republic, literally wiped out any embryonic notions of Kurdish nationalism that may have existed, politically paralysing the Kurdish people for the coming generation. Once Kemalism's external enemies had been defeated, Turkish nationalists rigorously forced through their modernizing reform agenda. On 1 November 1922, the Sultan was deposed; on 29 October 1923, the

Republic proclaimed; and on 3 March 1924, the Caliphate abolished – for good measure, associations on religious grounds were forbidden, all *medresses* (religious schools) closed, and all *tarikats* (Sufi orders), the cornerstone of folk-Islam in the Kurdish lands, were banned (Poulton 1997; Taspinar 2005; McDowall 2007; Hanioğlu 2011). Within 18 months, all bonds uniting Kurdish identity with the state were severed, all that the Kurds had fought for during the War of Independence was squashed, not by imperialist, Christian guns, but by the stroke of a pen from their nominal brothers in faith, the Kemalist reformers in Ankara.

It is impossible to underestimate the importance the abolishment of the Caliphate had on the development of Kurdish ethno-nationalism in Turkey. As a direct consequence, it triggered what Hakan Yavuz categorizes as 'the second stage in the construction and politicization of Kurdish ethno-nationalism in Turkey' (Yavuz 2001: 6). Both urban Kurdish nationalists and rural tribal leaders watched Turkish nationalists' doings with mounting concern. They felt betrayed by Ankara's 'sell-out' on the *Mosul vilayet* (Bozarslan 2003) – until recently portrayed by Atatürk as a constitutive part of *watan* never to be sacrificed, now bartered away for British comity, thus effectively tearing Kurdish lands apart (Cuthell 2004) – threatened by the increasing dominance of Turkishness, and its gradual elimination of the Kurdish element from the official domain. Above all, they were appalled by the Turkish nationalists' relentless dismantling of Ottoman institutions. Here, the sacrilege committed when abolishing the Caliphate mattered most to the predominantly pious Kurds in eastern Anatolia. It was the politico-religious dimension of the Caliphate, an implicit safeguard against ethno-centrist hegemonic ambitions within the *ummah*, which when banished, forged an alliance between urban Kurdish nationalists and tribal sheikhs (Olson 1989; Jwaideh 2006 [1960]; McDowall 2007). The ruthlessly imposed secularization and modernization reforms of the Kemalist regime thus forged an alliance between ideological antagonists that would have been inconceivable a few years earlier, and provoked a rebellion that shook the young Republic to the core.

In February 1925, the revered clergy, Sheikh Said of Piran, managed to rally 15,000 Zaza tribesmen behind his ethno-religious flag that took the Turkish Republic 52,000 soldiers to crush by mid-April (Olson 1989; van Bruinessen 1992; McDowall 2007; Üngör 2011). This rebellion has to be acknowledged as a turning point in the history of the Kurds in Turkey for three reasons. First, the failed Sheikh Said revolt forged and cemented the entente between urban nationalists and religio-tribal chieftains that was to determine the Kurdish proto-nationalist movement in Turkey for the next decade. Second, until 1938, in response to the mounting unparalleled suppression, it triggered a chain of more than three-dozen Kurdish insurrections, ranging from local skirmishes to full-scale military operations across international borders culminating in the doomed Kurdish Ararat Republic and the ethnocidal massacres of the Dersim campaign (van Bruinessen 1992, 1997; Nezan 1993; McDowall 2007; Üngör 2011). Eastern Anatolia had become a permanent war zone in a protracted ethnicized conflict, which in terms of territorial spread, destruction of livelihoods, human casualties, and costs in troops and resources for the Turkish state unseen since the War of Independence (van Bruinessen 1992, 1997; Nezan 1993; McDowall 2007; Üngör 2011). Third, and most lastingly, the Sheikh Said rebellion served as a pretext for the Turkish state[24] to unleash its arsenal of ethnic cleansing campaigns and Turkification-by-force programmes with the clear intent of destroying Kurdish ethnic identity (van Bruinessen 1997) – a textbook-like application of what Heather Rae has, as discussed earlier, called 'pathological homogenisation'. Nezan specifies that from 1925 until 1938, 'more than one and a half million Kurds were deported [or] massacred ... The entire area beyond the Euphrates ... was kept under a permanent state of siege until 1950' (Nezan 1993: 68).[25] In the years immediately before and after Dersim, the Turkish state, in addition to renaming Kurdish settlements with Turkish aliases and outlawing the Kurdish language,[26] systematized its ethnic cleansing campaigns by employing deportations, summary mass-executions, death marches, and the razing of hundreds of villages to the ground. From the perspective of the Turkish state, Kurds had become nonentities; they were to be either 'Turkified', i.e. assimilated as non-ethnic Turkish citizens, or eliminated outright. By 1940, the ethnocide of the Kurds in Turkey seemed complete.[27] Co-opted by force, deported, or summarily executed, Kurdish ethno-nationalism in Northern Kurdistan appeared to have vanished into thin air when the smoke over Dersim cleared. The decades between the massacre of Dersim and the gradual revival of Kurdish ethno-nationalism on the political stage in the 1960s may seem to have been lost, yet Hamit Bozarslan makes a compelling case for Kurdish ethnicized conscience, suppressed in the political arena, finding its niche in the cultural domain where it ensured Kurdish ethnic identity's survival and re-emergence, all the more forceful a generation after the last Kurdish rebellion had been crushed (Bozarslan 2007).

For Kurdish ethnic identity to gain ground, it required fundamental changes in the Turkish political system. Ironically then, it was political reforms, liberalization efforts, and the emergence of civil society in Turkey that encouraged the radicalization of Kurdish ethno-nationalism that would ultimately lead to the emergence of the PKK.

Commonalities and differences

Any attempt to summarize the vastly different dynamics and trajectories of state-formation in the twentieth century Middle East would go well beyond the confines of this study – in fact it is questionable whether, in light of the diverse genealogies of polities such as Turkey, Iraq, Syria, Egypt, Iran, Saudi Arabia, the Gulf States, etc., any such attempt is possible and whether, here, the generalizing categorization 'Middle East' is not as misplaced as in other contexts – which is why I refer to others for so copious a task (Ben-Dor 1983; Bromley 1994; Halliday 2000, 2005; Owen 2004; Ayubi 2008; Zubaida 2009; Milton-Edwards 2011), and will limit myself to *herausarbeiten* a few commonalities and differences in state-formation and Kurdish ethno-nationalism in Turkey and Iraq pertaining to this study:

1   'The impact of British rule in shaping modern Iraq has been second only to that of Ottoman rule', Phebe Marr (2011: 21) highlights the importance of the watershed moment that was the dissolution of the Ottoman Empire and the occupation of the territories between Suez and the Shat-el Arab by imperialist (British and French) forces in the aftermath of the First World War and the transformation of most of these territories into League of Nations-decreed mandates, administered by the imperialist powers. The 'Mandate System' constitutes a most peculiar synthesis of the Wilsonian doctrine of self-determination and the strategic interests of the imperialist powers, and while holding out independence for the future, for the time of the Mandate System, 'the creation of British and French mandates masked a de facto policy of colonial domination virtually indistinguishable from that found elsewhere in the British or French empires at the time' (Rear 2008: 151). Consequently, those polities that were created by and gained independence through the Mandate System, such as Iraq, can be considered post-colonial states.

2   Iraq, then, exhibits the triple-legacy of colonialism identified for post-colonial states earlier: an unresolved nationalities question due to the arbitrary imposition of state borders reflecting the strategic needs of the (quasi-)colonial power rather than the actual ethnic composition on the ground; a system-immanent authoritarianism due to the (quasi-)colonial power running an 'empire on the cheap' that ensured compliance through a 'divide-and-rule' maxim that played local elites and their constituencies off against each other; a system of lasting dependence on a volatile world market dominated by the 'capitalism-imperialism nexus' due to the collaboration of local elites in this nexus and the economic structure of the post-colonial state as a rentier state providing in unequal exchange cash crops, cheap labour, or, in the case of Iraq, oil for advanced technologies and FDI.

3   Turkey, on the other hand, is the only successor state of the Ottoman Empire that defended itself successfully against imperialist design and therefore, although closely associated with the West during the Cold War and as dependent on the volatile world market as the next state, can be considered to have experienced a more genuine national development that – despite differences – more closely resembles the process of state-formation in Western Europe than the post-colonial state. Owing to the dominant role of the military and the precursors of the CHP in the Turkish War of Independence, combined with the *Führerkult* around Atatürk, the political system in Turkey until well into the 1980s, however, can also be considered as inherently prone to authoritarianism, as illustrated in the quip of former President Süleyman Demirel that 'God first created the Turkish military and then He realized He had forgotten something and added the people as an afterthought'.[28]

4   Both Turkey and Iraq, though, were forced into the corset of the modern international system with its defining principle of the inviolability of state borders. This external imposition of a state system, an alien form of

governance, in whose formulation and configuration the new subjects had no say, markedly distinguishes the Western European experience in state-formation from most of the rest of the world, in particular the Middle East. Here,

> state makers [were compelled] ... to attempt to consolidate their power through the development of political institutions while simultaneously attempting to justify the existence of their various states and regimes to populations for whom the very idea of the territorial nation-state, the specific boundaries of existing states, and the concept of secular authority lack legitimacy.
>
> (Rear 2008: 153)

In Western Europe, on the other hand, 'the state developed conterminously with the state-system. As a result, there was no external intervention to impose boundaries upon the region' (Rear 2008: 153). In addition to the earlier detailed differences, this disparity between co-creator and recipients of the specious blessing of the principle of self-determination is what sets apart most profoundly the processes of state formation in Western Europe from the experience of the post-colonial state: the former was not only present at the creation of the modern state-system but actively took part in its design, while the latter was left with no alternative but to simply come to terms with it. Consequently, the stringent corset of state-centrism did not allow either Turkey and Iraq or the ethnic minorities within their borders to seek a solution for their unresolved nationalities questions outside this system, i.e. the redrawing of borders or secession.

5   As far as the nationalities question is concerned, in Iraq, one can identify a sectarian discourse based on the classic 'us' versus 'them' binary opposites of Kurds versus Arabs and Sunni versus Shi'a with each thus defined group struggling for influence in the post-1958 state. Aside from cursory and short-lived episodes, no ruler in Baghdad ever attempted a sincere project of nation-building, of crafting a new, more broadly defined and inclusive sense of communality. The doctrine of Turkification, on the other hand, can be understood as a peculiar form of racist 'civic nationalism' or 'pathological homogenization' that did not allow for any expressions of ethnic or religious pluralism. Ethnic and religious minorities in Turkey until the 1990s seen as fifth columns in the service of foreign agitators and interests, were either assimilated or annihilated.

6   As for the evolution of Kurdish ethno-nationalism, before the First World War, Kurdish nationalism was largely limited to cultural societies and literati circles in Istanbul, developing and becoming salient when the borders of the nationalizing states of Turkey, Iraq, Iran and Syria were already drawn. As a consequence thereof, the process of Kurdish identification has been oriented towards varying constitutive others and has been shaped by the political, social and economic contexts in the respective countries and

societies. While Kurds in Turkey were confronted by an effectively and ideologically strong nationalizing state that denied them their very identity, Kurds in Iraq faced a notoriously weak state which, lacking any coherent national legitimization, was torn apart by legion internal divisions. Consequently, while Kurds in Turkey became the victims of a cataclysmic ethnocide before their national consciousness became salient, Kurdish ethno-nationalism in Iraq blossomed along, and often in collaboration with the manifold currents of (pan-)Arab ethno-nationalism, which, until the second half of the 1970s, frequently bestowed upon Kurdish leaders the role of kingmakers in inner-Iraqi power struggles. This role was exacerbated by Iraq – unlike Turkey – becoming an early battlefield of super power rivalries during the Cold War, which had its Kurdish parties enjoy the dubious privilege of serving as their proxies.

Ultimately, while in Turkey the traditional Kurdish elites were either shattered early on, or largely co-opted by the nationalizing state, traditional societal structures in Iraq not only prevailed but tribal leaders often formed the vanguard of the Kurdish ethno-nationalist movement. In light of these different trajectories it then appears justifiable to conclude with Martin van Bruinessen, the only scholar who has conducted extensive ethnographic field work in all major parts of Kurdistan, 'it might, in fact, be more apt to consider the Kurds not as one, but as a set of ethnic groups' (van Bruinessen 2000: 14),[29] and to speak of Kurdish ethno-nationalisms in plural rather than a singular, which would imply an ethnic group defined by cross-border unity, communality and solidarity that is, in this case, absent. And yet it is such presupposed cross-border unity, and communality, by which the internationalization of the so-called 'Kurdish conflict' is explained by the ethnic alliance model and related groupist frameworks of explanatory IR.

Notes

1 Quoted in McDowall (2007: 464–465).
2 Hanioğlu (2006: 3). On the rise of Turkish national sentiment during the Hamidian era, which among other factors was greatly influenced by 'Western' Orientalist discourse and on which the CUP and its leading intellectuals built their ideology, see Kushner (1977) and Hanioğlu (2006, 2010).
3 On the politics of Turkification in the early years of the Republic, see Bali (2006).
4 On the fate of Jewish and Armenian minorities in the Turkish Republic in the 1920/30s, see Görgü-Guttstadt (2006) Akçam (2004) and Göçek (2011, 2013). On the Greek mass expulsion from Turkey, see, among many others, Clark (2006).
5 For example, in 1926, Turkish foreign minister, Tawfiq Rushdi Saracoğlu, put it in illustratively blunt terms:

> In [the Kurdish] case, their cultural level is so low, their mentality so backward, that they cannot be simply absorbed in the general Turkish body politic … they will die out, economically unfitted for the struggle for life in competition with the more advanced and cultured Turks … as many as can will emigrate into Persia and Iraq, while the rest will simply undergo the elimination of the unfit.
>
> (Quoted in McDowall 2007: 200)

6 Göçek (2011: 98) quotes a 2006 public opinion survey in Turkey, in which 57 per cent of those polled stated that the Copenhagen Criteria for Turkey's accession to the EU 'were similar to those required by the Sèvres Treaty' and 78 per cent opined that 'the West wants to divide and break up Turkey like they broke up the Ottoman Empire'.

7 Quoted in Jung and Piccoli (2001: 117).

8 Quoted in Göcek (2011: 154).

9 In this, Iraq resembled a well-established nineteenth-century practice of the European great powers imposing alien dynasties on states that had recently gained independence, the most prominent example being Otto from the Bavarian House of Wittelsbach who became King of Greece in 1832 by dictate of the United Kingdom, France, Russia, and Prussia.

10 Aside from personal connections the British had established with Faisal – T. E. Lawrence and Gertrude Bell acted as his most outspoken advocates with Winston Churchill – strategic considerations preponderated. After the French expelled Faisal from Syria in July 1920 – his reign as king of Greater Syria lasted only four months and 18 days – the Hashemites had to be indemnified somehow. Britain, the great power with the largest Muslim population, could ill afford to flout Hussein bin Ali, the Sharif of Mecca, the highest authority in Islam after Turkish Kemalists had abolished the Caliphate. The Hashemites were also needed as a counterweight against the power grabs of Ibn Saud and his *Ikhwan* (Paris 1998). Additionally, Gertrude Bell and Sir Percy Cox, the British High Representative in Mesopotamia, considered Shi'i incapable of government – Sir Percy being influenced by his recent experiences in Persia – and counted on ensuring Faisal's unquestioning loyalty by keeping him in a state of dependence as a non-native among a hostile populace (Olson 1992; Catherwood 2004; Sluglett 2007).

11 As early as 1919, one of the few dissenters of this policy, Major E. B. Soane, who favoured direct colonial administration for the Kurds, noted:

> Revival of the tribal system was … a retrograde movement. Already South Kurdistan had become largely detribalized and a measure of prosperity, in consequence, had been its lot in pre-war times. Now, the political officer, accepted the views of Sheikh Mahmoud, devoted his energies to re-tribalizing. Every man who could be labelled a tribesman was placed under a tribal leader. The idea was to divide South Kurdistan into tribal areas under tribal leaders … Ideal for the clansman but fatal for trade, civilization and tranquillity.
>
> (Quoted in McDowall 2007: 157)

12 Given the importance of oil in Iraq's recent history, a word needs to be said about the extent to which the oil riches of the Mosul *vilayet* influenced British imperialist design and its ultimate incorporation into the new state of Iraq (Kent 1976; Mejcher 1976; Gruen 2004). Advocates of black gold conspiracy theories may prefer to have it that all future Kurdish misfortune is rooted in imperialistic grabs for the Kirkuk field, a seemingly everlasting well of fortune that presently contributes almost half of Iraq's oil exports. At closer scrutiny, however, such arguments appear less clear-cut. Unlike the oil fields in Persia and at the confluence of the Euphrates and the Tigris, large deposits were suspected in Mosul province but were only confirmed in 1927 – in Churchill's considerations they are said to have played a minor role (Catherwood 2004), and are generally considered secondary by McDowall (2007), while Asadi (2007) quotes Council of Ministers minutes that emphasized the importance given to possible future oil discoveries.

13 The 'Brussels Line' was a provisional frontier between Turkey and Iraq suggested by Swedish diplomat Hjalmar Banting to a special session of the Council of the League of Nations convening in Brussels (Taha 2013).

14 For a general depiction of society in the Mosul *vilayet* in the years after the First World War and first-hand accounts of British policy via the Kurds, see Edmonds (1957) and Fieldhouse (2002).

15 On the same day Iraq joined the League of Nations as an independent state, 3 October 1932, the Anglo-Iraqi Treaty of June 1930 went into force, sustaining the relationship of dependency between the two unequal partners in exploitation, the puppet-regime in Baghdad and its string-pullers in London. The British Mandate of Mesopotamia had ended in name only.

16 Faisal II became the last king of Iraq in 1939 at the age of three after his father, Ghazi bin Faisal, had been killed in a mysterious car crash after only six turbulent years on the Hashemite throne. The unfortunate Faisal, gunned down with his entire family in the 14 July 1958 Revolution, was immortalized as the caricature of a spoilt royal brat in the Belgian comic series *The Adventures of Tintin* by Hergé (Farr 2001).

17 For an insightful, post-structuralist analysis of how the colonial legacy has and continues to shape the travails of the three most prominent 'hotspots' of the wider Middle East – Afghanistan, Palestine, and Iraq – see Gregory (2004).

18 The most notorious of these firebrands was Sheikh Mahmoud Barzinj, who the British had installed as *hukumdar* (governor) of Sulaymaniah. Sheikh Mahmoud interpreted his position quite differently and soon declared himself 'King of Kurdistan'. He kept challenging British quasi-colonial rule in successive revolts until the 1930s when he was finally defeated by the British Royal Air Force (Jwaideh 2006 [1960], McDowall 2007; Tripp 2007). On the effects of this tribal policy on Iraqi society in detail and on the RAF's air campaigns, see Dodge (2003).

19 On the Musa Dagh-like fate of the Republic of Mahabad, the standard works are still Eagleton (1963) and Ghassemlou (1965); see also Koohi-Kamali (2007) and Vali (2011).

20 The party's official name was *Kurdish Democratic Party* (KDP-I), the adjunct I for Iran is used to distinguish it from Mullah Mustafa's *Kurdish Democratic Party* in Iraq (KDP).

21 The name was changed to *Kurdistan Democratic Party* (KDP) at its Third Congress in January 1953. The KDP's founding, history, and evolution will be discussed in detail in the following chapter.

22 For a detailed account of the Kurdish wars, see O'Ballance (1973, 1996), Jawad (1981), and Ibrahim (1983).

23 The particularly short-lived Ba'athist rule from February until November 1963 was a prime example of the regime in Baghdad weakened by unsustainable confrontations with Mullah Mustafa until its competitors – this time Abdul Salam Arif – deposed it (Ghareeb 1981; Farouk-Sluglett & Sluglett 2003; Stansfield 2007a; Tripp 2007; Marr 2011). The socialist Ba'ath Party, an explicitly pan-Arab nationalist movement, was founded in the 1940s in Syria with a preponderant nucleus of Arab Christians, who viewed nationalist ideology of unification and advocacy of social equity as a means to transcend religious and cultural differences. Although its founding theoretician Michel Aflaq had originally endorsed democratic principles, the Ba'ath Party soon exhibited fascist tendencies, reminiscent of German nationalist socialism – from early on its *Weltanschauung* had been strongly influenced by Johann Gottlieb Fichte and Johann Gottfried Herder's concepts of a *Kulturnation* and etatism – after gaining power in Syria and Iraq in 1963, it became the ideological basis for the totalitarian regimes in both countries. Troubled by numerous internal divisions, of which the one between Soviet-oriented Syria and more centralist Iraq was the most prominent, Ba'athism became the major inner-Arab antagonist of non-aligned Nasserism during the 1950s and 1960s (Mahr 1971; Roberts 1987; Devlin 1991).

24 In (deliberate) misrepresentation of the true motives for the rebellion, 'the Kemalist leadership perceived the Sheikh Said rebellion as a counter-revolution which threatened the fledgling Turkish Republic' and the result of 'British agitation'. Yet, 'there

seems to be no evidence of British support for Kurdish nationalist uprisings after the proclamation of the Turkish Republic' (Taspinar 2005: 80–81). Indeed, once the final border between Turkey and Iraq had been agreed on and the *vilayet* of Mosul been assigned to the British mandate in Iraq, it was in London's best interest to win the Turkish Republic as an ally, not to foment Kurdish self-determination across the region. External conspiracies aimed at undermining the Turkish state and employing its ethnic minorities as 'fifth columns', against better knowledge, has continued to serve as a defining myth of Turkish nationalism well into the present.

25 Any figures on casualties or victims of deportation are to be treated with utmost caution. Jwaideh (2006 [1960]), for instance, by referring to a French scholar from the mid-1940s, indicates 40,000 Kurds killed during the actual Dersim campaign.

26 'In the 1930s, for instance, people who spoke Kurdish in public were fined five *kurus* per word' (Barkey & Fuller 1998: 19).

27 David McDowall (2007: 210) goes a step further in stating, 'Turkey had unmistakably intended genocide of the Kurdish people. In practice its intentions were defeated by the sheer size of the task'.

28 Quoted in Göçek (2011: 102).

29 Van Bruinessen (2000: 14).

5 The parties

The KDP

As outlined in the previous chapter, the origins of the KDP in Iraq were rooted in an alliance between Kurdish urban leftist movements and traditionalist rural tribesmen who felt excluded from the quasi-colonial systems of patronage the British had introduced to ensure compliance with the nascent Iraqi state and its underdeveloped political structures. The most prominent of these tribes was the Barzani clan, deriving its name from the village of Barzan in the remote Kurmanji-speaking mountain areas of northern Iraq, just south of the border with Turkey. In the turbulent era of the dissolution of the Kurdish emirates during the *tanzimat* reform era, the Barzani family, whose local authority derived from their religious status as sheiks of the *Naqshbandi* Sufi-order, had earned a reputation as a safe haven for political refugees, 'a sort of utopian society' that soon became 'a centre of emerging Kurdish nationalism' (Gunter 2010a: 58). Although it would be more correct to speak of a centre of political dissent – since, as detailed earlier, it would be a case of reading contemporary categories into the past to identify Kurdish nationalist sentiments prior to the dissolution of the Ottoman Empire – it can be argued that from the days of the division of the Kurdish lands in the Anglo-Turkish Treaty of 1926, the Barzanis acted as the leaders of a series of uprisings against the political order imposed on them by London, Baghdad and Ankara, and that the rebellion Sheikh Ahmad Barzani launched in 1931 against the Iraqi government can be read in the context of wider Kurdish rebellions in the region, most prominently the concurrent Ararat Rebellion in Turkey (Jwaideh 2006 [1960]).[1] In this campaign, Sheikh Ahmad's younger brother, Mulla Mustafa, earned his first military spurs; combat experience that led to Mulla Mustafa becoming the commander in the defence of the ultimately doomed Kurdish Republic of Mahabad in Iran (Ghareeb 1981; Entessar 1992; Gunter 1999a; Stansfield 2003a; Jwaideh 2006 [1960]; McDowall 2007). The frequency and apparent ease in which these cross-border alliances between various Kurdish movements were formed in the first decades after the imposition of the sovereign nation-state principle on the region not only attest to a notorious inability of the weak nationalizing states to control their territory, but also to the existence of a degree of solidarity among Kurdish tribes and movements transcending the recently established borders. To deduce from this degree of solidarity, however, common ethnicity as the independent variable determining relations between various segments of Kurdish societies in all four nationalizing states of Iraq, Turkey, Iran and Syria, as the ethnic alliance model and related groupist frameworks do in their reification of ethnic identities, would be a gross simplification of the complex dynamics within the matrix of interests, identities, and resulting behaviours of actors in this context.

The ambiguity and complexity of dynamics in these relations becomes apparent in Mulla Mustafa's machinations, who, while defending the KDP-I's Mahabad in Iran,[2] tried to capitalize on his involvement with the KDP-I for his own ends, namely to craft an umbrella organization uniting under his leadership the traditionalist tribal alliances in the rural hinterland and secular leftist movements such as *Komala-i-Liwen* (Young Men's Organisation), *Hiwa* (Hope), and *Shoresh* (Revolution) in the more cosmopolitan, educated, urban centres of Sulimaniyah and Kirkuk (Ghareeb 1981; Entessar 1992; Stansfield 2003a; Jwaideh 2006 [1960]; McDowall 2007; Tahiri 2007). Mulla Mustafa can be credited with the realization that, 'for a Kurdish movement to succeed, the tribes needed to work with the educated urban political parties, along the lines of the KDP-I' (Stansfield 2003a: 65). Yet, in these attempts though, Mulla Mustafa was opposed by the leader of the Iraqi branch of the KDP-I, Ibrahim Ahmed, whose loyalty to Mahabad and a more expansive pan-Kurdish nationalism cum socialism forbade his involvement in Mulla Mustafa's contrary, traditionalist and narrow ambitions, limited to self-determination within Iraq. The new KDP, officially formed at the party's first congress in Baghdad on 16 August 1946, thus could have remained a flash in the pan, had it not been for the fall of Mahabad and the execution of its leaders in March 1947 – dealing the KDP-I an almost lethal blow – that forced Ibrahim Ahmed to consider a merger with Mulla Mustafa's Iraqi KDP that was born out of competition with the very KDP-I Ahmed represented (Ghareeb 1981; Entessar 1992; Stansfield 2003a; Natali 2005; Jwaideh 2006 [1960]; McDowall 2007; Tahiri 2007). Ironically then, although the success of the KDP and Mulla Mustafa's rise to stardom with the Kurdish nationalist camp in Iraq was only made possible by the fall of Mahabad, the immediate effect of this military defeat meant for him individually a decade of exile in the Soviet Union;[3] an absence from the political scene in Iraq during which the new party's fate was determined by Ibrahim Ahmed.[4] Upon Mulla Mustafa's return from exile in the wake of the 1958 Free Officers coup in Iraq, animosities between his traditionalist tribal constituencies who thrived as feudal landholders and the socialist Politburo under Ahmed's leadership advocating for land reform, would gradually intensify, 'set[ting the scene] for the future internecine political fights which came to characterise Kurdish politics from then on' (Stansfield 2003a: 69).

One aspect that illustrates these internal divisions particularly well is the formation of the irregular Iraqi-Kurdish forces, the *peshmerga*, literally translated as 'those who face death' (Stansfield 2003a; Chapman 2011). When, in 1961, the Qassem regime resorted to direct military action against Barzani and the

KDP, the animosities between the KDP Politburo, 'ever wary of forming dependencies on the tribal militia of Barzani' (Stansfield 2003a: 70), and Mulla Mustafa, likewise, forbidding the KDP to operate in his tribal stronghold along the Turkish border, resulted in the establishment of an irregular force within the sphere of influence of the Politburo between Raniyah and Sulimaniyah, whose ranks were swelled by Kurdish deserters from the Iraqi army. Soon, 'the army cadres managed to develop [these guerrillas] into a rough mountain fighting force' (Stansfield 2003a: 71), superior in military knowhow and ideological motivation to Mulla Mustafa's tribal militias, and it is largely thanks to the *peshmerga* that the Kurds prevailed against Qassem's nominally more advanced forces (O'Ballance 1973, 1996).

These internal divisions within the KDP turned out no longer bridgeable and openly erupted to the surface in 1964. After initially having struck a compromise on Kurdish self-governance with Qassem's successor, the Ba'athist regime under Abdul Salam Aref and Ahmed Hassan al-Bakr, Mulla Mustafa was forced under military pressure to accept a political accord that made no mention of Kurdish autonomy; what made matters worse in the eyes of the KDP Politburo was the fact that Mulla Mustafa had not even bothered to consult the party before accepting a lesser deal on behalf of all Kurds in Iraq (Ghareeb 1981; Entessar 1992; Stansfield 2003a; Romano 2006; McDowall 2007; Tahiri 2007). When the Politburo revolted against his high-handedness, Mulla Mustafa had leading members of the body such as Ibrahim Ahmed and his son-in-law, Jalal Talabani, expelled and later persecuted into exile in Iran, where they formed a breakaway faction (Ghareeb 1981; Entessar 1992; Stansfield 2003a; Natali 2005; Romano 2006; McDowall 2007; Tahiri 2007), from which a decade later the PUK should emerge.

While the significance of the 1964-split and the resulting KDP-PUK rivalry cannot be emphasized strongly enough as the most decisive factor to determine the development of Kurdish ethno-nationalism in Iraq for four decades, the immediate consequences of the expulsion of the so-called 'Ahmed-Talabani faction' meant for Mulla Mustafa the freedom to assert his absolute control over the party by cleansing it from all internal opposition. In turn, his absolute dominance in the Kurdish nationalist movement in Iraq significantly strengthened his position via Baghdad, where the bloodless coup of July 1968 brought the Ba'athists to power for the second time in Iraq.[5] President Ahmad Hassan al-Bakr and his deputy, Saddam Hussein, had learned their lesson from their previous fray with Mulla Mustafa and tendered full recognition of Kurdish cultural and political rights in Iraq; in short, they bid 'the best deal ever offered to the Iraqi Kurds. At the time of signing, the agreement was hailed as a sincere move towards solving the Kurdish problem by all parties' (Stansfield 2003a: 75). This was precisely what the Ba'athists resolved to accomplish – not with the intent of truly crafting a multi-ethnic Iraqi nation but an accommodation of Kurdish demands dictated by necessity. Quite simply, the regime's survival depended on reconciling and appeasing the Kurds. The '11 March 1970 Manifesto', as the ground-breaking agreement came to be known, stipulated the Iraqi constitution would be amended to read 'the Iraqi people is made up of two nationalities, the Arab nationality and the Kurdish nationality' (O'Leary & Salih 2005: 34); promised to join all areas with a Kurdish majority in a self-governing unit, where Kurdish would be an official language; pledged to allocate generous special funds for the development of the Kurdish region along with the execution of overdue agrarian reform; and guaranteed proportional distribution of positions in government, bureaucracy and the armed forces, including a Kurd as vice-president of Iraq. Indeed, 'the period 1970–4 saw de facto autonomy throughout the region with the KDP effectively controlling it through the appointment of the governors. During this period, the Kurds learned the techniques of administration and government' (Stansfield 2003a: 75). No wonder the accord 'has remained the Kurds' favoured foundation stone for future relations with the rest of Iraq' (McDowall 2007: 327).

Much ink has been spent on why the newly found Ba'athist-Kurdish harmony was so short-lived. Ex post, both sides accused the other of having acted in bad faith and having failed to implement crucial stipulations of the deal from the beginning. Had the political space become ethnicized to an extent that made Arab–Kurdish reconciliation structurally impossible? Did the Ba'athists actually propose the accord as a ruse to lull the Kurds until they could consolidate power in Baghdad and felt strong enough to strike? Did Mulla Mustafa overplay his hand by insisting on the incorporation of oil-rich Kirkuk into the Kurdish administered area and, as Ghareeb (1981) suggests, maintain antagonism with the central government so his own position in Kurdistan could not be challenged by the Ahmed-Talabani faction? Most probably a combination of all the above factors played a role. What can be established beyond speculation is that the apple of discord poisoned relations soon after the ink had dried on the '11 March Manifesto'. In a strategic miscalculation, Mulla Mustafa entered an unholy alliance with the Shah of Iran, the United States and Israel against the pro-Soviet Ba'athist regime (Ghareeb 1981; Entessar 1992; Korn 1994; O'Ballance 1996; Stansfield 2003a; Natali 2005; Romano 2006; McDowall 2007; Tahiri 2007). Soon thereafter though, betrayed by his allies[6] – Iran struck a lucrative deal with Ba'athist Iraq in Algiers that secured its unrestricted access to the Schatt al Arab – and his forces routed by a determined and well-trained Iraqi Army, Mulla Mustafa's forces suffered a complete rout. More than a personal defeat – he died four years later of lung cancer in American exile (Korn 1994) – the reverse of 1975 signalled a changing of the guard within the Kurdish nationalist movement in Iraq. The era of Mulla Mustafa Barzani's dominance and the pre-eminence of local special interests over the reformist wing of the KDP had come to a drastic end. However, the fiasco of 1975, with the admitted benefit of hindsight, can also be interpreted in the vein of Stansfield (2003a) as a transition from one phase of Kurdish ethno-nationalism in Iraq to another; one in which the movement was set on a broader fundament with two parties, the KDP and the PUK – founded in the same year and as a direct consequence of Mulla Mustafa's miscalculations – competing for influence; a new phase in which Kurdish nationalism in Iraq was to ascend to a mass-scale movement encompassing all strata of society and, ultimately, blossoming into what became called the Kurdish de facto state in Iraq.

After a series of internal feuds, divisions and reunifications in the late 1970s and early 1980s as a result of the devastating defeat of 1975 and the systemic dissonance between 'traditionalists' and 'progressives' that had troubled the KDP ever since its founding, the KDP ultimately remained firmly within the grasp of the Barzani clan. After the death of Mulla Mustafa, his sons Idris and Massoud jointly led the KDP, restored in Iranian exile until, after Idris suffered a heart attack in 1984, Massoud became undisputed leader, supported by his nephew, Idris' son, Nechirvan Idris Barzani. The question of succession in the KDP after Massoud, from today's vantage point, seems limited to a competition between his son Masrour and his nephew Nechirvan Barzani. No wonder then that 'critics of the KDP claim that the KDP decision-making process is domi-nated by the immediate family of Massoud and Nechirvan Barzani, with the rest of the party being little more than the implementing agency of the family's wishes' (Stansfield 2003a: 107), and while giving itself a veneer of democratic-ally legitimated internal decision-making and elections for leadership at party congresses – the fact that 'the KDP is the only party in Iraqi Kurdistan that has had a continuous programme of party congresses and conferences' is promi-nently stressed by Massoud Barzani[7] – that these conferences and the party's main bodies such as the Central Committee are seen to merely act to rubber-stamp the decisions made by the party leadership, which is essentially the Barzani clan. 'When his enemies denounce him as a tribal, feudal man, they mean that Massoud [Barzani] does not distinguish between his own family's interest and those of the Kurdish people as a whole' (Gunter 1999a: 21). In fact, it would not be a gross exaggeration to view the KDP as a vehicle for the power politics and political ambitions of the Barzani clan, today exhibiting, rather than the 'democratic centralism' identified by Anderson (2007a) – see below – the 'dynastic republicanism' (Owtram 2012) of other (Arab) Middle Eastern states (Sadiki 2009, 2010). 'The post-colonial political orders and the ideologies that underpinned them, once emancipator vanguards on behalf of independence and republicanism, seem today to be regressing back into monarchism (read here as rule through hereditary succession),' Sadiki explains (2010: 101). In this, the KDP resembles Mubarak's Egypt or Ben Ali's Tunisia, which in light of recent developments in these countries as well as in Iraqi Kurdistan justifies elaborating on Sadiki's concept in some detail. What he calls the ' "privatization" of power' of the 'ruling complex' (*murakkab al-kursi* in Arabic, whereby the literal translation of *murakkab* as 'comfortably sat' or 'positioned' highlights 'the "free-rider" element involved in lubricating the wheel of political patronage-clientelism') is constituted by 'hereditary succession' and 'dynastic republican-ism' (Sadiki 2010: 101). Systemically connected to that ruling complex is a 'labyrinth of dependent or "parasitic" social forces', whether secular or religious, military or civilian, tribal or non-tribal, public or private, whether 'exist[ing] at … the apex [or the] bottom of the political pyramid' that have come to directly benefit from the preservation of the status quo and the continuing power of the ruling house. These parasitic forces, completely dependent on and owing their very existence to the ruling house, 'make the news; they guard the locus of power; they represent, endorse and defend the system; they occupy the market and the religious pulpit; and they close their minds to the possibility of an "alternative" order or rulers' (Sadiki 2010: 101) This stratum of *murakkab* forms the very basis on which the power of the ruling house rests, and they are handsomely rewarded for their 'supportive function … with the distributive rewards (status, resources, officialdom, self-preservation)' the system has to offer, 'deepening and nurturing their [lasting] dependence' (Sadiki 2010: 101).

The privatization of power based on patronage-clientelism, or as commonly referred to in the region as *wasta*, pervades every aspect of political and social life in Iraqi Kurdistan and is blatantly obvious to anybody conducting even a few days of field research there. On this aspect the PUK-controlled territories of Iraqi Kurdistan do not differ much from the KDP-dominated areas. What distinguishes the latter from the former, in addition to its rapid descent into authoritarianism with all the accompanying symptoms of human rights violations – routinely denounced by *Human Rights Watch* (2011, 2012) and other international human rights watchdogs (Reporters without Borders 2012), problematized in several media outlets (Dagher 2010; Artens 2011) as well as by governmental agencies (UK Border Agency 2011), and further discussed in Part III – is the aspect of 'dynastic republicanism' and the system of 'hereditary succession', not unlike the pre-'Arab Spring' regimes analysed by Sadiki, with all political power resting with one family, the Barzanis.

The PUK

> [When a]sking ardent backers of either the PUK or KDP what the policy and ideological differences between the two parties … I have yet to receive an answer that goes beyond the contention that one party fights more valiantly for the Kurdish cause, while the other allies itself with the hated central government more frequently. Iraqi Kurds not too closely attached to either party, however, tended to ascribe the differences to the leaders' personalities, interests, and old tribal rivalries.
>
> (Romano 2006: 197)

When confronted with this quote, one of the founders of the PUK, Omar Sheikhmous, had to admit that today the ideological differences between PUK and KDP are minimal – both promote a separatist Kurdish ethno-nationalism with the aim of wresting ever greater autonomy from the Iraqi state – but that the 'main difference between KDP and PUK is their style of leadership'.[8] Anderson (2007a) has identified 'democratic centralism' as the organizational principle of both parties. While, as detailed above, I argue the KDP is better characterized by 'dynastic republicanism' due to the dominance of the Barzani family and the principle of hereditary succession, I concur with Anderson that 'democratic centralism' best describes the organizational structures and decision-making processes of the PUK.

'Democratic centralism' as a political concept, 'was first formulated in the revolutionary movement in Russia. At that point it constituted simply a call both for organisational cohesion and for the adoption of democratic procedures in the Russian Social-Democratic Workers' Party' as the Bolsheviks had experienced them during their exile in Western Europe. 'To some extent [they] succeed[ed] in building these desiderata' – such as party elections and the freedom of expression – 'into their political practices' (Waller 1981: 4). Soon thereafter the imperative for internal cohesion, the centralist element came to supersede the democratic one, though. As Vladimir Lenin put it,

> the principle of democratic centralism ... implies universal and full freedom to criticise, so long as this does not disturb the unity of a defined action; it rules out all criticism which disrupts or makes difficult unity of action decided upon by the party.
>
> (Lenin 1978 [1905/6]: 433)

In practical political and organizational terms, this qualification meant that internal debate about policies in the designated bodies was tolerated, even encouraged, yet once a decision had been made by the party leadership it was expected to be implemented unconditionally and without further opposition. 'Once policy has been established by the party leadership, after vigorous internal debate, it must be implemented without dissent by the rank and file. Thus, the structure is democratic on the way up' – expressed in, for example, elections at routinely held party congresses, where 'the higher tiers are elected by the lower' – 'but authoritarian on the way down' (Anderson 2007a: 134). This inherent authoritarianism in policy implementation has a tendency to descend into rather dictatorial structures with a strongly centralized leadership cadre, who, if its actions are not to be questioned, is itself increasingly rarely challenged from within the party (Waller 1981; Tourish 1998; Anderson 2007a). One of the most prominent critics of Lenin's democratic centralism, Leon Trotsky – who ultimately paid for his dissent with his life – observed the pattern that, 'the party organization (the caucus) at first substitutes itself for the party as a whole; then the Central Committee substitutes itself for the organization; and finally a single "dictator" substitutes himself for the Central Committee'.[9] In other words, and this particularly holds true for the Stalinist era of democratic centralism, 'to criticise the leader is to betray the party and its ideals; thus the leader becomes infallible' (Anderson 2007a: 135); and party elections and congresses, once fora for a more or less open debate, become exercises in rubber-stamping pre-formulated policies and predetermined leadership cadres, the most prominent contemporary example being the National Congresses of the Communist Party of China, which meets at least once every five years to exercise the 'democratic element' of its version of democratic centralism. It has to be said, though, that the PUK, from its inception, constituted too heterogeneous a merger of diverse political movements and local power bases to ever achieve such a pure form of democratic centralism, yet in essence, at least until the *Gorran* split in 2009, the organizing principle of a somewhat more ambiguous democratic centralism than in contemporary China applies to it.[10]

As has been mentioned, the nucleus of the PUK was the progressive 'Ahmed-Talabani faction' of the Politburo that in 1964 split from the traditionalist majority of the KDP in defiance of Mulla Mustafa's authoritarian rule, and then lingered in exile for a decade. What moved them back onto the political stage in Iraq was the fatal blow the KDP had been dealt in 1975 resulting in the Kurdish nationalist movement in Iraq yearning for an alternative to Mulla Mustafa's brand.

> The collapse of the KDP in 1975 was such a traumatic event in Kurdish history, comparable to Mahabad; it affected Kurds in all parts, in Turkey, in Syria … everywhere there was a need for a new movement, not-aligned with the West [who had betrayed the KDP] and self-sustained,

Omar Sheikhmous summed up the public sentiment in Iraqi Kurdistan and beyond after this watershed moment.[11] Jalal Talabani and his followers, together with new KDP Politburo dissidents and more radical, 'third way' Maoist student movements, intended to capitalize on the public mood and the implosion of the KDP. In the late 1960s, with disillusion with Soviet-style Communism growing in the Third World, Maoist revisionism that put greater emphasis on nationalist liberation than its Soviet counterpart, rapidly gained ground among radical leftist NLMs in Asia, Latin America, Africa and the Middle East. These ideological shifts 'reached Iraqi Kurdistan through left-wing parties in Iran … who were against the old-style Communist parties, and through Palestinian parties and literature', Stansfield chronicles. The 'combination of socialism with Kurdish nationalism' that Maoism offered 'proved to be highly attractive' among Iraqi Kurdish activist youth, in particular 'when faced with the increasing autocracy of Barzani and the infighting within the KDP Political Bureau' (Stansfield 2003a: 81–82).

At the time of the March 1970 Manifesto, which these movements criticized as a concord between traditionalist Kurdish landholders and the dictatorial central government, these groups were little more than disparate cells lacking any overarching structure that could combine their 'third way' ideology into a more coherent political force. As with the KDP three decades earlier, it took a man from a rather traditionalist background, deeply embedded in the religio-tribalist structures of the Qadiri *tekiye* of Sufism (Gunter 1999a, 2010a), to band together these diverse elements into a political umbrella organization of his own design. In fostering contacts with Maoist student cells in Baghdad and Kurdistan in the late 1960s/early 1970s Jalal Talabani, or *Mam Jalal*, 'uncle Jalal' as he is affectionately called in Iraqi Kurdistan,[12] put to good use his connections and reputation from his student days, where 'in February 1953, he secretly [had] helped to establish the Kurdistan Student Union-Iraq and [had become] its secretary-general' (Gunter 1999a: 24). It was this rapport, which, from his exile in Damascus, he kept nourishing by keeping in contact with student groupings in

Iraq, that Talabani capitalized on when he played a crucial role in the formation of a single party, *Komala*, to unify these diverse student cells in June 1970 under the leadership of Newshirwan Mustafa, the editor of the influential Maoist student magazine *Rizgary*, who, in 2009, would fall out with Talabani and form the *Gorran* party.

Yet *Komala* was only meant to be the first step in Talabani's plan to form an alternative Iraqi Kurdish nationalist party to the KDP. In order to advance his designs the Maoist students had to be allied with KDP dissidents and those members of the politburo in opposition to Mulla Mustafa's authoritarian leadership – and for this alliance the 1975 collapse of Kurdish armed resistance and Mulla Mustafa's defeat proved the necessary catalyst. When, in March 1975, Mulla Mustafa gave the order to cease all hostilities against the central government, *Komala* and *peshmerga* units loyal to Talabani refused (Stansfield 2003a), while Talabani held secret meetings in Damascus, Beirut and Berlin to unite *Komala* with the KDP dissidents under a new umbrella organization. The co-founders – Jalal Talabani, Newshirwan Mustafa, Fouad Masoum, Kamal Fouad, Adil Murad, Omar Sheikhmous and Abdul-Razaq 'Faili' Mirza – first got together for preliminary discussions on 22 May 1975 in Talitla Restaurant in Damascus, a week later in a meeting in Berlin between Talabani, Newshirwan Mustafa and others the final decision for the formation of the PUK was reached,[13] and the party was officially established in Damascus on 1 June 1975 with the declared aim of:

> organising the revolutionary, patriotic and democratic forces of the Kurdish people in the form of a broad democratic and patriotic front that allows the fighting unity and coexistence of the different progressive tendencies under the leadership of a Kurdish revolutionary vanguard.[14]

The immediate success of the PUK can be explained mostly by two factors (Entessar 1992; Stansfield 2003a; Romano 2006; McDowall 2007): (1) when Mulla Mustafa had surrendered to the central government, they were the only Kurdish nationalist grouping with the manpower, logistics and organizational capacity to take up arms and continue the nationalist struggle against the Ba'athist regime; (2) the PUK constituted a radical alternative to the worn down, defeated KDP, Mulla Mustafa's high-handedness and his autocratic leadership that appeared to many Kurds to serve tribal-traditionalist interests first. Another factor that markedly distinguished the PUK from the KDP – and arguably made it more attractive to young radical nationalists who liked to think in non-hierarchical terms – was that 'the PUK was not a unified party in the sense of the KDP, but was more of a broad semi-front' (Stansfield 2003a: 80), a front that, rather than the KDP, who, arguably with limited success, had tried to unite disparate social and nationalist movements within one party, understood itself as an umbrella organization with the ambition and potential to harmonize these varying but often overlapping directions, to craft a certain nationalist unity out of diversity. Ultimately, though, 'too many ideological compromises were made to traditionalist elements ... and in order to gain mass appeal ... [from] land reform [to] women's rights ... [and] the PUK lost its ideological fervour with the negotiations in 1983'[15] between Talabani and Saddam Hussein. In the end, the PUK's Maoist nationalism turned out quite bourgeois, resulting in its ideological and nationalist direction becoming virtually indistinguishable from the KDP, as ascertained earlier by Romano.

Owing to its heterogeneous structure, the main difference between KDP and PUK is the latter's internal decision-making process, characterized by 'seemingly more opaque' structures, and with PUK politburo meetings being described as 'highly charged and chaotic', as being notoriously 'dominated by arguments and tense discussions' (Stansfield 2003a: 114). The heterogeneity of the party is also reflected in the fact that until the early 1990s the various groupings of the union held their own congresses, and 'that the first [actual] PUK Congress was [only] held in 1992, and was not followed until early 2001' (Stansfield 2003a: 114). The one element that holds these disparate elements together is Jalal Talabani, whose leadership style, rather surprisingly and unbefitting the role of *primus inter pares* he is often forced to play, is usually described as more mercurial and dictatorial than Massoud Barzani's (Gunter 1999a; Stansfield 2003a; Romano 2006). Nonetheless, Talabani managed to not only hold his PUK together but to field a formidable opposition to the resurgent KDP in the 1980/1990s. Little wonder then that when Talabani left the political stage of Iraqi Kurdistan to become President of Iraq in April 2005, his absence came to be keenly felt, and the party structures started to crumble until, in 2009, a disillusioned Newshirwan Mustafa split, along with many second-rank followers, to form their own party, *Gorran*, who in local elections in Iraqi Kurdistan in September 2013 defeated the PUK on its very home turf (Artens 2013a; BBC 2013; van Wilgenburg 2013a).

Another element that distinguishes the PUK from the KDP, of particular interest in the context of this study, is the more pan-Kurdish direction its founders originally intended. As a matter of fact, the imperative for an alternative to KDP's focus on limiting its nationalism to Iraq, that is reaching an accord with the central government on a generous autonomy status, had been one of the driving forces behind the negotiations on the formation of the PUK, with a strategic consideration to widen the nationalist struggle to Iran and Turkey explicitly discussed during the months leading up to June 1975. Future co-founders of the PUK such as Abdul Razaq Mirza reached out to the KDP-I in particular,[16] yet the Iranian Kurdish parties proved hesitant to enter an alliance with an Iraqi Kurdish movement just a few months after Mulla Mustafa had collaborated with the Shah's regime against them.[17] Likewise, and despite the fact that one of the co-founders of the PUK, Omar Sheikhmous, hailed from Syria, Talabani shied away from teaming up with Kurdish movements in Syria, which would have alienated his most influential external backer, the Assad regime in Damascus. For Sheikhmous, the final decision made by Talabani – 'he pushed for it', Sheikhmous recalled – to confine the PUK, like the KDP, to an 'Iraqi-Kurdistan only'-policy came as a particular disappointment.[18] However, even if a pan-Kurdish platform for the PUK was abandoned during its early days, the legacy of this debate is reflected, when compared with the KDP, in the PUK's more international orientation and its closer liaison with Kurdish nationalist movements in Iran and Turkey that occasionally could result in actual material cooperation,[19] most prominently and importantly in the context of this study, when the PUK came to save the PKK from sinking into insignificance in 1979. In fact, it is no exaggeration to say that the PUK contributed in no small fashion to the PKK becoming the most redoubtable ethno-nationalist insurgency in Kurdish history.

The PKK

The PKK was born out of the distinctive features of the socio-economic and political space in Turkey in the late 1960s/early 1970s. Perhaps at first rather surprisingly, the military coup of 1960 ushered in an era of political pluralism with a new constitution in the following year, safeguarding the principle of democratic checks and balances, the separation of powers, and civil liberties from elevated freedom of expression to granting trade unions the right to strike as well as constructing an electoral system conducive for governing coalitions in order to avoid single party rule, as during the *Demokrat Parti* (DP) era (Pope & Pope 1997; Jung & Piccoli 2001; Karpat 2004; Türsan 2004; Taspinar 2005; Zürcher 2009). While to some extent established party politics continued – such as the reliance of major parties on political machines in Eastern Anatolia headed by feudal Kurdish landholders that could guarantee votes (Natali 2005; Taspinar 2005) – on the other hand the political space, or one should rather say corset, was forced open by the emergence of the Workers Party of Turkey (*Türkiye İşçi Partisi*, TWP), the first official party positioned clearly outside Kemalist state doctrine and the first socialist party to win representation in parliament (Lipovsky 1992; Türsan 2004; Taspinar 2005); what is a more significant in the context of this study is that the TWP was the first political party in Turkey to acknowledge the Kurds as a distinct people with grievances and legitimate demands in Turkish society. 'For the first time since the founding of the republic, a legal political party had come to recognise the existence of a Kurdish minority within national borders' (Taspinar 2005: 92).

Among the reasons why the TWP proved so attractive to Kurdish voters – in the 1969 elections, four of the 15 TWP MPs were Kurds – was its openness towards emerging Kurdish ethnic consciousness and also the fact that it has to be seen as a function of the massive socio-economic changes Eastern Anatolia experienced during this decade. The Menderes government had already introduced a laissez-faire capitalist programme of free enterprise and import-substitution industrialization (Waterbury 1993) that, hand in hand with technological advances in the mechanization of the agricultural sector, hit the traditional stratum of Kurdish society – sharecroppers who paid the feudal land-lords an agreed proportion of the crop – exceptionally hard. The liberalized economic climate allowed feudal landlords to accumulate ever wider tracts of land,

and mechanization provided them with a leverage to force sharecroppers to accept ever more exploitative rent arrangements (White 1998, 2000; Natali 2005; McDowall 2007).

> Former sharecroppers in both the mountains and the plains of Turkey's Kurdish region increasingly became transformed into seasonal agricultural workers, or were forced to migrate either to Kurdish cities or to the West of Turkey, if not out of the country altogether.
>
> (White 2000: 98)

This rural exodus, with often the population of entire villages migrating to Izmir, Ankara and Istanbul, swelled urban shantytowns where inhabitants eked out a meagre existence under most precarious conditions – a development known in Turkish as *gecekondular*, entire districts of built-over-night shanty-neighbourhoods (Karpat 1976; Neuwirth 2004; Duyar-Kienast 2005). In the urban centres of Anatolia and the Mediterranean, Kurdish migrants came into contact with organized labour movements and were exposed to the teachings of Marxism-Leninism that promised them a better future under a socialist government. The mounting challenge of a radical, popular left, spurred on by events in Europe and the success of Marxist insurgencies in Asia, Africa and Latin America, momentously polarized the political space in Turkey and deeply unsettled the Kemalist establishment. In response to these challenges, Colonel Alpaslan Türkeş founded in 1965 the *Nationalist Action Party* (MHK, *Milliyetçi Hareket Partisi*), whose notorious youth wing, the *Grey Wolves*, attacked leftist movements in open street battles (Musil 2011).

By 1971, the programme of economic reform had demonstrably failed, the Turkish state was bankrupt (Waterbury 1993), and the politico-military establishment had lost tolerance with its experiment in democratic pluralism. For the second time in the history of the Turkish Republic the military intervened with the intent of imposing a cooling off phase on the country and cleansing the political system of radical leftist elements (Ahmad 1981, 1993; Hale 1994; Pope & Pope 1997; Jung & Piccoli 2001; Zürcher 2009); one of its first victims was the TWP, banned in 1971. For a short while the military could afford to lend itself to the illusion of having brought the situation under control: the 1961 Constitution had been amended, curtailing civil liberties and granting the *National Security Council* extended powers, special courts had been introduced to effectively do away with radical leftists, the *Grey Wolves* had been strengthened and trained by CIA instructors as part of 'Operation Gladio', martial law had been imposed in Eastern Anatolia, the media were gagged, and the autonomy of universities truncated (Ahmad 1981, 1993; Hale 1994; Pope & Pope 1997; Parla 1998; Jung & Piccoli 2001; Jacoby 2003; Zürcher 2009; Örnek & Üngör 2013). In 1973, the military felt confident enough to reintroduce parliamentary democracy and acquiesce into a general amnesty the following year (Nye 1977). Yet, if they had thought they could pacify the country and redirect the political space into well-trodden Kemalist channels, they were in for a surprise. If anything, the polarized political space turned out to be nothing but a precursor to the unprecedented political violence of the 1970s that reached almost civil war-like dimensions, pitting the state apparatus and the ultra-nationalist, paramilitary *Grey Wolves* against a myriad of radical leftist movements, who after 1974 came out of hiding and fought for such diverse ideals as enhancing civil liberties, workers' rights and economic equality, defeating the capitalist-imperialist nexus, or outright socialist world revolution (Dodd 1983; Harris 1985; Barkey 1990; Hale 1994; Pope & Pope 1997; Jung & Piccoli 2001; Zürcher 2009). It was in this polarized climate of proliferating political violence that the PKK was born, and its emergence can be understood as a combination of a complex of manifold but interrelated socio-economic and political factors, which can only be cursorily summarized here: from wider global phenomena,[20] the imposition of laissez-fare capitalism and top-down modernization programmes that on the one hand fuelled inequality in agrarian Eastern Anatolia but on the other hand radicalized migrant workers, the continuation of policies of Rae's 'pathological homogenization' with their outright denial of the existence of Kurdish identity, and 'opportunity structures' unique to the condition of the political space in Turkey (Romano 2006). On the one hand, the Kemalist politico-military establishment was no longer able to maintain the traditional order and in its attempts to re-establish order by force achieved little but a radicalization of its opponents, and on the other hand there was a progressive political opposition that mollified the worst excesses of the Kemalist establishment's repression and sought to widen the political space in order to potentially win the radical left as a partner in forcing open the Kemalist corset for democratic pluralism and eventually the creation of a more egalitarian society – the doctrine of a national democratic revolution or *milli demokratik devrim* (Landau 1974; Ahmad 1993; Zürcher 2009; Örnek & Üngör 2013). Those attempts quite naturally were bound to fail, since the radical left understood the legal opposition as not much different from the Kemalist establishment and used the widened political space for its own ends.

Given these parameters, it is easily discernible that 'the PKK does not have its political background in Kurdish politics ... but [was] born from the revolutionary left in Turkey' (Jongerden & Akkaya 2011: 126). Initially what became the most potent insurgency in Kurdish history was nothing more but a group of radicalized students in Ankara – three Kurds, Abdullah Öcalan, Ali Haydar Kaytan and Cemil Bayık; and three Turks, Kemal Pir, Haki Karer and Duran Kalkan – of whom some happened to cohabit and who spent their leisure time wallowing in revolutionary utopias (Jongerden & Akkaya 2011: 126). The part of town where they lived was a classic, predominantly Kurdish *gecekondu* with the potential of many sympathetic ears for their rhetoric of national liberation, class struggle and socialist revolution. Another important political platform for ideological exchange and the recruitment of sympathizers was the socialist student organization *Ankara Demokratik Yüksek Öğretim Derneği* (Ankara Democratic Higher Education Association, ADYÖD), of whose leadership committee Öcalan became a very proactive member (Çelik 2002; Özcan 2006; Marcus 2007a; Jongerden & Akkaya 2011; Gunes 2011). When

ADYÖD was closed down by the state authorities in December 1974, the group had learned the hard way that, in the contemporary political system, effecting revolutionary change by legal means and as part of an official movement was doomed to fail. They determined to go underground in rural Eastern Anatolia.

Given the group's urban background in student movements, this move may seem puzzling at first. Yet the relocation appears not motivated by nationalist liberation ideology, i.e. perceiving Turkey's Kurds as a distinct ethnic group that needed to be liberated from the assimilationist dominance of another ethnic group, the Turks, but born out of the Guevarist *foco*-theory (or 'nucleus' theory) of guerrilla warfare that put the disenfranchized peasants at the vanguard of the revolutionary struggle (Debray 1968; Weitz 1986; Wickham-Crowley 1991, 1992; Childs 1995; Guevara 1998 [1961]; Crouch 2009). In other words, at this time, Öcalan and his followers perceived the Kurdish peasants of rural Eastern Anatolia, analogous to the proletarian worker in Marxist-Leninism, in class terms first and ethnic terms second, and understood them as a vanguard in a class-based revolution turning Turkey as a whole into a socialist utopia (White 2000; Çelik 2002; Özcan 2006; Jongerden & Akkaya 2011; Gunes 2011). When the group, then operating under the name *Kurdistan Devrimcileri* ('Kurdistan Revolutionaries' or *Şoreşgerên Kurdistan* in Kurdish) or nicknamed *Apocular*, the 'followers of Apo', of 'uncle' Öcalan, reconvened in Ankara in late 1976 to assess their relocation to Kurdistan, the strategy was deemed a success. The group had attracted about 300 recruits, many of them

> university and teacher's school students or drop-outs. Their origins were rooted in the poor, mainly landless villagers that comprised the overwhelming majority of Kurdish society, families with close to a dozen children, illiterate ..., and a tough life based on small-scale farming and animal husbandry.
>
> (Marcus 2007a: 37)[21]

In his insightful discourse analysis of the PKK ideology, Cengiz Gunes (2011) surveys the major literature of the past two decades on the PKK. With an eye on the confines of this study, and since there is no need for reinventing the wheel, I will draw in my analysis on his observations. Aside from the official propaganda of the Turkish state apparatus and affiliated mouthpieces, it appears that recent scholarship is struggling to locate the PKK within the nationalist/ secessionist spectrum of contemporary NLMs. On the one hand, Kirişçi and Winrow argue,

> it would seem inappropriate to allocate to 'the Kurds' a particular label ... it would seem that the Kurds are an amalgam of Turkic, Armenian, and more dominant Indo-European groupings, ... the origins of the Kurds are hence somewhat obscure.
>
> (Kirişçi & Winrow 1997: 24)

It is an unease with applying the social category 'nation' to the Kurds – shared by White (2000) – that does not prevent Kirişçi and Winrow from explaining the PKK sanctuary in Iraqi Kurdistan along the lines of an ethnic alliance. On the other hand, Barkey and Fuller contest,

> the PKK's program mirrored the slogans of the extreme Left: Kurdistan with all of its four segments ... represented the weakest link in 'capitalism's chain' and the fight against imperialism was a fight to save Kurdistan's natural resources from exploitation.
>
> (Barkey & Fuller 1998: 23)

They continue:

> In fact, behind the left-wing rhetoric, the PKK had always been a nationalist movement. Its promise to save the exploited of the Middle East notwith-standing, its very formation represented a break with the Turkish Left and abandonment of the 'common struggle' ... Hence, its assumption of a nationalistic image is in fact not just in keeping with the times but also a return to its real self.
>
> (Barkey & Fuller 1998: 24)

As Gunes correctly criticizes, Barkey and Fuller seem to imply that nationalism and 'left-wing rhetoric' are contradictory ideologies, a somewhat astonishing claim given the long and well-established history of, for example, African and Asian NLMs, where both ideologies merged harmoniously, as did nationalism with liberalism in nineteenth century Europe. 'Nationalism is [always] strongly connected to other political ideologies and nationalist movements are involved in some other aspects of political demands.' In the Kurdish case this becomes evident for 'since the creation of Turkey, Kurdish national demands were articulated within various discourses; initially within the Islamist conservative discourse', then 'as a modernist discourse', a developmental discourse, a 'Marxist-Leninis[t], and, finally, [a pro-]democracy [discourse from] 1990 onward' (Gunes 2011: 11).

The significance of this observation, to which I will return shortly, cannot be underestimated since no ideology, be it nationalism, Communism, or liberalism, operates within a societal vacuum but always in tandem with and in opposition to other ideologies and discourses nor does it not change, fluctuate, develop over time and within an overall dynamic discourse – again the example of the union between nationalism and liberalism guiding the revolutions of 1848 and many national liberation movements in Europe since then is the example routinely referred to by modernist theoreticians, and in this case study, as elaborated earlier, the KDP and PUK are also instructive examples.

Earlier, it was outlined how the PKK emerged from the radicalized political left in Turkey in the 1960s and 1970s. By then a reading which situated the Kurdish peasant as the 'oppressed nation' in its abstracted form – trapped and exploited in a feudal structure of permanent dependence and in a dichotomous relationship with its constitutive other, the 'oppressor nation', that is the wider global capitalist-imperialist nexus and its local agents, the Turkish bourgeoisie and Kurdish *aghas* – was widely held among the Turkish radical left and emerging, more explicitly among Kurdish liberation movements (White 2000; Özcan 2006; McDowall 2007; Watts 2010; Gunes 2011). The issue that increasingly divided the emerging Kurdish liberation movements such as Kemal Burkay's *Socialist Party of Turkish Kurdistan* (TKSP, *Türkiye Kürdistan Sosyalist Partisi*) from its peers in the TWP was twofold: first, the debate on whether societal change was achievable in the socialist union of Turkish and Kurdish liberation movements and within the officially sanctioned channels of the political system, and second, a growing perception of Kurds in a national rather than merely abstracted form, whose liberation from oppression would have to include their dissociation from their Turkish 'brethren'. Already in 1974, Burkay declared, the Turkish bourgeois government reduced Kurdistan to the status of a colony.[22] By conceptualizing Kurdistan as a colony, the Turkish establishment as a colonialist power, as a co-protagonist in the global capitalist-imperialist nexus whose society overall benefited from the subjugation of the voiceless Kurdish masses, Burkay went a step further than the earlier 'oppressed nation'–'oppressor nation' dichotomy. He understood the 'Kurdish nation as,

> divided by the combined efforts of the imperialist, racist, and feudal reactionary forces, and which has been forced to live under the yoke. Because of this, in Kurdistan, the feudal relations have not been defeated and a bourgeois democratic revolution has not occurred. Therefore the main contradiction for the Kurdish people is national.[23]

In his writings, Burkay, one may say, thus equates Turkey's Kurds with those societies in Africa still under the colonial yoke – Portugal granted its colonies independence in the following year after decades of wars of liberation – who cannot follow the traditional Marxist-Leninist revolutionary trajectory of feudalism–capitalism–socialism since the system of colonial dependence, while having allowed Turkey to progress to the capitalist stage, still held them captive in feudalism. Burkay's concept of national liberation and the nation is therefore still class-based, with nations being defined according to what stage they occupy in the Marxist-Leninist revolutionary trajectory (Gunes 2011). Yet, despite this reasoning, Burkay did not advocate secession from Turkey. His TKSP's 'goal was to achieve a federal Kurdish state within Turkey' (Tahiri 2007: 225), very similar to the struggle for political autonomy advocated by the PUK in Iraq.

The PKK is therefore not the first Kurdish liberation movement in Turkey to have conceptualized the Kurds as a nation apart from Turks, nor is it the first to have called for a unification of the Kurdish lands to overcome the imperialist division, established at Lausanne, that was widely seen as the root cause for the Kurds' persistence in feudal dependence, nor to have identified the Kurdish *aghas* as the local collaborators with and greatest profiteers from the quasi-colonial system of feudal dependence – all these positions PKK and TKSP shared (White 2000; Watts 2010; Gunes 2011). What set the PKK apart from the TKSP and other similar organizations in Turkey's Kurdish political landscape are three factors: (1) the PKK's significant contributions to the Kurdish nationalist discourse in Turkey during the late 1970s/early 1980s becoming increasingly ethnicized – here Öcalan's writings reach from rather obscure, pseudo-historical attempts at establishing a connection between today's Kurds and the ancient Medes to the mythification of the annual *Newroz* (New Year)-celebrations (Özcan 2006; Marcus 2007a; Gunes 2011) – resulting in the conceptualization of the Kurdish nation altering in the 1980s from class-based to ethnic, thus converting the struggle for Kurdish liberation into an ethno-nationalist conflict; (2) the emphasis on the Turkish part of Kurdistan forming the vanguard in reuniting all Kurdish lands into an 'Independent, United and Democratic Kurdistan' (Gunes 2011: 90), as, for example, outlined in a 1982 Manifesto:

> Only the struggle in Centre-North-West Kurdistan in Turkey can lead the Kurdistan national liberation movement. This is because this part represents more than half the area and population of Kurdistan and more importantly it is the area where the new social forces have broken the backward old social structure and are the most developed.[24]

Therefore, although the PKK committed to the revolutionary trajectory that the liberation and unification of Kurdistan would constitute but a preliminary stage to the wider, regional (if not global) socialist revolution, it more explicitly than any other Kurdish NLM in Turkey entertained, at least in principle, the pursuit of secession. While it is important, in terms of the PKK's ideology, to put this pursuit of secession within the context of a wider socialist revolution – an aspect Barkey and Fuller seem to neglect in the above quoted passages – it can be ascertained, and in fact is crucial to strongly emphasize for the purpose of this study, that the PKK is the *only* modern Kurdish ethno-nationalist movement that not only advocated for secession and an actual (not just abstracted) unification of all Kurdish lands but actively fought for these principles in all four parts of Kurdistan. As will be detailed throughout Part III of this study, this constitutes the major difference between PKK and KDP/PUK and, naturally, had them become competitors and antagonists. Finally, (3) the PKK differed most profoundly from other Kurdish movements in Turkey, such as the TKSP, in allowing for the armed struggle, that is a guerrilla insurgency – to which all other parties only paid lip service, if at all – to be tantamount with its political work; in fact, the armed struggle was considered an integral part of it (Imset 1992; Kirişçi & Winrow 1997; Barkey & Fuller 1998; White 2000; Çelik 2002; Natali 2005; Taspinar 2005; Özcan 2006; Romano 2006; Ergil 2007; McDowall 2007; Marcus 2007a; Tahiri 2007; Brauns & Kiechle 2010; Eccarius-Kelley 2011, 2012; Gunes 2011). This guerrilla insurgency was to be directed against the organs of the Turkish state, the Kurdish *aghas* as imperialist profiteers from the system of feudal dependence in Kurdistan, (internal or external) collaborators with both agents, and competing Kurdish nationalist movements in Turkey that refused to accept a subordinate role to the PKK's dominance in the struggle for national liberation – given their ideological proximity and the PKK's ruthless pursuit of gaining dominance over all other Kurdish nationalist movements in the region, it should come then as no surprise that the PKK clashed with the TKSP as early as 1975 (White 2000; Özcan 2006; Marcus 2007a).

In the short duration from the group's departure from Ankara until the PKK's official founding on 27 November 1978, these ideological positions were developed and refined in the years thereafter. If one tries to identify a symbolic signifier to highlight the differences between the PKK, KDP and PUK, its founding moment may serve as well as any other: while the KDP was launched at an official congress in Baghdad, and the PUK initiated over the course of several meetings with its founding members jet-setting between Damascus, Beirut, and Berlin, the PKK was inaugurated in a clandestine gathering in the rural backwater of Fis village outside Diyarbakir, where Abdullah Öcalan was voted general secretary of the new party, and Cemil Bayık his deputy.[25] However, within less than a year of this historic meeting, the party faced complete annihilation. All through 1978/1979 the writing was on the wall that the Turkish military was gearing up for another coup – ominous signs that Abdullah Öcalan, who fled the country in July 1979, read correctly so that when on 12 September 1980 Chief of Staff General Kenan Evren announced military takeover, Öcalan listened to the broadcast from the safe distance of Lebanon (Ahmad 1981, 1993; Hale 1994; Parla 1998; Jung & Piccoli 2001; Çelik 2002; Jacoby 2003; Özcan 2006; Marcus 2007a; Tahiri 2007; Eccarius-Kelley 2011; Gunes 2011). Most of his unfortunate followers, less endowed with the gift of providence, were either killed or ended up in jail during the military crackdown immediately before, during or after the coup. For the PKK, the period of military rule from 1980 until 1983 constitutes a double-edged matter: on the one hand, the party gained widespread public recognition, with its members bravely defending their struggle for national liberation at show trials and enduring often fatal hunger strikes in prison (Çelik 2002; Özcan 2006; Romano 2006; Marcus 2007a; McDowall 2007; Tahiri 2007; Brauns & Kiechle 2010; Eccarius-Kelley 2011; Gunes 2011) – so that by 1983 the PKK as the sole 'true' defender of Kurdish self-determination was on everybody's lips. On the other hand, with most of its members killed, imprisoned or dispersed in exile, the 1980 coup left the PKK in dire peril, had it not been for the PUK lending it a helping hand in its hour of need.

Notes

1 On the nature of these early rebellions McDowall opines,

> Although sometimes described as a nationalist rebellion, the evidence indicated that it was not ... There is little solid evidence that Barzani has espoused the Kurdish cause during the course of his revolt ... If one looks at his actions ... it is more plausible that ... like any good tribal leader, he was constantly seeking to widen his regional authority.
>
> (McDowall 2007: 293)

Stansfield makes a similar point when noting,

> the major revolts of this period … are all characterized by tribal aims and support, with little, if any, thought for Kurdish nationalism or for alliance with the urban-based nationalists in Iran and Iraq. If nationalism became part of these struggles, it was usually as a means of mobilizing support for the benefit of the tribal rebellion.
>
> (Stansfield 2003a: 61–62)

2 Relations between Mulla Mustafa and the political leader of Mahabad and head of the KDP-I, Qazi Muhammad, were wrought with antagonisms (Ghareeb 1981; Entessar 1992; Stansfield 2003a; Jwaideh 2006 [1960]). Likewise, the KDP-I's attempt at self-governance in Mahabad was opposed by most of the Kurdish tribes in Iran, and its territorial control extended only to a few nearby villages and hamlets (Eagleton 1963; Ghassemlou 1965; Vali 2011), which makes it difficult to appreciate it as a genuine nationalist attempt at self-determination and separatism, let alone secession.

3 Mulla Mustafa escaped with 500 followers from Iraq in an epic three-week excursion through Iran, constantly harassed by the Iranian army; his time in the Soviet Union earned him the nickname the 'Red Mulla' (Ghareeb 1981; Entessar 1992; Stansfield 2003a; Jwaideh 2006 [1960]; McDowall 2007).

4 In 1957, many members of the *Iraqi Communist Party* (ICP) joined the KDP – by then renamed *Kurdistan Democratic Party* at its Third Congress in 1953 – which, for a while, was reflected in another name change into United-KDP (U-KDP) and gave the party an even more distinct socialist character (Stansfield 2003a).

5 The first Ba'athist regime had been deposed in a pro-Nasserist military coup on 18 November 1963. Between 1963 and the second Ba'athist coup of 1968 Iraq was ruled by the Nasserist Aref brothers, Abdul Salam and Abdul Rahman Aref.

6 A classified 'House Select Intelligence Report', published one year after the Kurdish defeat in *The Village Voice*, read,

> The recipients of U.S. arms and cash were an insurgent ethnic group fighting for autonomy [the Iraqi Kurds] in a country bordering our ally [Iran] (…) Documents in the Committee's possession clearly show that the President, Dr. Kissinger and the foreign head of state hoped that our clients would not prevail. They preferred instead that the insurgents simply continue a level of hostilities sufficient to sap the resources of our ally's neighbouring country (…) Even in the context of covert action, ours was a cynical enterprise.
>
> (Quoted in Korn 1994: 12)

7 Quoted in Stansfield (2003a: 107). His study provides an in depth overview on the political decision-making process of KDP and PUK and in this aspect can be considered the standard work on the politics of Iraqi Kurdistan until the 2003 Iraq War.

8 Interview with Omar Sheikhmous, Exeter, United Kingdom, 10 July 2012.

9 Quoted in Deutscher (2003: 74).

10 I had the privilege of attending as a guest the 2010 PUK Congress in Sulimaniyah and can attest that it was more controversial than its congresses had been before the Iraq War, with negotiations on party direction and leadership lasting for weeks.

11 Interview Sheikhmous op. cit.

12   There are at least two stories I was told about the origins of this name. One is that he was given it while young in memory of an admired maternal uncle who had recently died. The other story is that even as a young boy, Jalal took a very serious attitude, spoke well, and was accordingly given a name of distinction. The name 'Mam', however, is far from unique in Kurdish society.

> (Gunter 1999a: 23)

13 Interview Sheikhmous op. cit.

14 Quote from Patriotic Union of Kurdistan (1977) *Revolution in Kurdistan: The Essential Documents of the Patriotic Union of Kurdistan*, New York: PUK Publications, quoted in Stansfield (2003a: 80).

15 Interview Sheikhmous op. cit.

16 Interview with Abdul Razaq Mirza, Sulimaniyah, 11 June 2010.

17 Interview Sheikhmous op. cit.

18 Interview Sheikhmous op. cit.

19 This more international orientation is also reflected in the experiences of my own field research in Iraqi Kurdistan, where I found members of the PUK to be considerably more accessible and willing to engage in critical reflections on their party's history than were the KDP's members.

20 The influence on the radicalization of young Turkish exiles during military rule in Turkey from 1970 until 1973 through their exposure to radical youth movements and student organizations as well as clandestine cells of exiles of fraternal NLMs in Europe, Sweden and East/West Germany in particular – from the *Baader-Meinhof Group*, to *Brigate Rosse*, to the *Panhellenic Liberation Movement* (PAK), to a myriad of Palestinian groups, to the *Mozambique Liberation Front* (FRELIMO) – cannot be underestimated. On the PKK networks among the diaspora in Europe, see Wahlbeck (1998, 1999), Lyon and Uçarer (2001), Eccarius-Kelly (2002), Keeler (2007), and Grojean (2011). It would be no exaggeration to claim that the PKK had the most effective diaspora support network in Europe operating in the 1980s/1990s.

21 Two outspoken future PKK dissidents, Selim Çürükkaya and Selahettin Çelik, for example, illustrate this trajectory. While the parents of both hail from moderate rural milieu, Çürükkaya was a student at Tunceli Teachers School and Çelik studied engineering in Ankara. Both spoke fluent Turkish and had the skills and opportunities for promising careers, supposedly embodying the verisimilitude of Turkish nationalist ideology that if Turkey's ethnic minorities would 'accept' and 'live' their Turkishness they would be rewarded by society with wealth and status. What they ultimately came to embody, though, was the failure of the Turkish nationalist, assimilationist myth. Interview with Selahettin Çelik, San Louis, France, 9 May 2010.

22 Quoted in Gunes (2011: 72).

23 Quoted in Gunes (2011: 72).

24 Quoted in Gunes (2011: 90).

25 For a commensurate list of those attending and their fate in the years to come, see Çelik (2002).

Part III

6   The origins of relations

Early collaborations

The conventional narrative in most of the literature that deals with relations between the PKK and the Iraqi Kurdish parties – rather in passing and without much scrutiny ascribing it to either an ethnic alliance or instrumentalist explanatory model – has these relations start with the 'Declaration of Solidarity' between the PKK and KDP of 1983. One of the eminent authorities on the PKK in the 1980s, the Turkish journalist Ismet Imset, for example, states unequivocally, 'in fact, there was no major cooperation between the PKK and the Iraqi Kurds until 1983' (Imset 1992: 182). This view, however, is demonstrably wrong. As this study reveals, an Iraqi Kurdish party, the PUK, was in fact the very player that made the PKK's survival after the Turkish military coup of 12 September 1980 possible, whose vital support enabled the PKK to rise from the ashes of marginalization to become the most potent insurgency in Kurdish history.

By 1978, the Turkish state had imposed martial law in most south-eastern provinces, with the military penetrating every village in large numbers and thus making it increasingly difficult for PKK insurgents to carry out their, at first, rather amateurish operations. Although Öcalan claims that due to his foresight the organization managed to extract most of its top commanders from Turkey into the safety of neighbouring Syria just in time (Imset 1992), 'the military intervention did deliver a blow to the PKK ... Of the thousand or so detainees convicted of belonging to the PKK, a number were ... Central Committee members and included some of Öcalan's most trusted comrades'; many of them 'died in prison and others further weakened the organisation by becoming informers' (Imset 1992: 30). There can be little doubt that the radical left in Turkey had been dealt a devastating blow by police operations under martial law and the 12 September military coup; in security operations between 12 September 1980 and 31 March 1981,

> a total of 19,978 suspects were caught and put on trial in the three years of military rule and only 916 of these were from the right or extreme right organisations; ... 15,500 suspects were charged with membership in or engaging in the activities of the left-wing organisations ... [of which] the PKK took the largest toll.
>
> (Imset 1992: 29)

The PKK would have suffered a fate similar to sister organizations, like the TKSP, had it not established relations with a sympathetic foreign government, the regime of Hafez al-Assad in Syria. It is these relations with the Syrian government on which Imset focuses in his subsequent analysis, but without asking how they were established in the first place, how a political refugee and then no-name such as Abdullah Öcalan managed to secure for his newcomer organization the support of the mighty Syrian intelligence service, the *mukhabarat*? In July 1979, Öcalan fled to Syria via Lebanon, where, for three months, he came to stay with Adel Murad, one of the co-founders of the PUK. At the time, like most of the PUK leadership, Murad lived in exile, where from Beirut, in his day job, he covered political events in Iraq and Iran for Lebanese newspapers, yet in fact coordinated the PUK's activities in Lebanon. Murad recounts his first encounter with Öcalan:

> One evening I met with two of my Iranian contacts who told me that two persons had come from Turkey, that they were the new left there, important people I should meet ... They were very secretive, always concerned about security, even a bit scared ... we met then in my apartment at night, that was the first time I met Abdullah Öcalan. With him was a woman, her name was Myriam, I had no idea who she was, she only spoke Turkish, no Kurdish ... we sat down and Öcalan started talking, for an hour he kept going, but I could barely understand anything, his Kurdish was difficult [to understand], the Iranians, who spoke Turkish, had to translate ... I let Öcalan – his name was Ali then, nobody knew that it was Öcalan, and later I organised a passport for him on the name of Ali, a Jordanian passport – so I let Öcalan stay with me until I could find a translator ... Öcalan did not like the Iranians [translating] our talks, he later said he wanted to talk to me directly because I'm a Kurd ... so I got a translator, and Öcalan stayed with me ... in the end he stayed for three months in my apartment.[1]

Murad not only organized a translator but also sought approval for his talks with Öcalan from the PUK leadership.

> I wrote Mam Jalal [Talabani] and informed him about this new Turkish group, and that they wanted us to help them setting up contacts here in Lebanon. He answered that I should go ahead and help them but to proceed with caution because we had no clear idea who they were.[2]

Murad did as he was told and brought Öcalan in touch with Nayif Hawatmah's Syrian-backed *Democratic Front for the Liberation of Palestine* (DFLP). Murad attended the long conversations between Hawatmah and Öcalan, and recalls that at the end of the first meeting Hawatmah 'gave him ten Kalashnikovs and [later] promised him [more] assistance ... Within weeks dozens of young fighters of Öcalan's group came from Turkey, we received them and sent them on to the Palestinian camps in the Beqaa [Valley]'.[3]

Murad's portrayal of events appears plausible for three reasons. First, as will be shown shortly, the collaboration between the PKK and the Iraqi Kurdish parties, far from a credit one would seek to take in the current political discourse, is a matter the latter generally tend to downplay if not outright deny. To some extent then, Murad, who served as Iraq's Ambassador to Romania and at the time of the interview as general secretary of the PUK Central Committee – yet has no reputation of keeping his opinions about the fossilized and corrupt structures of the party to himself, when admitting to the crucial role his party played in accommodating the PKK in its hour of need – acted against the current discourse and the image that the Iraqi Kurdish parties generally tend to cultivate these days. Second, Murad can refer to a picture of himself with Öcalan taken during the days when the PKK leader stayed at his apartment in Beirut. The PUK was thus instrumental in throwing the enfeebled PKK a lifeline by facilitating contacts with the Palestinian NLMs operating in Lebanon in the early 1980s. Third, Aliza Marcus in her account of the PKK's early years hints to as much when she writes, 'in late 1979 or early 1980, Öcalan succeeded in getting a meeting in Beirut … with the DFLP. This meeting, probably arranged by Kurds Öcalan met in Beirut …' (Marcus 2007a: 55). For the first time in the literature on the PKK I can now substantiate and document that the Kurds in Beirut, to which Marcus refers, were Adel Murad and the PUK leadership.

Shortly after their first meetings, the DFLP agreed to host and train a small number of PKK fighters in its camps in the Syrian-controlled Beqaa Valley, most prominently the Helwe Camp.[4] 'The offer was not unusual. At various times, the DFLP trained Nicaraguan Sandinistas, Iranian leftists, Greek Communists, and even the odd Saudi' (Marcus 2007a: 55–56). In addition to wider ideological fraternity and solidarity among Marxist-Leninist NLMs,

> the DFLP likely also had more concrete reasons for helping. Giving shelter to other leftist revolutionaries allowed the DFLP to promote the image of an important, international revolutionary movement … and it helped them pad their numbers at a time of rising tensions with Israel.
>
> (Marcus 2007a: 56)[5]

By the time of the 12 September coup in Turkey, the numbers of PKK fighters the DFLP hosted had swelled to an extent that the DFLP could no longer accommodate them. But

> Öcalan, in the meantime, [had] successfully established similar training arrangements with other Palestinian organisations. This allowed the PKK to spread its people among the different Palestinian factions, including Yasir Arafat's Fatah, George Habash's *Popular Front for the Liberation of Palestine*, Samir Ghosheh's *Palestinian Popular Struggle Front*, and the Lebanese Communist Party.
>
> (Marcus 2007a: 57)

One of the PKK fighters who arrived in Lebanon via Syria in the wake of the coup was Selahettin Çelik. He recounts his journey:

> As soon as we crossed the border, [Syrian intelligence] knew about us … The Kurds in whose houses we stayed, they had to inform the authorities about us … We took Arab names, the Syrians gave us identity cards, … and we moved on to Lebanon … We felt bad about relying on [Syrian] help … They treated the[ir own] Kurds very badly, we knew that, we saw that … but there was nothing we could do about it. We needed [Syria's support] to get to Lebanon. We would not risk any trouble with them.[6]

What can be established at this point is that without the logistical support of the Syrian regime in channelling PKK fighters escaping Turkey to Lebanon and furnishing them with identity cards and that without the armed training and logistics the PKK received from the DFLP and other Palestinian NLMs, Abdullah Öcalan and his fledgling insurgency would have been finished. To Aliza Marcus, Selahettin Çelik summed it up:

> In reality, we were finished as an organisation after 1980. We had no strength in Europe, in Turkey we were in prison. But in Syria we could gather ourselves together. The minute we got money we used it to send people to Europe [to work in the Kurdish communities there]. From the Palestinians we learned things. We learned about making demonstrations for martyrs, about ceremonies. We did a lot of reading on a people's war [together], we also had armed training. They gave us clothing, cigarettes. We owe the Palestinians something.[7]

What can be further established is that the Assad regime in Syria had a long tradition of using regional NLMs as proxies to fight or at least to sting more powerful neighbours, many of which it had issues with. This practice reaches from its support of Palestinian organizations in the parts of Lebanon it controlled in both fighting Israel and also its antagonists in the Lebanese Civil War, to hosting Jalal Talabani and the PUK in Damascus to deal a blow to the Ba'athist regime in Baghdad with which it was at an ideological enmity, to today employing Hezbollah to fight the Syrian opposition in the Syrian Civil War since 2011. With its most powerful neighbour in the region, Turkey, the Syrian regime had many unsettled disputes, from Turkey's annexation of the province of Hatay in 1939, originally part of the French Mandate of Syria, to its *Güneydoğu Anadolu Projesi* (GAP) development project for south-eastern Anatolia with a series of hydro-electric dams and mass scale irrigation sapping the waters of the Euphrates and Tigris rivers, to its alleged shelter of the Muslim Brotherhood after the Hama insurrection in 1981 (Olson 1997, 2000, 2001; Marcus 2007a; Scheller 2013). Hosting the PKK in the Syrian-controlled parts of Lebanon, facilitating its collaboration with Syrian-backed Palestinian NLMs, and providing logistical support was a convenient tool to deal Turkey a blow by proxy, all the more

convenient since Syria's involvement came with the advantage of political deni-
ability (Imset 1992; Olson 1997, 2000, 2001; Çelik 2002; Byman 2005; Marcus
2007a; McDowall 2007; Tejel 2011; Scheller 2013).[8] In the years after 1980
both PKK–Syrian and PKK–Palestinian collaboration increased substantially, to
the extent that Öcalan, who had resettled to Damascus,

> was enjoying Syrian hospitality to the best of his benefit … he owned a villa
> in Damascus, travelled around in a red Mercedes provided for him from
> Syria and was protected by Syrian Kurds who are still his only bodyguards.
> In every way, he was living the life of a Syrian official.
>
> (Imset 1992: 32)

Likewise, the PKK presence in the Beqaa Valley had increased so much that it
had taken over control of the Helwe Camp, and in 1981 and 1982 the organization held its first two congresses abroad there (Imset 1992: 32; Çelik 2002;
Marcus 2007a). What is more, while Syria adamantly prohibited any agitation
against the regime among its own Kurdish population, it gave permission for the
PKK to recruit fighters from within their ranks, 'hoping this would redirect local
Kurdish attention away from fighting for change inside Syria' (Marcus 2007a:
100). On the phenomenon of Syrian Kurds being recruited by the PKK with the
encouragement of the Assad regime, Omar Sheikhmous, a Syrian Kurd,
recounts:

> [The PKK in Syria] had very good recruiters, especially among students and
> women. They were clever in recruiting youngsters, who were sent to
> Lebanon first and then to Turkey. For Syrian Kurds, the PKK was very
> attractive because the Syrian Kurdish community was corrupt and factional-
> ised and Syrian intelligence had infiltrated it … About 30–35% were
> recruited by government organs. It was mainly state security that worked as
> an initiator and organiser. They had a number of contacts in the Syrian com-
> munity, mainly in Ifrin, Damascus, Qamishli, and Aleppo. There was a clear
> agreement: 'You'll be sent to fight in Turkey and therefore you'll not be
> asked for military service, and after several years you come back' … When
> the recruits left Syria, security kept their identity cards. There were two con-
> siderations behind this: First of all, they could not easily return but needed
> permission of security to do so. Second, if they were killed or tracked in
> Turkey, there would be no reflection on Syria.[9]

Not even the fact that Öcalan was living the high life in Damascus courtesy of
the Syrian authorities illustrates the scope and depth of the support his group
received from the Assad regime as well as these practices of forcibly recruiting
Syrian Kurds into the ranks of the PKK.

The question remains as to what extent the PUK, another proxy Syria hosted
and supported generously since its founding, after its initial part in paving the
way for PKK-DFLP cooperation, played a role in further facilitating contacts

between Syrian authorities and the PKK. Sarkho Mahmoud, who lived as a student in Damascus during the 1980s and from 1985 on was one of the PUK's external representatives in charge of liaison with other Kurdish and non-Kurdish political parties there, observed on whether the PUK facilitated contacts between the PKK and the Syrian authorities: 'we made the door open for them ... through the Iraqi opposition in Syria, in which we were very strong, we helped them to set up talks with the Syrians'.[10] In the same interview he further claimed that PUK members had also assisted in establishing contacts between the PKK and the regime of Muammar Ghaddafi in Libya.[11] When I asked Adel Murad, Sarkho Mahmoud and Omar Sheikhmous why the PUK had lent a helping hand to the PKK, who, after all, just before the coup distinguished itself mostly by fighting Kurdish parties in Turkey, which the PUK had traditionally been affiliated with, such as Kemal Burkay's TKSP, they all gave more or less the same answer:

> We were young, we were naïve. We dreamt of building a large anti-imperialist front all over the Middle East, including many Kurdish parties and organisations from many countries. So, we reached out and helped any group we could work with ... and we hoped that [the PKK and other Kurdish parties in Turkey] would mend their differences.[12]

In light of these lofty declarations, the ethnic alliance model appears at first sight an apt explanatory framework to account for the PUK's support of the PKK in 1979/1980, therewith saving it from possible collapse. However, even though ideational factors appear to have determined the PUK's behaviour towards the PKK – material interests can be ruled out since the PUK had little to gain, and the PKK political refugees had nothing to give in terms of material benefits – a few important qualifications must be put in place that ultimately render untenable common ethnicity as the determining variable in explaining these acts of solidarity. First, the ethnic alliance model, strictly speaking, does not apply here since the PUK neither controlled a state of its own nor did it 'play a role in policy making' (Davis & Moore 1998: 93) in a neighbouring state; both PUK and PKK were political refugees, leading a paltry existence in exile, with little to lose from working together and equally dependent on the charity of others. During the time in question for our current analysis, nobody, neither the PUK, nor the DLFP, nor the Syrian government, could have foreseen the PKK's rise to becoming the most potent insurgency in Kurdish history within less than a decade; consequently, they must have thought their support of Öcalan's group of little, almost negligible consequence. Adel Murad makes a point when emphasizing that he 'saw no great difference' between offering Öcalan a couch to sleep on and facilitating contacts with the DFLP, since the consequences and extensive impact of his doing so were impossible to anticipate at this moment.[13] They were seen as simple acts of charity and hospitality towards an ideologically related Kurdish organization in need. The concurrence of two ideational factors, ethnicity and a radical leftist ideology, constitutes the second caveat to common ethnicity as the determining variable for categorizing their relations and to the ethnic alliance model serving as an applicable explanatory framework. Omar Sheikhmous' above remarks illustrate that for the PUK, the PKK's Marxist-Leninist pedigree counted as much as the fact that both were Kurdish organizations fighting for national self-determination. In particular, in light of both groups' collaboration with the Palestinian NLMs operating in Lebanon, who had no ethnic ties with the Kurds, I would find it very difficult if not impossible to draw a clear line between political ideology and ethnicity determining these groups' behaviours. This difficulty becomes even more apparent when extending the level of analysis to include the Syrian government, in whose case only instrumentalist but no ideational factors appear to have determined the behaviour of the Assad regime, the PKK and the PUK, with each availing themselves of the other for their own strategic and materialist ends; when bringing the Syrian Kurds and their prominence in the ranks of the PKK into the equation, the situation appears again less clear-cut, though. Here, a host of ideational factors[14] as well as material interests, i.e. avoiding conscription into the Syrian military, seem to account for their joining the PKK. In sum, I would argue that this first example of PKK collaboration with external actors, when considering the whole body of evidence at all levels of analysis – PKK-PUK, PKK-PUK-Palestinian NLMs-Syrian government, and PKK-Syrian government-Syrian Kurds constellations – in its entirety already attests as to why the simplifying reductionism of either the ethnic alliance model or instrumentalism fall short of convincingly explaining the PKK's various 'alliances'. Instead, it supports the case I have made in this study for appreciating these actors' relations as a complex, shifting and situational matrix of identities and interests, as advocated by Fierke (2007), in which each actor's motives ought to be studied individually as well as in their interaction with each other in order to get a workable grasp of the matrix's dynamics.

The PKK comes to Iraqi Kurdistan

When considering the dire conditions of the PKK in 1980 there can be no doubt that the PUK was instrumental in revitalizing Abdullah Öcalan's fledgling organization. Likewise, when considering the PKK's expansion in numbers, military strike capability and enhanced sophistication in tactics of guerrilla warfare through military training, equipment and overall professionalization between 1980 and August 1984, when it actively launched its insurgency in Turkey, there can be little doubt about the extent to which the support of the Syrian regime of Hafez al-Assad and the Palestinian NLMs operating in Syrian-controlled Lebanon proved instrumental in achieving this transformation. Not only had the collaboration with Syrian intelligence and Palestinian NLMs, facilitated by the PUK, provided the PKK with a second life, it allowed it to consider, in 1984, the transition from individual hit-and-run strikes to an elaborate guerrilla campaign based on the classic Maoist three-stage model of guerrilla warfare, later adapted by Vo Nguyen Giap, of (1) mobilization through targeted propaganda among the peasantry and contention of the authorities' security forces in the region through guerrilla warfare; (2) equilibrium through protracted conflict and mobile warfare, thus sapping the authorities' resources and public support; and (3) a general counteroffensive as part of mass-scale public uprising against the authorities (Sarkesian 1975; Snow 1997; Guevara 1998; Mao 2005 [1961]; Laqueur 2009). This transition is epitomized in the creation of the PKK's Vietcong-style armed wing, the *Hezen Rizgariya Kurdistan* (HRK, Kurdistan Freedom Unit),[15] renamed into *Arteşa Rizgariya Netewa Kurdistan*, (ARGK, People's Liberation Army of Kurdistan) in 1986 (Imset 1992; Çelik 2002; Özcan 2006; Marcus 2007a; Eccarius-Kelly 2011).

What the PKK dramatically lacked though was a strategically suitable geo-graphical launch pad for its first strikes into Turkish territory. The rather flat and arid terrain of the Turkish–Syrian border was incompatible with guerrilla warfare, and the Syrian regime proved hesitant to become that directly involved in the PKK's launch of military strikes (Imset 1992; Olson 1997; Çelik 2002; Marcus 2007a; Scheller 2013). When faced with this predicament of having a guerrilla ready to strike but no access to the theatre of operations, the second Iraqi Kurdish party, the KDP, stepped in to save the day for the PKK. In July 1983, at first sight perhaps surprisingly, the KDP and PKK signed an accord of mutual cooperation, entitled 'Principles of Solidarity' that was made public in the following year (Imset 1992; Gunter 1996; Marcus 2007a). In this 11-article long declaration, both parties committed to a joint effort, 'depend[ing] on the force of the Kurdish people' against 'every kind of imperialism and the struggle against the plans and plots of imperialism in the region'; they further pledged to seek and further 'cooperation with other revolutionary forces in the region and to effort the creation of new alliances'.[16] Wary of each other's past though, in article 10, KDP and PKK pledged not to interfere in each other's internal affairs, providing 'that the organisations would not side with actions which could damage the unity of the parties and that they should respect the organisational and political independence of each other' (Imset 1992: 184); if this principle were violated, the covenant foresaw a modus in which the aggrieved party would inform the other of its objection, then issue a warning, and if not altered, would be at liberty to terminate the compact (Imset 1992; Gunter 1996). In October 1984 Massoud Barzani and Abdullah Öcalan met in Damascus for the first and only time to publicly unveil their alliance, with the communiqué even translated into Arabic (Imset 1992; Gunter 1996).

To be sure, the history of Kurdish ethno-nationalism is full of ephemeral acts of cross-border cooperation between the various Kurdish ethno-nationalist parties and the four nationalizing states; rarely though has such cooperation, nor-mally rather dealt with in clandestine fashion, taken on such formal a character with public announcements and a detailed set of regulations. At least on paper, then, we can speak of a classic strategic alliance here between the two Kurdish parties that, although not explicitly including a clause of mutual defence or stip-ulations for collective military action, resembles a military alliance insofar as the KDP granted the PKK access to its territory and joint use of its infrastructure, i.e. camps, in Iraqi Kurdistan. Consequently, even before the accord was made public, the PKK established its largest base yet, called Lolan camp, in the inaccessible mountainous border area of Iraq and Turkey – a camp that, tellingly, also acted as the KDP's regional headquarter and clandestine radio station as well as a base camp for the Iraqi Communist Party (Imset 1992; Gunter 1996). The importance of this development cannot be underestimated, since by granting access to and sanctuary on its territory, the KDP provided the PKK with the one element Öcalan was missing in his strategy: a launch pad with direct access to the target state for projecting guerrilla operations into Turkey, in a territory as suitable for irregular warfare as the jungles of Vietnam or peaks of Afghanistan. This most advantageous position provided the PKK with the ideal conditions, in August 1984, to carry its guerrilla war into Turkey, a war that has lasted now for three decades, making it thus one of the longest examples of guerrilla warfare in modern history, and costing 50,000 lives – a war that arguably would have been difficult if not impossible to launch had the KDP not granted the PKK sanctuary. Conversely, though, the PKK sanctuary in Iraqi Kurdistan, together with Syria's support of Öcalan's group, allowed the Turkish politico-military establishment to portray the Kurdish uprising in southeast Anatolia as an external problem and the PKK as agents controlled from abroad by shadowy regional powers conspiring against Turkey (Pope & Pope 1997; Jung & Piccoli 2001; Lundgren 2007; Göçek 2011).

For any insurgency, the blessings of sanctuary are obvious and have been highlighted by guerrilla commanders from Mao Tse-tung to Ernesto Che Guevara, to Vo Nguyen Giap as well as theoreticians of insurgency and counter-insurgency (Brynen 1990; Galula 2006 [1964]; Laqueur 2009 [1976]; Kilcullen 2010), and I have detailed them together with providing a more nuanced model of insurgency-sanctuary state relations elsewhere (Artens 2012). Idean Salehyan (2007, 2008, 2009) is the latest in an array of analysts who has written extensively on the importance of international borders to shelter insurgencies from the jurisdiction of their target states. If we conceptualize the international system as a conglomerate of sovereign states that, as three main paradigms of explanatory IR would have it, exercise absolute power and control within their border but have little or no legal basis to prosecute subversive elements abroad, it is plainly clear why protest movements, NLMs or insurgencies find it attractive to evade persecution by relocating most of their operations into the territory of a neighbouring state well-disposed to their cause – geographical proximity being an additional factor in their favour, as insurgencies usually cannot project force across long distance. By going abroad, insurgencies thus not only successfully dodge the judicial, policing and military powers of the target state, they also significantly raise the stakes of the conflict by internationalizing it. They not only win a material and logistic supporter for their cause but also a potent patron in international fora and bodies that are, in most cases, 'states only clubs'. The insurgencies therewith also make it more costly for the target state to persecute them: doing so would violate the sovereignty of the neighbouring state and risk the condemnation in international bodies that comes with it, hazard an inter-state confrontation between two regular, more or less well-equipped armies, and even if the target state is willing to take that risk and intervene abroad, in most cases it would result in a lengthy and costly occupation to extirpate the insurgency and the neighbouring state's support of it (Salehyan 2009). Erin Jenne (2006) and Clayton Thyne (2006) demonstrate how the assistance of foreign governments and the higher costs resulting for the target state to combat them, significantly increases the bargaining position of the insurgents and may induce them to raise and radicalize their demands. 'Thus, the inclusion of additional parties to the bargaining environment can make it more difficult to find an acceptable settlement because external patronage alters expectations about the domestic balance of power' (Salehyan 2009: 49). Ironically then, the very principle of state sovereignty that holds international borders sacrosanct and, all too often, the internal affairs of states untouchable, to the same extent and when finding sanctuary in a neighbouring state, befits the (secessionist or separatist) insurgency that seeks to topple or revolutionize this order. In these aspects of sanctuary I agree with the cited analysts; what I do not agree with, and what I seek to problematize in this study, is the tendency to reduce the motives for political action of states, parties, NLMs or insurgencies – whether they are the recipients or givers of sanctuary – to singular explanatory factors such as common ethnicity or material interests and, by doing so, to reify these factors and the discourses from which they emerge.

For this study then, the central questions in this context are why the KDP, at first sight rather unexpectedly, reached out to the PKK, entered a formal alliance with Öcalan's group, granted it access to its territory and sanctuary, and even allowed it to share its infrastructure such as camps, supply lines and means of communication. As with the PUK, at cursory inspection a lot seems to speak for the ethnic alliance model as an explanatory framework. After all, when justifying his alliance with Öcalan, even Massoud Barzani himself boasted:

> For us, it is always a source of pride that in the regions that we have liberated with the cost of our blood, we have opened the area as a fortress for every Kurdish fighter. We signed the alliance with the PKK with this logic and for these reasons.[17]

At closer scrutiny, though, such lofty declarations are revealed as strategic essentialisms, maintaining an essentialized version of the group, the pretence of group cohesion and solidarity for strategic purposes. If we as scholars though, rather than calling it into question, adopt the strategic essentialisms of ethno-nationalist elites, like Massoud Barzani, as the basis of our enquiries or take on '*categories of ethnopolitical practice as our categories of social analysis*' (Brubaker 2004: 10, emphasis in original), as the ethnic alliance model and related explanatory frameworks propagate, we contribute to the reification and substantialization of the ethno-nationalist elites' primordialism and to the reproduction of its logic. Having said that, in order to reiterate the central point of critique of this study of the pre-eminent approaches of explanatory IR to explaining ethnic conflict, and before discussing alternative explanations, it appears only proper to clarify why

I am confident to discount Barzani's declaration of solidarity based on common ethnicity as a strategic essentialism.

Other than the PUK, where at least in its early stages and only to a certain degree are ideological congruities with the PKK identifiable, the ethno-nationalisms of KDP and PKK are strikingly dissimilar. As a matter of fact, up to 1983, more than anything else, KDP and PKK can be seen as antagonists. The PKK is the only modern Kurdish ethno-nationalist movement to advance a secessionist ethno-nationalist agenda, while the KDP's at best can be understood as separatist. This contrast, almost by default, would have put the former at odds with the KDP whose self-perception as the grand old party of Kurdish self-determination in Iraq would not have tolerated Öcalan's competition on its very home turf, while the PKK saw itself as the vanguard for the liberation and unification of all Kurdish lands. What is more, PKK and KDP can be located at the opposite ends of the spectrum of Kurdish ethno-nationalism. From even before the founding of the PKK, for Öcalan the KDP had embodied all that was wrong with Kurdish ethno-nationalism, the very reason for its failure, and he never tired of castigating Mulla Mustafa Barzani and his successors as adhering to a 'primitive' and 'defeatist' ideology in speech after speech.[18] Also, in its very founding declaration of 27 November 1978, the PKK explicitly positioned itself against the KDP's strategy of wresting from the state concessions for Kurdish autonomy, which, through acceptance and facilitation of the division of the Kurdish lands, it understood as nothing but attempts at playing into the hands of imperialist nationalizing states (Çelik 2002). Öcalan elaborated:

> The KDP program for autonomy is not accidental. This represents the special interests of Kurdish feudals, and it is an instrument to develop them into a bourgeoisie ... The feudal class cannot demand more than autonomy. They do not go against their interests. Independence is against the interests of the Kurdish feudals. The struggle for independence means the death of the Kurdish feudals. Only the forces of the proletariat can achieve independence.[19]

Given the opposing ideologies of PKK and KDP, these tirades and declarations were more than strategic essentialisms or examples of mere ethnic outbidding; the antagonism with the KDP was rooted in the very core of the PKK's perception of itself as a Marxist-Leninist NLM with the declared objective of liberating the oppressed Kurdish masses not only from the nationalizing states that denied them the expression of their ethnic identity but also the Kurdish tribal landlords that participated and profiteered from this system of oppression and exploitation. And, as has been detailed earlier, these Kurdish tribal landlords were the founding constituency of the KDP, and the Barzanis were not only prominent representatives of this stratum of Kurdish society but also the most potent champion of their interests. What is more, in this role, the Barzanis were not limited to Iraq but had inspired the founding of an affiliated party in Turkey, the KDP-T by Faik Bucak, one of the wealthiest landlords in the Siverek area (McDowall

2007). It was these very feudal landlords and Kurdish *aghas* who made a profit from collaborating with the Turkish state and who acted in elections as a political machine for the established parties that the PKK had designated its prime target during its early years of operation. As a matter of fact, nothing illustrates this ideological primacy and therewith the antagonism with the KDP better than the fact that, on 30 July 1979, the PKK dared as one of its signature feats an assassination attempt on Mehmet Celal Bucak, the head of the Bucak tribe – which had constituted the founding core of the KDP-T – and a deputy of in the governing coalition with the right-wing MHP (Gunter 1990; White 2000; Özcan 2006; Marcus 2007a; McDowall 2007).

It therefore seems not very plausible, as some authors claim (Marcus 2007a; McDowall 2007), that the KDP entered the alliance with the PKK in order to strengthen its pan-Kurdish credentials, deeply impaired after the collapse of Mulla Mustafa's 1975 revolt and the split with PUK. Why, of all organizations advocating Kurdish self-determination in Turkey, would the KDP have entered an alliance with the one most opposed to its own brand of Kurdish ethnonationalism? Why the only Kurdish NLM that laid claim to leading the Kurdish struggle for self-determination not only in Turkey but also in Iraq, where it would have competed with the KDP? Why then open the door to Iraqi Kurdistan for the PKK, giving it access to this political stage? Furthermore, the argument that the KDP sought to boost its pan-Kurdish credentials appears even less probable given the fact that, at the same time as Massoud Barzani extended his hospitality to the PKK, the KDP launched an attack on its sister organization in Iran, the KDP-I, on behalf of its ally, the Khomeini regime in Tehran, and as part of the wider Iran–Iraq War that had started with Iraq's invasion of 22 September 1980 (van Bruinessen 1986; Chubin & Tripp 1988; Hiro 1991; Entessar 1992; O'Ballance 1996; Stansfield 2003a, 2007a; Tahiri 2007). In light of these doubts and of the overall KDP–PKK antagonism, ideational factors appear to hold little purchase in explaining why the KDP entered an alliance with the PKK in 1983, and granted it access to and sanctuary on its territory. In addition, the ethnic alliance model and related frameworks seem questionable as a plausible explanatory model for these developments and the parties' motives. One additional caveat, already mentioned in the context of the PUK, also applies to the KDP's support of the PKK three years later: the KDP simply could not have foreseen the PKK's ascendance from second rank guerrilla in the pocket of the Assad regime to becoming the Middle East's most potent insurgency over the course of just a few years, and therefore can be excused for not fully appreciating what it actually bargained for.

Ensconced in its sanctuary in Iraqi Kurdistan and with direct access to the designated theatre of operations in Turkey, on 15 August 1984 the PKK began in earnest its peoples' war for the liberation of Kurdistan with dual attacks on the towns of Semdinli and Ehru, and in October of the same year, in a deliberate propagandistic strike, stepped up its activities with another widely publicized attack coinciding with President Kenan Evren's visit to the area (Imset 1992; Çelik 2002; Özcan 2006; Marcus 2007a; McDowall 2007; Eccarius-Kelly 2011);

in the spring of 1985 the PKK fought its as yet toughest battle in Siverek with 60 casualties among guerrilla, security forces and civilians (McDowall 2007). These successful attacks caught the Turkish politico-military establishment by complete surprise,[20] allowing the PKK, who by early 1985 was operating with at least 200 guerrillas active inside Turkey at any time, to intensify its propaganda among the Kurdish village population with the aim of persuading them to join the insurgency and to ultimately prepare the ground for a general mass uprising (Imset 1992; White 2000; Çelik 2002; Marcus 2007a; Eccarius-Kelly 2011). Yet, by mid-1985 the Turkish army had not only significantly stepped up its military presence in the area but also introduced the system of 'village guards', Kurdish villagers armed, paid, or at least as often press-ganged into the service of the army, to defend remote villages against guerrillas operating in the area, thus effectively creating state-sanctioned death squads and paramilitary services.[21] Within in a year, the PKK insurrection had turned into a full-scale civil war with tens of thousands perishing and millions becoming internally displaced.

If ideational factors cannot explain the KDP-PKK accord, what are the motives behind the parties' behaviour? In the current political discourse and climate, in which KRG politicians try their hardest to project the image of a reliable partner of the West and in which the Kurdistan Region is completely dependent on Turkey politically and economically, the KDP understandably would prefer their past alliance with PKK to be forgotten. These attempts at rewriting and whitewashing history sometimes take on a bizarre form, such as when I interviewed the Chief of Staff to President Barzani, Fuad Hussein, and he outright denied that the KDP 'had ever supported or collaborated with the PKK'.[22] Such brazen denials, in light of how well documented events are and the 'Principles of Solidarity' accord, make today's decision makers in the KRG appear surprisingly unprofessional in plying their political trade; indeed, rather than cloaking it, they offer insights into how uncomfortable they must be in coming to terms with their past. Alternatively Imset (1992) and McDowall (2007) suggest an instrumentalist explanation for why the KDP invited the PKK onto their territory. In May 1983, the Turkish military had launched a substantial raid in the Iraqi–Turkish border region in pursuit of Kurdish militants who had fled there from Turkey, but its attacks indiscriminately hit them and Barzani's *peshmerga* who had just returned there from Iran. Imset and McDowall hypothesize Barzani intended to create a buffer between his forces and the Turkish border, a buffer zone he planned the PKK to fill for him. This explanation, though, seems not very plausible. If Barzani had feared Turkish incursions into his territory, why would he invite an organization whose presence surely would trigger further retaliation from the Turkish military – a chain of events that unfolded precisely in this fashion once the PKK had pitched camp there.

A seemingly more plausible interpretation of the KDP's actions has the KDP–PKK alliance of 1983 rooted in the eternal rivalry between KDP and PUK and wider geo-political changes in the region. Since the PUK had sent *peshmerga* into the field to continue Iraqi Kurdish resistance against the regime of

Saddam Hussein in the wake of the collapse of Mulla Mustafa's uprising, KDP and PUK were embroiled in a de facto civil war, yet both sides were too weak to gain an upper hand (Entessar 1992; Stansfield 2003a; Asadi 2007; McDowall 2007). The situation dramatically changed when, in September 1980, Saddam Hussein invaded Iran and the entire region was flung into a war the like the Middle East had not witnessed since the First World War, with more than a million casualties. In this confrontation of titans, the KDP, scraping a living in exile in Iran, opposing Baghdad, and dependent on whoever was in power in Tehran, whether the Shah or Ayatollah Khomeini, took sides from early on, and since 1981 was employed by the Iranian Revolutionary regime against the KDP-I (van Bruinessen 1986; Entessar 1992; O'Ballance 1996; Stansfield 2003a; McDowall 2007).[23] For the PUK the outbreak of the war posed a profound predicament. Nominally allied with and dependent on Damascus and Tehran against Baghdad, it, on the other hand, was not keen on siding with its arch-enemy, the KDP against the KDP-I, who it still hoped to woo into a wider, more pan-Kurdish platform. In this decisive stage, Talabani, who had been encouraged in this move by KDP-I leader Ghassemlou, displayed shrewd brinkmanship by staking the fate of his party on one card: he accepted the overtures of Saddam Hussein for negotiations that, with Saddam Hussein driven into a corner, Talabani hoped could yield an even more generous autonomy statute than Mulla Mustafa Barzani's 1970 'March Manifesto' and cement his leadership of all Iraqi Kurds. In the spring of 1983, the PUK sided with the KDP-I against Iran, which in turn joined forces with the KDP in attacks on the PUK (Entessar 1992; Stansfield 2003a; McDowall 2007), and in December of the same year the PUK officially entered negotiations with the regime of Saddam Hussein. In a 2000 interview with PBS's *Frontline*, Talabani recalls that Saddam Hussein not only praised him for his patriotism in not siding with the Iranian 'invaders' but acknowledged that Talabani's effort should be all the more honoured and rewarded since he negotiated from a position of weakness. According to Talabani, he said, ' "Jalal, I will give you something, some Kurdish demand that will raise you not only in the eyes of Iraqi Kurds but with Iranian Kurds and Turkish Kurds" '.[24]

Yet for the PUK, Talabani's brinkmanship backfired dramatically. Not only did other Iraqi Kurdish groups such as the ICP refuse to heed his call for rapprochement with Baghdad, the negotiations opened rifts within his own party; the picture of Saddam Hussein and Talabani kissing cheeks remains until today one of the most iconic images of Iraqi Kurdish leaders betraying their own people,[25] while Saddam Hussein, who only played for time, dragged on the negotiations without committing to much, and the PUK was expelled from Syria in 1983 for its changing sides.[26] After more than a year of fruitless talks, and after having lost considerable public and inner-party support as well as major allies, most prominently the Assad regime, Talabani had to accept that he had been duped, and in 1986 he reluctantly reconciled with the KDP and the Iranian regime, accepted arms and provisions from the latter, and joined the fight against Saddam Hussein (Entessar 1992; Stansfield 2003a; McDowall 2007).

Yet, throughout 1983 and 1984, the prospect of a PUK–Baghdad alliance had posed a very clear and present danger to the KDP, an alliance with the potential to expel it from Iraqi Kurdistan for good and, if Talabani's negotiations for Iraqi Kurdish autonomy would have succeeded, would have doomed the KDP to a meagre existence at the margins of the Iraqi Kurdish ethno-nationalist discourse. McDowall, for example, states when discussing an April 1983 PUK attack on the KDP and ICP, 'in some circles the PUK was suspected of working in tandem with Baghdad, and possibly even Ankara' (McDowall 2007: 347). Given the dimension of this threat looming on the horizon during the crucial months of mid-1983, it seems conceivable that the KDP was eager to augment its military capacities by opening its territory to organizations that could be used for fending off an all-out attack by the PUK and the Iraqi army. It further seems logical that the PKK, whose ranks by then had grown substantially, was seen as having the potential to come to the KDP's assistance in times of need. A KDP–PKK alliance was therefore in the best strategic interest of the KDP, and the vital threat of a PUK alliance with Baghdad might have proven enough for the KDP to temporarily put aside their ideological differences with the PKK; likewise, the prospect of sanctuary in Iraqi Kurdistan and direct access to the designated theatre of operations on the eve of Abdullah Öcalan's intended launch of his military campaign surely would have outweighed his reservations to side with the, as he saw it, 'primitive', 'defeatist' and 'bourgeois' KDP. To identify the KDP–PUK antagonism and the shifting regional alliances during the early stages of the Iran–Iraq War as the driving force behind the KDP–PKK accord may gain even more plausibility when considering the fact that KDP and PKK shared the same external supporters. While the PUK's relations with the Assad regime deteriorated all through 1983 until it was formally expelled from Damascus at the end of the year, with the onset of the Iran–Iraq War, the KDP found itself on the same side as the regimes in Tehran and Damascus; likewise, the PKK's collaboration with the Khomeini regime can be documented for as early as mid-1979, when Adel Murad was approached in Beirut by Iranian agents on Öcalan's behalf, and had intensified since then (Olson 1998, 2001, 2004).[27] One could therefore hypothesize that KDP and PKK were encouraged to mend their differences by the nationalizing states backing them and that, at least to some extent, the KDP–PKK alliance was concocted in Tehran and Damascus. While naturally it has proved difficult to provide a smoking gun substantiating this rational for the KDP's behaviour, it is an interpretation that leading analysts of Kurdish ethno-nationalism I interviewed deem 'absolutely plausible'.[28] In sum then, it therefore seems that when analysing the relations between the PKK and the Iraqi Kurdish ethno-nationalist parties and the matrix of identities and interests that constitutes these relations, for this particular episode and for the timeframe under consideration (the years 1983/1984), materialist/strategic interests appear to outweigh ideational factors in determining both parties' decision making.

If Talabani's flirtation with Saddam Hussein did not pay off for the PUK, neither did Barzani's alliance with the PKK for the KDP. Turkey retaliated against the August 1984 PKK offensive with a vengeance. On 15 October 1984

Ankara and Baghdad signed a security protocol that allowed Turkish troops to penetrate Iraqi territory up to five kilometres in hot pursuit of PKK fighters, and in the following years launched several air raids on alleged PKK camps in Iraqi Kurdistan, the most severe occurred on 15 August 1986, killing 200, among them many Iraqi Kurdish civilians and KDP *peshmerga* (Imset 1992). By this time, the KDP had realized that instead of an ally – the PKK did no such thing as to join forces with the KDP against the PUK – they had incurred Turkey's wrath, resulting in heavy casualties in repeated indiscriminate Turkish air raids. Since 1984, the KDP had tried to persuade the PKK to abstain from operations that could provoke Turkish air raids, but the PKK proved undiscerning. Selahettin Çelik, who attended one of these meetings with the KDP in 1984 in Iran, recalled, 'we listened to Idris Barzani, assured them of our good intentions, and then chose to ignore them'.[29] Consequently, after another heavy Turkish attack, in May 1987, the KDP, as per the requirements of the 'Principles of Solidarity', issued a formal warning to the PKK, before severing relations completely and declaring the accord null and void.[30] Little surprise then that once the KDP–PKK alliance was severed, Öcalan reverted to his usual rhetoric, denouncing the Barzanis as 'traitors of the Kurdish movement, enemies of the Kurdish people'.[31] By then, the PKK had entrenched itself in several camps in Iraqi Kurdistan under its exclusive control, and there was precious little the KDP could do about it. The PKK had come to Iraqi Kurdistan to stay and still does so after 30 years.

Notes

1 Interview with Adel Murad, Erbil, Iraqi Kurdistan, 3 September 2010. The fact that the contact between Öcalan and Murad was facilitated by Iranian intelligence indicates that already a few months after the Iranian revolution Öcalan's PKK must have enjoyed good rapport with the new regime. On Iran's ambivalent relations with Turkey and how Tehran – whether under the Shah or under Khomeini – has often used Kurdish groups to destabilize its neighbour, see Olson (1998, 2004).

2 Interview Murad, op. cit.

3 Interview Murad, op. cit.

4 'Syria had occupied the Lebanese Bekaa Valley in 1976 to protect its own border', and as part of its wider intervention in the Lebanese Civil War (1975–1990), 'and Syrian heavy artillery ringed the nearby hills' (Marcus 2007a: 56).

5 In exchange for armed training and receiving clothing and other supplies, the PKK fighters committed to defending the camps in case of an Israeli raid (Marcus 2007a: 56).

6 Interview Çelik, op cit.

7 Quoted in Marcus (2007a: 58).

8 On the risk of the PKK becoming a proxy in Syria's regional power plays, Öcalan remarked in 1983, 'of course I know this, but I need time. I know they want to use me, but I will use them as well', quoted in Marcus (2007a: 74). According to Marcus the younger brother of Hafez al-Assad, Cemil, took a special interest in the PKK and visited its Helwe Camp in 1982.

9 Quoted in Scheller (2013: 101).

10 Interview with Sarkho Mahmoud, Sulimaniyah, Iraqi Kurdistan, 1 June 2010. At the time of the interview Mahmoud was no longer affiliated with the PUK but had become an official with *Gorran* who had split from the PUK the previous year.

11 While it can be considered established that the PKK also received support from Libya (Marcus 2007a; Eccarius-Kelly 2011), since this dimension would go beyond the scope of this study, I did not further investigate this claim.

12 Interview Sheikhmous, op cit.

13 Interview Murad, op cit.

14 There were multiple contributing factors, including a feeling of national solidarity, getting away from the social control of the elders, for women, freedom from the patriarchy, individual interests (access to material and symbolic resources), and the attraction of a movement advocating armed struggle as opposed to the Syrian Kurdish parties which were considered 'too moderate'.

(Tejel 2011: 135)

15 Even in its naming the HRK deliberately emulated Vo Nguyen Giap's first guerrilla, the Vietnam Freedom Unit (Çelik 2002).

16 Quoted in Imset (1992: 183) and Gunter (1996: 50–51).

17 Massoud Barzani in an interview with Turkish journalist Rafet Balli in 1993, quoted in Marcus (2007a: 70).

18 Quoted in Marcus (2007a: 34) and McDowall (2007: 422).

19 Quoted in Tahiri (2007: 2002).

20 Lieutenant General Kaya Yazgan, in charge of the Seventh Army Corps in southeast Anatolia in 1983, admitted:

It was an unexpected event … Up until then we didn't know Apo. His name was known, but he was not someone who was focused on. And besides, PKK militants were seen more as bandits … The politicians in Ankara did not believe that this event was the first sign of a big start.

(Quoted in Marcus 2007a: 83)

21 By March 2000, the number of village guards in southeast Anatolia had risen to about 70,000. On the phenomenon of village guards and the impact their creation is having on Kurdish society, most dramatically the salience of organized everyday violence and symbiosis with organized crime, see van Bruinessen (1996), Balta (2004), Jacoby (2005), and Jongerden (2007).

22 Interview with Fuad Hussein, Erbil, Iraqi Kurdistan, 21 September 2010. When confronted with evidence, he retracted, qualifying that 'these were different times then'.

23 Saddam Hussein exerted bloody revenge on the Barzanis for their 'treason' of siding with Iran. Already in 1975 Saddam Hussein had resettled large numbers of the Barzani tribe by force to south Iraq and then to a camp outside Erbil. In 1982, the Iraqi army raided this camp and seized all males over the age of 13 to be paraded through the streets of Baghdad before summary execution. According to McDowall (2007) up to 8000 Barzani males perished during this display of Saddam Hussein's thirst for vengeance.

24 Quoted in PBS (2000).

25 'With the negotiations in 1983/4 [the PUK] lost its innocence, we lost our moral and ideological superiority, we lost the trust of the people. After 1983/4 we no longer were what we used to be,' Omar Sheikhmous reminisced. Interview Sheikhmous, op cit.

26 Interview Mahmoud, op cit.

27 According to Imset (1992) the alliance with the KDP also allowed the PKK to set up a camp on Iranian territory in the Urumiye region.

28 Interviews with Henri Barkey, Bethlehem, USA, 1 February 2011; Robert Olson, Lexington, USA, 9 March 2011; Michael Gunter, Cookeville, USA, 11 March 2011; Doğu Ergil, Istanbul, Turkey, 25 October 2011; Abbas Vali, Istanbul, Turkey, 8 May 2012.

29 Interview Çelik, op cit.

30 The full text of the KDP communiqué detailing their many grievances with the PKK is quoted in Imset (1992: 186).

31 Quoted in Imset (1992: 187).

7   Iraqi Kurdistan and the PKK in the 1990s

The Iraqi Kurdish 'de facto state'

In the final stages of the Iran–Iraq War the regime of Saddam Hussein perpetrated a genocidal ethnic cleansing campaign against the Kurdish minority in northern Iraq. The *Anfal* campaign, named after the eighth sura of the Qu'ran on the spoils of war, lasted from March 1987, when Ali Hassan al-Majid was appointed Saddam Hussein's viceroy in northern Iraq, until 1989, and comprised targeted ground and aerial bombing of villages with chemical agents, the systematic destruction of villages, mass deportations, and the operation of concentration camps (Human Rights Watch 1993, 1995; Randal 1998; Hiltermann 2007; Stansfield 2007a; Tripp 2007; Marr 2011). According to Human Rights Watch (1993, 1995), during the campaign the Iraqi authorities and their local willing executioners killed 50,000 to 100,000 civilians, destroyed 4500 villages in Iraqi Kurdistan, attacked 250 villages with chemical weapons, and removed tens of thousands from their homesteads by force.[1] A distinct component of the *Anfal* campaign was a programme of 'Arabization' that expelled Kurdish inhabitants from northern villages and cities – most prominently oil rich Kirkuk – and replaced them with Arab settlers from southern and central Iraq, a factor that significantly contributes to the current ethnic tensions in the affected areas (*The Economist* 2007; Natali 2008; Anderson & Stansfield 2009). The tragic climax of the *Anfal* campaign was the attack on the town of Halabja on 16 March 1988 with mustard gas, VX and sarin, in which 5000 civilians, mostly women and children were killed.

To dispel any notions of ethnic group solidarity once and for all, the PKK watched the juggernaut of Saddam Hussein's genocidal ethnic cleansing campaign from the sidelines; what is more, it directly profited from it. With the KDP, PUK and any non-organized Iraqi Kurdish resistance broken, with their armed forces ground down to a nub, and with their leaders' backs to the wall, desperately holding on to the last vestiges of territory or being pushed across the borders into Iran, the PKK reigned supreme in Iraqi Kurdistan. By 1988/1989, with the PKK able to field several thousand fighters (Gunter 1990; Gürbey 1996), no one, not even the mighty Iraqi army, could contest the PKK for its absolute control over the Iraqi–Turkish border region. In fact, the Iraqi army had no intention of doing so; on the contrary, the demise of KDP and PUK, the

PKK's absolute control over the border region, and the formidable challenge it posed to the Turkish state, had raised Baghdad's interest in Abdullah Öcalan's group and encouraged it to intensify its attempts at establishing lines of communication with the PKK. This PKK–Baghdad link became public when, in 1991 during the chaos of the Iraqi Kurdish uprising in the wake of the Gulf War, the PUK came upon a series of top secret Iraqi documents that it passed to the *Turkish Daily News* and the London-based Arabic daily *Al Hayat*. The *Turkish Daily News'* article from 12 August 1992, detailed how a PKK official, identified as a certain Baran Ahmed, and supposed to be in charge of PKK operations in the Hakkari, Semdinli and Cukurca regions and in direct contact with Abdullah Öcalan, met with members of the Iraqi *mukhabarat* and offered his party's cooperation in intelligence gathering. According to the documents, marked top secret, Ahmed offered intelligence on American troop levels at Incirlik Air Force Base near Adana and emphasized his party's readiness to fight the KDP.

> In exchange [for] this information and readiness for cooperation Baran reportedly asked ... for all Iraqi troops in the region to ignore the presence of the PKK and for Baghdad to provide [them] with printing facilities and weapons, i.e. BCKs, RPGs, and 60 mm mortars. He even said that the PKK was willing to pay for these supplies.[2]

These documents gave substantial weight to what the Iraqi Kurdish parties had suspected of the PKK for several years: that the PKK, in exchange for equipment, weaponry and the Iraqi army turning a blind eye to the their activities, provided the very regime that had just perpetrated genocide against the Iraqi Kurds with intelligence on them, indeed, even offered to fight them for Baghdad.

This picture corresponds with the information I gathered in interviews with PKK dissidents. They all indicate that between 1985/1986, when relations with Barzani's KDP deteriorated, and until the 'Principles of Solidarity' accord was formally renounced in May 1987, relations between the PKK and Iraqi army and intelligence services subsisted on a low, informal level, with neither side committing to anything substantial and, from 1987/1988 on, gradually intensified.[3] However, both the sequence of events as well as the nature of the information the PKK provided to Iraqi intelligence are crucial here. Until 1990, in the run up to Iraq's invasion of Kuwait, Saddam Hussein would have had little interest in intelligence on US air force deployment in Turkey and, while intelligence on Turkey was always welcome, Iraqi intelligence was primarily interested in gathering information on the KDP – an understandable prioritization since it was fighting the KDP (and PUK since 1986) in the life and death struggle that was the Iran–Iraq War. The implications of this chronology and the fact that it is conceivable that the PKK provided Iraqi security services with intelligence on the KDP in 1987/1988, however, are nowhere mentioned in the literature and are too woeful even for PKK dissidents to contemplate, which is why they all remained reticent about details in my interviews with them. For it would mean appreciating that the organization they belonged to, believed in, fought and sacrificed so much for, through sharing intelligence, assisted the regime of Saddam Hussein in perpetrating genocide against other Kurds, that this intelligence was used by Iraqi security services and armed forces in executing the *al Anfal* campaign. The mere possibility and plausibility alone of the PKK providing Iraqi security services with intelligence on the KDP during the genocidal *al Anfal* campaign – or at the very least to directly benefit from it – reveals any attempts by IR scholars to label the PKK sanctuary in Iraqi Kurdistan an ethnic alliance and to belabour ethnic group solidarity between PKK and KDP/PUK as the main explanatory factor for interpreting the relations between the PKK and the Iraqi Kurdish parties as factually certifiably untenable.

Yet, in 1991, out of the debris of utter defeat and the suffering and grief of genocide, like a phoenix from the ashes, the Kurds in Iraq emerged almost born again, and, virtually overnight, came to determine their own fate by crafting the most independent political entity in Kurdish history. The chain of events leading up to 1991 was triggered by Saddam Hussein's occupation of Kuwait in the previous year, and his transmogrification from courted ally of the international community against revolutionary Iran, to pariah against whom an international military alliance was forged. To be sure, though, the beginning of the year did not augur any such auspicious developments for the Iraqi Kurds. On the contrary, the year started with them suffering another devastating defeat.

On 15 February 1991, in the midst of the Allied air campaign and about a week before the launch of the ground campaign to liberate Kuwait, US President George H. W. Bush addressed the Iraqi people via *Voice of America*:

> There is another way for the bloodshed to stop: and that is for the Iraqi military and the Iraqi people to take matters into their own hands and force Saddam Hussein, the dictator, to step aside and then comply with the United Nations' resolution and rejoin the family of peace-loving nations.[4]

Similar appeals were made by US political and military leaders as well as US-funded radio stations in Saudi Arabia and Egypt all through February, and yet when the Iraqi people heeded this call and took matters into their own hands, it came as a complete and inconvenient surprise to the Gulf War Allies (Gunter 1992, 2002, 2011b; Jabar 1992; Graham-Brown 1999; Stansfield 2007a; Tripp 2007; Charountaki 2010; Shareef 2010; Marr 2011). Equally surprised were the leaders of KDP and PUK, Massoud Barzani and Jalal Talabani, who since 1988 had joined forces in the *Iraqi Kurdistan Front* (IKF), in their exile in Iran, when, beginning with Raniyah on 4 March, the Kurdish population in Iraq rose in a spontaneous and uncoordinated mass uprising, called *Repareen*, that encompassed every strata of Kurdish society, even the detested *jash* – literally 'donkey', a derogatory term for Iraqi Kurds who had been cooperating with the Saddam Hussein regime (Gunter 1992; Human Rights Watch 1992; Jabar 1992; Laizer 1996; Randal 1998; Stansfield 2003a; Romano 2006; Asadi 2007; McDowall 2007). Within days the *peshmerga* of the IKF had joined the public and liberated every city in northern Iraq except Kirkuk and Mosul, and Talabani was dreaming of marching on Baghdad (Jabar 1992). Yet, with the uprising failing to spread to the Sunni Arab centre of Iraq and international aid not materializing,[5] Saddam Hussein was at liberty to launch a counter-offensive by the end of the month, which crushed the Kurdish resistance, similar to the failed Shi'a revolt in the south, within days (Gunter 1992; Human Rights Watch 1992; Jabar 1992; Laizer 1996; Randal 1998; Stansfield 2003a; Romano 2006; Asadi 2007; McDowall 2007; Tahiri 2007). The onslaught of Saddam Hussein's troops on Kurdish civilians and the refusal of the US administration to impose restraints on his indiscriminate attacks triggered a wave of up to 2.5 million refugees heading for the Turkish and Iranian borders (Gunter 1992, Laizer 1996; Randal 1998; Stansfield 2003a).

This turn of events came as a shock to Turkey. Finding himself between a rock and a hard place, either having CNN broadcast the Turkish military refusing a million civilian refugees entry into Turkey and safety – thus leaving them at Saddam Hussein's mercy or freezing to death in wintry mountains – or adding hundreds of thousands of Kurds to Turkey's south-eastern Anatolia, already on the brink of its own Kurdish mass uprising, and thus rendering the security situation there completely uncontrollable, President Turgut Özal personally intervened with President Bush and British PM John Major for a quick solution to the humanitarian crisis (Kirişçi 1993, 1996; Aydin 1998; 2002; Hale 2003, 2007; Robins 2003a; Natali 2005; Yildiz 2007; Gunter 2011a). The significance of this development and sea change in Turkish foreign policy cannot be underestimated. For more than four decades Turkey had cooperated with whatever regime held power in Iraq in suppressing the struggle for self-determination and political autonomy of its Kurdish population, as well as all too often indirectly collaborated in Baghdad's military offensives and pogroms against them (Lundgren 2007). Now, in the aftermath of the Gulf War and the failed Iraqi Kurdish uprisings, Turkey, *nolens volens* and almost overnight, found itself occupying the unusual role of senior champion of the fate of Iraq's Kurds in the international arena. What is more, Turkey, the hitherto implacable opponent to any form of Kurdish political autonomy in the entire region, against its will but pushed into this role by rapidly developing events, was to play midwife to the emergence and survival of the most independent political entity in Kurdish history.

Urged by Turkey, France and Iran, and with the US abandoning its reservations due to Turkish-French-British pressure, on 5 April, the UN passed Security Council Resolution 688 that demanded from Iraq an end to the violent repression of its people and assistance for the international humanitarian organizations in gaining access to the refugee population, as well as for Iraq to cooperate in all international efforts to alleviate the suffering of the affected population. It is worth noting that Resolution 688 made no mention of the no-fly zones the Gulf War Allies established north of the 36th and south of the 32nd parallel, and that the military aspects of what became known as 'Operation Provide Comfort' – or 'Operation Safe Haven' (its British name) – were based on the Allies' liberal interpretation of the wording in the resolution (Frelick 1992; Graham-Brown 1999; Di Prizio 2002; Romano 2004; Rudd 2004). Provide Comfort not only prevented Saddam Hussein from capitalizing on his victory by dealing the Iraqi

Kurds the final blow, but over a few months it also forced him to recognize the futility of seeking a military solution (Gunter 1992; Laizer 1996; Randal 1998; Graham-Brown 1999; Stansfield 2003a). At the eleventh hour, the Iraqi Kurds had been rescued by the most unlikely and most self-serving saviour, Turkey.[6] I concur with Frelick (1992) and Kirişçi (1996) that Provide Comfort served for the main part the security interests of states, and that the needs of the Iraqi Kurdish refugees were of secondary importance; for if Turkey had not perceived this onrush of refugees as a security threat – and since Turkey, with the world's attention centred on Iraq after the Gulf War, could not afford to cold-shoulder the refugees as it had done just three years earlier during the *Anfal* campaign – it is highly questionable whether the international community would have come to the rescue of the Iraqi Kurds. What is more, as will be discussed in the next section, visionary President Turgut Özal had his own ideas for a rapprochement between Turkey and the Iraqi Kurdish parties, a vision for which his intervention during the 1991 refugee crisis was just a first step.

When, in October 1991, the negotiations between the Iraqi Kurdish parties and Baghdad on an autonomy statute broke down without result, Saddam Hussein, demonstrably a man of questionable strategic acumen, took a most unusual step. In an attempt to starve the Iraqi Kurds into submission he imposed an economic and administrative embargo on northern Iraq by withdrawing the entire bureaucratic apparatus of the state – from policemen to tax collectors, from civil servants to teachers – freezing the salaries of Kurdish employees and stripping anybody who sought to enter northern Iraq of fuel and food supplies, thus essentially forcing the Iraqi Kurdish population to subsist under a double embargo, an external one imposed by the UN on the whole of Iraq and an internal one levied by Saddam Hussein on the Iraqi Kurds (Gunter 1992; Laizer 1996; Randal 1998; Graham-Brown 1999; Stansfield 2003a, 2007a; Natali 2005; Romano 2006; Asadi 2007; McDowall 2007; Tahiri 2007). Saddam Hussein calculated that the harsh conditions of winter combined with the burden of more than a million refugees and IDPs would over-exert the international community's assistance and the IKF's political and organizational capabilities, forcing the latter to accept an autonomy agreement largely on his terms. This, however, proved a strategic miscalculation second only to his invasion of Kuwait the previous year. He withdrew his forces to a line running from the Syrian border to south of Dohuk and Erbil, west of Chamchamal, and southwest of Kifri, thus abandoning considerably more territory than designated either as the safe haven imposed by the international community or the no-fly zone north of the 36th parallel – thus voluntarily relinquishing control over the area that roughly corresponds with today's Kurdistan Region of Iraq. What is more important, his blockade created a political vacuum in northern Iraq, a new political space the Iraqi Kurds, for the first time in history, could potentially frame and organize on their own, without consultation or confrontation with the central government in Baghdad.

In this, though, the Iraqi Kurdish parties knew they would have to tread with extreme caution since any step towards wider self-determination would be interpreted by their neighbours and the West as an attempt at independence, in the worst case leading them to reconsider their protection of the safe haven and no fly zone as well as their economic and developmental assistance, on both of which the IKF and the Iraqi Kurdish population depended wholesale (Gunter 1992; Laizer 1996; Graham-Brown 1999; Stansfield 2003a; Romano 2004; Asadi 2007; McDowall 2007). Barzani and Talabani therefore must not have taken lightly the step to hold general elections for a legislative assembly in order to provide the people with a democratically elected administration that could fill the void Saddam Hussein had left behind, and they were routinely warned against 'go[ing] down the road of elections' by US military on the ground and officials in Washington.[7] Despite the risk of losing their precious international support, KDP and PUK proposed holding elections for a legislative assembly for 3 April. After a month's delay the elections were actually held on 19 May 1992, resulting in 45 per cent for the KDP and 43.6 per cent for the PUK in the 105-seat parliament, and on 4 June the *Kurdistan Regional Government* (KRG) was formed, run jointly by KDP and PUK (Gunter 1992; Laizer 1996; Graham-Brown 1999; Stansfield 2003a, 2005, 2007a; Romano 2006; Asadi 2007; McDowall 2007).[8]

The election of 19 May, 'for all the haste in its preparation and the occasional cases of fraud and malpractice [was] an historic moment', not only because 'it demonstrated almost uniquely outside Israel and Turkey, the ability of a Middle Eastern electorate to conduct a peaceful, multi-party election' (McDowall 2007: 381), but also, and more importantly, it can be considered the birth hour of Kurdish self-rule in Iraq as well as, in the political science literature, the Kurdish de facto state in Iraq (Stansfield 2003a; Anderson & Stansfield 2005; Gunter 1993, 2007, 2011c; Romano 2004, 2006; Chorev 2007; Natali 2010; Wolff 2010; Caspersen 2012; Caspersen & Stansfield 2011; Voller 2014). It has to be emphasized, though, that this Kurdish self-rule in Iraq came about entirely by accident, and can be considered the singular, outstanding aberration of historic patterns of the regional and international powers dealing with Iraq's Kurdish minority, a true *annus mirabils* that would have been impossible without the profound sea change in the political dynamics of the Middle East generated by the Gulf War. As in Kosovo, the international community had created a so-called de facto state by accident, rendered the autonomy of the Iraqi Kurdish people possible through their intervention but without plan or intent. In actual fact, in light of the historic trajectories outlined in Part II, the decisions by the Turkish state, however it saw its hands forced by events beyond its control, to mutate almost overnight, from an opponent to a backer of the Iraqi Kurds in the international arena, and Saddam Hussein's choice to leave them to their own devices, can be understood as the most momentous event in Iraqi Kurdish history since the implosion of the Ottoman Empire. This event, which unexpectedly resulted in Iraqi Kurdish self-rule, however, came at the price of complete dependence of the Iraqi Kurdish parties and the fate of their political entity on external actors, most prominently Turkey – a dependence that has shaped Iraqi Kurdish politics ever since, in particular the KDP and PUK's dealing with the PKK.[9]

The Kurdish wars of the 1990s

If 1991 was the *annus mirabils* for the Iraqi Kurds, then 1990 was the year in which the PKK reached the zenith of its power. To be sure, the military confrontation with the mighty Turkish state, combined with its strategy of forced depopulation of hundreds of villages in south-eastern Anatolia and the paramilitary system of village guards, had repeatedly dealt the insurgency heavy blows (Imset 1992; Gürbey 1996; Gunter 1997; Kirişçi & Winrow 1997; Barkey & Fuller 1998; White 2000; Çelik 2002; Özcan 2006; Marcus 2007a; Eccarius-Kelly 2011; Gunes 2011). On the diplomatic front, Turkey's pressure on Syria to curb its support for the PKK finally appeared to bear fruit when, in 1987, both countries signed a security protocol, after which the PKK was no longer able to conduct raids into Turkey from Syrian territory (Imset 1992; Olson 1997, 2000, 2001).[10] This, however, was compensated for by the strategic position the PKK had gained in Iraqi Kurdistan, where, after the accord with the KDP had broken down, they had struck a similar deal with the PUK in May 1988 (Imset 1992; Gunter 1996, 1997; Ibrahim 2000; Çelik 2002; Marcus 2007a). As has been shown, though, by 1988 the PKK enjoyed unrestrained control over the Iraqi–Turkish border and was no longer in need of collaboration with the Iraqi Kurdish ethno-nationalist parties. What is more, the dynamics of the armed struggle in Turkey itself changed. On 13 March 1990, the PKK had conducted a raid in the Mardin-Savur region in which 13 guerrillas died. The funeral procession of one of these fallen insurgents turned into an outpouring of public anger, which law enforcement tried to muzzle by force, lighting a spark that triggered a wave of public demonstrations in the tens of thousands throughout the entire region (Imset 1992; Gürbey 1996; Gunter 1997; Çelik 2002; Özcan 2006; Marcus 2007a; Eccarius-Kelly 2011; Gunes 2011). This people's uprising, often called the Kurdish Intifada or *Serhildan*, fundamentally altered the dynamics and nature of the guerrilla campaign in Turkey, propelling the PKK insurgency, to their great surprise and without taking an active role in this spontaneous development,[11] from the first stage of guerrilla warfare, discussed earlier, to what appeared to be the brink of the third and final stage: a general counter-offensive as part of a mass-scale public uprising against the authorities. With the *Serhildan*,

> the guerrilla fight had taken on a mass character. Urban centres became a theatre of daily guerrilla operations. The numbers of guerrilla fighters multiplied … there was no part of Kurdistan, in which the guerrilla could not operate and carry out raids.
>
> (Çelik 2002: 128)[12]

For a brief moment, the PKK appeared to have brought the mighty Turkish state to its knees.

In the end, though, the PKK failed to capitalize on the potential of the *Serhildan*:

In fact the PKK had little capability to guide or move these demonstrations forward ... One reason was the difficulty of operating in an urban environment ... [where the PKK yet] had not placed special emphasis on establishing themselves ... [another is that] it seems logical to assume that PKK commanders, who saw themselves as leading the Kurdish fight, also were concerned that these protests might somehow draw attention and people away from the guerrillas' struggle.

(Marcus 2007a: 143)[13]

Whatever the PKK's reasons for not sufficiently making strategic use of the public uprising that erupted in 1990 and continued until 1994 with noticeable sparks in demonstrations during the annual *Newroz* celebrations, the events in the aftermath of the Gulf War that fundamentally reconfigured the power constellations of the Middle East proved as much a watershed moment for the PKK as for the Iraqi Kurdish ethno-nationalist parties. The most immediate and, for the PKK, most dramatic change wrought by the events in March/April 1991 was that the Iraqi Kurds had become completely dependent on the PKK's opponent, Turkey. Not only did the Turkish parliament have to approve the use of Incirlik AFB by Allied fighter jets for patrolling the no fly zone in Northern Iraq as part of Operation Provide Comfort (Kirişçi 1993, 1996; Barkey 1996; Aydın 1998, 2002; Graham-Brown 1999; Di Prizio 2002; Rudd 2004; Hale 2003, 2007), but also virtually all international development aid for the destitute Iraqi Kurdish population had to pass through Turkey. Hoshyar Zebari, a KDP foreign policy spokesman and future Foreign Minister of Iraq, summed up the Iraqi Kurds' plenary dependence on Turkey aptly:

Turkey is our lifeline to the West and the whole world in our fight against Saddam Hussein. We are able to secure allied air protection and international aid through Turkey. If [Operation Provide Comfort] is withdrawn, Saddam's units will again reign in this region and we will lose everything.[14]

As a result of this novel and yet absolute dependence on Turkey, KDP/PUK could ill afford any move that might antagonize their benefactor – all the more since this benefactor had already developed a queasy feeling about Iraqi Kurdish self-rule increasing by the day, a development for which it saw itself as, at least indirectly and partially, to blame. The Iraqi Kurdish ethno-nationalist parties therefore had to drastically reconsider their relations with the PKK since, they correctly assumed, Turkey would not tolerate backing an incipient Iraqi Kurdish political entity whose emergence was anyway anathema to Ankara, to continue its support or indulgence of the PKK on its territory. These strategic considerations were given further impetus by the unprecedented attempt of Turkish President Turgut Özal in reaching out and establishing quasi-formal relations with KDP/PUK in the spring of 1991.

Much speculation has been devoted to whether Özal, a true visionary ahead of his time, merely reacted to rapidly unfolding events or pursued a grand vision that, in addition to drawing on the good offices of the Iraqi Kurdish parties to open a channel to the PKK, even allegedly intended to bring Iraqi Kurdistan, the former *vilayet* of Mosul, back under Turkey's orbit (Robins 2003a; Lundgren 2007); according to Robins,

> Özal argued, Turkey should bring the impoverished northern Iraqi economy into its orbit, as a way of maximizing Turkish influence in the territory. Özal believed that for as little as $30–40 million Turkey could create a relationship of dependence.
>
> (Robins 2003a: 321)

While discussing these speculations more substantially would go beyond the scope of this study, suffice it to say here that in the talks detailed below Jalal Talabani allegedly repeatedly offered Iraqi Kurdish collaboration if Turkey wished to annex Iraqi Kurdistan in the aftermath of the Gulf War (Gunter 1996, 1997, 2011a; Randal 1998) – an offer that, to put it mildly, would put his understanding of national self-determination at odds with the modernist and explanatory IR definition discussed earlier – and that today, as will be detailed subsequently, this relationship of dependence appears widely accomplished.

Based on interviews with the actors involved, what appears safer to establish is that as early as 20 February 1991 – four days before Coalition forces entered Kuwait – the public relations officer of President Özal, Kaya Toperi, called the Kurdish journalist Qamran Qaradaghi of *Al Hayat* at his office in London and asked him to communicate to Jalal Talabani that President Özal wished for him to come to Ankara for a meeting. Qaradaghi, who enjoyed close personal relations with Talabani and later became his press secretary, recalls that during an interview a week earlier, it had been Özal who had done most of the questioning, showing great interest in Qaradaghi's opinion on the rapidly developing situation in Iraq, the political positions of KDP and PUK as well as their relations with the PKK, to which Qaradaghi replied, 'Mr. President, if you are that interested in all these issues, may I suggest, why not reach out and establish direct contact with Jalal Talabani and Massoud Barzani. I am certain they would welcome such a move.'[15] A week later Qaradaghi had Özal's answer, on which he acted quickly. On 8 March Talabani and Mosheen Dezayee, Massoud Barzani's representative, 'arrived together in Istanbul on a flight from Damascus and were immediately flown to Ankara's military airport by personnel of the National Intelligence Organisation (MIT)' (Gunter 2011a: 90) to meet with the under-secretary in the Foreign Ministry, Ambassador Tugay Özceri, on Özal's behalf. The fact that Talabani left Iraqi Kurdistan in the midst of the *Repareen* illustrates the importance he accorded to this meeting, a sensational diplomatic breakthrough he appraised as, 'a new page … turned in relations between Turkey and the Kurds of Iraq'.[16] Further,

> he stated that he had assured the Turkish officials that the Kurds did not want to establish an independent state in northern Iraq and then explained

that, 'Turkey has for years been putting forth effective and significant obstacles to the struggle we have been waging in northern Iraq. We wanted to explain our goals and eliminate Turkey's opposition ... We were received with understanding'.[17]

If, for Jalal Talabani, this first official engagement at the highest level of Turkish officials with representatives of the Iraqi Kurds – followed by a second meeting two weeks later when the *Repareen* was about to collapse (Gunter 2011a: 90) – was the diplomatic sea change he portrayed it to be, it also lets President Özal's initiative on behalf of the Iraqi Kurds and his role in bringing about Operation Provide Comfort appear in a different light, as part of a greater strategy not only to save the Iraqi Kurds from Saddam Hussein but also to ensure their dependence on and solid establishment in Turkey's geo-strategic orbit (Robins 2003a). To some extent, one may say that with these meetings, the establishment of the safe haven and Operation Provide Comfort on Özal's initiative, together with the fact that all international aid for Iraqi Kurdistan passed through Turkey and that the Turkish parliament had to renew, every six months, permission for Operation Provide Comfort allied fighter jets to operate from Incirlik AFB, the first steps towards an Iraqi Kurdish client relationship with Turkey were laid – a client relationship that closely resembles the economic and strategic dependence President Özal allegedly had in mind for them.

For Özal's representative, though, the main issue of interest in these first talks was the PKK and what role the Iraqi Kurdish parties could play as intermediaries in the process of national reconciliation Özal planned, and in which he, overall, acted independent of and in opposition to the Turkish politico-military establishment (Pope & Pope 1997; Lundgren 2007; Marcus 2007a; Gunter 2011a). Özal, an economist by trade who had recently begun to refer in public to his own Kurdish ancestry, perceived the so-called 'Kurdish Question' in Turkey as mainly a problem of cultural divides and structural underdevelopment, which he thought could not be addressed militarily but by massive official investment programmes in southeast Anatolia and by granting the Kurdish population of Turkey certain cultural rights (Gunter 1997, 2011a; Pope & Pope 1997; Barkey & Fuller 1998; White 2000; Lundgren 2007; Marcus 2007a). In recognition of the potential of the *Serhildan* to widen into a mass scale uprising, for a brief window of opportunity Turkish officials were willing to experiment with gestures of opening the political space for dialogue. In an unprecedented move, on 7 June 1990, Turkish authorities had permitted the formation of the first explicit Kurdish political party, *Halkın Emek Partisi* (HEP or People's Labour Party) after seven Kurdish MPs had split from the SHP,[18] and President Özal called for a lift on the ban on the use of Kurdish language in public everyday but not official discourse (Gunter 1997, 2011a; Pope & Pope 1997; Barkey & Fuller 1998). Özal intended to now expand on this window of opportunity by reaching out to Abdullah Öcalan, who likewise had shown signs of distancing himself from his maximal demand for Kurdish independence. After lauding Özal for his initiative – 'To tell the truth, I did not expect [Özal] to display such courage ... In this context, he shamed us ... He has taken an important step'[19] – Öcalan announced in an interview with AFP that the PKK 'might opt for a diplomatic-political solution', that he would consider holding 'conditional' negotiations with Turkish authorities, and 'the PKK no longer sought independence, just "free political expression" for Turkey's Kurds'.[20]

To broaden and expand on this opening Özal required an intermediary of renown and with direct access to Öcalan in Damascus. He found this intermediary in Jalal Talabani, who, conveniently, was also politically dependent on Turkey. The first personal meeting between Talabani and Özal took place in Ankara in June 1991, where the KDP/PUK were given permission to open liaison offices in Ankara and, to ease the Iraqi Kurdish leaders' travel restrictions, both Barzani and Talabani were given Turkish diplomatic passports[21] Thus, well equipped, Talabani assumed his role as mediator and repeatedly met Öcalan for talks in Damascus during October, and in November announced that the PKK was willing to declare a four-months ceasefire (Gunter 1996, 1997).[22] Such promising announcements turned out to be grossly premature, though. Not only were the talks between Talabani and Öcalan complicated by the Turkish military continuing its incursions into northern Iraq in pursuit of PKK fighters – Imset (1992) lists five major raids by the Turkish air force for the period between August and October alone, at the very time when Talabani was trying to get Öcalan to agree to and announce a ceasefire – but also by the fact that President Özal considered a unilateral PKK ceasefire as a first conciliatory step to pave the ground for political consultations, while Öcalan saw a ceasefire as his ultimate concession after Turkey met some of his demands. In sum, it has to be said, that 'Özal had many good intentions but no concrete plans whatsoever' on how to practically engage the PKK in talks and what specific issues such talks should cover.[23] Not only that, but Özal, after his rapprochement with the Iraqi Kurdish leaders had become public, increasingly acted in isolation from the politico-military establishment, the MIT, the media, and PM Demirel,[24] and it was questionable whether he could muster the political backing to implement any concessions made (Imset 1992; Gunter 1996, 1997; Pope & Pope 1997; Barkey & Fuller 1998).

What further exacerbated the situation was that, while Özal may have deemed Talabani the ideal intermediary, Öcalan saw him as merely a puppet of the Turkish state willing to do Ankara's bidding in exchange for protection and international backing of the emergent Iraqi Kurdish polity.

> Öcalan sarcastically declared that Talabani had written him from Ankara to 'lay down your arms unilaterally, accept a ceasefire, come to Ankara and sit at the table with obscure people, and be thankful and grateful for whatever you are given'.
>
> (Gunter 1996: 53)

Talabani's attempts at intimidating Öcalan into a more compromising stance led to the IKF issuing an ultimatum in February 1992 that 'if the PKK failed to cease activities against Turkey [from Iraqi Kurdish territory], it would be purged from the region',[25] which only further antagonized Öcalan. He went on to denounce, as had become routine by then, Barzani as a 'collaborator ... reactionary, feudal person, and a primitive nationalist', and accused him and Talabani of 'trying to stab the PKK in the back by cooperating with Turkey ... The first thing we must do is remove these leeches ... They espouse the views of the fascist Turks. These two leaders are now our enemies'.[26]

With Öcalan increasingly feeling cornered – on 25 December 1991 the Soviet Union had dissolved, putting a successful Marxist-Leninist world revolution in greater doubt than ever before, the Turkish military, as part of Operation Provide Comfort, had gained access to Iraqi Kurdistan, and a military alliance between KDP/PUK and Turkey appeared an ever-greater possibility –there was a storm brewing between the PKK and the Iraqi Kurdish parties. Öcalan must have felt as if his room to manoeuvre became more limited by the day, and the condition of the PKK camps, caught between the Turkish border and international troops operating in Iraqi Kurdistan together with the KDP/PUK *peshmerga*, more desperate.

> He must have felt like losing control of events, in Turkey and Southern Kurdistan. In Turkey we did not know how to react to the [mass protests], how to respond to the public sentiment, how to make use of it for our struggle, how to channel it. In Southern Kurdistan he feared losing the leadership in the Kurdish struggle [for self-determination] to Talabani and Barzani. He feared them joining forces with Turkey against the PKK.[27]

With the tide of international and regional events turning against him, Öcalan decided to take the bull by the horns and embark on a path of escalation. In an interview with the Turkish daily *Milliyet* on 26 March 1992, Öcalan announced the founding of a regional affiliate for Iraqi Kurdistan, the *Partiya Azadiya Kurdistan* (PAK or Kurdistan Liberation Party), designated to politically challenge KDP/PUK on their home turf (Gunter 1996, 1997, Çelik 2002). Although even Çelik admits that the PAK 'never exceeded its marginal existence' (Çelik 2002: 151), and PUK representatives, with the benefit of hindsight, have discounted the PKK's regional branch as a 'non-issue',[28] at the time the founding of PAK must have appeared to Talabani and Barzani as an intolerable provocation. Graver than that though were the ever-increasing small-scale military clashes between the PKK and Iraqi Kurdish *peshmerga*, mainly of the KDP. Those isolated clashes came to a head when, in Zakho on 29 June 1992, the KDP reportedly ordered the killing of the Sindi tribal leader Sadik Omer for joining PAK; in retaliation the PKK assassinated the local KDP commander in Dohuk, which again was answered by the KDP launching a full-scale offensive against the Sindi tribe and attempting to blockade the PKK camps at the Turkish border (Gunter 1996). On 24 July, Öcalan retaliated by 'successfully placing an embargo on trade between Turkey and northern Iraq' (Gunter 1996: 54) by shelling the Harbur border through which virtually all international aid and imports for Iraqi Kurdistan passed.

This PKK-imposed ban threatened to cut the Iraqi Kurds' economic lifeline, as local drivers, in fear of the consequences, stopped taking supplies to northern Iraq. Soon a shortage of foodstuffs and medicine resulted, and prices doubled and tripled. The PKK asserted that it would lift the trade ban only if Barzani would remove his blockade of the PKK camps.

(Gunter 1996: 54)

If the founding of PAK had been merely a political provocation, and the clashes with the Sindi tribe can still be understood as brawls at the tribal level, the PKK's embargo of the Harbur border posed an existential threat to the survival of Iraqi Kurdistan. 'The effects [of the PKK's] actions were felt immediately', Mohammed Tawfiq, then a PUK official in Dohuk near the border crossing, remembered,

every day less goods came from Turkey, there were shortages of food, of fuel, of medicine. Prices went up, people could no longer afford the most basic goods ... We were very vulnerable then, completely dependent on imports from Turkey and [international] aid. The PKK tried to exploit this, tried to turn our people against us, have them lose faith in our government ... less than a month after the first free government in Kurdistan was formed we had to fight for our survival.[29]

It was a fundamental challenge the KRG could not afford to leave unanswered, and Barzani and Talabani took up the gauntlet. Barzani declared:

Öcalan's men acted as if they were the authorities and started to control roads and collect taxes ... [they] threatened to expel the government and parliament from Erbil. They said they would hang all those 'who sold out the homeland' ... They even threatened to expel us from Dohuk and Suli-maniyah and started to form espionage, terrorism, and sabotage networks inside cities. It has unequivocally been proven that they are conspiring and planning to undermine the existing situation in Kurdistan and its experiment in democracy and national self-determination.[30]

On 30 September 1992, the war of words escalated to an actual armed confrontation with the IKF forces launching a major offensive against the PKK all through Iraqi Kurdistan, and on 26 October the Turkish army joined the fray (Gunter 1996, 1997; Laizer 1996; Randal 1998; Celik 2002; Asadi 2007; Marcus 2007a; Tahiri 2007). Laizer delineates the frontline:

The fighting was focused on two main fronts – the area around Bahdinan known as Haftanin and the Xarkuk/Biradost region close to the Iranian border where the PKK guerrillas were being sandwiched ... between Turkish warplanes on bombing missions and peshmerga forces, mainly from the KDP, PUK, and the Biradost tribe's own militia on the ground,

Laizer (1996: 62)

Yet, 'apart from the aerial bombardments by the Turks, most of the action in this war was concentrated after dark, peshmerga against guerrilla' (Laizer 1996: 66).[31] Cornered between the Turkish military and the *peshmerga* of KDP and PUK, the PKK formally surrendered to the latter on 30 October. Osman Öcalan was transported with a small delegation to Erbil where he signed a ceasefire agreement obliging the PKK to cease all activities of a military nature in the territory controlled by the KRG, to abandon all its camps along the Turkish border and acquiesce in being removed to camps to be designated by the KRG, as well as to stop all its involvement in political activities aimed against or agitating against the Kurdistan Regional Government and the parties comprising it.[32] In exchange, about 1700 PKK fighters were resettled to Zaleh camp north of Sulimaniyah were they were allowed to keep all their weapons, ammunition, and supplies, as well as to continue their peaceful political activities for as long as they did not oppose the activities and policies of the KRG.[33]

When analysing the brief war between the IKF and the PKK, two aspects require further scrutiny. The PKK has always claimed that the KDP and PUK had formed an alliance with Turkey to crush them,[34] and Çelik (2002) contends that, since June 1992, Talabani and Barzani had repeatedly met with the commander of the Turkish Gendarmerie in the region, General Eşref Bitlis, and the commander of *Jandarma İstihbarat ve Terörle Mücadele* (JITEM, Gendarmerie Intelligence and Counter-Terrorism Organization), General Cem Ersever, in Erbil and in army barracks in Silopi to prepare and coordinate their forces for their attack on the PKK. The PUK vociferously denies these claims, and refers to a KRG public statement from 28 October calling for Turkey to withdraw its forces from Iraqi Kurdish territory.[35] However, when examining the events that led up to the war, in particular in light of the rapprochement and closer political ties between the Özal presidency and KDP/PUK leaders, the role Özal had intended for Talabani as an intermediary between himself and Öcalan, the role Turkey played in establishing and policing the Iraqi Kurdish safe haven – with Turkish military on the ground – and the gradual and entirely predictable escalation of the conflict between KDP/PUK and PKK, Henri Barkey concludes, 'from a military perspective, it would have been grossly negligent if [Turkey and the IKF] had not coordinated their actions, politically it is difficult to imagine that they did not'[36] – an assessment with which I completely agree. Once Talabani's mediation efforts had proven fruitless and relations between the PKK and the KRG had deteriorated rapidly, it simply would have made no sense for the IKF to take on the PKK on its own with the Turkish military across the border alert and ready to strike.

The second concern relates to the generous terms with which the PUK allowed the PKK to surrender – relocation to camps in PUK-controlled territory and the PKK fighters keeping all their weaponry and ammunition – terms of surrender that had not been discussed with the KDP, and about which Barzani, who wanted to finish off the PKK, was reportedly furious.[37] What is more, when the PKK fighters were transported to Zaleh camp, the PUK commander Mustafa Chawrash, of his own accord and 'as a gesture of goodwill', he declared, even equipped them with additional light weapons and ammunition from PUK stocks.[38] Why, if the PKK were forbidden to carry out any military activities on Iraqi Kurdish territory, would the PUK allow the guerrilla fighters to keep their weaponry? Why did the PUK, after acting in alliance with the KDP during the conflict and when facing the unique opportunity of ridding themselves once and for all of the PKK, accept a unilateral ceasefire with the PKK not only without informing its coalition partner but presenting Barzani with a fait accompli? One cannot help but speculate that, while individual field commanders such as Chawrash might have acted on their own initiative, he must have still done so within a discourse, an overall sentiment in the PUK, propagated by its leadership, that did not want the PKK to be finished off. If that is the case one has to wonder what motivated this discourse, what interests and identities bred this sentiment? Could the notion of ethnic group solidarity explain the PUK's change of heart? While such subjective feelings of relatedness and kinship ties again may have played a role at the individual level, it seems somewhat implausible that after a month's heavy fighting Talabani suddenly came to perceive the PKK as 'kin'. It seems more plausible that if the PKK had been annihilated in October 1992, Talabani, the designated intermediary of President Özal, would have been considerably less useful to Turkey. In the lopsided relationship of complete dependence on Turkey, the Iraqi Kurds had very little to give, no leverage worth speaking of except for the influence they supposedly could exert on the PKK. Would it not make sense then to keep this factor in play for as long as possible, to have the PKK card up their sleeve for future use, to continue exerting this one leverage on Turkey for as long as the situation permitted? Furthermore, as developments just 18 months later would prove, the harmony between the PUK and KDP during the *Repareen* and the first two years of the Kurdistan Regional Government proved short lived. There were already signs on the horizon that the proverbial antagonism between both parties would erupt again – as it did with a vengeance in 1994. Is it not conceivable then that Talabani shrewdly kept the PKK alive, against his allies' wishes, and relocated them, fully armed, to a camp in PUK controlled territory to be able to draw on this formidable fighting force in case of new tensions with the KDP? Admittedly, such a reading of events is done with the benefit of hindsight, but it not only fits the historic pattern outlined here so far but it again, when discussed, is deemed plausible by other authorities on the politics of the Iraqi Kurdish parties.[39]

If Talabani indeed pursued such brinkmanship, it paid off for him almost instantly. In December he took up his mediation efforts with Öcalan in Damascus again, allowing him on 8 March 1993 to present President Özal with the Öcalan's surprisingly conciliatory terms for a ceasefire:

(1) I am giving up the armed struggle. I will wage a political struggle in the future. (2) I am withdrawing my past conditions for holding talks to resolve the Kurdish problem. Turkish officials can hold talks with Kurdish deputies in the National Assembly. (3) We agree to live within Turkey's existing borders if the necessary democratic conditions are created to allow us to do so.[40]

Without waiting for a Turkish response, Öcalan even went a step further and on 17 March 1993, together with Jalal Talabani, declared a unilateral PKK ceasefire at a historic press conference in Lebanon (Gürbey 1996; Gunter 1997; White 2000; Çelik 2002; Özcan 2006; Marcus 2007a; Tahiri 2007; Gunes 2011). Öcalan proclaimed:

[Turkey's Kurds] want peace, dialogue, and free political action within the framework of a democratic Turkish state ... We hope that the Turkish authorities will understand that this question cannot be resolved militarily, and that the Kurdish people, their existence, their language, their identity, and their rights cannot be ignored ... We are not working to partition Turkey. We are demanding the Kurds' human rights (cultural, political, and so on) in the framework of one homeland.[41]

The importance of the monumental step of the PKK declaring a unilateral and unconditional ceasefire cannot be underestimated. With it,

the PKK intended to issue two signals ... its readiness for negotiations, and, on the other [hand], the turning back from its ultimate aim of creating a Kurdish state. The PKK no longer insists on this demand but instead strives toward the aim of finding a federalist [re]solution [to the conflict] within Turkey.

(Gürbey 1996: 23–24)

It therefore constitutes not only a fundamental shift in the PKK's nationalist ideology but also the most auspicious window of opportunity for a peaceful solution to the PKK conflict in Turkey in the 1990s. Alas, this unique opportunity came to naught with the untimely death of Turgut Özal of a heart attack on 17 April 1993, after which the Turkish politico-military establishment, which had always been wary of his initiative, reverted to a hard, militaristic line towards the PKK.

This episode in relations between the PKK and KDP/PUK clearly shows that the ethnic alliance model has no explanatory value for understanding actors' behaviour in this internationalized ethno-nationalist conflict. As an explanatory model for analysing and conceptualizing the relations between an insurgency and a supposedly 'co-ethnic' political entity where it found sanctuary, in the case of the PKK sanctuary in Iraqi Kurdistan from 1991 until 1993, it has no analytical purchase, not only because instead of an alliance, the parties were fighting each other, but for the reasons as to why the fighting occurred. The ethnic alliance model claims that

conflict between a state and an ethnic group will escalate to the international level when other elite members of that same ethnic group play a role in policy making in another state and that state finds the first state to be politically relevant.

(Davis & Moore 1998: 93)

If we put aside for a moment the fact that the PKK and KDP/PUK, as has been argued throughout this study, cannot and should not be categorized as belonging to the same ethnic group, what is particularly striking here is that at the very moment when the KDP/PUK played the most significant role in policy making in the territory and political space where the PKK had found sanctuary – that is when they crafted a political entity not nominally independent from but acting and performing statecraft independently from Baghdad as a so-called de facto state – which is when the ethnic alliance model is supposed to become most relevant, they turned on the PKK. And, it can be argued, they turned on the PKK to protect that very political relevance the ethnic alliance model lists as a prerequisite for an ethnic alliance. In other words, dependent on Turkey and the international community for their very survival, KDP/PUK had to confront the factor that could jeopardize their newly gained political relevance; that is, they fought the PKK because it posed a vital threat to their political relevance.

When both KDP and PUK were just one of dozens of insurgencies operating in the 1980s' Middle East, they did not have much to lose from forming a temporary alliance with the PKK. Yet, when their status changed in 1991, when they gained political relevance as the recipient of international aid and diplomatic as well as military backing, precisely because they feared they could lose this political relevance, they had to turn on the PKK. As Rex Brynen (1990) has detailed, and I have expanded on elsewhere (Artens 2012), a sanctuary state will always have to consider whether hosting an insurgency on its territory enhances its sovereignty or puts it at risk. For example, it can be argued that, at least temporarily, Honduran strongman General Gustavo Álvarez benefited from hosting on its territory the CIA-backed Contras during the 1980s (Shepherd 1984; La Feber 1993; Schulz & Schulz 1994; Sobel 1995; Kinzer 2001), while Jordan hosting the Palestinian *fida'iyyin* not only threatened to undermine the Hashemite dynasty's hold on power but the very survival of Jordan as a state, which is why they were expelled by force in 1970/1971 in what became known as the 'Black September' (Quandt *et al.* 1973; Bailey 1984; Shemesh 1988; Cobban 1992). While I will argue that in the 2000s the KRG performed such brinkmanship, trying to gain political capital via Turkey from the PKK's presence on its territory, in 1991/1992 the emergent Iraqi Kurdish political entity, however defined, was in no position and too dependent on Ankara and the international community to dare any such tightrope walks. In addition, from 24 July 1992 on, when the PKK imposed an embargo on traffic between Turkey and Iraqi Kurdistan, it not only posed an indirect threat to the political relevance of the KDP/PUK – potentially provoking Turkey to sever its ties with them or to intervene militarily – but directly menaced the very survival of the Kurdistan Regional Government just a month after its inauguration.

In the literature, the 30 days war between the PKK and KDP/PUK in 1992 is often referred to as the first stage of *birakuji* or 'fratricidal war' that came to define Iraqi Kurdish history in the 1990s (Laizer 1996; Gunter 1996, 1997, 1999a; Özcan 2006; Tahiri 2007), and in the case of Özcan and Tahiri is used as an example of the manifold 'internal divisions' that have prevented the Kurds from gaining statehood. Yet, as I have continually maintained throughout this study, it would be wrong for us analysts to categorize Kurds from Turkey, Iraq, Iran, and Syria as belonging to the same ethnic group. For this reason, it would likewise be wrong to portray the conflict between the Kurds of Iraq, the KDP and PUK, and Kurds from Turkey and Syria, the PKK, as an 'intra-group ethnic conflict' or a 'fratricidal war'; by the same token, theories of factionalism do not apply to this case since if they do not belong to the same group, they cannot be factions of it. Likewise, manifestations of the conflict such as the strategic essentialisms of ethnic outbidding should not be misinterpreted as the conflict's causes. To be sure, Öcalan never tired of decrying Barzani and Talabani as 'collaborators, reactionaries, feudal persons, primitive nationalists', and 'leeches', who collaborated with the 'fascist Turks', and, as cherished in PKK ideology, may have genuinely believed that his organization fought on behalf of and for the national self-determination of all Kurds, and that he could speak with greater authority on their behalf than either Barzani and Talabani. Yet, to infer ethnic groupness from these acts of ethnic outbidding, from these strategic essentialisms, would amount to taking Öcalan's beliefs and preaching as gospel – something the intended audience, brainwashed for years in PKK training camps or persecuted by assimilationist nationalizing states may have done sincerely with their hearts and minds or out of necessity, but which we scholars, for whom such restraints do not apply, should be hesitant to do. The strategic essentialisms and calculated radicalization of ethnic outbidding do not make an ethnic group, as the Manichean categorization of being 'with us, or against us' does not make those who opposed George Bush's invasion of Iraq in 2003 sympathizers of terrorism.

If these attempts at explaining ethnic conflict with ethnicity hold little purchase, instrumentalist explananda appear to better capture the dynamics of relations between the PKK and KDP/PUK and what motivated their actions. To be sure, the actions of these parties during the first half of 1992, which led to the 30 days war of October, can be reduced to material, in this case security, interests. The PKK feared an emerging IKF–Turkish alliance, and the KRG feared that the PKK's presence on its territory would either antagonize Turkey or that the PKK would directly challenge their authority, as it did when it shut down border traffic in July. While these realist accounts are accurate, I feel they do not capture the whole picture, and that it would be not only reductionist but also erroneous to completely discard identity as an explanatory factor. For I would argue that, in 1991/1992 Iraqi Kurdish identity, if such a generalization can be made, entered a critical period of transformation that is still ongoing today. Over the course of just a few months the Iraqi Kurds, until then either ignored or (ab)used by the international community, saw their fates altered from being the victims of a genocidal campaign of ethnic cleansing to becoming the fosterlings of the international community; they had to come to terms with and adjust their perceptions as well as their behaviours towards the very power, Turkey, that until then had opposed Kurdish autonomy in Iraq most ardently becoming their benefactor; and finally, they came to exercise the first cautious steps in crafting a political entity, however defined, of their own control and acting independently from the Iraqi government that had oppressed them for generations. Certainly, such a fundamental transformation in their self-perception altered their interests, as, in turn, did the strategic interests of having to adapt to rapidly changing developments affect the transformative process of their identities. Arguably, one would be hard pressed to determine a causality in these developments, of either identities shaping interests or interests being a function of identity, but would argue that both went hand in hand as a complex matrix of identities and interests shaping actors' behaviour and actions – and I therefore would make a strong case for studying them as such.

If, to explain the first stage of what is commonly, and as has been shown, wrongly referred to as *birakuji* or Kurdish 'fratricidal war', we have to belabour a complex matrix of shifting interests and emergent identities, for the second stage, terms such as 'intra-group conflict' or 'civil war' seem more appropriate and the traditional instrumentalist arsenal of explanatory IR suffices to explain the conflict between KDP and PUK that turned violent in the first half of 1994. Naturally, both parties accused each other of bad faith, of betraying the national unity of the Kurdistan Regional Government, and of selling out the Kurdish people and Iraqi Kurdish self-determination to external forces. 'The PUK called the KDP "international traitors" and counter-revolutionaries, the betrayers of Kurdish nationalism for party interests' (Laizer 1996: 137). The KDP proved in no way inferior in their heated rhetoric:

> The *Jalalis'* [followers of Jalal Talabani] are this time more than any time against the Kurdish people and their interests. The PUK and Jalal Talabani have established a culture of *jashati* [treason] in Kurdish history. The PUK's attack is a careful plan in coordination with the enemies of the Kurds to destroy the Kurdish Regional Government in Iraqi Kurdistan ... If the KDP is attacked by the enemies of Kurdistan, the Kurdish heroes will smash them ... long live the peshmerga of the KDP and Barzani.[42]

Such exercises in ethnic outbidding and strategic essentialisms, as instructive as they are for discourse analysis, should not disguise the fact that they are merely expressions and manifestations of the conflict that must not be mistaken as its causes. Virtually all analysts agree that in the on-and-off conflict between KDP and PUK from 1994 until 1998, ideological and ideational factors played no role (Gunter 1999a; Stansfield 2003a, 2007a; Natali 2005, 2010; Romano 2006; Asadi 2007; McDowall 2007), that it can be best described by theories of factionalism.[43] Any appeals to national unity were appeals to a myth, since, despite auspicious beginnings in 1992, 'essentially, the elected parliament had been carrying out decisions made at the party headquarters of the KDP and the PUK, rather than in the KRG legislature. Both parties' administrations were based on clientelism' (Romano 2006: 209). At the end of the day, this civil war was nothing more and nothing less than a power struggle over supremacy in Iraqi Kurdistan, in which the decades-old antagonisms between both parties, detailed in Part II, openly came to the surface. Additionally, very material interests resulting from the configuration of the political space in Iraqi Kurdistan since 1992 played a major role. The 1992 elections – which, although as Jalal Talabani had put it, 'everyone ended up dissatisfied with the results', 'all Kurdish parties accepted, albeit reluctantly, in order to safeguard the unity of Kurdish ranks and to portray the Kurds as civilised people before the world'[44] – had produced a 50:50 power-sharing deal between both parties. However, when in December 1992 a smaller party merged with the KDP this carefully calibrated equilibrium threatened to come out of balance.

> These changes did indeed send shockwaves through the PUK camp and altered the balance between the groupings partaking in the already strained power-sharing system of governance ... The inclusion of the smaller parties created a sharp polarization between the PUK and the KDP.
>
> (Stansfield 2003a: 151, 152)

The KDP, who had already fared slightly better in the 1992 election, was eager to exploit this advantage.

> In January 1994, the Central Committee of the KDP met and, believing to have been strengthened by coalescing with the smaller parties, decided that the 50:50 system was no longer the favoured method of power-sharing. Massoud [Barzani] subsequently proposed ... that a new election should take place in the immediate future.
>
> (Stansfield 2003a: 152)

Other factors also turned out to the PUK's long-term detriment. One of the major sources of income for both parties were the duties collected at the Harbur border gate as well as revenues from smuggling goods from and into Turkey, Iran and Syria. Of those borders, the PUK controlled only parts of the one with Iran, and had for long suspected the KDP of not declaring and submitting all duties from Harbur to the KRG institutions, thus leaving the PUK at a precarious financial disadvantage.[45] With the KDP eyeing snap elections and a majority government, the PUK ran the risk of losing millions of dollars in revenue, putting the party's survival in question. What aggravated the PUK perhaps most, though, was that while virtually all of the KDP's territory was protected by the internationally patrolled no-fly zone, the majority of PUK territory, including its stronghold Sulimaniyah, lay south of the 36th parallel, and therefore was at constant risk from the Iraqi army. In sum, in almost every aspect the PUK felt either short changed or that the political space since 1992 had developed to its distinct disadvantage.

> The PUK felt itself being gradually squeezed out of power and starved of finances. Hence the PUK was probably the party that initiated the 1994 civil war, in an attempt to redress the worsening balance of power in Iraqi Kurdistan.
>
> (Romano 2006: 209–210)

The first round of fighting in May 1994 was triggered by a banality,[46] but

> by the beginning of June more than 600 civilian and military deaths had occurred in fighting throughout much of Kurdistan. In late May PUK forces seized the Kurdish parliament building in Erbil ... [and] the fighting threatened the continuation of much needed international aid.
>
> (Gunter 1999a: 76)

Over the next four years, thousands of Iraqi Kurds came to perish in the civil war that escalated into a regional conflagration, drawing in all of the Kurdistan Region's neighbours and major powers further afield. Initially, all regional powers, who after the turmoil of the Gulf War saw a stabilized Iraqi Kurdistan as a strategic priority, tried to prevent the civil war in Iraqi Kurdistan from getting out of hand.

> Turkey, Iran, and, ironically, even Baghdad also offered to mediate ... while in late January 1995, U.S. President Bill Clinton sent a message to both Barzani and Talabani in which he warned, 'We will no longer cooperate with the other countries to maintain security in the region if the clashes continue'.
>
> (Gunter 1999a: 80, 81)

Over the course of the next three years the US repeatedly threatened to cut off its international aid and even end its military protection of the Iraqi Kurds through Operation Provide Comfort. Kenneth Pollack, then Director for Near East and South East Asian Affairs of the *National Security Council* (NSC), recalls:

> We used everything we got to get them to stop their fighting each other that only played into the hands of Saddam. We used incentives and disincentives, threatening to terminate our military engagement in the CTF [Combined Task Force for OPC I and II and from 1997 on Operation Northern Watch]. That message was absolutely sent. We clearly said, we're not going to support you, if you keep fighting each other, if you keep bringing in the Iranians and Saddam.[47]

It seems that by late 1994 the war had gained a momentum of its own, with the antagonisms between the KDP and PUK, built-up over decades, fully unloading, and no party able or willing to give ground, and even their most powerful external supporters, the US and Turkey, proving unable to bring their clients under control for longer than the ink on another futile peace agreement took to dry.[48] Of all regional powers, it was Turkey that most feared a long-term destabilized Iraqi Kurdistan.

> Turkey saw harmony among the Iraqi Kurds as a way to prevent the ... PKK from raiding Turkey from Iraqi Kurdish territory. Civil War between the

KDP and PUK, however, created opportunities for the PKK to [re-]establish camps in northern Iraq.

(Gunter 1999a: 78)

Consequently, Turkey pursued a dual strategy of stepping up its military incursions into northern Iraq – with two major offensive from March until May and then again in July 1995 – to prevent the PKK from regaining lost ground, while at the same time acting as a mediator in two major rounds of talks between KDP and PUK in Silopi in the summer of 1994 and in Ankara in 1996/7 (Gunter 1999a; Robins 2003a; Lundgren 2007). Turkey's fears proved well-founded since the PKK not only managed to take advantage of the chaos of war and regained the camps at the Turkish border it had abandoned in 1992 but, on 26 August 1995, also launched a major offensive against the KDP (Gunter 1996, 1999a; Çelik 2002; Marcus 2007a). The PKK claims that it acted on its own accord – its press organs announced that the KDP had 'to be wiped out because it was backing Turkey's bid to crush the PKK' and for 40 years had been 'in league with the Turkish intelligence services'[49] – and denies that it attacked the KDP in concert with the PUK.[50] This, however, seems as unconvincing as the KDP/PUK claiming they had not coordinated their 1992 attacks on the PKK with Turkey. Both PKK and PUK received support from the same external actors, Iran and Syria, and the PKK prepared its assault on the KDP from PUK territory.

For their own ulterior motives such regional powers as Syria and Iran, as well as the PUK, apparently encouraged the PKK. The former two states acted because they did not want to see their U.S. enemy successfully broker an end to KDP-PUK strife … while Talabani sought in effect to open a second front against Barzani.

(Gunter 1999a: 84)

On a short term basis, it seemed as if Talabani's brinkmanship of letting the PKK live to fight another day from three years earlier had paid off. As he should have expected, though, in the long run, the PKK's offensive against the KDP provoked Turkey to intervene directly in the conflict on the side of the KDP. On 14 May 1997, Turkey invaded northern Iraq with 50,000 troops, and in September, with its tanks advancing to within a few miles of Erbil, even shelled PUK positions along the strategic Hamilton Road.[51] For what may somewhat be euphemistically coined Turkey's 'partisan peace-making' (Robins 2003a), Talabani had stronger words. For him, 'Turkey has discarded its neutral role and is now an ally of Barzani.'[52]

The civil war's darkest hour occurred when, on 31 August 1996, Barzani joined forces with Saddam Hussein against the PUK and their combined forces took Erbil, and later on its own (but generously equipped by the Iraqi Army) conquered the PUK stronghold Sulimaniyah, to which the US responded with cruise missile strikes on command and control facilities in Iraq proper

(Graham-Brown 1999; Gunter 1999a; Byman 2000; Byman & Waxman 2000; Stansfield 2003a, 2007a; Asadi 2007; Tahiri 2007; Lawrence 2009). For many Kurds, this 1996 KDP–Iraqi army alliance against the PUK is Iraqi Kurdistan's day that will live on in infamy; for Kurdish-born analysts such as Tahiri (2007), it is further testimony of Kurdish tribalist 'backwardness' and their nationalist parties' incapacity for national unity, and Ali Kemal Özcan even goes so far as to identify '"treason" as *an inseparable element of the Kurdish ethnic personality'* (Özcan 2006: 5, my emphasis).

Such juxtapositions of arbitrary values such as 'tribalist' and 'backward' versus 'modern' and 'civilized' are troublesome for their blatant normativism alone. As Ernest Gellner observed:

Nationalisms are simply those tribalisms, or for that matter any other kind of group, which through luck, effort or circumstances succeed in becoming an effective force under modern circumstances. They are only identifiable *ex post factum*. Tribalism never prospers, for when it does, everyone will respect it as true nationalism, and no one will dare call it tribalism.

(Gellner 2006: 84)

What is even more troublesome for the historic baggage such normativisms carry, and what in my opinion becomes neither intellectually nor ethically justifiable, is when we scholars as categorizers start ascribing certain derogatory psychological or social connotations and characteristics such as 'backward', 'treasonous' or 'fratricidous' as cultural attributes or traits to whole ethnic groups, nations or people. Not only are such normativisms pseudo-scientific, they have the potential of getting us dangerously close to a cultural stereotyping of what should be a bygone era in the social sciences.

Ultimately, in 1998, the US and Turkey reached two separate crucial diplomatic breakthroughs, each with a major impact on Kurdish history. In early September the US finally succeeded in bringing Talabani and Barzani to the negotiation table in Washington. After two days of heated negotiations both leaders reached an accord, hailed as the 'Washington Agreement' that ended the Iraqi Kurdish civil war and was presented with great fanfare and under the aegis of Secretary of State Madeleine Albright to the world on 17 September 1998 (Gunter 1999a; Stansfield 2003a; Natali 2005, 2010; Asadi 2007). While it is difficult to establish a direct relation,[53] it is quite striking that a month later President Bill Clinton signed the *Iraq Liberation Act* into law, adopting an official US policy for regime change in Iraq and designated certain groups in Iraq as recipients of covert funding to bring about the toppling of Saddam Hussein's regime.[54] On 4 February 1999, President Clinton revealed what groups would qualify for US assistance with both KDP and PUK featuring prominently on the list. The fact that the bill was introduced for a vote in the House of Representatives on 29 September (Freedman 1999; Gunter 1999b; Byman 2000; Byman & Waxman 2000; Davis 2006; Ritchie & Rogers 2007; Charountaki 2010), less than two weeks after Barzani and Talabani had signed their peace accord, is too conspicuous for coincidence, and leads one to believe that the 'Washington Agreement' was sweetened by the promise of millions of dollars of covert funding and the KDP/PUK being enhanced to the status of quasi-official allies in US efforts to bring about regime change in Iraq.[55]

For the PKK the 'Washington Agreement' was bad news. The PKK had demonstrably benefited from the civil war between the KDP and PUK and regained most of the ground lost in 1992, which is why Gunter's (1997, 1999a) theory that the PKK deliberately attacked the KDP to torpedo the Drogheda peace talks between both parties could very well hold some merit. For as long as the two Iraqi Kurdish parties were fighting they would not interfere with the PKK setting up camp at the Turkish border again, and the PKK could shape the outcome of the struggle by strategically throwing its weight behind one combatant as the situation required. The prospect of the KDP and PUK reaching a lasting settlement and returning to Washington's and presumably Ankara's good graces was therefore inherently against the PKK's interest. In the same weeks as Barzani and Talabani were making peace in Washington, though, the PKK was dealt a much heavier blow when, after more than 15 years, Turkish diplomatic, and in this case even overt military, pressure finally paid off, and the Syrian government expelled Abdullah Öcalan on 9 October 1998 (Olson 2001; Marcus 2007a). With that dramatic turn of events began the PKK leader's four months desperate odyssey through Europe until his capture by Turkish intelligence in Kenya on 15 February 1999.

Notes

1 Human Rights Watch (1993, 1995). According to Iraqi prosecutors during the 2007 trial of Ali Hassan al-Majid, 180,000 Kurds were killed during the *Anfal* campaign (Sinan 2007).

2 Quoted in Imset (1992: 190). Together with Izmir AFB Incirlik AFB was the major NATO AFB in Turkey, with routinely about 50 US reconnaissance planes, fighters and bombers stationed there. Saddam Hussein correctly anticipated that Incirlik AFB would serve as the major site of operations for deploying USAF in a potential second northern front during the coming Gulf War.

3 Interview Çelik op. cit.; see also interviews with Osman Öcalan, Koy Sanjaq, Iraqi Kurdistan, 12 and 16 September 2010 as well as with Nizamettin Taş and Halil Ataç, Erbil, Iraqi Kurdistan, 23 October 2011.

4 Quoted in Human Rights Watch (1992: 38).

5 On the reasons for the US failure to support the popular uprisings of March 1991, see Graham-Brown (1999), Charountaki (2010), Shareef (2010), and Gunter (2011b). Essentially US decision makers feared that the international alliance they had crafted for the liberation of Kuwait would not hold together in pursuit of regime change in Iraq. Additionally, the US did not seem eager to replace a strong Iraq, on which it still relied as a regional counterweight to revolutionary Iran, with a country plunged into seemingly endless sectarian strife, a civil war that potentially would require the US to commit troops to stabilize the country. President Bush, Secretary of Defense Dick Cheney and other US political and military decision makers had repeatedly made clear that this was a price for regime change they were not willing to consider. This reading of US motives is further substantiated by the autobiography of then CJCS General Colin Powell (1996), and in an interview with General Norman Schwarzkopf

(Arango 2011), then Commander in Chief of CENTCOM and of the international coalition during the Gulf War, who expressed his regrets for the US role during the 1991 uprisings that was dictated by balance of power considerations with Iran.

6 While it is true that British PM John Major, when faced with the plight of Kurdish refugees in the icy mountains of the Iraqi–Turkish border, also exerted considerable pressure on the US to intervene and for the first time formally proposed the idea of a humanitarian 'safe haven' at an EC Summit on 8 April 1991, this idea had been first suggested to him by Turgut Özal (Kirişçi 1996; Di Prizio 2002; Robins 2003a; Gunter 2011a).

7 Interview with Najmaldin Karim, Sulimaniyah, Iraqi Kurdistan, 6 September 2010, then the unofficial representative of the PUK in Washington, later the personal physician of Jalal Talabani, and today the Governor of Kirkuk.

8 Both KDP and PUK went to great lengths in emphasizing in their election campaigns the stability of the Iraqi state, illustrated in, for example, the KDP's slogan, 'autonomy for Kurdistan, democracy for Iraq' (McDowall 2007: 380).

9 Economically, for example, the Kurdistan Region since 1991/1992 has become so dependent on relief supplies in the first instance, and food imports today, that very few agricultural products are grown there competitively today – based on my own observations, even watermelons are imported from Turkey. On how international aid since 1991 has shaped the economy and society of Iraqi Kurdistan, see Graham-Brown (1999), Leezenberg (2000, 2003, 2005), and Stansfield (2003a).

10 Until then Syria had flatly denied that the PKK operated within Syrian controlled territory (including Lebanon) at all. When, in 1992, during another bilateral meeting in Damascus, Turkish intelligence MIT confronted Syrian officials with videos showing Abdullah Öcalan going in and out of official buildings in Damascus, such cover ups were no longer supportable (Imset 1992). Since then, Syria, after the collapse of the Soviet Union and in the wake of the Gulf War eager to establish better relations with the West, stepped up its efforts to limit PKK activities, at least to a degree that they were not easily verifiable, which ultimately resulted in Öcalan's expulsion in 1998.

11 The PKK was as surprised as the state by the strength of the protests ... The PKK, which did not realise how much pent-up support it had in urban centres, had no plan for how to react to such an outburst. 'The demonstrations broke out without any involvement of the PKK,' insisted former PKK commander Sari Baran, whose claim was repeated by other PKK members.

(Marcus 2007a: 142–143)

12 Author's translation from the original German.

13 I, for one, tend to side with this interpretation of events. Given Abdullah Öcalan's personality, I believe he in particular must have been reluctant to loosen his grip and dominance of the nationalist struggle and discourse by permitting a conflation of the armed guerrilla fight with an uncontrollable public uprising – a reading of events that is supported by the PKK's behaviour throughout the 2000s.

14 Quoted in Gunter (1996: 52).

15 Interview with Qamran Qaradaghi, London, UK, 21 April 2011.

16 Quoted in Gunter (2011a: 89).

17 Quoted in Gunter (2011a: 90).

18 On the question of the extent to which HEP had been infiltrated by the PKK and can be understood as merely a political front for the insurgency, see White (2000) and Marcus (2007a). HEP was banned by the Turkish Constitutional Court in July 1993 after a strong showing in parliamentary elections in 1991.

19 Abdullah Öcalan in an interview with Turkish journalist Mehmet Ali Birand, quoted in Gunter (2011a: 93).

20 Quoted in Gunter (2011a: 93).

21 Interview Qaradaghi op. cit. The fact that Talabani and Barzani were travelling on Turkish diplomatic passports is widely mentioned in the literature on Kurdish nationalism and exploited by certain authors (Tahiri 2007) to illustrate that their nationalism was not genuine.

22 In the course of these negotiations, Gunter (1996, 1997) claims that Abdullah Öcalan in December 1991 travelled to Iraqi Kurdistan to meet with Talabani. I tried to verify this claim among my contacts of PKK dissidents – interviews with Çelik, Öcalan, Taş and Ataç op. cit. – who all denied it. When confronted with these findings Gunter (interview op. cit.) corrected it. It therefore can be considered as established that Abdullah Öcalan has never been to Iraqi Kurdistan.

23 Interview Qaradaghi op. cit.

24 Nonetheless, PM Demirel met Talabani twice in Ankara in early 1992 and in August of the same year, and once held direct talks with Massoud Barzani (Imset 1992).

25 Quoted in Gunter (1996: 53).

26 Quoted in Gunter (1996: 53–54).

27 Interview Çelik op. cit.

28 Interview with Ahmed Saadi Pire, Sulimaniyah, Iraqi Kurdistan, 10 June 2010.

29 Interview with Mohammed Tawfiq, Sulimaniyah, Iraqi Kurdistan, 4 June 2010. At the time of the interview Tawfiq had left the PUK and become a spokesman for *Gorran*.

30 Quoted in Gunter (1996: 54).

31 Laizer (1996: 62, 66). As is common in guerrilla wars, any figures for casualties have to be treated with utmost caution. In the immediate days after the war the Turkish Chief of Staff General Doğan Güreş claimed that the PKK had lost up to 5000 fighters (Gunter 1996) while the PKK publication *Serxwebun* spoke of 193 guerrillas killed in action (Laizer 1996). Based on figures in Gunter (1996, 1997), Laizer (1996), Randal (1998), it appears prudent to estimate that all three parties to the conflict – the Turkish military, PKK, and KDP/PUK – lost several hundred fighters each during the conflict.

32 Interview Öcalan op. cit.

33 For the exact wording of the ceasefire agreement, see Laizer (1996: 68–69).

34 Interviews Çelik, Öcalan, Taş and Ataç op. cit.

35 Interview Pire op. cit.

36 Interview Barkey op. cit.

37 Interview Gunter op. cit.

38 Interview Mustafa Chawrash, Sulimaniyah, Iraqi Kurdistan, 31 May 2010.

39 Interviews Barkey, Gunter, Ergil, Olson, Vali op. cit.

40 Quoted in Gunter (1997: 75).

41 Quoted in Gunter (1997: 75–76).

42 KDP radio broadcast from 15 October 1997, quoted from Tahiri (2007: 282).

43 See also interviews with Barkey, Gunter, Olson, op. cit. McDowall (2007) and Tahiri (2007), on the other hand, belabour theories of tribalism, that in Tahiri's overall questionable approach supposedly explain Kurdish ideological 'backwardness'.

44 Quoted in Gunter (1999a: 29, 30). Both Talabani and Barzani demonstrated their dissatisfaction with the election results by refusing to hold any senior office in the KRG, which undermined the legitimacy and credibility of the unified governmental structures.

45 Interview with Chato Hawesi, a veteran PUK politburo member, Sulimaniyah, Iraqi Kurdistan, 7 June 2010.

46 The first blood in what was to become a four-year civil war was drawn in a dispute over a plot of land belonging to a KDP official and his PUK tenants (Gunter 1999a).

47 Interview with Kenneth Pollack, Washington, USA, 21 March 2011.

48 It has to be said though, that the regional powers were also to blame for the failure of consecutive peace agreements. Turkey, for example, took issue with the US-sponsored talks in Drogheda, Ireland, because the accord reached there did not sufficiently address the PKK sanctuary in Iraqi Kurdistan, and Iran, then allied with the PUK,

torpedoed the implementation of the same talks because it sought to counter growing US influence in the region (Gunter 1999a; Robins 2003a).

49 Quoted in Gunter (1996: 56, 57).

50 Interviews Celik and Öcalan op. cit.

51 Interview with Omar Abdullah, veteran PUK member and head of the military wing of the PUK until 1991, Sulimaniyah, Iraqi Kurdistan, 13 June 2010, who routinely liaised with Abdullah Öcalan on behalf of Jalal Talabani in Damascus throughout 1996/1997.

52 Quoted in Gunter (1999a: 88). As expected the KDP of course denies any formal alliance or coordination of military activities with Turkey, interview with the then KDP representative in Ankara, Safeen Dizayee, Erbil, 19 September 2010.

53 Kenneth Pollack hinted at the possibility of an at least indirect link between the Washington Agreement and the Iraq Liberation Act and the millions of dollars in covert funding that would come with it, having helped to change Talabani's and Barzani's mind in the negotiations. Interview Pollack op. cit.

54 The change in the Clinton administration's policy towards Iraq from containment to regime change can, to some extent, be explained by increasing neo-conservative pressure in Congress, the media, and from right-wing think tanks. One of the most prominent here was the *Project for a New American Century* (PNAC), who in January 1998 sent an open letter to President Clinton calling for a change of policy in support of regime change; many of the PNAC signatories of 1998 would hold influential positions in the George W. Bush administration and were key in setting the US on the road to war in 2002/2003 (Altheide & Grimes 2005; Halper & Clarke 2005; Bialasiewicz *et al.* 2007; Burgos 2008; Dumbrell 2008).

55 An earlier episode of PUK involvement in a failed attempt by the CIA to orchestrate a coup against Saddam Hussein is detailed in Baer (2002), whose claims, though, should be taken with the grain of salt that such first-hand accounts of covert operations require.

8   Iraqi Kurdistan and the PKK in the post-2003 Middle East

Crafting Iraqi Kurdish national self-determination

The Iraqi Kurdish ethno-nationalist parties entered the new century as divided as they had spent the previous one. The Washington Agreement had put an end to the armed confrontation but left the so-called Iraqi Kurdish de facto state partitioned into two power blocks corresponding to the two segments of territory that KDP and PUK had militarily and politically controlled since 1996. Those two regions were run as separate political entities. In Erbil, the KDP administered its territory through a third KRG cabinet, and in Sulimaniyah the PUK established its own third cabinet; virtually every executive and legislative structure, government ministry, bureaucratic institution, and civil service existed in double (Stansfield 2003a, 2003b, 2005, 2006, 2010; Natali 2005, 2010; Ahmed 2007, 2012; Olson 2007), resulting not only in a disproportionately inflated bureaucratic apparatus cum cumbersome decision making process but also a solidification and protraction of the proverbial factionalism between both parties. On the other hand, once the fighting had stopped, the two KRGs could refer to a gradually improving economy (Leezenberg 2003; Olson 2007) as well as to learning, practising and, to a certain degree, mastering apart what they had failed to execute together: running an increasingly efficient political and bureaucratic administration (Stansfield 2003a, 2003b, 2005, 2006, 2010; Ahmed 2007, 2012; Olson 2007). The qualified success of the two KRGs leads Stansfield (2005) to conclude that not only would a unified administration have been unfeasible at this stage, but that the era of peaceful division actually yielded tangible benefits for the Iraqi Kurdish political system and the people both parties governed. 'The executive governmental structures have matured considerably under the divided political system … [and] the capability of Kurds to govern their own country has obviously been enhanced by' their division (Stansfield 2005: 204).

Yet, again, as in 1991, the Iraqi Kurdish ethno-nationalist parties were forced by external actors and events to put aside their differences and cooperate. And, as in 1991, at the outset of the second US invasion of Iraq, prospects for the Iraqi Kurds to benefit from this campaign again looked dire. Understandably, in its war plans for Iraq, the Bush administration conceded greater importance to Turkey and the opportunity to open a second, northern front than to the quibbling Iraqi Kurdish ethno-nationalist parties. In Ankara, in 2002, a new political party, the *Adalet ve Kalkınma Partisi* (AKP, Justice and Development Party), had come to power that not only substantially differed in its composition, ideology and constituency from any previous mainstream Turkish party but soon was to revolutionize and lastingly alter the Kemalist consensus on which the Turkish political system had rested since the founding of the Republic.[1] The dilemma the new Turkish government posed for the Bush administration was not so much about the price Washington would have to pay to win Ankara over for its invasion of Iraq, but that even if Washington were to pay what was asked of it, the AKP leadership could not guarantee whether it could get enough of its MPs in line to back, in parliament, the stationing of US troops on Turkish soil, where a majority viewed what they saw as an 'imperialist crusade' against a fellow Muslim country, without legitimization or justification, extremely critically (Park 2003, 2005; Robins 2003a, 2003b; Güney 2005; Rubin 2005; Kapsis 2006; Hale 2007). With tens of thousands of US troops waiting off Turkish ports to disembark, crucial time in the run up to the vote ticked away while Turkey haggled over what it expected in compensation, and US diplomats tried to square the circle of getting the Iraqi Kurds to agree to a Turkish troop presence in a buffer zone extending up to 40 kilometres into Iraqi Kurdistan – as expected, the Turkish military was keen to make the best of an inevitable war it opposed in principle by extending operations against the PKK – which Massoud Barzani threatened to meet by force (Park 2003, 2005; Stansfield 2003b; Robins 2003a, 2003b; Güney 2005; Rubin 2005; Kapsis 2006; Hale 2007; Lawrence 2009). For the Iraqi Kurds, when war loomed on the horizon in February 2003, it did not so much promise the downfall of their nemesis in Baghdad as it did threaten the possible end of their de facto independent polity and their exercise in self-government at the hands of a Turkish occupation.

Despite these seemingly insurmountable obstacles, it came as a surprise to everyone involved when, in a historic and extremely narrow vote on 1 March 2003, the Turkish parliament rejected the US request for a second, northern front to be staged from Turkish soil.[2] With some pathos but not lacking in accuracy the most fortunate incident of the vote of the Turkish parliament against taking an active role in the US-led Iraq War can be considered the second birth hour of the Kurdistan Region of Iraq.

> For the Kurds of Iraq the outcome of 2003 could be seen as a best case scenario, since it removed the hated Saddam Hussein and kept the Turkish army out of their territory. Since they were the only group in Iraq which firmly supported US policy, and had substantial forces on the ground which Turkey lacked, it was the Iraqi Kurds, rather than the Turks, who emerged as America's most effective local allies.
>
> (Hale 2007: 124)[3]

Consequently, they became the main beneficiaries of US state-building in Iraq once Turkey had taken itself out of the equation and removed itself from having any say in the unfolding political future of its southern neighbour.

The March 2003 invasion, subsequent occupation, and resulting endeavour of crafting a new political and constitutional order for Iraq posed a seemingly insurmountable problem for Western scholars and policy-makers alike. Namely, what to do with a society with no prior feeling of communality or shared sense of national unity, that had deep ethnic and sectarian divisions, and where, for most of its existence as a state, its centripetal forces had been held together by a form of authoritarian governance that can only be described as a massive apparatus of coercion, unmitigated oppression, and ethnic cleansing to the extent of genocide. In short, and as outlined earlier, they were confronted with an entity that throughout its history had never been a functioning state or nation at all. Within the scholarly community Liam Anderson and Gareth Stansfield (2005), after deliberating alternative options, were among the first to argue for a 'managed partition of Iraq', in which the state would be divided by the *Coalition Provisional Authority* (CPA) that administered the US and British-led occupation and governance of Iraq from April 2003, into three autonomous regions corresponding to the existing ethno-religious divisions of a Kurdish north, Sunni Arab centre, and Shi'a Arab south. As a first step this would result in 'three autonomous units governed under the loose auspices of a single state', and with each individual region 'governed through existing structures' (Anderson & Stansfield 2005: 214). For a second step, the authors proposed a plebiscite to determine whether these three units wished to coexist and cooperate within a single federal state, a secession of the Kurdish north to become an independent state via a second, predominantly Arab state, or whether Iraq would break up altogether into three independent states along the pre-existing regions. While one is compelled to agree with Anderson and Stansfield (2005: 224) that 'the managed partition of Iraq is far from an ideal solution to the dilemma that currently confronts the US [in Iraq] … but there are no good options left, only less bad options', and one can even see the merit of their proposed plebiscite on the future of Iraq – in which 'the Iraqi people themselves [would be given] the opportunity to decide on the issue' (Anderson & Stansfield 2005: 214), for the first time in history – their argument is evidently driven by the authors' pro-Kurdish bias and a state-centric ontology that analytically equates ethnic groups and nations with states. This pro-Kurdish bias is neither surprising given their background as area studies experts having conducted years of extensive and invaluable field research among Iraq's Kurds, nor is it in itself something to epistemologically take issue with, since, in rejection of the false idol of scientific objectivism discussed in Part I, all of us engaging in scholarly analysis are inherently biased and our take on political matters is inherently subjective and shaped by our pre-conceived notions, values, experiences and world views. Another scholar deeply immersed in these matters through his writings, advocacy and role as an advisor to the Kurdistan Regional Government during the negotiations on the *Transitional Administrative Law* (TAL) in 2004 and the Iraqi constitution of 2005, Brendan O'Leary, openly admits to this bias when regarding himself, Stansfield, Michael Gunter, Peter Galbraith and other contributors to their edited volume also discussed and referenced here, among the ranks of 'honorary Kurdistanis' (O'Leary *et al.* 2005: XIX), internationals who share a deep professional and scholarly commitment to Iraqi Kurdistan, take 'the existence of Kurdistan as a political entity as a desirable given' (O'Leary *et al.* 2005: XVII), and acknowledge the 'compelling moral case for Kurdish statehood' (Anderson & Stansfield 2005: 220). In this sense then, Anderson and Stansfield's proposal for a 'managed partition' of Iraq amounts to nothing less than an organized, and democratically sanctioned transition from a unitary, artificial, and allegedly nonviable state of Iraq into two independent states – a Kurdish north and an Arab south – and they clearly commit themselves to identifying this as the 'most likely outcome' (Anderson & Stansfield 2005: 216).

Perhaps the most outspoken proponent for Iraqi Kurdish independence among this group of scholars, the so-called 'honorary Kurdistanis', is Peter Galbraith. In 2006, Galbraith condensed his advocacy for an independent Kurdish state into a book, entitled *The End of Iraq* (2006). After identifying 'an unrealistic and futile commitment to preserving the unity of [the Iraqi] state' as the 'main error' of US policy in Iraq since the fall of Saddam Hussein (Galbraith 2006: 12), Galbraith assured his readers that 'almost certainly, Kurdistan's full independence is just a matter of time' (Galbraith 2006: 206), and, in light of mounting US casualties before the so-called 'surge' of 2007, argued that the most viable strategy for the US to extract itself from the Iraqi quagmire was to reverse course and support the breakup of Iraq into two, potentially three, independent states.

> Partition works as a political solution to Kurdistan, the Shiite south, and the Sunni Arab centre because it formalizes what has already taken place. Partition is the reason Kurdistan is stable and the south relatively so. It is an Iraqi solution, embodied in the constitution, and not an imposed one. By contrast, the American effort to build a unified state with a non-sectarian, nonethnic police and army has not produced the result nor made any progress toward it. If the US were to try seriously, it would destabilize the parts of Iraq that are today secure.
>
> (Galbraith 2006: 222)

Once partition had been implemented, Galbraith advocated that the US should permanently station a troop contingent in Iraqi Kurdistan to protect its population from neighbouring countries and to serve as a base for US interventions in the region, a suggestion already made by Anderson and Stansfield (2005). Another prominent voice to join the chorus advocating partition of Iraq along ethnic lines, was the grand doyen of ethnic partition theory, Chaim Kaufmann (2006).

However, such prominent scholars advocating for partition of Iraq are not acting within a political vacuum, solely in the ivory towers of academia; their work and expertise carries considerable weight and has substantial public impact among policy makers and the media. They are the experts decision makers and journalists turn to for advice on policy formulation as well as strategic and contingency planning, or merely to get a comprehensive background on contemporary developments in a part of the world they know little about. As mentioned earlier, in the Foucauldian power-knowledge nexus they therefore hold positions of profound significance. President Clinton, for instance, allegedly declared Robert Kaplan's *Balkan Ghosts* mandatory reading for his administration struggling with the conflicts in the former Yugoslavia in the 1990s (Joras & Schetter 2004) and President Kennedy was famously influenced by Barbara Tuchman's *The Guns of August* during the Cuban Missile Crisis. In a reverse example, when expert advice is sought but not followed on by political decision makers, the so-called 'six wise men', British academics with a profound knowledge of the Middle East, counselled PM Tony Blair against an invasion on the eve of the Iraq War (Moreton 2015) – as we all know, in vain and with devastating consequences for Iraq, the wider region, the British government, and world politics at large. Even though we know of a few individual cases, in general, the direct impact of scholars on political decision making is rarely conclusively measurable. Yet, the fact that a phenomenon is difficult to quantify, does not mean that it is not significant.

Having said that, from the body of explanatory IR scholars who have written extensively on Iraqi Kurdistan, we can at least guess at their level of influence from positions they held as political advisors for international organizations, Western governments and the KRG itself, as well as their prominence as experts in leading Western media outlets. For example, the curriculum vitae of Brendan O'Leary, Lauder Professor of Political Science at the University of Pennsylvania and former director of its research institute on ethnic conflict, who has distinguished himself as an expert on federalism and power-sharing in ethnic conflicts from his involvement in the Northern Ireland peace process on, lists him as a UN, EU and UK Department for International Development and, as mentioned earlier, KRG constitutional and political advisor in conflicts in the Middle East and beyond, as well as a regular contributor on these issues for the BBC, CNN, NBC, *Voice of America*, the *Guardian*, the *Independent*, *Globe & Mail* and the *Financial Times* (UPenn 2015). Likewise, Gareth Stansfield, aside from his positions at the *Royal United Services Institute for Defence and Security Studies* (RUSI) and Chatham House, is prominently listed as a leading contributor to the 2014/2015 UK House of Commons Foreign Affairs Committee Report 'UK Government Policy on the Kurdistan Region of Iraq' (University of Exeter 2015). When trying to ascertain the degree of influence of scholars on the policy formulation process in the context of the US crafting a new political order for Iraq, the example of Peter Galbraith is, again, quite instructive. In this process, Galbraith, a former US diplomat and professor at the US Naval War College (Galbraith 2015), wore two hats, on the one hand advising the KRG on constitutional design while on the other hand acting as a lobbyist and consultant among the Washington foreign policy elite. In both roles he could draw on a sterling network of contacts, counting the late Richard Holbrooke as a close friend, and acting as a foreign policy advisor for the presidential campaigns of John Kerry in 2004 and Joe Biden in 2008 (Glanz 2009).[4] Given these connections, it should come as little surprise that the so-called 'Biden Plan' of a three-state solution for

Iraq (Biden 2006), with which the presidential candidate toured the country during the campaign, and which he had developed together with Leslie Gelb (Gelb 2003), President Emeritus of the *Council on Foreign Relations*, bore conspicuous resemblance to what Galbraith had been advocating.[5] By the same token, it is no stretch of the imagination to interpret these connections – together with a wider network of lobbyists the Iraqi Kurdish representation in Washington employed, strikingly portrayed by the *Washington Post's* Rajiv Chandrasekaran (2007) of *Imperial Life in the Emerald City* fame – as authoritative sources of influence whose expertise and advocacy could and indeed *did* shape public and professional perceptions of Iraqi Kurdistan and therewith the discourse on its future political status. This influence can be quite overt as in the case of Peter Galbraith who openly admits,

> I realized that the Kurdish leaders had a conceptual problem in planning for a federal Iraq. They were thinking in terms of devolution of power – meaning that Baghdad grants them rights. I urged the equation to be reversed. In a memo I sent [to Barham Salih and Nechirvan Barzani] … Kurdistan, I wrote, should take the initiative by writing its own constitution before the Iraqi constitutional process began … which clearly defined the powers of the Kurdistan Government as against those of the government of Baghdad … [Kurdistan] should, I argued manage its own resources … I urged that the Kurdistan constitution explicitly guarantee Kurdistan 'the power to establish, maintain, regulate, and control, a Kurdistan self-defense force' … I wrote … in the event of a conflict … the Constitution of Kurdistan … is the supreme law of Kurdistan. Any conflict between laws of Kurdistan and the laws of or Constitution of Iraq shall be decided in favour of the former.
>
> (Galbraith 2006: 160–161)

As elaborated in Part I, in general, though, the perceptions of a social phenomenon by political decision makers, journalists, and the general public – in this case the nature of an ethnic group and its political status – is shaped more subtly and over time by authoritative voices and accounts making reference to beliefs and world views the audience already holds or considers common sense. The world views of bureaucrats working in the service of the state, as discussed earlier, are unsurprisingly inherently state-centric, which is why the state-centric and groupist representations of explanatory IR scholars, whose expertise those bureaucrats are familiar with from previous accounts of the subject, policy briefings, expert testimonials and personal encounters, is valued. It constitutes knowledge that a specific audience holds in esteem and considers authoritative, all the more since it resonates with already held wider perceptions of the social world. If one already adheres in general to the perception of nations as organic, static, substantive, distinct, homogeneous and bounded units that constitute a precursor to the nation state, in other words as states-in-waiting, those scholars' portrayal of Kurds in Iraq as the Arabs' constitutive other and of the ethno-sectarian lines of division that tear the country apart as factual with each group vying for a maximum of political representation, if not outright national self-determination, makes sense. It is in this state-centric ontology, grounded in the analytical equation of ethno-nationalist groups with (proto-)states – more than merely a pro-Kurdish bias – where the representations of explanatory IR scholars of the nature, status and alleged political demands of the Iraqi Kurds, become problematic.

As has been detailed, those explanatory IR scholars advocating ethnic partition for Iraq tend to portray themselves as the voices of reason and pragmatism, who merely acknowledged the already existing ethnic and sectarian fault lines within Iraqi society and understood their proposals for the future political order of Iraq as simply implementing those 'realities' in a constitutional order. Peter Galbraith, for example, claimed, 'partition works as a political solution to Kurdistan, the Shiite south, and the Sunni Arab centre because it [would] formalise what has already taken place' (Galbraith 2006: 222), and since this constituted the supposedly factual point of departure for any deliberations on Iraqi Kurdistan's future political status, he asserted that 'almost certainly, Kurdistan's full independence is just a matter of time' (Galbraith 2006: 206). This, of course, is not to say that those explanatory IR scholars created the ethnic lines of division in Iraq – as has been outlined, an ethnicized discourse has dominated the Iraqi political space since the 1930s and has intensified ever since. It does suggest though, that by reading the political space of Iraq exclusively through a state-centric and groupist lens, by declaring this ethnicized discourse hegemonic in Iraq, that is, superseding all other forms of political discourse, and by portraying ethnic lines of division as inviolable factual reality rather than socio-political constructs, those scholars have not only dismissed alternative interpretations of Iraq's political space but, deliberately or not, contributed to the reification, substantialization, and essentialization of these ethnicized discourses and ethnic lines of division.

As an alternative to these representations, Toby Dodge, for example, takes issue with the simplistic, essentialist and groupist reading of Galbraith *et al.* that Iraq has 'three distinct communities' (Dodge 2005: 45). He goes on to invoke the Iran–Iraq War, in which '80 percent of the rank and file and 20 percent of the officer corps of the Iraqi army were Shias, yet they fought loyally for Iraq throughout the gruelling eight-year war with Iran, a state with a Shia majority' (Dodge 2005: 46). For him, 'explanations of this phenomenon cannot simply concentrate on ethnic identity, but must instead acknowledge the strength of Iraqi nationalism' (Dodge 2005: 46–47), even if that nationalism was constructed and propagated by the regime of Saddam Hussein. More recently, Fanar Haddad (2011) magisterially deconstructs the often belaboured Sunni-Shi'ia sectarian divide and gives a commendable account of the varied ambiguities of Iraqi identities, in conclusion reflecting on the potential for an Iraqi communality that counters the groupist perspective of explanatory IR. Yet, in the discourse on the future political order of Iraq in 2003/2004 such alternative accounts that would have facilitated inter-ethnic alliances and explored non-ethnic expressions of communality were sidelined, with ethnic solutions for an ethno-sectarian conflict dominating the debate.

The CPA under US 'Viceroy' Paul Bremer, who ran Iraq from 11 May 2003 by mandate of the United Nations until governance could be handed over to a democratically legitimized Iraqi government, had in principle agreed to a federalist structure, yet while Bremer intended for 'specific consideration being given to ethnic, sectarian and gender diversity' (Marr 2011: 266), he wished for the national dialogue on the future of Iraq to be as broadly based as feasible under the conditions of occupation, reflecting the neo-conservative Wilsonian idealism of transforming Iraq into a paragon of democracy with the potential to act as a model for the entire region (Heinze 2008; Dodge 2009, 2010, 2013; Ikenberry *et al.* 2009; Owens 2009; Miller 2010; Smith 2011). Yet, aside from quickly unravelling in light of the rapidly deteriorating security situation, the neo-conservative utopia too, had a distinctly groupist element. 'The [CPA] tried to right Saddam's wrongs by engaging in social engineering, favouring the once oppressed Shiites and Kurds at the expense of the once ruling Sunnis' (Chandrasekaran 2010: 217), another aspect in which the discourse reflected previously held beliefs of the CPA decision makers: the Sunni Arabs, as a group, as the perpetrators and Kurds and Shi'ia Arabs, also as ethno-sectarian groups, as the victims of a dictatorial regime. Chandrasekaran (2010: 218) continues,

> the result was a governing council that had strict quotas: thirteen Shiite Arabs, five Sunni Arabs, five Sunni Kurds, one Christian and one Turkmen. To some Iraqis, who placed national identity over religious or ethnic affiliation, it looked like the Americans were adopting a version of the troubled political system in Lebanon that divided government posts among several religious groups. 'We never saw each other as Sunnis or Shiites first. We were Iraqis first', said Saad Jawad, a professor of political science at Baghdad University. 'But the Americans changed all that. They made a point of categorizing people as Sunni or Shiite or Kurd'.

With Iraq descending into civil war, each faction in the political power struggle increasingly forming their own militia, and the US government, under pressure with upcoming elections in 2004, pushing for Bremer to abandon his drawn out process of nation building in favour of an accelerated transition to Iraqi rule, ethnic and sectarian divisions soon came to overshadow any voices for Iraqi or Arab unity (International Crisis Group 2005a, 2005b, 2006; Hashim 2006; Dodge 2006, 2012; Allawi 2007; Ricks 2007; Stansfield 2007a; Chandrasekaran 2010; Haddad 2011; Marr 2011). The final hour of those in support of creating a stronger central state based on civil rights, Islam as a unifying factor and a vague notion of Iraqi identity, came during the negotiations for the TAL, which was supposed to formalize an interim structure of governance until a new permanent constitution had been approved by the public. They foundered against overwhelming KRG opposition, which threatened to veto any compromise that did not guarantee the current autonomous status of the Kurdistan Region

(Chandrasekaran 2010), and Bremer 'had to ... essentially set[ting] up a separate negotiation track for the Kurds' (Marr 2011: 281).

The KRG representatives presented Bremer and the Iraqi negotiators in Baghdad with a fait accompli, and in the end, the KRG got all it had bargained for, with a 'highly decentralized' system that 'gave the Kurds a victory by recognizing KRG control in the north and allowing it to continue government functions in these regions, to retain control over police and security, and to tax in KRG areas' (Marr 2011: 281). Ironically, the biggest negotiation victory for the KRG in the TAL had originally been intended to placate the Sunni Arabs (Stansfield 2007a), who felt left out of the dialogue on the future order of Iraq, by granting a provision for a two-thirds majority vote in three governorates to block the adoption of a new constitution, thus providing the KRG with an iron-clad veto on any future political arrangement that would not enshrine the principle of ethnic federalism in the constitution.[6] The Iraqi Constitution of 2005 then merely cast in stone the principle of ethnic federalism for which the TAL had already prepared the ground.[7]

> On this issue, the Kurds won virtually all the arguments. They insisted on a distribution of power between the central government and regions, which gave the latter priority. The Kurds worked to weaken the authority of the central government ... they managed to get a weak central government and a highly decentralized polity.
>
> (Marr 2011: 293)

Following Gabraith's above-quoted advice, Article 111 of the constitution turned out to stipulate that 'in case of a conflict between regional and national legislation, the region would prevail ... [in sum,] the federal government was given few exclusive authorities' (Marr 2011: 294–295).[8]

For the Iraqi Kurdish ethno-nationalist parties, the prevalence of the principle of ethnic federalism that enshrined in the Iraqi Constitution their national self-governance in the three governorates of Dohuk, Erbil and Al Sulaimaniyah constitutes unquestionably the greatest accomplishment in their 70-year struggle for national self-determination. For the rest of Iraq it turned out an unmitigated disaster. Not so much because the KRG had managed to codify the self-governance they had enjoyed since 1991 in the current constitutional structure of Iraq, but because during the entire constitutional process ethnic lines of division between Kurds and Arabs had been reified, essentialized and substantialized – therewith never giving the alternative of developing an Iraqi identity based on factors other than sectarian divisions and groupist thinking, any realistic chance to evolve. What is worse, the principle of ethnic federalism, groupist thinking, the Iraqi Kurdish leaders' negotiation strategy, together with the dynamics resulting from the ethno-sectarian strife cum civil war left the rest of Iraq with such a weak and powerless central government inherently prone to paralysis that it should have come as no surprise it proved utterly incapable of dealing with the challenges it faced in all but the Kurdish parts of Iraq.[9]

It may appear futile to speculate as to what would have come of Iraq had the CPA wholeheartedly embraced ethnic partition as advocated by Anderson, Stansfield, O'Leary, Galbraith and others, ultimately resulting in an independent Kurdish state or a genuine three-state solution. The true tragedy of Iraq may very well be that after the toppling of Saddam Hussein's regime, foreign invasion and occupation, and more than two years of an ethnicized discourse, exacerbated by the policies the CPA imposed on the country and ultimately culminating in a full-scale civil war, the ethno-sectarian divides had become so wide and the frontlines so hardened that indeed complete partition would have been the least bad option, as Anderson and Stansfield argued. Catastrophically, Iraq has become the case study par excellence of the contradictions inherent to state-centrism and ethnic partition – whether it is admitted to be ethnic partition or euphemistically called regional federalism is of secondary importance. On the one hand, groupism and state-centrism presuppose ethno-nationalist groups as organic, static, substantive, distinct, homogeneous and bounded units, ascribe social agency to them, reify and substantialize them together with their claims for national self-determination, which, in a state-centric world, is all too often equated with territorial sovereignty. On the other hand, though, it considers existing sovereign states and their borders as sacrosanct and inviolable. When between 2003 and 2005, the CPA, through its policies and designs for the future political order of Iraq, advanced the former but at the same time upheld its commitment to the latter, the two contradicting principles inevitably came to clash. If, at the outset, the assessment of the 'honorary Kurdistanis' had been factual, had been the only conceivable interpretation of the socio-political space in Iraq in 2003 – that Iraq is divided into three distinct ethno-sectarian groups and that these pre-existing divisions ran so deep that a peaceful coexistence in one state would have been impossible – the CPA should have allowed these groups to pursue independence. If, on the other hand, the international community intended to stay true to its commitment to the sovereignty and territorial integrity of Iraq, as voiced by President Bush, PM Tony Blair and other US/UK decision makers before the invasion and repeatedly during the occupation (Bush 2003; Bush & Blair 2003; Bush & Aznar 2003; Williams & Roach 2006; Ricks 2007; Elden 2009; Elden & Williamson 2007), the CPA should have vigorously opposed the discourse propagated by Iraq's ethno-sectarian elites and instead strengthened those political forces working on the preservation of Iraq as a unitary state, a dialogue of inclusion and a common Iraqi identity with perhaps Islam as a unifying factor. By striking a *media via*, an incomplete partition based on ethnic federalism that exacerbated the existing ethno-sectarian divides yet at the same time forced the ethno-sectarian groups vying for power to remain within the corset of a sovereign state, the CPA doomed Iraq and its people to suffer from competing ethno-sectarian forces, strengthened and emboldened by the provisions of the TAL, a notoriously weak central government, and foreign powers playing Iraq's various ethno-sectarian factions off against each other.

In order to fully appreciate this argument about the inherent contradictions and complete failure of the CPA's state-building in Iraq and its devastating consequences it is worth recalling what governing structure Anderson and Stansfield had advocated for Iraq in 2005:

> The governing of Iraq does not need to be enshrined immediately in a set of inviolate constitutional principles; government can be regionally organised, flexible, and sensitive to the diverse social structures on the ground. Some form of loosely organised, largely powerless central government can be established to provide an umbrella over the whole. This can be made deliberately powerless and given to the Iraqi exile community to run, or can be constitutionally engineered to produce paralysis. A replication of the constitution of Bosnia perhaps.
>
> (Anderson & Stansfield 2005: 215)

Yet, they saw their 'loosely, organised, largely powerless central government' as a precursor to ethnic partition, to the break-up of Iraq, a situation that was from their point of view inevitable and ultimately desirable. Earlier, they themselves had admitted that 'by all accounts, the Bosnian constitution has been a disaster for all concerned, and has served to heighten rather than reduce ethnic tensions' (Anderson & Stansfield 2005: 194); they never argued for a central government perpetually paralysed by ethnic division, à la Bosnia, having to run the affairs of Iraq indefinitely, but understood it as a temporary vehicle to administer the 'managed partition of Iraq'; an eventuality which they advocated for Iraq's future together with the plebiscite legitimizing that partition. Anderson and Stansfield's central government, powerless by intent and design, only makes sense in the context the authors had intended, as a provisional and transitional arrangement, not as permanent institution of good governance. And yet, the dreaded precedent of Bosnia is precisely what the Iraqi Constitution and its architects bestowed upon Iraq in 2005, with an autonomous Kurdistan Region reminiscent of Republika Srpska vis-à-vis a system-immanently dysfunctional central government. The main difference from Bosnia, which makes the application of this model to Iraq all the more tragic, is that the intentionally powerless central government in Iraq – save the Kurdistan Region – has to cope day in, day out with a level of violence Bosnia experienced before, not after, the Dayton accords.

This interpretation also puts into perspective the role explanatory IR scholars such as the 'honorary Kurdistanis' played in the process of crafting a new political order for Iraq. As has been repeatedly emphasized throughout this study, when identifying them as co-protagonists in the ethno-nationalist conflicts they set out to describe, this does not mean that they brought into existence the ethnosectarian lines of division that increasingly dichotomized Iraqi society. On the contrary, in Part II, the evolution of these divisions from the early 1930s onwards was described in detail. Nor does this study claim that such scholars propagating a groupist and modernist reading of ethno-nationalism are responsible for the political structure of Iraq that developed after 2003 and that has been identified as the single most important factor for the inherent weakness of the central government, the collapse of governance at large, the hardening of ethno-sectarian fault lines and the ensuing civil war (Jawad 2013). That responsibility rather rests with the ethno-nationalist elites in Iraq, the CPA, its sponsors primarily in the US government and the international community at large, who, each for their own reason, promoted an ethnic solution for an ethno-nationalist conflict and exacerbated the existing ethno-sectarian lines of division, while at the same time forcing those ethno-nationalist elites and the Iraqi population to coexist in a unitary sovereign state that existed on paper only. It is this contradiction of principles, manifest in the imposition of a flawed-by-design political order à la Dayton on Iraq, that spelled disaster for the country and the wider region. The role some explanatory IR scholars played in these developments, which renders them co-protagonists in Iraq's ethno-sectarian conflicts, is that through their essentialist reading of the socio-political space of Iraq prior to and immediately after the invasion, together with their normative prescriptions for the country's future political order based on these groupist accounts, they reified and substantialized ethno-sectarian divides that were not factual but socially constructed. Furthermore, through their representations, they occasionally legitimized the claims to authority and territorial sovereignty of certain ethno-nationalist elites and contributed to the overall shaping of particular perceptions among Western decision makers of Iraq's socio-political landscape – a portrayal in which the ethnicized discourse is presupposed and depicted as predominant at the expense of more inclusionary approaches that would have emphasized aspects of communality rather than us versus them dichotomies. This, in conclusion of this section, is the ontological case made against explanatory IR in this study. Curiously then, at the same time as the principle of ethnic federalism with all its devastating consequences was enshrined in the Iraqi constitution, it was the PKK, one of the objects of study of these scholars, one of the supposedly essentialist ethno-nationalist elites, that developed an interesting alternative to the modernist reading on Kurdish national self-determination.

The PKK after the capture of Abdullah Öcalan

For an insurgency like the PKK, so strictly structured around a *Führerprinzip*, in which Öcalan's often seemingly endless ideological musings were considered gospel and his orders dogma, the capture, show trial, and life sentence for its leader amounted to the most severe blow the group had to endure in its history, and it appears a miracle that it survived this at all. The more so since, to many of its rank and file, Öcalan's 'conversion' during the trial must have appeared as a betrayal of all they had fought and often given their and their families' lives for. At first Öcalan declared an end to the two-decades-long armed struggle and encouraged his guerrillas to lay down arms:

> I want to make an important appeal. I want to offer a peace congress to the PKK. If the government extends a hand to us for peace, the PKK will become the state's most powerful ally … I am calling for an end to the

armed struggle. The PKK should stop resisting the democratic state ... My authority in the organization is unbroken. If the government gives me a chance, I can make the PKK fighters come down from the mountains within three months.[10]

For any PKK fighter in the field this alone must have been difficult to come to terms with. Not only did Öcalan call for a unilateral ceasefire and promised the Turkish authorities his and his cadres' full cooperation, he called the Turkish state – who tens of thousands of Kurds in decades of PKK indoctrination had come to see as the relentlessly assimilationist and oppressive enemy – a 'democratic state'. And yet Öcalan went even further in a statement of 2 August 1999, in which he questioned the armed struggle of the PKK over the past two decades itself, and tried to portray himself as a reasonable man of peace while blaming others within the organization for the escalation of the conflict since the 1980s:

> It can hardly be said that military activities under the leadership of the PKK had developed into a proper guerrilla warfare in terms of basic strategy and tactics. Even more wrong would it be to suppose that the way of warfare of the high-ranking responsible persons had been the way I wanted it to be ... Especially in 1997, under the name of an offensive against village guards, there were attacks on civilians, among them women and children, that should never [have been] the target of military attacks ... I find it important that people know that I was involved in quite a tough struggle against this from 1987–97 ... It is not difficult to find out that the activities that harmed the PKK most have mainly happened in that period and by the hands of people like these who tried to take control by themselves.[11]

What is surprising is that these barely disguised attempts by the PKK leader to save his own skin and avoid the death penalty by portraying himself as the man who can persuade the PKK insurgents to lay down arms, and therefore be of greater use to the Turkish state alive, were heeded by his followers. The PKK command, although at first issuing orders that Öcalan, who was feared to be influenced by the Kurdish state apparatus, were to be ignored, in the end obeyed his command and implemented a unilateral ceasefire from 1 September 1999 on that lasted until 1 June 2004 (Özcan 2006; Marcus 2007a; Tahiri 2007; Uslu 2007; Brauns & Kiechle 2010; Akkaya & Jongerden 2011, 2012; Eccarius-Kelly 2011; Gunter 2011c; Gunes 2011).

At this stage, though, when analysing the PKK's evolution from the capture of Abdullah Öcalan until today, one has to ask, in the words of Doğu Ergil,

> when we say 'the PKK', who are we talking about today? Are we talking about Öcalan on İrmalı, the fighters in the mountains in Qandil, the TAK [*Teyrêbazên Azadiya Kurdistan* or Kurdistan Freedom Falcons], the criminal networks that sustain the organisation and profiteer from trading drugs, weapons, and smuggling, or the many affiliated organisations in the diaspora

in Europe? And where do the legal Kurdish political parties like the BDP [*Barış ve Demokrasi Partisi*, in Kurdish *Partiya Aştî û Demokrasiyê* or Peace and Democracy Party] fit into the picture?[12]

The best answer may be that to a greater or lesser extent all of the above actors need to be taken into consideration. This heterogeneity and multi-layeredness not only makes the post-1999 PKK so difficult to analyse but also complicates the on and off peace process since the Turkish state not only has no clearly identifiable interlocutor with which to negotiate but also, once a comprehensive deal had been struck, it is not at all certain whether all the various actors subsumed under the today rather vague term 'PKK' would abide by it. This heterogeneity is a result of the chaotic period from 1999 until 2004/2005, in which the organization tried to respond to the capture of its leader, his demands for a political reorientation towards political dialogue with the Turkish state, mass scale defections of prominent cadre members, and an increasingly hostile international environment in the wake of the global 'War on Terror', the consolidation of the Iraqi Kurdish polity, the US invasion of Iraq in 2003, and the rise of the AKP in Turkey. It is reflected in a rapid succession of party congresses that often ended in heated disputes, divisions, prominent defections and power struggles between the group's leaders, attempts at re-branding and re-naming the movement, and giving it a new ideological direction that took until 2003 to gain consistency and logical clarity. After the PKK, at its Eight Congress in April 2002, changed its name to *Kongreya Azadî û Demokrasiya Kurdistanê* (KADEK, Kurdistan Freedom and Democracy Congress) in order to emphasize its commitment to non-violent struggle for Kurdish cultural and civil rights within the democratic framework of the Turkish state, in November 2003 KADEK abolished itself and was re-launched as *Kongra Gelê Kurdistan* (Kongra-Gel, People's Congress of Kurdistan) in order to make the party more politically inclusive, allowing for former *Demokrasi Partisi* (DEP, Democracy Party) MPs to hold prominent positions within its ranks, only for the organization to re-establish itself as PKK in 2005 (Özcan 2006; Brauns & Kiechle 2010; Akkaya & Jongerden 2011; Akkaya 2012, 2013; Eccarius-Kelly 2011; Gunter 2011c; Gunes 2011). Naturally, these organizational and ideological revisions, shifts and new orientations did not come unopposed; the most prominent of these defections occurred in August 2004, when, after losing out in a power struggle with the faction around Murat Karaylian and Cemil Bayik, Osman Öcalan and Nizamettin Taş left the PKK to found a rival organization, the *Partiya Welatparêzên Demokratên Kuristan* (PWD, Patriotic and Democratic Party of Kurdistan), with former *Halkın Demokrasi Partisi* (HADEP, People's Democracy Party) MP Hikmet Fidan, which among other differences with the Karaylian/Bayik faction, advocated for a closer cooperation with KDP and PUK. After Fidan was assassinated in Diyarbakir in July 2005, and two other prominent party leaders killed in a car bomb in Iraqi Kurdistan the following year – Osman Öcalan and Nizamettin Taş harbour no doubt that the PKK was behind the assassinations – the party descended into obscurity.[13]

As significant as these structural shifts, factional feuds, and defections are for political analysis, the prime concern here is with the PKK's ideological re-orientation after 1999, and in particular its re-conceptualization of national self-determination. The ideological paradigm shift that started to emerge from Öcalan's prison writings (2008, 2011a, 2011b, 2012) constitutes an amalgam of anarchist conceptualization of society cum critique of the nation state, utopian socialism, feminism, and a rather obscure Mesopotamian historicism (Brauns & Kiechle 2010; Akkaya & Jongerden 2011; Akkaya 2012, 2013; Casier 2011; Gunes 2011). Central to the post-1999 PKK ideology are the concepts of 'radical democracy' and 'democratic confederalism' developed by nineteenth-century anarchist theoreticians Pierre-Joseph Proudhon, Mikhail Bakunin, and Peter Kropotkin (Fowler 1972; Hyams 1979; Crowder 1991; Ward 1992; Prichard 2010; Carter 2012). Those writers conceptually opposed the ideology of liberal, democratic nationalism prevalent in nineteenth-century Europe, and developed an alternative model to the centralizing nation state for how society is rooted in a purportedly 'truer' form of democracy, federalism, and regionalism. While Proudhon recognized that the liberal, mass democratic, and centralized nation state had the potential of turning into a majority-sanctioned despotism of elites promoting ever more comprehensive homogenization of society in order to maximize their control over it (Hyams 1979; Crowder 1991; Ward 1992; Prichard 2010), Bakunin developed the utopian concept of a global federalism replacing individual, competing and authoritarian nation states. Taking the pre-1848 Swiss Confederation as an example, Bakunin envisioned a federalism that is rooted in an individualist and regionalist conceptualization of society, resulting in a bottom-up and voluntary collectivization of people, goods, and means of production into communes, and, in the long run, into a global confederation (Bakunin 1973). He emphasized, though, the completely voluntary character of any political federation and formation into a polity; a community that could be as freely dissolved by its members as it was formed:

> Just because a region has formed part of a state, even by voluntary accession, it by no means follows that it incurs any obligation to remain tied to it forever. No obligation in perpetuity is acceptable to human justice … The right of free union and equally free secession comes first and foremost among all political rights; without it, confederation would be nothing but centralisation in disguise.
>
> (Bakunin 1973: 96)

This anarchist conceptualization of a democratic, communally-based, organized society in confederation with other equally structured societies is in direct opposition to the liberal, modernist understanding of nation and state advocated by explanatory IR, as discussed in Part I. It challenges the hegemonic concept of nation, national self-determination, and the state on four fundamental levels (Akkaya & Jongerden 2011, 2012, 2013): (1) similar to Marxism, it argues that the formation of political units, i.e. modern sovereign nation states, advanced by modern liberal nationalism is a (bourgeois) elite project and therefore not truly democratic, contradicting the equation of liberal democracy and modern nationalism that constitutes the key criteria of the modernist understanding of nationhood; (2) instead of the top-down implementation of nationhood and state sovereignty, it argues for a voluntary association of free individuals at the grassroots level that, if desired, pursue an equally voluntary project of confederation with other like-minded communities that is at any time reversible; (3) due to the fact that any political community is voluntarily entered, it can as freely be dissolved or abandoned, therefore, unlike the modern nation state and the state-centric system, valorizing the right to secession as one of its founding principles – in other words, to them, self-determination only makes sense with an implicit and comprehensive right to secession, an ideal, as has been shown, the liberal modernist understanding of the principle of explanatory IR denies; finally, (4) in particular, Proudhon argues that such a voluntary confederation of individuals is better suited to accommodating diversity within society than the assimilationist and pathologically homogenizing nation state.

Öcalan, who identifies the organization of societies into states as the 'original sin' of humanity (Akkaya & Jongerden 2011, 2012, 2013), argues that the 'democratic confederalism' he advocates, 'builds on the self-government of local communities, and is organised in the form of open councils, town councils, local parliaments and larger congresses. The citizens themselves are agents of this kind of self-government, not state-based authorities' (Öcalan 2008: 32). These local councils and various forms of self-governance in the Bakunian sense, united in a democratic confederation, Öcalan sees as the prime driving force behind Kurdish liberation and unification. I therefore agree with Akkaya and Jongerden (2011) and Akkaya (2012, 2013), who argue that authors such as Özcan (2006) err when claiming that the PKK has abandoned the struggle for an independent and united Kurdistan. The post-1999 PKK ideology therefore,

> does not mean the abandonment of the ideal for a united Kurdistan, but rather that this ideal is aimed at in a different way. The ultimate aim of independence is no longer embodied in the realisation of a classical state, but in the establishment and development of self-government … Instead of a classical state-building process, that is, from above, establishing the overarching structures of governance, a process of constructing Kurdistan from below is being attempted, that is, a genuinely democratic confederalism.
>
> (Akkaya & Jongerden 2011: 156)

Even more central to Öcalan's thinking and post-1999 PKK ideology than the classics of anarchist thought are the writings of the American anarchist and libertarian socialist author Murray Bookchin who, most prominently in *The Ecology of Freedom* (2005) and *The Next Revolution* (2015), advocated the decentralization of societies along principals of environmentalism, egalitarianism, communalism, municipalism and direct democracy (Biehl 2012, 2015; de Jong 2016).[14] Bookchin, while critical of the simplistic and primitive dismissal and overt hostility towards the state of US political libertarianism, conceptualized a system of organizing societies he called 'libertarian municipalism', where libertarian institutions, vested with and empowered by directly democratic assemblies, would self-govern communalist municipalities, these municipalities would form federations that, confronted with environmental catastrophe, would ultimately replace the nation state, which Bookchin, like Bakunin and other classic anarchists since him, understand to be not only an impediment but an actual confinement of true freedoms (Bookchin 2005, 2015; Biehl 2015).

> To bring about this society, Bookchin favoured a combination of political action and prefigurative organising – the creation in the here and now of structures such as cooperatives and democratic associations that could foreshadow a better society. Political action and these experiments would, Bookchin argued, begin to empower ordinary people in their communities … Öcalan's lawyers shared his [adaptations of Bookchin's] ideas with the PKK, who embraced it and radically reformed the organisation's theory and practice.
>
> (de Jong 2016)

While de Jong himself doubts Öcalan's conversion from absolutist and merciless guerrilla leader to social reformer embracing peaceful activism and direct democracy – which in today's PKK remains as unrealized as in the days when he directly commanded the insurgency – many of Bookchin's ideas are said to be implemented today in *Rojava*, Syrian Kurdistan (discussed in the final chapter), where the local PKK-offshoot, the PYD, fights to establish a system of autonomous self-governance on the principles of democratic confederalism.

Having said that, I agree with Akkaya and Jongerden that the PKK today advocates in theory a compelling alternative to the hegemonic state-centric international system of assimilationist and pathologically homogenizing modern nation states for whom sovereignty all too often means the suppression of democracy and self-determination. The post-1999 PKK therefore not only 'successfully reinvented itself' but 'Öcalan's critique of the (classical) concept of the nation-state brings him to a fresh conceptualization of politics. He considers the nation-state as outdated, and instead pleads for a system named democratic confederalism as an alternative to the state' (de Jong 2016: 157). Consequently, it would be wrong, to apply, as Özcan does, to the post-1999 PKK the same understanding of nationalism, national self-determination, and independence as to the pre-1999 PKK, for while the latter can be conceived with the traditional understanding of these principles of explanatory IR, the former revolutionizes and ontologically challenges them. It has to be said, though, that as intellectually intriguing as this alternative concept of political communal organization is, in practice, the PKK, with its authoritarian organizational structure and its ongoing attempts to monopolize the Kurdish political discourse, remains as much an obstacle to its realization as the nationalizing states it opposes.

In practical terms, from 2000 until its return to the armed struggle in 2004, the PKK tried to facilitate a national democratic dialogue on cultural and democratic rights for Turkey's Kurds, in which it was assisted by the affiliated *Demokratik Toplum Partisi* (DTP, *Partiya Civaka Demokratîk* in Kurdish or Democratic Society Party), who until its ban by the Turkish Constitutional Court in 2009, propagated an ideologically related 'Project for Democratic Autonomy' (Watts 2006, 2010; Çandar 2009; Casier *et al.* 2011; Gunes 2011; Erdem 2013). In terms of organizational structure, the novel concept of democratic confederalism is implemented in the PKK encouraging the formation of regional sister-organizations such as *Partiya Jiyani Azadi Kurdistan* (PJAK, Kurdistan Free Life Party) in Iran, *Partiya Yekita ya Demokratik* (PYD, Democratic Union Party) in Syria, and *Partiya Careseriya Demokratik a Kurdistane* (PCDK, Kurdistan Democratic Solution Party) in Iraqi Kurdistan, united under the umbrella organization *Koma Civaken Kurdistan* (KCK, Kurdistan Democratic Confederation). This re-conceptualization of national self-determination through democratic confederalism, though, not only brought the PKK into conflict with the nationalizing states as well as with the US state-building project in Iraq, but also reignited its ideological antagonism with KDP and PUK.

Notes

1 On the AKP, see Atasoy (2009), Yavuz (2009), Zürcher (2009), Hale & Özbudun (2010), Öktem (2011), Park (2012a), and White (2012).
2 264 MPs voted in favour, 251 against, with 19 abstentions. Yet since Turkish parliamentary regulations allow a measure to pass only with a majority supporting it, the 'nays' and abstentions combined outweighed the 'yes's (Kapsis 2006).
3 On the military dimension of the 2003 Iraq War and the immediate aftermath, see Woodward (2004), Packer (2005), Phillips (2005), Gordon & Trainor (2007), Ricks (2007) and Chandrasekaran (2010). On the role of the Iraqi Kurdish *peshmerga* during the war, see Lawrence (2009).
4 According to the *New York Times'* James Glanz (2009) and the Norwegian investigative journalist who uncovered his remuneration, Galbraith was rewarded for his consultancy in Iraqi Kurdistan with a 5 per cent share in the exploits of the Tawke oil field, for which the Norwegian oil company DNO had secured licences, also thanks to Galbraith lobbying on their behalf via the KRG.
5 It should be noted, though, that the 'Biden Plan' did not argue for Iraq to partition into three independent states but rather advocated for ever wider degrees of autonomy beyond what the 2005 constitution had already admitted the regions, which potentially could lead to a region declaring independence in the future (Harrer 2014). In this more moderate approach it resembled the trajectory Anderson and Stansfield (2005) had outlined earlier rather than Galbraith's finite course for secession.
6 On the principle of ethnic federalism, see McGarry (2005a, 2005b), McGarry and O'Leary (2005), Herther-Spiro (2007), Erk & Anderson (2009), Fessha (2011).
7 Detailed analyses of the process of negotiating and drafting the Iraqi Constitution are given in International Crisis Group (2005a, 2005b), Morrow (2005), Allawi (2007), McGarry and O'Leary 2007; Arato (2009), Elden (2009), and Jawad (2013). Anderson (2007b) wants the principle of 'regional federalism' as introduced in the 2005 Iraqi Constitution understood as a 'flexible hybrid' between 'ethnic federalism', that usually accentuates ethnic divisions, and 'territorial federalism', that, at least in theory, 'manufactur[es] pluralism' (Anderson 2007b: 224). Given the fact that, according to Fathi Al Mudaris, a statistician at the KRG Ministry of Trade and Industry, the population of the Kurdistan Region is estimated 90 per cent ethnic

Kurdish (Interview Al Mudaris, Erbil, Iraqi Kurdistan, 20 October 2011), and that the KRG intends to incorporate those areas with a significant Kurdish population outside its jurisdiction – the so-called 'contested territories' – into the Kurdistan Region, Anderson's hybrid, to put it euphemistically, appears ostensibly lopsided towards 'ethnic federalism'. Herther-Spiro (2007), for example, positively recognizes post-2005 as a clear-cut case of 'ethnic federalism'.

8 The draft Iraqi Constitution was approved in a public referendum on 15 October 2005. Overall turnout was 63 per cent, and while the three main Sunni Arab provinces of Anbar, Salah al-Din, and Niniveh rejected the constitution, in the other provinces it was affirmed by more than 90 per cent. The TAL had specified that the constitutional draft would fail if two-thirds of the electorate in any three provinces rejected it in the referendum; since Niniveh only rejected it by 55 per cent it passed, constitutionally speaking, not in terms of overall approval in sheer numbers, but by a hair's breadth (Dawisha & Diamond 2006; Allawi 2007; Stansfield 2007a; Marr 2011).

9 As in this study, Jawad (2013: 1) identifies the 'excessive concessions granted to the Kurds on the issues of federal government' as one of the main factors explaining the weakness of the Iraqi state and its system-immanent inability to effectively deal with the myriad political and security challenges it came to face after 2005. See also International Crisis Group (2005b), Morrow (2005), Elden (2009) and Elden and Williams (2007) for a similar assessment.

10 Quoted in Tahiri (2007: 244).

11 Quoted in Tahiri (2007: 259–260). In response to his about-turn, one of Öcalan's lawyers, Ahmet Zeki Okcuoglu, resigned from his defence team and declared, 'For dictators, their own lives are more important than everything … There is nothing that can't be sacrificed for this.' Quoted in Marcus (2007a: 285). Öcalan's long-time political opponent Kemal Burkay, had as much to say:

> He is a coward … It is possible that since being arrested, Abdullah Öcalan thinks that he has been mistaken and that he has accepted [the idea of] a peaceful solution … But Öcalan's statements to the court and to the state that 'whatever you want, I will do' and his extending his respects to the Turkish Republic, and stressing many times his wish to be of service, this shocked Kurds and [the PKK's] members.
>
> (Quoted in Tahiri 2007: 284)

12 Interview Ergil op. cit. The TAK is considered a radical splinter group from the PKK (Brandon 2006b; Marcus 2007b; Casier 2010); the BDP, until 2014, was the then incarnation of the legal Kurdish political parties that have been routinely outlawed by Turkish state institutions and then re-founded under a new name (Watts 2010; Kubicek 2011).

13 Interviews Öcalan, Taş, and Ataç op. cit.

14 In 2004, Öcalan, who referred to himself as a disciple of Bookchin, even tried to arrange through his lawyers a meeting with the anarchist iconoclast in his prison on Imrali, which – aside from the Turkish authorities being unlikely to grant this request – Bookchin, who passed away in 2006, was too frail to accept (Biehl 2012).

9 Iraqi Kurdistan, the PKK and Turkey

The Iraqi Kurdistan – Turkey rapprochement

The historic decision by the Turkish parliament to deny the US a second, northern front in its 2003 invasion of Iraq not only saved the Kurdistan Region of Iraq from Turkish occupation, it also resulted in an unprecedented period of strained relations between Washington and Ankara that extended to the US client polity in Erbil.[1]

> For five years, between 2003 and 2008, Turkey refused to have any dialogue with us, they simply did not talk to us, they did not even talk to the US … there were no political consultations, no talks on how to deal with the PKK, no negotiations on Kirkuk or on the post-conflict order of Iraq … only silence. We wanted to engage them in dialogue on many issues but could not get them [to talk to us].[2]

By imposing a de facto political embargo on Iraqi Kurdistan and pursuing a stubborn, and ultimately self-defeating refusal to engage in any meaningful political dialogue with the Bush administration – who after what it considered a betrayal in 2003 was not keen to amend relations either – the Erdoğan government virtually took itself out of the equation of having any say in the post-war restructuring of Iraq (Barkey 2005, 2011; Olson 2005a, 2005b, 2009; Park 2005, 2012a, 2012b; Fuller 2008). By 2007 the AKP leadership had to realize that its obstructionism was leading nowhere and was no longer sustainable. This recognition had four primary reasons.

1   First, it illustrates recognition by the Turkish government of the dramatically altered nature and political status of the Kurdistan Region in the post-2003 order of Iraq, outlined earlier. Of equal importance, and both an expression as well as a function of Iraqi Kurdistan's altered political status, was the fact that every day that the rest of Iraq descended more into the chaos of ethno-sectarian civil war, Erbil came to be seen in Washington as the only stable and reliable partner in Iraq. Turkish foreign policy simply could no longer afford to ignore that the Kurdistan Region had become a key US ally in the region, nor

that even when it limited its relations to the Iraqi government, its main interlocutors – President Jalal Talabani and Foreign Minister Hoshyar Zebari – were Iraqi Kurds and naturally represented Iraqi Kurdish interests to a perhaps greater extent than Iraqi positions.

2   Due to several setbacks in Turkish foreign policy since the AKP had come to power, and in response to the dramatic changes in regional power constellations that the US occupation of Iraq had brought about, Turkish political scientist and then advisor to PM Erdoğan, Ahmet Davotoğlu, hailed in 2010 by *Foreign Policy* as the 'brains behind Turkey's global reawakening' and number seven of its top 100 'thinkers' with a global impact (*Foreign Policy* 2010), developed a paradigm shift that would revolutionize Turkish foreign policy; subsumed under the catchword 'strategic depth' the new, less paranoid Turkish foreign policy doctrine, instead of perceiving Turkey's neighbours as an inherent threat, sought to engage them in projects of mutual interests and to capitalize on the rich legacy of the Ottoman Empire in the Middle East and beyond (Murinson 2006; Walker 2007; Aras 2009; Davotoğlu 2010; Sözen 2010).

3   The Turkish military-politico establishment, with the PKK conflict again intensifying since 2004, would have to rely on US acquiescence, if not active cooperation for carrying out any cross-border operations into Iraq.

4   While the Turkish politico-military establishment kept snubbing the Kurdistan Region of Iraq, Turkish business there not only had stayed on but was booming, and Turkish business associations increasingly exerted pressure on the AKP government to abandon its obstructionism and back up Turkish investments in the region with a diplomatic rapprochement (Gunter 2011c; Ahmed 2012).

Many opinion makers and scholars cum retired politicians in the US policy world bemoaned the deterioration of relations with as crucial an ally as Turkey and behind the scenes prepared the ground for reconciliation and a reinvigorated partnership that would also include the KRG.[3] Their efforts bore fruit when during a state visit to Washington on 5 November 2007 PM Erdogan managed to convince President Bush that both countries were allies in the 'War on Terror' and that the PKK was a vital threat to the two countries' strategic interests in the Middle East; both sides reached an agreement on military intelligence cooperation and, it is safe to assume in light of developments in the following month, tacit US approval of limited Turkish incursions into northern Iraq in pursuit of the PKK (BBC 2007; Myers 2007; Purvis 2007; Flanagan & Brannen 2008). 'In effect, America would now give a green light to Turkish operations in northern Iraq, provided they were limited to attacks on the PKK and did not cause unnecessary civilian casualties' (Hale & Özbudun 2010: 135). Thus, well provided for with US political backing and 'real time intelligence', the Turkish Air Force flew the first sorties against PKK camps in Iraqi Kurdistan since the Iraq War. on 16 December 2007, which were followed by a substantial ground incursion in February 2008 (Al Jazeera 2007; Reuters 2008a; *Der Spiegel* 2008; Tavernise 2008). Although the KRG engaged in the usual pro forma condemnation of the attacks (Xinhua Daily News 2008; Reuters 2008b), Iraqi Kurdish leaders' consternation appears less convincing with Jalal Talabani capitalizing on improved relations and intelligence cooperation between the US and Turkey and visiting Ankara in his capacity as President of Iraq on 7 March 2008 (Ahmed 2012), merely a week after Turkey had withdrawn its troops from northern Iraq. Indeed, *Wikileaks* cables from the US embassy in Ankara indicate that US support with real-time intelligence of Turkish military operations in northern Iraq was conditional to Turkey mending its differences with the KRG (ICG 2011). During Talabani's visit it stands to reason then that he made use of his unique position as President of Iraq and leader of the PUK to prepare the ground for a Turkish–KRG rapprochement. In sum, then, the diplomatic build up to the 2007/2008 Turkish incursion into northern Iraq in its seemingly endless war with the PKK, via Washington's good offices, resulted in Turkey abandoning its policy of isolating the KRG and entering into a political dialogue with the Iraqi Kurdish parties after five years of strained relations.

Without the political cover that the American help provided, the [AKP] government would have faced even fiercer domestic opposition to extending any olive branch to Iraqi Kurds. Iraqi Kurds for their part toned down their criticisms of Turkey and especially of the air strikes.

(Barkey 2011: 56)

After February 2008, which in retrospect can be identified as a watershed moment, relations between Ankara and Erbil improved profoundly and, at least until 2014, persistently. The first direct meeting at the highest political level since the days of Turgut Özal between representatives of the Iraqi Kurdish parties and the Turkish government took place in Baghdad on 1 May 2008, when KRG PM Nechirvan Barzani met with Turkish Foreign Minister Ahmet Davotoğlu and the Turkish Special Envoy Murat Özçelik, in which both sides reached an accord on improving political and economic ties and, in foresight of the AKP's 'Kurdish Initiative' in the following year, agreed on jointly working towards a political solution of the 'Kurdish Question' in southeast Anatolia (Ahmed 2012; Charountaki 2012), an agreement that was further substantiated by the establishment in November 2008 of a Trilateral Commission between the US, Turkey, and Iraq – prominently represented by the KRG – with a joint command centre in Erbil to facilitate security cooperation between all parties in setting active steps against the PKK (Kardaş 2009; *Today's Zaman* 2009; Charountaki 2012; Park 2012b). These first substantial steps towards strategic cooperation and political rapprochement between Turkey and Iraqi Kurdistan were followed up by even higher level contacts when, during the 'Kurdish Initiative' and in acknowledgement of the KRG's role in it, Foreign Minister Davotoğlu met President Barzani in October 2009 in Erbil, and there was the first personal meeting by President Barzani with PM Erdoğan in Ankara on 4

June the following year, and these ultimately culminated in the historic first visit of a Turkish Prime Minister to the Kurdistan Region of Iraq in March 2011, when, with much pomp, they jointly inaugurated the new Erbil International Airport and the Turkish Consulate in Erbil (Ayhan 2010; Ahmed 2012; Charountaki 2012; Kurd.net 2013a). In light of Turkey's relations with the Iraqi Kurdish nationalist parties since the creation of the state of Iraq and subsequently the Kurdish political entity in northern Iraq as outlined in this study, it is impossible to underestimate the historic significance of this rapprochement between the KRG and Turkey's AKP government. This sea change signals nothing less than, at least in relation to the Kurdistan Region, the AKP overcoming the 'Sèvres Syndrome' that has determined Turkish identity and foreign policy ever since the founding of the Republic. Today, the Kurdistan Region of Iraq is no longer seen by the decision makers in the AKP as pursuing pan-Kurdish separatism or as an external agent inciting ethnic divisions among Turkey's Kurdish population but as a strategic partner in the region with largely complimentary interests and policies. This paradigm shift in perceptions becomes even more momentous given the relatively short time frame in which it evolved, from utter political boycott in 2007, when PM Erdoğan announced, 'I met with the Iraqi President and Prime Minister. I won't meet with any tribal leader … I won't meet with Barzani,'[4] to declaring during Barzani's Ankara visit less than three years later:

> We [Erdogan and Barzani] will build together a very solid bridge in bilateral relations between Iraq and Turkey and between the Kurdistan Region and Turkey especially. We will be in touch. We will also engage in economic cooperation. We will act together on energy and infrastructure.[5]

The climactic improvement of relations is all the more astonishing since on the one issue that has determined Turkey's perception of and interaction with the Iraqi Kurdish political parties, their ambivalent relations with the PKK and its presence on Iraqi Kurdish territory, very little actual progress beyond symbolic gestures was made. True, the KRG initiated policies that restricted the freedom of movement of PKK political representatives in Iraqi Kurdistan and made it more difficult for journalists to reach the PKK camps in the Qandil mountains.[6] By the same token, Iraq (which in this case can effectively be equated with the KRG since the influence of the central Iraqi government at the Iraqi–Turkish border is practically nil), Turkey and the US have established a political dialogue and operational infrastructure to combat the PKK on Iraqi territory, yet seven years after this mechanism has been set up its effectiveness remains to be seen. The fact is that the PKK is still entrenched in its stronghold in the Qandil mountains, and the KRG has not done significantly more to change this fact since 2008 than before the KRG-AKP rapprochement. Yet if the thawing of relations and paradigm shift in Turkey's perception of its Iraqi Kurdish neighbours cannot be accounted for by the very issue that dominated them for three decades, what other factors brought about this dramatic sea change?

I would argue that an overriding trope may be the changed self-perception of Turkey, both at the political level but also in the public discourse, together with a growth in self-confidence since the AKP came to power. Turkey in the 2000s has been a regional, geo-strategic and economic powerhouse, a member of the G20, who has actively shaped politics in the Middle East and beyond, whose Turkish Airlines have become a major carrier transporting Turkish investors to every part of the globe (Bank & Karadag 2012; Ergin 2012; IMF 2012; Turkish Airlines 2013; Elliott 2014), and who, at least during the early stages of the 'Arab Spring', has been hailed by Western and Turkish media alike as a model to be emulated by the democratic regimes hoping to gain power in Tunisia, Egypt, Libya, Syria, and Yemen (Cook 2011; Le Vine 2011; *The Economist* 2011; Kenyon 2012; Öniş 2012; Kardaş 2013; Oğuzlu 2013). The AKP brand offered to optimists a promising version of how Islam, capitalism, traditional values and democratic freedoms can be successfully merged; the fact that this optimism has waned both in Turkey and the countries in the region who were supposed to emulate it does not negate the fact that for a while Turkey was seen as a regional model, which had a profound effect on Turkish identity, self-perception and foreign policy. An equally compelling interpretation may be the fact that the AKP, while not being the first Turkish government to recognize that its 'Kurdish Question' cannot be solved by military means, was the first government not only willing to go where no other Turkish mainstream party had gone before but also, due to its own eternal strife with the Turkish military, the Kemalist 'Deep State' and the Turkish judiciary, was able to outplay those forces traditionally opposed to any democratic reforms or engagement with Turkey's explicitly Kurdish parties, interest groups and political movements. The AKP, until it reversed into authoritarianism, can be seen as fundamental in bringing both these changes about, thus altering Turkish society more radically – at first for the better, at present for the worse – more than any political party since the days of Atatürk.

As far as relations between the AKP and the KRG are directly concerned, I would hypothesize that the AKP recognized the wisdom in the old colonialist adage that the flag, i.e. politics, follows trade. What is remarkable is that despite the political embargo Ankara had imposed on the KRG from 2003 until 2008, economic relations between both trade partners kept booming:

> By early 2007, the volume of bilateral trade between Turkey and northern Iraq had grown to an estimated $5 billion a year. In addition, Turkish contractors had secured an estimated $2 billion worth of construction contracts, including large infrastructure projects such as airports, highways, universities, housing complexes and even the new KDP headquarters. By early 2007 there were estimated to be 1,200 Turkish companies in northern Iraq, creating 14,000 jobs for Turkish citizens in northern Iraq and employment for several hundred thousand more back in Turkey.
>
> (Jenkins 2008: 18)

As Jenkins (2008) notes further, booming trade relations directly benefited the elites on both sides of the border. Close relatives of Massoud Barzani established a network of companies in south-eastern Anatolia and Turkey's financial hubs, while major AKP donors and big wigs did the same in Iraqi Kurdistan. Those special interests increasingly exerted pressure on the Erdoğan government to assist them in making gains in this important foreign market rather than continually posing obstacles to the inroads Turkish businesspeople made (Gunter 2010b, 2011c; Klein 2011; Ahmed 2012; Charountaki 2012). This factor gained even greater significance with the Kurdistan Region transforming from an importer to a major supplier of energy to Turkey (Ahmed 2012; Charountaki 2012; Park 2012b, 2012c; UPI 2012; Dombey 2013; Pamuk & Coskun 2013; Okumuş 2014). Today, there can be no doubt that Turkey effectively dominates the Iraqi Kurdish market:

> Economic relations between Turkey and the Kurdistan Region are excellent, and both sides are enjoying substantial benefits from our close economic cooperation. Today, about 20,000 Turkish citizens are permanently living and doing business here. Half of all foreign companies registered in the Kurdistan Region are Turkish. Five major Turkish banks are operating here, 20 Turkish schools and institutions of higher education are educating the future generation of Turkish citizens living here and of the local population, 600 Turkish construction companies are involved in large-scale infrastructure projects, and Turkish Airlines and other private Turkish carriers operate daily flights between several major Turkish airports and Erbil and Sulimaniyah, which has boosted tourism and contributed to easing business relations. Overall, Turkey has a trade volume with Iraq of about $12 billion last year, of which 70 percent is with the Kurdistan Region.[7]

As a matter of fact, to put this in perspective, for two consecutive years in 2011 and 2012 Iraq was Turkey's second biggest export market after the EU (Republic of Turkey, Ministry of Economy 2013), which, if 70 per cent and counting of this trade is accounted for by the Kurdistan Region, underscores the paramount importance bilateral trade has for both polities and consequently for their relations. I would even go so far to argue that the Kurdistan Region of Iraq and Turkey's southeast Anatolia by now constitutes one of the economically most integrated areas in the Middle East.

This alignment of economic interests has been accompanied by an increasing consonance of strategic interests in the region, in particular in Syria, where both the KRG and the AKP government from early on have taken an unambiguous stance against the Assad regime, and, as will be detailed in the following chapter, Barzani and Erdoğan have tirelessly worked towards a KDP-controlled alternative to the current Democratic Union Party (*Partiya Yekita ya Demokratik*, PYD) dominance among Syria's armed Kurdish opposition. There, up to 2014, the AKP leadership has tried to avail themselves of Barzani's pan-Kurdish appeal to reduce the PYD's influence to a sufferable limit and, through the Iraqi

Kurdish KDP and its Syrian Kurdish allies, at least have a say in the political future of Syria's Kurds.

Ironically, south-eastern Anatolia became the very arena where the AKP has already clearly tried, and arguably succeeded in capitalizing on and exploiting for its own ends the image of Iraqi Kurdistan as a beacon of hope for wider Kurdish political and cultural aspirations and of Massoud Barzani as a Kurdish leader the AKP not only can work with but also as an alternative to Abdullah Öcalan's radicalism. Under pressure by the 2013 Gezi Park Protests widening to a wave of mass civil society protests engulfing Turkey's major cities (Berlinski 2013; Kotsev 2013; Letsch 2013; Shafak 2013; Steinvorth & Zand 2013), PM Erdoğan landed perhaps his as yet greatest PR-coup by meeting with President Barzani in Diyarbakir, the 'spiritual centre' of Kurdish ethno-nationalism in Turkey, on 18 November 2013. There, Erdoğan not only broke the taboo of referring for the first time in a public address to 'Kurdistan' as a territorial concept and listened to Barzani addressing the crowds in Kurdish, both statesmen also enjoyed the performance of Shivan Perwer, another legendary figurehead of Kurdish ethnic identity, who after 37 years in exile had returned with Barzani to his homeland. Barzani, in turn, concluded his speech with shouting in Turkish, 'Long live Turk-Kurd brotherhood, long live freedom, long live peace' (Çandar 2013; Çengiz 2013; *Hürriyet Daily News* 2013; Mert 2013; Reuters 2013; Tuysuzoğlu 2013). At this stage it was not clear whether both leaders have formed a genuine, albeit temporary partnership designed to ensure their mutual political survival and intend to form a united front of conservative parties against the PKK and the BDP, who threatened to cost Erdoğan dearly in the upcoming 2014 elections, or whether it was just another attempt at both sides manipulating each other. What I would argue is that Barzani lending the struggling Erdoğan a helping hand in the very 'spiritual capital' of Kurdish nationalism in Turkey for decades dominated by the PKK and BDP (and its pre- and successors) was a deliberate snub of both movements, and that Barzani increasingly intends to extend his appeal as the leader of the freest political entity in Kurdish history, and the promise of self-determination – however defined – that the Iraqi Kurdish experiment holds for so many Kurds beyond the borders of the Kurdistan Region. Ultimately, both sides appear to have entered a true marriage of mutual conveniences then: the AKP instrumentalizes Barzani and Iraqi Kurdistan's pan-Kurdish appeal and significance in the Kurdish ethno-nationalist discourse in Turkey and beyond, and by doing so not only keeps the PKK and BDP (today HDP) at bay but also tries to influence this discourse in line with its interests, and Barzani enjoys and tries to expand on his role of pan-Kurdish figurehead by the grace of the AKP.[8]

What was also remarkable about this marriage of mutual conveniences is that both sides have reached this point by bracketing the very issue that had dominated their relations for the past three decades, the PKK's status in Iraqi Kurdistan,[9] and by doing so reached a mutual understanding on how to jointly deal with this issue. To this extent then, the KRG–AKP rapprochement at the end of the 2000s can be understood as a textbook case of de-securitization. Securitization theory (Wæver 1993, 1995; Buzan *et al.* 1997; Williams 2003; Balzacq 2005, 2011; Taureck 2006; Stritzel 2007; Peoples & Vaughan-Williams 2010), in a nutshell, holds that very few issues in the social world are per se threats or security issues, but that what we come to perceive as threats or security issues is contextual, contingent and part of a social process and discourse. Not unlike ethnic identity as a social category, a security issue then is constructed through perceptions and performatively enacted, first and foremost by labelling it a security issue or a threat in the political discourse through a speech act:

> By saying security something is done (as in betting, giving a promise, naming a ship). By uttering 'security', a state representative moves a particular development into a specific area, and thereby claims a special right to use whatever means are necessary to block it.
>
> (Wæver 1995: 35)

Proponents of securitization theory therefore argue that 'issues can become security issues by virtue of their presentation and acceptance as such, rather than because of any innate threatening qualities per se' (Peoples & Vaughan-Williams 2010: 78). Securitization is then the 'shifting [of] an issue out of the realm of "normal" political debate into the realm of emergency politics by presenting it as an existential threat' (Peoples & Vaughan-Williams 2010: 76), and, if the social agent who does the securitizing of the relevant issue is seen by the public as someone who speaks with authority, such as the military, scholars, or the government, the public is likely to accept this transformation from non-security to security issue and the measures introduced to meet this existential threat as justified. In other words, the process of securitization not only covers the speech act of labelling something a security issue but the entire social process and discourse that comes with and results from it. De-securitization then is the reverse of the process of securitization, as it describes the social discourse in which an issue is shifted back from 'the realm of securitization and emergency politics ... into the realm of "normal" or technical political debate' (Peoples & Vaughan-Williams 2010: 78).[10]

In our case, for decades since the founding of the Turkish Republic, the Turkish politico-military establishment has perceived and portrayed the possible emergence of a Kurdish autonomous political entity, let alone an independent state, in a neighbouring country as an existential threat to the territorial and political integrity of the Turkish *watan*, mostly because it was feared that such a polity would first fuel the desire for separatism among Turkey's Kurdish minority and then lend political and perhaps even military support to their struggle for national self-determination. Yet, as we have seen, the desire for national self-determination among Turkey's Kurds and the insurgency of the PKK for those ends predate the emergence of an autonomous Kurdish polity at Turkey's borders, and in the two and a half decades since the Kurdistan Region de facto became autonomous, one would be hard pressed to argue that the existence of such a polity per se has increased the risk to the territorial integrity of

Turkey – on the contrary, while before 1991 northern Iraq was a notorious source of unrest, lawlessness and political chaos, once the KRG established its control there, Turkey at least has an interlocutor to address with its security concerns, hold accountable, and can, as has been demonstrated, cooperate with on several issues.

By the same token, Turkey defined its relations with the KRG until 2008 primarily through a security lens; that is, what determined relations between Erbil and Ankara was almost exclusively the presence of the PKK on Iraqi Kurdish territory and how to deal with it. Here, again, while the Turkish politico-military establishment could have chosen to focus on other, non-threatening issues such as economic cooperation – as it ultimately did – for over 15 years it chose not to, determined to perceive the KRG exclusively within the realm of a security issue. What the AKP accomplished then after 2008 by, to some extent, bracketing the PKK issue from its relations with the KRG and focusing instead on areas where cooperation was easily achievable and mutually beneficial, is shifting the issue at hand – relations with the KRG – from the realm of securitization or emergency politics to a level of a 'normal', more technical, and economically as well as politically lucrative discourse. In other words, it desecuritized Turkey's relations with Iraqi Kurdistan. What is even more remarkable than this respectable feat in itself is the dynamic that developed from it. For the issue of relations with the KRG got desecuritized, in two ways: (1) by bracketing the most controversial aspect – the PKK presence on Iraqi Kurdish territory – by first instead focusing on areas of mutual interest such as trade relations and strategic cooperation in Syria; (2) both sides (the AKP and KRG) paved the ground for political cooperation on the very issue Turkey had always feared in the context of an autonomous Kurdish political entity at its borders: how such an entity would affect its own Kurdish population and their desire for national self-determination. If the period between 2008 and 2014 is anything to go by, the answer must have turned out reassuringly for the Turkish politico-military establishment since KRG leaders not only proved willing to assist the AKP in shaping the Kurdish ethno-nationalist discourse in Turkey in a direction in line with AKP thinking, but both sides, the KRG and AKP leadership, even discovered that their strategic interests via the Kurdish ethno-nationalist discourse in Turkey corresponded, offering ample room for collaboration in imprinting their partnership on this identity discourse. The AKP leadership believed that through Massoud Barzani, who is politically and economically dependent on Turkey in Iraqi Kurdistan, they could influence the Kurdish ethno-nationalist discourse at home. Both sides clearly benefited from holding up Barzani as a moderate and conservative alternative to the PKK's radicalism as well as to the BDP with whom the AKP had to compete for votes in southeast Anatolia, and both sides intended through their partnership to shape Kurdish ethnic identity in Turkey as sympathetic to the AKP. In sum, I would say, using Lord Ismay's famous maxim for NATO as an allegory, the purpose of their partnership in the ethnic discourse among Turkey's Kurds was to keep Barzani in, the BDP down and the PKK out.

As in the theoretical section, I argue here that instead of a causal sequence between identities and interests, in which either interests determine one's identity or for interests to be a function of an agent's identity, identities and interests should be conceptualized as a complex matrix with no identifiable sequence or hierarchy. I, for one, in the pre-2015 ethnicized discourse in southeast Anatolia, would be hard pressed to determine where precisely Massoud Barzani's strategic interests to exert his influence beyond Iraqi Kurdistan and to collaborate with the AKP end, and his self-perception as a (pan-)Kurdish leader with wider nationalist appeal who feels an evolving degree of communality and solidarity with Kurds across the border begins. The complex dynamics of this situational, shifting and ambiguous matrix should be seen as one important aspect of Iraqi Kurdish identity at the outset of the twenty-first century, at least the one central to understanding the relations between the KRG and the PKK in this period.

The PKK and the Iraqi Kurdish ethno-nationalist parties in the 2000s

Relations between the Iraqi Kurdish ethno-nationalist parties and the PKK in the early 2000s were as much defined by complex ambiguities and ambivalences as they had been in the early 1990s. While on the one hand rumours were spreading that while on the run in Rome Abdullah Öcalan might be offered asylum by the PUK in Iraqi Kurdistan,[11] less than two years later PUK and PKK were fighting again. The reasons for this round of hostilities between September and December 2000 remain opaque.

> The reason never was clear – the PKK claimed Talabani's PUK party attacked first, the PUK accused the PKK of breaking an agreement to stay in its mountain redoubts – but it probably had a lot to do with maintaining group unity and giving PKK fighters some sort of armed focus,

Marcus (2007a: 289) speculates. Gunter (2001) as well as Brauns and Kiechle (2010), on the other hand, argue that the PUK had been pressured by Turkey into attacking the PKK. The Turkish military certainly showed no willingness to agree to the unilateral ceasefire the PKK had declared in September 1999; on the contrary, it seemed as though after the capture of Öcalan the Turkish military-politico establishment was determined to defeat the PKK once and for all – illustrated by a series of cross-border incursions throughout 1999, in which the Turkish military was assisted by the KDP (Immigration and Refugee Board of Canada 2001). In line with its ceasefire of September 1999 the PKK formally asked the KDP to cease hostilities in November 1999, and Cemil Bayık pledged that 'despite the attacks launched by the KDP, the PKK had no intention of responding' ((Immigration and Refugee Board of Canada 2001); yet the KDP chose to ignore the PKK overtures for peace. Interestingly, this episode of KDP–PKK fighting is not mentioned in the pertinent literature; on the contrary, Gunter (2001) portrays the PUK–PKK fighting of September and December

2000 as an isolated incident, which the KDP refused to join, and in which the PUK tried to remove the PKK from the Qandil mountains, where they had established themselves in 1998, in order to open the area for a direct trade route with Turkey.[12] One possible interpretation may be that after dragging its feet for two years after the Washington Agreement, the PUK had finally been persuaded by Turkey through incentives and disincentives to join its operations to kill off the PKK;[13] why the KDP sided with Turkey in 1999, yet refused to join the Turkish-PUK alliance in its fight against the PKK in September and December 2000 remains a mystery, though.

While this episode fits the already established historic pattern of rapidly shifting temporary alliances and antagonisms between the Iraqi Kurdish nationalist parties and the PKK, what profoundly altered the dynamics of their relations, as it did for the entire Middle East, was the Iraq War. It had not been lost on the PKK that, unlike in 1991, the US invaded Iraq in March 2003 to stay as an occupying force. Doubtlessly, it had also noted with a sigh of relief that Turkey had taken itself out of the picture with its parliament's refusal to grant US forces the opening of a second, northern front. Finally, the PKK, like the rest of the world, must have conjectured that after the initial quick victory, the US was about to fundamentally re-shape the political order of the Middle East and would not refrain, if necessary, from toppling one hostile regime after the other with Syria and Iran being the most likely next candidates on the list, which would leave the PKK with nowhere to go. With the US the dominant power in the Middle East in the spring of 2003, it would not seem far-fetched to venture the guess that the PKK would have been eager to reach some kind of accommodation with the new hegemon that would allow it at least to remain in Qandil. It is in this context that the proverbial sphinx of Kurdish ethno-nationalist movements, PJAK, comes into play, whose nature analysts are still struggling to comprehensively portray.

On the face of things PJAK is a sister-organization of the PKK operating under the KCK umbrella and within the concept of democratic confederalism to advance, by military means if forced to, Kurdish cultural and civil rights within a confederal Iran. That is at least how today's PKK and PJAK want it understood, with the PKK admitting that they and PJAK share logistics, facilities, supplies and men in their mutually operated bases in the Qandil mountains at the Iraqi–Turkish–Iranian border, yet are to be seen as separate but equal (Brandon 2006a; Cuffe 2007; Kutschera 2008; Renard 2008; Flood 2009; Elik 2011; Rudaw 2013a; Di Stefano Pironti 2014), similar to, as will be discussed in the next chapter, the PKK's sister organization PYD in Syria. PJAK asserts its aims are to 'unite the Kurdish and Iranian opposition, to change the oppressive Islamic regime in Iran and to establish a free democratic confederal system for the Kurds and the Iranian peoples'.[14] For the Turkish politico-military establishment PKK and PJAK are essentially the same, two sides of the same coin (Elik 2011; TREND 2011), which, based on the principle the enemy of my enemy is my friend, has led to increased Iranian-Turkish anti-terror cooperation, despite the Iranian Regime's past support of the PKK (Cagaptay & Eroğlu 2007; Elik 2011). At the same time, the blogosphere and Iranian media are brimming over with allegations that the US has used PJAK as a proxy to destabilize Iran, a conspiracy theory also detailed in more respectable publications (Escobar 2007; Oppel 2007; Rand 2007; Renard 2008; Di Stefano Pironti 2014), and, as could be expected, by the peerless Seymour Hersh (2008). However, as is the nature of the beast with covert operations, all claims are hardly ever sufficiently substantiated and often amount to not much more than, for example, a local security official in the border area in 2007, when asked whether the CIA or US Special Forces were covertly training PJAK fighters, answering with a smile, 'I'm allowed to say no, but I'm not allowed to say yes.'[15]

One angle none of these sources mention and that is also absent from the sparse scholarly literature on PJAK is what I came across in my field research. Two prominent PKK dissidents, Osman Öcalan and Nizamettin Taş, independently of each other, claim that when PJAK was founded in 2003 it was their brainchild with the explicit agenda of gradually transforming the PKK into PJAK and winning US support for continuing a peaceful political dialogue with Turkey, while simultaneously using PKK fighters to destabilize the Iranian regime for the Bush administration.[16] In that they intended to copy the *Mojahedin-e-Khalq* (MEK, People's Mujahideen of Iran), a dissident group cum micro insurgency Saddam Hussein had hosted at Camp Ashraf near Baghdad, and for whom more substantial evidence exists that the US at least toyed with the idea of using them as proxies against the regime in Tehran in their post-2003 hubris (Cafarella 2005; Khalaji 2007; Fayazmanesh 2008; Hersh 2008; Takeyh 2009; Rogin 2011; Wilkie 2011). Unlike what the official PKK party line asserts, that PJAK is an expression of democratic confederalism and the regional branch of the KCK, Öcalan and Taş – who fell out with each other while still in the PKK and again after their PWD alternative project failed – claim that during the chaotic days before 2003/2004 when the PKK tried to formulate a coherent strategy and ideology, PJAK was conceived as a means to continue the political dialogue with Turkey under tacit US backing, while, quid pro quo, providing PKK fighters for the Bush administration's clandestine war against Iran. In other words, they intended for the PKK to become PJAK, and only when they had been forced out of the PKK in August 2004 and driven to pursue their third way project with the PWD, had PJAK been appropriated by the PKK leadership and integrated into its democratic confederalism strategy.[17] Asked whether this initiative bore any fruits, whether they managed to reach out to American officials to get support for PJAK, Nizamettin Taş remembers:

N.T.: In the second half of 2003 and the first half of 2004 we met with many Americans in Mosul, in Baghdad, here in Hewler for talks. We asked them for money, for supplies, and weapons to fight in Iran.

Q.: Who were these Americans you met?

N.T.: They were military commanders and intelligence officers working here in Iraq.

Q.: Do you remember what organization or institutions they worked for? What their functions in Iraq were, what their ranks were?

N.T.: No, I don't remember [those details], but they were high-ranking American military intelligence. We had about ten meetings with them, and we had the Americans agreeing to our proposal ... But in these days all strategic decisions had to be approved by [Abdullah Öcalan], and he said no to our meetings.

Q.: So you are saying that in these talks you were close to reaching an agreement with the Americans you met to supply you with weapons to fight in Iran, but that nothing came of it because Öcalan forbade it?

N.T.: Yes, the Americans agreed to supply PJAK, they wanted us to work with them, but Öcalan disagreed with it ... That's why we left the PKK.

Q.: Why did Öcalan disagree with this initiative? Would it not have been good for the PKK to receive American support?

N.T.: It was not Öcalan speaking. He was controlled by Ergenekon. It was not him making decisions, it was Ergenekon.[18]

The scope of this study did not allow me to pursue this angle further and I do not advocate any specific theories or interpretations on PJAK, but, if Taş' account is credible, it would explain the sporadic meetings between US officials and PKK leaders which so many sources report, why it took the US until 2009 when the Obama administration came to office, to designate PJAK a terrorist organization (Kardaş & Özcan 2009; *Turkish Weekly* 2009),[19] and why, in the period of 2003 until 2007, during which Ankara had fallen out of Washington's graces, all remained quiet on the KDP/PUK-PKK front: the two Iraqi Kurdish nationalist parties may have waited to see what their major external backer, the US, had in plan for PKK/PJAK.

By the same token, is it conceivable that during this period of insecurity from 2003 until 2008, when relations between Ankara and Erbil improved, and while the Iraqi Kurdish nationalist parties were negotiating in Baghdad over the scope, contours and boundaries of their political entity within a federal Iraq, they preferred to keep the PKK as an ace up their sleeves, as a form of leverage that could be employed if Turkey were to oppose the political structure of the new Iraq that turned out distinctly in the KRG's favour? Until 2008, when Turkey *nolens volens* came to terms with the enhanced status of the Kurdistan Region, KDP and PUK knew that any increase in Iraqi Kurdish autonomy was anathema for the Turkish politico-military establishment that would see it as a first step towards future independence – these Turkish fears applied in particular to the inclusion of oil-rich Kirkuk into the Kurdistan Region, which it was presumed, would provide Erbil with the economic muscle to declare independence in the future (Barkey 2005, 2011; Olson 2005a, 2005b; Park 2005; Yavuz 2005; Lundgren 2007; ICG 2008; Romano 2010; Gunter 2011c; Ahmed 2012). The Iraqi Kurdish nationalist parties had very little to counter this perception. No matter how often their leaders went on the record that they did not intend to pursue a unilateral declaration of independence and were not preparing for it, the Turkish politico-military establishment would not abandon the almost pathological impression – dating back, as has been shown, to the post-First World War era

– that its Kurdish minority together with Kurds abroad were conspiring with external actors, in this case the US, to divide the Turkish *watan*. If Turkish decision makers could not be convinced of the Iraqi Kurds' non-secessionist intentions, KDP and PUK logic might have dictated, Ankara would have to be offered something else to appreciate their willingness to cooperate with Turkey in a restructured Iraq, and to acquiesce into the KRG gaining political and territorial ground in this as yet to be constructed polity. Of the little leverage KDP and PUK had on Turkey, the PKK card would have been the strongest, either played by offering their good offices in finding a political solution to the conflict or by collaborating in a final military assault on the PKK, in exchange for Turkey not posing an insurmountable obstacle in the pro-Kurdish political reconstitution of Iraq (Eccarius-Kelly 2011). Naturally, most KRG officials reject any notions that the Iraqi Kurdish nationalist parties would have considered the PKK presence on their territory a leverage to be used against Turkey when the situation called for it. The paraphrased official post-2005 KRG line on the PKK is:

> The PKK is an issue external to the Kurdistan Region of Iraq. It is a domestic issue for the Turkish state, and therefore any solution to it has to be found in Turkey, and primarily by Turkey. We believe and advocate for this position to be a peaceful, political dialogue, and pledge to do anything in our power to assist such a dialogue, but there is nothing we can do against the PKK in the mountains at our border with Turkey.[20]

When reminded that since the KRG claims to be in quasi-sovereign control of its territory it has an obligation to neighbouring states to prevent attacks from insurgencies from its territory on neighbouring countries, the usual paraphrased response is either, 'we are part of the federal state of Iraq and share this responsibility with the Iraqi state' – an astonishing attempt at having it both ways, since the KRG would not tolerate Iraqi troops policing its border with Turkey – or,

> we fought the PKK in the 1990s, suffered many casualties in these wars, but failed to dislodge them – as did the Turkish military on dozens of occasions. How are we to succeed in a task, in which the mighty Turkish military failed? … There is no military solution to the PKK's presence in the mountains, only a political one. But this political solution cannot come from us, it has to come from Turkey, we can only assist in it.[21]

One high-ranking official representing the KRG abroad with whom I talked, while denying that the KRG has used the PKK as leverage on Turkey in the past, at least considered the potential for the PKK presence to be used as leverage in future KRG-Turkish negotiations:

> As a government, and [Turkey] too, any two parties, they would leverage anything they have, they would be dumb not to … I'm not saying that we use it as a leverage, … on all these issues such as the status of Kirkuk there

was no dialogue with Turkey [between 2003 and 2008], Turkey refused to engage with us or the Iraqi government, but now that relations [with Turkey] are good ... I think we should leverage everything, that's would you do as a government negotiating with other governments.[22]

Naturally, the Turkish government disagrees with the official KRG line on the PKK presence on its territory:

Even if we accept that the KRG cannot prevent the PKK from carrying out attacks on Turkey from Iraqi territory – to which the Iraqi state, of which the Kurdistan Region of Iraq is a part, would be obligated by international law – there are many ways the KRG could limit the PKK's freedom to operate on Iraqi territory. My government has very openly and repeatedly stated that we think the KRG has not done enough in this regard, but we appreciate that recently they have been putting means into place that limit the PKK's capabilities.[23]

Notwithstanding the means the KRG put in place in 2011 to limit the PKK's freedom to operate on its territory, such as curtailing access for journalists to Qandil – which prevented me from conducting interviews there – I find it hard to believe that a joint military operation of Turkey, the US and the KRG after 2008, when these parties had mended their differences, would not be able to dislodge the PKK from its mountain strongholds.

The question is not whether the KRG can do this together with Turkey and the US, but whether they want to do it. The KRG lacks the political will to enter such an alliance to fight the PKK. It is not in their interest,

agrees Denise Natali, an authority on Iraqi Kurdistan who lived there for many years.[24] Several Iraqi Kurdish journalists I talked to in Erbil and Sulimaniyah share this view that if there had been the political will of the KRG to join an alliance with Turkey and the US to expel the PKK from its territory, they could have accomplished it, but that the KRG has no interest in doing so. Yet, opinions differ on why the KRG lacks the political will to confront the PKK as part of an international alliance. Some say that Iraqi Kurdish and Kurdish opinion worldwide would not tolerate KRG *peshmerga* fighting fellow Kurds on Turkey's behest, while others argue that such a war would claim too many lives, and yet others again agree with the position that it is politically more expedient for the KRG to have a weakened PKK on its territory, where it can be controlled and potentially used in a trade-off with Turkey.[25]

I would argue that, when reasoning for using the PKK as leverage in future negotiations with Turkey, the above-quoted KRG official got the sequence of strategic thinking wrong. During the period when Turkey boycotted the KRG from 2003 until 2008, it would make sense to keep the PKK card up one's sleeve, not as leverage – since hardly any contacts took place between both parties – but to use as an asset in case Turkey's boycott would transform into outright obstruction. In the early 2010s, on the other hand, since Turkey–KRG relations were excellent, trade was booming and both governments cooperated on a host of economic and strategic issues, from joint energy projects to supporting the same clients in the Syrian Civil War, exerting leverage with the PKK would be counterproductive. What is more, in the then political discourse, with the KRG trying to portray itself globally in costly media and lobbying campaigns as an island of peace and prosperity open for business and investment, the PKK was no longer an asset but a disturbing factor. This became apparent when I interviewed the KRG Minister of Trade, Sinan Abdulkhalq Ahmed Chalabi, and reminded him that we had met the previous year with a student delegation from the University of Exeter, of which a good number were Kurds from Turkey. The minister was in a foul mood since, on a screen behind us, CNN was broadcasting images into the world of Turkish fighter jets bombing PKK positions on Iraqi Kurdish territory while he was preparing to host the Erbil International Trade Fair, the biggest economic event the Kurdistan Region had staged in its history. 'Yes, I remember, you were here with these militants,' the minister grumbled. 'They kept saying, "we are from Northern Kurdistan". Why use the same language as these militants?' he said and pointed at the screen. 'Why not say, we are Kurds from Turkey?'[26] Intriguingly, here we had a minister from the freest political entity in Kurdish history using the same semantic line of argument the Turkish state had employed for decades, objecting to Kurds using the word Kurdistan. He then kept taking issue with the 'reckless militancy' of the PKK jeopardizing everything the Kurds in Iraq had accomplished, compromising relations with Turkey, driving away business and foreign investors, and discrediting the Kurdistan Region as an economic hub for the region.[27] In October 2011, when this interview was conducted, the strategic thinking of KRG decision makers was primarily investment-oriented, and the PKK was seen as bad for business;[28] in this world view the PKK's presence in Iraqi Kurdistan is certainly not seen as an ace up their sleeves but, at the very least, a disruptive element.

Again, though, I believe the relations between the Iraqi Kurdish nationalist parties and the PKK in post-2008 Iraqi Kurdistan cannot be captured by instrumentalist *explananda* alone; that is, by being reduced to material interests. If that were the case, since the PKK was a disruptive element to the peace and progress of the Kurdistan Region, the KRG would join forces with Turkey to rid themselves once and for all from them. That they have not taken military action against them since 2000 – given the incessant fighting of the 1980s and 1990s, this decade of peace appears almost an eternity – I believe, is a function of the evolving identity of Iraqi Kurdistan that is currently in a process of rapid transformation, and therefore is one facet to the variations of Kurdish identity of the Iraqi Kurdish nationalist parties. Aliza Marcus concludes her study on the PKK with the observation:

'Turkey's Kurds used to face Istanbul,' remarked ... Tayfun Mater, a former activist in the militant Turkish left, and an often prescient commentator.

He meant that many Kurds, whether or not they backed the PKK, once believed the answer to the Kurdish problem lay in the multicultural streets of Istanbul, that Kurds and Turks may jointly come up with a mutually agreeable solution. 'But these days, they face Iraq,' he said.

(Marcus 2007a: 301)

A similar point is made by Akkaya and Jongerden (2011: 154), representative of many accounts on the post-2005 Kurdistan Region, that 'Iraqi Kurdistan ... as an autonomous, self-ruling territory ... turned out to be a center of attraction for many Kurds'. In 2010, I attended a presentation of the KRG Representative to the UK, Bayam Abdul Rahman at SOAS in London, where she was beseeched by the mostly Kurdish audience for the KRG to advocate on this group's behalf with the Iranian government, to be more outspoken on the dragging 'Kurdish Initiative' with Ankara, to demand Damascus grant Syrian Kurds citizenship, to plea with the Danish government to stop its indictment against ROJ-TV, etc.[29] – demands very often beyond the KRG's level of influence with regional or European governments, and yet, still in 2010, despite critical voices starting to question the KRG's potential to act as a saviour for Kurds throughout the region,[30] the narrative of hope that the freest political entity in Kurdish history would advocate on the behalf of Kurds everywhere had persisted among many. Ever since the days of Mulla Mustafa, while strategically pursuing an Iraqi Kurds-first policy, Iraqi Kurdish leaders have basked in the glory of being seen as spiritual figureheads of the Kurdish struggle for self-determination in all parts of what is called Kurdistan, yet in the late 2000s/early 2010s, when this allure had actually become part of the perception of the Kurdistan Region by other Kurds and had aroused very real demands and expectations, this role seemed to often ask too much of Iraqi Kurdish leaders. 'There are so many expectations of our leadership by Kurds everywhere,' Abdul Rahman admitted later.

Expectations we cannot always live up to ... we will always be sympathetic to Kurds struggling for human or cultural rights everywhere in the region and here in Europe and will never tire to advocate on their behalf but first and foremost we are committed to the well being of [our] people in Iraqi Kurdistan ... [which] sometimes puts limitations on what we can do.[31]

These limitations became particularly acute when the Iraqi Kurdish evolving identity as the freest political entity in Kurdish history, and the wider Kurdish expectations that come with that perception, clashed with the strategic interests of the KRG to maintain Turkey's goodwill towards the Kurdistan Region. The resulting complex matrix of identities and interests often mirrored a tightrope walk or 'delicate balance' the KRG is compelled to strike, as Michael Gunter (2011c) observed. In other words, identity did matter in PKK–KDP/PUK relations in the 2000s but not in the simplistic notion that the ethnic alliance model suggests of the Iraqi Kurdish nationalist parties forming an alliance with the PKK against Turkey – which has been soundly disproven with this study.

Instead, these relations operated in a more complex matrix of shifting interests and evolving identities that can explain why the KRG, despite material interests suggesting it, could not afford to act militarily against the PKK on Turkey's behest: to do so would have run counter to the configurations of the complex matrix of Iraqi Kurdish identities and interests in the 2000s, and as such the refusal of the KRG to engage the PKK militarily is to be seen as part of this matrix in a permanent flux.

This tightrope walk of balancing identities and interests that constituted the meaning of Iraqi Kurdish identity in the late 2000s/early 2010s both via Turkey but also Kurdish expectations in the region and diaspora, became apparent with the KRG's attempts to assist the 2009 'Kurdish Initiative' of the AKP government with a pan-Kurdish peace conference aimed at facilitating a peaceful solution to the PKK conflict. Just within its first two years in power the AKP government had implemented more far-reaching reforms of Kurdish minority rights than any previous Turkish government – from lifting the state of emergency in the provinces of Southeast Anatolia where it was still enforced to removing restrictions on the use of Kurdish language in public, to permitting limited radio broadcasting on private channels and tolerating Kurdish language education at private schools.

> While those reforms were not new and indeed most were introduced before the AKP took office [by previous governments in order to prepare the ground for accession talks with the EU], it was the AKP that turned them into a coherent reform agenda, had the political will and talent to sell them to an often sceptical public, and allocated the financial and other resources that were needed to implement them ... For the most part, the AKP ... has carefully crafted its reform agenda around the concepts of individual rights and general minority rights rather than Kurdish collective rights as such – a position that also happens to be aligned with the predominant EU approach to such matters.
>
> (Bahcheli & Noel 2011: 115, 117)

The AKP's reforming zeal stalled, though, when the PKK ended its unilateral ceasefire in 2004. With military casualties in southeast Anatolia mounting and TAK carrying out terrorist attacks on civilian targets and tourist infrastructure in Istanbul and Turkey's coastal resorts in the summer of 2006 (Brandon 2006b; Grossbongardt 2006; Kirby & Turgut 2006; Casier 2010; Eccarius-Kelly 2011), the government of PM Erdoğan was forced to launch a series of major offensives into Iraqi Kurdistan in late 2007 and early 2008, that, although militarily ineffective, as discussed earlier, brought the US government and the KRG back on Turkey's side. The military impasse, combined with the AKP competing with the DTP for the 'Kurdish vote' and a new, less paranoid foreign policy doctrine that, instead of perceiving Turkey's neighbours as an inherent threat, sought to engage them in projects of mutual interests, led to a shift in the public discourse with civil society organizations and business associations – most prominently the

Türkiye Ekonomik ve Sosyal Etüdler Vakfı (Turkish Economic and Social Studies Foundation, TESEV) – demanding a reconsideration of the state's approach to Kurdish minority rights and the PKK conflict. Although at first hesitantly, the AKP took up the cue,[32] and under the leadership of the Minister of the Interior Beşir Atalay started to engage in a far-reaching dialogue with civil society organizations to prepare the ground for extensive political, social and economic reforms – since July 2009 dubbed the 'Kurdish Initiative' – that were supposed to culminate in a grandiose 'National Unity Initiative' and, a pet project the AKP had pursued since 2007, the drafting of a new constitution embracing the diversity of Turkish society (Çandar 2009; Olson 2009; Casier *et al.* 2011; Eccarius-Kelly 2011; Gunter 2011c; ICG 2011, 2012a; Park 2012a; Çiçek 2013). Despite such auspicious openings, 'it soon became evident … that the AK Party had not thought out its Kurdish Initiative very well and then proved rather inept in trying to implement it' (Gunter 2011c: 178–179). While 'representatives of Kurdish civil society, Kurdish intellectuals, and leftist political activists expressed frustration about the glacial pace of progress, and the ease with which demands for increased democratic rights had been framed as ethno-nationalist, divisive, or separatist in spirit' (Eccarius-Kelly 2011: 162), the PKK misused the government's offer of amnesty for a publicity stunt that scared the Turkish public away from considering more far-reaching concessions and eroded popular support for the Kurdish Initiative.[33] It is debatable whether the AKP ever sincerely pursued a reformist agenda with the potential of breaking the three-decade long stalemate between the Turkish state and the PKK (Casier *et al.* 2011; Çiçek 2013), and whether the PKK with its various sub-divisions and competing decision-making bodies was ever willing and able to respond to conciliatory gestures and a genuine national dialogue for peace in kind. The fact is that by the end of 2009 the AKP had lost interest in pursuing its Kurdish Initiative any further; the banning of the DTP by the Constitutional Court on 11 December was merely the death blow to an already wasted away momentum (Al Jazeera 2009; Tait 2009).

All throughout 2009, though, Iraqi Kurdish and international media were abuzz with the proposal for a pan-Kurdish peace conference to be held in Erbil and hosted by the KRG, that not only for the first time would bring together all main Kurdish parties to discuss ethno-nationalist conflicts in all four parts of wider Kurdistan but also to accompany the Kurdish Initiative of the AKP government (Azadi 2009; Kurd.net 2009; Sadjadi 2009; UPI 2009).[34] Simultaneously, the possibility of Scandinavian countries granting high-ranking PKK leaders asylum was explored (Uslu 2009), and allegedly CIA officers even went to Qandil to persuade the PKK to lay down their arms (Artens 2009). There were clear indications that a substantial international effort was under way to find a peaceful solution to the PKK conflict and for confidence building measures between the KRG and the AKP government that appeared to follow the script of a 2007 report by David Phillips, a US scholar held in high regard by policymakers in both Erbil and Ankara, in which he had laid out precisely such a roadmap for peace (Phillips 2007; Artens 2009); in April 2009 Phillips and the

Atlantic Council of the United States hosted a first promising workshop between Turkish and Iraqi Kurdish delegates in Washington (Phillips 2009). However, as in Turkey, by the end of 2009 the momentum suddenly petered out and the initiative disappeared from the headlines. Theories for the failure of the KRG supporting the AKP's Kurdish Initiative with a pan-Kurdish summit abound, the most obvious being that the KRG abandoned the idea when the AKP aborted its own Kurdish Initiative, which it was supposed to accompany. Phillips believes that Turkey's whole 'Kurdish Initiative amounts to nothing ... that the AKP never was sincere about it, never put the necessary political capital behind it,' and in addition that 'any PKK presence at such a conference [in Iraqi Kurdistan] would have legitimised the PKK, an impossible scenario for Turkey ... when they realised that they pulled the plug'.[35] Others believe that Turkey, after initial support, backed off from approving the summit at the eleventh hour when it realized the risks that would inevitably come with dozens of Kurdish delegates from all four countries coming together discussing their right to national self-determination. 'I think it was typical of Nechirvan Barzani, one of his many over-ambitious projects that was not thought through enough, not discussed with all parties, and lacked political backing and planning,' Abbas Vali evaluated the KRG plans for a pan-Kurdish conference.[36] One of my Iraqi Kurdish journalist contacts concurred, 'it was a vanity project. And when the Turks saw where this was heading, they shut it down.'[37] In retrospect the KRG plan to host a pan-Kurdish conference in Erbil may seem to have lacked planning and did not sufficiently take into account Turkey's reaction to the idea of dozens of Kurdish delegates congregating in Erbil to discuss the future of Kurdish national identity on a national and supra-national level. However, it might have been more than just one of the many KRG vanity projects. I would argue it looks like a genuine attempt to bring the centripetal forces that constitute the dynamic matrix of shifting interests and evolving identities of the then Iraqi Kurdish political space into harmony, to square the circle of strategic interests via Turkey, and taking a more active role as a figurehead in the Kurdish nationalist discourse to satisfy the expectations of so many Kurds abroad. The fact that the KRG-sponsored pan-Kurdish summit ultimately fell through then does not diminish its illustrative value in showing the workings of the matrix of identities and interests that constitutes the nature of Iraqi Kurdish political space and the nationalist discourse in the late 2000s.

Notes

1 Relations between Turkey and the US were further compromised by the so-called 'Hood Incident', when in July 2003 US forces captured a team of Turkish special forces operating in northern Iraq – allegedly either planning an assassination attempt on the Iraqi-Kurdish governor of Kirkuk or to arm the *Iraqi Turkoman Front* (ITF), a Turkmen political movement opposing Iraqi Kurdish rule over Kirkuk – paraded them with hoods over their heads, detained and interrogated them for about three days (*The Economist* 2003; Howard & Goldenberg 2003; Barkey 2005).
2 Interview Abdul Rahman op. cit.

3 One key player was retired US Air Force General Joseph Ralston, who enjoyed excellent connections to the Turkish military and business circles as well as among Iraqi Kurdish leaders, and was appointed US Special Envoy for Countering the PKK in a good will gesture in August 2006 (Flanagan & Brannen 2008). Another influential pundit engaging in behind the scenes shuttle-diplomacy between Washington, Ankara, and Erbil was the *Atlantic Council's* David Phillips, see interview Phillips op. cit.

4 Quoted in Charountaki (2012: 191).

5 Quoted in Charountaki (2012: 199).

6 Interviews Bakir, Chalabi, Dizayee, Hussein, Karim, and Pire op. cit.

7 Interview Aydin Selcin, then Turkish Consul General in Erbil, Erbil, Iraqi Kurdistan, 19 October 2011.

8 Of course, it goes without saying that this marriage of mutual conveniences celebrated in Diyarbakir did not go unopposed. The BDP and many Kurdish civil society organizations in Turkey criticized Barzani and Shivan Perwer for selling out when allowing the AKP to exploit them (Çandar 2013; Tuysuzoglu 2013).

9 As Hugh Pope, the International Crisis Group chief analyst in Turkey, observed,

> what is remarkable in this context ... in the relations between the KRG and the PKK via Turkey since the Kurdish Initiative faltered in 2009 is not so much what the KRG could do to actively support a political solution to Turkey's Kurdish problem but how inactive the KRG has been over the past three years ... one gets the impression that they are content with watching developments in Turkey from the sidelines.
> (Interview with Hugh Pope, Istanbul, Turkey, 6 May 2012)

At the time this interview took place I agreed with Pope, but the Diyarbakir episode in November 2013 and, as will be detailed subsequently, events in Syria up to 2014, were illustrating that the KDP was more prominently taking sides with the AKP against the PKK and affiliated political parties such as the BDP, even in the political discourse in Turkey proper.

10 For an interesting application of de-securitization theory to Turkey's relations with pre-2011 Syria and Iran, see Aras and Polat (2008).

11 Çelik (2002) claims that when Öcalan arrived in Moscow for the second time in January 1999 during his European odyssey for asylum, his escape plan foresaw 'Southern Kurdistan', i.e. northern Iraq, as its final destination, which he intended to reach via Iran. In our interview he specifies that Newshirwan Mustafa had been voicing the possibility of the PUK granting Öcalan refuge on its territory (interview Çelik op. cit.). I failed to secure an interview with Mustafa but one high-ranking PUK representative in Europe who visited Öcalan during his stay in Rome, Ahmed Barmani, denied that any such discussion had taken place or that any such offer had been made (interview with Ahmed Barmani, Sulimaniyah, Iraqi Kurdistan, 11 June 2010). In my opinion, granting Öcalan refuge in the heated international atmosphere after his expulsion from Syria, with even Italy and Germany, Russia, and several other European states, due to combined US and Turkish pressure, considering Öcalan too hot a commodity to deal with, and only a few months after the Washington Agreement had been signed, in which KDP/PUK committed to an anti-PKK line, it would have been political suicide for the PUK to harbour Öcalan on its territory. I would go so far as to speculate that such a move would have invited a Turkish invasion – surely Turkey would not be reluctant to take such a dramatic step in northern Iraq since it had actively considered it for Syria, certainly a more formidable opponent than the PUK – and therefore think it implausible that the PUK leadership ever actively considered such an offer.

12 It is worth remembering that the KDP-PUK civil war of 1994, to some extent, had started because the KDP controlled the only trade route with Turkey at the Harbur border crossing; ever since then opening an alternative route from PUK controlled territory was high on Talabani's agenda.

13 To further complicate matters, an expert on Kurdish inter-party relations who had visited Öcalan in Rome at the end of 1998, and who wishes to remain unnamed due to the sensitivity of the information, related to me that during the visit Öcalan had kept ranting about the PUK's betrayal in Washington after the PKK had, for years, paid the PUK millions of dollars in quasi protection money for allowing the PKK to re-establish itself after the 1992 defeat on PUK territory. As significant as this allegation is, I was unable to verify it during my field research since, as expected, all PUK interviewees vehemently denied any such payments. Only Osman Öcalan hinted at the fact that during the KDP–PUK civil war, when the PUK faced defeat after the joint Iraqi–KDP forces' conquest of Erbil and was hard pressed for assets, the PKK purchased supplies and ammunition from the PUK at above market prices to help them out, interview Öcalan op. cit.

14 PJAK Press Release of 7 May 2008, quoted in Renard (2008).

15 Quoted in Rand (2007).

16 Interviews Öcalan and Taş op. cit.

17 Interviews Öcalan and Taş op. cit.

18 Interview Taş op. cit. Ergenekon was an alleged ultra-nationalist conspiracy against the AKP government in Turkey, comprising of high ranking military, police, and intelligence officials, whose origins were supposed to date back to Operation Gladio's counter-guerrillas during the Cold War, and who were generally considered part of the Turkish so-called 'Deep State'. Since 2008, dozens of legal proceedings have been launched against alleged members of Ergenekon, yet these trials and investigations have also been criticized as attempts by the AKP government to rid themselves of domestic critics and, in general, to curtail civil freedoms (Kaya 2009; Cizre & Walker 2010; Hale & Özbudun 2010; Aydinli 2011; Öktem 2011; Straw 2013).

19 David Phillips, an expert on Turkey and Iraqi Kurdistan, when asked what he thinks about alleged PJAK–US intelligence meetings and possible small-scale cooperation, thinks 'the Bush administration absolutely capable of such a folly', interview with David Phillips, New York, USA, 11 February 2011.

20 Interviews Dizayee, Hussein, and Pire op. cit., as well as interviews with Falah Mustafa Bakir, the de facto Foreign Minister of the KRG, Erbil, Iraqi Kurdistan, 27 May 2010, and with Sinan Abdulkhalq Ahmed Chalabi, the KRG Minister for Trade and Industry, Erbil, Iraqi Kurdistan, 20 October 2011, and with the KRG foreign representatives, aka de facto ambassadors, to the UK, Bayan Abdul Rahman, London, UK, 5 July 2010, and to the US, Qubad Talabani, Washington, USA, 25 February 2011.

21 Interviews Abdul Rahman, Bakir, Chalabi, Dizayee, Hussein, Pire, and Talabani op. cit.

22 This part of the interview was given off the record which is why the identity of this KRG official is not disclosed.

23 Interview Selcin op. cit.

24 Interview with Denise Natali, Washington, USA, 21 March 2011. The KRG's political will to confront the PKK is also questioned by Joost Hiltermann, the International Crisis Group analyst on Iraq, interview with Joost Hiltermann, Washington, USA, 9 February 2011.

25 Four interviews with not-to-be-named Iraqi Kurdish journalists in Erbil and Sulimaniyah, Iraqi Kurdistan, during 2010 and 2011.

26 Interview Chalabi op. cit.

27 Interview Chalabi op. cit.

28 This view is shared by several of the journalists critical of the KRG regime I talked to in Iraqi Kurdistan during 2010 and 2011.

29 ROJ-TV is an international Kurdish satellite television channel widely considered to be a PKK propaganda organ. In January 2012 a Danish court determined that the station is 'financed and controlled' by the PKK and fined it for 'promoting terrorism' (Reuters 2012).

30 Naqishbendi (2011), Kurd.net (2013b), Mohammed (2013), Wood (2013).
31 Interview Abdul Rahman op. cit. A similar point was made by Qubad Talabani, interview Talabani op. cit.
32 The first major concession the AKP made was the launch of a 24 hours Kurdish language state-run television channel, TRT 6, in January 2009 (Zeydanlioğlu 2013).
33 In October 2009 the AKP had negotiated with the PKK the return to Turkey and amnesty of 34 guerrillas and sympathizers from the PKK-controlled Makhmour refugee camp in Iraq. When the PKK fighters arrived at the Harbur border in their uniforms, the DTP had arranged for thousands to welcome them in displays of public affection that could easily be interpreted as victory celebrations for the PKK.

> The Turkish authorities, who thought they had agreed with the PKK that the returnees would go quietly back to their villages, felt betrayed, angry and undermined as sensationalist Turkish media broadcast what appeared to western Turkish opinion as PKK victory celebrations. AKP's attempt to use the rhetorical symbolism of brotherhood [and] the high casualties on both sides … in a way that included both Turks and Kurds backfired and began to be used against it in Turkish street rallies at substantial political cost.
>
> (International Crisis Group 2011: 8–9)

34 A conference sponsored by the Gülen movement, that until 2013 was closely associated with the AKP, entitled 'Searching for Peace and a Future Together', held in Erbil in February 2009 and attended by Kurdish delegates from Turkey and Iraqi Kurdistan as well as representatives of Turkish religious and civil society organizations and journalists, can be considered a precursor to the envisioned pan-Kurdish summit and an attempt by both sides, the KRG and, indirectly through the Gülen movement, the AKP, to test the waters for a more prominent initiative (Olson 2009). On the Gülen movement, see Bilici (2006), Ebaugh (2010), Park (2012a), and a series of articles from a conference on the topic held in October 2007 at Leeds Metropolitan University, edited by Barton (2013).
35 Interview Phillips op. cit.
36 Interview Vali op. cit.
37 Interview with a to-remain-unnamed Iraqi Kurdish journalist in Erbil, Iraqi Kurdistan, in 2011.

10 The Kurds in the war against ISIS

The peculiar status of Iraqi Kurdistan

As argued in the previous chapter, one factor that has come to increasingly shape the matrix of identities and interests in other parts of what is called wider Kurdistan, and has a significant impact on the relations between the KRG and Kurdish ethno-nationalist parties elsewhere, is the image of the Kurdistan Region of Iraq as a beacon of hope, a source of emulation or a model case for, and potential supporter of, Kurdish national self-determination beyond Iraq. In order to appreciate the significance of this image and to evaluate its political and ideational potential in a wider ethnicized Kurdish discourse cum struggle for national self-determination, one needs to return to the question of the nature and status of the current Kurdistan Region of Iraq. In other words, one needs to ask what is actually meant today by 'the freest political entity in Kurdish history', what are its freedoms and constraints, and how those are expressed in political practice.

Strictly speaking, from a perspective of international law only, the case of Iraqi Kurdistan is quite straightforward: it is an autonomous region within the federal Republic of Iraq. In terms of political realities, though, the case is all but clear-cut. For what kind of autonomy or federative status are we talking about here? The degree of autonomy the Kurdistan Region enjoys in Iraq surpasses all comparable international cases of federally structured states, whether the US, Russia, the regions of Flanders and Wallonia in Belgium, the Basque region in Spain – none of these international precedents can claim a degree of autonomy and self-governance comparable to the Kurdistan Region.

> The Kurdistan Region has its own parliament, and its President Massoud Barzani ... is the commander in chief of the Iraqi Kurdish armed forces ... estimated 127,000 deployable men that, despite this being stipulated in the constitution, have not yet been integrated into the Iraqi Army and likely never will.
>
> (Artens 2013b)

Back in 2013, 'with an annual GDP of $20 billion, the Kurdistan Region, in sheer economic figures, plays in the same league as independent states like Albania, Cambodia, and North Korea,' and when it was still seen as the most promising market in the Middle East after Turkey and the Gulf States, 'international investors [kept] flock[ing] there, major European carriers like Lufthansa operate[d] direct flights to its capital Erbil, where five star hotels run by the Kempinski and Hyatt group [we]re mushrooming,' and what is perhaps most significant, 'all major EU countries as well as the US, Korea, Japan, and Russia ha[d] consulates or interest sections there. The Kurdistan Region itself entertain[d] representations that are de facto embassies in three dozen countries' (Artens 2013b). In light of its rapid economic development during the second half of the 2000s, vast opportunities for international investors, and its political stability, Iraqi Kurdistan was widely hailed as the 'sole success story' of the Iraq War (Zakaria 2006; CBS 2007; Hitchens 2007), *National Geographic* (2011) listed it as one of its must-see destinations for 2011 and, in 2012, the *Arab Council of Tourism* named Erbil its Tourism Capital for 2014 (Newton-Small 2012). All this is in stark contrast to rest of the country being torn apart by ethno-sectarian violence and the infighting of an ineffective central government.[1] When, taking a snapshot in the early second decade of the twenty-first century, evaluating the degree of autonomy the Kurdistan Region enjoyed in Iraq, including its de facto autonomous foreign representation, the control of its own armed forces, and its booming economy, one could indeed not help but agree with Brendan O'Leary (2009: X) that 'Kurdistan [is] freer within Iraq than any member state within the European Union'.

In light of these promising developments and at the same time persistent political disputes with the central government in Baghdad, it was only a matter of time until those explanatory IR scholars who had advocated ethnic partition in the run up to the Iraqi constitution of 2005 came to question the limitations the constitution imposed on Iraqi Kurdistan and thus to revisit the theme of its eventual independence. Gareth Stansfield, for example, after initially embracing the federal/regional principle for Iraq (Stansfield 2007b), appeared to have increasing doubts as to whether the Kurdistan Region's status was not merely a transitional state towards full independence. After declaring that 'the Kurdistan Region has matured into an institutionalised reality in territorial, political, and economic terms', he outlined a scenario for the Kurdistan Region to declare independence by 2016, that although 'hypothetical' was 'constructed on facts and events that have come to pass in recent years' (Stansfield 2013: 260–261). Tellingly, in Stansfield's scenario, it was Turkey that came to the KRG's rescue with a military intervention, after the latter suffered a rout at the hands of the Iraqi army in an armed conflict over the status of Kirkuk (Stansfield 2013). By the same token, Ofra Bengio speculated that Barzani was pursuing a 'creeping independence … until the Kurdish leadership is sure that Ankara and Washington would accept Kurdish independence as a fait accompli' (Bengio 2012a) a scenario she further elaborated in a monograph (Bengio 2012b). Indeed, their confidence in its political maturity and stability, eventual destiny as an independent state, and the fact that Turkey, if not outright supporting it, would at least one day tacitly approve Iraqi Kurdish secession from Iraq, was a view shared by Iraqi Kurdish leaders. In December 2012, PM Nechirvan Barzani alluded to as much when he was interviewed on the possibility of Iraqi Kurdish independence:

I believe, yes, we have a very good opportunity. But we have a lot of challenges as well. How we can – I mean an independent Kurdistan – first of all we have to convince at least one country around us. Without convincing them, we cannot do this. Being landlocked we have to have a partner, a regional power to be convinced and internationally, a major power to be convinced to support that.[2]

While, as subsequent events would prove, Barzani might have been overly optimistic in hoping that the 'one country around us' he is referring to, which was obviously Turkey, would eventually support Iraqi Kurdish independence, the degree of Turkish–KRG collaboration against Baghdad had reached such a level that the power who originally conceived of and nurtured their rapprochement, became increasingly concerned. Francis Ricciardone, US ambassador to Turkey warned:

Turkey and Iraq have no choice but to pursue strong ties if they want to optimize the use of Iraq's resources and export them via Turkey. If Turkey and Iraq fail to optimize their economic ties, the failure could be worse than that. There could be a more violent conflict in Iraq and [the chances of] disintegration of Iraq could be [strengthened].[3]

On most points of issue between Iraqi Kurdistan and the central government, from the status of the so-called 'contested territories' (areas with a significant Kurdish population outside the KRG's direct jurisdiction), to Erbil's unrestricted control over its natural resources, Turkey has, since 2008, come to either indirectly back the KRG via Baghdad, directly profit from it, as in the case of energy supplies, or has at least rescinded obstacles it had posed previously to thwart Iraqi Kurdish expansionism – all to the extent that some Turkish commentators lamented that the AKP had sacrificed good relations with Baghdad to support the KRG (Cagaptay & Evans 2012; Pamir 2013), and for Bill Park (2012c) to conclude that, 'indeed, the KRG now appears as an almost isolated beacon of Turkey's "zero-problems" approach to its neighbours'. With respect to Kirkuk, Ankara, for whom the city and its oil resources incorporation into the Kurdistan Region had long constituted a red line, downgraded the support for its local proxy, the Iraqi Turkmen Front (ITF, *Irak Türkmen Cephesi*) (Barkey 2011). As of today, the most brazen Kurdistan Region–Turkish joint venture in defiance of nominal Iraqi sovereignty occurred in early 2012 when PM Erdoğan announced that the two governments, together with Exxon Mobil, would build a new network of pipelines directly linking Turkey to the Kurdistan Region's rich oil and gas reserves (Cagaptay & Evans 2012; Park 2012c; Gemici 2013; Pamir 2013). Until then, most of the Iraqi Kurdish oil and gas exports had reached Turkey through the Kirkuk–Ceyhan pipeline, outside the KRG's territorial control, so this step indicated a major shift in Ankara's thinking towards recognition of Erbil's sovereign control of its natural resources at the expense of the Iraqi central government. Given this degree of diplomatic exposure, and in a most ironic twist of fate, it appears understandable that Iraqi Kurdish politicians and so many international analysts and commentators believed that the AKP government in Turkey had replaced the US after the American troop withdrawal in 2011 as the main external backer of Iraqi Kurdish autonomy via Baghdad.

The prospect of Iraqi Kurdish secession, international advocacy for independence, together with Turkey's possible support of it, and the incessant stand offs between Erbil and Baghdad came to a head when, in the most momentous event in the region since the US invasion of 2003, the Islamist insurgency *Islamic State of Iraq and al-Sham* (ISIS) took Mosul, Iraq's second biggest city, in June 2014 (Al Jazeera 2014a; Chulov *et al.* 2014; Reuters 2014a).[4] In Baghdad, the embattled government of PM Nouri al-Maliki reacted to the fall of Iraq's second biggest city and ISIS's subsequent Blitzkrieg-like advance on the capital with complete political paralysis. Two months earlier Maliki had enjoyed a surprisingly strong showing at parliamentary elections, yet the sectarian divisions paralysing the political process seemed irreconcilable, the Kurdish MPs boycotted the first sessions of parliament in protest against Maliki, and it was this antagonism and clash of interests that ISIS exploited. While the central government in Baghdad proved too divided to even declare a state of emergency, the Iraqi Kurds exploited the political vacuum while their *peshmerga* occupied the so-called 'contested territories' – most prominently the oil-rich city of Kirkuk – that the Iraqi army had abandoned when taking flight from ISIS (Černy 2014b; Chulov & Hawramy 2014; Johnson 2014; Parkinson 2014). Emboldened by their territorial gains, the Iraqi state's disintegration before everyone's eyes, and the international community's identification of Maliki, his divisive leadership and stubborn refusal to relinquish power as the main culprit for the political paralysis and the rout of the Iraqi army, the Kurds reiterated a commitment to their conquest and to holding a referendum on Iraqi Kurdish independence (Al Arabiya 2014a; BBC 2014a; Černy 2014b; Lake 2014).

To be sure, the weeks immediately following ISIS's capture of Mosul may perhaps have constituted the most auspicious window of opportunity for a unilateral declaration of independence in Iraqi Kurdish history. The Iraqi Kurds had gained control of all territories with a substantial Kurdish population outside their nominal jurisdiction. Even more importantly, they had accomplished this feat without the risk of being blamed for causing Iraq's disintegration. Iraq's ultimate collapse as a state in June 2014 was evidently brought about by ISIS, the fact that substantial numbers of alienated Sunni Arab communities in central Iraq had joined the Islamist insurgency, the ineptitude and unwillingness of the US-trained and equipped Iraqi army to defend the country, and an embattled sectarian leader, whose divisive rule was widely blamed for the dysfunction of Iraq's political system – in fact, at this stage, even the Islamic Republic of Iran had abandoned Maliki, its long-time protégé (BBC 2014b). All this lent plausible credence to Massoud Barzani's claim that Iraq had already been effectively partitioned:

Independence is a natural right of the people of Kurdistan … the goal of Kurdistan is independence. Now, of course, conditions are ripe, in reality, Iraq is partitioned … we can't go back to the previous situation … but it's not me who will decide the future of Kurdistan, it's the people. We will hold a referendum in Kurdistan, and we will respect and be bound by the decision of our people and hope that others will do likewise … I will work with parliament to establish a timeline [for the referendum] … it's a question of months.[5]

Yet, as Barzani continued to emphasize, the implosion of Iraq had been brought about by others, not the Kurds, and they would merely hold on and defend what was left of the country against what virtually all regional powers and the international community had quickly come to agree was the gravest threat the region had come to face, a millennialist insurgency of tens of thousands of fighters that would stop at nothing to bring down the regional order they had tried to uphold for almost a century. In fact, the Iraqi Kurdish *peshmerga* were seen by many commentators and military analysts as the only force left in Iraq that could hold its ground against ISIS' advance (Černy 2014b; Filkins 2014; Friedman & Salih 2014; Krajeski 2014a; Salih 2014a). Due to the ISIS threat and the complete failure of the institutions (i.e. the central government and the army) the international community had so far backed in attempts to preserve the unity of the Iraqi state, the supposedly secessionist Kurds, over night, had become a most coveted ally. This key role was captured by Peter Galbraith, who argued that when declaring independence in this constellation Barzani would not be seen as the gravedigger but saviour of Iraq, and then called on the Obama administration to face reality and accept Iraqi Kurdish independence in exchange for the *peshmerga* fighting ISIS:

If the United States wants the peshmerga to join the fray [against ISIS], it will have to pay a price … Kurdistan will … want something to fight for, and that is independence. To convert their current de facto independence into full independence, the Kurds need diplomatic recognition. And this the United States can provide. So, here is the basis of a bargain: US recognition of an independent Kurdistan in exchange for peshmerga troops joining a US air campaign against ISIS and helping to stabilize what used to be Iraq.

(Galbraith 2014)

Yet, this time around, those explanatory IR scholars and commentators advocating Iraqi Kurdish independence were no longer an influential minority but constituted the majority discourse. In the wake of the shock of the ISIS advance, the international *Kommentariat* was full of arguments in support of Iraqi Kurdish independence, hailing Iraqi Kurdistan as the world's '194th state' (Wright 2014); or, in contrast, politicians wary of such a development, such as German Foreign Minister Frank Walter Steinmeier, argued that the West arming the *peshmerga* would set Iraqi Kurdistan irreversibly on a path towards independence

(*Der Spiegel* 2014). What counts most though, is that officials of other governments voiced their tacit acceptance of, or even outright support for, an independent Iraqi Kurdish state. Prime Minister Benjamin Netanyahu, went on record that Israel would be the first country to recognize an independent Kurdistan (Ravid 2014), and its Foreign Minister, Avigdor Lieberman, declared an independent Iraqi Kurdistan as much as a 'foregone conclusion' (Williams 2014). In Turkey, where until a decade ago the mere utterance of the word Kurdistan had been anathema, AKP officials suggested that, 'if Iraq is divided and it is inevitable', Turkey may resign itself to accepting Iraqi Kurdish independence.[6] In sum then, the weeks after the fall of Mosul constituted a uniquely auspicious window of opportunity, a set of conducive factors for Iraqi Kurdish leaders to actively push for independence:

1   The swift collapse of the very institutions the West had created, sustained, and pinned their hopes on for keeping Iraq together, while the multiparty central government and the army had manifestly demonstrated to the world the futility of such an endeavour.

2   These state institutions were brought down not by Kurdish secessionism but centrifugal internal and external forces – ISIS and disenfranchized Sunni Arab tribes – that proved beyond control, together with an inherently dysfunctional government led by a divisive sectarian autocrat, thus lending credence to the Kurdish argument that they could not possibly remain in a house so divided.

3   The Iraqi Kurds had managed to unite all territories beyond their borders without, as they claimed, bloodshed and with only verbal protests from Baghdad.

4   Confronted with the seemingly unstoppable advance of ISIS on central Iraq, the international community relied on the Iraqi Kurds to integrate their *peshmerga* into a joint operation to stop ISIS, all the more since the *peshmerga* were widely seen as the only military force in the region left capable of confronting the Islamist insurgency.

5   Advocacy for an independent Kurdish state to emerge among academia and the international *Kommentariat* from the ruins of Iraq was no longer limited to an influential fringe but had become mainstream.

6   Finally, and in a state-centric world most importantly, even though key allies such as the US, UK, France or Germany still opposed or at best remained noncommittal towards independence, powerful players in the region – most crucially Turkey, who, as detailed above, some Iraqi Kurdish leaders and international advocates saw replacing the US as the most potent possible backer of eventual Iraqi Kurdish independence, signalled that they may recognize an independent Kurdistan in the wake of a breakup of Iraq.

And yet, despite this auspicious set of conditions, this unique window of opportunity closed without the Iraqi Kurdish leaders capitalizing on the conditions; on the contrary, just a few weeks after Barzani had announced the referendum, the prospect of Iraqi Kurdish independence came to appear more distant than at any time in the past decade. In fact, it was revealed that on the same day, 2 July 2014, Barzani informed the Iraqi Kurdish parliament of his intention to hold a referendum on independence in Iraqi Kurdistan, his representatives in Washington assured Vice-president Joe Biden and Secretary of State John Kerry that the Iraqi Kurds would give a national unity government in Baghdad one last try (Slavin 2014; Phillips 2015a). In a press conference after the meetings President Barzani's Chief of Staff, Fuad Hussein assured his American audience that the Iraqi Kurds would pursue a dual strategy, on the one hand continuing to collaborate in efforts to form a new government in Baghdad while at the same time ensuring 'an independent economic life' for Iraqi Kurdistan;[7] both he and KRG de facto Foreign Minister Fallah Mustafa Bakir also kept emphasizing to their US counterparts that any referendum on Iraqi Kurdish independence would have declaratory character only – a message that sounded noticeably different and significantly watered down from what Massoud Barzani was telling the Iraqi Kurdish audience at home. It can be assumed that in these meetings the outlines of a deal that evidently came to pass in the following weeks were sketched out: the Iraqi Kurds were rewarded for their restraint with Western military equipment and Western military trainers instructing the *peshmerga* on the ground in Iraqi Kurdistan (Parkinson & Nissenbaum 2014; Berman 2015; Salih 2015) and the Iraqi Kurds installing as President of Iraq one of their own, Fuad Masoum, one of the legendary founders of the PUK (Morris 2014; Reuters 2014b), who a few weeks later finally succeeded in pushing Nouri al-Maliki out and replacing him with the consensus candidate Haider al-Abadi as new Iraqi Prime Minister (BBC 2014c; Harding 2014). Consequently, in September 2014, the Iraqi Kurdish leadership announced then that an independence referendum would be postponed indefinitely until the political and security situation allowed it (Parkinson & Entous 2014).

How is one to interpret this sequence of events, in which once again the Iraqi Kurdish leadership voluntarily decided not to pursue independence at a moment when countless international analysts and commentators were already writing it into existence and the conditions arguably were more encouraging than at any time since the creation of the Iraqi Kurdish 'de facto state' in 1991? It has been detailed in Part II that the discourse on national self-determination in Iraqi Kurdistan prior to 2003 did not feature independence as a declared political objective, that throughout their history both Iraqi Kurdish ethno-nationalist parties, KDP and PUK, rather sought accommodation by Baghdad of a generously defined autonomy status. Only recently has the KDP adopted demands for a unilaterally pursued independence into its rhetoric; PUK and *Gorran*, while also hailing independence as the Iraqi Kurds' ultimate destiny, are more cautious in their pleas, putting emphasis on political reforms at home preceding any such endeavour which ultimately, they argue, can only be pursued in accordance with Baghdad (Chomani 2014). Could it be then that the incessant holding out of soon-to-be independence by KDP elites is merely a rhetoric device, a political tool to establish the KDP as the true party of Iraqi Kurdish independence and shore up support for it at home, while using the threat of the same as political leverage via the central government in Baghdad and Iraqi Kurdistan's international partners abroad? Could it further be that Massoud Barzani, ever the shrewd pragmatist, has recognized that, strategically, independence is not achievable (and was not even in the promising regional climate of June/July 2014) as long as the United States is unwilling to give it its blessing and support? While one wonders what more opportune conditions he would then be waiting for, such a pragmatist reading of the discourse in Iraqi Kurdistan, in which President Barzani for the time being has effectively written off independence as an achievable goal, yet capitalizes on holding out the promise of it in domestic politics, cannot be easily discarded. I have repeatedly questioned elsewhere whether independence is what the Iraqi Kurds are actually after (Artens 2013b; Černy 2014c, 2014d, forthcoming), both arguing the above pragmatist reading shared by other authorities on Iraqi Kurdistan (Barkey 2014a; Hiltermann 2012; Hassan 2015; Natali 2015), yet also proposing an alternative interpretation, based on the findings of my ethnographic-inspired fieldwork in Iraqi Kurdistan and combining Kurdish historical tradition with Weberian 'charismatic authority', the socioeconomic model of the 'rentier state', and Sadiki's 'dynastic republicanism' discussed earlier. This alternative interpretation argues that Massoud Barzani may hold an altogether different understanding of sovereignty than the normativist state-centrism of explanatory IR that regards the nation as a precursor to the sovereign, independent state. In fact, it is an opinion routinely encountered in the cafes of Iraqi Kurdistan when sitting together with journalists, political activists, or students critical of the KRG and Barzani's leadership that the Iraqi Kurdish president has no intention of pursuing independence but is actually content to emulate the Kurdish emirates of early modern times, where hereditary rulers enjoined a considerable degree of autonomy from the Sublime Porte (van Bruinessen 1992, 2002; Özoğlu 1996; 2004; Finkel 2005; Eppel 2008; Imber 2009).

In the many military clashes between the Ottoman and Safavid Empires of the sixteenth and seventeenth centuries, the border region inhabited by the Kurdish tribal federations became of paramount strategic importance to both sides. 'As a result, Kurdish allegiance to the two empires fluctuated during the [sixteenth] century, indicating that the Kurds were not passive partners in the state-tribe interaction' (Özoğlu 2004: 49), allowing Kurdish tribal leaders, often successfully, to play their temporary imperial overlords off against each other. One prominent example is Sharaf Khan IV of Bitlis – whose grandson, Sharaf Khan V, authored the famous *Şerefname* on the history of Kurdish dynasties in eastern Anatolia. Other examples include,

> when in the war of 1578–90, the Kurdish lords of Bitlis and Hakkari were able to use their allegiance to the Ottomans to extend their own territories. In 1605, however, the defection of some of the Kurdish leaders to the Safavids was a factor in Shah Abbas' victory.

> (Imber 2009: 177)

Successive Ottoman dynasties tried to bring the wayward Kurdish principalities under closer central control. They introduced a system of *sancaks* (district), governed by a *sancakbeyi*, and several *sancaks* constituted an *eyalet* or *beylerbeyilik* (province), where executive authority lay with the *beylerbeyi*, later *vali* (governor) as the representative of the sultan (van Bruinessen 1992; Özoğlu 1996, 2004; Finkel 2005; Imber 2009). In general, 'the beys of frontier regions enjoyed greater autonomy than the beys who ruled sancaks closer to the center' (Özoğlu 2004: 53) – with the most remote *sancaks*, bordering a hostile empire, such as Safavid Iran, enjoying the greatest degree of autonomy. In order to better control the vacillating Kurdish emirs and to further integrate their dominions into the administrative structure of the empire,

> hereditary succession was granted to the Kurdish beys loyal to the Ottoman state, an exceptional privilege in the Ottoman administration, ... and the Ottoman state was extremely careful to ensure that power remained in the hands of the same ruling families.
>
> (Özoğlu 2004: 54)

In a few cases of *sancaks*, referred to as *hükümets* at the Iranian border, the degree of self-rule went even further:

> The state preferred not to interfere in their succession and internal affairs, and contented itself with recognising the authority of the rulers. The sultan issued official diplomas of investiture to show his approval ... They neither paid taxes to the Ottoman state nor provided regular military forces to the *sipahi* army.
>
> (Özoğlu 2004: 57)

The more these autonomous Kurdish principalities became integrated into the administrative structure of the empire and the more the central government succeeded in asserting its authority there through the *beylerbeyi*, the more Kurdish self-rule at the border came to fade during the second half of the seventeenth century, culminating in the last Kurdish emirate of Botan being abolished by force in 1847 as part of the *tanzimat* reform process (van Bruinessen 1992, 2002; Özoğlu 2004; Finkel 2005; Eppel 2008; Imber 2009, Hanioğlu 2010; Ghalib 2011; Klein 2011; Ateş 2013).

Is it conceivable then that Massoud Barzani pursues a more traditional, historically grounded understanding of national self-determination that, while at odds with the modernist paradigm of the independent sovereign nation state being the end to all nationalist means, is more in tune with Kurdish cultural tradition and is distinguished by the principle of hereditary succession, mirrored in Sadiki's 'dynastic republicanism' that, as has been outlined earlier, defines the KDP. In contrast to the modernist reading of nationalism that establishes a linear trajectory and development from nation as proto-state to sovereign nation state and views nationalism as a Renanian 'daily plebiscite' (Renan 1994 [1882];

Finlayson 1998; Yack 1999; Smith 2004; Roshwald 2015), in which the democratic will of the people for unity, communality and solidarity is channelled into political action in the pursuit of national coherence and territorial integrity, here instead an autocratic, benevolent ruler instrumentalizes nationalism to legitimize the dynastic principle of leadership via his constituency and via the suzerains of larger units 'his' polity is nominally and loosely part of or enjoys relations with; something akin to a protective power. Relations between the ruler and his constituency are not clearly delineated and static but inherently ambiguous, in constant flux, and require to be continually renegotiated in the context of shifting personal and political dynamics. Legitimacy and authority are not so much derived from the ballot box and the impersonal institutionalization of nationalist principles into bodies of governance but, in application of Weberian 'charismatic authority', from the personal prowess of the ruler and the extent to which he embodies and champions these nationalist principles. By living and fulfilling his role as the 'father of the nation' the leader attains and maintains the consent of the governed.

Weber (2009 [1924]) famously differentiated between three types of legitimate authority: (1) traditional authority, in which a social group, due to historically established or hereditary structures, accepts its subordination to an individual or elite as can be found among priesthood, family clans, tribes, etc.; (2) rational or legal authority, where leadership is regulated and legitimized through norms on which at least a majority of the group (democratically) agrees; and (3) charismatic authority, where it is the 'charismatically qualified leader as such who is obeyed by virtue of personal trust in him and his revelation, his heroism or his exemplary qualities so far as they fall within the scope of the individual's belief in his charisma' (Weber 2009 [1924]: 328). Weber understood charisma as 'a certain quality of an individual personality, by virtue of which he is set apart from ordinary men and treated as endowed with supernatural, superhuman, or at least specifically exceptional powers or qualities' (Weber 2009 [1924]: 358). However, Weber rightly comprehended charismatic authority, that is 'resting on devotion to the exceptional sanctity, heroism or exemplary character of an individual person, and of the normative patterns or order revealed or ordained by him' (Weber 2009 [1924]: 328) as a discursive process, as a social phenomenon which only gains meaning through the discourse, that is through the relationship between the leader and his 'followers' or 'disciples' (Weber 2009 [1924]: 359). In other words, and as already elucidated by Foucault (1980, 1983, 1984),

> charisma is not a thing that can be possessed by an individual. Neither does it emerge automatically from certain circumstances regardless of individual qualities and initiative. Stated more precisely, charisma is a process that exists only in social relationships. It is a product of the qualities and actions of individuals and situational factors, but the nature of the situation is its most important determinant.
>
> (Jermier 1993: 221)

After identifying the phenomenon as a discursive process, Weber devotes his analysis to the ways in which charismatic authority becomes routinized and institutionalized, since 'for Weber, it was not the moral teachings that become routinised but the personal authority of the charismatic individual once he transferred his command to an impersonal, stratified order' (Lee 1992: 42). In *The Theory of Social and Economic Organization*, Weber (2009 [1924]) convincingly explains that it is primarily in the interest of the administrative or bureaucratic strata of the group or organization for the charismatic authority of the leader to become institutionalized, since these strata derive their own authority by reference to the leader's charismatic qualities; in other words, their authority rests on the reification of the leader's charisma, a process Lee calls 'the ramifications of an individualised hegemony' (Lee 1992: 43). It needs to be emphasized that when applying Weber's 'charismatic authority' to an ethno-nationalist discourse, what is institutionalized and routinized here is, unlike in Renanian modernism, not the abstract idea of nation and state itself nor the principles of democracy, rule of law, and good governance per se, but the charisma of the ruler, his political prowess, his capacity to benevolently and charitably administer to the needs of the populace – often reduced to the recipients of subsidies in exchange for political support and allegiance – and the extent to which he embodies and champions the nationalist principles. By extension, the model of dynastic republicanism the process of institutionalization and routinization of charismatic authority is not limited to a single individual, though, but broadened to the clan over which he presides.

The socio-economic aspect of the relationship between the charismatic ruler and his constituency is best captured in the 'rentier state' framework. The defining feature of a rentier state is not the dependence of a country's economy on a single cash crop or commodity per se – a situation that would thus render it extremely vulnerable to the variations in the international market on which the state has little or no influence – but rather how the socio-economic space in a society, in particular in relation to dynamics of power and authority between public and ruler, is structured (Mahdavy 1970; Herb 2005; Luciani 2013; Luciani & Beblawi 1987). Proponents of the rentier state paradigm ever since Mahdavi developed the concept juxtapose it to 'production states', in which society in itself is the main source of income for a state, which generates a surplus through taxation, duties or other levies on society's productivity. In exchange for their material contribution to the common good the people demand a say in how to define that common good as well as on the portion their contributions amount to. In other words, the production state requires a form of a social contract, a set of regulations about who has the authority to levy and spend the citizenry's taxes, and how much tax is acceptable, which is usually realized in some form or another of political representation of the taxed citizenry in the decision-making bodies of the state. Thus, the socio-economic structuration of the production state is said to lead à la longue to the development of democratic institutions. The rentier state, on the other, derives most of its income not from the productive activities of its citizenry but from selling a commodity on the international market, and then benevolently distributing among the citizenry the surplus thus accrued. The process of income generation and distribution does not require the material and political participation or productivity of the people, who consequently are also excluded from decisions on how to spend the national income; without political representation or a social contract that structures society, the citizenry here is reduced to the role of a mere recipient of handouts of a state that does not govern in consultation with the people but has become their magnanimous benefactor. Thus, the old adage that 'oil is bad for democracy' (Herb 2005: 297) holds some truth, for Iraqi Kurdistan as much as for any other petro state; yet, In Iraqi Kurdistan, that particular curse predates the oil boom of the second half of the 2000s since the structuration of society along the lines of a rentier state was already established in the 1990s when the rent was derived from humanitarian aid (Leezenberg 2000, 2003).

The same principles that determine relations between the charismatic ruler and his constituency – ethno-nationalism, charismatic authority, dynastic republicanism, and the rentier state framework – also shape relations between the charismatic ruler and his suzerain or protective power. It is his status as the 'father of the nation' that allows him to formulate relations with the latter on behalf of the people, and to switch allegiance between suzerains if one threatens to violate these nationalist principles and the freedoms that come with them, i.e. regional autonomy, his ability to distribute sinecures, and the like. The extent of relations are not clearly delineated as in a mere vassal–overlord relationship, the legal stipulations of a constitutional compact in a federalized state, or the specifications of a codified alliance, but are more ambiguous, changeable, and dependent on the ever-shifting interpersonal, political, and regional context. The autonomous ruler expects the suzerain or protective power to honour the fundamentals that allow him to act within his role, i.e. not to challenge his local authority, the means to distribute sinecures, etc., while the suzerain or protective power gains from the partnership nominal, shared control over the territory, populace and resources of the ruler's domain. In other words, their relations are on the one hand exclusively based on material interests – whether political, economic, or strategic – yet at the same time are highly personalized since they are a function of an individual leader or his clan's authority and the interpersonal rapport the suzerain or protective power maintain with the autonomous ruler. Needless to say then, associations wholly based on material interests and interpersonal relations are as unstable as those interests and relations are ephemeral, with the suzerain or protective power tirelessly trying to exert more control over the local potentate, while the autonomous ruler is ever more keen on expanding his autonomy, to renegotiate the terms of mutuality to his advantage, and in pursuit of this to shift allegiances or play suzerain and protective power off against each other.

Such an interpretation of Massoud Barzani's possible understanding of sovereignty and national self-determination has led analysts such as Hussein Tahiri (2007) to decry his nationalist brand as 'Medieval', 'tribalist' and 'backward'. As I have argued elsewhere (Černy 2014d), 'alternatively, his ideology can be described as post-modern, where several layers of sovereignty overlap ..., complement each other', and are constantly renegotiated, re-enacted and adapted to the requirements of a given context or constellation. Rather than linear trajectories from nation to state and static normative absolutes of the existence of sovereignty or its lack, it is acknowledged here that sovereignty can take many forms, can be shared, divided, and renegotiated according to context. The flexibility of such an ambiguous and vague political status, in essence the extension of what has been called a 'temporary anomaly' in the context of 'de facto states' into perpetuity – and arguably exemplified for decades now by Taiwan – would allow Barzani to shift allegiances and readjust as he sees fit relations with the central government in Baghdad, Turkey, the US and, to a lesser extent, even non-state actors such as the oil giant Exxon Mobil, in his pursuit of expanding Iraqi Kurdistan's autonomy without ever bringing it to the conclusion of full independence. In sum, 'Barzani may be quite content with indefinitely preserving the status quo – "his" state-like polity remaining within but at the same time apart from Iraq' (Černy 2014d), or in other words, for the time being at least, he may be perfectly satisfied with the 'smaller slice of a larger pie Kurdish autonomy in Iraq offers [rather] than staking everything on one card, the larger slice of a smaller pie of independence' (Černy 2014c). For in one crucial aspect – aside from the fact that any historic analogy from Medieval or early modern times should be treated with extreme caution when discussed in the context of twenty-first century statecraft – Massoud Barzani's position in today's Iraqi Kurdistan as a frontier region between Iraq, Turkey, Iran and Syria differs significantly from the historic cases discussed earlier. Unlike the Kurdish emirs, today's Iraqi Kurdish leaders not only dominate politics at the periphery in their autonomous region, but also hold considerable sway at the centre of the polity of which Iraqi Kurdistan is nominally part. While the Kurdish emirs had little or no influence on politics in the capital of the Ottoman Empire beyond issues directly affecting their domains, Iraqi Kurds, during the 2010–2014 Maliki government, held several key offices of state, the presidency and foreign ministry among them.

What is more, and quite ironically in light of developments thereafter, Nouri al-Maliki would not have been prime minister of Iraq had it not been for Massoud Barzani throwing his weight behind him after an arduous eight months of horse-trading, when the March 2010 elections at first produced the secular, cross-sectarian *Iraqiyya* alliance of former PM Iyad Allawi as numerical winner at the polls (ICG 2010; Marr 2011; Dodge 2012).[8] Such a temporary collaboration between Barzani and Maliki may appear at first sight perplexing, yet Toby Dodge points out that both Maliki's *Islamic Dawaa Party* and the KDP belong to the political elite that had benefited and thrived on the *muhasasa* principle, 'the division of cabinet posts according to sectarian quotas, with its assertion of religious and ethnic identity, its defence of elite interests and its encouragement of both personal and political corruption and government incoherence' (Dodge 2012: 156). To this 'elite pact' the polling victory of a movement with an explicitly secular, non-sectarian platform whose agenda was to transform the political landscape in Iraq away from ethno-sectarian binary opposites towards a more pronounced Iraqi identity, 'was a direct threat' (Dodge 2012: 155), which is why Maliki and Barzani cooperated in neutralizing *Iraqiyaa* in yet another government of national unity (Dodge 2012; Alaaldin 2010; Fadel 2010).[9] As a result of these complex dynamics, not only had ethno-sectarian divisions and those politically benefiting from them again triumphed, but relations between the Kurdistan Region and the central government in Iraq are now not exclusively antagonistic but considerably more ambiguous than commonly portrayed. I would argue, it is these inner-Iraqi power constellations and machinations that have provided a convincing argument against a unilateral declaration of independence of the KRG: for as long as the Kurdistan Region nominally remains part of Iraq, its leaders can influence the political space and process within its perceived constitutive other – a luxury no so-called 'de facto state' has, and the KRG would relinquish with independence.

As has been shown, in the summer of 2014, the KRG again traded the pursuit of independence for the role of kingmaker in Baghdad. It seems the price Massoud Barzani demanded for his restraint on secession and for cooperating with the capital in the attempt to form a government of national reconciliation was securing the presidency for the Iraqi Kurds. In turn, it was then an Iraqi Kurd, President Fuad Masoum, who finally succeeded in pushing Nouri al-Maliki out of office and nominating the consensus candidate, Haider al-Abadi. These developments illustrate that in the current ambiguous constellation, Iraqi Kurdish elites enjoy the best of both worlds: their president and de facto Foreign Minister is received by governments of major powers such as Turkey, the US, the UK and Germany as an equal, their armed forces, the *peshmerga*, are seen as a key ally in the fight against ISIS and are trained and equipped by coalition armies, they negotiate with international oil giants such as Exxon Mobil exploration contracts as if they were in undivided control of their natural resources, yet at the same time it is they who determine who becomes prime minister of Iraq. No doubt, the indeterminateness of their status allows them privileges independence would not offer.

Admittedly, what has been outlined here is merely one possible interpretation of the position of the Iraqi Kurdish leadership in the discourse on national self-determination and potential independence. But so is the 'explanation' of explanatory IR scholars that these elites are pursuing independence, with, as it turns out, little to substantiate that claim beyond the rhetoric and strategic essentialisms of those elites. As has been shown in the summer of 2014, when a plethora of analysts, commentators and decision makers portrayed Iraqi Kurdish independence as merely 'a matter of time', as 'a foregone conclusion', and began referring to it as the world's '194th state', Barzani did little more to bring statehood about than announce yet another referendum; once the *peshmerga* had brought the contested territories under their control, Barzani apparently relented and struck yet another deal with Baghdad and Washington that expanded Iraqi Kurdish autonomy but deferred independence. This time, however, those analysts, commentators and decision makers, in their representations, went beyond reifying and substantializing the strategic essentialisms of ethno-nationalist elites. In their normativist and essentialist categorizations that professed a linear trajectory from nation to sovereign nation state, analytically equated ethno-nationalist groups with states, and averred an ambition for sovereign control, i.e. independence, as the defining criterion for a nation, they presupposed a desire and assumed political action in pursuit of that goal where demonstrably the evidence to support their assertions was tenuous at best. In doing so, they not only altered the discourse but adopted a more prominent role in it. Given the incongruence between their representations and the actual behaviour of the ethno-nationalist elites, they could no longer claim to merely reflect realities on the ground in their writings but actually wrote a reality into existence, and one that not even the ethno-nationalist elites, whose behaviour they sought to explain, were pursuing. At this stage at the latest then, they undeniably had become very active co-protagonists of the ethno-nationalist conflict they purported to merely describe and explain.

For the Iraqi Kurds, their leader's reservations and brinkmanship ultimately paid off, though. When, by the end of July, what was left of the Iraqi army and Shi'ia militias had finally managed to slow the advance of ISIS in central Iraq, the Islamist insurgency pivoted to the north and overran the *peshmerga* defensive positions in a matter of days. By 6 August, ISIS had come as close as 40 km to the Iraqi Kurdish capital, Erbil, and on the following day it briefly captured the strategic town of Makhmour on the road between Mosul and Kirkuk, a mere 30 km southeast of Erbil (Al Arabiya 2014b), while east of Mosul it had taken most of the Sinjar region, threatening to commit genocide on its Yazidi population (Arango 2014; Packer 2014). The prospect of mass killings of Iraq's Christian communities and the threat to Erbil with its thousands of international residents finally propelled the Obama administration into action, and on 8 August the US air force flew its first sorties against ISIS in the Erbil area (Carter *et al.* 2014; De Young & Morris 2014; Kliff 2014; Shear 2014). American air cover allowed the *peshmerga* and PKK fighters from Iraq, Turkey and Syria to regain Makhmour on 10 August and to evacuate up to 50,000 Yazidi civilians stranded on the Sinjar mountains (Cooper & Shear 2014; Deutsche Welle 2014; Shelton 2014). Although the potential catastrophe of Erbil's fall had been averted at the eleventh hour, the ISIS assault on Iraqi Kurdistan came as an unprecedented shock to its people, politicians and the military alike. Against all expectations, the revered *peshmerga*, in the end, had turned out to be no match for ISIS, and Turkey, on whom so many Iraqi Kurdish politicians had pinned their hopes to become a potent backer of eventual Kurdish independence, had not done so much as lift a finger in its defence when ISIS advanced to the gates of Erbil. In the end, Iraqi Kurdistan was once again saved by the United States military, soundly demonstrating to any advocates of secession that Iraqi Kurdistan could not go it alone.

Today, one and a half years later, Iraqi Kurdistan is in no position to contemplate independence. Its political institutions are paralysed by a profound constitutional crisis over term-limited President Barzani's attempts to extend his tenure in office into perpetuity. After parliament had already granted him a two year extension in 2013, in August 2015, Barzani, in violation of the Iraqi Kurdish constitution yet backed by a dubious court decision, unilaterally invoked emergency powers that would allow him to remain in office until 2017, resulting in a political stalemate and street protests in Sulimaniyah that were violently put down by security forces (Bozarslan 2015a; Černy 2015; Hassan 2015; Natali 2015; Pollack 2016). Concomitantly, Iraqi Kurdistan is hit by the worst economic crisis in its history. The effects of decades of mismanagement, corruption, and nepotism, together with a dramatic drop in oil prices, the drain on international capital in the wake of the ISIS threat, and the Iraqi government finally acting on its threats to withhold funds if Iraqi Kurdistan continued to unilaterally sell oil on the international market, have worked together to plunge the region into a full grown recession (Bozarslan 2015a; Černy 2015; Hassan 2015; Kalin 2015; Natali 2015; Pollack 2016). After a balanced budget in the previous year, in 2014 the KRG had to account for a US$22 billion deficit and saw itself unable to pay public salaries for months. As a consequence, 'thousands of local businesses have closed, IOC payments remain in arrears, new investment has halted, and nearly 25,000 Kurds, mainly educated youth, have fled the Kurdistan Region over the past eight months' (Natali 2015). As has been observed on numerous occasions before, and currently in Venezuela, a rentier state runs into trouble when its coffers are empty. For a production state a systemic and extensive deficit may herald times of painful austerity, which does not necessarily mean the erosion of the social contract per se or the very fundaments society is built upon. Yet a rentier state that is not founded on the principles of democratic cooperation, solidarity and participation, but on a benevolent ruler purchasing the consent of the governed, is, when threatened by bankruptcy, challenged at the very core of its functionality. The Iraqi Kurdistan of 2015 is just another case in point. In light of these recent developments then, Kenneth Pollack (2016) observed that today's Iraqi Kurdistan is a far cry from its reputation as the island of stability and prosperity it enjoyed for a decade from 2003 on; on the contrary, with 'Kurdish politics … fragmenting in a mirror image of Iraq's splintering polity'. Iraqi Kurdistan has increasingly come to resemble the dysfunctional state of the rest of Iraq.

In June 2014, PM Nechirvan Barzani had declared that for Iraqi Kurdistan there existed a time before and after the fall of Mosul, and that after the implosion of the Iraqi state when faced with the ISIS advance, it was impossible for the Iraqi Kurds to go back to a reality overtaken by events. For Iraqi Kurdistan the immediate time after the fall of Mosul constitutes a double-edged outcome at best. On the credit side, it has gained control of Kirkuk and all the contested territories, and the Iraqi state appears too weak for the foreseeable future to challenge its supremacy there. Likewise, even though the *peshmerga* proved not capable of defending the Iraqi Kurdish territory on their own, Iraqi Kurdistan has established itself as an indispensable partner in the international coalition to fight ISIS, its military is trained and equipped by Western forces and closely cooperates with them in all strategic matters. On the negative, the consensus candidate Haider al-Abadi, brought to office with the help of the Iraqi Kurds, proved as unrelenting as his predecessor in accepting Iraqi Kurdish autonomy to further erode Iraq's sovereignty. What is worse, the ISIS shock assault on Erbil demonstrated that Iraqi Kurdistan is too weak, in the context of an inhospitable regional climate, to dare the ultimate act of brinkmanship for unilateral secession, a move that would alienate the one power that has repeatedly guaranteed its survival and on whom it remains utterly dependent: the US. This continued dependence, together with a profound feeling of betrayal by Turkey and the domestic political cum economic crisis, has dealt Iraqi Kurdish national consciousness and identity a serious blow, making any pursuit of independence at present appear not only unrealistic but also undesirable.[10]

The ISIS war in the wider Kurdish regional context

As it turned out, it was not the glorified Iraqi Kurdish *peshmerga* but another Kurdish militia that dealt ISIS its first major defeat on the battle field: the Syrian Kurdish PYD and its armed wing, *Yekîneyên Parastina Gel* (YPG, Peoples' Protection Units). Their prominence in the ISIS war, eminence in the wider contemporary Kurdish discourse on national self-determination, relations with the KRG, and the fact that of the four regional movements operating within the KCK umbrella the PYD can be considered the most successful as yet in implementing PKK ideology in actual forms of governance, necessitates a brief organizational sketch on the origins, structure, and ideology of the PYD.

Today's significance of so-called 'Western Kurdistan' or *Rojava* in the discourse on Kurdish national self-determination, constitutes a historic anomaly. Until the regional conflagration of the 'Arab Spring' that triggered the Syrian Civil War, and with it the rise of the PYD, *Rojava* was widely treated as an afterthought in most scholarly accounts of Kurdish ethno-nationalism. Editors felt compelled to add a chapter on Syria's Kurds for completeness' sake, yet, with few exceptions (Lowe 2007, 2010; Tejel 2011; Allsopp 2015), those accounts rarely added something to the better understanding of this remote border region and its people beyond a distressing chronicle of utter marginalization and consummate state oppression. The reasons for this neglect were varied. Of the four countries in the Middle East with a Kurdish population, Syria's is the smallest with about two million or roughly 10 per cent of the overall Syrian population (Lowe 2007, 2010; Tejel 2011; Allsopp 2015; Gunter 2014; Schmidinger 2014). Their historic lands consist of a triangular-shaped territory, the Jazira, stretching from the Tigris at the Turkish–Iraqi border to the city of al-Hasakah, and three separate sizeable pockets on the banks of the artificial Lake Assad, an area stretching from the Turkish border to Aleppo, encompassing Kobani and Jarablus, and finally a hilly territory in the Levant, bordering what used to be Hatay or the Sanjak of Alexandretta around the city of Afrin. These disconnected enclaves, historically disjointed by the Arab majority population and additionally isolated by deliberate policies of the Assad regime of Arab re-settlement at the borders in order to curb local populations' interactions with Kurds in Iraq

and Turkey (Lowe 2007, 2010; Tejel 2011; Allsopp 2015; Gunter 2014; Schmidinger 2014), naturally impeded the evolution of a Kurdish identity of communality and solidarity and any sentiment of, let alone political ambitions
towards national self-determination. Overall, it is no exaggeration to assert that
the oppressive Assad regime – rather than Heather Rea's pathological homogenization, pursuing a policy of de facto denying Syria's Kurds any socio-political
existence at all – has been the most ruthless and successful of all the four states
with a Kurdish population in inhibiting the incipiencies of any political organization among them, even withholding Syrian citizenship for large numbers and
depriving them of any civil rights,[11] and making it exceedingly difficult if not
genuinely impossible for scholars to conduct purposeful field research there.[12]
'For all the reasons', concludes Gunter (2014: 2), 'little was heard about the
Kurds in Syria'.

This depiction of complete isolation of Syria's Kurds comes with one crucial
caveat, though. As has been detailed earlier, during the era in which the Assad
regime played host to Abdullah Öcalan, from the early 1980s until his expulsion in 1998, the regime not only encouraged but actively supported PKK
recruitment among Syria's Kurdish communities in a process akin to military
conscription, allegedly in exchange for the PKK curbing any separatist tendencies or ideas hostile to the Assad regime among its populace (Scheller 2013;
Savelsberg 2014). Thus, while it is true that the PYD is a relative new comer to
the Syrian Kurdish political theatre, with thousands of PKK fighters and many
of its mid-level commanders originating from Syria, the PYD could draw on
vast resources of personnel and local knowledge – in addition to them being
seasoned guerrilla fighters with superior weaponry – all of which gave the PYD
a head start over its competitors. As has also been outlined, the origins of the
PYD date back to 2003, when the PKK was restructured along the principles of
democratic confederalism into an umbrella organization, the KCK, and local
quasi-autonomous branches, such as the PKK in Turkey, PJAK in Iran, and the
PYD in Syria. Given this organizational structure, the fact that almost all YPG
commanders at some point had also served in the PKK, and that the PYD
pursues the implementation of KCK/PKK ideology on the ground in Syria, it
appears rather pointless to debate to what extent PKK and PYD are related:
they are clearly two sides of the same coin and share ideological orientation,
personnel, logistics, training facilities, equipment, finances, etc. (Lowe 2010,
2014; Lowe & Gunes 2015; Caves 2012; ICG 2013, 2014a; Gunter 2014; Savelsberg 2014; Schmidinger 2014; Allsopp 2015; Barfi 2016; Üstündağ 2016).[13]
Thus, complaints by the Turkish government that any Western military assistance for the YPG also boosts the PKK cannot be easily dismissed. To deduce
from this though that 'the PKK leadership in the Qandil mountains and Abdullah Öcalan in Imrali are the ones who really rule [in *Rojava*] through various
PKK/PYD commanders responsible for different areas' (Gunter 2014: 111),
may be an over simplification. In accordance with Doğu Ergil,[14] I have argued
already for the 2000s that it is exceedingly difficult to ascertain who actually
runs the PKK and whether it is possible to speak of the PKK as a distinctly

bounded, monolithic group with a linear command and clearly defined organizational structure. Even more scepticism seems judicious when characterizing the PKK-PYD relationship. It would appear questionable to appreciate the PYD as merely a Syrian extension of the PKK who obligingly implements locally what has been decided far off in Qandil or Imrali, given that today it is the PYD who arguably can chalk up a greater victory in realizing the principle of democratic self-governance and a degree of autonomy for Syria's Kurds the PKK never even got close to. Such an oversimplified portrayal would seem even less credible, given that it is the PYD's armed wing, the YPG, who receives weaponry and support from Western powers while the PKK is still persona non grata in international diplomacy, and, most importantly, given that the PYD/YPG has established itself as the only force on the ground in Syria who not only can hold its own against ISIS but also forms the vanguard in Syria in the international coalition's attempts to regain ground from the radical Islamist insurgency. Is it plausible that the PYD and its leader Salih Muslim would sacrifice all these gains for Öcalan negotiating better detention conditions for himself or, if ordered to, give ground by the field commanders in Qandil? Rather than such an alleged direct line of command, I would argue that since 2011 and the PYD's ascent to regional influence, the centre of decision making and authority within the KCK has gradually started to shift in the PYD's favour, and while the PKK and the PYD's objectives have not yet been at odds, it will be interesting to see what happens when they inevitably become incompatible. Thus, the image of the KCK as a multi-headed hydra appears more apt (Eccarius-Kelly 2011); a hydra, of which, until recently, Qandil was the dominant head. Today though, given Qandil's embattled status versus the PYD's unprecedented freedom of action, we may witness – possibly by strategic necessity – a conspicuous shift towards a more decentralized structure with increased local autonomy in far-reaching decision making.

By the same token, it would be quite a simplification, as alleged by the *Encûmena Niştimanî ya Kurdî li Sûriyê* (KNC, Kurdish National Council in Syria) – see below – the Turkish politico-military establishment, and some authors, to portray the PYD as an ally of the Assad regime in the Syrian civil war, and, when assessing its form of governance in de facto autonomous *Rojava*, to evaluate it as not fundamentally different from previous Baathist rule (Savelsberg 2014).[15] For the rise of the PYD for example, Eva Savelsberg (2014) narrates a version of events according to which, in September 2011, Jalal Talabani, the then President of Iraq and leader of the PUK, forged a deal between the regimes in Tehran and Damascus and the PKK, with the latter ceasing the armed resistance in Iran through PJAK in exchange for its fighters, equipped by Iran, to move into *Rojava* in order to monopolize state-like power there on behalf and in collaboration with the Assad regime. She concludes, 'thus armed, the PYD began to prevent the Kurdish population from effectively participating in the revolution' (Savelsberg 2014: 98).

While it was not possible to verify Talabani's involvement in the rise to dominance of the PYD in Syria, up to this point, Savelsberg's description appears plausible. Previous instances of collaboration between the PKK and the Assad regime, as has been detailed, are a historic fact, and virtually all authorities on Syria's Kurdish ethno-nationalist movements agree that the speed and ease with which the PYD exploited the popular uprising[16] and took control of *Rojava* in the first half of 2012 could have only happened with the tacit acquiescence if not outright complicity of the Assad regime (Lowe 2014; Lowe & Gunes 2015; Caves 2012; ICG 2013, 2014a; Gunter 2014; Savelsberg 2014; Schmidinger 2014; Allsopp 2015; Barfi 2016; Üstündağ 2016). What is more, even once the PYD declared *Rojava's* official autonomy within Syria in January 2014, the Syrian army retained forces in their barracks in Qamishli and al-Hasakah, exercised some form of joint administration of these cities with the PYD, and continued to pay the salaries of public officials there (Lowe 2014; Lowe & Gunes 2015; ICG 2014a; Gunter 2014; Savelsberg 2014; Allsopp 2015; Barfi 2016; Üstündağ 2016). The advantages of this collaboration for both sides are obvious. The PYD, it allowed to get the better of its Kurdish ethno-nationalist competitors and take control of *Rojava* with very little resistance, while for the Assad regime it was expedient to hand over governance and security in north-eastern Syria to a known quantity, thus allowing it to concentrate and deploy its resources and forces in Aleppo and elsewhere. Having said that, there is no reason to believe that this alliance will prove more lasting than any other in the Syrian Civil War. 'A shared fear of the [FSA] rebels and IS has rendered the regime and the PYD "frenemies"', Barfi (2016) aptly concludes, 'each deeply distrusts the other, but they are nevertheless warier of their common adversaries. To this end, they have a modus vivendi that closely resembles a nonbelligerency pact.' Indeed, after collaborating in repelling an ISIS attack on al-Hasakah during the summer of 2015 (Al Rifai 2015; Moore 2015), this quasi nonbelligerency pact came to an end, when, since April 2016 the YPG and Syrian security forces together with pro-government militias have repeatedly clashed there and in Qamishli (Reuters 2016; van Wilgenburg 2016).

By the same token, it is indisputable that since 2012 there have been several instances of systematic human rights violations in PYD-controlled *Rojava*, including arbitrary arrests and expulsions, torture, forced conscription of minors, and allegations of ethnic cleansing, primarily levelled at the YPG (Human Rights Watch 2014; Rosenthal 2015; Smith 2015). Likewise, the implementation of the democratic element of 'democratic confederalism' – unilaterally announced with great fanfare by the PYD on 29 January 2014 in the so-called Constitution of Rojava, that gained considerable international attention (Graeber 2014; Aretaios 2015; Barnett 2015; Enzinna 2015; Ross 2015; Tax 2015) with its explicit affirmation of minority rights, gender equality, direct democracy along the principles outlined by Abdullah Öcalan and Murray Bookchin, as well as a commitment to the territorial integrity of Syria – leaves much to be desired. It would do injustice to the PYD experiment, though, to equate these shortcomings and a questionable human rights record with a history of decades of brutal oppression during the Assad era. Lowe (2014) and Allsopp (2015) are more balanced in their verdict on the PYD's accomplishments, acknowledging that when locked in a life-and-death struggle with ISIS may not yet be an appropriate time to realize the lofty principles of Bookchin and Bakunin, and with Lowe observing:

> Following decades of stifling repression, there has been a great hubbub of activity: political, civic, and cultural. Political discourse has found unprecedented freedom and Kurds have begun exploring and debating the possibilities of developing local government. The relaxation of pressure from the Syrian regime has also allowed a flowering of cultural activities and notable efforts to teach and promote the banned Kurdish language.
>
> (Lowe 2014: 228–229)

If the direct involvement of Jalal Talabani in Syrian affairs in 2011 is difficult to establish, there can be no doubt about the key role played by Massoud Barzani. The oldest Kurdish ethno-nationalist party in Syria has been the KDP-S, a sister party of Iraq's KDP, founded in 1957, yet who, like all Kurdish ethno-nationalist movements during the Assad regime, carved out a feeble existence at the margins until the public uprising in 2011 (Tejel 2011; ICG 2013; Gunter 2014; Schmidinger 2014; Allsopp 2015). By then, though, the rise of the PYD had forced the KDP-S and other movements associated with Barzani and/or wary of the PYD's dominance to unite under the umbrella of the *Encûmena Niştimanî ya Kurdî li Sûriyê* (Kurdish National Council, KNC), founded in October 2011 and headquartered in Erbil 'with the goals of profiting from the popularity of the [rebellious] youth groups, unifying the Kurdish political parties programmatically, and more effectively representing Kurdish demands' (Savelsberg 2014: 95). There can be no doubt, though, that a prime rationale for the founding of the KNC was to keep at bay the rising influence of PYD, who consequently refused to participate in it (Lowe 2014; Lowe & Gunes 2015; Caves 2012; ICG 2013, 2014a; Gunter 2014; Savelsberg 2014; Schmidinger 2014; Allsopp 2015; Barfi 2016; Üstündağ 2016). In his efforts to counter the PYD, Barzani was actively encouraged and supported by the AKP government in Turkey (Park 2012a, 2012b, 2012c; Tol 2012; Mert 2013; Tuysuzoglu 2013; Gunter 2014; ICG 2014b; Lowe & Gunes 2015), thus further cementing their strategic partnership; for the AKP, a PYD-controlled autonomous *Rojava* was, reasonably or not, anathema, since from Ankara's point of view this would amount to a PKK-run quasi-state at its southern border. Inevitably, tensions between the KNC and the PYD rose when the latter, in accordance with the Assad regime, exerted its control over *Rojava* during the first half of 2012, forcing Barzani to broker the Erbil Agreement of July 2012 between the antagonists, in which the basis was laid for a unified military command for the Kurdish militias operating in Syria and a power-sharing deal for jointly administering *Rojava* (Ates 2012; Kurd.net 2012; ICG 2013, 2014a; Gunter 2014; Lowe 2014; Lowe & Gunes 2015; Allsopp 2015). As with countless power-sharing agreements between squabbling Kurdish ethno-nationalist parties before, the spirit of the Erbil Agreement remained limited to paper only, its failure being best illustrated by the PYD moving towards a unilateral declaration of autonomy in November 2013 without consultation of the KNC (Rudaw 2013b; van Wilgenburg 2013b; Abdulla 2014; ICG 2014a).

The squabbling between Barzani, KNC and PYD over supremacy in *Rojava* might have continued endlessly, had it not been for two unexpected events like no other since the capture of Abdullah Öcalan, events that had an impact on the dynamics between the Iraqi Kurdish ethno-nationalist parties and the PKK: ISIS assault on the KRG in the summer of 2014, and the epic siege of Kobane during the fall/winter 2014/2015. When, in August 2014, ISIS advanced on Erbil, and took the city of Makhmour, it not only directly threatened the survival of the Kurdish autonomous region but also one of the strongest PKK bases in the region. The Makhmour refugee camp, founded in 1998 and housing up to 12,000 Kurdish refugees from Turkey, has been one of the prime recruitment grounds for the PKK in Iraqi Kurdistan; the insurgency even maintains a prominent remembrance site there, called 'Garden of the Martyrs', where relatives can pray for their fallen family members (Gee 2009; Eccarius-Kelly 2012; Harris 2014).[17] The potential massacre of thousands of refugees and the possible fall of Erbil propelled the PKK into action, to cast aside its differences with the Iraqi Kurdish ethno-nationalist parties, and come to the rescue of Iraqi Kurdistan. While the *peshmerga* withdrew, the PKK held the outskirts of Makhmour against ISIS, and thus not only prevented the slaughter of the unarmed refugees but also blocked the Islamist insurgency's advance on Erbil until they were relieved by US-airforce-backed *peshmerga* returning on 10 August. In the following days and weeks, PKK fighters and YPG volunteers were also instrumental in joint operations with the Iraqi Kurdish *peshmerga* in breaking the ISIS siege of Mount Sinjar (Beck 2014; Jacinto 2014; Malek 2014; Salih 2014b, 2014c; Solomon & Dombey 2014; Zaman 2014a; van Wilgenburg 2014; Shelton 2014; Schirra 2015). In a most ironic twist of fate then, while the revered *peshmerga* failed to protect the Kurdish homeland and the supposed ally, Turkey's Recep Tayyip Erdoğan, refused to lift a finger in the defence of Iraqi Kurdistan, it is no exaggeration to assert that it was the US air force and, in arguably equal measure, the PKK who saved the Iraqi Kurdish capital from falling into the hands of ISIS. Even Massoud Barzani, who for more than three decades had fought on several fronts to limit the PKK's influence across the Kurdish lands, had to grudgingly express his respect and gratitude for the PKK's contribution in the defence of Iraqi Kurdistan, when visiting Makhmour a week later (van Wilgenburg 2014; Schirra 2015).

The second event, the epic siege of Kobane, is one of those mythical moments in a nation's history the late Anthony Smith (1998, 1999, 2000, 2008, 2009) has made a core theme of his ethno-symbolist approach to nationalism. Indeed, how, in a five months siege of intense urban combat, a hopelessly outnumbered Kurdish force turned what was initially dubbed the 'Kurdish Alamo' (Dettmer 2014; Wilkens 2014) into ISIS's Stalingrad truly is the stuff legends are made of, and doubtlessly will live on in Kurdish nationalist narratives beyond Syria for a long time to come. When the battle was still raging, Henri Barkey (2014b) wrote:

Whether it falls or survives, Kobani is likely to become for Syrian and Turkish Kurds ... a defining moment of nationhood and identity ... Kobani will have two different effects on the region. First and foremost, it will be an important marker in the construction and consolidation of Kurdish nationhood. The exploits of Kobani's defenders are quickly joining the lore of Kurdish fighting prowess. After all, the Iraqi Kurdish forces, not to mention the Iraqi army, folded in the face of a determined IS onslaught only a couple of months ago. The longer the city resists, the greater will be the reputational impact ... [it has already] mobilized Kurds across the world.

Of equal importance is the effect the heroic resistance of Kobane's defenders had on an international, non-Kurdish audience. When ISIS closed in on the strategic border town in September, based on previous experience in Iraq, virtually every commentator expected the city to fall within weeks, and wrote the YPG's commitment to holding the city off as a brave, but ultimately futile and militarily meaningless attempt. Indeed, one month into the siege, US Secretary of State John Kerry explained away America's inaction to come to the Kurds' assistance, with preventing ISIS from taking Kobane 'not [to be] a priority' for the US anti-ISIS war in Syria, even though it presented the US air force with plenty of sitting duck-like ISIS targets (Ditz 2014; Salih, C. 2014), while the Turkish army, after initially admitting 180,000 refugees from Kobane, idly watched from a safe distance across the border as ISIS encroached on the city (Dettmer 2014; De Young & Sly 2014; Nazish 2014; Ozcan 2014; Park 2014). What is more, the Turkish military actively prevented Kurdish volunteers with tear gas volleys from crossing the border to participate in the defence of the city (Çandar 2014; Dettmer 2014; Letsch & Traynor 2014; Ozcan 2014; Zaman 2014b). While utterly repugnant from a humanitarian perspective, politically there can be little doubt that the Turkish politico-military establishment saw it as expedient for the YPG to get slaughtered in Kobane, and the US remained passive out of fear of alienating its key NATO ally.[18]

By 13 October, though, at the eleventh hour, as ISIS had managed to capture 40 per cent of the city, and the YPG defenders faced annihilation, the level of pressure from international public opinion became untenable and the US finally cast Turkish sensitivities aside, flying its first sustained bombing campaigns on ISIS positions, coordinated with YPG forces on the ground in target identification, and a week later started dropping small arms and ammunition in aid of the YPG (Al Jazeera 2014b; Letsch 2014; Pinar 2014). Less than a week after declaring it not a 'strategic objective' for the US to aid the YPG in Kobane, Secretary of State, John Kerry, now explained the American air campaign without being troubled by the irony in his statement, arguing,

It would be irresponsible for us, as well [as] morally very difficult to turn our back on a community fighting ISIL as hard as it is at this particular moment.[19]

While the battle for Kobane would rage another three months it was in these days in October that the tide began to turn for Kobane's Kurdish defenders. It was also in these days that a strategic shift of unprecedented proportion in regional Kurdish politics and beyond occurred, when the US, who had toed Turkey's line on the PKK for decades, acknowledged a sister organization of the PKK as the most potent force in the region to counter ISIS and started supplying this very organization with arms, strategically coordinated air sorties with it, and actively assisted it militarily and logistically in future operations; the YPG has even assigned a representative to the US-led situation room in Erbil that coordinates the Kurdish units in the war against ISIS – all over Turkey's vociferous objections (Cunningham 2015; Phillips 2015b; Gladstone 2016; Rogin & Lake 2016; Zaman 2016).[20] It seems that for pragmatic reasons the Obama administration had decided to simply decouple the PYD from the PKK, thus discounting the Turkish argument that they are two sides of the same coin and that any arms supplies for the YPG will inevitably also end up in the hands of the PKK, who could then direct them at Turkish soldiers. Abdulla (2016: 94) sums up Washington's reasoning as follows: 'to Washington the PYD is an independent Syrian Kurdish group that deserves US military support because of its effectiveness in fighting ISIL'. One cannot overstate the enhancement experienced by the PYD in their international profile with this collaboration – and therewith indirectly the PKK's as well – from pariah to strategic partner in the Western anti-ISIS coalition, which constitutes a watershed moment in recent Kurdish history and its significance for regional developments.

It would go well beyond the scope of this book to analyse with the depth such a complex subject merits the sea changes in Turkish foreign and domestic politics during and since the Arab Spring. Suffice it to say that in contrast to the clear and comprehensive vision of Ahmed Davotoğlu that guided it during the second half of the 2000s, today's Turkish foreign policy cannot be interpreted as anything but utter chaos. Ankara's foreign relations appears as much determined by knee-jerk reactions grounded in a unwholesome paranoia about the potential emergence of a Kurdish state-like entity run by the PYD in Syria, a resurgence of the Sèvres Syndrome, the no less pathological obsession of its megalomaniac strong man, Recep Tayyip Erdoğan, with toppling the Assad regime – as a consequence of these factors, Turkey's by now well documented support for ISIS (Cockburn 2014; De Bellaigue 2014; Guiton 2014; Phillips 2014; Ackerman 2015; Bekdil 2015; Bertrand 2015; Chulov 2015; Norton 2016)[21] – and Erdoğan's attempts at consolidating his power by forcing through a constitutional change that would transform Turkey into a presidential republic (Phillips 2012; Cagaptay 2013, 2016; ICG 2014b; Idiz 2015; Khan 2015; Kuru 2015; Traynor & Letsch 2015; Kardaş 2016; Der Spiegel 2016a). Turkey's complicity in the rise of ISIS, in an unprecedented step for NATO allies, was publicly acknowledged and condemned by US Vice President Joe Biden in a speech at Harvard University, where he stated:

My constant cry was that our biggest problem is our allies — our allies in the region were our largest problem in Syria … when it came to Syria and the effort to bring down President Bashar Assad there, those allies' policies wound up helping to arm and build allies of al Qaeda and eventually the terrorist 'Islamic State' ... They were so determined to take down Assad and essentially have a proxy Sunni-Shia war, what did they do? They poured hundreds of millions of dollars and tens, thousands of tons of weapons into anyone who would fight against Assad — except that the people who were being supplied were al Nusra and al Qaeda and the extremist elements of jihadis coming from other parts of the world.[22]

By the same token, it is no longer tenable to call present day Turkey a democracy even on paper. As with its foreign and overall policy failures since 2011, the steps the AKP government has taken in the past years to erode democratic institutions, the state of law, and civil liberties will be the topic of myriads of accounts to come – from 'jailing hundreds ... journalists, university rectors, military officers, aid workers ... on trumped-up charges and fabricated evidence', to 'crushing the remnants of a free press' (Filkins 2016), to the arbitrary shut down of civil society organizations and the arrest of its members, the co-option of the independent judiciary and campaigns of intimidation against state prosecutors, to overseeing a system of state-sponsored racketeering that directly benefits AKP grandees and their families,[23] to plans for a new constitution that, according to Turkish constitutional law experts, would amount to a 'one-man rule with no mechanisms of checks and balances'.[24] With hindsight, one can identify the brutal crackdown by the security apparatus on the Gezi Park protests in the summer of 2013 (Berlinski 2013; Kotsev 2013; Letsch 2013; Shafak 2013; Steinvorth & Zand 2013) as the moment when Turkey crossed the line from democracy to autocratic rule with increasingly fascist tendencies. By the spring of 2016, even President Obama admitted as much, when he lamented that once he had seen his Turkish counterpart as a 'moderate Muslim leader who would bridge the divide between East and West – but ... now considers [Erdoğan] a failure and an authoritarian' (Goldberg 2016).

Turkey's Kurdish community came to bear the brunt of state repression when protests against Turkey preventing Kurdish volunteers from Turkey and Europe joining the YPG in the defence of Kobane turned violent (Gurcan 2014; Letsch & Traynor 2014; Keles 2014; Ozcan 2014; Reuters 2014c) – a particularly cynical gambit in light of Ankara allowing for years its Syrian border to be turned into a 'jihadist highway' for future ISIS fighters from Europe travelling to Syria (Gursel 2014). When in response, Kurdish political representatives of the HDP, Abdullah Öcalan and leading PKK commanders threatened to abandon the peace process launched in 2012, the Turkish military answered in a deliberate provocation by carrying out air strikes against PKK fighters in Hakkari Province, the first since the beginning of the peace process. (ICG 2014c; Krajeski 2014b). The tense standoff was de-escalated when, at the end of October 2014, the AKP government allowed a convoy of Iraqi Kurdish *peshmerga* to cross Turkey in aid of the YPG defenders of Kobane – see below – but, after the YPG, assisted by American bombers, had liberated the town of Al Abayd in June 2015, thus consolidating its control over a coherent territory now stretching from the Iraqi border to the banks of the Euphrates, President Erdoğan reaffirmed his determination to oppose the PYD from gaining more ground in Syria when he declared that he would 'never allow the establishment of a Kurdish state in Syria'.[25]

It was in this heated climate that the Turkish public went to the polls on 7 June 2015 to vote for a new parliament. And yet the people bravely presented the AKP with the bill for years of systematic corruption, authoritarianism, police state brutality, an assault on democracy and the state of law, a foreign policy in tatters, and the country's alienation from virtually all its international partners, with the party losing more than 50 seats and its majority, mostly at the expense of the Kurdish HDP, who gained 13 per cent of the vote (Gürbey 2015a; Uras 2015a). Erdoğan refused to accept this outcome and, from that day on, torpedoed the constitutionally required talks to form a coalition government with the intention of forcing the country into snap elections (Bender 2015; Cagaptay & Bhaskar 2015; Tattersall & Coskun 2015; Zirngast 2015). In order for his party to succeed then, the ground had to be prepared by delegitimizing the HDP and raking up ethnic tensions that would allow for a national climate of fear and a siege mentality among AKP supporters to emerge. Tragically, ISIS and the PKK provided Erdoğan with the justification he needed for plunging the country into a renewed civil war for the sole purpose of ensuring a parliamentary majority for his AKP that was required to keep his ambition for a new constitution alive. On 20 July, ISIS suicide bombers attacked a congregation of Kurdish peace activists in Suruç, killing 33 and wounding more than a hundred (Letsch 2015; Sayman 2015; Uras 2015b). Both the HDP and the PKK argued that this attack could not have been carried out without the connivance of Turkey's security apparatus – made worse by the fact that of hundreds of 'terror suspects' arrested in the aftermath of the bombing, the majority were Kurdish activists (*Hürriyet Daily News* 2015; Robinson 2015) – and two days later the PKK killed two police officers in nearby Ceylanpinar in retaliation (Bohn 2015; Bozarslan 2015b; Gurcan 2015; Robinson 2015).

In response to these attacks, on 24 July 2015, Turkey actively entered the regional war with its air force flying sorties against ISIS in Syria and the PKK in Turkey and Iraqi Kurdistan, with strikes on the latter amounting to 155 sorties against 400 targets flown within the first three days of the campaign (Bohn 2015; Bozarslan 2015b; Gurcan 2015; Robinson 2015; Albayrak 2015; Gürbey 2015b). Even though the US complained about Turkey's war on the PKK indirectly weakening the PYD, the most effective ally of the US in fighting ISIS in Syria, Washington resigning itself to Turkey's war against the PKK was achieved by Turkey offering the international alliance use of its Incirlik AFB in the war against ISIS – which it had previously denied in October 2014 – in exchange (Almukhtar & Wallace 2015; Bohn 2015; Callimachi 2015; Çandar 2015; Cockburn 2015a, 2015b; Whitney 2015). Yet, even that concession came at a price with Ankara demanding Washington agree to the establishment of a 'safe zone' along its border, stretching about 90 km west from Jarablus, which would be liberated from ISIS but which the US would also prevent its PYD ally from entering (Almukhtar & Wallace 2015; Bohn 2015; Callimachi 2015; Çandar 2015; Cockburn 2015a, 2015b; Whitney 2015). The obvious sole purpose of this 'safe zone' was to prevent the PYD from connecting the territory it held east of the Euphrates with the Kurdish dominated lands around Afrin, thus ensuring that the Kurdish-controlled territory in Syria would remain divided indefinitely. Although this part of the Washington–Ankara deal was quickly broken by all sides, America's Kurdish allies in Syria were understandably furious about America's yielding to Turkey's demands, and Patrick Cockburn (2015a) wondered whether Washington's betrayal of the Kurds amounted to its 'worst error in the Middle East since the Iraq War'. Cockburn's question appears appropriate, for the Ankara–Washington deal of July 2015 has led to the paradoxical situation that the US is supplying the YPG with weapons to fight ISIS, which it uses for that purpose but also without fail shares with the PKK for attacks on America's NATO ally Turkey, while Turkey in turn kills PKK fighters that otherwise could have been used in YPG offensives against ISIS. Given that during the first two weeks of its so-called 'two-pronged war against terror', Turkey has hit the PKK 300 times with combined air and artillery strikes, yet ISIS with only three confirmed strikes (Dyke & Blaser 2015), the 'two-pronged war' seems suspiciously one-sided, and it appears apt to conclude that Turkey's participation is once again causing more harm than good to the international community's war against ISIS.

Yet, with the stage thus set, for Erdoğan his cynical electoral gambit paid off. With the national state of fear further exacerbated by another horrific ISIS suicide bombing of peace activists in Ankara on 10 October, claiming three times as many casualties as the Suruç attack (Al Jazeera 2015; Vick 2015), the AKP regained its majority in parliamentary elections on 1 November (Henley *et al.* 2015; Uras 2015c). The price for his scrupulous brinkmanship and politics of stirring ethnic conflict for electoral gain could not have been higher though. Not only did Erdoğan's machinations end the three-year-long 'peace and solution process' with the PKK that, despite several setbacks, had constituted the most sincere attempt by both sides at finding a peaceful solution to the almost four decade long conflict, his 'two-pronged war against terror' – of which the second prong was as much directed against the YPG as against ISIS – plunged the country back into civil war, with Turkey's south-east becoming a ravaged battlefield, a level of violence and destruction unseen since the worst days of the late 1980s, devastating Kurdish cities and towns, and reminding more than one commentator of Syria (Gursel 2016). Indeed, contrary to earlier phases of the PKK war, this renewed conflict is mostly fought in south-eastern Anatolia's cities with the urban civilian population bearing the brunt of the military's artillery shelling, aerial bombardments, street-to-street fighting, and the PKK's retaliatory bomb attacks (Gursel 2016; Deutsche Welle 2016; ICG 2016; Leverink 2016; Kuntz 2016; Worth 2016). A year into the war, the International Crisis Group (2016) estimates casualties of at least 2,000, with more than a quarter being civilian deaths, and up to 350,000 internally displaced persons. In June 2016, German human rights lawyers filed a 200-page lawsuit against President Erdoğan and members of the military for mass murder and crimes against humanity in the latter's conduct of 'anti-terror operations' in Turkey's south-east; the indictment focused mostly on the so-called 'basement massacre', perpetrated in the city of Cizre in February 2016, in which Turkish security forces had allegedly deliberately set fire to three residential basements where civilians were hiding, killing 178 – the lawsuit came a week after the Turkish parliament had passed a new law giving security personnel immunity from prosecution for human rights abuses committed during the conflict (Deutsche Welle 2016). While the nature of the war may have changed, the politics and rhetoric of Turkey's politico-military establishment remained the same as in the 1980s, with President Erdoğan declaring that there is 'no Kurdish question', just a 'terror problem', vowing that 'combating terror will continue until doomsday', and that 'the martyr's hills will never be vacant'.[26] With the frontlines between the Turkish state and the PKK more hardened than at any time since the AKP came to power, the conflict appears unlikely to end any time soon; on the contrary, with the PYD/YPG gaining ever more ground in Syria, the prevention of which, after domestic considerations, is the second objective of Turkey's war, the conflict seems likely to further escalate in the near future, and, in my opinion, it is only a matter of time until the Turkish military will be dispatched to fight the YPG directly in Syria.

As concerns relations between the PKK and the Iraqi Kurdish ethno-nationalist parties during this latest stage, the current situation is too fluid for an exhaustive interpretation. On the one hand, old patterns persist. In what may have been his last act of political brinkmanship, Jalal Talabani allegedly forged a deal between the regimes in Damascus and Tehran and the PKK that allowed for a large number of PKK fighters to be transferred to Syria, where, with the acquiescence of the Assad regime, they, as the PYD, came to control *Rojava*; likewise, Massoud Barzani's reaction to Turkish incursions into northern Iraq since the summer of 2015 (Al Shibeeb 2015) resemble the many token protests over the violation of Iraqi Kurdish sovereignty he has previously issued on similar occasions. Both behaviours appear primarily motivated by strategic calculations. In the case of Talabani's intermediary role, if such a deal occurred, he may have sought to limit the PKK presence in Qandil and ease tensions with Iran while, at the same time, sensing an opportunity to weaken his rival Barzani's influence in Syria. In the case of Barzani's token protests, he could ill afford antagonizing Ankara with too outspoken an objection in 2015 as, in previous instances, when Turkey's air force had attacked PKK camps on Iraqi Kurdish territory. What is more, even though relations between KDP and PKK have changed for the better since August 2014, the breakdown of the peace process in Turkey that, if successful, would have strengthened the PKK and HDP, cannot have been unwelcome for Barzani (Barkey 2015).

On the other hand, new patterns have emerged, I would argue, because the identity of the respective actors has evolved. Today's Iraqi Kurdistan is no longer the beacon of hope it was merely five years ago among Kurds in the region and throughout the diaspora. Even in Iraqi Kurdistan itself, disillusioned youth are flocking to the banners of the PKK (Otten 2015), and international media as well as the Kurdish blogsphere are abuzz with reports on the latest military exploits of the YPG or on the unique social and political experiment in self-governance the PYD seeks to implement in *Rojava*. For young Kurds in the region and among the diaspora, Iraqi Kurdistan's leaders are old news, more associated with systemic corruption and calculating deal-making than with advancing the cause of national self-determination, and even among his Western allies, Barzani's increasingly autocratic regime is no longer seen as Iraq's sole success story and is unofficially coming to be characterized in the way Franklin Delano Roosevelt allegedly described Anastasio Somoza in 1939, of whom he is supposed to have said, 'he's a son of a bitch, but he's our son of a bitch'.[27]

Currently, the future of Kurdish national self-determination appears to be with the PYD and its YPG fighters, perhaps just because that future is so precarious and perhaps because they unexpectedly ascended to this moment of glory from so previously neglected a corner of Kurdistan. Tales of their rise, prowess, determination, and perseverance against all odds culminate in narratives of the epic siege of Kobane, an event that has already entered the sphere of mythology in Kurdish nationalist lore, conceivably in the not too distant future ranking in equal significance to the Battle of Isandlwana for the Zulu nation or Adwa for Ethiopians. The importance of Kobane and the momentum of the PYD have not escaped Massoud Barzani, who in the last weeks of October decided to dispatch a convoy of 150 *peshmerga* with heavy weaponry to aid in the city's defence. In a development that, until then, would have appeared inconceivable to any observer, Turkey granted the armed convoy free passage through its territory, and on 30 October the 20 vehicle-strong relief force, commanded by the President's brother, Sihad Barzani (Whitcomb 2014), arrived in Kobane amidst frenetic cheers from its defenders (Al Jazeera 2014c; Barbarani & Stephens 2014; BBC 2014d; Ozcan 2014; Saleh 2014; Lowe & Gunes 2015).[28] The motives for this extraordinary show of solidarity with a force Barzani had considered until a few months earlier a foe, with whom he had fought over supremacy in Kurdistan for three decades, can certainly be ascribed to strategic calculations or material interests. That is doubtlessly applicable for Turkey who acutely needed a gesture of generosity to counter the bad international press it received over its behaviour during the siege of Kobane, and who could once again demonstrate to its Kurdish population that there are Kurds with whom the AKP is willing to work – Barzani – and that collaboration with Erdoğan's regime pays off. Likewise, Barzani may have computed that his reputation would suffer from the Iraqi Kurds watching from the sidelines as the greatest and first truly pan-Kurdish contest of resistance unfolded, all the more since the PKK had come to the Iraqi Kurds' aid in their hour of need two months earlier. Such a relatively cynical interpretation may be reinforced by the fact that Barzani only dispatched the *peshmerga* once the US had decided to throw their lot in with the YPG in defiance of Turkey, and once the tide of the battle already began to turn in the Kurds' favour – then again, it is difficult to tell how long it took Barzani to persuade Turkey to grant his *peshmerga* free passage and whether talks on it started before or after the US flew its first sorties in support of Kobane's defenders. Be that as it may, even if Barzani's reasoning for coming to the aid of the YPG was primarily motivated by material, i.e. strategic interests, and the episode constitutes yet another example of his propensity for striking shady deals with his Turkish counterpart, the trigger for this action was one of the most significant events formative of Kurdish identity in our times, the epic defence of Kobane. Given this interplay between identity and interests, I would contend that this instance is but the most recent illustration of why a prioritization of either in explaining the behaviour of these actors – i.e. taking identity or interests as the dependent/independent variables – falls short of that objective, and why, as has been argued throughout this book, an approach grounded in perceiving both identity and interest as components of a fluid, situational matrix without supremacy yields a more comprehensive picture of such a complex interaction.

Notes

1 In 2006 the *Kurdistan Development Corporation* (KDC) launched a multimillion dollar advertising campaign in the US – and to a lesser extent in the UK – executed by the public relations firm *Russo, Marsh and Rogers* with close links to the Republican party, and entitled 'Kurdistan: The Other Iraq' with the dual objective of emphasizing the gratitude of the Iraqi Kurdish people for their liberation from the dictatorship of Saddam Hussein and to promote the Kurdistan Region for international investment and tourism (Glantz 2006; Kamen 2006; Flood 2009b).

2 Quoted in Pamir (2013).

3 Quoted in Pamir (2013).

4 On ISIS see Atwan (2015), McCants (2015), Cockburn (2015), Wood (2015).

5 Quoted in BBC (2014a).

6 Huseyin Çelik, AKP spokesman, quoted in Dombey (2013).

7 Quoted in Slavin (2014).

8 For a portrayal of the *Iraqiyya* alliance that has considerably lost influence after 2011, see International Crisis Group (2012b).

9 The other force whose eleventh hour backing secured Maliki's victory in the negotiations on a coalition was the Sadrist Movement of Shi'ite cleric Muqtada al-Sadr (Escobar 2010; Marr 2011).

10 Series of Skype interviews with several Iraqi Kurdish journalists in the autumn of 2015.

11 The origins of this policy of denial predate the Assad regime. In 1962, the Syrian government conducted an unannounced census, in which it deemed about 120,000, or 20 per cent of the Kurdish population, not as Syrians but refugees from Turkey, and were consequently denied citizenship. Worse than these 'aliens', or *ajanib*, was the fate of those not present at their dwellings at the time of the census. These unregistered Kurds, or *maktumin*, were considered non-existent by the state. 'Their basic rights to education, employment, property ownership, political participation, and legal marriage were severely limited, relegating them to the outermost margins of Syrian civil society' (Tejel 2011: 51). Their properties were seized and given to Arabs for resettlement, thus providing the basis for the above-mentioned Arab corridors along the border that separated Kurds from their kin in Iraq and Turkey. Since this political non-status was inheritable, by 2011 when the policy was finally revoked, it affected more than 400,000 people.

12 The degree of isolation of the Kurdish territories even within Syria is perhaps best illustrated by the fact that during his entire rule Hafez al-Assad did not consider it expedient to visit them even once (Scheller 2013).

13 PYD commanders, on the other hand, take great pains to draw a more nuanced picture. Alan Semo, the foreign affairs representative of the PYD, for example, declared in 2012 (quoted in ICG 2013),

> The PYD is a Syrian Kurdish party with its own leader, organisations, structures, exclusive councils and leadership. The PYD only shares the ideology of democratic self-governance with the KCK, similar to how other Syrian Kurdish parties share the ideology of the KDP or PUK.

14 Interview Ergil op. cit.

15 The alleged similarities in authoritarian rule of the PYD and the Assad regime also formed the core argument of an unpublished paper by Rana Marcel Khalaf at a conference at the University of Exeter, UK, in early May 2016, entitled 'The New World of Kurdish Politics'.

16 As with the *Repareen* in Iraq in 1991 and the Qamishli riots of 2004, the sudden public uprising took the Kurdish ethno-nationalist parties in Syria by surprise and it took them months to instrumentalize, co-opt and control the public's zeal of anti-regime sentiment (ICG 2013, 2014a; Gunter 2014; Savelsberg 2014; Schmidinger 2014; Allsopp 2015). On the earlier Qamishli riots, see Lowe (2006), Human Rights Watch (2009), Tejel (2011), Gunter (2014), Savelsberg (2014), Schmidinger (2014), and Allsopp (2015).

17 Further information on the camp can be accessed at the website of the Makhmour Women's Charity (www.wjmexmur.com/en/).

18 While the fight for Kobane was raging *Foreign Policy* ran a story, based on leaked State Department cables and interviews with former US officials in Syria, that claimed the US government had been engaged in indirect talks with the PYD since 2012 via its embassy in Paris, while at the same time encouraging and supporting Massoud Barzani's efforts to strengthen the KNC as an alternative power to the PYD (Hess 2014). According to the US official interviewed, the American government took great pains to coordinate this dual strategy with the Turkish politico-military establishment that had its own backchannel talks with the PYD (Hess 2014).

19 John Kerry on 20 October 2014, quoted in Abdulla (2016: 95).

20 In May 2016 photos were revealed that showed US Special Forces commandos operating in Syria even wearing insignia of the YPG. When challenged on this practice by Turkey, Pentagon Spokesman Peter Cook explained that it was standard operating procedure for US commandos 'to blend in with local partners' (BBC 2016).

21 On 25 August 2015, the Turkish newspaper *Burgün* exposed an incident of Turkish officials transferring weapons and ammunition to ISIS at the Turkish-Syrian border; a few days later the office of *Koza Ipek Media Group*, the owner of *Burgün*, in Istanbul were raided and shut down by police (Ant *et al.* 2015). After the editorial deadline for this book, the German government, based on an assessment of the German intelligence service, the *Bundesnachrichtendienst* (BND), in a leaked, non-official parliamentary enquiry for the first time admitted to have a substantial body of evidence for the AKP government's support of Islamist insurgencies and terrorist organizations such as the Muslim Brotherhood, Hamas, and non-specified radical Islamist movements operating in Syria from 2011 until the present (*Der Spiegel* 2016b).

22 US Vice-President Joe Biden on 2 October 2014, quoted in Dickey (2014). Diplomatic etiquette forced Biden to subsequently apologize for his remarks to the Turkish government.

23 The 2013 corruption scandal implicated the director of the state-owned *Halkbank*, several children and relatives of AKP ministers, and even the sons of President Erdoğan himself to be involved in systematic corruption, bribery, fraud, money laundering and gold smuggling (Orucoglu 2015). While in Turkey, under political pressure, Erdogan's sons were removed from the list of suspects, Italian state prosecutors in February 2016 launched an investigation against Bilal Erdoğan for money laundering, which led him to abandon his PhD studies at Bologna (Day 2016).

24 Ergun Ozbudun quoted in Cengiz (2015).
25 Quoted in *The Economist* (2015).
26 Quoted in Kuntz (2016) and Gursel (2016) respectively.
27 The origins of this saying remain as unclear due to how frequently it has been used in political writing ever since. Various sources ascribe its first use to FDR, Cordell Hull, Dean Acheson or John Foster Dulles characterizing Anastasio Somoza, Rafael Leonidas Trujillo or even Francisco Franco. Be that as it may, Massoud Barzani joining this illustrious tradition of US-sponsored dictators appears increasingly fitting.
28 Aside from its significance for Kurdish inter-party relations, this development constitutes yet another instance when Barzani rode roughshod over the prerogatives of the Iraqi central government and parliament, who, according to the Iraqi constitution, has the sole authority to send troops abroad. However, Baghdad's protests once again fell on deaf ears (Al Jazeera 2014c).

Conclusion

The objective of this study has been to deconstruct explanatory IR's representation, frameworks and concepts of ethnic conflict by employing a constitutive theory-grounded approach. In the theory section the focus has been on a critical reading of the discourses and narratives on ethnic conflict constructed and established by explanatory IR. Those narratives and discourses are characterized by a positivist, essentialist, and substantialist belief that the social world can be divided, measured and categorized into organic, static, substantive, distinct, homogeneous and bounded units and that ethnic groups and nations can be analytically equated with states, thus ascribing them with social agency as unitary or unitarily acting protagonists of ethnic and ethno-nationalist conflict. In its examinations of ethnic conflict, explanatory IR operationalizes ethnic identity as either the dependent variable, merely a political tool utilized by ethnic elites and entrepreneurs (and the masses) in their pursuit of mostly material interests, and thus of only extrinsic value in attempts to comprehend and capture the dynamics of ethnic conflict, or as the independent variable, where ethnic conflict is tautologically explained with ethnicity. Not only have the epistemologies, ontologies and methodologies of this discourse been exposed as fallacious, it has also been shown how closely they correspond with the narratives set forth by the ethnic elites and entrepreneurs these studies set out to study. By reifying ethnic groups, presenting them as factual, static, substantive, distinct, homogeneous and bounded units of the social world that can be ascribed with social agency, explanatory IR scholars not only play into the hands of ethnic elites and their claims to represent the group in an antagonistic relationship with the other, but through their way of portraying the composition of the social world they often further accentuate and substantiate those ideational lines of division that supposedly constitute ethnic groups and nations, and occasionally even write them into existence.

However, this argument should not be misunderstood as a claim that explanatory IR scholars are doing the bidding of ethnic elites. Some explanatory IR scholars may at a personal level sympathize with an oppressed minority's struggle for national self-determination, as is the case with the self-declared 'honorary Kurdistanis' discussed in the case study. In some very rare cases scholars may accrue a material benefit from their representations and advocacy, as for example in the case of Peter Galbraith, also discussed, but the vast majority of explanatory IR scholars represent ethnic groups and nations in groupist and state-centric terms as a result of their genuinely held groupist and state-centric worldviews. Such deliberations on the epistemologies of explanatory IR have led to hypotheses on why explanatory IR does what it does, i.e. on the motives behind groupist and state-centric epistemologies. In these inferences I have drawn on the central dictum of Critical Theory as applied to IR by Robert Cox (1981: 129), that 'all theory is always for someone and for some purpose', and combined the juxtaposition of traditional versus critical theory with a Bourdieuian conceptualization of IR as a social (sub-)field. This perspective has not only allowed me to identify (neo-)realism, (neo-)liberalism, and systemic constructivism as traditional, Coxian problem-solving, or in the terminology of this study *status-quo maintaining theory*, but also to interpret the ontologies that are at the core of explanatory theory, groupism and state-centrism, as *doxa*. Similar to Gramscian cultural hegemony, *doxa* in Bourdieu's theory is

> the point of view of the dominant, which presents and imposes itself as a universal point of view, the point of view of those who dominate by dominating the state and who have constituted their point of view as universal by constituting the state.
>
> (Bourdieu 1998a: 57)

While the state is constituted first and foremost by the common belief in it, the questions are what structures and agents dominate the discourses and practices of the state to an extent that they can shape and sustain this commonly held belief in the state, and which social fields yield such considerable (symbolic) power that the state and the international domain as a system of states can become common sense? The answer lies in Michel Foucault's power–knowledge nexus: those who produce, negotiate and disperse knowledge about the state, which are, in addition to state institutions, bureaucrats, and the media, scholars who write about, analyse and seek to explain the state and the international system of states. Those scholars who in their scholarship affirm the state, share with state institutions, the bureaucracy and mainstream media a particular habitus, most prominently expressed in the shared belief in the existence of and need for the preservation of the state. Yet, they not only exist with those fields in a symbiotic relationship, due to their expertise, they are seen by these fields and the general public as being in a position to speak with authority on matters of the state, and thus contribute to groupism and state-centrism becoming *doxa*. What is more, as voices of the orthodoxy they act as gatekeepers in this discursive formation who keep dissenting opinions, alternative views on the state, i.e. representations of the heterodoxy at bay. To do so is a result of their habitus, their genuinely held worldviews and the social roles they occupy, in other words it is an expression of their identities and interests, which again – like those of ethnonationalist elites – should be studied as a complex, fluid and historically contingent matrix.

These themes and points of critiques have been taken up in the case study, in which, by way of examining the relations between the Iraqi Kurdish ethno-nationalist parties and the PKK from the early 1980s until the present, I have shown the concepts, models and frameworks of explanatory IR on ethnic conflict, in particular the ethnic alliance model, instrumentalism and state-centrism to fail in adequately explaining the dynamics and complexities of their relations. The ethnic alliance model operationalizes ethnic identity as the independent variable and, more explicitly than any other explanatory IR framework, analytically equates the ethnic group with the state; instrumentalism, on the other hand, which deploys ethnic identity as the dependent variable, all too often reduces it to merely a political tool with which shrewd and calculating ethnic elites manipulate the docile masses in pursuit of material interests, thus admitting it only extrinsic value. While one could say that both are thus situated at opposite ends of the spectrum of explanatory IR's approach to ethnic conflict, I have argued that a systemic constructivism and instrumentalism in particular exhibits a tendency of reifying the structure via the agent.

In the case study, I have demonstrated that neither instrumentalism nor ethnicity as the independent variable, on their own, comprehensively explain the motives and behaviour of the actors determining the relations between the Iraqi Kurdish ethno-nationalist parties, KDP and PUK, and the PKK. There are instances where instrumentalism, that is predominantly interests shaping policies and identities being reduced to political or propaganda tools, proves of use, as for example when the KDP granted the PKK sanctuary on its territory in the early 1980s either on the order of its external backers in Iran and Syria or in a failed attempt to win the PKK as a potential ally against its nemesis, the PUK. Likewise, the civil wars of the 1990s between KDP/PUK and the PKK and later PUK/PKK and KDP can be understood as violent expressions of regional rivalries and factionalisms in the case of the latter, and as dictated by the complex political necessities of the first Kurdish de facto state and its dependence on Turkey and the international community at large. Yet, instrumentalism cannot sufficiently explain why the Iraqi Kurdish ethno-nationalist parties started to collaborate in the first place – after the military coup in Turkey, the PUK literally saved the PKK from a shadowy existence at the margins of the Kurdish ethno-nationalist discourse – nor, as I have argued, the complex dynamics and shifting alliances of today's Iraqi Kurdistan both within Iraq and all the more when adopting a wider geographical lens and including both the KDP and PKK's attempts at positioning themselves as regional champions of wider, perhaps even pan-Kurdish aspirations for national self-determination in Turkey and Syria,

The case against the ethnic alliance model is even more clear-cut. First, as I have demonstrated by way of an extensive historical excursus in Part II, aside from epistemological objections, it would be untenable to categorize the Kurds in the Middle East as one ethnic group, that is Kurds in Iraq, Turkey, Iran and Syria all belonging to the same ethnic group with common ideational boundaries and constitutive others and characterized by networks of intra-ethnic solidarity and mutual commitments. On the contrary, I have shown in the historical excursus that Kurds in Iraq and Turkey are defined by their relations and boundaries towards different constitutive others – the Kemalist and Ba'athist regimes in Ankara and Baghdad respectively – and followed a completely different trajectory in their processes of becoming and being nationalist. Second, given the almost proverbial rivalry between KDP and PUK it would be completely fallacious to conceive of the Iraqi Kurds as a unitary actor or unitarily acting political entity that can be analytically equated with a state. Third, and perhaps most confutative of any attempts to showcase the PKK sanctuary in Iraqi Kurdistan as an example of an ethnic alliance, as is routinely done in the literature, is that the relations between PKK and KDP/PUK are more often determined by rivalry and armed conflict than by solidarity and cooperation. As a matter of fact, at the very moment when the ethnic alliance model is supposed to have come into effect, when Iraqi Kurdistan became a state-like entity – however defined and open to debate – or its main protagonists came to dominate the political discourse and exercised territorial control, in the wake of the Gulf War, KDP and PUK did not reach out to the oppressed 'co-ethnic' minority in Turkey and its empowered incumbent, the PKK, but, in alliance with Turkey, attacked Öcalan's group. With that episode at the very least the case against the ethnic alliance model and ethnic group solidarity to explain 'intra-ethnic' relations and the internationalization of ethnic conflict can rest as disproven.

Yet the purpose of this case study has not only been to show why the main frameworks of explanatory IR fail to explain the formation of ethnic identities in ethnic conflict, but also to illustrate how ethnicity works in these contexts. Grounded in constitutive theory, I have argued why I believe that instead of explaining the relations between and within so-called ethnic groups through factual, static, substantive, distinct, homogeneous and bounded categories and an artificially measurable division of identities and interests that can be operationalized as dependent and independent variables, the social world is better conceived of as a fluid, ever-shifting, open-ended and complex matrix of identities and interests. At each stage in the analysis of the relations between the Iraqi Kurdish ethno-nationalist parties and the PKK I have paused and made a case against explaining it by employing dependent and independent variables and pleading for a processual approach that views them as an intricate, never completed, eternally unfolding matrix. This, in my opinion, becomes most apparent when examining the shifting sands of identities and interests in post-2003 Iraqi Kurdistan and what it means to be an Iraqi Kurd in the twenty-first century. This dense, web-like mosaic of competing sovereignties with the freest political entity in Kurdish history existing in permanent transition within but at the same time apart from Iraq, pan-Kurdish and parochial identities pulling in often opposite directions, and strategic considerations and material interests at the local, regional and geo-political level dictating restraint while at the same time autonomy has gained a momentum of its own that pulls Iraqi Kurdish leaders – sometimes perhaps against their will – towards ever wider national self-determination, constitutes an ideal and incredibly rich case study to investigate not so much what ethnic identity is but how ethnic identity works. In terms of identities and interests Iraqi Kurdistan is constituted and at the same time internally split by centrifugal and centripetal forces and ideologies. Large strata of the Kurdish diaspora in Europe, at least until very recently, have seen the freest political entity in Kurdish history as a beacon of hope and champion of Kurdish rights for national self-determination across the entire region, an aspiration Iraqi Kurdish leaders fear and simultaneously try to exploit for their own ends; they try to walk a fine line between expanding their polities' autonomy and not antagonizing their external backers together with the status as Washington's most reliable ally, yet the relative freedom Iraqi Kurdistan enjoys and a mainly young population that has never come to know Arab rule increasingly questions why they have to continue coexisting in an artificial state with Arabs towards whom they feel no solidarity, commonality or shared identity. Concomitantly, the ambiguous status of ever-wider autonomy allows Iraqi Kurdish leaders to strengthen their hold onto power at home, where they play the ethno-nationalist card against the central government in Baghdad and perpetually hold out the promise of independence to their constituency – a promise they may never be in a position or want to fulfil – yet at the same time their influence in Baghdad allows them to play kingmaker in the formation of every Iraqi government for the past decade; likewise, they remain economically and strategically dependent on Turkey, who, aside from Baghdad, quite contradictorily poses the biggest obstacle to Iraqi Kurdish independence out of fear that it might set a precedent for its own Kurdish population to demand a similar status, yet at the same time the Erdoğan AKP has shrewdly utilized the pan-Kurdish reputation and nationalistic pull of Massoud Barzani to sway Kurdish voters in Turkey. With both, Iraqi Kurdistan and the PKK through its regional affiliate, the PYD, being key allies on the ground of the international coalition fighting ISIS in Iraq and Syria, and with Turkey having started an all-out war against the latter while failing to support the former against ISIS (yet, at the time of writing, featuring a sizable troop presence in Iraqi Kurdistan), the picture has become even more convoluted. Given these ambiguities, complex dynamics and contradictions – of which I have just elaborated the most obvious – that constitute the matrix of identities and interests in contemporary Iraqi Kurdistan and beyond, I would hazard the guess, that even the most ardent positivist would struggle to comprehensively explain them by allocating dependent and independent variables, divining a definite line parting identities from interests and ideational from material motives for actors' behaviour, let alone translate those into quantifiable data.

Exercising a modernist interpretation of nationalism that views the ethnic group as a precursor to an ethnically defined nation and the nation as a proto-state, explanatory IR often analytically equates the ethnic group with the state, thus not only endowing it with social agency but portraying as it as a unitary actor or unitarily acting entity. Again, Iraqi Kurdistan serves as a powerful case in point why such an equation is untenable. Given the notorious rivalry between the KDP and PUK, with each side even joining forces with their constitutive other – the genocidal regime of Saddam Hussein, for example, in the case of the KDP – against their opponent, and their on-and-off alliances and hostilities with the PKK, the myth of the ethnic group as unitary actor is easily refutable. What is more interesting though, and supported by previous scholarship, is that the sovereign nation state is as much a social construct and discursive formation as the ethnic group or nation; a social construct, like the ethnic group or nation, based on a constructed dichotomy of internal versus external, of order and rule of law at home versus anarchy abroad. The complexities, ambiguities and contradictions of sovereignty at work in the indeterminate political space of today's Iraqi Kurdistan illustrate not only that the presupposed linear development from ethnic group to nation to state, may not be at all linear but curvy, oscillating, interrupted and, in fact, for intrinsic reasons, may never reach its supposed conclusion, but it also highlights the constructed nature of sovereignty better than in so-called established states. In established states sovereignty is said to exist, period. Iraqi Kurdistan, whose sovereignty is contested, provides a much richer case to study how sovereignty actually works, how it is enacted through foreign policy, how it harmonizes national identit(ies) with national interest(s), and that, ultimately, in the post-modern world of universal neo-liberal consensus, it can be more important to strike a deal on the exploitation of national resources with ExxonMobil or offer your constituency the dubious blessings of international brands opening a branch in their local shopping mall than being recognized by say Nicaragua – as in the case of Abkhazia – as a peer.

Explanatory IR theory purports to depict the social world as it is, as factual, grounded in reality, empirically measurable. Rejecting the false idol of scientific objectivism that claims to be capable of a detached and rational analysis of how the social world works, constitutive theory posits all of us researchers that study social relationships as co-protagonists of these relations. Contrary to explanatory theory that purports to tell *the* definitive story about how the social world works, constitutive theory maintains that there are myriad interpretations and takes on social issues, that the ones presented as factual and common-sense are but one possible reading of things and that we social scientists will by our very nature as human beings always be biased and partisan in the narratives we tell. Yet, even though we are all co-protagonists of the social world we try to understand and analyse, it makes a difference whether we present our findings as one possible reading of actors' motives and behaviour or as the definitive account of social interactions and relations; it makes a difference whether we have the intellectual honesty to acknowledge our roles in influencing and shaping the narratives and discourses about our objects of analysis or purport to deliver a scientifically verified singular truth that remains irrefutable irrespective of the researcher's ideological disposition and level of engagement with its subject. For, last but not least, it makes a great difference to what extent we become involved with our subject of analysis, whether we manage to maintain the very minimum of a critical attitude or increasingly come to advocate a certain direction or cause in our writings, research, lectures and testimonials as experts at public hearings and parliamentary inquiries. At the very least, we social scientists cannot have it both ways; that is, on the one hand hold up the principles of a detached scientific objectivism – an intellectual fallacy in any case – and at the same time through our ontologies and methodologies, such as the selection of variables or our categorization of ideational groups as social agents, directly or indirectly adopt the narratives of our subjects of analysis and thus substantiate their claims to legitimacy on the other. The ambition of this study is thus to act as the impetus for us IR scholars to be more cognizant of and forthright about our own subjectivity and our roles within the discourse on the subject matter we set out to describe, as it is a reminder to our audiences that our expertise is not the truth but merely opinion – however well informed – and one particular point of view, one possible interpretation of the social, political and economic dynamics in, say, Iraq, Turkey, Syria and beyond, that is a product of our worldviews. This does not mean that the legendary editor of the *Guardian* newspaper, C. P. Scott, erred when he wrote, 'comment is free but facts are sacred', but that what is presented as fact – which all too often is common sense advanced as fact – should always be up for (re-)interpretation, that it is our duty as scholars and critical readers to question, scrutinize and, if necessary, challenge. After all, in a more emancipatory understanding of the role of scholarship, as advanced by Critical Theory, to do so is the essence of speaking (an alternative) truth to power.

These are but some of the issues I have raised in my critique of positivist explanatory IR's approaches to ethnic conflict and state sovereignty. I do not claim to have provided a definitive account of ethnic identity formation and so-called intra-ethnic relations, state sovereignty or Kurdish ethno-nationalism, nor for my findings and insights to have universal applicability. However, bearing in mind this subjectivity, I have offered a solid and comprehensive deconstruction of the epistemologies, ontologies, models, frameworks and methodologies of explanatory IR's approach to ethnic conflict and state sovereignty at the theoretical and empirical level. What I offer here is a well-wrought and subjective interpretation of scholars' roles as co-protagonists of ethnic conflict, a possible reality among many and not *the* reality of the development of Kurdish ethnonationalism, an account of the relations between the Iraqi Kurdish ethnonationalist parties and the PKK that can stand up to scholarly scrutiny without needing to rely on supposedly universal truth claims.

Further studies are called for, those that critically examine and deconstruct the reification and essentialization of groupness in the discourse on ethnic and ethno-nationalist conflict, both at the level of ethnic elites as well as focusing on the scholarship on these conflicts, and either by scrutinizing the intra-group level, as V. P. Gagnon has demonstrated for the former Yugoslavia, or by questioning the inter-group level, as is the lens through which this present study approaches the issue. More generally, while this study furnished an in-depth overview of the problem of reification of groupness in the study of ethnic and ethno-nationalist conflict in explanatory IR literature, more detailed theoretical inquiries into individual aspects and effects of this practice would be desirable; say, for example, how they shape the paradigm of consociationalism in ethnic conflict resolution or how the research-policy nexus, the interplay between scholarship and policy formulation in, for example, think tanks shape Western doctrine and playbooks for nation- and state-building in the majority world. In addition to my commitment to the ethical concerns I have raised throughout the book, I would consider it a great accomplishment for this study to have acted as an incentive and point of departure for such promising future inquiries.

References

Monographs and articles in journals, edited volumes and institutional reports

Aalberts, T. (2012) *Constructing Sovereignty between Politics and Law*, London: Routledge.

Abdulla, N. (2016) 'How ISIL Advanced Kurdish Nationalism', *Turkish Policy*, 14(4), pp. 89–97.

Adamson, F. B. (2013) 'Mechanisms of Diaspora Mobilization and the Transnationalisation of Civil War', in J. T. Checkel (ed.), *Transnational Dynamics of Civil War*, Cambridge: Cambridge University Press, pp. 63–88.

Adler, E. (1997) 'Seizing the Middle Ground: Constructivism in World Politics', *European Journal of International Relations*, 3(3), pp. 319–363.

Adler, E. (2010) 'Constructivism in International Relations: Sources, Contributions, and Debates', in: W. Carlsnaes, T. Risse & B. Simmons (eds), *Handbook of International Relations*, 2nd edn, London: Sage, pp. 95–118.

Adler, E. & Pouliot, V. (2011) 'International Practices: Introduction and Framework', in E. Adler & V. Pouliot (eds), *International Practices*, Cambridge, UK: Cambridge University Press, pp. 3–35.

Adler-Nissen, R. (2011) 'Opting Out of an Ever Closer Union: The Integration *Doxa* and the Management of Sovereignty', *West European Politics*, 34(5), pp. 1092–1113.

Agnew, J. (2009) *Globalization and Sovereignty*, Lanham: Rowman & Littlefield.

Ahmad, F. (1981) 'Military Intervention and the Crisis in Turkey', *MERIP Reports*, 11(1), pp. 5–24.

Ahmad, F. (1993) *The Making of Modern Turkey*, London: Routledge.

Ahmed, M. A. (2007) 'Laying the Foundation for a Kurdistani State in Iraq, 1991–2006', in M. A. Ahmed & M. Gunter (eds), *The Evolution of Kurdish Nationalism*, Costa Mesa: Mazda Press, pp. 149–185.

Ahmed, M. A. (2012) *Iraqi Kurds and Nation-Building*, Basingstoke: Palgrave Macmillan.

Akçam, T. (2004) *From Empire to Republic: Turkish Nationalism and the Armenian Genocide*, London: Zed Books.

Akkaya, A. H. & Jongerden, J. (2011) 'The PKK in the 2000s: Continuity through Breaks?' In M. Casier & J. Jongerden (eds), *Nationalisms and Politics in Turkey: Political Islam, Kemalism and the Kurdish Issue*, London: Routledge, pp. 143–162.

Akkaya, A. H. & Jongerden, J. (2012) 'Reassembling the Political: The PKK and the Project of Radical Democracy', *European Journal of Turkish Studies* 14, available at: http://ejts.revues.org/pdf/4615.

Akkaya, A. H. & Jongerden, J. (2013) 'Confederalism and Autonomy in Turkey: The Kurdistan Worker's Party and the Reinvention of Democracy', in C. Gunes & W. Zeydanlioglu (eds), *The Kurdish Question in Turkey: New Perspectives on Violence, Representation, and Reconciliation*, London: Routledge, pp. 186–204.

Alavi, H. (1972) 'The State in Post-Colonial Societies: Pakistan and Bangladesh', *New Left Review*, 74, pp. 59–81.

Ali, O. (1997) 'The Kurds and the Lausanne Peace Negotiations 1922–23', *Middle Eastern Studies*, 33(3), pp. 521–534.

Alker, H. & Biersteker, T. (1984) 'The Dialectics of World Order: Notes for an Archaeologist of International Savoir Faire', *International Studies Quarterly* 28(2), pp. 121–142.

Allawi, A. A. (2007) *The Occupation of Iraq: Winning the War, Losing the Peace*, New Haven: Yale University Press.

Allsopp, H. (2015) *The Kurds of Syria*, 2nd edn, London: I.B. Tauris.

Altheide, D. L. & Grimes, J. N. (2005) 'War Programming: The Propaganda Project and the Iraq War', *The Sociological Quarterly*, 46(4), pp. 617–643.

Amin-Khan, T. (2012) *The Post-Colonial State in the Era of Capitalist Globalization: Historical, Political, and Theoretical Approaches to State Formation*, London: Routledge.

Anderson, B. (2006) *Imagined Communities: Reflections on the Spread and Origins of Nationalism*, 3rd edn, London: Verso.

Anderson, C. A. (1983) 'Abstract and Concrete Data in the Perseverance of Social Theories: When Weak Data Lead to Unshakable Beliefs', *Journal of Experimental and Social Psychology*, 19(2), pp. 93–108.

Anderson, C. A., Lepper, M. R., & Ross, L. (1980) 'Perseverance of Social Theories: The Role of Explanation in the Persistence of Discredited Information', *Journal of Personality and Social Psychology*, 39(6), pp. 1037–1049.

Anderson, L. (2007a) 'The Role of Political Parties in Developing Kurdish Nationalism', in M. Ahmad & M. Gunter (eds), *The Evolution of Kurdish Nationalism*, Costa Mesa: Mazda Press, pp. 123–148.

Anderson, L. (2007b) 'The Non-Ethnic Regional Model of Federalism: Some Comparative Perspectives', in R. Visser & G. Stansfield (eds), *An Iraq of Its Regions: Cornerstones of a Federal Democracy?* London: Hurst, pp. 205–256.

Anderson, L. & Stansfield, G. (2005) *The Future of Iraq: Democracy, Dictatorship or Division?* Basingstoke: Palgrave Macmillan.

Anderson, L. & Stansfield, G. (2009) *Crisis in Kirkuk: The Ethnopolitics of Conflict and Compromise*, Philadelphia: University of Pennsylvania Press.

Anderson, P. (1974) *Lineages of the Absolutist State*, London: New Left Books.

Anghie, A. (2007) *Imperialism, Sovereignty and the Making of International Law*, 2nd edn, Cambridge: Cambridge University Press.

Aras, B. (2009) 'The Davotoğlu Era in Turkish Foreign Policy', *Insight Turkey*, 11(3), pp. 127–142.

Aras, B. & Polat, R. (2008) 'From Conflict to Cooperation: Desecuritization of Turkey's Relations with Syria and Iran', *Security Dialogue* 39(5), pp. 495–515.

Arato, A. (2009) *Constitution Making under Occupation: The Politics of Imposed Revolution in Iraq*, New York: Columbia University Press.

Artens, H. (2012) 'Sanctuary State-Insurgency Relations in Ethnic Conflicts: A New Explanatory Model', *Oficina do CES Working Paper Series* 392, Center for Social Studies, University of Coimbra.

Asadi, A. (2007) *Der Kurdistan-Irak-Konflikt: Der Weg zur Autonomie seit dem Ersten Weltkrieg*, Berlin: Schiler.

Ashley, R. (1984) 'The Poverty of Neorealism', *International Organisation*, 38(2), pp. 225–286.

Ashley, R. (1987) The Geopolitics of Geopolitical Space: Toward a Critical Social Theory of International Politics', *Alternatives*, 12, pp. 403–434.

Ashley, R. (1988) 'Untying the Sovereign State. A Double Reading of the Anarchy Problematique', *Millennium*, 17(2), pp. 227–262.

Atasoy, Y. (2009) *Islam's Marriage with Neoliberalism: State Transformation in Turkey*, Basingstoke: Palgrave Macmillan.

Ateş, S. (2013) *Ottoman-Iranian Borderlands: Making a Boundary, 1843–1914*, Cambridge: Cambridge University Press.

Atwan, A. B. (2015) *Islamic State: The Digital Caliphate*, Berkeley: University of California Press.

Aydın, M. (1998) 'Turkish Foreign Policy during the Gulf War of 1990–91', *Cairo Papers in Social Science*, 21(1), pp. 1–87.

Aydın, M. (2002) 'Ten Years After: Turkey's Gulf Policy (1990–91) Revisited', Center for Eurasian Strategic Studies, *Ankara Paper*, 3, London: Frank Cass.

Aydinli, E. (2011) 'Ergenekon, New Pacts, and the Decline of the Turkish "Inner State"', *Turkish Studies*, 12(2), pp. 227–239.

Ayoob, M. (1995) *The Third World Security Predicament: State Making, Regional Conflict and the International System*, Boulder: Lynne Rienner.

Ayubi, N. N. (2008) *Over-stating the Arab State: Politics and Society in the Middle East*, 5th edn, London: I.B. Tauris.

Azar, E. (1982) 'Conflict and Peace Databank (COPDAB), 1948–1978, 2nd release, study No. 7767', Ann Arbor: Interuniversity Consortium for Political and Social Research, available at: www.icpsr.umich.edu/icpsrweb/ICPSR/studies/07767.

Baer, R. (2002) *See No Evil: The True Story of a CIA Ground Soldier in the CIA's War on Terrorism*, London: Arrow Books.

Bahcheli, T. & Noel, S. (2011) 'The Justice and Development Party and the Kurdish Question', in in M. Casier & J. Jongerden (eds), *Nationalisms and Politics in Turkey: Political Islam, Kemalism and the Kurdish Issue*, London: Routledge, pp. 101–120.

Bailey, C. (1984) *Jordan's Palestinian Challenge 1948–1983: A Political History*, Boulder: Westview Press.

Bakunin, M. (1973) *Selected Writings*, London: Jonathan Cape.

Bali, R. N. (2006) 'The Politics of Turkification during the Single Party Period', in H. L. Kieser (ed.) *Turkey beyond Nationalism: Towards Post-Nationalist Identities*, London: I.B. Tauris, pp. 43–49.

Balta, E. (2004) 'Causes and Consequences of the Village Guard System in Turkey', unpublished paper presented at Mellon Fellowship for Humanitarian and Security Affairs Conference, CUNY – Graduate Center, New York.

Balzacq, T. (2005) 'The Three Faces of Securitization: Political Agency, Audience and Context', *European Journal of International Relations*, 11(2), pp. 171–201.

Balzacq, T. (2011) 'A Theory of Securitization: Origins, Core Assumptions, and Variants', in T. Balzacq (ed.) *Securitization Theory: How Security Problems Emerge and Dissolve*, London: Routledge, pp. 1–30.

Bank, A. & Karadag, R. (2012) 'The Political Economy of a Regional Power: Turkey under the AKP', German Institute for Global and Area Studies (GIGA), *Working*

Papers 204, available at: www.giga-hamburg.de/en/system/files/publications/wp204_ bank-karadag.pdf.

Barfi, B. (2016) 'Ascent of the PYD and SDF', The Washington Institute for Near East Policy, *Research Notes* 32, available at: www.washingtoninstitute.org/uploads/ Documents/pubs/ResearchNote32-Barfi.pdf.

Barkey, H. (1990) 'Why Military Regimes Fail: The Perils of Transition', *Armed Forces and Society*, 16, pp. 169–192.

Barkey, H. (1996) 'Under the Gun: Turkish Foreign Policy and the Kurdish Question', in R. Olson (ed.) *The Kurdish Nationalist Movement in the 1990s: Its Impact on Turkey and the Middle East*, Lexington: University of Kentucky Press, pp. 65–83.

Barkey, H. (2005) 'Turkey and Iraq: The Perils (and Prospects) of Proximity', United States Institute for Peace, *Special Report* 141, available at: www.usip.org/publications/ turkey-and-iraq-the-perils-and-prospects-of-proximity.

Barkey, H. (2011) 'A Transformed Relationship: Turkey and Iraq', in H. Barkey, S. B. Lasensky & P. Marr (eds), *Iraq, Its Neighbours, and the United States: Competition, Crisis, and the Reordering of Power*, Washington, DC: United States Institute for Peace Publications, pp. 45–72.

Barkey, H. (2015) 'On the KRG, the Turkish-Kurdish Peace Process and the Future of the Kurds', Woodrow Wilson International Center for Scholars, *Working Paper* 12, available at: www.iai.it/sites/default/files/gte_wp_12.pdf.

Barkey, H. & Fuller, G. (1998) *Turkey's Kurdish Question*, Lanham: Rowman & Littlefield.

Barr, J. (2012) *A Line in the Sand: Britain, France, and the Struggle that Shaped the Middle East*, New York: Simon & Schuster.

Barrington, L. (1997) ' "Nation" and "Nationalism": The Misuse of Key Concepts in Political Science', *Political Science and Politics*, 30(4), pp. 712–716.

Bartelson, J. (1995) *A Genealogy of Sovereignty*, Cambridge, UK: Cambridge University Press.

Barth, F. (1998 [1969]) *Ethnic Groups and Boundaries: The Social Organization of Cultural Difference*, 2nd edn, Long Grove: Waveland Press.

Barton, G. (2013) *The Muslim World and Politics in Transition: Creative Contributions of the Gülen Movement*, London: Bloomsbury.

Batatu, H. (1978) *The Old Social Classes and the Revolutionary Movements of Iraq: A Study of Iraq's Old Landed and Commercial Classes and of its Communists, Baathists, and Free Officers*, Princeton: Princeton University Press.

Bekdil, B. (2015) 'Turkey's Double Game with ISIS – Timeline', *Middle East Quarterly* 22(3), available at: www.meforum.org/5317/turkey-isis.

Bellamy, A. (2009) *Responsibility to Protect: The Global Effort to End Mass Atrocities*, Cambridge: Polity Press.

Ben-Dor, G. (1983) *State and Conflict in the Middle East*, New York: Praeger.

Bengio, O. (2012b) *The Kurds of Iraq: Building a State within a State*, Boulder: Lynne Rienner.

Berdal, M. (2003) 'How "New" Are "New Wars"? Global Economic Change and the Study of Civil War', *Global Governance*, 9, pp. 477–502.

Berger, P. L. & Luckmann, T. (1991) *The Social Construction of Reality: A Treatise in the Sociology of Knowledge*, rev edn, London: Penguin.

Berman, L. (2015) 'The Status of Western Military Aid to Kurdish Peshmerga Forces', Jerusalem Center for Public Affairs, 11 May, available at: http://jcpa.org/article/the-status-of-western-military-aid-to-kurdish-peshmerga-forces/.

Bhabha, H. (1990) *Nation and Narration*, London: Routledge.

Bialasiewicz, L., Campbell, D., Elden, S., Graham, S., Jeffrey, A. & Williams, A. (2007) 'Performing Security: The Imaginative Geographies of Current US Strategy', *Political Geography*, 26(4), pp. 405–422.

Biehl, J. (2012) 'Bookchin, Öcalan, and the Dialectics of Democracy', paper presented at the conference 'Challenging Capitalist Modernity: Alternative Concepts and the Kurdish Question', Hamburg, Germany, February, available at: http://new-compass. net/articles/bookchin-%C3%B6calan-and-dialectics-democracy.

Biehl, J. (2015) *Ecology or Catastrophe: The Life of Murray Bookchin*, Oxford: Oxford University Press.

Biersteker, T. (2009) 'The Parochialisms of Hegemony: Challenges for "American" International Relations', in A. Tickner & O. Wæver (eds), *International Relations Scholarship around the World*, London: Routledge, pp. 308-327.

Biersteker, T. (2010) 'State, Sovereignty and Territory', in W. Carlsnaes, T. Risse & B. A. Simmons (eds), *Handbook of International Relations*, 2nd edn, London: Sage, pp. 157–176.

Biersteker, T. & Weber, C. (1996) *State Sovereignty as Social Construct*, Cambridge, UK: Cambridge University Press.

Bigo, D. (2011) 'Pierre Bourdieu and International Relations: Power of Practices, Practices of Power', *International Political Sociology*, 5(3), pp. 225–258.

Bilici, M. (2006) 'The Fethullah Gülen Movement and Its Politics of Representation in Turkey', *The Muslim World*, 96(1), pp. 1–20.

Blommaert, J. (2005) *Discourse: A Critical Introduction*, Cambridge: Cambridge University Press.

Bookchin, M. (2005) *The Ecology of Freedom: The Emergence and Dissolution of Hierarchy*, Palo Alto: Cheshire Books.

Bookchin, M. (2015) *The Next Revolution: Popular Assemblies and the Promise of Direct Democracy*, London: Verso.

Booth, K. (1999) 'Three Tyrannies', in T. Dunne & N. Wheeler (eds), *Human Rights in Global Politics*, Cambridge: Cambridge University Press, pp. 31–70.

Booth, K. & Smith, S. (1995) *International Relations Theory Today*, Cambridge: Polity Press.

Bottomore, T. B. (1964) *Elites and Society*, New York: Basic Books.

Bourdieu, P. (1977) *Outline of a Theory of Practice*, Cambridge, UK: Cambridge University Press.

Bourdieu, P. (1990) *The Logic of Practice*, Stanford: Stanford University Press.

Bourdieu, P. (1991) *Language and Symbolic Power*, Cambridge, MA: Harvard University Press.

Bourdieu, P. (1994) 'Rethinking the State: Genesis and Structure of the Bureaucratic Field', *Sociological Theory*, 12(1), pp. 1–18.

Bourdieu, P. (1998a) *Practical Reason: On the Theory of Action*, Cambridge: Polity.

Bourdieu, P. (1998b) *The State Nobility: Elite Schools in the Field of Power*, Cambridge: Polity.

Bourdieu, P. (2000) *Pascalian Meditations*, Cambridge: Polity.

Bourdieu, P. (2003) *Firing Back: Against the Tyranny of the Market*, London: Verso.

Bourdieu, P. (2008) *Political Interventions: Social Science and Political Action*, London: Verso.

Bourdieu, P. & L. Wacquant (1992) *An Invitation to Reflexive Sociology*, Cambridge: Polity.

Bozarslan, H. (2003) 'Kurdish Nationalism in Turkey: From Tacit Contract to Rebellion 1919–1925', in A. Vali (ed.) *Essays on the Origins of Kurdish Nationalism*, Costa Mesa: Mazda Press, pp. 163–190.

Bozarslan, H. (2007) 'Kurdish Nationalism under the Kemalist Republic: Some Hypotheses', in M. Ahmad & M. Gunter (eds), *The Evolution of Kurdish Nationalism*, Costa Mesa: Mazda Publishers, pp. 36–51.

Brass, P. (1985) *Ethnic Groups and the State*, London: Croom Helm.

Brass, P. (1991) *Ethnicity and Nationalism: Theory and Comparison*, New Delhi: Sage.

Brass, P. (1993) 'Elite Competition and the Origins of Ethnic Nationalism', in J. G. Beramendi, R. Máiz & X. M. Nuñez (eds), *Nationalism in Europe: Past and Present*, Santiago de Compostela: University of Santiago de Compostela, pp. 111–126.

Brauns, N. & Kiechle, B. (2010) *PKK: Perspektiven des kurdischen Freiheitskampfs*, Stuttgart: Schmetterlings Verlag.

Breuilly, J. (1993) *Nationalism and the State*, 2nd edn, Manchester: Manchester University Press.

Breuilly, J. (2001) 'The State and Nationalism', in: M. Guibernau & J. Hutchinson (eds), *Understanding Nationalism*, Cambridge: Polity, pp. 32–52.

Breuilly, J. (2005) 'Dating the Nation: How Old Is an Old Nation?' In A. Ichijo & G. Uzelac (eds), *When Is a Nation? Towards an Understanding of Theories of Nationalism*, London: Routledge, pp. 15–39.

Bromley, S. (1994) *Rethinking Middle East Politics: State Formation and Development*, Cambridge: Polity.

Brown, C. & Ainley, K. (2009) *Understanding International Relations*, 4th edn, Basingstoke: Palgrave Macmillan.

Brown, G. K. & Langer, A. (2010) 'Conceptualizing and Measuring Ethnicity', *Oxford Development Studies*, 38(4), pp. 411–436.

Brown, M. (1996) *The International Dimensions of Internal Conflict*, Cambridge, MA: Center for Science and International Affairs.

Brown, P. M. (1924) 'From Sévres to Lausanne', *The American Journal of International Law*, 18(1), pp. 113–116.

Brubaker, R. (1996) *Nationalism Reframed: Nationhood and the National Question in the New Europe*, Cambridge: Cambridge University Press.

Brubaker, R. (2004) *Ethnicity without Groups*, Cambridge, MA: Harvard University Press.

Brubaker, R. (2009) 'Ethnicity, Race, and Nationalism', *Annual Review of Sociology*, 35, pp. 21–42.

Brynen, R. (1990) *Sanctuary and Survival: The PLO in Lebanon*, Boulder: Westview Press.

Buhaug, H., Cederman, L. E., & Rød, J. K. (2008) 'Disaggregating Ethno-Nationalist Civil Wars: A Dyadic Test of Exclusion Theory', *International Organization*, 62(3), pp. 531–551.

Bull, H. (2002) *The Anarchical Society: A Study of Order in World Politics*, 3rd edn, New York: Columbia University Press.

Burgos, R. A. (2008) 'Origins of Regime Change: "Idealpolitik" on the Long Road to Baghdad, 1993–2000', *Security Studies*, 17(2), pp. 221–256.

Bush, K. (2003) *The Intra-Group Dimension of Ethnic Conflict in Sri Lanka*, Basingstoke: Palgrave Macmillan.

Bush, K. & Keyman, F. (1997) 'Identity-Based Conflict: Rethinking Security in a Post-Cold War World', *Global Governance*, 3(3), pp. 311–328.

Buzan, B. (1991) *People, States & Fear: An Agenda for International Security Studies in the Post-Cold War Era*, 2nd edn, Colchester, ECPR Press.

Buzan, B., Jones, C., & Little, R. (1993) *The Logic of Anarchy: Neorealism to Structural Realism*, New York: Columbia University Press.

Buzan, B., Wæver, O., & de Wilde, J. (1997) *Security: A New Framework for Analysis*, Boulder: Lynne Rienner.

Buzan, B. (2015) *The Global Transformation: History, Modernity and the Making of International Relations*, Cambridge, UK: Cambridge University Press.

Buzan, B. & Little, R. (2000) *International Systems in World History: Remaking the Study of International Relations*, Oxford. Oxford University Press.

Byman, D. (1998) 'The Logic of Ethnic Terrorism', *Studies in Conflict and Terrorism*, 21(2), pp. 149–169.

Byman, D. (2000) 'After the Storm: US Policy toward Iraq since 1991', *Political Science Quarterly*, 115(4), pp. 493–516.

Byman, D. (2005) *Deadly Connections: States that Sponsor Terrorism*, Cambridge, UK: Cambridge University Press.

Byman, D. & Waxman, M. C. (2000) *Confronting Iraq: U.S. Policy and the Use of Force since the Gulf War*, Washington: RAND Corporation.

Cagaptay, S. (2013) 'Ankara's Middle East Policy Post-Arab Spring', Washington Institute for Near East Policy, *Policy Notes* 16, available at: www.washingtoninstitute.org/uploads/Documents/pubs/PolicyNote16_Cagaptay2.pdf.

Cagaptay, S. & Evans, T. (2012) 'Turkey's Changing Relations with Iraq: Kurdistan Up, Baghdad Down', The Washington Institute for Near East Policy, *Policy Focus* 122, available at: www.washingtoninstitute.org/ uploads/Documents/pubs/PolicyFocus122.pdf.

Calhoun, C. (1993) ''Nationalism and Ethnicity', *Annual Review of Sociology*, 19, pp. 211–239.

Calhoun, C. (1997) *Nationalism*, Minneapolis: University of Minnesota Press.

Cameron, D., Ranis, G., & Zinn, A. (2006) *Globalization and Self-Determination: Is the Nation State under Siege?* London: Routledge.

Camilleri, J. (2008) 'Sovereignty Discourse and Practice – Past and Future', in T. Jacobson, C. Sampford & R. Thakur (eds), *Re-envisioning Sovereignty: The End of Westphalia?'* Aldershot: Ashgate, pp. 33–50.

Campbell, D. (1998a) *National Deconstruction: Violence, Identity and Justice in Bosnia*, Minneapolis: University of Minnesota Press.

Campbell, D. (1998b) *Writing Security: United States Foreign Policy and the Politics of Identity*, 2nd edn, Manchester: Manchester University Press.

Campbell, D. (1999) 'Apartheid Cartography: The Political Anthropology and Spatial Effects of International Diplomacy in Bosnia', *Political Geography*, 18, pp. 395–435.

Campbell, D. (2009) 'Discourse', in D. Gregory, R. Johnson & G. Pratt (eds), *The Dictionary of Human Geography*, 5th edn, Malden: Blackwell, pp. 166–168.

Campbell, D. & Shapiro, M. (1999) *Moral Spaces. Rethinking Ethics and World Politics*, Minneapolis: University of Minnesota Press.

Çandar, C. (2009) 'The Kurdish Question: The Reasons and Fortunes of the "Opening" ', *Insight Turkey* 11(4), pp. 13–19.

Canterbury, D. C. (2005) *Neoliberal Democratization and New Authoritarianism*, Aldershot: Ashgate.

Caputo, J. (1997) *Deconstruction in a Nutshell: A Conversation with Jaques Derrida*, New York: Fordham University Press.

Carayannis, E. & Pirzadeh, A. (2014) *The Knowledge of Culture and the Culture of Knowledge*, Basingstoke: Palgrave Macmillan.

Cardoso, F. H. & Faletto, E. (1979) *Dependency and Development in Latin America*, Berkeley: University of California Press.

Carr, E. H. (2001 [1939]) *The Twenty Years' Crisis 1919–1939: An Introduction to International Relations*, rev. edn, Basingstoke: Palgrave Macmillan.

Carter, A. (2012) *The Political Theory of Anarchism*, London: Routledge.

Casier, M. (2010) 'Designated Terrorists: The Kurdistan Workers' Party and Its Struggle to (Re-)Gain Political Legitimacy', *Mediterranean Politics*, 15(3), pp. 393–413.

Casier, M. (2011) 'Beyond Kurdistan? The Mesopotamia Social Forum and the Appropriation and Re-imagination of Mesopotamia by the Kurdish Movement', *Journal of Balkan and Near Eastern Studies*, 13(4), pp. 417–432.

Casier, M., Jongerden, J., & Walker, N. (2011) 'Fruitless Attempts? The Kurdish Initiative and Containment of the Kurdish Movement in Turkey, *New Perspectives on Turkey*, 44, pp. 103–127.

Caspersen, N. (2010) *Contested Nationalism: Serb Elite Rivalry in Croatia and Bosnia in the 1990s*, Oxford: Berghahn.

Caspersen, N. (2012) *Unrecognised States: The Struggle for Sovereignty in the International System*, Cambridge: Polity.

Caspersen, N. & Stansfield, G. (2011) *Unrecognised States in the International System*, London: Routledge.

Castells, M. (1996) *The Rise of the Network Society, The Information Age: Economy, Society, and Culture, vol. I*, Oxford: Blackwell.

Castells, M. (1997) *The Power of Identity, The Information Age: Economy, Society, and Culture, vol. II*, Oxford: Blackwell.

Castells, M. (1998) *End of Millennium, The Information Age: Economy, Society, and Culture, vol. III*, Oxford: Blackwell.

Catherwood, C. (2004) *Winston's Folly: Imperialism and the Creation of Modern Iraq*, London: Constable & Robinson.

Caves, J. (2012) 'Syrian Kurds and the Democratic Union Party (PYD)', Institute for the Study of War, *Backgrounder*, available at: http://understandingwar.org/sites/default/files/Backgrounder_SyrianKurds.pdf.

Cederman, L. E. (1997) *Emergent Actors in World Politics: How States and Nations Develop and Dissolve*, Princeton: Princeton University Press.

Cederman, L. E. (2010) 'Nationalism and Ethnicity', in W. Carlsnaes, T. Risse & B. A. Simmons (eds), *Handbook of International Relations*, 2nd edn, London: Sage, pp. 409–428.

Cederman, L. E. & Girardin, L. (2007) 'Beyond Fractionalization: Mapping Ethnicity onto Nationalist Insurgencies', *American Political Science Review*, 101(1), pp. 173–185.

Cederman, L. E., Buhaug, H., & Rød, J. K (2009a) 'Ethno-Nationalist Dyads: A GIS-Based Analysis', *Journal of Conflict Resolution*, 53(4), pp. 496–525.

Cederman, L. E., Girardin, L., & K. S. Gleditsch (2009b) 'Ethno-Nationalist Triads: Assessing the Influence of Kin Groups on Civil Wars', *World Politics*, 61(3), pp. 403–437.

Cederman, L. E., Wimmer, A., & Min, B. (2010) 'Why Do Ethnic Groups Rebel? New Data and Analysis', *World Politics*, 62(1), pp. 87–119.

Cederman, L. E., Gleditsch, K.S., Salehyan, I. & Wucherpfenning, J. (2013) 'Transborder Ethnic Kin and Civil War', *International Organization*, 67(2), pp. 389–410.

Çelik, S. (2002) Den Berg Ararat versetzen. Die politischen, militärischen, ökonomischen, und gesellschaftlichen Dimensionen des aktuellen kurdischen Aufstands, Frankfurt/Main: Zambon Verlag.

Černy, H. (2014a) 'Ethnic Alliances Deconstructed: The PKK Sanctuary in Iraqi Kurdistan and the Internationalisation of Ethnic Conflict Revisited', *Ethnopolitics* 13(4), pp. 328–354.

Černy, H. (forthcoming) 'Writing Statehood into Existence: Explanatory IR, the War against ISIS, and Discourses on Kurdish National Self-determination', *Middle East Critique*.

Cetinyan, R. (2002) 'Ethnic Bargaining in the Shadow of Third-Party Intervention', *International Organization*, 56(3), pp. 645–677.

Chandler, D. (2000) *Bosnia. Faking Democracy after Dayton*, London: Pluto Press.

Chandra, K. (2004) *Why Ethnic Parties Succeed: Patronage and Ethnic Headcounts in India*, Cambridge, UK: Cambridge University Press.

Chandra, K. (2006) 'What Is Ethnic Identity and Why Does It Matter?' *Annual Review of Political Science*, 9, pp. 397–424.

Chandrasekaran, R. (2010) *Green Zone: Imperial Life in the Emerald City*, rev. edn, London: Bloomsbury.

Chapman, D. P. (2011) *Security Forces of the Kurdistan Regional Government*, Costa Mesa: Mazda Press.

Charountaki, M. (2010) *The Kurds and US Foreign Policy: International Relations in the Middle East since 1945*, London: Routledge.

Charountaki, M. (2012) 'Turkish Foreign Policy and the Kurdistan Regional Government', *Perceptions*, 17(4), pp. 185–208.

Chatterjee, P. (1993) *The Nation and its Fragments: Colonial and Postcolonial Histories*, Princeton: Princeton University Press.

Chatterjee, P. (1999) 'Anderson's Utopia', *Diacritics*, 29(4), pp. 128–134.

Checkel, J. (1998) 'The Constructivist Turn in International Relations Theory', *World Politics*, 50(2), pp. 324–348.

Childs, M. D. (1995) 'An Historical Critique of the Emergence and Evolution of Ernesto Guevara's Foco Theory', *Journal of Latin American Studies*, 27(3), pp. 593–624.

Chopra, R. (2003) 'Neo-liberalism as Doxa: Bourdieu's Theory of the State and the Contemporary Indian Discourse on Liberalization and Globalization', *Cultural Studies*, 17(3/4), pp. 419–444.

Chorev, M. (2007) 'Iraqi Kurdistan: The Internal Dynamics and the Statecraft of a Semistate', *Al Nakhlah: The Fletcher School Online Journal for Issues Related to Southwest Asia and Islamic Civilization* Fall Issue, available at: http://kms1.isn.ethz.ch/service engine/Files/ISN/48034/ichaptersection_singledocument/3D351A1EADCF451798D29 21A4615DC01/en/3_Matan_Chorev_AN.pdf.

Chouliaraki, L. & Fairclough, N. (1999) *Discourse in Late Modernity. Rethinking Critical Discourse Analysis*, Edinburgh: University of Edinburgh Press.

Christia, F. (2012) *Alliance Formation in Civil Wars*, Cambridge, UK: Cambridge University Press.

Chubin, S. & Tripp, C. (1988) *Iran and Iraq at War*, Boulder: Westview Press.

Çiçek, C. (2013) 'Elimination or Integration of Pro-Kurdish Politics: Limits of the AKP's Democratic Initiative', in C. Gunes & W. Zeydanlioğlu (eds) *The Kurdish Question in Turkey: New Perspectives in Violence, Representation, and Reconciliation*, London: Routledge, pp. 245–257.

Cizre, U. & Walker, J. (2010) 'Conceiving the New Turkey after Ergenekon', *The International Spectator: Italian Journal of International Affairs*, 45(1), pp. 89–98.

Clark, B. (2006) *Twice a Stranger: How Mass Expulsion Forged Modern Greece and Turkey*, London: Granta.

Claude, I. (1989) 'The Balance of Power Revisited', *Review of International Studies*, 15(2), pp. 77–86.

Coakley, J. (2008) 'Ethnic Competition and the Logic of Party System Transformation', *European Journal of Political Research*, 47(6), pp. 766–793.

Cobban, H. (1992) *The Palestinian Liberation Organisation: People, Power and Politics*, 6th edn, Cambridge: Cambridge University Press.

Cockburn, P. (2015) *The Rise of Islamic State: ISIS and the New Sunni Revolution*, London: Verso.

Cohen, A. (1974) *Two-Dimensional Man: An Essay on the Anthropology of Power and Symbolism in Complex Societies*, London: Routledge.

Cohen, J. (2012) *Globalization and Sovereignty: Rethinking Legality, Legitimacy, and Constitutionalism*, Cambridge, UK: Cambridge University Press.

Cohen, Y., Brown, B. R., & Organski, A. F. (1981) 'The Paradoxical Nature of Statemaking: The Violent Creation of Order', *American Political Science Review*, 75(4), pp. 901–910.

Connolly, W. (1991a) 'Democracy and Territoriality', *Millennium*, 20(3), pp. 463–484.

Connolly, W. (1991b) *Identity/Difference: Democratic Negotiations of Political Paradox*, Ithaca: Cornell University Press.

Connor, W. (1993) *Ethnonationalism: The Quest for Understanding*, Princeton: Princeton University Press.

Conversi, D. (2004) *Ethnonationalism in the Contemporary World: Walker Connor and the Study of Nationalism*, London: Routledge.

Cordell, K. & Wolff, S. (2009) *Ethnic Conflict: Causes, Consequences, and Responses*, Cambridge: Polity Press.

Cox, R. (1981) 'Social Forces, States, and World Orders: Beyond International Relations Theory', *Millennium*, 10(2), pp. 126–155.

Cox, R. (1992) 'Multilateralism and World Order', *Review of International Studies*, 18(2), pp. 161–180.

Craig, G. & George, A. L. (1995) *Force and Statecraft: Diplomatic Problems of Our Time*, 3rd edn, Oxford: Oxford University Press.

Crouch, C. (2009) *Managing Terrorism and Insurgency: Regeneration, Recruitment and Attrition*, London: Routledge.

Crowder, G. (1991) *Classical Anarchism: The Political Thought of Godwin, Proudhon, Bakunin, and Kropotkin*, Oxford: Clarendon Press.

Cunliffe, P. (2011) *Critical Perspectives on the Responsibility to Protect: Interrogating Theory and Practice*, London: Routledge.

Cuthell, D. (2004) 'A Kemalist Gambit: A View of the Political Negotiations in the Determination of the Turkish-Iraqi Border', in R. Spector-Simon and E. Tejirian (eds), *The Creation of Iraq 1914–1921*, New York: Columbia University Press, pp. 80–94.

Daddow, O. (2013) *International Relations Theory: The Essentials*, 2nd edn, London: Sage.

Dann, U. (1969) *Iraq under Qassem: A Political History 1958–1963*, New York: Praeger.

Daston, L. & Galison, P. (2007) *Objectivity*, New York: Zone Books.

David, S. (1997) 'Internal War: Causes and Cures', *World Politics*, 49(4), pp. 552–576.

Davidson, B. (1992) *The Black Man's Burden: Africa and the Curse of the Nation-State*, Melton: James Currey.

Davis, D. & Moore, W. (1997) 'Ethnicity Matters: Transnational Ethnic Alliances and Foreign Policy Behaviour', *International Studies Quarterly* 41: 171–184.

Davis, D. & Moore, W. (1998) 'Transnational Ethnic Ties and Foreign Policy', in D. Lake and D. Rothchild (eds), *The International Spread of Ethnic Conflict: Fear, Diffusion, and Escalation*, Princeton: Princeton University Press, pp. 89–104.

Davis, J. (2006) 'Infighting in Washington: The Impact of Bureaucratic Politics on US Iraq Policy', in J. Davis (ed.) *Presidential Policies and the Road to the Second Iraq War*, Aldershot: Ashgate, pp. 92–123.

Dawood, H. (2003) 'The "State-ization" of the Tribe and the Tribalisation of the State: The Case of Iraq', in F. A. Jabar & H. Dawood (eds), *Tribes and Power: Nationalism and Ethnicity in the Middle East*, London: Saqi Books, pp. 110–135.

Dawisha, A. & Diamond, L. (2006) 'Iraq's Year of Voting Dangerously', *Journal of Democracy*, 17(2), pp. 89–103.

Deane, S. M. (2004) *Negotiating Peace Agreements: Elite Bargaining and Ethnic Conflict Regulation in Northern Ireland and Israel-Palestine*, unpublished PhD thesis, London School of Economics.

Debray, R. (1968) *Revolution in the Revolution? Armed Struggle and Political Struggle in Latin America*, London: Penguin.

De Dreu, C. & van Knippenberg, W. (2005) 'The Possessive Self as a Barrier to Conflict Resolution: Effects of Mere Ownership, Process Accountability, and Self-Concept Clarity on Competitive Cognitions and Behaviour', *Journal of Personality and Social Psychology*, 89(3), pp. 345–357.

Deer, C. (2014) 'Doxa', in M. J. Grenfell (ed.), *Pierre Bourdieu: Key Concepts*, 2nd edn, London: Routledge, pp. 114–125.

Deleuze, G. (1988) *Foucault*, Minneapolis: University of Minnesota Press.

Derrida, J. (1978) *Writing and Difference*, London: Routledge.

Derrida, J. (1981a) *Dissemination*, London: Athlone Press.

Derrida, J. (1981b) *Positions*, London: Athlone Press.

Derrida, J. (1982) *Margins of Philosophy*, Chicago: University of Chicago Press.

Derrida, J. (1998) *Of Grammatology*, Baltimore: The Johns Hopkins University Press.

Derrida, J. (2004) 'Living On: Border Lines', in H. Bloom *et al.* (eds), *Deconstruction and Criticism*, 3rd edn, London: Continuum Publishing, pp. 62–142.

Deutscher, I. (2003) *The Prophet Armed: Trotsky 1879–1921*, London: Verso.

Devetak, R. (2009) 'Post-structuralism', in S. Burchill *et al.* (eds), *Theories of International Relations*, 4th edn, Basingstoke: Palgrave Macmillan, pp. 183–211.

De Votta, N. (2005) 'From Ethnic Outbidding to Ethnic Conflict: The Institutional Bases for Sri Lanka's Separatist War', *Nations and Nationalism*, 11(1), pp. 141–159.

Devlin, J. (1991) 'The Ba'ath Party: Rise and Metamorphosis', *The American Historical Review*, 96(5), pp. 1396–1407.

Diez, T. (2014) 'Postmodern Approaches', in S. Schieder & M. Spindler (eds), *Theories of International Relations*, London: Routledge, pp. 287–303.

Di Leonardo, M. (1998) *Exotics at Home: Anthropologists, Others, American Modernity*, Chicago: University of Chicago Press.

Di Prizio, R. (2002) *Armed Humanitarianism: U.S. Interventions from Northern Iraq to Kosovo*, Baltimore: Johns Hopkins University Press.

Dodd, C. H. (1983) *The Crisis of Turkish Democracy*, Walkington: Eothen Press.

Dodge, T. (2003) *Inventing Iraq: The Failure of Nation Building and a History Denied*, London: Hurst.

Dodge, T. (2005) *Iraq's Future: The Aftermath of Regime Change*, London: International Institute for Strategic Studies, *Adelphi Papers*, 372.

Dodge, T. (2006) 'War and Resistance in Iraq: From Regime Change to Anarchy', in R. Hinnebusch & R. Fawn (eds), *The Iraq War: Causes and Consequences*, Boulder: Lynne Rienner, pp. 211–224.

Dodge, T. (2009) 'Coming Face to Face with Bloody Reality: Liberal Common Sense and the Ideological Failure of the Bush Doctrine in Iraq', *International Politics* 46(2–3), pp. 253–275.

Dodge, T. (2010) 'The Ideological Roots of Failure: The Application of Kinetic Neo-Liberalism to Iraq', *International Affairs*, 86(6), pp. 1269–1286.

Dodge, T. (2012) *Iraq: From War to a New Authoritarianism*, London: International Institute for Strategic Studies, *Adelphi Papers*, 434.

Dodge, T. (2013) 'Interventions and Dreams of Exogenous Statebuilding: The Application of Liberal Peacebuilding in Afghanistan and Iraq', *Review of International Studies*, 39(5), pp. 1189–1212.

Doty, R. L. (1997) 'Aporia: A Critical Exploration of the Agent-Structure Problematique in International Relations Theory', *European Journal of International Relations*, 3(3), pp. 365–392.

Duffy-Toft, M. (2005) *The Geography of Ethnic Violence: Identity, Interests, and the Indivisibility of Territory*, Princeton: Princeton University Press.

Dumbrell, J. (2008) 'The Neoconservative Roots of the War in Iraq', in J. P. Pfiffner & M. Phythian (eds), *Intelligence and National Security Policymaking on Iraq: British and American Perspectives*, Manchester: Manchester University Press, pp. 19–39.

Duyar-Kienast, U. (2005) *The Formation of Gecekondu Settlements in Turkey: The Case of Ankara*, Münster: LIT Verlag.

Eagleton, T. (1991) *Ideology: An Introduction*, London: Verso.

Eagleton, W. (1963) *The Kurdish Republic of 1946*, London: Oxford University Press.

Ebaugh, H. R. (2010) *The Gülen Movement: A Sociological Analysis of a Civic Movement Rooted in Moderate Islam*, New York: Springer.

Eccarius-Kelly, V. (2002) Political Movements and Leverage Points: Kurdish Activism in the European Diaspora', *Journal of Muslim Minority Affairs*, 22(1), pp. 91–118.

Eccarius-Kelly, V. (2011) *The Militant Kurds: A Dual Strategy for Freedom*, Santa Barbara: Praeger.

Eccarius-Kelly, V. (2012) 'Surreptitious Lifelines: A Structural Analysis of the FARC and the PKK', *Terrorism and Political Violence*, 24(2), pp. 235–258.

Edkins, J. (1999) *Poststructuralism and International Relations: Bringing the Political Back In*, Boulder: Lynne Rienner.

Edmonds, C. J. (1957), *Kurds, Turks and Arabs: Politics, Travels, and Research in North-Eastern Iraq*, London: Oxford University Press.

Egan-Sjölander, A. & Gunnarsson-Payne, J. (2011) *Tracking Discourses: Politics, Identity and Social Change*, Lund: Nordic Academic Press.

Eifert, B., Miguel, E., & Posner, D. N. (2010) 'Political Competition and Ethnic Identification in Africa', *American Journal of Political Science*, 54(2), pp. 494–510.

Elden, S. (2009) *Terror and Territory: The Spatial Extent of Sovereignty*, Minneapolis: University of Minnesota Press.

Elden, S. & Williams, A. J. (2007) 'The Territorial Integrity of Iraq, 2003–2007: Invocation, Violation, Viability', *Geoforum*, 40, pp. 407–417.

Elik, S. (2011) *Iran-Turkey Relations, 1979–2011: Conceptualising the Dynamics of Politics, Religion, and Security in Middle-Power States*, London: Routledge.

Elliot, M. (1996) *'Independent Iraq': The Monarchy and British Influence 1941–1958*, London: I.B. Tauris.

Entessar, N. (1992) *Kurdish Ethnonationalism*, Boulder: Lynne Rienner.

Eppel, M. (2008) 'The Demise of the Kurdish Emirates: The Impact of Ottoman Reforms and International Relations on Kurdistan during the First Half of the Nineteenth century', *Middle Eastern Studies*, 44(2), pp. 237–258.

Erdem, D. (2013) ,The Representation of the Democratic Society Party (DTP) in the Mainstream Turkish Media', in C. Gunes & W. Zeydanlioglu (eds) *The Kurdish Question in Turkey: New Perspectives on Violence, Representation, and Reconciliation*, London: Routledge, pp. 47–67.

Ergil, D. (2007) 'PKK: Partiya Karkarên Kurdistan', in M. Heiberg, B. O'Leary & J. Tirman (eds), *Terror, Insurgency, and the State: Ending Protracted Conflicts*, Philadelphia: University of Pennsylvania Press, pp. 323–358.

Eriksen, T. H. (2002) *Ethnicity and Nationalism: Anthropological Perspectives*, 2nd edn, London: Pluto.

Erk, J. & Anderson, J. (2009) 'The Paradox of Federalism: Does Self-Rule Accommodate or Exacerbate Ethnic Divisions?', *Regional and Federal Studies*, 19(2), pp. 191–202.

Escobar, A. (1995) *Encountering Development: The Making and Unmaking of the Third World*, Princeton: Princeton University Press.

Esmark, A. (2004) 'Systems and Sovereignty: A Systems Theoretical Look at the Transformation of Sovereignty', in M. Albert & L. Hilkermeier (eds), *Observing International Relations: Niklas Luhmann and World Politics*, London: Routledge, pp. 121–141.

Evans, S. (1982) *The Slow Rapprochement: Britain and Turkey in the Age of Kemal Atatürk, 1919–38*, Walkington: Eothen Press.

Fagan, M., Glorieux, L., Hasimbegovic, I. & Suetsugu, M. (2007) *Derrida: Negotiating the Legacy*, Edinburgh: Edinburgh University Press.

Fairclough, N. (2001a) Critical Discourse Analysis as a Method in Social Scientific Research', in R. Wodak & M. Meyer (eds), *Methods of Critical Discourse Analysis*, London: Sage, pp. 121–138.

Fairclough, N. (2001b) *Language and Power*, 2nd edn, Harlow: Pearson Education.

Fairclough, N. (2003) *Analysing Discourse: Textual Analysis for Social Research*, London: Routledge.

Fairclough, N. (2010) *Critical Discourse Analysis: The Critical Study of Language*, 2nd edn, Harlow: Pearson Education.

Fairclough, N. & Wodak, R. (1997) 'Critical Discourse Analysis', in T. van Dijk (ed.) *Discourse as Social Interaction*, London: Sage, pp. 258–284.

Fairclough, N. & Fairclough, I. (2012) *Political Discourse Analysis: A Method for Advanced Students*, London: Routledge.

Farouk-Sluglett, M. & Sluglett, P. (2003) *Iraq Since 1958: From Revolution to Dictatorship*, 3rd edn, London: I.B. Tauris.

Farr, M. (2001) *Tintin: The Complete Companion*, London: John Murray.

Fattah, H. (2003) 'The Question of the "Artificiality" of Iraq as a Nation-State', in S. C. Inati (ed.), *Iraq: Its History, People and Politics*, Amherst: Humanity Books, pp. 49–62.

Fayazmanesh, S. (2008) *The United States and Iran: Sanctions, Wars, and the Policy of Dual Containment*, London: Routledge.

Fearon, J. D. (2003) 'Ethnic and Cultural Diversity by Country', *Journal of Economic Growth*, 8, pp. 195–222.

Fearon, J. D. (2004a) 'Ethnic Mobilization and Ethnic Violence', unpubl. paper, available online at: www.seminario2005.unal.edu.co/Trabajos/Fearon/Ethnic%20mobilization%20and%20ethnic%20violence.pdf.

Fearon, J. D. (2004b) 'Separatist Wars, Partition, and World Order', *Security Studies*, 13(4), pp. 394–415.

Fearon, J. D. & Laitin, D. (1996) 'Explaining Interethnic Cooperation', *American Political Science Review*, 90(4), pp. 715–735.

Fearon, J. D. & Laitin, D. (2000) 'Violence and the Social Construction of Ethnic Identity', *International Organization*, 54(4), pp. 845–877.

Fenton, S. (2004) 'Beyond Ethnicity: The Global Comparative Analysis of Ethnic Conflict', *International Journal of Comparative Sociology*, 45(3–4), pp. 179–194.

Fenton, S. (2010) *Ethnicity*, 2nd edn, Cambridge: Polity.

Fernea, R. & Louis, R. (1991) *The Iraqi Revolution of 1958: The Old Social Classes Revisited*, London: I.B. Tauris.

Fessha, Y. T. (2011) *Ethnic Diversity and Federalism: Constitution Making in South Africa and Ethiopia*, Aldershot: Ashgate.

Fieldhouse, D. (2002) *Kurds, Arabs and Britons: The Memoir of Col. W. A. Lyon in Kurdistan 1918–1945*, London: I.B. Tauris.

Fierke, K. (2005) *Diplomatic Interventions: Conflict and Change in a Globalising World*, Basingstoke: Palgrave Macmillan.

Fierke, K. (2007) *Critical Approaches to International Security*, Cambridge: Polity.

Fierke, K. (2010) 'Constructivism', in T. Dunne, M. Kurki & S. Smith (eds), *International Relations Theory: Discipline and Diversity*, 2nd edn, Oxford: Oxford University Press, pp. 166–184.

Finkel, C. (2005) *Osman's Dream: The Story of the Ottoman Empire, 1300–1923*, London: John Murray.

Finlayson, A. (1998) 'Ideology, Discourse and Nationalism', *Journal of Political Ideologies*, 3(1), pp. 99–118.

Flanagan, S. J. & Brannen, S. J. (2008) 'Turkey's Shifting Dynamics: Implications for U.S.-Turkey Relations', Center for Strategic & International Studies, *Report of the U.S.-Turkey Strategic Initiative*, available at: http://csis.org/files/media/csis/pubs/080606_turkeyshiftingdyn.pdf.

Foucault, M. (1972) *The Archaeology of Knowledge*, London: Tavistock.

Foucault, M. (1974) *The Order of Things: Archaeology of the Human Sciences*, London: Tavistock.

Foucault, M. (1980) *Power/Knowledge: Selected Interviews and Other Writings 1972–77*, edited by C. Gordon, New York: Harvester Wheatsheaf.

Foucault, M. (1983) 'The Subject and Power', in H. Dreyfus & P. Rabinow (eds), *Beyond Structuralism and Hermeneutics*, Chicago: University of Chicago Press, pp. 208–226.

Foucault, M. (1984) *The History of Sexuality, vol. II: The Uses of Pleasure*, London: Penguin.

Fowler, M. & Bunk, J. (1995) *Law, Power, and the Sovereign State: The Evolution and Application of the Concept of Sovereignty*, University Park: Penn State Press.

Fowler, R. B. (1972) 'The Anarchist Tradition of Political Thought', *Political Research Quarterly*, 25(4), pp. 738–752.

Frank, A. G. (1979) *Dependent Accumulation and Underdevelopment*, London: Palgrave Macmillan.

Frank, A. G. (1981) *Crisis in the Third World*, New York: Holmes & Meier.

Frankel, J. (1973) *International Politics: Conflict and Harmony*, Baltimore: Penguin Books.

Freedman, R. O. (1999) 'U.S. Policy toward the Middle East in Clinton's Second Term', *MERIA – Middle East Review of International Affairs*, 3(1), pp. 55–79.

Freij, H. Y. (1998) 'Alliance Patterns of a Secessionist Movement: The Kurdish Nationalist Movement in Iraq', *Journal of Muslim Minority Affairs*, 18(1), pp. 19–37.

Frelick, B. (1992) 'The False Promise of Operation Provide Comfort: Protecting Refugees or Protecting State Power?' MERIP, *Middle East Report*, 176, pp. 22–27.

Friedman, G. & Starr, H. (2006) *Agency, Structure, and International Politics from Ontology to Empirical Enquiry*, 2nd edn, London: Routledge.

Fromkin, D. (2009) *A Peace to End All Peace: The Fall of the Ottoman Empire and the Creation of the Modern Middle East*, 3rd edn, New York: Henry Holt.

Fukuyama, F. (1989) 'The End of History?' *The National Interest*, available at: http://ps321.community.uaf.edu/files/2012/10/Fukuyama-End-of-historyarticle.pdf.

Fuller. G. (2008) *The New Turkish Republic: Turkey as a Pivotal State in the Muslim World*, Washington, DC: United States Institute for Peace Press.

Gagnon, V. P. (2004) *The Myth of Ethnic War: Serbia and Croatia in the 1990s*, Ithaca: Cornell University Press.

Galbraith, P. (2006) *The End of Iraq: How American Incompetence Created a War without End*, New York: Simon & Schuster.

Galula, D. (2006 [1964]) *Counterinsurgency Warfare: Theory and Practice*, New York: Praeger.

Ganguly, R. (1998) *Kin State Intervention in Ethnic Conflicts: Lessons from South Asia*, London: Sage.

Gellner, E. (2006) *Nations and Nationalism*, 2nd edn, Malden: Blackwell.

Ghani, A. & Lockhart, C. (2009) *Fixing Failed States: A Framework for Rebuilding a Fractured World*, Oxford: Oxford University Press.

Ghalib, S. A. (2011) *The Emergence of Kurdism with Special Reference to the Three Kurdish Emirates within the Ottoman Empire, 1800–1850*, unpublished PhD thesis, University of Exeter.

Ghareeb, E. (1981) *The Kurdish Question in Iraq*, Syracuse: Syracuse University Press.

Ghassemlou, A. R. (1965) *Kurdistan and the Kurds*, Prague: Czechoslovak Academy of Science.

Giddens, A. (1979) *Central Problems in Social Theory: Action, Structure and Contradiction in Social Analysis*, London: Macmillan.

Giddens, A. (1984) *The Constitution of Society: Outline of the Theory of Structuration*, Cambridge: Polity.

Giddens, A. (1985) *A Contemporary Critique of Historical Materialism, Volume II: The Nation State and Violence*, Cambridge: Polity.

Gleditsch, K. S., Salehyan, I., & Schultz, K. (2008) 'Fighting at Home, and Fighting Abroad: How Civil Wars Lead to International Disputes', *Journal of Conflict Resolution*, 52(4), pp. 479–506.

Göçek, F. M. (2011) *The Transformation of Turkey: Redefining State and Society from the Ottoman Empire to the Modern Era*, London: I. B. Tauris.

Göçek, F. M. (2013) *A Question of Genocide: Armenians and Turks at the End of the Ottoman Empire*, 2nd edn, Oxford: Oxford University Press.

Goodman, L. (1961) 'Snowball Sampling', *The Annals of Mathematical Statistics*, 32(1), pp. 148–170.

Gordon, M. & Trainor, B. (2007) *Cobra II: The Inside Story of the Invasion and Occupation of Iraq*, 2nd edn, London: Atlantic Books.

Görgü-Guttstadt, C. (2006) 'Depriving Non-Muslims of Citizenship as Part of the Turki-fication Policy in the Early Years of the Turkish Republic: The Case of Turkish Jews and Its Consequences during the Holocaust', in H. L. Kieser (ed.), *Turkey beyond Nationalism: Towards Post-Nationalist Identities*, London: I.B. Tauris, pp. 50–56.

Gourevitch, P. (2000) *We Wish to Inform You that Tomorrow We Will Be Killed with Our Families: Stories from Rwanda*, London: Picador.

Graham-Brown, S. (1999) *Sanctioning Saddam: The Politics of Intervention in Iraq*, London: I.B. Tauris.

Gramsci, A. (1992) *Prison Notebooks*, 2nd edn, New York: Columbia University Press.

Gray, C. (2009) *National Security Dilemmas: Challenges and Opportunities*, Washington: Potomac Books.

Gregory, D. (2004) *The Colonial Present: Afghanistan, Palestine, Iraq*, Malden: Blackwell.

Grenier, F. (2012) 'Conversations In and On IR: Labelling, Framing and Delimiting IR Discipline', *Bridges: Conversations in Global Politics*, 1(1), available online at: http://digitalcommons.mcmaster.ca/cgi/viewcontent.cgi?article=1000&context=bridges.

Grojean, O. (2011) 'Bringing the Organization Back In: Pro-Kurdish Protest in Europe', in J. Jongerden & M. Casier (eds), *Nationalism and Politics in Turkey: Political Islam, Kemalism, and the Kurdish Issue*, London: Routledge, pp. 182–196.

Gruen, G. E. (2004) 'The Oil Resources of Iraq: Their Role in the Policies of the Great Powers', in R. Spector-Simon and E. Tejirian (eds), *The Creation of Iraq 1914–1921*, New York: Columbia University Press, pp. 110–124.

Guevara, E. (1998 [1961]) *Guerrilla Warfare: A Method*, Lincoln: Bison Books.

Guibernau, M. (2000) *Nations without States: Political Communities in a Global Age*, 2nd edn, Cambridge: Polity.

Guibernau, M. & Hutchinson, J. (2004) *History and National Destiny: Ethnosymbolism and its Critics*, Oxford: Blackwell.

Gunes, C. (2011) *The Kurdish National Movement in Turkey: From Protest to Resistance*, London: Routledge.

Güney, A. (2005) 'An Anatomy of the Transformation of the US-Turkish Alliance: From "Cold War" to "War on Iraq"', *Turkish Studies*, 6(3), pp. 341–359.

Gunter, M. (1990) *The Kurds in Turkey: A Political Dilemma*, Boulder: Westview Press.

Gunter, M. (1992) *The Kurds of Iraq: Tragedy and Hope*, New York: St. Martin's Press.

Gunter, M. (1993) 'A De facto Kurdish State in Northern Iraq', *Third World Quarterly*, 14(2), pp. 295–319.

Gunter, M. (1996) 'Kurdish Infighting: The PKK-KDP Conflict', in R. Olson (ed.), *The Kurdish Nationalist Movement in the 1990s: Its Impact on Turkey and the Middle East*, Lexington: University Press of Kentucky, pp. 50–62.

Gunter, M. (1997) *The Kurds and the Future of Turkey*, Basingstoke: Palgrave Macmillan.

Gunter, M. (1999a) *The Kurdish Predicament in Iraq: A Political Analysis*, Basingstoke: Macmillan.

Gunter, M. (1999b) 'The Iraqi Opposition and the Failure of U.S. Intelligence', *International Journal of Intelligence and Counterintelligence*, 12(2), pp. 135–167.

Gunter, M. (2001) 'The Bane of Kurdish Disunity', *Orient*, 42(4), pp. 605–616.

Gunter, M. (2002) 'After the War: President Bush and the Kurdish Uprising', in M. Bose & R. Perotti (eds), *The Foreign Policy of George H. W. Bush*, Westport: Greenwood Press, pp. 507–520.

Gunter, M. (2007) 'The Modern Origins of Kurdish Nationalism', in M. M. Ahmed & M. Gunter (eds), *The Evolution of Kurdish Nationalism*, Costa Mesa: Mazda Press, pp. 1–17.

Gunter, M. (2010a) *Historical Dictionary of the Kurds*, 2nd edn, Lanham: Scarecrow Press.

Gunter, M. (2010b) 'Prospects for the Kurdish Future in Iraq and Turkey', in R. Lowe & G. Stansfield (eds), *The Kurdish Policy Imperative*, London: Chatham House, pp. 192–206.

Gunter, M. (2011a) 'Turgut Özal and the Kurdish Question', in J. Jongerden & M. Casier (eds), *Nationalism and Politics in Turkey: Political Islam, Kemalism and the Kurdish Issue*, London: Routledge, pp. 85–100.

Gunter, M. (2011b) 'The Five Stages of American Foreign Policy towards the Kurds', *Insight Turkey*, 13(2), pp. 93–106.

Gunter, M. (2011c) *The Kurds Ascending: The Evolving Solution to the Kurdish Problem in Iraq and Turkey*, Basingstoke: Palgrave Macmillan.

Gunter, M. (2014) *Out of Nowhere: The Kurds of Syria in Peace and War*, London: Hurst.

Gürbey, G. (1996) 'The Kurdish Nationalist Movement in Turkey since the 1980s', in R. Olson (ed.), *The Kurdish Nationalist Movement in the 1990s: Its Impact on Turkey and the Middle East*, Lexington: University of Kentucky Press, pp. 9–37.

Gurr, T. R. (1993) *Minorities at Risk*, Washington: United States Institute for Peace.

Gurr, T. R. & Harff, B. (1994) *Ethnic Conflict in World Politics*, Boulder: Westview Press.

Guzzini, S. (2013) 'Power', in R. Adler-Nissen (ed.), *Bourdieu in International Relations*, London: Routledge, pp. 78–92.

Habyarimana, J., Humphreys, M., Posner, D. & Weinstein, J. M. (2007) 'Does Ethnic Diversity Undermine Public Goods Provision?' *The American Political Science Review*, 101(4), pp. 709–725.

Haddad, F. (2011) *Sectarianism in Iraq: Antagonistic Visions of Unity*, London: Hurst.

Hale, W. (1994) *Turkish Politics and the Military*, London: Routledge.

Hale, W. (2003) *Turkish Foreign Policy since 1774*, 2nd edn, London: Frank Cass.

Hale, W. (2007) *Turkey, the US and Iraq*, London: Saqi.

Hale, W. & Özbudun, E. (2010) *Islamism, Democracy, and Liberalism in Turkey: The Case of the AKP*, London: Routledge.

Halliday, F. (2000) *Nation and Religion in the Middle East*, London: Saqi Books.

Halliday, F. (2005) *The Middle East in International Relations: Power, Politics and Ideology*, Cambridge: Cambridge University Press.

Hall, R. B. (1999) *National Collective Identity: Social Constructs and International Systems*, New York: Columbia University Press.

Hall, S. (1995) 'Fantasy, Identity, Politics', in E. Carter, J. Donald & J. Squires (eds), *Cultural Remix: Theories of Politics and the Popular*, London: Lawrence & Wishart, pp. 63–69.

Hall, S. (1996) 'Introduction: Who Needs "Identity"?', in S. Hall & P. du Gay (eds), *Questions of Cultural Identity*, London: Sage, pp. 1–18.

Hall, S. (1997) 'The Work of Representation', in S. Hall (ed.), *Representation: Cultural Representations and Signifying Practices*, London: Sage, pp. 13–74.

Hall, S. (2003a) 'Foucault: Power, Knowledge, and Discourse', in M. Wetherell, S. Taylor & S. Yates (eds), *Discourse Theory and Practice*, 3rd edn, London: Sage, pp. 72–81.

Hall, S. (2003b) 'The Spectacle of the Other', in M. Wetherell, S. Taylor & S. Yates (eds), *Discourse Theory and Practice*, 3rd edn, London: Sage, pp. 324–344.

Halper, S. & Clarke, J. (2005) *America Alone: The Neo-conservatives and the Global Order*, Cambridge, UK: Cambridge University Press.

Hamati-Ataya, I. (2012) 'IR Theory as International Practice/Agency: A Clinical/Cynical Bourdieusian Perspective', *Millennium*, 40(3), pp. 625–646.

Hamilton, P. (2014) *Knowledge and Social Structure*, 2nd edn, London: Routledge.

Hanioğlu, M. S. (2006) 'Turkism and the Young Turks, 1889–1908', in H. L. Kieser (ed.), *Turkey beyond Nationalism: Towards Post-Nationalist Identities*, London: I.B. Tauris, pp. 3–19.

Hanioğlu, M. S. (2010) *A Brief History of the Late Ottoman Empire*, Princeton: Princeton University Press.

Hanioğlu, M. S. (2011) *Atatürk: An Intellectual Biography*, Princeton: Princeton University Press.

Hansen, L. (2006) *Security as Practice: Discourse Analysis and the Bosnian War*, London: Routledge.

Hansen, L. (2013) 'Poststructuralism', in J. Baylis, S. Smith & P. Owens (eds), *The Globalization of World Politics: An Introduction to International Relations*, 6th edn, Oxford: Oxford University Press, pp. 169–183.

Hansen, T. & Stepputat, F. (2001) *States of Imagination: Ethnographic Explorations of the Postcolonial State*, Durham: Duke University Press.

Haraway, D. (1988) 'Situated Knowledges: The Science Question in Feminism and the Privilege of Partial Perspective', *Feminist Studies*, 14(3), pp. 575–599.

Hardt, M. & Negri, A. (2000) *Empire*, Cambridge: Harvard University Press.

Harris, G. S. (1985) *Turkey: Coping with Crisis*, Boulder: Westview Press.

Harvey, D. (2003) *The New Imperialism*, Oxford: Oxford University Press.

Hashim, A. (2006) *Insurgency and Counter-Insurgency in Iraq*, London: Hurst.

Hassan, K. (2015) 'Kurdistan's Politicized Society Confronts a Sultanistic System', Carnegie Middle East Center, *Briefing Paper* 18 August, available at: http://carnegie-mec. org/2015/08/17/kurdistan-s-politicized-society-confronts-sultanistic-system/ieta.

Hechter, M. (1998) *Internal Colonialism: The Celtic Fringe in British National Development*, 2nd edn, Piscataway: Transaction Publishers.

Hechter, M. (2001) *Containing Nationalism*, Oxford: Oxford University Press.

Heinze, E. A. (2008) 'The New Utopianism: Liberalism, American Foreign Policy, and the War in Iraq', *Journal of International Political Theory*, 4(1), pp. 105–125.

Held, D. (1995) *Democracy and the Global Order: From the Modern State to Cosmopolitan Governance*, Stanford: Stanford University Press.

Held, D. (2000) 'Regulating Globalization? The Reinvention of Politics', *International Sociology*, 15(2), pp. 394–408.

Helmreich, P. (1974) *From Paris to Sèvres: The Partition of the Ottoman Empire at the Peace Conference 1919–1920*, Columbus: Ohio State University Press.

Helsing, J. (2004) 'The Regionalization, Internationalization and the Perpetuation of Conflict in the Middle East', in S. Lobell & P. Mauceri (eds), *Ethnic Conflict and International Politics: Explaining Diffusion and Escalation*, Basingstoke: Palgrave Macmillan, pp. 133–164.

Herb, M. (2005) 'No Representation without Taxation? Rents, Development, and Democracy', *Comparative Politics*, 37(3), pp. 297–316.

Herther-Spiro, N. B. (2007) 'Can Ethnic Federalism Prevent "Recourse to Rebellion"? A Comparative Analysis of the Ethiopian and Iraqi Constitutional Structures', *Emory International Law Review*, 21(1), pp. 321–372.

Herz, J. (1950) 'Idealist Internationalism and the Security Dilemma', *World Politics*, 2(2), pp. 157–180.

Hinsley, F. H. (1986) *Sovereignty*, 2nd edn, Cambridge: Cambridge University Press.

Hiltermann, J. R. (2007) *A Poisonous Affair: America, Iraq, and the Gassing of Halabja*, Cambridge: Cambridge University Press.

Hiltermann, J. R. (2012) 'Revenge of the Kurds', *Foreign Affairs*, 91(6), pp. 16–22.

Hiro, D. (1991) *The Longest War: The Iran-Iraq Military Conflict*, London: Routledge.

Hirt, E. R. & Sherman, S. J. (1985) 'The Role of Prior Knowledge in Explaining Hypothetical Events', *Journal of Experimental and Social Psychology*, 21, pp. 519–543.

Hobsbawm, E. (1990) *Nations and Nationalism since 1780: Programme, Myth, Reality*, Cambridge, UK: Cambridge University Press.

Hobsbawm, E. & Ranger, T. (1984) *The Invention of Tradition*, Cambridge: Cambridge University Press.

Hobson, J. (2000) *The State and International Relations*, Cambridge, UK: Cambridge University Press.

Hobson, J. (2012) *The Eurocentric Conception of World Politics: Western International Theory, 1760–2010*, Cambridge, UK: Cambridge University Press.

Holsti, K. (2002) 'Interview with Kal Holsti by A. Jones', *Review of International Studies*, 28(3), pp. 619–633.

Holzgrefe, J. L. & Keohane, R. (2003) *Humanitarian Intervention: Ethical, Legal, and Political Dilemmas*, Cambridge, UK: Cambridge University Press.

Horowitz, D. (2001) *Ethnic Groups in Conflict*, 2nd edn, Berkeley: University of California Press.

Horowitz, S. (2008) 'Mapping Pathways of Ethnic Conflict Onset: Preferences and Enabling Conditions', *Ethnopolitics*, 7(2–3), pp. 307–320.

Houston, C. (2009) 'An Anti-History of a Non-People: Kurds, Colonialism, and Nationalism in the History of Anthropology', *Journal of the Royal Anthropological Institute*, 15, pp. 19–35.

Human Rights Watch (1992) *Endless Torment: The 1991 Uprising in Iraq and Its Aftermath*, New York: Human Rights Watch, available at: www.hrw.org/legacy/reports/1992/Iraq926.htm.

Human Rights Watch (1993) 'Genocide in Iraq: The Anfal Campaign against the Kurds', *Middle East Watch Report*, New York: Human Rights Watch.

Human Rights Watch (1995) *Iraq's Crime of Genocide: The Anfal Campaign against the Kurds*, New Haven: Yale University Press.

Human Rights Watch (2009) *Group Denial: Repression of Kurdish Political and Cultural Rights in Syria*, New Haven: Yale University Press.

Huntington, S. (2002) *The Clash of Civilizations*, 2nd edn, New York: Simon & Schuster.

Hurd, I. (2008) 'Constructivism', in C. Reus-Smit & D. Snidal (eds), *The Oxford Handbook of International Relations*, Oxford: Oxford University Press, pp. 298–316.

Husain, M. Z. & Shumock, S. (2006) 'Kurdish Ethnonationalism: A Concise Overview', in: S. Saha (ed.), *Perspectives on Contemporary Ethnic Conflict: Primal Violence or the Politics of Conviction*, Lanham: Lexington Books, pp. 269–294.

Hutchinson, J. (2004) *Nations as Zones of Conflict*, London: Sage.

Huysman, M. (2016) 'Communities of Practice: Facilitating Social Learning while Frustrating Organisational Learning', in H. Tsoukas & N. Mylonopoulos (eds), *Organisations as Knowledge Systems: Knowledge, Learning, and Dynamic Capabilities*, Basingstoke. Palgrave Macmillan, pp. 67–85.

Hyams, E. (1979) *Pierre-Joseph Proudhon*, London: John Murray.

Ibrahim, F. (1983) *Die kurdische Nationalbewegung im Irak: Eine Fallstudie zur Problematik ethnischer Konflikte in der Dritten Welt*, Berlin: Klaus Schwarz Verlag.

Ikenberry, G., Knock, T., Slaughter, A. M. & Smith, T. (2009) *The Crisis of American Foreign Policy: Wilsonianism in the Twenty-first century*, Princeton: Princeton University Press.

Imber, C. (2009) *The Ottoman Empire, 1300–1650: The Structure of Power*, 2nd edn, Basingstoke: Palgrave Macmillan.

Imset, I. G. (1992) *The PKK: A Report on Separatist Violence in Turkey 1973–1992*, Ankara: Turkish Daily News Publications.

International Crisis Group – ICG (2005a) 'Iraq: Don't Rush the Constitution', *Middle East Report* 42, available at: www.crisisgroup.org/~/media/Files/Middle%20East%20 North%20Africa/Iraq%20Syria%20Lebanon/Iraq/Iraq%20Dont%20Rush%20the%20 Constitution.pdf.

International Crisis Group – ICG (2005b) 'Unmaking Iraq: A Constitutional Process Gone Awry', *Middle East Briefing* 19, available at: www.crisisgroup.org/~/media/ Files/Middle%20East%20North%20Africa/Iraq%20Syria%20Lebanon/Iraq/Iraq%20 Dont%20Rush%20the%20Constitution.pdf.

International Crisis Group – ICG (2006) 'The Next Iraqi War? Sectarianism and Civil Conflict', *Middle East Report* 52, available at: www.crisisgroup.org/~/media/Files/ Middle%20East%20North%20Africa/Iraq%20Syria%20Lebanon/Iraq/52_the_next_ iraqi_war_sectarianism_and_civil_conflict.

International Crisis Group – ICG (2008) 'Turkey and Iraqi Kurds: Conflict or Cooperation?' *Middle East Report* 81, available at: www.crisisgroup.org/~/media/ Files/Middle%20East%20North%20Africa/Iraq%20Syria%20Lebanon/Iraq/81Turkey %20and%20Iraqi%20Kurds%20Conflict%20or%20Cooperation.pdf.

International Crisis Group – ICG (2010) 'Iraq's Uncertain Future: Elections and beyond', *Middle East Report* 94, available at: www.crisisgroup.org/~/media/Files/Middle%20 East%20North%20Africa/Iraq%20Syria%20Lebanon/Iraq/94_iraq_s_uncertain_ future___elections_and_beyond.pdf.

International Crisis Group – ICG (2011) 'Turkey: Ending the PKK Insurgency', *Europe Report* 213, available at: www.crisisgroup.org/~/media/Files/europe/turkeycyprus/ turkey/213%20Turkey%20%20Ending%20the%20PKK%20Insurgency.pdf.

International Crisis Group – ICG (2012a) 'Turkey: The PKK and a Kurdish Settlement', *Europe Report* 219, available at: www.crisisgroup.org/~/media/Files/europe/turkey- cyprus/turkey/219-turkey-the-pkk-and-a-kurdish-settlement.pdf.

International Crisis Group – ICG (2012b) 'Iraq's Secular Opposition: The Rise and Decline of Al-Iraqiya', *Middle East Report*, 127, available at: www.crisisgroup.org/~/media/ Files/Middle%20East%20North%20Africa/Iraq%20Syria%20Lebanon/Iraq/127-iraqs- secular-opposition-the-rise-and-decline-of-al-iraqiya.pdf.

International Crisis Group – ICG (2013) 'Syria's Kurds: A Struggle within a Struggle', *Middle East and North Africa Report* 136, available at: www.crisisgroup.org/middle- east-north-africa/eastern-mediterranean/syria/syria-s-kurds-struggle-within-struggle.

International Crisis Group – ICG (2014a) 'Flight of Icarus? The PYD's Precarious Rise in Syria', *Middle East and North Africa Report* 151, available at: www.crisisgroup.org/ middle-east-north-africa/eastern-mediterranean/syria/flight-icarus-pyd-s-precarious- rise-syria.

International Crisis Group – ICG (2014b) 'The Rising Costs of Turkey's Syrian Quag- mire', *Europe Report* 230, available at: www.crisisgroup.org/europe-central-asia/ western-europemediterranean/turkey/rising-costs-turkey-s-syrian-quagmire.

International Crisis Group – ICG (2014c) 'Turkey and the PKK: Saving the Peace Process', *Europe Report* 234, available at: https://d2071andvip0wj.cloudfront.net/ turkey-and-the-pkk-saving-the-peace-process.pdf.

International Crisis Group – ICG (2016) 'Turkey's PKK Conflict: The Rising Toll', regularly updated interactive feature, accessed 30 June, available at: www.crisisgroup.be/interactives/turkey/.

Isajiw, W. (2000) 'Approaches to Ethnic Conflict Resolution: Paradigms and Principles', *International Journal of Intercultural Relations*, 24(1), pp. 105–124.

Izady, M. (1992) *The Kurds: A Concise Handbook*, Washington: Crane Russak.

Jabar, F. A. (1992) 'Why the Uprisings Failed', MERIP, *Middle East Report*, 176, available at: www.merip.org/mer/mer176/why-uprisings-failed.

Jackson, R. (1996) *Quasi-States: Sovereignty, International Relations and the Third World*, 2nd edn, Cambridge: Cambridge University Press.

Jackson, R. (2007) *Sovereignty: The Evolution of an Idea*, Cambridge: Polity Press.

Jackson, R. & Sørensen, G. (2012) *Introduction to International Relations: Theories and Approaches*, 5th edn, Oxford: Oxford University Press.

Jacoby, T. (2003) 'For the People, of the People and by the Military: The Regime Structure of Modern Turkey', *Political Studies*, 51(4), pp. 669–685.

Jacoby, T. (2005) 'Semi-Authoritarian Incorporation and Autocratic Militarism in Turkey', *Development and Change*, 36(4), pp. 641–665.

James, A. (1999) 'The Practice of Sovereign Statehood in Contemporary International Society', *Political Studies*, 47(3), pp. 457–473.

Jawad, S. N. (1981) *Iraq and the Kurdish Question 1958–1970*, London: Ithaca Press.

Jawad, S. N. (2013) 'The Iraqi Constitution: Structural Flaws and Political Implications', *London School of Economics Middle East Centre Paper Series* 1, available at: www.lse.ac.uk/middleEastCentre/publications/PaperSeries/ SaadJawad.pdf.

Jenkins, R. (2002) *Pierre Bourdieu*, London: Routledge.

Jenkins, R. (2008a) *Rethinking Ethnicity: Arguments and Exploration*, 2nd edn, London: Sage.

Jenkins, R. (2008b) *Social Identity*, 3rd edn, London: Routledge.

Jenne, E. (2006) *Ethnic Bargaining: The Paradox of Minority Empowerment*, Ithaca: Cornell University Press.

Jenne, E. (2009) 'The Paradox of Ethnic Partition: Lessons from De facto Partition in Bosnia and Kosovo', *Regional and Federal Studies*, 19(2), pp. 273–289.

Jenne, E. (2010) 'Ethnic Partition under the League of Nations: The Cases of Population Exchanges in the Interwar Balkans', in E. Chenoweth & A. Lawrence (eds), *Rethinking Violence: States and Non-State Actors in Conflict*, Cambridge, MA: MIT Press, pp. 117–140.

Jenne, E. (2012) 'When Will We Part with Partition Theory? Flawed Premises and Improbable Longevity of the Theory of Ethnic Partition', *Ethnopolitics*, 11(3), pp. 255–267.

Jermier, J. M. (1993) 'Introduction: Charismatic Leadership – Neo-Weberian Perspectives', *The Leadership Quarterly*, 4(3–4), pp. 217–233.

Jervis, R. (1978) *Perception and Misperception in International Politics*, Princeton: Princeton University Press.

Jesse, N. & Williams, K. (2010) *Ethnic Conflict: A Systematic Approach to Cases of Conflict*, Washington: CQ Press.

Johnson, B. (1981) 'Translator's Introduction', in J. Derrida (ed.), *Dissemination*, Chicago: University of Chicago Press.

Jones, S. (2006) *Antonio Gramsci*, London: Routledge.

Jongerden, J. (2007) *The Settlement Issues in Turkey and the Kurds: An Analysis of Spatial Politics, Modernity and War*, Leiden: Brill.

Jongerden, J. & Akkaya, A. H. (2011) 'Born from the Left: The Making of the PKK', in J. Jongerden & M. Casier (eds), *Nationalism and Politics in Turkey: Political Islam, Kemalism and the Kurdish Issue*, London: Routledge, pp. 123–142.

Joras, U. & Schetter, C. (2004) 'Hidden Ties: Similarities between Research and Policy Approaches to Ethnic Conflicts', in A. Wimmer *et al.* (eds), *Facing Ethnic Conflicts. Towards a New Realism*, Lanham: Rowman & Littlefield, pp. 315–332.

Jung, D. (2001) 'The Sèvres Syndrome: Turkish Foreign Policy and Its Historical Legacy', in B. Muller (ed.), *Oil and Water: Cooperative Security in the Persian Gulf*, London: I.B. Tauris, pp. 131–159.

Jung, D. & Piccoli, W. (2001) *Turkey at the Crossroads: Ottoman Legacies and a Greater Middle East*, London: Zed Books.

Jwaideh, W. (2006 [1960]) *The Kurdish National Movement: Its Origins and Development*, Syracuse: Syracuse University Press.

Kaldor, M. (2007) *New and Old Wars: Organised Violence in a Global Era*, 2nd edn, Cambridge: Polity.

Kalyvas, S. N. (2001) '"New" and "Old" Civil Wars: A Valid Distinction?', *World Politics*, 54(1), pp. 99–118.

Kaplan, R. (1994) *Balkan Ghosts: A Journey through History*, 2nd edn, New York: St. Martin's Press.

Kapsis, J. E. (2006) 'The Failure of US-Turkish Pre-Iraq War Negotiations: An Overconfident United States, Political Mismanagement, and a Conflicted Military', *Middle East Review of International Affairs*, 10(3), pp. 33–45.

Kardaş, S. (2013) 'Turkey: A Regional Power Facing a Changing International System', *Turkish Studies*, 14(4), pp. 637–660.

Kardaş, S. (2016) 'Between a Hard Place and the United States: Turkey's Syria Policy ahead of the Geneva Talks', The German Marshall Fund of the United States, *On Turkey*, 3 February, available at: www.gmfus.org/publications/between-hard-place-and-united-states.

Karpat, K. (1976) *The Gecekondu: Rural Migration and Urbanization*, Cambridge, UK: Cambridge University Press.

Karpat, K. (2004) *Studies on Turkish Politics and Society: Selected Articles and Essays*, Leiden: Brill.

Kaufman, S. (1996a) 'An "International" Theory of Inter-Ethnic War', *Review of International Studies*, 22(2), pp. 149–171.

Kaufman, S. (1996b) 'Spiraling to Ethnic War: Elites, Masses, and Moscow in Moldova's Civil War', *International Security*, 21(2), pp. 108–138.

Kaufman, S. (2001) *Modern Hatreds: The Symbolic Politics of Ethnic War*, Ithaca: Cornell University Press.

Kaufman, S., Little, R., & Wohlforth, W. (2007) *The Balance of Power in World Politics*, Basingstoke: Palgrave Macmillan.

Kaufmann, C. (1996) 'Possible and Impossible Solutions to Ethnic Civil Wars', *International Security*, 20(4), pp. 136–175.

Kaufmann, C. (1998) 'When All Else Fails: Ethnic Population Transfers and Partitions in the Twentieth Century', *International Security*, 23(2), pp. 120–156.

Kaufmann, C. (2006) 'Separating Iraqis, Saving Iraq', *Foreign Affairs*, 85(4), pp. 156–160.

Kaya, S. (2009) 'The Rise and Decline of the Turkish "Deep State": The Ergenekon Case', *Insight Turkey*, 11(4), pp. 99–113.

Keane, F. (1996) *Seasons of Blood: A Rwandan Journey*, London: Penguin Books.

Kecmanovic, D. (1996) *The Mass Psychology of Ethnonationalism*, New York: Plenum Press.

Kecmanovic, D. (2002) *Ethnic Times. Exploring Ethnonationalism in the Former Yugoslavia*, Westport: Praeger.

Kedourie, E (1994 [1960]) *Nationalism*, 4th edn, Oxford: Blackwell.

Keeler, S. (2007) *'There Has Been Enough Crying and now I Want to Dance': Belonging, Cosmopolitanism and Resistance in London's Kurdish Diasporic Spaces*, unpublished PhD thesis, University of Kent.

Kent, M. (1976) *Oil and Empire: British Policy and Mesopotamian Oil, 1900–1920*, London: Macmillan.

Keohane, R. (1984) *After Hegemony: Cooperation and Discord in the World Political Economy*, Princeton: Princeton University Press.

Keohane, R. (1989) *International Institutions and State Power: Essays in International Relations Theory*, Boulder: Westview Press.

Keohane, R. & Nye, J. (2001) *Power and Interdependence*, 3rd edn, New York: Longman.

Khan, S. (2015) 'The Transformation of Turkish Foreign Policy towards the Middle East', *Policy Perspectives*, 12(1), pp. 31–50.

Kilcullen, D. (2010) *Counterinsurgency*, London: Hurst.

Kirişçi, K. (1993) '"Provide Comfort" and Turkey: Decision Making for Refugee Assistance', *Low Intensity Conflict and Law Enforcement*, 2(2), pp. 227–253.

Kirişçi, K. (1996) 'Security for States vs. Refugees: Operation Provide Comfort and the 1991 Mass Influx of Refugees from Northern Iraq into Turkey', *Refuge: Canada's Journal on Refugees*, 15(3), pp. 18–22.

Kirişçi, K. (2006) 'Turkey's Foreign Policy in Turbulent Times', *Chaillot Paper*, Nr. 92.

Kirişçi, K. & Winrow, G. (1997) *The Kurdish Question and Turkey: An Example of a Trans-state Ethnic Conflict*, London: Frank Cass.

Kissinger, H. (2003) *Diplomacy*, 5th edn, New York: Simon & Schuster.

Klein, J. (2011) *The Margins of Empire: Kurdish Militias in the Ottoman Tribal Zone*, Stanford: Stanford University Press.

Knutsen, T. (1999) *The Rise and Fall of World Orders*, Manchester: Manchester University Press.

Koohi-Kamali, F. (2007) 'The Kurdish Republic in Mahabad: Formation of a National Movement', in M. Ahmed & M. Gunter (eds), *The Evolution of Kurdish Nationalism*, Costa Mesa: Mazda Publishers, pp. 225–259.

Korn, D. (1994) 'The Last Years of Mustafa Barzani', *The Middle East Quarterly*, 1(2), pp. 12–27.

Kowert, P. (2012) 'Completing the Ideational Triangle: Identity, Choice, and Obligation in International Relations', in V. Shannon & P. Kowert (eds), *Psychology and Constructivism in International Relations*, Ann Arbor: University of Michigan Press, pp. 30–56.

Krasner, S. (1983) *International Regimes*, Ithaca: Cornell University Press.

Krasner, S. (1999) *Sovereignty: Organized Hypocrisy*, Princeton: Princeton University Press.

Krasner, S. (2009) *Power, the State, and Sovereignty: Essays on International Relations*, London: Routledge.

Kreijen, G. (2004) *State Failure, Sovereignty and Effectiveness*, Leiden: Martinus Nijhoff Publishers.

Kristeva, J. (1993) *Nations without Nationalism*, New York: Columbia University Press.

Kubicek, P. (2011) 'The 2011 Elections and Prospects for Change in Turkey', *Mediterranean Politics*, 16(3), pp. 443–448.

Kuhn, T. (1996 [1962]) *The Structure of Scientific Revolutions*, 3rd edn, Chicago: University of Chicago Press.

Kumar, R. (1997) 'The Troubled History of Partition', *Foreign Affairs*, 76(1), pp. 22–34.

Kurki, M. (2008) *Causation in International Relations: Reclaiming Causal Analysis*, Cambridge: Cambridge University Press.

Kuru, A. (2015) 'Turkey's Failed Policy toward the Arab Spring: Three Levels of Analysis', *Mediterranean Quarterly*, 26(3), pp. 94–116.

Kushner, D. (1977) *The Rise of Turkish Nationalism 1876–1908*, London: Frank Cass.

Lacher, H. (2003) 'Putting the State in Its Place: The Critique of State-centrism and Its Limits', *Review of International Studies*, 29, pp. 521–541.

Laclau, E. & Mouffe, C. (1985) *Hegemony and Socialist Strategy: Towards a Radical Democratic Politics*, London: Verso.

Laclau, E. & Mouffe, C. (1990) *New Reflections on the Revolution of Our Time*, London: Verso.

Laclau, E. & Mouffe, C. (2001) 'Hegemony: The Genealogy of a Concept', in S. Seidman & J. Alexander (eds), *The New Social Theory Reader: Contemporary Debates*, London: Routledge, pp. 76–87.

La Feber, W. (1993) *Inevitable Revolutions: The United States in Central America*, 3rd edn, New York: W. W. Norton.

Laitin, D. & Posner, D. (2001) 'The Implications of Constructivism for Constructing Ethnic Fractionalization Indices', American Political Science Association, *Comparative Politics Newsletter*, 12(1), pp. 13–17.

Laizer, S. (1996) *Martyrs, Traitors and Patriots: Kurdistan after the Gulf War*, London: Zed Books.

Lake, D. (2008) 'The State and International Relations', in C. Reus-Smit & D. Snidal (eds), *The Oxford Handbook of International Relations*, Oxford: Oxford University Press, pp. 41–61.

Lake, D. & Rothchild, D. (1996) 'Containing Fear: The Origins and Management of Ethnic Conflict', *International Security*, 21(2), pp. 41–75.

Landau, J. (1974) *Radical Politics in Modern Turkey*, Leiden: Brill.

Lane, J. (2012) *Bourdieu's Politics: Problems and Possibilities*, 2nd edn, London: Routledge.

Laqueur, W. (2009 [1976]) *Guerrilla Warfare: A Historical and Critical Study*, 7th edn, New Brunswick: Transaction Publishers.

Lawrence, Q. (2009) *Invisible Nation: How the Kurds' Quest for Statehood is Shaping Iraq and the Middle East*, New York: Walker & Co.

Lee, R. L. M. (1992) 'Two Faces of Charisma: Structure, System, and Praxis in Islam and Hinduism', *Journal for the Theory of Social Behaviour*, 22(1), pp. 41–62.

Leezenberg, M. (2000) 'Humanitarian Aid in Iraqi Kurdistan', *Cahiers d'études sur la Méditerranée orientale et le monde turco-iranien* 29, available at: http://kurdish congress.org/data/upimages/subfolders/PDF/Economics%20Leezenberg2000%20 Humanitarian%20Aid%20in%20Iraqi%20Kurdistan.pdf.

Leezenberg, M. (2003) 'Economy and Society in Iraqi Kurdistan: Fragile Institutions and Enduring Trends', in T Dodge & S. Simon (eds), *Iraq at the Crossroads: State and Society in the Shadow of Regime Change*, London: International Institute for Strategic Studies, *Adelphi Papers*, 354, pp. 149–160.

Leezenberg, M. (2005) 'Iraqi Kurdistan: Contours of a Post-Civil War Society', *Third World Quarterly*, 26(4–5), pp. 631–647.

Legro, J. (2005) *Rethinking the World: Great Power Strategies and International Order*, Ithaca: Cornell University Press.

Lenin, V. I. (1978 [1905/6]) *Collected Works, vol. X*, London: Lawrence & Wishart.

Leoussi, A. & Grosby, S. (2006) *Nationalism and Ethnosymbolism: History, Culture and Ethnicity in the Formation of Nations*, Edinburgh: Edinburgh University Press.

Lessa, L. (2006) 'Discursive Struggles within Social Welfare: Restaging Teen Motherhood', *British Journal of Social Work*, 36(2), pp. 283–298.

Linklater, A. (1990) *Men and Citizens in the Theory of International Relations*, 2nd edn, Basingstoke: Macmillan.

Linklater, A. (1996) 'Citizenship and Sovereignty in the Post-Westphalian State', *European Journal of International Relations*, 2(1), pp. 77–103.

Linklater, A. (1998) *The Transformation of Political Community: Ethical Foundations of the Post-Westphalian Era*, Cambridge: Polity Press.

Linklater, A. (2001) 'Citizenship, Humanity, and Cosmopolitan Harm Conventions', *International Political Science Review*, 22(3), pp. 261–277.

Lipovsky, I. (1992) *The Socialist Movement in Turkey 1960–1980*, Leiden: Brill.

Little, R. (1989) 'Deconstructing the Balance of Power: Two Traditions of Thought', *Review of International Studies*, 15(2), pp. 87–100.

Little, R. (1997) 'The Growing Relevance of Pluralism?' In S. Smith, K. Booth & M. Zalewski (eds), *International Theory: Positivism and Beyond*, 2nd edn, Cambridge: Cambridge University Press, pp. 66–86.

Little, R. (2007) *The Balance of Power in International Relations: Metaphors, Myths and Models*, Cambridge, UK: Cambridge University Press.

Locke, T. (2004) *Critical Discourse Analysis*, London: Continuum.

Louis, R. & Owen, R. (2002) *A Revolutionary Year: The Middle East in 1958*, London: I.B. Tauris.

Lowe, R. (2006) 'The Syrian Kurds: A People Discovered', The Royal Institute of International Affairs at Chatham House, *Middle East Programme Briefing Paper*, 6(1), pp. 1–7.

Lowe, R. (2007) 'Kurdish Nationalism in Syria', M. Ahmad & M. Gunter (eds), *The Evolution of Kurdish Nationalism*, Costa Mesa: Mazda Press, pp. 287–308.

Lowe, R. (2010) 'The *Serhildan* and the Kurdish National Story in Syria', in R. Lowe & G. Stansfield (eds), *The Kurdish Policy Imperative*, London: Chatham House, pp. 161–179.

Lowe, R. (2014) 'The Emergence of Western Kurdistan and the Future of Syria', in D. Romano & M. Gunes (eds), *Conflict, Democratization, and the Kurds in the Middle East: Turkey, Iran, Iraq, and Syria*, Basingstoke: Palgrave Macmillan, pp. 225–245.

Lowe, R. &. Gunes, C. (2015) 'The Impact of the Syrian War on Kurdish Politics across the Middle East', The Royal Institute of International Affairs at Chatham House, *Research Paper*, July, available at: www.chathamhouse.org/sites/files/chathamhouse/field/field_document/20150723SyriaKurdsGunesLowe.pdf.

Lundgren, Å. (2007) *The Unwelcome Neighbour: Turkey's Kurdish Policy*, London: I.B. Tauris.

Luciani, G. (2013) 'Oil and Political Economy in the International Relations of the Middle East', in L. Fawcett (ed.), *International Relations of the Middle East*, 3rd edn, Oxford: Oxford University Press, pp. 103–126.

Luciani, G. & Beblawi, H. (1987) *The Rentier State*, London: Croom Helm.

Lyon, A. J. & Uçarer, E. M. (2001) 'Mobilizing Ethnic Conflict: Kurdish Separatism in Germany and the PKK', *Ethnic and Racial Studies*, 24(6), pp. 925–948.

Mahdavy, H. (1970) 'The Patterns and Problems of Economic Development in Rentier States: The Case of Iran', in M. Cook (ed.), *Studies in the Economic History of the Middle East*, Oxford: Oxford University Press.

Mahr, H. (1971) *Die Baath Partei: Portrait einer panarabischen Bewegung*, München: G. Olzog.

Malešević, S. (2004) *The Sociology of Ethnicity*, London: Sage.

Malešević, S. (2006a) *Identity as Ideology: Understanding Ethnicity and Nationalism*, Basingstoke: Palgrave Macmillan.

Malešević, S. (2006b) 'Ethnicity Without Groups, Reviewed by Siniša Malešević', *Nations and Nationalism*, 12(4), pp. 699–700.

Malešević, S. (2010) *The Sociology of War and Violence*, Cambridge: Cambridge University Press.

Malmvig, H. (2006) *State Sovereignty and Intervention: A Discourse Analysis of Interventionary and Non-Interventionary Practices in Kosovo and Algeria*, London: Routledge.

Mamdani, M. (2001) *When Victims Become Killers: Colonialism, Nativism, and the Genocide in Rwanda*, Princeton: Princeton University Press.

Mann, M. (1983) *The Macmillan Student Encyclopaedia of Sociology*, New York: Macmillan.

Mann, M. (1986) *The Sources of Social Power, Volume I: A History of Power from the Beginning to AD 1760*, Cambridge: Cambridge University Press.

Mann, M. (1993) *The Sources of Social Power, Volume II: The Rise of Classes and Nation States, 1760–1914*, Cambridge: Cambridge University Press.

Mao, T. (2005 [1961]) *On Guerrilla Warfare*, 5th edn, Champaign: University of Illinois Press.

Maoz, Z. (1997) 'Domestic Political Change and Strategic Response: The Impact of Domestic Conflict on State Behaviour, 1816–1986', in D. Carment & P. James (eds), *Wars in the Midst of Peace: The International Politics of Ethnic Conflict*, Pittsburgh: University of Pittsburgh Press, pp. 116–147.

Marcus, A. (2007a) *Blood and Belief: The PKK and the Kurdish Fight for Independence*, New York: New York University Press.

Marcus, A. (2007b) 'Turkey's PKK: Rise, Fall, Rise Again?' *World Policy Journal*, 24(1), pp. 75–84.

Marr, P. (2011) *The Modern History of Iraq*, 3rd edn, Boulder: Westview Press.

McCants, W. (2015) *The ISIS Apocalypse: The History, Strategy, and Doomsday Vision of the Islamic State*, New York: Palgrave Macmillan.

McDowall, D. (2007) *A Modern History of the Kurds*, 3rd edn, London: I.B. Tauris.

McGarry, J. (2005a) 'Can Federalism Help to Manage Ethnic and National Diversity?' *Federations*, 5(A1), pp. 15–17, available at: www.forumfed.org/libdocs/Federations/V5N1SEen-int-McGarry.pdf.

McGarry, J. (2005b) 'Canadian Lessons for Iraq', in B. O'Leary, J. McGarry & K. Salih (eds), *The Future of Kurdistan in Iraq*, Philadelphia: University of Pennsylvania Press, pp. 92–115.

McGarry, J. & O'Leary, B. (1993) *The Politics of Ethnic Conflict Regulation: Case Studies of Protracted Ethnic Conflicts*, London: Routledge.

McGarry, J. & O'Leary, B. (2005) 'Federation as a Method of Ethnic Conflict Regulation', in S. Noel (ed.) From Power Sharing to Democracy: Post-Conflict Institutions in Ethnically Divided Societies, Toronto: McGill-Queens University Press, pp. 263–296.

McGarry, J. & O'Leary, B. (2007) 'Iraq's Constitution of 2005: Liberal Consociation as Political Prescription', *International Journal of Constitutional Law*, 5(4), pp. 670–698.

McQuillan, M. (2009) 'Introduction: Five Stages for Deconstruction', in M. McQuillan (ed.), *Deconstruction: A Reader*, Edinburgh: University of Edinburgh Press, pp. 1–46.

McSweeney, B. (1996) 'Identity and Security: Buzan and the Copenhagen School', *Review of International Studies*, 22(1), pp. 81–93.

McSweeney, B. (1999) *Security, Identity, and Interests: A Sociology of International Relations*, Cambridge: Cambridge University Press.

Mearsheimer, J. (2001) *The Tragedy of Great Power Politics*, New York: W.W. Norton.

Mejcher, H. (1976) *Imperial Quest for Oil: Iraq 1910–1928*, London: Ithaca Press.

Melander, E., Öberg, M., & Hall, J. (2009) 'Are "New Wars" More Atrocious? Battle Severity, Civilians Killed and Forced Migration before and after the End of the Cold War, *European Journal of International Relations*, 15(3), pp. 505–536.

Melvern, L. (2000) *A People Betrayed: The Role of the West in Rwanda's Genocide*, London: Zed Books.

Meyer, J. W., Boli, J., Thomas, G. & Ramirez, F. (1997) 'World Society and the Nation-State', *American Journal of Sociology*, 103(1), pp. 144–181.

Michels, R. (1915) *Political Parties*, New York: Hearst's International Library.

Miller, B. (2010) 'Explaining Changes in US Grand Strategy: 9/11, the Rise of Offensive Liberalism, and the War in Iraq', *Security Studies* 19(1), pp. 26–65.

Milton-Edwards, B. (2011) *Contemporary Politics in the Middle East*, 3rd edn, Cambridge: Polity.

Milton-Edwards, B. & Hinchcliffe, P. (2008) *Conflicts in the Middle East since 1945*, 3rd edn, London: Routledge.

Morgenthau, H. J. (2005 [1951]) *Politics among Nations: The Struggle for Power and Peace*, 7th edn, New York: McGraw-Hill.

Morrow, J. (2005) 'Iraq's Constitutional Process II: An Opportunity Lost', United States Institute of Peace, *Special Report* 155, available at: www.usip.org/publications/iraqs-constitutional-process-ii-opportunity-lost-arabic-edition.

Morton, S. (2007) *Gayatri Spivak: Ethics, Subalternity and the Critique of Postcolonial Reason*, Cambridge: Polity.

Mosca, G. (1939) *The Ruling Class*, New York: McGraw Hill.

Müller, A., Tausch, A. & Zulehner, P. (2000) *Global Capitalism, Liberation Theology and the Social Sciences: An Analysis of the Contradictions of Modernity at the Turn of the Millennium*, Hauppauge: Nova Science Publishers.

Münkler, H. (2005) *The New Wars*, Cambridge: Polity.

Murinson, A. (2006) 'The Strategic Depth Doctrine of Turkish Foreign Policy', *Middle Eastern Studies*, 42(6), pp. 945–964.

Musil, P. A. (2011) *Authoritarian Party Structures and Democratic Political Setting in Turkey*, Basingstoke: Palgrave Macmillan.

Nagata, J. (1981) 'In Defense of Ethnic Boundaries: The Changing Myths and Charters of Malay Identity', in C. F. Keyes (ed.), *Ethnic Change*, Seattle: University of Washington Press, pp. 87–118.

Nairn, T. (1981) *The Break-up of Britain: Crisis and Neo-nationalism*, 2nd edn, London: Verso.

Natali, D. (2005) *The Kurds and the State: Evolving National Identity in Iraq, Turkey, and Iran*, Syracuse: Syracuse University Press.

Natali, D. (2008) 'The Kirkuk Conundrum', *Ethnopolitics* 7(4), pp. 433–443.

Natali, D. (2010) *The Kurdish Quasi-State: Development and Dependency in Post-Gulf War Iraq*, Syracuse: Syracuse University Press.

Natali, D. (2015) 'Stalemate, not Statehood for Iraqi Kurdistan', The Brookings Institution, *Markaz – Middle East Policy & Politics* 2 November, available at: www. brookings.edu/blogs/markaz/posts/2015/11/02-stalemate-not-statehood-iraqi-kurdistan.

Neumann, I. B. (1996) 'Self and Other in International Relations', *European Journal of International Relations*, 2(2), pp. 139–174.

Neumann, I. B. (2002) 'Returning Practice to the Linguistic Turn: The Case of Diplomacy', *Millennium*, 31(3), pp. 627–651.

Neumann, I. B. (2007) '"A Speech that the Entire Ministry May Stand for," or Why Diplomats Never Produce Anything New', *International Political Sociology*, 1(2), pp. 183–200.

Neumann, I. B. (2012) *At Home with the Diplomats: Inside a European Foreign Ministry*, Ithaca: Cornell University Press.

Neuwirth, R. (2004) *Shadow Cities: A Billion Squatters, a New Urban World*, London: Routledge.

Newman, E. (2004) 'The "New Wars" Debate: A Historical Perspective is Needed', *Security Dialogue*, 35(2), pp. 173–189.

Nezan, K. (1993) 'Kurdistan in Turkey', in G. Chaliand (ed.), *A People without a Country: The Kurds and Kurdistan*, 2nd edn, London: Zed Press, pp. 38–71.

Norris, C. (2002) *Deconstruction*, London: Routledge, 3rd edition.

Nye, R. P. (1977) Civil-Military Confrontation in Turkey: The 1973 Presidential Election', *International Journal of Middle East Studies*, 8(2), pp. 209–228.

O'Ballance, E. (1973) *The Kurdish Revolt 1961–1970*, London: Faber & Faber.

O'Ballance, E. (1996) *The Kurdish Struggle, 1920–1994*, Basingstoke: Palgrave Macmillan.

Öcalan, A. (2008) *War and Peace in Kurdistan*, London: Transmedia Publishing.

Öcalan, A. (2011a) *Prison Writings: The PKK and the Kurdish Question in the 21st century*, London: Transmedia Publishing.

Öcalan, A. (2011b) *The Road Map to Negotiations*, Neuss: Mesopotamien Verlag.

Öcalan, A. (2012) *Democratic Confederalism*, London: Transmedia Publishing.

Öktem, K. (2011) *Angry Nation: Turkey since 1989*, London: Zed Books.

O'Leary, B. (2009) 'Preface', in B. O'Leary, J. McGarry & K. Salih (eds), *The Future of Kurdistan in Iraq*, Philadelphia: University of Pennsylvania Press, pp. XI–XXI.

O'Leary, B., McGarry, J., & Salih, K. (2005) *The Future of Kurdistan in Iraq*, Philadelphia: University of Pennsylvania Press.

O'Leary, B. & Salih, K. (2005) 'The Denial, Resurrection, and Affirmation of Kurdistan', in B. O'Leary, J. McGarry & K. Salih (eds), *The Future of Kurdistan in Iraq*, Philadelphia: University of Pennsylvania Press, pp. 3–45.

Olson, R. (1989) *The Emergence of Kurdish Nationalism and the Sheikh Said Rebellion, 1880–1925*, Austin: University of Texas Press.

Olson, R. (1992) 'Battle for Kurdistan: The Church-Cox Correspondence Regarding the Creation of the State of Iraq 1921–1923', *Kurdish Studies*, 5(1/2), pp. 29–44.

Olson, R. (1997) 'Turkey-Syria Relations since the Gulf War: Kurds and Water, *Middle East Policy*, 5(2), pp. 168–193.

Olson, R. (1998) *The Kurdish Question and Turkish-Iranian Relations: From World War I to 1998*, Costa Mesa: Mazda Press.

Olson, R. (2000) 'Turkish and Syrian Relations since the Gulf War: The Kurdish Question and the Water Problem', in F. Ibrahim & G. Gürbey (eds), *The Kurdish Conflict in Turkey: Obstacles and Chances for Peace and Democracy*, Münster: LIT Verlag, pp. 119–150.

Olson, R. (2001) *Turkey's Relations with Iran, Syria, Israel, and Russia: The Kurdish and Islamist Questions*, Costa Mesa: Mazda Press.

Olson, R. (2004) *Turkey-Iran Relations, 1979–2004: Revolution, Ideology, War, Coups and Geopolitics*, Costa Mesa: Mazda Press.

Olson, R. (2005a) *The Goat and the Butcher: Nationalism and State-Formation in Kurdistan-Iraq since the Iraqi War*, Costa Mesa: Mazda Press.

Olson, R. (2005b) 'Turkey and Kurdistan-Iraq Relations: The Consolidation of Iraqi Kurdish Nationalism, 2003–2004', in M. Gunter & M. A. Ahmed (eds), *The Kurdish Question and the 2003 Iraqi War*, Costa Mesa: Mazda Press, pp. 97–122.

Olson, R. (2007) 'Kurdish Nationalism, Capitalism, and State Formation in Kurdistan-Iraq', in M. A. Ahmed & M. Gunter (eds), *The Evolution of Kurdish Nationalism*, Costa Mesa: Mazda Press, pp. 186–224.

Olson, R. (2009) *Blood, Belief, and Ballots: The Management of Kurdish Nationalism in Turkey, 2007–2009*, Costa Mesa: Mazda Press.

Olzak, S. (2006) *The Global Dynamics of Racial and Ethnic Mobilization*, Stanford: Stanford University Press.

Öniş, Z. (2012) 'Turkey and the Arab Spring: Between Ethics and Self-Interest', *Insight Turkey*, 14(3), pp. 45–63.

Onuf, N. (1989) *World of Our Making: Rules and Rule in Social Theory and International Relations*, Columbia: University of South Carolina Press.

Örnek, C. & Üngör, Ç. (2013) 'Turkey's Cold War: Global Influences, Local Manifestations', in C. Örnek & Ç. Üngör (eds), *Turkey in the Cold War: Ideology and Culture*, Basingstoke: Palgrave Macmillan, pp. 1–20.

O'Shea, M. (2004) *Trapped between the Map and Reality: Geography and Perceptions of Kurdistan*, London: Routledge.

Owen, R. (2004) *State, Power and Politics in the Making of the Modern Middle East*, 3rd edn, London: Routledge.

Owens, M. T. (2009) 'The Bush Doctrine: The Foreign Policy of Republican Empire', *Orbis*, 53(1), pp. 23–40.

Owtram, F. (2012) 'The Kurdistan Region of Iraq: Ethnic Conflict and the Survival of Dynastic Republicanism in a De facto State', in H. Artens (ed.), 'De facto States and Ethnic Conflict', *P@x Online Bulletin* 21, Centre for Social Studies, University of Coimbra, pp. 13–15, available at: www.ces.uc.pt/publicacoes/ p@x/pdf/P@x21en.pdf.

Özcan, A. K. (2006) *Turkey's Kurds: A Theoretical Analysis of the PKK and Abdullah Öcalan*, London: Routledge.

Özkirimli, U. (2010) *Theories of Nationalism: A Critical Introduction*, Basingstoke: Palgrave Macmillan.

Özoğlu, H. (1996) 'State-Tribe Relations: Kurdish Tribalism in the 16th and 17th century Ottoman Empire', *British Journal of Middle Eastern Studies*, 23(1), pp. 5–27.

Özoğlu, H. (2004) *Kurdish Notables and the Ottoman State: Evolving Identities, Competing Loyalties, and Shifting Boundaries*, Albany: State of New York University Press.

Packer, G. (2005) *The Assassin's Gate: America in Iraq*, New York: Farrar, Straus & Giroux.

Pareto, V. (1976 [1902–1903]) *Sociological Writings*, 2nd edn, Oxford: Blackwell.

Pareto, V. (2009 [1901]) *The Rise and Fall of Elites: An Application of Theoretical Sociology*, 8th edn, New Brunswick: Transaction Publishers.

Paris, T. J. (1998) 'British Middle East Policy-Making after the First World War: The Lawrentian and Wilsonian Schools', *The Historical Journal*, 41(3), pp. 773–793.

Park, B. (2003) 'Strategic Location, Political Dislocation: Turkey, the United States, and Northern Iraq', *Middle East Review of International Affairs*, 7(2), pp. 11–23.

Park, B. (2005) *Turkey's Policy towards Northern Iraq: Problems and Perspectives*, London: International Institute for Strategic Studies, *Adelphi Papers*, 374.

Park, B. (2012a) *Modern Turkey: People, State, and Foreign Policy in a Globalised World*, London: Routledge.

Park, B. (2012b) 'Turkey, the US, and the KRG: Moving Parts and the Geopolitical Realities', *Insight Turkey*, 14(3), pp. 109–125.

Parla, T. (1998) 'Mercantile Militarism in Turkey, 1960–1998', *New Perspectives on Turkey* 19, pp. 29–52.

Parry, G. (1977) *Political Elites*, 5th edn, London: George Allen & Unwin.

Pascoe, P. (1990) *Relations of Rescue: The Search for Female Moral Authority in the American West 1874–1939*, Oxford: Oxford University Press.

Patrick, S. (2011) *Weak Links: Fragile States, Global Threats and International Security*, Oxford: Oxford University Press.

Pecheux, M. (1982) *Language, Semantics and Ideology*, New York: St. Martin's Press.

Peoples, C. & Vaughan-Williams, N. (2010) *Critical Security Studies: An Introduction*, London: Routledge.

Peters, G. (1998) *Comparative Politics: Theory and Methods*, New York: New York University Press.

Petersen, K. (2004) 'A Research Note: Reexamining Transnational Ethnic Alliances and Foreign Policy Behaviour', *International Interactions*, 30, pp. 25–42.

Phillips, C. (2012) 'Into the Quagmire: Turkey's Frustrated Syria Policy', The Royal Institute of International Affairs at Chatham House, *Briefing Paper*, December, available at: www.chathamhouse.org/sites/files/chathamhouse/public/Research/Middle%20East/1212bp_phillips.pdf.

Phillips, D. (2005) *Losing Iraq: Inside the Post-War Reconstruction Fiasco*, Boulder: Westview Press.

Phillips, D. (2007) 'Disarming, Demobilising, and Reintegrating the Kurdistan Workers' Party', National Committee on American Foreign Policy, Policy Paper.

Phillips, D. (2009) 'Confidence Building between Turks and Iraqi Kurds', Atlantic Council of the United States, Policy Report.

Phillips, D. (2015a) *The Kurdish Spring: A New Map of the Middle East*, New Brunswick: Transaction Publishers.

Piazza, A. (2008) 'Incubators of Terror: Do Failed States and Failing States Promote Transnational Terrorism?' *International Studies Quarterly*, 52(3), pp. 469–488.

Pope, N. & Pope, H. (1997) *Turkey Unveiled: Atatürk and After*, London: John Murray.

Porter, T. (1995) *Trust in Numbers: The Pursuit of Objectivity in Science and Public Life*, Princeton: Princeton University Press.

Posen, B. (1993) 'The Security Dilemma and Ethnic Conflict', in M. Brown (ed.), *Ethnic Conflict and International Security*, Princeton: Princeton University Press, pp. 103–124.

Posner, D. (2005a) 'The Implications of Constructivism for Studying the Relationship between Ethnic Diversity and Economic Growth', Paper delivered at the 2004 Annual Conference of the American Political Science Association, available at: www.sscnet.ucla.edu/ polisci/wgape/papers/7Posner.pdf.

Posner, D. (2005b) *Institutions and Ethnic Politics in Africa*, Cambridge: Cambridge University Press.

Potts, T. (2010) *Pierre Bourdieu*, London: Routledge.

Powell, C. L. (1996) *My American Journey*, New York: Ballantine Books.

Pouliot, V. (2008) 'The Logic of Practicality: A Theory of Practice of Security Communities', *International Organization*, 62(2), pp. 257–288.

Poulton, H. (1997) *Top Hat, Grey Wolf and the Crescent: Turkish Nationalism and the Turkish Republic*, London: Hurst.

Premnath, G. (2003) 'The Weak Sovereignty of the Postcolonial Nation-State', in A. Kumar *et al.* (eds), *World Bank Literature*, Minneapolis: University of Minnesota Press, pp. 253–264.

Prichard, A. (2010) 'David Held is an Anarchist: Discuss', *Millennium*, 39(2), pp. 439–459.

Putnam, R. (1976) *The Comparative Study of Political Elites*, Englewood Cliffs, NJ: Prentice-Hall.

Quandt, W., Jabber, F., & Lesch, A. M. (1973) *The Politics of Palestinian Nationalism*, Berkeley: University of California Press.

Rae, H. (2002) *State Identities and the Homogenisation of Peoples*, Cambridge: Cambridge University Press.

Randal, J. C. (1998) *Kurdistan: After such Knowledge, what Forgiveness?* London: Bloomsbury.

Rashid, A. & Shaheed, F. (1993) 'Pakistan: Ethno Politics and Contending Elites', Geneva: UN Research Institute for Social Development, available at: www.unrisd.org/80256B3C005BCCF9/%28httpPublications%29/49E58DAD1F9390B680256B6500565470?OpenDocument.

Rattansi, A. (1999) 'Racism, "Postmodernism", and Reflexive Multiculturalism', in S. May (ed.), *Critical Multiculturalism: Rethinking Multicultural and Antiracist Education*, London: Falmer Press, pp. 84–123.

Rear, M. (2008) *Intervention, Ethnic Conflict and State Building in Iraq: A Paradigm for the Postcolonial State*, London: Routledge.

Renan, E. (1994 [1882]) 'Qu'est-ce qu'une nation?' In J. Hutchinson & A. Smith (eds), *Nationalism: A Reader*, Oxford: Oxford University Press, pp. 17–18.

Reus-Smit, C. (2009) 'Constructivism', in S. Burchill *et al.* (eds), *Theories of International Relations*, 4th edn, Basingstoke: Palgrave Macmillan, pp. 212–236.

Ricks, T. E. (2007) *Fiasco: The American Military Adventure in Iraq*, London: Penguin Books.

Ritchie, N. & Rogers, P. (2007) *The Political Road to War with Iraq: Bush, 9/11, and the Drive to Overthrow Saddam*, London: Routledge.

Roberts, D. (1987) *The Ba'ath and the Creation of Modern Syria*, New York: St. Martin's Press.

Robins, P. (2003a) *Suits and Uniforms: Turkish Foreign Policy since the Cold War*, London: Hurst.

Robins, P. (2003b) 'Confusion at Home, Confusion Abroad: Turkey between Copenhagen and Iraq', *International Affairs*, 79(3), pp. 547–566.

Robinson, A. (2006) 'Towards an Intellectual Reformation: The Critique of Common Sense and the Forgotten Revolutionary Project of Gramscian Theory', in A. Bieler & A. Morton (eds), *Images of Gramsci: Connections and Contentions in Political Theory and International Relations*, London: Routledge, pp. 75–88.

Robinson, R. (1986) 'The Excentric Idea of Imperialism with or without Empire', in W: J. Mommsen & J. Osterhammel (eds), *Imperialism and After: Continuities and Discontinuities*, London: Allen & Unwin, pp. 267–289.

Roe, P. (1999) 'The Intrastate Security Dilemma: Ethnic Conflict as a 'Tragedy'?' *Journal of Peace Research*, 36(2), pp. 183–202.

Roe, P. (2004) *Ethnic Violence and the Societal Security Dilemma*, London: Routledge.

Romano, D. (2004) 'Safe Havens as Political Projects: The Case of Iraqi Kurdistan', in P. Kingston & I. S. Spears (eds), *States within States: Incipient Political Entities in the Post-Cold-War Era*, Basingstoke: Palgrave Macmillan, pp. 153–166.

Romano, D. (2006) *The Kurdish Nationalist Movement: Opportunity, Mobilization, and Identity*, Cambridge: Cambridge University Press.

Romano, D. (2010) 'The Kurds and Contemporary Regional Political Dynamics', in R. Lowe & G. Stansfield (eds), *The Kurdish Policy Imperative*, London: Chatham House, pp. 42–57.

Rose, G. (1998) 'Neoclassical Realism and Theories of Foreign Policy', *World Politics*, 51(1), pp. 144–172.

Rose, R. (1991) 'Comparing Forms of Comparative Analysis', *Political Studies*, 39(3), pp. 446–462.

Roshwald, A. (2015) 'The Daily Plebiscite as Twenty-first century Reality', *Ethnopolitics* 14(5), pp. 443–450.

Rotberg, R. (2002) *State Failure and State Weakness in a Time of Terror*, Washington: Brookings Institution Press.

Rotberg, R. (2010) *When States Fail: Causes and Consequences*, Princeton: Princeton University Press.

Rouse, J. (2005) 'Power/Knowledge', in G. Gutting (ed.), *The Cambridge Companion to Foucault*, 2nd edn, Cambridge: Cambridge University Press, pp. 95–122.

Rubin, A. (2007) 'Abd al-Karim Qasim and the Kurds of Iraq: Centralisation, Resistance and Revolt, 1958–63', *Middle Eastern Studies*, 43(3), pp. 353–382.

Rubin, M. (2005) 'A Comedy of Errors: American-Turkish Diplomacy and the Iraq War', *Turkish Policy Quarterly* Spring issue, available at: www.meforum.org/701/a-comedy-of-errors-american-turkish-diplomacy.

Rudd, G. (2004) *Humanitarian Intervention: Assisting the Iraqi Kurds in Operation Provide Comfort, 1991*, Washington, United States Army Center of Military History.

Ruggie, J. (1983) 'Continuity and Transformation in the World Polity: Toward a Neo-Realist Synthesis', *World Politics*, 36(2), pp. 261–285.

Sadiki, L. (2009) 'Like Father, Like Son: Dynastic Republicanism in the Middle East', Carnegie Endowment for International Peace, *Policy Outlook* 52, available at: http://carnegieendowment.org/files/ dynastic_republicanism.pdf.

Sadiki, L. (2010) 'Whither Arab "Republicanism"? The Rise of Family Rule and the "End of Democratization" in Egypt, Libya, and Yemen', *Mediterranean Politics* 15(1), pp. 99–107.

Said, E. (2003 [1978]) *Orientalism*, 25th edn, London: Penguin Books.

Saideman, S. (1998) 'Is Pandora's Box Half Empty or Half Full? The Limited Virulence of Secessionism and the Domestic Sources of Disintegration', in D. Lake and D. Rothchild (eds), *The International Spread of Ethnic Conflict: Fear, Diffusion, and Escalation*, Princeton: Princeton University Press, pp. 127–150.

Saideman, S. (2001) *The Ties that Divide: Ethnic Politics, Foreign Policy, and International Conflict*, New York: Columbia University Press.

Salehyan, I. (2007) 'Transnational Rebels: Neighbouring States as Sanctuary for Rebel Groups', *World Politics*, 52(2), pp. 217–242.

Salehyan, I. (2008) 'No Shelter Here: Rebel Sanctuaries and International Conflict', *Journal of Politics*, 70(1): 54–66.

Salehyan, I. (2009) *Rebels without Borders: Transnational Insurgencies in World Politics*, Ithaca: Cornell University Press.

Sambanis, N. (2000) 'Partition as a Solution to Ethnic War. An Empirical Critique of the Theoretical Literature', *World Politics*, 52 (4), pp. 437–483.

Sampson, R. V. (1968) *The Psychology of Power*, New York: Vintage Books.

Sarajlic, E. (2010) 'The Convenient Consociation: Bosnia and Herzegovina, Ethnopolitics and the EU', *Transitions*, 51(1–2), pp. 61–80.

Sarkesian, S. C. (1975) *Revolutionary Guerrilla Warfare*, Chicago: Precedent Publishing.

Sassoon, A. (1987) *Gramsci's Politics*, Minneapolis: University of Minnesota Press.

Sassoon, J. (1987) *Economic Policy in Iraq, 1932–1950*, London: Frank Cass.

Savelsberg, E. (2014) 'The Syrian-Kurdish Movements: Obstacles rather than Driving Forces for Democratization', in D. Romano & M. Gunes (eds), *Conflict, Democratization, and the Kurds in the Middle East: Turkey, Iran, Iraq, and Syria*, Basingstoke: Palgrave Macmillan, pp. 85–110.

Scheller, B. (2013) *The Wisdom of Syria's Waiting Game: Foreign Policy under the Assads*, London: Hurst.

Schirra, B. (2015) *ISIS: Der Global Dschihad*, Berlin: Ullstein Verlag.

Schmidinger, T. (2014) *Krieg und Revolution in Syrisch-Kurdistan: Analysen und Stimmen aus Rojava*, Vienna: Mandelbaum Verlag.

Schroeder, P. (1989) 'The Nineteenth century System: Balance of Power or Political Equilibrium?' *Review of International Studies*, 15(2), pp. 135–154.

Schulz, D. E. & Schulz, D. S. (1994) *The United States, Honduras, and the Crisis in Central America*, Boulder: Westview Press.

Schweller, R. L. (2006) *Unanswered Threats: Political Constraints on the Balance of Power*, Princeton: Princeton University Press.

Shapiro, M. (1981) *Language and Political Understanding: The Politics of Discursive Practices*, New Haven: Yale University Press.

Shapiro, M. (1988) *The Politics of Representation: Writing Practices in Biography, Photography and Political Analysis*, Madison: University of Wisconsin Press.

Shapiro, M. (2003) 'Textualizing Global Politics', in M. Wetherell, S. Taylor & S. Yates (eds), *Discourse Theory and Practice*, 3rd edn, London: Sage, pp. 318–323.

Shareef, M. J. M. (2010) *President George W. Bush's Policy towards Iraq: Continuity or Change?* Unpublished PhD thesis, University of Durham.

Shemesh, M. (1988) *The Palestinian Entity 1959–1974: Arab Politics and the PLO*, London: Frank Cass.

Shepherd. P. L. (1984) 'The Tragic Course and Consequences of U.S. Policy in Honduras', *World Policy Journal*, 2(1), pp. 109–154.

Shields, S. (2004) 'Mosul Questions: Economy, Identity, and Annexation', in R. Spector-Simon & E. Tejirian (eds), *The Creation of Iraq 1914–1921*, New York: Columbia University Press, pp. 50–60.

Simpson, G. (2008) 'The Guises of Sovereignty', in T. Jacobsen, C. Sampford & R. Thakur (eds), *Re-envisioning Sovereignty: The End of Westphalia?* Aldershot: Ashgate, pp. 51–72.

Simpson, P. & Mayr, A. (2010) *Language and Power: A Resource Book for Students*, London: Routledge.

Singer, J. D. (1961) 'The Level of Analysis Problem in International Relations', *World Politics*, 14(1), pp. 77–92.

Sluglett, P. (2007) *Britain in Iraq: Contriving King and Country*, 2nd edn, London: I.B. Tauris.

Smith, A. (1995) *Nations and Nationalism in a Global Era*, Cambridge: Polity.

Smith, A. (1998) *Nationalism and Modernism: A Critical Survey of Recent Theories of Nations and Nationalism*, London: Routledge.

Smith, A. (1999) *Myths and Memories of the Nation*, Oxford: Oxford University Press.

Smith, A. (2000) *The Nation in History: Historiographical Debates about Ethnicity and Nationalism*, Cambridge: Polity.

Smith, A. (2004) *Nationalism: Theory, Ideology, History*, 3rd edn, Cambridge: Polity.

Smith, A. (2008) *The Cultural Foundations of Nations: Hierarchy, Covenant, and Republic*, Hoboken: Wiley-Blackwell.

Smith, A. (2009) *Ethno-symbolism and Nationalism: A Cultural Approach*, London: Routledge.

Smith, S. (1995) 'The Self-Images of a Discipline: A Genealogy of International Relations Theory', in K. Booth & S. Smith (eds), *International Relations Theory Today*, Cambridge: Polity, pp. 1–37.

Smith, S. (2000) 'The Discipline of International Relations: Still an American Social Science', *British Journal of Politics and International Relations*, 2(3), pp. 374–402.

Smith, T. (2011) 'From Woodrow Wilson in 1902 to the Bush Doctrine in 2002: Democracy Promotion as Imperialism', *International Politics*, 48, pp. 229–250.

Snow, D. M. (1997) *Distant Thunder: Patterns of Conflict in the Developing World*, 2nd edn, Armonk: M.E. Sharpe Publishers.

Snyder, J. (1991) *Myths of Empire: Domestic Politics and International Ambition*, Ithaca: Cornell University Press.

Sobel, R. (1995) 'Contra Aid Fundamentals: Exploring the Intricacies and the Issues', *Political Science Quarterly*, 110(2), pp. 287–306.

Sørensen, G. (2001) *Changes in Statehood: The Transformation of International Relations*, Basingstoke: Palgrave Macmillan.

Sözen, A. (2010) 'A Paradigm Shift in Turkish Foreign Policy: Transition and Challenges', *Turkish Studies*, 11(1), pp. 103–123.

Spivak, G. (1987) *In Other Worlds: Essays in Cultural Politics*, London: Routledge.

Spruyt, H. (2005) *Ending Empire: Contested Sovereignty and Territorial Partition*, Ithaca: Cornell University Press.

Stack, J. (1997) 'The Ethnic Challenge to International Relations Theory', in: D. Carment & P. James (eds), *Wars in the Midst of Peace: The International Politics of Ethnic Conflict*, Pittsburgh: University of Pittsburgh Press, pp. 11–25.

Stansfield, G. (2003a) *Iraqi Kurdistan: Political Development and Emergent Democracy*, London: Routledge.

Stansfield, G. (2003b) 'The Kurdish Dilemma: The Golden Era Threatened', in T Dodge & S. Simon (eds), *Iraq at the Crossroads: State and Society in the Shadow of Regime Change*, London: International Institute for Strategic Studies, *Adelphi Papers*, 354, pp. 131–148.

Stansfield, G. (2005) 'Governing Kurdistan: The Strength of Division', in B. O'Leary, J. McGarry & K. Salih (eds), *The Future of Kurdistan in Iraq*, Philadelphia: University of Pennsylvania Press, pp. 195–218.

Stansfield, G. (2006) 'Finding a Dangerous Equilibrium: Internal Politics in Iraqi Kurdistan – Parties, Tribes, and Ethnicity Reconsidered', in F. A. Jabar & H. Dawood (eds), *The Kurds: Nationalism and Politics*, London: Saqi, pp. 258–276.

Stansfield, G. (2007a) *Iraq: People, History, Politics*, Cambridge: Polity.

Stansfield, G. (2007b) 'Conclusion', in R. Visser & G. Stansfield (eds), *An Iraq of Its Regions: Cornerstones of a Federal Democracy?*, London: Hurst, pp. 257–266.

Stansfield, G. (2010) 'From Civil War to Calculated Compromise: The Unification of the Kurdistan Regional Government in Iraq', in R. Lowe & G. Stansfield (eds), *The Kurdish Policy Imperative*, London: Chatham House, pp. 130–144.

Stansfield, G. (2013) 'The Unravelling of the Post-First World War State System? The Kurdistan Region of Iraq and the Transformation of the Middle East', *International Affairs*, 89(2), pp. 259–282.

Steans, J., Pettiford, L., Diez, T. & El-Anis, I. (2010) *An Introduction to International Relations Theory*, 3rd edn, Harlow: Pearson Education.

Stein, D. (1997) *Cognitive Science and the Unconscious*, Washington: American Psychiatric Press.

Stepan, A., Linz, J. J., & Yadav, Y. (2011) *Crafting State-Nations: India and Other Multinational Democracies*, Baltimore: Johns Hopkins University Press.

Sterling-Folker, J. (2013) 'Neoliberalism' in T. Dunne, M. Kurki & S. Smith (eds), *International Relations Theories: Discipline and Diversity*, 3rd edn, Oxford: Oxford University Press, pp. 114–131.

Strang, D. (1990) 'From Dependency to Sovereignty: An Event History Analysis of Decolonization, 1870–1987', *American Sociological Review*, 55(6), pp. 846–860.

Strang, D. (1996) 'Contested Sovereignty: The Social Construction of Colonial Imperialism', in T. Biersteker & C. Weber (eds), *State Sovereignty as Social Construct*, Cambridge: Cambridge University Press, pp. 22–49.

Straw, D. (2013) *Human Rights Violation in Turkey: Rethinking Sociological Perspectives*, Basingstoke: Palgrave Macmillan.

Stritzel, H. (2007) 'Towards a Theory of Securitization: Copenhagen and beyond', *European Journal of International Relations* 13(3), pp. 357–383.

Suny, R. (1993) *The Revenge of the Past: Nationalism, Revolution, and the Collapse of the Soviet Union*, Stanford: Stanford University Press.

Taha, M. (2013) 'Self-determination, Oil and Islam in the Face of the League of Nations: The Mosul Dispute and the "Non-European" Legal Terrain', in D. French (ed.), *Statehood and Self-determination: Reconciling Tradition and Modernity in International Law*, Oxford: Oxford University Press, pp. 324–348.

Tahiri, H. (2007) *The Structure of Kurdish Society and the Struggle for a Kurdish State*, Costa Mesa: Mazda Press.

Takeyh, R. (2009) *Guardians of the Revolution: Iran and the World in the Age of the Ayatollahs*, Oxford: Oxford University Press.

Tansey, O. (2009) 'Process Tracing and Elite Interviewing: A Case for Non-probability Sampling', in S. Pickel *et al.* (eds), *Methoden der vergleichenden Politik- und Sozialwissenschaft: Neue Entwicklungen und Anwendungen*, Wiesbaden: VS Verlag, pp. 481–496.

Taras, R. & Ganguly, R. (2006) *Understanding Ethnic Conflict: The International Dimension*, 3rd edn, New York: Pearson.

Taspinar, Ö. (2005) *Kurdish Nationalism and Political Islam in Turkey: Kemalist Identity in Transition*, London: Routledge.

Taureck, R. (2006) 'Securitization Theory and Securitization Studies', *Journal of International Relations and Development*, 9, pp. 53–61.

Taylor, C. C. (1999) *Sacrifice as Terror: The Rwandan Genocide 1994*, Oxford: Berg.

Tejel, J. (2011) *Syria's Kurds: History, Politics and Society*, London: Routledge.

Tetlock, P. E. (2006) *Expert Political Judgement: How Good Is It? How Can We Know?* Princeton: Princeton University Press.

Thomson, P. (2014) 'Field', M. J. Grenfell (ed.), *Pierre Bourdieu: Key Concepts*, London: Routledge, 2nd edition, pp. 65–82.

Thyne, C. (2006) 'Cheap Signals with Costly Consequences: The Effect of Interstate Relations on Civil War', *Journal of Conflict Resolution*, 50(6), pp. 937–961.

Tilly, C. (1975) *The Formation of National States in Western Europe*, Princeton: Princeton University Press.

Tilly, C. (1990) *Coercion, Capital, and European States*, Malden: Blackwell.

Tiunov, O. (1993) 'The International Legal Personality of States: Problems and Solutions', *Saint Louis University Law Journal*, 37, pp. 323–336.

Tourish, D. (1998) 'Ideological Intransigence, Democratic Centralism and Cultism: A Case Study from the Political Left', *Cultic Studies Journal*, 15(1), pp. 33–67.

Tripp, C. (2007) *A History of Iraq*, Cambridge: Cambridge University Press.

Türsan, H. (2004) *Democratisation in Turkey: The Role of Political Parties*, Brussels: Peter Lang.

Üngör, U. (2011) *The Making of Modern Turkey: Nation and State in Eastern Anatolia, 1913–1950*, Oxford: Oxford University Press.

Uslu, E. (2007) 'Turkey's Kurdish Problem: Steps towards a Solution', *Studies in Conflict & Terrorism*, 30(2), pp. 157–172.

Üstündağ, N. (2016) 'Self-defence as a Revolutionary Practice in Rojava, or How to Unmake the State', *South Atlantic Quarterly*, 115(1), pp. 197–210.

van Bruinessen, M. (1986) 'The Kurds between Iran and Iraq', *MERIP Middle East Report*, 141, pp. 14–27.

van Bruinessen, M. (1992) *Agha, Shaikh and State: The Social and Political Structures of Kurdistan*, London: Zed Books.

van Bruinessen, M. (1996) 'Turkey's Death Squads', *Middle East Report*, 199, pp. 20–23.

van Bruinessen, M. (1997) 'Genocide in Kurdistan? The Suppression of the Dersim Rebellion in Turkey (1937–8) and the Chemical War against the Iraqi Kurds (1988)', in G. Andreopoulos (ed.), *Genocide: Conceptual and Historical Dimensions*, Philadelphia: University of Pennsylvania Press, pp. 141–170.

van Bruinessen, M. (2000) *Kurdish Ethno-Nationalism versus Nation Building States*, Istanbul: Isis Press.

van Bruinessen, M. (2002) 'Kurds, States, and Tribes', in F. A. Jabar & H. Dawood (eds), *Tribes and Power: Nationalism and Ethnicity in the Middle East*, London: Saqi, pp. 165–183.

van Creveld, M. (1991) *The Transformation of War*, New York: Free Press.

van Creveld, M. (2008) *The Culture of War*, New York: Presidio Press.

van den Berghe, P. (1978) 'Race and Ethnicity: A Sociobiological Perspective', *Ethnic and Racial Studies*, 1(4), pp. 401–411.

van den Berghe, P. (1981) *The Ethnic Phenomenon*, New York: Elsevier.

van den Berghe, P. (1999) 'Racism, Ethnocentrism and Xenophobia: In Our Genes or in Our Memes?', in K. Thienpont & R. Cliquet (eds), *In-Group/Out-Group Behaviour in Modern Societies: An Evolutionary Perspectives*, Brussels: NIDI CBGS Publications, pp. 21–36.

van Dijk, T. (1993) *Elite Discourse and Racism*, London: Sage.

van Dijk, T. (2008) *Discourse and Power*, Basingstoke: Palgrave Macmillan.

van Evera, S. (1994) 'Hypotheses on Nationalism and War', *International Security*, 18(4), pp. 5–39.

Vali, A. (2011) *Kurds and the State in Iran: The Making of Kurdish Identity*, London: I.B. Tauris.

Varshney, A. (2002) *Ethnic Conflict and Civic Life: Hindus and Muslims in India*, New Haven: Yale University Press.

Varshney, A. (2003) 'Nationalism, Ethnic Conflict, and Rationality', *Perspectives on Politics*, 1(1), pp. 85–99.

Vasquez, J. (2003) *Realism and the Balancing of Power: A New Debate*, Upper Saddle River: Prentice Hall.

Vincent, R. J. (1974) *Nonintervention and International Order*, Princeton: Princeton University Press.

Voller, Y. (2014) *The Kurdish Liberation Movement in Iraq: From Insurgency to Statehood*, London: Routledge.

Wæver, O. (1993) *Identity, Migration, and the New Security Agenda in Europe*, London: Pinter.

Wæver, O. (1995) 'Securitization and Desecuritization', in R. D. Lipschutz (ed.), *On Security*, New York: Columbia University Press, pp. 46–86.

Wæver, O. (1997) 'The Rise and Fall of the Inter-Paradigm Debate', in S. Smith, K. Booth & M. Zalewski (eds), *International Theory: Positivism and Beyond*, 2nd edn, Cambridge: Cambridge University Press, pp. 149–185.

Wæver, O. (2007) 'Still a Discipline after All These Debates?' In T. Dunne, M. Kurki & S. Smith (eds), *International Relations Theories: Discipline and Diversity*, 2nd edn, Oxford: Oxford University Press, pp. 306–328.

Wagner, R. H. (1993) 'The Causes of Peace', in R. Licklider (ed.), *Stopping the Killing: How Civil Wars End*, New York: New York University Press, pp. 257–263.

Wahlbeck, Ö. (1998) *Transnationalism and Diasporas: The Kurdish Example*, unpublished paper, International Sociological Association XIV World Congress of Sociology, Montreal.

Wahlbeck, Ö. (1999) *Kurdish Diasporas: A Comparative Study of Kurdish Refugee Communities*. Basingstoke: Palgrave Macmillan.

Walker, J. W. (2007) 'Learning Strategic Depth: Implications of Turkey's New Foreign Policy Doctrine', *Insight Turkey*, 9(3), pp. 32–47.

Walker, R. B. J. (1993) *Inside/Outside: International Relations as Political Theory*, Cambridge: Cambridge University Press.

Walker, R. B. J. (1995) 'International Relations and the Concept of the Political', in K. Booth & S. Smith (eds), *International Relations Theory Today*, Cambridge: Polity, pp. 306–327.

Waller, M. (1981) *Democratic Centralism: An Historical Commentary*, Manchester: Manchester University Press.

Wallerstein, I. (1974) *The Modern World System, vol. I.: Capitalist Agriculture and the Origins of the European World Economy in the Sixteenth century*, New York. Academic Press.

Wallerstein, I. (1980) *The Modern World System, vol. II: Mercantilism and the Consolidation of the European World Economy, 1600–1750*, New York: Academic Press.

Wallerstein, I. (1989) *The Modern World System, vol. III: The Second Great Expansion of the Capitalist World Economy, 1730–1840s*, New York: Academic Press.

Walt, S. (1985) 'Alliance Formation and the Balance of World Power', *International Security*, 9(4), pp. 3–43.

Walt, S. (1990) *The Origin of Alliances*, Ithaca: Cornell University Press.

Waltz, K. (1979) *Theory of International Politics*, New York: Random House.

Waltz, K. (2001 [1959]) *Man, the State, and War: A Critical Analysis*, new revised edition, New York: Columbia University Press.

Ward, C. (1992) 'The Anarchist Sociology of Federalism', *Freedom* June/July issue, available at: http://theanarchistlibrary.org/library/colin-ward-the-anarchist-sociology-of-federalism.

Waterbury, J. (1993) *Exposed to Innumerable Delusions: Public Enterprise and State Power in Egypt, India, Mexico, and Turkey*, Cambridge: Cambridge University Press.

Watts, N. (2006) 'Activists in Office: Pro-Kurdish Contentious Politics in Turkey', *Ethnopolitics*, 5(2), pp. 125–144.

Watts, N. (2010) *Activists in Office: Kurdish Politics and Protest in Turkey*, Seattle: University of Washington Press.

Weber, C. (1995) *Simulating Sovereignty: Intervention, the State and Symbolic Exchange*, Cambridge: Cambridge University Press.

Weber, C. (1998) 'Performative States', *Millennium*, 27(1), pp. 77–95.

Weber, C. (2010) *International Relations Theory: A Critical Introduction*, 3rd edn, London: Routledge.

Weber, M. (1970 [1919]) 'Politics as Vocation', in H. Gerth & C. Wright Mills (eds), *From Max Weber: Essays in Sociology*, London: Routledge, pp. 77–128.

Weber, M. (1978 [1922]) *Economy and Society*, 2nd edn, Berkeley: University of California Press.

Weber, M. (2009 [1924]) *The Theory of Social and Economic Organization*, New York: Free Press.

Weitz, R. (1986) 'Insurgency and Counterinsurgency in Latin America, 1960–1980', *Political Science Quarterly*, 101(3), pp. 397–413.

Welsh, J. (2003) *Humanitarian Intervention and International Relations*, Oxford: Oxford University Press.

Wendt, A. (1987) 'The Agent-Structure Problem in International Relations Theory', *International Organization*, 41(3), pp. 335–370.

Wendt, A. (1992) 'Anarchy Is What States Make of It: The Social Construction of Power Politics', *International Organization*, 46(2), pp. 391–425.

Wendt, A. (1999) *Social Theory of International Politics*, Cambridge: Cambridge University Press.

Wendt, A. (2003) 'Why a World State Is Inevitable', *European Journal of International Relations*, 9(4), pp. 491–542.

White, J. (2012) *Muslim Nationalism and the New Turks*, Princeton: Princeton University Press.

White, P. (1998) 'Economic Marginalization of Turkey's Kurds: Failed Promise of Modernization and Reform', *Journal of Muslim Minority Affairs* 18(1), pp. 139–158.

White, P. (2000) *Primitive Rebels or Revolutionary Modernisers: The Kurdish Nationalist Movement in Turkey*, London: Zed Books.

Wickham-Crowley, T. (1991) *Exploring Revolution: Essays on Latin American Insurgency and Revolutionary Theory*, New York: M.E. Sharpe.

Wickham-Crowley, T. (1992) *Guerrillas and Revolution in Latin America: A Comparative Study of Insurgents and Regimes since 1956*, Princeton: Princeton University Press.

Wight, C. (2006) *Agents, Structures and International Relations: Politics as Ontology*, Cambridge: Cambridge University Press.

Wight, C. (2010) 'Philosophy of Social Science and International Relations', in: W. Carlsnaes, T. Risse & B. A. Simmons (eds), *Handbook of International Relations*, 2nd edn, London: Sage, pp. 29–56.

Williams, J. & Roach, T. (2006) 'Security, Territorial Borders, and British Iraq Policy: Buying a Blair Way to Heaven', *Geopolitics*, 11(1), pp. 1–23.

Williams, M. C. (2003) 'Words, Images, Enemies: Securitization and International Politics', *International Studies Quarterly*, 47(4), pp. 511–531.

Wimmer, A. (2008) 'The Making and Unmaking of Ethnic Boundaries: A Multilevel Process Theory', *American Journal of Sociology*, 113(4), pp. 970–1022.

Wimmer, A. (2012) *Waves of War: Nationalism, State Formation, and Ethnic Exclusion in the Modern World*, Cambridge: Cambridge University Press.

Wimmer, A., Cederman, L. E., & Min, B. (2009) 'Ethnic Politics and Armed Conflict: A Configurational Analysis of a New Global Dataset', *American Sociological Review*, 74(2), pp. 316–337.

Wimmer, A. & Feinstein, Y. (2010) 'The Rise of the Nation-State Across the World, 1816–2001', *American Sociological Review*, 75(5), pp. 764–790.

Wodak, R. (2001) 'What CDA Is about: A Summary of Its History, Important Concepts, and Its Developments', in R. Wodak & M. Meyer (eds), *Methods of Critical Discourse Analysis*, London: Sage, pp. 1–13.

Wohlforth, W. (1993) *Elusive Balance: Power and Perception during the Cold War*, Ithaca: Cornell University Press.

Wohlforth, W. (2012) 'Realism and Foreign Policy', in: S. Smith, A. Hadfield & T. Dunne (eds), *Foreign Policy: Theories, Actors, Cases*, 2nd edn, Oxford: Oxford University Press, pp. 35–53.

Wolfers, A. (1962) *Discord and Collaboration: Essays on International Politics*, Baltimore: Johns Hopkins University Press.

Wolff, S. (2010) 'The Relationship between States and Non-States Peoples: A Comparative View of the Kurds', in R. Lowe & G. Stansfield (eds), *The Kurdish Policy Imperative*, London: Chatham House, pp. 16–26.

Woodward, B. (2004) *Plan of Attack*, New York: Simon & Schuster.

Woodwell, D. (2004) 'Unwelcome Neighbours: Shared Ethnicity and International Conflict during the Cold War', *International Studies Quarterly*, 48(1), pp. 197–223.

Yack, B. (1999) 'The Myth of the Civic Nation', in R. Beiner (ed.), *Theorising Nationalism*, Albany: State University of New York Press, pp. 103–118.

Yavuz, M. H. (2001) 'Five Stages of the Construction of Kurdish Nationalism in Turkey', *Nationalism and Ethnic Politics*, 7(3), pp. 1–25.

Yavuz, M. H. (2005) 'Turkey's Kurdish-Centered Iraqi Policy', in M. Gunter & M. A. Ahmed (eds), *The Kurdish Question and the 2003 Iraqi War*, Costa Mesa: Mazda Press, pp. 163–173.

Yavuz, M. H. (2009) *Secularism and Muslim Democracy in Turkey*, Cambridge: Cambridge University Press.

Yildiz, K. (2007) *The Kurds in Iraq: Past, Present and Future*, 2nd edn, London: Pluto Press.

Young, C. (1994) *The African Colonial State in Comparative Perspective*, New Haven: Yale University Press.

Young, C. (2012) *The Postcolonial State in Africa: Fifty Years of Independence, 1960–2010*, Madison: University of Wisconsin Press.

Youngs, G. (1999) *International Relations in a Global Age: A Conceptual Challenge*, Cambridge: Polity.

Youngs, G. & Kofman, E. (2008) *Globalization: Theory and Practice*, London: Continuum International Publishing Group.

Zalewski, M. & Enloe, C. (1995) 'Questions about Identity in International Relations', in: K. Booth & S. Smith (eds), *International Relations Theory Today*, Cambridge: Polity Press, pp. 279–305.

Zehfuss, M. (2002) *Constructivism in International Relations: The Politics of Reality*, Cambridge: Cambridge University Press.

Zehfuss, M. (2006) 'Constructivism and Identity: A Dangerous Liaison', in S. Guzzini & A. Leander (eds), *Constructivism and International Relations*, London: Routledge, pp. 93–117.

Zehfuss, M. (2009) 'Jaques Derrida', in J. Edkins & N. Vaughan-Williams (eds), *Critical Theorists and International Relations*, London: Routledge, pp. 137–149.

Zeydanlioğlu, W. (2013) 'Repression or Reform? An Analysis of the AKP's Kurdish Language Policy', in C. Gunes & W. Zeydanlioğlu (eds), *The Kurdish Question in Turkey: New Perspectives in Violence, Representation, and Reconciliation*, London: Routledge, pp. 162–185.

Zubaida, S. (2009) *Islam, the People, and the State: Political Ideas and Movements in the Middle East*, 4th edn London: I.B. Tauris.

Zürcher, E. J. (2009) *Turkey: A Modern History*, 9th edn, London: I.B. Tauris.

Non-referenced newspaper, magazine and online articles, bulletins and briefings

Abdulla, N. (2014) 'The Rise of Syria's Kurds', *Al Jazeera* 23 January, available at: www.aljazeera.com/indepth/opinion/2014/01/rise-syria-kurds-201412353941189707.html.

Ackerman, E. (2015) 'Erdogan's ISIS Opportunism', *The New Yorker*, 12 August, available at: www.newyorker.com/news/news-desk/erdogans-isis-opportunism.

Alaaldin, R. (2010) 'Kurds Are Iraq's Kingmakers', the *Guardian* 18 October, available at: www.theguardian.com/commentisfree/2010/oct/18/kurds-iraqpoliticalstalemate.

Al Arabiya (2014a) 'Iraq's Barzani Says Kurdish Self-Rule in Kirkuk to Stay', 27 June, available at: http://english.alarabiya.net/en/News/2014/06/27/Iraq-s-Barazani-says-Kurdish-self-rule-in-Kirkuk-to-stay-.html.

Al Arabiya (2014b) 'Kurdish Forces, ISIS Clash near Arbil', 6 August, available at: http://english.alarabiya.net/en/News/middle-east/2014/08/06/U-N-condemns-ISIS-attacks-in-Iraq.html.

Albayrak, A. (2015) 'Turkey Strikes Kurdish Militant Positions in Northern Iraq', *Wall Street Journal*, 26 July, available at: www.wsj.com/articles/turkey-strikes-pkk-targets-in-northern-iraq-1437819823.

Al Jazeera (2007) 'Turkey Continues Raids into Iraq', 23 December, available at: http://english.aljazeera.net/NR/exeres/3B6368C5-6EED-4B5A-B5F6-E654ADC4FA   0A.htm.

Al Jazeera (2009) 'Violence Follows DTP Ban in Turkey', 13 December, available at: www.aljazeera.com/news/europe/2009/12/20091213615 2398809.html.

Al Jazeera (2014a) 'Iraqis Flee Mosul after Fighters Seize City', 11 June, available at: www.aljazeera.com/news/middleeast/2014/06/thousands-iraqis-flee-after-mosul-seized-20146102344498723.html.

Al Jazeera (2014b) 'Fighting Rages for Control of Syria's Kobane', 18 October, available at: www.aljazeera.com/news/middleeast/2014/10/syria-kobane-isil-2014101714131737 0535.html.

Al Jazeera (2014c) 'Iraqi Kurds to Send Forces to Syria's Kobane', 23 October, available at: www.aljazeera.com/news/middleeast/2014/10/iraqi-kurds-peshmerga-syria-kobane-2014 1022132341576698.html.

Al Jazeera (2015) 'Nearly 100 Dead as Ankara Peace Rally Rocked by Blast', 11 October, available at: www.aljazeera.com/news/2015/10/explosions-hit-turkey-ankara-peace-march-151010073827607.html.

Almukhtar, S. & Wallace, T. (2015) 'Why Turkey is Fighting the Kurds Who Are Fighting ISIS', *New York Times*, 12 August, available at: www.nytimes.com/interactive/ 2015/08/12/world/middleeast/turkey-kurds-isis.html?ref=world.

Al Rifai, D. (2015) 'ISIL Makes Major Advance on Syria's Hasakah', *Al Jazeera*, 5 June, available at: www.aljazeera.com/news/2015/06/isil-syria-hasakah-kurds-kurdish-15060 4140013137.html.

Al Shibeeb, D. (2015) 'Iraq's Kurdistan Slams Airstrikes on PKK', *Al Arabiya* 25 July, available at: http://english.alarabiya.net/en/News/middle-east/2015/07/25/Turkey-justifies-Syria-air-strikes-in-letter-to-U-N-.html.

Ant, O., Hacaoğlu, S., & Finkel, I. (2015) 'Turkey Escalates Gulen Witch Hunt with Koza Ipek Raids', *Bloomberg News*, 1 September, available at: www.bloomberg.com/ news/articles/2015-09-01/turkish-police-raid-gulen-linked-koza-ipek-on-terrorism-charges.

Arango, T. (2011) 'A Long-Awaited Apology for Shiites, but the Wounds Run Deep', the *New York Times*, 8 November, available at: www.nytimes.com/ 2011/11/09/world/middle east/iraqi-shiite-anger-at-united-states-remains-strong.html ?pagewanted=all&_r=0.

Arango, T. (2014) 'Sunni Extremists in Iraq Seize Three Towns from Kurds and Threaten Major Dam', *New York Times*, 3 August, available at: www.nytimes.com/2014/08/04/ world/middleeast/iraq.html.

Aretaios, E. (2015) 'The Rojava Revolution', *Open Democracy*, 15 March, available at: www.opendemocracy.net/arab-awakening/evangelos-aretaios/rojava-revolution.

Artens, H. (2009) ' "Plan Obama" to Disarm PKK Imperiled', *World Politics Review*, 21 May, available at: www.worldpoliticsreview.com/ articles/3791/plan-obama-to-disarm-pkk-imperiled.

Artens, H. (2011) 'Kurdistan Protests Could Drive Iraq to the Brink', *World Politics Review*, 29 March, available at: www.worldpoliticsreview.com/articles/8340/kurdistan-protests-could-drive-iraq-to-the-brink.

Artens, H. (2013a) 'Iraqi Kurdistan Elections Cement Barzani's Role as Regional Power-broker', *World Politics Review*, 30 September, available at: www.worldpoliticsreview. com/articles/13256/iraqi-kurdistan-elections-cement-barzani-s-role-as-regional-powerbroker.

Artens, H. (2013b) 'What the Peculiar Case of the Kurdistan Region Can Teach Us about Sovereignty', *E-International Relations*, 13 August, available at: www.e-ir. info/2013/08/13/what-the-peculiar-case-of-the-kurdistan-region-can-teach-us-about-sovereignty/.

Ates, H. (2012) 'Barzani Unites Syrian Kurds against Assad', *Al Monitor*, 16 July, available at: www.al-monitor.com/pulse/politics/2012/07/barzani-grabs-assads-kurdish-car. html.

Ayhan, V. (2010) 'An Analysis of Massoud Barzani's Visit to Turkey', *Today's Zaman*, 6 July, available at: http://todayszaman.com/news-215263-100-an-analysis-of-massoud-barzanis-visit-to-turkey.html.

Azadi, M. (2009) 'The Kurdish Summit', *The Kurdish Aspect*, 22 March, available at: www.kurdishaspect.com/doc032209MA.html.

Barbarani, S. & Stephens, M. (2014) 'Peshmerga Entrance into Kobane Strengthens Kurdish Ties', *Middle East Eye*, 28 October, available at: www.middleeasteye.net/news/150-peshmerga-enter-kobane-regions-kurds-strengthen-ties-544054810.

Barkey, H. (2014a) 'Kurdish Independence: One Day, but Certainly not Now', *The American Interest*, 8 August, available at: www.the-american-interest.com/2014/08/08/kurdish-independence-one-day-but-certainly-not-now/.

Barkey, H. (2014b) 'The Meaning of Kobane', *The American Interest*, 18 October, available at: www.the-american-interest.com/2014/10/18/the-meaning-of-kobani/.

Barnett, A. (2015) 'The Rojava Spirit Spreads', *Dissent*, 25 February, available at: www.dissentmagazine.org/online_articles/turkey-erdogan-putin-rojava-kurdish-democracy.

Beck, J. (2014) 'Meet the PKK "Terrorists" Battling the Islamic State on the Frontlines of Iraq', *VICE News*, 22 August, available at: https://news.vice.com/article/meet-the-pkk-terrorists-battling-the-islamic-state-on-the-frontlines-of-iraq.

Bender, J. (2015) 'Turkey's President is Making a Machiavellian Move', *Business Insider*, 3 August, available at: www.businessinsider.sg/tradeoff-that-will-let-the-us-strike-isis-from-turkey-2015-7/#CdvHFfbdtKso6YfO.97.

Bengio, O. (2012a) 'Will the Kurds Get Their Way?' *The American Interest*, November/December issue, available at: www.the-american-interest.com/article.cfm? piece=1323.

Berlinski, C. (2013) 'Turkey's Agony: How Erdoğan Turned a Peaceful Protest into a Violent Nightmare', *The Spectator*, 15 June, available at: www.spectator.co.uk/features/8934351/turkeys-agony-the-view-from-taksim-square/.

Bertrand, N. (2015) 'Senior Western Official: Links between Turkey and ISIS are Now "Undeniable"', *Business Insider*, 28 July, available at: www.businessinsider.com/links-between-turkey-and-isis-are-now-undeniable-2015-7?IR=T.

Biden, J. (2006) 'Iraq: The Way Forward, a Conversation with Senator Joe Biden', *Council on Foreign Relations, Podcast*, 20 September, available at: www.cfr.org/iraq/iraq-way-forward-conversation-senator-joseph-biden-audio/p12023.

Bohn, L. (2015) '"All Our Young People Have Gone to the Mountains"', *The Atlantic*, 18 August, available at: www.theatlantic.com/international/archive/2015/08/turkey-kurds-pkk-syria/401624/.

Bozarslan, M. (2015a) 'Iraqi Kurdistan's Brewing Crisis', *Al Monitor*, 20 October, available at: www.al-monitor.com/pulse/originals/2015/10/turkey-iraq-kurdistan-economic-political-crisis-kdp-goran.html#.

Bozarslan, M. (2015b) 'Turkey Drawn into Vortex of Violence', *Al Monitor*, 26 July, available at: www.al-monitor.com/pulse/originals/2015/07/turkey-suruc-bombing-violence.html.

British Broadcasting Corporation – BBC (2007) 'US "to Help Turkey Combat Rebels"', 5 November, available at: http://news.bbc.co.uk/1/hi/world/europe/7079391.stm.

British Broadcasting Corporation – BBC (2013) 'Iraqi Kurdistan Opposition Party Beats PUK in Elections', 2 October, available at: www.bbc.co.uk/news/world-middle-east-24362864.

British Broadcasting Corporation – BBC (2014a) 'Iraqi Kurdistan Independence Referendum Planned', 1 July, available at: www.bbc.com/news/world-middle-east-28103124.

British Broadcasting Corporation – BBC (2014b) 'Why Iran Has Finally Let Go of Maliki', 13 August, available at: www.bbc.com/news/world-middle-east-28777142.

British Broadcasting Corporation – BBC (2014c) 'Haider al-Abadi: A New Era for Iraq?' 9 September, available at: www.bbc.com/news/world-middle-east-28748366.

British Broadcasting Corporation – BBC (2014d) 'Islamic State: Turkey to Let Iraqi Kurds Join Kobane Fight', 20 October, available at: www.bbc.com/news/world-middle-east-29685830.

British Broadcasting Corporation – BBC (2016) 'Syria War: Turkey Angry over US Commando Photos', 27 May, available at: www.bbc.com/news/world-middle-east-36396248.

Brandon, J. (2006a) 'Iran's Kurdish Threat: PJAK', Jamestown Foundation, *Terrorism Monitor*, 4(12), available online at: http://intersci.ss.uci.edu/wiki/eBooks/Articles/Jamaats%202%20Terrorism%20Monitor.pdf.

Brandon, J. (2006b) 'The Kurdistan Freedom Falcons Emerge as a Rival to the PKK', Jamestown Foundation, *Terrorism Focus*, 3(40), 17 October, available online at: www.jamestown.org/single/?no_cache= 1&tx_ttnews[tt_news]=936.

Bush, G. W. (2003) 'Full Text: George Bush's Speech to the American Enterprise Institute', the *Guardian*, 27 February, available at: www.theguardian.com/world/2003/feb/27/usa.iraq2.

Bush, G. W. & Aznar, J. M. (2003) 'Text: The Azores Summit Statement', *BBC News*, 16 March, available at: http://news.bbc.co.uk/1/hi/world/ middle_east/2855567.stm.

Bush, G. W. & Blair, T. (2003) 'Joint Statement by President George W. Bush and Prime Minister Tony Blair on Iraq', *The White House, Office of the Press Secretary*, 8 April, available at: http://2001-2009.state.gov/p/eur/rls/rm/2003/19406.htm.

Cagaptay, S. (2016) 'Erdogan's Nationalist Path to a Full Presidential System', Washington Institute for Near East Policy, *Policywatch* 2620, 24 May, available at: www.washingtoninstitute.org/policy-analysis/view/erdogans-nationalist-path-to-a-full-presidential-system.

Cagaptay, S. & Bhaskar, M. (2015) 'Why Erdogan Could Push for Early Elections', The Washington Institute for Near East Policy, *Policywatch* 2451, 7 July, available at: www.washingtoninstitute.org/policy-analysis/view/why-erdogan-could-push-for-early-elections-turkeys-regulatory-bodies-in-a-n.

Cagaptay, S. & Eroğlu, Z. (2007) 'The PKK, PJAK, and Iran: Implications for US-Turkish Relations', The Washington Institute for Near East Policy, *Policywatch* 1244, 13 June, available at: www.washingtoninstitute.org/policy-analysis/view/the-pkk-pjak-and-iran-implications-for-u.s.-turkish-relations.

Callimachi, R. (2015) 'Inside Syria: Kurds Roll Back ISIS, but Alliances Are Strained', *New York Times*, 10 August, available at: www.nytimes.com/2015/08/10/world/middle east/syria-turkey-islamic-state-kurdish-militia-ypg.html?action=click&contentCollecti on=Middle%20East&region=Footer&module=WhatsNext&version=WhatsNext& contentID=WhatsNext&moduleDetail=undefined&pgtype=Multimedia.

Çandar, C. (2013) 'Erdoğan-Barzani Diyarbakir Milestone Encounter', *Al Monitor*, 20 November, available at: www.al-monitor.com/pulse/ originals/2013/11/erdogan-barzani-kurdistan-diyarbakir-political-decision.html.

Çandar, C. (2014) 'Turkish Government Plays with Kurdish Fire', *Al Monitor*, 1 October, available at: www.al-monitor.com/pulse/security/2014/10/turkey-syria-kurds-kobane-isis-coalition-1.html.

Çandar, C. (2015) 'Violence in Turkey Could Push US to Pick Sides in Turkey, PKK Battle', *Al Monitor*, 19 August, available at: www.al-monitor.com/pulse/originals/2015/08/turkey-united-states-syria-kurds-pkk-isis-crossroads.html.

Cafarella, N. (2005) 'Mujahideen-e-Khalq Dossier', Center for Policing Terrorism, 15 March, available at: www.nejatngo.org/Storage/file/Book_EN/CPT_MKO_Dossier.pdf.

Calderwood, J. (2011) 'Iraq's Kurds Content to Wait for Their State', *The National*, 21 June, available at: www.thenational.ae/news/world/middle-east/iraqs-kurds-content-to-wait-for-their-state.

Carter, C., Cohen, T., & Starr, B. (2014) 'U.S. Jet Fighters, Drones Strike ISIS Fighters, Convoys in Iraq', *CNN*, 9 August, available at: http://edition.cnn.com/2014/08/08/world/iraq-options/index.html?hpt=hp_t1.

Columbia Broadcasting System – CBS (2007) 'Kurdistan: The Other Iraq', *60 Minutes*, 16 February, available at: www.cbsnews.com/news/kurdistan-the-other-iraq/.

Cengiz, O. K. (2015) 'Turkey's Path to Dictatorship', *Al Monitor*, 12 November, available at: www.al-monitor.com/pulse/originals/2015/11/turkey-erdogan-executive-president-sultan-or-caliph.html.

Çengiz, S. (2013) 'Erdogan, Barzani See Eye to Eye on Four Issues in Diyarbakir Visit', *Today's Zaman*, 19 November, available at: www.todayszaman.com/news-331684-erdogan-barzani-see-eye-to-eye-on-four-issues-in-diyarbakir-visit.html.

Cerny, H. (2014b) 'As ISIS Chaos Grows, Iraqi Kurds Must not Overplay Their Hand', *World Politics Review*, 24 June, available at: www.worldpoliticsreview.com/articles/13878/as-isis-chaos-grows-iraqi-kurds-must-not-overplay-their-hand.

Cerny, H. (2014c) 'Islamic State Threat Puts Independence on Hold for Iraq's Kurds', *World Politics Review*, 16 September, available at: www.worldpoliticsreview.com/articles/14064/islamic-state-threat-puts-independence-on-hold-for-iraq-s-kurds.

Cerny, H. (2014d) 'Amidst ISIS War, Kurdish Discourses on National Self-determination', *Open Democracy*, 29 October, available at: www.opendemocracy.net/arab-awakening/hannes-černy/amidst-isis-war-kurdish-discourses-on-national-selfdetermination.

Cerny, H. (2015) 'Unrest Threatens Sheen of Stability in Iraq's Kurdistan Region', *World Politics Review*, 21 October, available at: www.worldpoliticsreview.com/articles/16995/unrest-threatens-sheen-of-stability-in-iraq-s-kurdistan-region.

Chandrasekaran, R. (2007) 'Kurds Cultivating Their Own Bonds with US', *Washington Post*, 23 April, available at: www.washingtonpost.com/wpdyn/content/article/2007/04/22/AR2007042201568.html.

Chomani, K. (2014) 'Push for Kurdish Independence Divides Iraqi Kurds', *Al Monitor*, 9 July, available at: www.al-monitor.com/pulse/originals/2014/07/iraq-kurdistan-barzani-puk-division-independence-iran-turkey.html.

Chulov, M. (2015) 'Turkey Sends in Jets as Syria's Agony Spills over Every Border', *The Observer*, 26 July, available at: www.theguardian.com/world/2015/jul/26/isis-syria-turkey-us?CMP=share_btn_tw.

Chulov, M & Hawramy, F. (2014) 'Iraqi Kurds Strengthen Their Position while ISIS Advances on Baghdad'. the *Guardian*, 26 June, available at: www.theguardian.com/world/2014/jun/26/iraqi-kurds-strengthen-position-kirkuk-isis.

Chulov, M., Hawramy, F., & Ackerman, S. (2014) 'Iraqi Army Capitulates to ISIS Militants in Four Cities', the *Guardian*, 12 June, available at: www.theguardian.com/world/2014/jun/11/mosul-isis-gunmen-middle-east-states.

Cockburn, P. (2014) 'Whose Side Is Turkey on?' *London Review of Books*, 6 November, available at: www.lrb.co.uk/v36/n21/patrick-cockburn/whose-side-is-turkey-on.

Cockburn, P. (2015a) 'Turkey Conflict with Kurds: was Approving Air Strikes against the PKK America's Worst Error in the Middle East since the Iraq War?' *The Independent*, 26 July, available at: www.independent.co.uk/news/world/middle-east/turkey-conflict-with-kurds-was-approving-air-strikes-against-the-pkk-americas-worst-error-in-the-10417381.html.

Cockburn, P. (2015b) 'Obama's Deal with Turkey Is a Betrayal of Syrian Kurds and May not even Weaken ISIS', *The Independent*, 1 August, available at: www.independent. co.uk/voices/turkey-kurdish-conflict-obamas-deal-with-ankara-is-a-betrayal-of-syrian-kurds-and-may-not-even-10432524.html.

Cook, S. A. (2011) 'Arab Spring, Turkish Fall', *Foreign Policy*, 5 May, available at: www.foreignpolicy.com/articles/2011/05/05/ arab_spring_turkish_fall.

Cooper, H. & Shear, M. (2014) 'Militants' Siege on Mountain in Iraq is Over, Pentagon Says', *New York Times*, 13 August available at: www.nytimes.com/2014/08/14/world/ middleeast/iraq-yazidi-refugees.html?_r=0.

Cuffe, J. (2007) 'Iraq's Other Kurdish Rebel Group', *BBC News*, 19 December, available at: http://news.bbc.co.uk/1/hi/world/middle_east/ 7148405.stm.

Cunningham, E. (2015) 'Turkey Summons U.S. Envoy amid Reports of Weapons Aid to Syrian Kurds' *Washington Post*, 14 October, available at: www.washingtonpost.com/ world/middle_east/turkey-summons-us-envoy-amid-reports-of-weapons-aid-to-syrian-kurds/2015/10/14/10bdf322-7272-11e5-ba14-318f8e87a2fc_story.html.

Dagher, S. (2010) 'Abducted Kurdish Writer Is Found Dead in Iraq', *New York Times*, 6 May, available at: www.nytimes.com/2010/05/07/world/middleeast/07erbil.html?_r=3&.

Davotoğlu, A. (2010) 'Turkey's Zero-Problems Foreign Policy', *Foreign Policy*, 20 May, available at: http://jft-newspaper.aub.edu.lb/reserve/data/s11244/s11244.pdf.

Day, M. (2016) 'Bilal Erdoğan: Italy Names Turkish President's Son in Money Launder-ing Investigation Allegedly Connected to Political Corruption', *The Independent*, 17 February, available at: www.independent.co.uk/news/world/europe/bilal-erdogan-italy-investigates-turkish-presidents-son-over-money-laundering-allegedly-connected-to-a6879871.html.

De Bellaigue, C. (2014) 'Turkey's Double Game in Syria', *New York Review of Books*, 14 October, available at: www.nybooks.com/daily/2014/10/14/turkey-double-game-syria/.

De Jong, A. (2016) 'The New-Old PKK', *Jacobin*, 18 March, available at: www.jacobin-mag.com/2016/03/pkk-ocalan-kurdistan-isis-murray-bookchin/.

Dettmer, J. (2014) 'Impotent Airstrikes, Passive Turks, and an ISIS Triumph', *The Daily Beast*, 3 October, available at: www.thedailybeast.com/articles/2014/10/03/impotent-u-s-airstrikes-passive-turks-and-an-isis-triumph.html.

Deutsche Welle (2014) 'Kurds Break Mount Sinjar Siege against "Islamic State", Free Yazidis', 19 December, available at: www.dw.com/en/kurds-break-mount-sinjar-siege-against-islamic-state-free-yazidis/a-18140706.

Deutsche Welle (2016) 'German Lawsuit Accuses Turkey of "War Crimes" in Military Operations against Kurds', 27 June, available at: www.dw.com/en/german-lawsuit-accuses-turkey-of-war-crimes-in-military-operations-against-kurds/a-19361089.

De Young, K. & Morris, L. (2014) 'U.S. Airstrikes Target Islamic State Militants in Northern Iraq', *Washington Post*, 8 August, available at: www.washingtonpost.com/ world/middle_east/islamic-state-militants-seize-christian-town-in-northern-iraq-thousands-flee/2014/08/07/942a553a-1e2b-11e4-ab7b-696c295ddfd1_story.html? hpid=z1.

De Young, K. & Sly, L. (2014) 'U.S. Frustration Rises as Turkey Withholds Military Help from Besieged Kobane', *Washington Post*, 8 October, available at: www. washingtonpost.com/world/national-security/us-frustration-rises-as-turkey-withholds-military-help-from-besieged-kobane/2014/10/08/311cb190-4f0e-11e4-babe-e91da 079cb8a_story.html.

Dickey, C. (2014) 'VP Biden Apologizes for Telling the Truth about Turkey, Saudi and ISIS', *The Daily Beast*, 5 October 2014, available at: www.thedailybeast.com/articles/2014/10/05/vp-biden-apologizes-for-telling-truth-about-turkey-saudi-and-isis.html.

Di Stefano Pironti, A. (2014) 'Iranian Repression of Kurds behind Rise of Militant PJAK', *Rudaw*, 23 January, available at: http://rudaw.net/english/middleeast/iran/23012014.

Ditz, J. (2014) 'Kerry: Stopping Kobane Takeover "Not a Priority"', *Anti War.com*, 8 October, available at: http://news.antiwar.com/2014/10/08/kerry-stopping-kobani-takeover-not-a-priority/.

Dombey, D. (2013) 'Turkey Agrees Energy Deal with Kurdish North Iraq', *Financial Times*, 13 May, available at: www.ft.com/cms/s/0/bbde0bf6-a859-11e2-8e5d00144 feabdc0.html #axzz2wiDh8hvR.

Dyke, J. & N. Blaser (2015) 'Is Turkey Using ISIS as an Excuse to Fight the Kurds?' *IRIN News Agency*, 11 August, available at: http://newirin.irinnews.org/fact-check-turkey-isis-pkk/.

The Economist (2003) 'Turkey and the United States: A Partnership at Risk?' 10 July, available at: www.economist.com/node/1914570.

The Economist (2007) 'Iraq and the Kurds: The Other Jerusalem', 4 April, available at: www.economist.com/node/8976641.

The Economist (2011) 'The Turkish Model: A Hard Act to Follow', 6 August, available at: www.economist.com/node/21525408.

The Economist (2015) 'Syria's Conflict: Drawing in the Neighbours', 4 July, available at: www.economist.com/news/middle-east-and-africa/21656692-turkey-and-jordan-are-considering-setting-up-buffer-zones-war-scorched.

Elliott, L. (2014) 'Mint Condition: Countries Tipped as the Next Economic Power-houses', the *Guardian*, 9 January, available at: www.theguardian.com/business/2014/jan/09/mint-condition-countries-tipped-economic-powerhouses.

Enzinna, W. (2015) 'A Dream of Secular Utopia in ISIS' Backyard', the *New York Times Magazine*, 24 November, available at: www.nytimes.com/2015/11/29/magazine/a-dream-of-utopia-in-hell.html?_r=0.

Ergin, Y. (2012) 'Meet the People behind Turkey's "Miracle"', *Global Post*, 16 April, available at: www.globalpost.com/dispatch/news/regions/europe/turkey/120411/meet-the-people-behind-turkeys-economic-miracle.

Escobar, P. (2007) 'Double-Crossing in Kurdistan', *Asia Times Online*, 2 November, available at: www.atimes.com/atimes/Middle_East/IK02Ak01.html.

Escobar, P. (2010) 'And the Winner is … Muqtada', *Asia Times Online*, 20 October, available at: www.atimes.com/atimes/Middle_East/LJ20Ak03.html.

Fadel, L. (2010) 'Iraq's Kurds Set to Be Kingmakers again', the *Washington Post*, 16 October, available at: www.washingtonpost.com/wp-dyn/content/article/2010/10/15/AR2010101506096.html.

Filkins, D. (2014) 'The Fight of Their Lives'. *The New Yorker*, 29 September, available at: www.newyorker.com/magazine/2014/09/29/fight-lives.

Filkins, D. (2016) 'Erdoğan's March to Dictatorship in Turkey', *The New Yorker*, 31 March, available at: www.newyorker.com/news/news-desk/erdogans-march-to-dictatorship-in-turkey.

Flood, D. H. (2009a) 'Between the Hammer and the Anvil: An Exclusive Interview with PJAK's Agiri Rojhilat', Jamestown Foundation, *Terrorism Monitor*, 7(31), available at: www.jamestown.org/single/?tx_ttnews[swords]=8fd5893941d69d0be3f378576261a e3e&tx_ttnews[any_of_the_words]=PJAK&tx_ttnews[tt_news]=35638&tx_ttnews [backPid]=7&cHash=e7f9626b0770af932d3d3994c8d82f8f#.UwNf_c5X-So.

Flood, D. H. (2009b) 'The "Other" Kurdistan Seethes with Rage', *Asia Times Online*, 16 October, available at: www.atimes.com/atimes/Middle_East/ KJ16Ak01.html.

Foreign Policy (2010) 'The FP Top 100 Global Thinkers', 10 December, available at: www.foreignpolicy.com/2010globalthinkers.

Friedman, D. & Salih, C. (2014) 'Kurds to the Rescue'. *Foreign Affairs*, 17 June, available at: www.foreignaffairs.com/articles/iraq/2014-06-17/kurds-rescue.

Galbraith, P. (2014) 'House of Kurds', *Politico*, 17 June, available at: www.politico.com/ magazine/story/2014/06/iraq-independent-kurdistan-107958.html#.U8-i0EAcOSo.

Galbraith, P. (2015) 'Peter W. Galbraith', Biographical Page on Galbraith's personal blog on *Wordpress*, available at: http://peterwoodardgalbraith. wordpress.com/about/.

Gee, H. (2009) 'Forgotten Refugees of Northern Iraq', *RNW Media*, 27 May, available at: www.rnw.org/archive/forgotten-refugees-northern-iraq.

Gelb, L. H. (2003) 'The Three-State Solution', the *New York Times*, 23 November, available at: www.nytimes.com/2003/11/25/opinion/the-three-state-solution.html.

Gemici, H. (2013) 'Turkey, Exxon Mobil Going Ahead with Gas Project in Iraqi Kurdistan', *Al Monitor*, 20 May, available at: www.al-monitor.com/pulse/business/2013/05/ turkey-and-exxon-explore-oil-in-iraqi-kurdistan.html.

Gladstone, A. (2016) 'Dispute over Kurds Threatens U.S.-Turkey Alliance', *New York Times*, 19 February, available at: www.nytimes.com/2016/02/19/world/middleeast/ dispute-over-kurds-threatens-us-turkey-alliance.html.

Glantz, A. (2006) 'Kurdish "Thank You" a Republican Stunt?', *Inter Press Service News Agency*, 31 July, available at: www.ipsnews.net/ 2006/07/politics-us-kurdish-thank-you-a-republican-stunt/.

Glanz, J. (2009) 'US Advisor to Kurds Stands to Reap Oil Profits', the *New York Times*, 11 November, available at: www.nytimes.com/2009/11/12/world/middleeast/12 galbraith.html?pagewanted=all&_r=2&.

Goldberg, J. (2016) 'The Obama Doctrine', *The Atlantic*, April Issue, available at: www. theatlantic.com/magazine/archive/2016/04/the-obama-doctrine/471525/#1.

Graeber, D. (2014) 'Why Is the World Ignoring the Revolutionary Kurds in Syria?' the *Guardian*, 8 October, available at: www.theguardian.com/commentisfree/2014/oct/08/ why-world-ignoring-revolutionary-kurds-syria-isis.

Grossbongardt, A. (2006) 'Terrorism in Turkey: Who's Bombing Tourists?' *Der Spiegel International*, 7 September, available at: www.spiegel.de/international/spiegel/terrorism-in-turkey-who-s-bombing-tourists-a-435494.html.

Guiton, B. (2014) ' "ISIS Sees Turkey as Its Ally": Former Islamic State Member Reveals Turkish Army Cooperation', *Newsweek*, 7 November, available at: http://europe. newsweek.com/isis-and-turkey-cooperate-destroy-kurds-former-isis-member-reveals-turkish-282920?rm=eu.

Gürbey, G. (2015a) 'Parlamentswahlen in der Türkei: Politischer Aufbruch oder Stagnation?' *EurActiv*, 11 June, available at: www.euractiv.de/section/eu-aussenpolitik/ opinion/parlamentswahlen-in-der-turkei-politischer-aufbruch-oder-stagnation/.

Gürbey, G. (2015b) 'Gegen den "Zeitgeist": Die türkische Militäroffensive gegen die PKK und die Kurden', *EurActiv*, 25 August, available at: www.euractiv.de/section/eu-aussenpolitik/opinion/gegen-den-zeitgeist-die-turkische-militaroffensive-gegen-die-pkk-und-die-kurden/.

Gurcan, M. (2014) 'Kurdish Activist Violence Brings Kobani Conflict to Turkish Streets', *Al Monitor*, 8 October, available at: www.al-monitor.com/pulse/originals/2014/10/ turkey-syria-kurds-kobani-pkk-street-violence.html.

Gurcan, M. (2015) 'Is PKK Real Target of Turkish Strikes?' *Al Monitor*, 27 July, available at: www.al-monitor.com/pulse/originals/2015/07/turkey-syria-iraq-pkk-kurds-pyd-ypg-two-front-conflict.html.

Gursel, K. (2014) 'Turkey Paying Price for Jihadist Highway on Border', *Al Monitor*, 13 June, available at: www.al-monitor.com/pulse/originals/2014/06/gursel-al-qaeda-isis-turkey-mosul-iraq-syria-consulate.html.

Gursel, K. (2016) 'Turkey's Southeast Beginning to Resemble Syria', *Al Monitor*, 13 June, available at: www.al-monitor.com/pulse/originals/2016/06/turkey-syria-kurdish-militants-terror-spilled-major-cities.html.

Harding, L. (2014) 'Haider al-Abadi: From Exile in Britain to Iraq's Next Prime Minister', the *Guardian*, 11 August, available at: www.theguardian.com/world/2014/aug/11/haider-al-abadi-profile-iraqs-next-prime-minister.

Harrer, G. (2014) 'Der geflickte Irak', *Der Standard*, 10 February, available at: http://derstandard.at/1389859851281/Der-geflickte-Irak.

Harris, W. (2014) 'Chaos in Iraq: Are the Kurds Truly Set to Win?' *Small Wars Journal*, 28 August, available at: http://smallwarsjournal.com/jrnl/art/chaos-in-iraq-are-the-kurds-truly-set-to-win.

Henley, J., Shaheen, K., & Letsch, C. (2015) 'Turkey Election: Erdogan and AKP Return to Power with Outright Majority', the *Guardian*, 2 November, available at: www.theguardian.com/world/2015/nov/01/turkish-election-akp-set-for-majority-with-90-of-vote-counted.

Hersh, S. M. (2008) 'Preparing the Battlefield: The Bush Administration Steps up its Secret Moves against Iran', *The New Yorker*, 7 July, available at: www.newyorker.com/reporting/2008/07/07/080707fa_fact_hersh.

Hess, J. (2014) 'Washington's Secret Backchannel Talks with Syria's Kurdish "Terrorists"', *Foreign Policy*, 7 October, available at: http://foreignpolicy.com/2014/10/07/washingtons-secret-back-channel-talks-with-syrias-kurdish-terrorists/.

Hiltermann, J. (2014) 'Kurdish Independence: Harder than it Looks', *The New York Review of Books*, 10 July, available at: www.nybooks.com/blogs/nyrblog/2014/jul/10/kurdish-independence-harder-than-it-looks/.

Hitchens, C. (2007) 'Letter from Kurdistan: Holiday in Iraq', *Vanity Fair*, April issue, available at: www.vanityfair.com/politics/features/2007/04/hitchens200704.

Howard, M. & Goldenberg, S. (2003) 'US Arrest of Soldiers Infuriates Turkey', the *Guardian*, 8 July, available at: www.theguardian.com/world/2003/jul/08/turkey.michaelhoward.

Human Rights Watch (2011) 'Iraqi Kurdistan: Growing Efforts to Silence Media', 24 May, available at: www.hrw.org/news/2011/05/24/iraqi-kurdistan-growing-effort-silence-media.

Human Rights Watch (2012) 'World Report 2012: Iraq', available at: www.hrw.org/world-report-2012/world-report-2012-iraq.

Human Rights Watch (2014) 'Syria: Abuses in Kurdish-Run Enclaves', 18 June, available at: www.hrw.org/news/2014/06/18/syria-abuses-kurdish-run-enclaves.

Hürriyet Daily News (2013) 'Iraqi Kurdish Leader Barzani Urges Support for Peace Process in Diyarbakir Rally with Turkish PM', 16 November, available at: www.hurriyetdailynews.com/iraqi-kurdish-leader-barzani-urges-support-for-peace-process-in-diyarbakir-rally-with-turkishpm.aspx?PageID=238&NID=58028&NewsCatID=338.

Hürriyet Daily News (2015) 'Turkey Arrests some 1300 PKK-Linked Suspects, Less than 300 ISIL-Linked Suspects since Late July', 20 October, available at: www.hurriyet

dailynews.com/turkey-arrests-some-1300-pkk-linked-suspects-less-than-300-isil-linked-suspects-since-late-july.aspx?pageID=238&nID=90118&NewsCatID=509.

Idiz, S. (2015) 'Erdogan Aims to Create Stronger Presidential System', *Al Monitor*, 3 June, available at: www.al-monitor.com/pulse/tr/contents/articles/originals/2015/02/turkey-erdogan-presidential-system-campaign.html.

Immigration and Refugee Board of Canada (2001) *Iraq: Relations between the Kurdistan Workers Party (PKK) and the Kurdish Democratic Party (KDP) in northern Iraq (1999–2000)*, 16 June, available at: www.refworld.org/docid/ 3df4be4c8.html.

International Monetary Fund – IMF (2012) 'World Economic Outlook Database', October version, available at: www.imf.org/external/pubs/ft/weo/2012/02/weodata/index.aspx.

Jacinto, L. (2014) 'Strange Bedfellows: Terror Groups, Kurdish Factions Unite against ISIS', *France 24*, 15 August, available at: www.france24.com/en/20140815-kurds-isis-pkk-terror-group-iraq-turkey-usa.

Jenkins, G. (2008) 'Turkey and Northern Iraq: An Overview', Jamestown Foundation, *Occasional Paper*, July, available at: www.jamestown.org/uploads/media/Jamestown-JenkinsTurkeyNIraq.pdf.

Johnson, K. (2014) 'The Revenge of the Kurds'. *Foreign Policy*, 12 June, available at: http://foreignpolicy.com/2014/06/12/revenge-of-the-kurds/.

Kalin, S. (2015) 'Iraqi Kurdistan's Cash Crisis Hits Banks – and the Region's Promise', *Reuters*, 4 December, available at: http://uk.reuters.com/article/us-iraq-kurds-economy-idUKKBN0TN0FT20151204.

Kamen, A. (2006) 'The Iraq We Haven't Seen', the *Washington Post*, 26 July, available at: www.washingtonpost.com/wp-dyn/content/article/2006/07/25/AR2006072501254.html.

Kardaş, S. (2009) 'Turkish-Iraqi-American Trilateral Security Mechanism Focuses on PKK Terrorism', Jamestown Foundation, *Eurasia Daily Monitor*, 6(70), available at: www.turkishnews.com/en/content/2009/04/13/turkish-iraqi-american-trilateral-security-mechanism-focuses-on-pkk-terrorism/.

Kardaş, S. & Özcan, N. A. (2009) 'PJAK, Iran and the United States: Kurdish Militants Designated Terrorist Organisation by the United States', Jamestown Foundation, *Terrorism Monitor*, 7(7), available at: www.jamestown.org/single/?tx_ttnews[swords]= 8fd5893941d69d0be3f378576261ae3e&tx_ttnews[any_of_the_words]=PJAK&tx_ ttnews[tt_news]=34759&tx_ttnews[backPid]=7&cHash=a115ff6979084b0209205e32 cbbc5319#.UwN99M5X-So.

Keles, J. (2014) 'The European Kurds Rallying to Fight IS', *Open Democracy*, 10 December, available at: www.opendemocracy.net/opensecurity/janroj-yilmaz-keles/european-kurds-rallying-to-fight-is.

Kenyon, P. (2012) 'The Turkish Model: Can It Be Replicated?' *National Public Radio*, 6 January, available at: www.npr.org/2012/01/06/144751851/the-turkish-model-can-it-be-replicated.

Khalaji, M. (2007) 'US Support for the Iranian Opposition', *The Washington Institute for Near East Policy, Policywatch* 1258, 9 July, available at: www.washingtoninstitute.org/policy-analysis/view/u.s.-support-for-the-iranian-opposition.

Kinzer, S. (2001) 'Our Man in Honduras', *New York Review of Books*, 48(14), pp. 40–43.

Kirby, T. & Turgut, P. (2006) 'Kurdish Separatists Claim Deadly Attack on Popular Holiday Resorts, *The Independent*, 29 August, available at: www.independent.co.uk/news/world/europe/kurdish-separatists-claim-deadly-attack-on-popular-holiday-resorts-413752.html.

Kliff, S. (2014) 'President Obama's Full Statement on the Iraq Crisis', *Vox.com*, 7 August, available at: www.vox.com/2014/8/7/5981449/president-obamas-full-statement-on-the-iraq-crisis.

Kotsev, V. (2013) 'How the Protests Will Impact Turkey at Home and Abroad', *The Atlantic*, 2 June, available at: www.theatlantic.com/international/archive/2013/06/how-the-protests-will-impact-turkey-at-home-and-abroad/276456/.

Krajeski, J. (2014a) 'In Northern Iraq, Kurds Mobilize for War against ISIS', *The Nation*, 23 June, available at: www.thenation.com/article/northern-iraq-kurds-mobilize-war-against-isis/.

Krajeski, J. (2014b) 'What Kobani Means for Turkey's Kurds', *The New Yorker*, 8 November, available at: www.newyorker.com/news/news-desk/kobani-means-turkeys-kurds.

Kurd.net (2009) 'Turkey's DTP May Call for "Kurdish Conference" in Iraqi Kurdistan', 15 September, available at: www.ekurd.net/mismas/articles/misc2009/9/turkey kurdistan2258.htm.

Kurd.net (2012) 'Erbil Agreement Yet to Be Fully Implemented in Syrian Kurdistan', 24 October, available at: www.ekurd.net/mismas/articles/ misc2012/10/state6581.htm.

Kurd.net (2013a) 'Turkish PM in First Visit to Kurdistan Region of Iraq', 29 February, available at: www.ekurd.net/mismas /articles/misc2011/3/ state4916.htm.

Kurd.net (2013b) 'Turkey, Iran Influence Iraqi Kurdish Politics', 23 November, available at: www.ekurd.net/mismas/articles/misc2013/11/state7510.htm.

Kuntz, K. (2016) 'Children of the PKK: The Growing Intensity of Turkey's Civil War', *Der Spiegel*, 12 February, available at: www.spiegel.de/international/world/escalating-turkish-civil-war-sees-young-fighters-on-front-a-1076663.html.

Kutschera, C. (2008) 'Hajji Ahmadi: PJAK Fights for a Confederal Iran', *The Middle East Magazine*, August/September issue, available at: www.chris-kutschera.com/A/PJAK.htm.

Lake, E. (2014) '"Practically Speaking, Iraq Has Broken Apart"', *The Daily Beast*, 15 June, available at: www.thedailybeast.com/articles/2014/06/15/practically-speaking-iraq-has-broken-apart.html.

Le Vine, M. (2011) 'Is Turkey the Best Model for Arab Democracy?' *Al Jazeera*, 19 September, available at: www.aljazeera.com/indepth/opinion/2011/09/2011916843569952 73.html.

Letsch, C. (2013) 'Turkey Protests Unite a Colourful Coalition of Anger against Erdogan', the *Guardian*, 3 June, available at: www.theguardian.com/world/2013/ jun/03/turkey-protests-coalition-anger-erdogan.

Letsch, C. (2014) 'US Drops Weapons and Ammunition to Help Kurdish Fighters in Kobani', the *Guardian*, 20 October, available at: www.theguardian.com/world/2014/ oct/20/turkey-iraqi-kurds-kobani-isis-fighters-us-air-drops-arms.

Letsch, C. (2015) 'Turkey Releases Bombing Suspect Details as Twitter Temporarily Shut Down', the *Guardian*, 22 July, available at: www.theguardian.com/world/2015/ jul/22/turkey-blocks-twitter-to-stop-broadcast-of-suruc-bombing-images.

Letsch, C. & Traynor, I. (2014) 'Kobani: Anger Grows as Turkey Stops Kurds from Aiding Militias in Syria', the *Guardian*, 8 October, available at: www.theguardian. com/world/2014/oct/08/kobani-isis-turkey-kurds-ypg-syria-erdogan.

Leverink, J. (2016) 'Turkey Descends into Civil War as Conflict in Southeast Escalates', *Inter Press Service News Agency*, 4 February, available at: www.ipsnews.net/2016/02/ turkey-descends-into-civil-war-as-conflict-in-southeast-escalates/.

Malek, A. (2014) 'After Repelling ISIL, PKK Fighters Are the New Heroes of Kurdistan', *Al Jazeera*, 17 October, available at: http://america.aljazeera.com/articles/2014/ 10/17/pkk-s-rise-in-iraqikurdistan.html.

Mert, N. (2013) 'The Erdogan-Barzani Alliance: A Turkish Policy Classic', *Hurriyet Daily News*, 18 November, available at: www.hurriyetdailynews.com/the-erdogan-barzani-alliance-a-turkish-policyclassic.aspx?pageID=449&nID=58056&NewsCat ID=406.

Mohammed, B. (2013) 'Barzani's Foreign Policy Risks Kurdistan's Long Term Future', *The Kurdish Aspect*, 3 February, available at: www.kurdishaspect.com/doc020413BM.html.

Moore, J. (2015) 'Report: ISIS Ousted from Syrian City of Hasakah', *Newsweek*, 30 June, available at: http://europe.newsweek.com/report-isis-ousted-syrian-city-hasakah-330957.

Moreton, C. (2015) 'Iraq Invasion 2003: The Warnings Six Wise Men Gave to Tony Blair as He Planned to Launch Poorly Planned Campaign', *The Independent*, 25 January, available at: www.independent.co.uk/news/uk/politics/iraq-invasion-2003-the-bloody-warnings-six-wise-men-gave-to-tony-blair-as-he-prepared-to-launch-10000839.html#gallery.

Morris, L. (2014) 'Veteran Kurdish Politician Elected President of Iraq', *Washington Post*, 24 July, available at: www.washingtonpost.com/world/middle_east/veteran-kurdish-politician-elected-president-of-iraq/2014/07/24/28448523-487b-4091-a4f1-fb7eefb87899_story.html.

Myers, S. L. (2007) 'Bush Pledges to Help Turkey on Intelligence', the *New York Times*, 5 November, available at: www.nytimes.com/ 2007/11/06/world/europe/06prexy. html?_r=0.

Naqishbendi, R. (2011) 'The Time is Right to Bring the Two Kurdish Leaders Talabani and Barzani to the Court of Justice', *Kurdish Media.com*, 20 February, available at: www.kurdmedia.com/article.aspx?id=16641.

National Geographic (2011) '20 Best Trips of 2011', available at: http://travel.national geographic.com/travel/best-trips-2011-photos/#/20-ulaanbaatar-mongolia-gandan-monastery_30422_600x450.jpg.

Nazish, K. (2014) 'Turkey "There just to Watch" in Kobane', *Al Jazeera*, 4 October, available at: www.aljazeera.com/news/middleeast/2014/10/turkey-there-just-watch-kobane-201410481243432189.html.

Newton-Small, J. (2012) 'Destination Kurdistan: Is this Autonomous Iraqi Region a Budding Tourist Hot Spot?' *Time Magazine*, 31 December, available at: http://world. time.com/2012/12/31/destination-kurdistan-is-this-autonomous-iraqi-region-a-budding-tourist-hotspot/.

Norton, B. (2016) 'Turkey's "Double Game" on ISIS and Support for Extremist Groups Highlighted after Horrific Istanbul Attack', *Salon.com*, 30 June, available at: www.salon.com/2016/06/30/turkeys_double_game_on_isis_and_support_for_extremist_groups_highlighted_after_horrific_istanbul_attack/.

Oğuzlu, T. (2013) 'Arab Spring and the Day after: What Went Wrong for Turkey?' *Today's Zaman*, 29 September, available at: www.todayszaman.com/news-327521-arab-spring-and-the-day-after-what-went-wrong-for-turkey.html.

Okumuş, O. (2014) 'Turkey Energy Deal with KRG Lacks Transparency', *Al Monitor*, 8 January, available at: www.al-monitor.com/pulse/originals/2014/01/turkey-krg-energy-deal-oil-pipeline-agreement.html.

Oppel, R. A. (2007) 'In Iraq, Conflict Simmers on a Second Kurdish Front', the *New York Times*, 23 October, available at: www.nytimes.com/2007/10/23/world/middleeast/23kurds.html?_r=2&oref=slogin&.

Orucoglu, B. (2015) 'Why Turkey's Mother of All Corruption Scandals Refuses to Go Away', *Foreign Policy*, 6 January, available at: http://foreignpolicy.com/2015/01/06/why-turkeys-mother-of-all-corruption-scandals-refuses-to-go-away/.

Otten, C. (2015) 'ISIS in Iraq: Young Kurds Flock to PKK to Take up Arms against Militants after Becoming Disillusioned with Their Government', *The Independent*, 8 September, available at: www.independent.co.uk/news/world/middle-east/isis-in-iraq-young-kurds-flock-to-pkk-to-take-up-arms-against-militants-after-becoming-disillusioned-10492171.html.

Ozcan, N. A. (2014) 'Understanding Turkey's Hesitation over Kobane Crisis', Jamestown Foundation, *Terrorism Monitor*, 12(21), 7 November, available at: www.jamestown.org/programs/tm/single/?tx_ttnews%5Btt_news%5D=43061&cHash=c3dc7746bc7c653e48989690e278684a#.V8bQgxJYDYg.

Packer, G. (2014) 'A Friend Flees the Horror of ISIS', *The New Yorker*, 6 August, available at: www.newyorker.com/news/daily-comment/friend-flees-horror-isis.

Pamir, N. (2013) 'Turkey Contributes to Fragmentation of Iraq', *Al Monitor*, 20 February, available at: www.al-monitor.com/pulse/originals/2013/02/turkey-krg-relations-strain-future-iraq-oil-interests.html.

Pamuk, H. & Coskun, O. (2013) 'Turkey, Iraqi Kurdistan Clinch Major Energy Pipeline Deals', *Reuters*, 6 November, available at: http://uk.reuters.com/article/2013/11/06/uk-turkey-iraq-kurdistan-idUKBRE9A50HN20131106.

Park, B. (2012c) 'Turkey, Kurds, Iraq, Syria: A New Regional Dynamic', *Open Democracy*, 30 August, available at: www.opendemocracy.net/bill-park/turkey-kurds-iraq-syria-new-regional-dynamic.

Park, B. (2014) 'Why Won't Turkey Save Kobane from Isil?' *Daily Telegraph*, 10 October, available at: www.telegraph.co.uk/news/worldnews/europe/turkey/11153852/Why-wont-Turkey-help-save-Kobane-from-Isil.html.

Parkinson, J. (2014) 'Kurds' Takeover of Iraqi City of Kirkuk Strengthens Their Hand'. *Wall Street Journal*, 20 June, available at: www.wsj.com/articles/kurds-takeover-of-strategic-city-strengthens-their-hand-1403238922.

Parkinson, J. & Entous, A. (2014) 'How Kurds Came to Play Key Role in U.S. Plans to Combat Islamic State', *Wall Street Journal*, 8 September, available at: www.wsj.com/articles/in-iraq-kurds-are-key-part-of-u-s-strategy-against-islamic-state-1410229982.

Parkinson, J. & Nissenbaum, D. (2014) 'U.S., Allies Training Kurds on Sophisticated Weaponry against Islamic State', *Wall Street Journal*, 21 September, available at: www.wsj.com/articles/u-s-allies-training-kurds-on-using-sophisticated-weaponry-against-islamic-state-1411339625.

Phillips, D. (2014) 'ISIS-Turkey Links', Columbia University, Institute for the Study of Human Rights, Research Paper, 11 September, available at: www.huffingtonpost.com/david-l-phillips/research-paper-isis-turke_b_6128950.html.

Phillips, D. (2015b) 'U.S. and Turkey on a Collision Course in Syria', *Huffington Post*, 11 February, available at: www.huffingtonpost.com/david-l-phillips/us-and-turkey-on-a-collis_b_8452606.html.

Pinar, M. (2014) 'Pentagon: U.S. Believes Several Hundred Militants Killed in Kobani Strikes', *Chicago Tribune*, 15 October, available at: www.chicagotribune.com/news/nationworld/chi-islamic-state-airstrikes-kobani-20141015-story.html.

Pollack, K. (2016) 'Iraq Situation Report, Part III: Kurdistan', The Brookings Institution, *Markaz – Middle East Policy & Politics*, 30 March available at: www.brookings.edu/blog/markaz/2016/03/30/iraq-situation-report-part-iii-kurdistan/.

Public Broadcasting Service – PBS (2000) 'The Survival of Saddam – An Interview with Jalal Talabani', *Frontline*, 8 February, available at: www.pbs.org/wgbh/pages/frontline/shows/ saddam/interviews/talabani.html.

Purvis, A. (2007) 'Erdogan Talks Turkey in Washington', *Time Magazine*, 4 November, available at: http://content.time.com/time/world/article/0,8599,1680526,00.html.

Rand, N. (2007) 'US Wages Covert War on Iraq-Iran Border', *Asia Times Online*, 28 November, available at: www.atimes.com/atimes/MiddleEast/IK28Ak01.html.

Ravid, B. (2014) 'Netanyahu Calls for Kurdish Independence from Iraq', *Haaretz*, 30 June, available at: www.haaretz.com/israel-news/.premium-1.601997.

Renard, T. (2008) 'PJAK in Northern Iraq: Tangled Interests and Proxy Wars', Jamestown Foundation, *Terrorism Monitor*, 6(10), available at: www.jamestown.org/programs/gta/single/?tx_ttnews%5Btt_news%5D=4924&tx_ttnews%5BbackPid%5D=167&no_cache=1.

Reporters without Borders (2012) 'Black December for Media Freedom in Iraqi Kurdistan', 3 January, available at: http://en.rsf.org/iraq-black-december-for-media-freedom-03-01-2012,41621.html.

Republic of Turkey, Ministry of Economy (2013) 'Countries and Regions – Middle East – Iraq', Country Reports and Indices, July version, available at: www.economy.gov.tr/index.cfm?sayfa=countriesandregions&country=IQ&region=4.

Reuters (2008a) 'Turkey Launches Major Land Offensive into N. Iraq', 22 February, available at: http://uk.reuters.com/article/homepageCrisis/idUKL22614485._CH_.242020080222.

Reuters (2008b) 'Interview: "Turkey Targets Iraq Kurds, not just Rebels," Kurd PM', 28 February, available at: www.reuters.com/article/2008/02/28/idUSL2882159.

Reuters (2012) 'Danish Court Fines Kurd TV for Promoting Terrorism', 13 January, available at: www.reuters.com/article/2012/01/13/us-denmark-tv-turkey-idUSTRE80C1EU20120113.

Reuters (2013) 'Iraqi Kurdish President in Turkey to Back PM's Peace Effort', 16 November, available at: www.reuters.com/article/2013/11/16/us-turkey-kurdistan-idUSBRE9AF05L20131116.

Reuters (2014a) 'Mosul Falls to Militants, Iraqi Forces Flee Northern City', 10 June, available at: www.reuters.com/article/us-iraq-security-idUSKBN0EL1H520140610.

Reuters (2014b) 'Iraq Parliament Elects Senior Kurdish Politician President', 24 July, available at: www.reuters.com/article/us-iraq-president-idUSKBN0FT1GC20140724.

Reuters (2014c) 'Renwed Assault on Kobani; 21 Dead in Turkey as Kurds Rise' 8 October, available at: www.reuters.com/article/us-mideast-crisis-idUSKCN0HX0XF20141008.

Reuters (2016) 'Battle between Syrian government, Kurdish Forces Kill 26: Kurdish Official', 21 April, available at: www.reuters.com/article/us-mideast-crisis-syria-hasaka-idUSKCN0XI1G6.

Robinson, N. (2015) 'Turkey Is Using ISIS as Cover for Its War against Kurdish Activists', *The Nation* 26 August, available at: www.thenation.com/article/turkey-is-using-isis-as-cover-for-its-war-against-kurdish-activists/.

Rogin, J. (2011) 'MEK Rally Planned for Friday at State Department', *Foreign Policy, The Cable*, 25 August, available at: http://thecable.foreignpolicy.com/posts/2011/08/25/mek_rally_planned_for_friday_at_state_department.

Rogin, J. & Lake, E. (2016) 'Obama Administration Argues over Support for Syrian Kurds', *Bloomberg News*, 23 February, available at: www.bloomberg.com/view/articles/2016-02-23/obama-administration-fights-itself-over-role-of-syrian-kurds.

Rosenthal, M. (2015) 'US-Backed Forces in Syria Accused of Human Rights Violations', *Mother Jones*, 9 November, available at: www.motherjones.com/politics/2015/11/us-kurds-syria-human-rights-abuses.

Ross, C. (2015) 'Power to the People: A Syrian Experiment in Democracy', *Financial Times*, 23 October, available at: www.ft.com/intl/cms/s/2/50102294-77fd-11e5-a95a-27d368e1ddf7.html#axzz4IXnlHiCW.

Rudaw (2013a) 'Prominent PKK Leader Leaves Group', 25 December, available at: http://rudaw.net/english/kurdistan/251220131.

Rudaw (2013b) 'President Barzani Slams PYD in Syria, Rejects Autonomy Declaration', 15 November, available at: http://rudaw.net/english/ kurdistan/14112013.

Sadjadi, G. (2009) 'Interview with Dr. Fuad Hussein, Chief of Staff to the Presidency of the Kurdistan Regional Government', *The Kurdish Herald*, May issue, available at: www.kurdishherald.com/issue/001/article02.php.

Saleh, J. (2014) 'The Battle for Kobane Is also Political', The Washington Institute for Near East Policy, *Fikra Forum*, 5 December, available at: www.washingtoninstitute. org/policy-analysis/view/the-battle-for-kobane-is-also-political1.

Salih, C. (2014) 'Why Did the U.S. Help the Kurds in Iraq but Leave ISIS to Massacre Them in Syria?', the *Guardian*, 7 October, available at: www.theguardian.com/ commentisfree/2014/oct/07/us-kurds-iraq-isis-massacre-syria-kobani.

Salih, M. (2014a) 'The Kurds Are Coming', *Foreign Policy*, 16 June, available at:.http:// foreignpolicy.com/2014/06/16/the-kurdish-are-coming/.

Salih, M. (2014b) 'PKK Forces Impress in Fight against Islamic State', *Al Monitor*, 1 September, available at: www.al-monitor.com/pulse/originals/2014/09/pkk-kurdish-fight-islamic-state.html.

Salih, M. (2014c) 'Meet the Badass Women Fighting the Islamic State', *Foreign Policy*, 12 September, available at: http://foreignpolicy.com/2014/09/12/meet-the-badass-women-fighting-the-islamic-state/.

Salih, M. (2015) 'New Units Step toward Reforming Kurdish Peshmerga', *Al Monitor*, 2 July, available at: www.al-monitor.com/pulse/originals/2015/07/iraq-new-peshmerga-brigades-kurdistan-us-isis.html.

Sayman, Y. (2015) 'ISIS Bombs Turkey', *The Daily Beast*, 20 July, available at: www. thedailybeast.com/articles/2015/07/20/isis-bombs-turkey.html.

Shafak, E. (2013) 'The View from Taksim Square: Why Is Turkey now in Turmoil?', the *Guardian*, 3 June, available at: www.theguardian.com/world/2013/jun/03/taksim-square-istanbul-turkey-protest.

Shear, M. (2014) 'Obama Says Iraq Airstrike Effort Could Be Long-Term', *New York Times* 9 August, available at: www.nytimes.com/2014/08/10/world/middleeast/us-airstrikes-on-militants-in-iraq.html?_r=0.

Shelton, T. (2014) 'If It Wasn't for the Kurdish Fighters, We Would Have Died Up There', *Public Radio International*, 29 August, available at: www.pri.org/stories/2014-08-29/if-it-wasn-t-kurdish-fighters-we-would-have-died-there.

Sinan, O. (2007) 'Iraq's "Chemical Ali" Sentenced to Hang', *Washington Post*, 24 June, available at: www.washingtonpost.com/wp-dyn/content/article/2007/06/24/AR2007 062400823_pf.html.

Slavin, B. (2014) 'Iraqi Kurdish Officials Describe "Different Country" after Mosul', *Al Monitor*, 2 July, available at: www.al-monitor.com/pulse/originals/2014/07/us-kurdish-independence-hopes-baghdad-collapse-power-share.html.

Smith, H. L. (2015) 'Thousands of Arabs Driven Out by Kurds' Ethnic Cleansing', *The Times*, 1 June, available at: www.thetimes.co.uk/tto/news/world/middleeast/article 4456567.ece.

Solomon, E. & Dombey, D. (2014) 'PKK "Terrorists" Crucial to Fight against ISIS', *Financial Times* 15 August, available at: www.ft.com/cms/s/0/4a6e5b90-2460-11e4-be8e-00144feabdc0.html#axzz4If1DJB1A.

Der Spiegel (2008) 'Ankara's Intentions: What Is behind Turkey's Invasion of Northern Iraq', 25 February, available at: www.spiegel.de/international/world/ankara-s-intentions-what-is-behind-turkey-s-invasion-of-northern-iraq-a-537554.html.

Der Spiegel (2014) 'Vor Abstimmung im Bundestag: Steinmeier befürchtet Gründung eines kurdischen Staates', 1 September, available at: www.spiegel.de/politik/ deutschland/ nordirak-steinmeier-warnt-vor-gruendung-eines-kurdischen-staates-a-989135.html.

Der Spiegel (2016a) 'Türkei: Der schwierige Partner – wie Präsident Erdoğan mit dem Westen spielt', 2 April, available at: https://magazin.spiegel.de/SP/2016/14/143908087/ index.html?utm_source=spon&utm_campaign=centerpage.

Der Spiegel (2016b) 'Vertrauliches Dokument: Bundesregierung wirft Türkei Terrorunterstützung vor', 16 August, available at: www.spiegel.de/politik/deutschland/ bundesregierung-wirft-tuerkei-terror-unterstuetzung-vor-a-1107915.html.

Steinvorth, D. & Zand, B. (2013) 'A Country Divided: Where Is Turkey Headed?', *Der Spiegel*, 24 June, available at: www.spiegel.de/international/world/protests-reveal-the-deep-divisions-in-turkish-society-a-907498.html.

Tait, R. (2009) 'Turkey Bans Main Kurdish Party over Alleged Terror Links', the *Guardian*, 12 December, available at: www.theguardian.com/world/2009/dec/12/ turkey-bans-main-kurdish-party.

Tattersall, N. & Coskun, O. (2015) 'Turkey's Erdoğan Gambles on Using Crisis to Consolidate Power', *Al Arabiya*, 17 August, available at: www.businessinsider.com/ r-turkeys-erdogan-gambles-on-using-crisis-to-consolidate-power-2015-8?IR=T.

Tavernise, S. (2008) 'Turkey Says it Has Sent Ground Troops into Iraq', the *New York Times*, 22 February, available at: www.nytimes.com/2008/02/22/world/middleeast/22iraq. html?_r=4&hp&oref=slogin&oref=slogin&oref=slogin&oref=slogin.

Tax, M. (2015) 'The Revolution in Rojava', *Dissent*, 22 April, available at: www.dissentmagazine.org/online_articles/the-revolution-in-rojava.

Today's Zaman (2009) 'Trilateral Roadmap with US, Iraq Ready for Steps against PKK', 22 December, available at: www.todayszaman.com/tz-web/news-196258-trilateral-road-map-with-iraq-us-ready-for-steps-against-pkk.html.

Tol, G. (2012) 'Syria's Kurdish Challenge to Turkey', *Foreign Policy*, 29 August, available at: http://mideastafrica.foreignpolicy.com/posts/2012/08/29/syrias_kurdish_challenge_to_turkey.

Traynor, I. & Letsch, C. (2015) 'Turkey at a Crossroads as Erdogan Bulldozes His Way to Lasting Legacy', the *Guardian*, 2 June, available at: www.theguardian.com/ world/2015/jun/02/turkish-election-recep-tayyip-erdogan-legacy.

TREND (2011) 'PJAK, PKK One Terrorist Group with Two Names, Turkish Deputy PM', 26 August, available at: http://en.trend.az/regions/met/turkey/1923185.html.

Turkish Airlines (2013) 'Investor Relations, Fact Sheet', September version, available at: http://investor.turkishairlines.com/documents/ThyInvestorRelations/download/ icerikler/turkish_airlines_fact_sheet_eng_ver1.pdf.

Turkish Weekly (2009) 'US Brands PKK's Iran Branch, PJAK, "Terrorist Organisation"', 5 February, available at: www.turkishweekly.net/news/64144/us-brands-pkk-39-s-iran-branch-pjak-quot-terrorist-organization-quot-.html.

Tuysuzoğlu, G. (2013) 'Realities between Historic Erdogan-Barzani Meeting', *Al Monitor*, 29 November, available at: www.al-monitor.com/pulse/politics/2013/11/ reality-historic-meeting-barzani-erdogan-turkey-kurdistan.html.

UK Border Agency – Home Office (2011) 'Iraq', *Country of Origin Information, COI Report*, 30 August, available at: www.refworld.org/cgi-bin/texis/vtx/rwmain?docid= 4e5f69202.

United Press International – UPI (2009) 'Kurdish Groups May Call for Conference', 14 September, available at: www.upi.com/Top_News/Special/2009/09/14/Kurdish-groups-may-call-for-conference/UPI-10761252951711/.

United Press International – UPI (2012) 'Turkey Keen on KRG Oil', 17 July, available at: www.upi.com/Business_News/Energy-Resources/2012/07/17/Turkey-keen-on-KRG-oil/UPI-16461342521310/.

University of Exeter (2015) 'Professor Gareth Stansfield – staff profile', available at: http://socialsciences.exeter.ac.uk/iais/staff/stansfield/.

University of Pennsylvania (2015) 'Brendan O'Leary – curriculum vitae', available at: www.sas.upenn.edu/polisci/sites/tengu.sas.upenn.edu.psci-test/files/2015%20BOL%20 CV%20December.pdf.

Uras, U. (2015a) 'Ruling Party Loses Majority in Turkey Elections', *Al Jazeera*, 8 June, available at: www.aljazeera.com/news/2015/06/ak-party-leads-turkish-parliamentary-polls-150607161827232.html.

Uras, U. (2015b) 'Blast Kills Kurdish Activists in Turkish Town', *Al Jazeera*, 20 July, available at: www.aljazeera.com/news/2015/07/turkey-syria-explosion-suruc-150720 093632908.html.

Uras, U. (2015c) 'Turkey's AK Party Wins Back Majority in Snap Elections', *Al Jazeera*, 2 November, available at: www.aljazeera.com/news/2015/11/turkey-ruling-akp-leads-crucial-snap-elections-151101160104190.html.

Uslu, E. (2009) 'Kurds May Ask the PKK to Lay Down Its Arms', Jamestown Foundation, *Eurasia Daily Monitor*, 6(51), available at: www.jamestown.org/single/?no_ cache=1&tx_ttnews[tt_news]=34716#.UwdPdc5X-So.

van Wilgenburg, W. (2013a) 'Talabani's Party Stung by Loss in Iraqi Kurdistan Elections', *Al Monitor*, 11 October, available at: www.al-monitor.com/pulse/originals/ 2013/10/talabani-loses-kurdistan-elections.html.

van Wilgenburg, W. (2013b) 'Kurds Divided over Syrian Autonomy', *Al Monitor*, 19 November, available at: www.al-monitor.com/pulse/originals/2013/11/syrian-autonomy-divides-kurds.html.

van Wilgenburg, W. (2014) 'Kurdish Rivals Unite to Fight Islamic State', *Al Jazeera*, 16 August, available at: www.aljazeera.com/news/middleeast/2014/08/iraq-turkey-kurds-fight-islamic-state-201481581133776796.html.

van Wilgenburg, W. (2016) 'From the Frontline of Assad's Strike on the Kurds', *The Daily Beast*, 22 April, available at: www.thedailybeast.com/articles/2016/04/22/from-the-frontlines-of-assad-s-strike-on-the-kurds.html.

Vick, K. (2015) 'The Ankara Bombing Reveals Scary Political Rifts in Turkey', *Time*, 12 October, available at: http://time.com/4069951/ankara-bombing-erdogan-role-turkey/.

Whitcomb, A. (2014) 'Kurdish President's Brother to Lead Kobane Relief Force', *Rudaw*, 25 October, available at: http://rudaw.net/english/middleeast/syria/25102014.

Whitney, M. (2015) 'The Politics of Betrayal: Obama Backstabs Kurds to Appease Turkey', *Counterpunch*, 29 July, available at: www.counterpunch.org/2015/07/29/the-politics-of-betrayal-obama-backstabs-kurds-to-appease-turkey/.

Wilkens, K. (2014) 'A Kurdish Alamo: Five Reasons the Battle for Kobane Matters', Carnegie Endowment for International Peace, *Syria in Crisis Series*, 10 October, available at: http://carnegieendowment.org/syriaincrisis/?fa=56905.

Wilkie, C. (2011) 'Mujahideen-e-Khalq: Former US Officials Make Millions Advocating for Terrorist Organisation', *The Huffington Post*, 8 August, available at: www.huffingtonpost.com/2011/08/08/mek-lobbying_n_913233.html.

Williams, D. (2014) 'Israel Tells US Kurdish Independence is Foregone Conclusion', *Reuters*, 26 June, available at: www.reuters.com/article/2014/06/26/us-iraq-crisis-israel-kurds-idUSKBN0F111520140626.

Wood, G. (2015) "What ISIS Really Wants", *The Atlantic*, March Issue, available at: www.theatlantic.com/magazine/archive/2015/03/what-isis-really-wants/384980/.

Wood, P. (2013) 'Democracy in Kurdistan: More Losers than Winners', *Open Democracy*, 27 October, available at: www.opendemocracy.net/arab-awakening/philip-wood/democracy-in-kurdistan-more-losers-than-winners.

Worth, R. (2016) 'Behind the Barricades of Turkey's Hidden War', *New York Times*, 24 May, available at: www.nytimes.com/2016/05/29/magazine/behind-the-barricades-of-turkeys-hidden-war.html.

Wright, R. (2014) 'The 194th State: The Kurds' Bid for Nationhood', *The New Yorker*, 17 July, available at: www.newyorker.com/news/news-desk/the-194th-state-the-kurds-bid-for-nationhood.

Xinhua Daily News (2008) 'Iraqi Kurds Condemn Turkey Incursion, Call for Troops Withdrawal', 23 February, available at: http://news.xinhuanet.com/english/2008-02/23/content_7655337.htm.

Zakaria, F. (2006) 'Rethinking Iraq: The Way Forward', *Newsweek*, 11 May, available at: www.newsweek.com/zakaria-rethinking-iraq-way-forward-107037.

Zaman, A. (2014a) 'Fight against IS Helps PKK Gain Global Legitimacy' *Al Monitor*, 16 September, available at: www.al-monitor.com/pulse/originals/2014/09/turkey-kurdistan-iraq-syria-us-isis-pkk-global-legitimacy.html.

Zaman, A. (2014b) 'Turkey's Leaders See Kobane as Opportunity, not Threat', *Al Monitor*, 7 October, available at: www.al-monitor.com/pulse/originals/2014/10/turkey-syria-kobane-kurds-erdogan-assad.html.

Zaman, A. (2016) 'Mission Impossible? Triangulating U.S.-Turkish Relations with Syria's Kurds', Wilson Center, Middle East Program, 13 April, available at: www.wilsoncenter.org/publication/mission-impossible-triangulating-us-turkish-relations-syrias-kurds.

Zana, L. (2009) 'Leyla Zana's Speech to the Diyarbakir Criminal Court', *Kurdish Media.com*, 20 April, available at: www.kurdmedia.com/article.aspx?id=15643.

Zirngast, M. (2015) 'Erdoğan's Bloody Gambit', *Jacobin*, 3 August, available at: www.jacobinmag.com/2015/08/turkey-nato-isis-hdp-kpp-suruc/

Interviews

(In addition to interviews with about a dozen Iraqi Kurdish journalists and NGO workers who, for their own safety, will remain unnamed)

Abdul Rahman, B., KRG Representative to the UK, London, UK, 5 July 2010.

Abdullah, O., Former PUK military commander, Sulimaniyah, Iraqi Kurdistan, 13 June 2010.

Al Mudaris, F. A., Statistician in the KRG Ministry of Trade, Erbil, Iraqi Kurdistan, 20 October 2011.

Ataç, H., PKK dissident, Erbil, Iraqi Kurdistan, 23 October 2011.

Bakir, F. M., Head of the KRG Department of Foreign Relations, Erbil, Iraqi Kurdistan, 27 May 2010.

Barkey, H., Scholar, Bethlehem, USA, 1 February 2011.

Barmani, A. Veteran PUK functionary and former Iraqi Ambassador to Sweden and Norway, Sulimaniyah, Iraqi Kurdistan, 11 June 2010.

Çelik, S. PKK dissident and author, San Louis, France, 9 May 2010.

Chalabi, S. A., KRG Minister of Trade, Erbil, Iraqi Kurdistan, 20 October 2011.

Chawrash, M., Former PUK military commander, Sulimaniyah, Iraqi Kurdistan, 31 May 2010.

Dizayee, S., KRG Minister of Education, former KRG Representative to Turkey, Erbil, Iraqi Kurdistan, 19 September 2010.

Ergil, D., Scholar, Istanbul, Turkey, 25 October 2011.

Gunter, M., Scholar, Cookeville, USA, 11 March 2011.

Hawesi, C., Veteran PUK functionary, Sulimaniyah, Iraqi Kurdistan, 7 June 2010.

Hiltermann, J., ICG Country/Region Director for the Middle East and North Africa, Washington, USA, 8 February 2011.

Hussein, F., Chief of Staff to the Kurdistan Region Presidency, Erbil, Iraqi Kurdistan, 21 September 2010.

Karim, N., Former PUK representative to the U.S., personal physician of Iraqi President Jalal Talabani, current governor of the Governorate of Kirkuk, Sulimaniyah, Iraqi Kurdistan, 6 September 2010.

Mahmoud, S., Former PUK official stationed in Syria, currently *Gorran* functionary, Sulimaniyah, Iraqi Kurdistan, 1 June 2010.

Mirza, A. R., PUK co-founder, Sulimaniyah, Iraqi Kurdistan, 11 June 2010.

Murad, A., PUK co-founder, former Iraqi Ambassador to Romania, currently Secretary General of PUK Central Council, Erbil, Iraqi Kurdistan, 3 September 2010.

Natali, D., Scholar, Washington, USA, 21 March 2011.

Öcalan, O., Former PKK commander, brother of Abdullah Öcalan, Koysinjaq, Iraqi Kurdistan, 12 & 16 September 2010.

Olson, R., Scholar, Lexington, USA, 9 March 2011.

Phillips, D., Scholar, New York, USA, 11 February 2011.

Pire, S., Veteran PUK functionary, Sulimaniyah, Iraqi Kurdistan, 10 June 2010.

Pollack, K., Former Director for Near East and South East Asian Affairs of the National Security Council in the Clinton administration, currently Director of Research at the Brookings Institution's Saban Center for Middle East Policy, Washington, USA, 21 March 2011.

Pope, H., Scholar, ICG Country/Region Director for Turkey, Istanbul, Turkey, 6 May 2012.

Qaradaghi, Q., Iraqi Kurdish journalist, former press secretary to Iraqi President Jalal Talabani, London, UK, 21 April 2011.

Selçen, A., Turkish Consul General in Erbil, Erbil, Iraqi Kurdistan, 19 October 2011.

Sheikhmous, O., PUK co-founder, Exeter, UK, 10 July 2012.

Talabani, Q., KRG Representative to the USA, son of Jalal Talabani, Washington, USA, 25 February 2011.

Tawfiq, M., Former PUK official in Dohuk, currently *Gorran* spokesman, Sulimaniyah, Iraqi Kurdistan, 4 June 2010.

Taş, N., PKK dissident, Erbil, Iraqi Kurdistan, 23 October 2011.

Vali, A., Scholar, Istanbul, Turkey, 8 May 2012.

Index

Taylor & Francis eBooks

Helping you to choose the right eBooks for your Library

Add Routledge titles to your library's digital collection today. Taylor and Francis ebooks contains over 50,000 titles in the Humanities, Social Sciences, Behavioural Sciences, Built Environment and Law.

Choose from a range of subject packages or create your own!

Benefits for you
» Free MARC records
» COUNTER-compliant usage statistics
» Flexible purchase and pricing options
» All titles DRM-free.

Benefits for your user
» Off-site, anytime access via Athens or referring URL
» Print or copy pages or chapters
» Full content search
» Bookmark, highlight and annotate text
» Access to thousands of pages of quality research at the click of a button.

REQUEST YOUR FREE INSTITUTIONAL TRIAL TODAY

Free Trials Available
We offer free trials to qualifying academic, corporate and government customers.

eCollections – Choose from over 30 subject eCollections, including:

Archaeology	Language Learning
Architecture	Law
Asian Studies	Literature
Business & Management	Media & Communication
Classical Studies	Middle East Studies
Construction	Music
Creative & Media Arts	Philosophy
Criminology & Criminal Justice	Planning
Economics	Politics
Education	Psychology & Mental Health
Energy	Religion
Engineering	Security
English Language & Linguistics	Social Work
Environment & Sustainability	Sociology
Geography	Sport
Health Studies	Theatre & Performance
History	Tourism, Hospitality & Events

For more information, pricing enquiries or to order a free trial, please contact your local sales team: www.tandfebooks.com/page/sales

Routledge
Taylor & Francis Group

The home of
Routledge books

www.tandfebooks.com